CONSUMER GUIDE®

2005 CARS

pil

Publications International, Ltd.

CONTENTS

INTRODUCTION

WELCOME TO CONSUMER GUIDE'S® *2005 CARS*

With evaluations, prices, and specifications for nearly 200 cars, minivans, and SUVs, *2005 Cars* helps you find the information you need to make the right car-buying decision. Our auto editors comb the carmakers' data sheets; interview automotive designers, engineers, and executives; and test drive hundreds of vehicles per year to bring you our reports and ratings.

BEST BUYS AND RECOMMENDED

The Auto Editors of Consumer Guide® select Best Buys as the top overall vehicles in their model categories. This is our highest ranking. Models labeled Recommended also merit serious consideration. Neither ranking is based solely on point totals. Rather, they reflect overall value for the money compared to the competition. There may be more than one Best Buy or Recommended pick per model class.

VEHICLE CLASSES

To help you compare direct competitors, we place each vehicle we cover into one of 16 classes based on size, price, and market position. Each vehicle's class is listed at the top of its report. The classes are:

COMPACT CARS These range from tiny economy models to slightly larger popularly priced sedans, hatchbacks, and wagons.

PREMIUM COMPACT CARS Similar in size to the larger compact cars, but more expensive. Upscale in equipment and image.

MIDSIZE CARS The heart of the U.S. car market. Price-sensitive, conservatively designed, family oriented sedans and wagons.

PREMIUM MIDSIZE CARS Luxury, performance, and prestige without excess bulk. Among the fastest-growing categories.

LARGE CARS Big, inside and out. Includes the only 6-passenger cars. Lots of metal for the money. Domestic brands dominate.

PREMIUM LARGE CARS Top-of-the-line size and luxury. Flagship showcases for technology. Some have 6-figure price tags.

SPORTY/PERFORMANCE CARS Two-seat roadsters, 4-cyl hatchbacks, V8 muscle cars. Emphasis is affordable performance.

PREMIUM SPORTY/PERFORMANCE CARS High power, high style, high price. Two-passenger convertibles, 4-seat coupes rule.

COMPACT SUVS Least-costly, most-efficient SUVs. Five seats max. Most use car-type chassis, are not designed for off-road.

MIDSIZE SUVS A mix of car- and truck-type construction, V6 and V8 power, up to 8-passenger seating. Includes crossovers.

PREMIUM MIDSIZE SUVS Many are gilded versions of vehicles in midsize SUV category, others are exclusive upscale designs.

LARGE SUVS Workhorse wagons with brawny chassis, ample towing ability, lots of space, and mostly abysmal fuel economy.

PREMIUM LARGE SUVS Supersized luxury liners. Some use less-costly large SUVs as their basis. All are powerful and pricey.

MINIVANS Easily the smartest use of space for passengers and cargo. The best blend comfort, convenience, and safety features.

RATINGS GUIDELINES

Acceleration

Rating	0-60 mph	Rating	0-60 mph
1	over 12.0 sec	6	7.1-8.0 sec
2	11.1-12.0 sec	7	6.1-7.0 sec
3	10.1-11.0 sec	8	5.1-6.0 sec
4	9.1-10.0 sec	9	4.6-5.0 sec
5	8.1-9.0 sec	10	under 4.6 sec

Fuel Economy

Rating	Miles Per Gallon	Rating	Miles Per Gallon
1	under 10.1	6	22.0-24.9
2	10.1-13.9	7	25.0-29.9
3	14.0-15.4	8	30.0-34.9
4	15.5-17.9	9	35.0-49.9
5	18.0-21.9	10	over 49.9

Cargo space

Rating	Cubic Feet	Rating	Cubic Feet
1	under 8.0	6	17.0-49.8
2	8.0-12.9	7	49.9-75.8
3	13.0-14.4	8	75.9-99.9
4	14.5-15.9	9	100-149
5	16.0-16.9	10	over 149

SHOPPING TIPS

DO

- Keep your eye on the bottom-line cost you'll pay for the vehicle, including fees, taxes, and financing charges. This is your true cost, and the number you should compare to see which dealer is offering the best deal.
- Research which type of vehicle best suits your needs, which model your budget can comfortably accommodate, and what equipment you'll actually use. Do this homework before venturing out to compare the new models.
- Shop for the best rate on auto financing at a bank or other lending institution before you shop for a car. Ask the dealer to meet or beat that rate.
- Shop at least three dealers to compare prices on the same model with the same equipment. Let each dealer know you are shopping around.
- Test drive the exact model and equipment you intend to buy.
- Bargain up from the dealer-invoice price, not down from the manufacturer's suggested retail price. Research what additional customer incentives in the form of manufacturer cash rebates or cut-rate financing might be available. Also research what incentives the manufacturer may be offering the dealer on the vehicle you're shopping. This will help you bargain for the best price. Information on these incentives is online at **http://auto.consumerguide.com.**
- Get written price quotes that are good next week, not just today. If a dealer won't give you a price in writing, go elsewhere.
- Keep your trade-in separate from new-car price negotiations. Get a written

trade-in value on your old car after you settle on a price for the new one. If you have an old car you intend to sell, you'll almost always get more money by selling it yourself instead of trading it in. However, balance this potential profit against the pitfalls of temporarily becoming a used-car salesperson.

- Keep discussions of financing and lease terms separate from negotiations about the bottom-line price. Salespeople may attempt to confuse you by juggling these numbers, appearing to lower some while secretly raising others.
- Get all promises in writing before leaving the dealership.

Don't

- Waste time and energy arguing with the dealer sales representative about the price of each and every item or charge on the vehicle. The dealer has more time and energy than you do. Keep your eye on the bottom-line price.
- Have your heart set unwaveringly on a specific model, color, or equipment—or at least don't be obvious about it to the salesperson. This limits your bargaining power. Being flexible frees you to snare a deal on a vehicle the dealer may have on hand and might be willing to offer at a bargain price.
- Put down a deposit to get a price quote or test drive. If the salesperson should make such an unethical demand, go to another dealer.
- Tell a salesperson how much you're willing to pay, either as a bottom-line figure or as a monthly payment. You may be forfeiting your chance to get a lower price. Make the salesperson quote you the dealer's bottom-line price.
- Just "add 4 percent to the invoice price" and refuse to budge from there. There is no formula for calculating a "good deal." Real-world selling prices depend on supply and demand for a particular model in your area, and on competition among dealers. This is why it's vital that you shop around.
- Shop for a monthly payment before you secure the bottom-line price for the vehicle. By focusing on monthly payments instead of overall costs, dealers can easily manipulate you into paying a higher total or into buying a vehicle you might not be able to afford.
- Pay a separate "advertising fee." Advertising is part of the dealer's cost of doing business and should be rolled into the price they're asking for the vehicle, allowing you to consider their bottom-line price against those offered by competing dealers. (Advertising fees are not included in our price lists because they vary by region, and not all dealers try to pass advertising fees on to customers.)
- Purchase rustproofing, paint or fabric sealant, or other dealer add-ons. These dealer profit-padders are unnecessary on today's modern vehicles.

LEASING

Leasing may be right for you if you:

- Like to drive a more-expensive car than you might be able to buy, or you like to drive a new car every few years.
- Can afford a substantial initial payment, often called a "capital cost reduction." These can amount to thousands of dollars, but are usually less than the typical down payment required on a purchase. You'll also likely pay an "acquisition fee" to the lessor when you sign the lease, and may be hit with a "disposition fee" when you return the car.
- Are looking to lower your monthly payment. Monthly lease payments are generally less than monthly loan payments for an equivalent car.
- Take reasonably good care of your vehicle.
- Consult a financial advisor before leasing. This is the best way to determine leasing's advantages and disadvantages in your specific situation.

Leasing may not be right for you if you:

- Don't realize that unless you eventually buy a car, you'll always be making a monthly payment.
- Drive a lot. Most leases have mileage limits, typically 15,000 miles annually. Unless you stay within these limits or negotiate some arrangement before you lease, you'll be charged for exceeding the limits.
- Don't take reasonably good care of your vehicle. At the end of the lease, you'll be liable for "excessive wear" as determined by the lessor. And you may be charged for prepping the car for resale.
- Don't budget for sales taxes. If you buy the car at the end of the lease, you may have to pay sales tax on the purchase price. And, at the lease inception, some states demand sales tax on the full suggested retail price of the car. Try to roll these taxes into your monthly payment.

All sport-utility vehicles (SUVs) and pickup trucks are available with some form of 4-wheel drive, and some cars and minivans are as well. But there are significant differences in the types of 4WD systems offered.

AN EXPLANATION OF 4-WHEEL DRIVE AND ALL-WHEEL DRIVE

For those who don't do severe off-roading, the most important factor to consider is whether the 4WD system on the vehicle you are contemplating can be left engaged on dry pavement. Some 4WD systems are designed to be used only on loose surfaces, and may be damaged if used on dry pavement. Others can be left engaged on dry pavement, a convenience that relieves the driver of deciding when 4WD is needed. In some cases, more than one system is available for a given vehicle. Here is how we refer to the various systems, and a brief discussion of what each means to you:

4WD that should not be left engaged on dry pavement

This is the most-basic system and is sometimes referred to as "part-time 4WD." It provides a choice of settings, usually 2WD, 4WD High, and 4WD Low. Such systems can be shifted from 2WD to 4WD High while driving. But 4WD should not be left engaged while driving on dry pavement. Leaving 4WD engaged on dry pavement causes mechanical wear—and eventual damage to the drivetrain. Repairs are expensive. (4WD Low is appropriate for severe off-road driving. Most vehicles must be brought to a complete stop before it can be engaged.)

4WD that can be left engaged on dry pavement

This system is more advanced—and more convenient. It is sometimes referred to as full-time 4WD. Such systems have a choice of settings, usually 2WD, 4WD High, and 4WD Low. Some add settings labeled Automatic 4WD or Full-time 4WD. These systems can be switched between 2WD and 4WD High, Automatic 4WD, or full-time 4WD while under way. More importantly, they allow you to leave 4WD engaged while driving on dry pavement without fear of mechanical damage.

All-wheel drive (AWD)

This system distributes power to all four wheels automatically when it detects wheel slippage. The system is always in AWD, so the driver doesn't have to bother deciding when it is necessary to switch in and out of 2WD. Some AWD systems in SUVs and pickup trucks offer low-range gearing for serious off-road work.

It is important to note that while 4WD and AWD help you "go in the snow," they do little to aid cornering ability and virtually nothing for braking.

Many drivers, finding they can accelerate in snow as quickly as on dry roads, assume they can also corner and stop just as well. This is untrue.

USING THIS GUIDE

1 **Best Buy:** The top pick in its class, based on value, performance, and reliability. **Recommended:** A good alternate choice. There may be more than one Best Buy or Recommended per class.

2 Vehicle class, based on size, price, and market position (see "Vehicle Classes" on page 4).

3 The wheels or combination of wheels that propel the vehicle.

4 Base price of the least- and most-expensive models in the lineup, not including options. "Built in" identifies the country in which the vehicle is assembled.

5 A sample of other vehicles in this class that merit your consideration.

6 Important vehicle details. Highlights noteworthy changes to the vehicle for the model year, lists the available body styles, trim lines, engines, transmissions, and significant standard equipment and optional features.

7 Vehicle ratings and evaluation based on test drives by the auto editors. Noted at the top of each numerical ratings column is the specific model tested and any equipment that has a bearing on its performance or accommodations. Vehicles tested are furnished by the manufacturers. We evaluate vehicles the same way owners would: commuting, shopping, family vacations, highway travel, stop-and-go city driving.

Ratings values are in 10 categories on a 1-10 scale, with 10 being the best. It's important to note that with the exception of Value Within Class, these ratings numbers reflect how the model we tested compares with all vehicles, not solely with other models in its class.

Ratings numbers and comments are based on the subjective evaluations of our test drivers. However, we have established quantitative guidelines for three ratings categories: acceleration, fuel economy, and cargo space (see "Ratings Guidelines" on page 5). These are guidelines only not the exclusive basis for our ratings in these categories.

Our fuel-economy ratings are based on the driving our editors do, not EPA fuel-economy estimates.

Cargo ratings are based on the vehicle's maximum cargo volume, meaning with all rear seats folded or removed, when possible.

8 Value Within Class judges the tested models on a value-for-money basis solely against competitors within their market category. If you read nothing else in this book, be sure to read the text associated with Value Within Class.

9 The average total for all vehicles in that class provides an idea of how the tested models scored relative to others in their vehicle class.

10 Engines available for the vehicle

KEY: ohv overhead valve design; **sohc** single overhead camshaft design; **dohc** dual overhead camshaft design; **I** inline arrangement of cylinders; **V** cylinders in a V configuration; **H** horizontally opposed cylinders; **W** V-configured cylinders in staggered rows, **I4/electric** "hybrid" with both a gas engine and an electric motor; **Size, liters/cu. in.** engine displacement in liters and cubic inches; **rpm** revolutions per minute; **S** Standard; **O** Optional

11 Environmental Protection Agency (EPA) fuel-economy estimates in miles per gallon city/highway for that engine and transmission combination
automatic transmission; **manual** transmission; **CVT** continuously variable (automatic) transmission; **SMT** sequential manual transmission; **NA** information not available.

12 Prices for each vehicle trim level at the time of publication. **Retail Price** is the manufacturer's suggested retail price for each trim level. The dealer is free to ask more or less. **Dealer Invoice** is the price the dealer pays the factory for the vehicle. The actual amount the dealer pays can be affected by incentives and other financial arrangements between the manufacturer and the dealer. **Destination charge** is the cost the dealer pays to have the vehicle shipped to the dealership

Automakers can change their prices at any time. If the retail prices we publish do not match those on the vehicle's factory window sticker, the manufacturer has probably altered the price since this book was printed. If a dealer claims our prices are incorrect, or if the information in this book doesn't match what you see in showrooms, check out Web site at **http://auto.consumerguide.com** or write or e-mail us at *info@consumerguide.com* and we'll try to help.

13 Lists each model designation within the vehicle line and the standard equipment included on that model.

14 Options available by model and their retail- and dealer-invoice price. To find the true cost the dealer paid for a vehicle, add the invoice price of the options to the invoice price of the trim level and the destination charge. **NC** No charge. ***Manufacturer's Discount Price*** Price of the option after the manufacturer's discount is calculated.

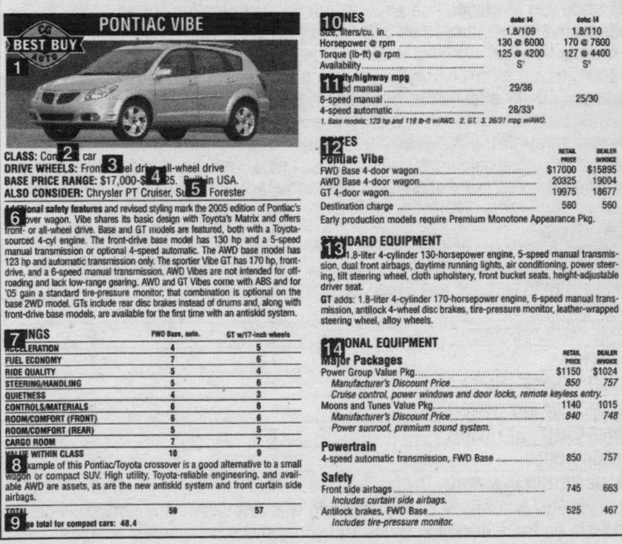

PONTIAC VIBE

CG BEST BUY AUTO

[1]

CLASS: Co [2] car
DRIVE WHEELS: Fron [3] el dr… ll-wheel drive
BASE PRICE RANGE: $17,000-$ [4] 25. … in USA.
ALSO CONSIDER: Chrysler PT Cruiser, Su [5] Forester

[6] …**onal safety features** and revised styling mark the 2005 edition of Pontiac's …over wagon. Vibe shares its basic design with Toyota's Matrix and offers front- or all-wheel drive. Base and GT models are featured, both with a Toyota-sourced 4-cyl engine. The front-drive base model has 130 hp and a 5-speed manual transmission or optional 4-speed automatic. The AWD base model has 123 hp and automatic transmission only. The sportier Vibe GT has 170 hp, front-drive, and a 6-speed manual transmission. AWD Vibes are not intended for off-roading and lack low-range gearing. AWD and GT Vibes come with ABS and for '05 gain a standard tire-pressure monitor; that combination is optional on the base 2WD model. GTs include rear disc brakes instead of drums and, along with front-drive base models, are available for the first time with an antiskid system.

[7] …INGS	FWD Base, auto.	GT w/17-inch wheels
…ELERATION	4	5
FUEL ECONOMY	7	6
RIDE QUALITY	5	4
STEERING/HANDLING	5	6
QUIETNESS	4	3
CONTROLS/MATERIALS	6	6
ROOM/COMFORT (FRONT)	6	6
ROOM/COMFORT (REAR)	5	5
CARGO ROOM	7	7
…E WITHIN CLASS	10	9

[8] …xample of this Pontiac/Toyota crossover is a good alternative to a small wagon or compact SUV. High utility, Toyota-reliable engineering, and available AWD are assets, as are the new antiskid system and front curtain side airbags.

TOTAL	59	57

[9] …e total for compact cars: 48.4

[10] …NES	dohc I4	dohc I4
…, liters/cu. in.	1.8/109	1.8/110
Horsepower @ rpm	130 @ 6000	170 @ 7600
Torque (lb-ft) @ rpm	125 @ 4200	127 @ 4400
Availability	S[1]	S[2]
[11] …ity/highway mpg		
…ed manual	29/36	
6-speed manual		25/30
4-speed automatic	28/33[3]	

1. Base models; 123 hp and 116 lb-ft w/AWD. 2. GT. 3. 26/31 mpg w/AWD.

[12] …ES

Pontiac Vibe	RETAIL PRICE	DEALER INVOICE
FWD Base 4-door wagon	$17000	$15895
AWD Base 4-door wagon	20325	19004
GT 4-door wagon	19975	18677
Destination charge	560	560

Early production models require Premium Monotone Appearance Pkg.

[13] …DARD EQUIPMENT

… 1.8-liter 4-cylinder 130-horsepower engine, 5-speed manual transmission, dual front airbags, daytime running lights, air conditioning, power steering, tilt steering wheel, cloth upholstery, front bucket seats, height-adjustable driver seat.

GT adds: 1.8-liter 4-cylinder 170-horsepower engine, 6-speed manual transmission, antilock 4-wheel disc brakes, tire-pressure monitor, leather-wrapped steering wheel, alloy wheels.

[14] …ONAL EQUIPMENT

…r Packages	RETAIL PRICE	DEALER INVOICE
Power Group Value Pkg.	$1150	$1024
Manufacturer's Discount Price	*850*	*757*
Cruise control, power windows and door locks, remote keyless entry.		
Moons and Tunes Value Pkg.	1140	1015
Manufacturer's Discount Price	*840*	*748*
Power sunroof, premium sound system.		
Powertrain		
4-speed automatic transmission, FWD Base	850	757
Safety		
Front side airbags	745	663
Includes curtain side airbags.		
Antilock brakes, FWD Base	525	467
Includes tire-pressure monitor.		

ACURA MDX

CLASS: Premium midsize sport-utility vehicle
DRIVE WHEELS: All-wheel drive
BASE PRICE RANGE: $36,700-$43,775. Built in Canada.
ALSO CONSIDER: Cadillac SRX, Lexus RX

Added entertainment features lead 2005 news for this popular SUV. Acura's parent-company Honda uses MDX's underskin for its Pilot SUV. But MDX holds seven passengers instead of eight and has slightly less cargo room. Its 2nd- and 3rd-row seats fold flat to create a flat load floor. MDX shares Pilot's V6 engine, but with 265 hp vs. 255. It has a 5-speed automatic transmission and all-wheel drive without low-range gearing. ABS and antiskid system are standard. So are front side airbags and head-protecting curtain side airbags, which cover all seating rows and are designed to deploy in both side impacts and rollovers. MDX comes as a base model and as upscale Touring versions with rear DVD entertainment, navigation system, or both, priced as separate models. All have standard satellite radio for '05, plus a larger fuel tank. Tourings add Acura's new HandsFreeLink, a wireless connection for using cell phones through the audio system. OnStar assistance is newly standard with navigation, which includes voice control and a rearview camera that uses the dashboard screen to show what's behind with the transmission in Reverse.

RATINGS	Base	Touring w/nav. sys.
ACCELERATION	6	6
FUEL ECONOMY	3	3
RIDE QUALITY	5	5
STEERING/HANDLING	6	6
QUIETNESS	7	7
CONTROLS/MATERIALS	7	6
ROOM/COMFORT (FRONT)	8	8
ROOM/COMFORT (REAR)	7	7
CARGO ROOM	8	8
VALUE WITHIN CLASS	10	9

Acura's SUV is a highly desirable blend of competence and convenience. Its ride can be truck lumpy at times and some rivals have newer designs, but

RATINGS (cont.)

	Base	Touring w/nav. sys.
MDX shines for overall refinement, generous standard equipment, and keen pricing. That's why it's a Best Buy—and seldom discounted.		
TOTAL	67	65

Average total for premium midsize sport-utility vehicles: 59.6

ENGINES

	sohc V6
Size, liters/cu. in.	3.5/212
Horsepower @ rpm	265 @ 5800
Torque (lb-ft) @ rpm	253 @ 3500
Availability	S
EPA city/highway mpg	
5-speed automatic	17/23

PRICES

Acura MDX

	RETAIL PRICE	DEALER INVOICE
Base 4-door wagon	$36700	$33062
Touring 4-door wagon	39525	35605
Touring w/DVD player 4-door wagon	41025	36955
Touring w/navigation 4-door wagon	42275	38079
Touring w/navigation and DVD player 4-door wagon	43775	39430
Destination charge	570	570

STANDARD EQUIPMENT

Base: 3.5-liter V6 engine, 5-speed automatic transmission, all-wheel drive, dual front airbags, front side airbags, curtain side airbags, antilock 4-wheel disc brakes, antiskid system, tire-pressure monitor, front and rear air conditioning w/front and rear automatic climate controls, power steering, tilt leather-wrapped steering wheel w/radio controls, cruise control, leather upholstery, 7-passenger seating, heated front bucket seats, 8-way power driver seat, center console, cupholders, 2nd- and 3rd-row stowable split folding bench seats, heated power mirrors, power windows, power door locks, remote keyless entry, power sunroof, AM/FM/cassette/CD player, satellite radio (requires monthly fee), digital clock, tachometer, illuminated visor mirrors, universal garage-door opener, automatic day/night rearview mirror, outside-temperature indicator, trip computer, map lights, rear defogger, intermittent rear wiper/washer, automatic headlights, floormats, theft-deterrent system, rear privacy glass, fog lights, 235/65R17 tires, alloy wheels.

Touring adds: 8-way power passenger seat, memory system (driver seat, mirrors), passenger-side tilt-down back-up-aid mirror, Bose AM/FM/cassette w/in-dash 6-disc CD changer, hands-free cellular telephone link, rain-sensing wipers, roof rack.

Touring w/navigation adds: navigation system w/voice recognition, rearview camera, OnStar assistance system w/one-year service.

Options are available as dealer-installed accessories.

ACURA NSX

CLASS: Premium sporty/performance car
DRIVE WHEELS: Rear-wheel drive
2004 BASE PRICE: $89,000. Built in Japan.
ALSO CONSIDER: Chevrolet Corvette, Porsche 911

The midengine sports car from Honda's premium division is unchanged for 2005. NSX comes with a lift-off "targa" roof panel, a 290-hp 3.2-liter V6, and a 6-speed manual transmission. A 4-speed automatic transmission with manual-shift feature is available by special order and teams with a 252-hp 3.0-liter V6. Standard are ABS, traction control, and 17-inch wheels, plus leather upholstery, keyless entry system, and trunk-mounted CD changer. Side airbags are unavailable.

RATINGS

	Base, man.
ACCELERATION	9
FUEL ECONOMY	6
RIDE QUALITY	2
STEERING/HANDLING	10
QUIETNESS	4
CONTROLS/MATERIALS	7
ROOM/COMFORT (FRONT)	5
ROOM/COMFORT (REAR)	0
CARGO ROOM	1
VALUE WITHIN CLASS	4

This sophisticated, well-built high performer provides plenty of thrills, yet is a fairly practical day-to-day car. But it also costs a mint, and aluminum-intensive construction means expensive repairs for even minor damage.

TOTAL	48

Average total for premium sporty/performance cars: 48.3

ENGINES

	dohc V6	dohc V6
Size, liters/cu. in.	3.0/181	3.2/194
Horsepower @ rpm	252 @ 6600	290 @ 7100
Torque (lb-ft) @ rpm	210 @ 5300	224 @ 5500
Availability	O	S

 Specifications begin on page 547.

ENGINES (cont.)

	dohc V6	dohc V6
EPA city/highway mpg		
6-speed manual		17/24
4-speed automatic	17/24	

2005 prices unavailable at time of publication.

2004 PRICES

Acura NSX	RETAIL PRICE	DEALER INVOICE
Base 2-door coupe, automatic	$89000	$79213
Base 2-door coupe, manual	89000	79213
Destination charge	765	765

STANDARD EQUIPMENT

Base automatic: 3.0-liter V6 engine, 4-speed automatic transmission w/manual-shift capability, traction control, dual front airbags, antilock 4-wheel disc brakes, air conditioning w/automatic climate control, power steering, tilt/telescope leather-wrapped steering wheel, cruise control, leather upholstery, 4-way power bucket seats, center console, cupholders, power mirrors, power windows, power door locks, remote keyless entry, Bose AM/FM/cassette, 6-disc CD changer, digital clock, tachometer, variable-intermittent wipers, rear defogger, remote fuel-door and decklid releases, floormats, theft-deterrent system, removable roof panel, rear spoiler, xenon headlights, 215/40ZR17 front tires, 255/40ZR17 rear tires, alloy wheels.

Base manual adds: 3.2-liter V6 engine, 6-speed manual transmission.

Options are available as dealer-installed accessories.

ACURA RL

CLASS: Premium midsize car
DRIVE WHEELS: All-wheel drive
BASE PRICE RANGE: $48,165-$48,900. Built in Japan.
ALSO CONSIDER: Audi A6, Infiniti G35, Mercedes-Benz E-Class

Acura redesigns its flagship sedan for 2005. The new RL is four inches shorter in wheelbase and overall length than its 1996-2004 predecessor, but gains standard all-wheel drive, more power, fresh styling, and additional safety and convenience features. It comes in one trim level with no options. The sole engine is again a 3.5-liter V6, but with 300 hp vs 225. The only transmission is a 5-speed automatic with steering-wheel-mounted paddle shifters for manual operation. Acura calls the AWD system Super Handling All-Wheel Drive (SH-AWD). It is designed to transfer power to the outside rear wheel in turns to help rotate the RL around a corner. Front side airbags and head protecting curtain side airbags are standard. So are antilock 4-wheel disc brakes, antiskid control, steering-linked xenon headlights, and keyless access and ignition. Also included is the AcuraLink system, which displays maintenance reminders, operating tips, diagnostic information, and vehicle recalls on a dashboard screen. A navigation system is standard and can alert the driver to traffic conditions and accidents in major urban areas. This evaluation is based on preview test drives.

RATINGS

	Base
ACCELERATION	7
FUEL ECONOMY	4
RIDE QUALITY	8
STEERING/HANDLING	8
QUIETNESS	8
CONTROLS/MATERIALS	8
ROOM/COMFORT (FRONT)	8
ROOM/COMFORT (REAR)	7
CARGO ROOM	3
VALUE WITHIN CLASS	7

The RL impresses with efficient design, smart engineering, and a sporty personality. Standard AWD, great interior decor, and Acura's reputation for reliability and resale value are other attributes. It's not slow, but there are rivals in the $50,000 price bracket that offer V8 power and more sheetmetal—important touchstones for some premium-car buyers.

TOTAL	68

Average total for premium midsize cars: 61.7

ENGINES

	sohc V6
Size, liters/cu. in.	3.5/212
Horsepower @ rpm	300 @ 6200
Torque (lb-ft) @ rpm	260 @ 5000
Availability	S
EPA city/highway mpg	
5-speed automatic	18/26[1]

1. Manufacturer estimates.

PRICES

Acura RL

	RETAIL PRICE	DEALER INVOICE
Base 4-door sedan	$48900	$43536
Base 4-door sedan Alaska/Hawaii	48165	42882
Destination charge	570	570

Satellite radio w/traffic information not available in Alaska and Hawaii. Navigation system not available in Alaska.

STANDARD EQUIPMENT

Base: 3.5-liter V6 engine, 5-speed automatic transmission w/manual-shift capability, all-wheel drive, traction control, dual front airbags, front side airbags, curtain side airbags, antilock 4-wheel disc brakes, brake assist, antiskid system, tire-pressure monitor, daytime running lights, emergency inside trunk release, air conditioning w/dual-zone automatic climate controls, power steering, power tilt/telescope leather-wrapped steering wheel w/radio controls, cruise control, leather upholstery, heated front bucket seats w/lumbar adjustment, 8-way power driver seat, 4-way power passenger seat, center console, cupholders, memory system (driver seat, mirrors, steering wheel), trunk pass-through, wood interior trim, active noise cancellation, power-folding rear headrests, heated power mirrors w/turn signals and tilt-down back-up aid, power windows, power door locks, remote keyless entry, remote starting, power sunroof, OnStar assistance system w/one-year service, navigation system w/voice recognition, Bose AM/FM radio w/in-dash 6-disc CD/DVD changer, satellite radio w/traffic information, digital clock, hands-free cellular telephone link, tachometer, trip computer, automatic day/night rearview mirror, variable-intermittent wipers, illuminated visor mirrors, universal garage-door opener, map lights, power rear sunshade, rear defogger, automatic headlights, floormats, theft-deterrent system, steering-linked adaptive xenon headlights, fog lights, 245/50VR17 tires, alloy wheels.

Options are available as dealer-installed accessories.

ACURA RSX

CLASS: Sporty/performance car
DRIVE WHEELS: Front-wheel drive
BASE PRICE RANGE: $20,175-$23,570. Built in Japan.
ALSO CONSIDER: Mini Cooper, Scion tC

Freshened styling and sporty-model upgrades mark Acura's entry-level car for 2005. RSX is a 2-dr hatchback coupe sold in base and higher-performance Type-S trim. Both have a 2.0-liter 4-cyl engine. The 160-hp base model offers 5-speed manual or 5-speed automatic transmissions. The Type-S comes only with a 6-speed manual and for '05 gains 10 hp, to 210. Both get revised suspension, steering, and brakes, plus a minor facelift, more heavily bolstered front seats, and extra interior accents in chrome and faux titanium. The Type-S has a firmer suspension, and for '05 increases wheel size to 17 inches from 16. The base model retains 16s. Every RSX includes antilock 4-wheel disc brakes and front side airbags, sunroof, and heated mirrors. Leather upholstery is standard for the Type-S and available on the base. Type-S also comes with an in-dash CD changer and adds a rear spoiler for '05.

RATINGS

RATINGS	Base, man.	Base, auto.	Type-S
ACCELERATION	6	5	6
FUEL ECONOMY	7	6	6
RIDE QUALITY	5	5	4
STEERING/HANDLING	8	8	9
QUIETNESS	4	4	3
CONTROLS/MATERIALS	8	8	8
ROOM/COMFORT (FRONT)	5	5	5
ROOM/COMFORT (REAR)	2	2	2
CARGO ROOM	5	5	5
VALUE WITHIN CLASS	8	7	8

RSX is fun to drive, stoutly built, and competitively priced Best Buy. Driving enthusiats will want a Type-S, but the lower-cost base model appeals too. Maximum satisfaction requires working any RSX slightly hard, so consider the Scion tC for performance that's easier to access in another high-value sporty coupe.

TOTAL	58	55	56

Average total for sporty/performance cars: 48.5

ENGINES

	dohc I4	dohc I4
Size, liters/cu. in.	2.0/122	2.0/122
Horsepower @ rpm	160 @ 6500	210 @ 7800
Torque (lb-ft) @ rpm	141 @ 4000	143 @ 7000
Availability	S[1]	S[2]
EPA city/highway mpg		
5-speed manual	27/34	
6-speed manual		23/31
5-speed automatic	25/34	

1. Base. 2. Type-S.

PRICES

Acura RSX	RETAIL PRICE	DEALER INVOICE
Base 2-door hatchback, manual	$20175	$18397
Base 2-door hatchback, automatic	21075	19217
Base w/leather 2-door hatchback, manual	21250	19376
Base w/leather 2-door hatchback, automatic	22150	20195
Type-S 2-door hatchback, manual	23570	21488
Destination charge	570	570

Specifications begin on page 547.

STANDARD EQUIPMENT

Base: 2.0-liter 4-cylinder 160-horsepower engine, 5-speed manual or 5-speed automatic transmission w/manual-shift capability, dual front airbags, front side airbags, antilock 4-wheel disc brakes, air conditioning w/automatic climate control, interior air filter, power steering, tilt leather-wrapped steering wheel, cruise control, cloth upholstery, front bucket seats w/driver-seat height and lumbar adjustment, center console, cupholders, split folding rear seat, heated power mirrors, power windows, power door locks, remote keyless entry, power sunroof, AM/FM/CD player, digital clock, tachometer, variable-intermittent wipers, map lights, visor mirrors, cargo cover, rear defogger, intermittent rear wiper/washer, floormats, theft-deterrent system, 205/55VR16 tires, alloy wheels.

Base w/leather adds: leather upholstery.

Type-S adds: 2.0-liter 4-cylinder 210-horsepower engine, 6-speed manual transmission, Bose AM/FM/cassette w/in-dash 6-disc CD changer, rear spoiler, sport suspension, 215/45VR17 tires.

Options are available as dealer-installed accessories.

ACURA TL

CLASS: Premium midsize car
DRIVE WHEELS: Front-wheel drive
2004 BASE PRICE RANGE: $32,650-$34,850. Built in USA.
ALSO CONSIDER: Audi A6, Cadillac CTS, Infiniti G35 sedan

The best-selling car at Honda's upscale Acura division gets no changes of note for 2005. The TL is based on the Honda Accord platform, but has different styling and powertrains and more upscale features. The only engine is a 270-hp V6 with a choice of a 5-speed automatic transmission with manual shift gate or a 6-speed manual. TLs with manual transmission include a firmer suspension, Brembo-brand front brakes, and limited-slip differential. They're also available with performance tires instead of all-season treads. Every TL comes with 17-inch wheels, antilock 4-wheel disc brakes, antiskid system, plus front side airbags and head-protecting curtain side airbags. Also standard are leather upholstery with heated front seats, aluminum interior trim, sunroof, satellite radio, and an in-dash CD changer that plays DVD-Audio discs. The TL also comes with Acura's HandsFreeLink, which employs the audio system as a hands-free, wireless link to cell phones. A navigation system with voice command is optional.

RATINGS

RATINGS	Base, auto.	Base w/nav. sys., man.	Base w/nav. sys. and perf. tires, man.
ACCELERATION	7	7	7
FUEL ECONOMY	6	5	5
RIDE QUALITY	7	6	5
STEERING/HANDLING	7	7	8
QUIETNESS	8	8	7
CONTROLS/MATERIALS	9	8	8
ROOM/COMFORT (FRONT)	7	7	7
ROOM/COMFORT (REAR)	4	4	4
CARGO ROOM	3	3	3
VALUE WITHIN CLASS	10	9	9

This Acura is an impressive blend of sport and luxury, but annoying torque steer with manual transmission compromises dynamic ability and driving ease. Still, it's a solid Best Buy, offering high refinement, solid workmanship, and lots of features at hard-to-beat prices.

TOTAL	68	64	63

Average total for premium midsize cars: 61.7

ENGINES

	sohc V6
Size, liters/cu. in.	3.2/196
Horsepower @ rpm	270 @ 6200
Torque (lb-ft) @ rpm	238 @ 5000
Availability	S
EPA city/highway mpg	
6-speed manual	20/30
5-speed automatic	20/28

2005 prices unavailable at time of publication.

2004 PRICES

Acura TL	RETAIL PRICE	DEALER INVOICE
Base 4-door sedan, manual	$32650	$29755
Base 4-door sedan w/performance tires, manual	32850	29937
Base 4-door sedan w/navigation, manual	34650	31575
Base 4-door sedan w/navigation and performance tires, manual	34850	31758
Base 4-door sedan, automatic	32650	29755
Base 4-door sedan w/navigation, automatic	34650	31575
Destination charge	545	545

STANDARD EQUIPMENT

Base: 3.2-liter V6 engine, 6-speed manual or 5-speed automatic transmission w/manual-shift capability, limited-slip differential (manual), dual front airbags, front side airbags, curtain side airbags, antilock 4-wheel disc brakes, brake assist, upgraded brakes (manual), antiskid system, emergency inside trunk

 Specifications begin on page 547.

release, air conditioning w/dual-zone automatic climate controls, power steering, tilt/telescope leather-wrapped steering wheel w/radio controls, cruise control, leather upholstery, heated front bucket seats, 10-way power driver seat, 4-way power passenger seat, memory system (driver seat, mirrors), center console, cupholders, trunk pass-through, heated power mirrors w/tilt-down backup aid, power windows, power door locks, remote keyless entry, power sunroof, AM/FM/cassette/CD/DVD player, satellite radio, digital clock, hands-free cellular telephone link, automatic day/night rearview mirror, universal garage-door opener, illuminated visor mirrors, map lights, variable-intermittent wipers, rear defogger, automatic-off headlights, floormats, theft-deterrent system, fog lights, xenon headlights, sport suspension (manual), 235/45WR17 tires, alloy wheels. Options are available as dealer-installed accessories.

ACURA TSX

CLASS: Premium compact car
DRIVE WHEELS: Front-wheel drive
2004 BASE PRICE RANGE: $26,490-$28,490. Built in Japan.
ALSO CONSIDER: Audi A4, BMW 3-Series, Saab 9-3

Satellite radio is one of several new 2005 standard features for the entry-level sedan at Honda's upscale division. The TSX is a premium compact slotting between Acura's RSX coupe and TL sedan. A 200-hp 2.4-liter 4-cyl engine teams with a 6-speed manual transmission or an optional 5-speed automatic with manual shift gate. Antilock 4-wheel disc brakes, antiskid system, and 17-inch alloy wheels are standard. So are head-protecting curtain side airbags and front torso side airbags. The TSX also includes leather upholstery, sunroof, automatic climate control, tilt/telescope steering wheel, in-dash CD changer, power driver seat, and xenon headlamps. Besides satellite radio, the '05 models add a power passenger seat and heated power door mirrors. The only option is a navigation system, which is priced as a separate model and includes voice recognition for some navigation, audio, and climate functions. Also for '05, night lighting is added to the standard steering-wheel audio/cruise-control buttons.

RATINGS

	Base w/nav. sys., man.
ACCELERATION	6
FUEL ECONOMY	6

RATINGS (cont.)

	Base w/nav. sys., man.
RIDE QUALITY	6
STEERING/HANDLING	8
QUIETNESS	6
CONTROLS/MATERIALS	8
ROOM/COMFORT (FRONT)	7
ROOM/COMFORT (REAR)	4
CARGO ROOM	3
VALUE WITHIN CLASS	10

The TSX delivers the same solid quality and high features-per-dollar quotient as Acura's larger TL, but ups the fun-to-drive factor with a trimmer, lighter package. Automatic transmission may cost some scoot, but the TSX is a Best Buy premium compact sedan in every way.

TOTAL	64

Average total for premium compact cars: 57.5

ENGINES

	dohc I4
Size, liters/cu. in.	2.4/144
Horsepower @ rpm	200 @ 6800
Torque (lb-ft) @ rpm	166 @ 4500
Availability	S
EPA city/highway mpg	
6-speed manual	21/29
5-speed automatic	22/31

2005 prices unavailable at time of publication.

2004 PRICES

Acura TSX	RETAIL PRICE	DEALER INVOICE
Base 4-door sedan, manual	$26490	$24147
Base 4-door sedan, automatic	26490	24147
Base 4-door sedan w/navigation, manual	28490	25967
Base 4-door sedan w/navigation, automatic	28490	25967
Destination charge	545	545

STANDARD EQUIPMENT

Base: 2.4-liter 4-cylinder engine, 6-speed manual or 5-speed automatic transmission w/manual-shift capability, traction control, dual front airbags, front side airbags, curtain side airbags, antilock 4-wheel disc brakes, antiskid system, air conditioning w/dual-zone automatic controls, interior air filter, power steering, tilt/telescope leather-wrapped steering wheel w/radio controls, cruise control, leather upholstery, heated front bucket seats, 8-way power driver seat w/memory, center console, cupholders, split folding rear seat, power mirrors, power windows, power door locks, remote keyless entry, power sunroof, AM/FM radio w/in-dash 6-disc CD changer, digital clock, tachometer, outside-temperature indicator, automatic day/night

Specifications begin on page 547.

rearview mirror, universal garage-door opener, illuminated visor mirrors, variable-intermittent wipers, map lights, rear defogger, automatic-off headlights, floormats, theft-deterrent system, high-intensity-discharge headlights, 215/50VR17 tires, alloy wheels.

Base w/navigation adds: navigation system w/voice recognition.

Options are available as dealer-installed accessories.

AUDI A4

CLASS: Premium compact car
DRIVE WHEELS: Front-wheel drive, all-wheel drive
BASE PRICE RANGE: $25,800-$55,150. Built in Germany.
ALSO CONSIDER: Acura TSX, BMW 3-Series, Infiniti G35

Audi's best-selling line gets only minor changes for 2005. The A4 comes in sedan, Avant wagon, and Cabriolet convertible body styles. The 1.8T versions use a turbo 4-cyl engine, the 3.0 models a V6. Sedans and convertibles offer front-wheel drive or Audi's quattro all-wheel drive; all Avants have quattro. Three transmissions are available. Quattros use a 6-speed manual or a conventional 5-speed automatic. Convertibles and the front-drive V6 sedan have a continuously variable automatic transmission. This CVT is available for the front-drive 1.8T sedan in lieu of a 5-speed manual. The CVT provides variable drive ratios, plus six preset "gears" selected from the floor shift or steering-wheel buttons.

The high-performance S4 sedan, wagon, and convertible models have quattro, a V8 engine, and 6-speed manual or 6-speed automatic transmission, plus unique trim, sport suspension, and 18-inch wheels. Other A4s come with 16-inch wheels; 17s and 18s are part of Sport Package options that also include a firmer suspension. Every A4/S4 includes antilock 4-wheel disc brakes and antiskid system. Sedans and Avants add head-protecting curtain side airbags and front torso side airbags; rear torso side airbags are available. Cabriolets have front side airbags that provide head and torso protection, plus rear support bars that pop up automatically to protect occupants in a rollover. They include a power-folding top with heated glass rear window.

A navigation system is optional for V6 and S4 models. Dealer-installed satellite radio is available for all. For '05, optional OnStar assistance is dropped, and the xenon headlamps available for A4 sedans and Avants switch from high-beam to dual-beam units.

RATINGS

RATINGS	1.8T Avant w/Sport Pkg., man.	1.8T sdn, CVT	3.0 sdn w/quattro, man.	3.0 Cabriolet
ACCELERATION	6	5	7	6
FUEL ECONOMY	6	5	5	5
RIDE QUALITY	6	7	7	7
STEERING/HANDLING	7	7	7	7
QUIETNESS	6	7	7	6
CONTROLS/MATERIALS	8	8	8	8
ROOM/COMFORT (FRONT)	7	7	7	7
ROOM/COMFORT (REAR)	4	4	4	3
CARGO ROOM	7	3	3	2
VALUE WITHIN CLASS	8	9	9	7

The A4 matches or beats most any class rival for refinement, performance, features, and variety of body styles. BMW, Infiniti, Jaguar, Mercedes-Benz, and Volvo also offer AWD models, but none has an AWD convertible or counters Audi's impressive CVT.

TOTAL	65	62	64	58

Average total for premium compact cars: 57.5

ENGINES

ENGINES	Turbocharged dohc I4	dohc V6	dohc V8
Size, liters/cu. in.	1.8/109	3.0/182	4.2/255
Horsepower @ rpm	170 @ 5900	220 @ 6300	340 @ 7000
Torque (lb-ft) @ rpm	166 @ 1950	221 @ 3200	302 @ 3500
Availability	S[1]	S[2]	S[3]
EPA city/highway mpg			
5-speed manual	22/31		
6-speed manual	21/30	17/26	15/21
5-speed automatic	20/28	18/25	
6-speed automatic			18/24
CVT automatic	23/29	20/28	

1. 1.8T. 2. 3.0. 3. S4.

PRICES

Audi A4

Audi A4	RETAIL PRICE	DEALER INVOICE
A4 1.8T 4-door sedan, manual	$25800	$23823
A4 1.8T 4-door sedan, CVT	27000	24995
A4 1.8T Cabriolet 2-door convertible, CVT	35750	32958
A4 1.8T quattro 4-door sedan, manual	28150	26137
A4 1.8T quattro 4-door sedan, automatic	29350	27309
A4 1.8T Avant quattro 4-door wagon, manual	29150	27047
A4 1.8T Avant quattro 4-door wagon, automatic	30350	28219
A4 3.0 4-door sedan, CVT	31950	29500
A4 3.0 Cabriolet 2-door convertible, CVT	42300	38918
A4 3.0 quattro 4-door sedan, manual	33590	31087
A4 3.0 quattro 4-door sedan, automatic	34790	32259
A4 3.0 Avant quattro 4-door wagon, manual	34590	31997

 Specifications begin on page 547.

PRICES (cont.)

	RETAIL PRICE	DEALER INVOICE
A4 3.0 Avant quattro 4-door wagon, automatic	$35790	$33169
A4 3.0 quattro Cabriolet 2-door convertible, automatic	44250	40868
S4 quattro 4-door sedan, manual	45850	42244
S4 quattro 4-door sedan, automatic	47050	43416
S4 Avant quattro 4-door wagon, manual	46850	43154
S4 Avant quattro 4-door wagon, automatic	48050	44326
S4 quattro Cabriolet 2-door convertible, manual	53950	49615
S4 quattro Cabriolet 2-door convertible, automatic	55150	50787
Destination charge	720	720

S4 w/manual transmission adds $1700 Gas-Guzzler Tax.

STANDARD EQUIPMENT

A4 1.8T: 1.8-liter turbocharged 4-cylinder engine, 5-speed manual or continuously variable automatic transmission (CVT) w/manual-shift capability, traction control, front limited-slip differential, dual front airbags, front side airbags, curtain side airbags, antilock 4-wheel disc brakes, brake assist, antiskid system, air conditioning w/dual-zone automatic climate controls, interior air filter, power steering, tilt/telescope leather-wrapped steering wheel, cruise control, cloth upholstery, front bucket seats w/height adjustment, center console, cupholders, split folding rear seat, heated power mirrors, power windows, power door locks, remote keyless entry, AM/FM/CD player, digital clock, tachometer, rear defogger, illuminated visor mirrors, map lights, variable-intermittent wipers w/heated washer nozzles, floormats, theft-deterrent system, headlight washers, front and rear fog lights, full-size spare tire, 215/55HR16 tires, alloy wheels.

A4 1.8T Cabriolet adds: automatic roll bars, front-seat power lumbar adjustment, trunk pass-through w/ski sack, AM/FM/cassette w/in-dash 6-disc CD changer, trip computer, outside-temperature indicator, power convertible top. *Deletes:* curtain side airbags, split folding rear seat.

A4 1.8T quattro adds to A4 1.8T: all-wheel drive, 6-speed manual or 5-speed automatic transmission w/manual-shift capability, front and rear limited-slip differentials, AM/FM/cassette w/in-dash 6-disc CD changer, trip computer, outside-temperature indicator, cargo cover (wagon), rear wiper/washer (wagon), roof rails (wagon).

A4 3.0 adds to A4 1.8T: 3.0-liter V6 engine, continuously variable automatic transmission (CVT) w/manual-shift capability, vinyl/leather upholstery, 12-way power front seats w/power lumbar adjustment, wood interior trim.

A4 3.0 quattro adds: all-wheel drive, 6-speed manual or 5-speed automatic transmission w/manual-shift capability, front and rear limited-slip differentials, AM/FM/cassette w/in-dash 6-disc CD changer, trip computer, outside-temperature indicator, cargo cover (wagon), rear wiper/washer (wagon), roof rails (wagon).

S4 adds: 4.2-liter V8 engine, 6-speed manual or 6-speed automatic transmission w/manual-shift capability, automatic roll bars (Cabriolet), leather upholstery, trunk pass-through w/ski sack (Cabriolet), power convertible top (convertible), bi-xenon headlights, sport suspension, 235/40ZR18 tires.

Deletes: curtain side airbags (Cabriolet), split folding rear seat (Cabriolet).

A4 3.0 Cabriolet adds to A4 3.0: automatic roll bars, power convertible top, AM/FM/cassette w/in-dash 6-disc CD changer, trip computer, outside-temperature indicator, trunk pass-through w/ski sack. *Deletes:* curtain side airbags, split folding rear seat.

A4 3.0 quattro Cabriolet adds: all-wheel drive, 5-speed automatic transmission w/manual-shift capability, front and rear limited-slip differentials.

OPTIONAL EQUIPMENT

Major Packages	RETAIL PRICE	DEALER INVOICE
Sport Pkg., 1.8T, 1.8T quattro	$950	$865
3.0, 3.0 quattro, A4 Cabriolet	800	728
Aluminum trim (1.8T sedan/wagon, 1.8T quattro sedan/wagon), sport suspension, 235/45HR17 all-season tires or 235/45YR17 performance tires.		
Ultra Sport Pkg., sedan, wagon	3000	2730
Perforated leather-wrapped steering wheel, aerodynamics pkg. aluminum trim, sport suspension, 225/40YR18 tires. NA S4.		
Premium Pkg., 1.8T, 1.8T quattro	2000	1820
Vinyl/leather upholstery, 12-way power driver seat w/power lumbar adjustment, power sunroof, universal garage-door opener, driver information center. NA Cabriolet.		
Premium Pkg., 1.8T Cabriolet	1700	1547
Vinyl/leather upholstery, 12-way power driver seat w/power lumbar adjustment, adjustable headrests, universal garage-door opener, wind deflector.		
Premium Pkg., 3.0 Cabriolet, 3.0 quattro Cabriolet	1550	1411
3.0 sedan	2300	2139
3.0 quattro sedan/wagon	2500	2275
S4 sedan/wagon	1650	1502
S4 Cabriolet	900	819
Power sunroof (3.0 sedan, 3.0 quattro sedan/wagon, S4 sedan/wagon), automatic day/night rearview and outside mirrors, compass, power-folding outside mirrors, driver-seat and mirror memory, steering-wheel radio and climate controls (Cabriolet), universal garage-door opener, wind deflector (Cabriolet), automatic headlights, approach lights, xenon headlights (Cabriolet), bi-xenon headlights (3.0/3.0 quattro sedan, wagon).		
Enhanced Interior Pkg., S4 sedan/wagon	NC	NC
Leather/alcantara upholstery, exterior aluminum trim.		
Audio Pkg.	1000	910
Bose sound system, satellite radio (includes one-year service). NA 1.8T sedan.		
Lighting Pkg., 1.8T/1.8T quattro sedan/wagon	950	865
1.8T Cabriolet	750	683
Automatic headlights, approach lights, automatic day/night rearview mirror, compass, xenon headlights (Cabriolet), bi-xenon headlights (sedan, wagon).		
Cold Weather Pkg.	650	592
Heated front seat, ski sack. NA Cabriolet, S4.		

Safety	RETAIL PRICE	DEALER INVOICE
Rear side airbags	$350	$319
NA Cabriolet.		

Comfort & Convenience Features

Navigation system, 3.0, 3.0 quattro, 3.0 Cabriolet, 3.0 quattro cabriolet, S4	1350	1241
Leather upholstery, 3.0, 3.0 quattro, 3.0 Cabriolet, 3.0 quattro Cabriolet	1000	910
Leather upholstery w/sport seats, 3.0 Cabriolet, 3.0 quattro Cabriolet	1500	1365
Heated front seats, Cabriolet, S4	450	410
Bose sound system, 1.8T sedan, 3.0 sedan	900	819
Includes 6-disc CD changer.		
Satellite radio	350	319
Includes one-year service.		
Steering-wheel radio and climate controls, S4	150	137
Telephone provisions	306	254
Phone cradle and bracket. S4 requires Infotainment Pkg. NA Cabriolet.		
Power rear and manual side sunshades, 3.0/3.0 quattro/S4 sedan	400	364
Manual side sunshades, 3.0 quattro/S4 wagon	150	137

Appearance & Special Purpose

235/45HR17 tires, A4	500	455

AUDI A6/ALLROAD QUATTRO

CLASS: Premium midsize car
DRIVE WHEELS: Front-wheel drive, all-wheel drive
BASE PRICE RANGE: $40,250-$50,500. Built in Germany.
ALSO CONSIDER: BMW 5-Series, Lexus LS 430, Mercedes-Benz E-Class

Audi redesigns its A6 sedan for 2005, giving it new styling, more room, and more power. Wheelbase grows by 3.2 inches compared to the 1998-2004 A6, but other exterior dimensions are virtually unchanged. The ’05 sedan comes in 3.2 and 4.2 models, both with Audi’s quattro all-wheel drive and a 6-speed automatic transmission with manual-shift capability. The 3.2 has a 255-hp V6, the 4.2 a 335-hp V8. Both adopt a version of Audi's MMI operating system that uses a single console-mounted control knob and combines minor radio functions with the trip computer and navigation system.

Carried over for 2005 using the 1998-2004 design is Audi's SUV-flavored allroad wagon. The 2.7T model has a turbocharged 2.7-liter V6 and a 6-speed manual transmission or a 5-speed automatic with manual-shift capability. The 4.2 model has a 300-hp V8 and 5-speed automatic. Both come with quattro.

All A6s have front side airbags and head-protecting curtain side airbags; rear torso side airbags are optional. Also standard are antilock 4-wheel disc brakes and an antiskid system. Xenon headlamps are standard for 4.2 models, optional for 3.2 sedans and 2.7T allroads. The 3.2 sedan is available with 16-, 17-, and 18-inch wheels. The 4.2 sedan is available with 17s or 18s. Among allroads, the 2.7T has 17s and the 4.2 has 18s. Available features include a navigation system, satellite radio, and, for sedans, steering-linked adaptive headlights. This evaluation of the 2005 A6 sedan is based on preview test drives.

RATINGS	3.2 sdn w/17-in. whls., nav. sys.	4.2 sdn w/17-in. whls., nav. sys.	2.7T allroad quattro, man.
ACCELERATION	7	8	7
FUEL ECONOMY	5	5	5
RIDE QUALITY	7	7	7
STEERING/HANDLING	8	8	6
QUIETNESS	7	7	7
CONTROLS/MATERIALS	6	6	8
ROOM/COMFORT (FRONT)	8	8	8
ROOM/COMFORT (REAR)	7	7	7
CARGO ROOM	4	4	7
VALUE WITHIN CLASS	6	6	6

Though the MMI system complicates some control functions, the A6's luxurious interior detailing, capable quattro AWD, overall refinement, and cool sophistication earn it a place on any luxury-shopper's list. The older-design allroads still appeal for utility, all-weather capability, and a touch of SUV style.

TOTAL	65	66	68

Average total for premium midsize cars: 61.7

ENGINES	Turbocharged dohc V6	dohc V6	dohc V8	dohc V8
Size, liters/cu. in.	2.7/163	3.2/191	4.2/255	4.2/254
Horsepower @ rpm	250 @ 5800	255 @ 6500	300 @ 6200	335 @ 6600
Torque (lb-ft) @ rpm	258 @ 1850	243 @ 3250	295 @ 3000	309 @ 3500
Availability	S[1]	S[2]	S[3]	S[4]
EPA city/highway mpg				
6-speed manual	16/23			
5-speed automatic	16/22		16/21	
6-speed automatic		19/26		17/23

1. 2.7T allroad quattro. 2. 3.2 sedan. 3. 4.2 allroad quattro. 4. 4.2 sedan.

 Specifications begin on page 547.

PRICES

Audi A6/allroad quattro

	RETAIL PRICE	DEALER INVOICE
3.2 4-door sedan, automatic	$40900	$37847
4.2 4-door sedan, automatic	50500	46583
2.7T allroad quattro 4-door wagon, manual	40250	37255
2.7T allroad quattro 4-door wagon, automatic	40250	37255
4.2 allroad quattro 4-door wagon, automatic	47250	43625
Destination charge	720	720

STANDARD EQUIPMENT

3.2: 3.2-liter V6 engine, 6-speed automatic transmission w/manual-shift capability, all-wheel drive, front and rear limited-slip differentials, dual front airbags, front side airbags, curtain side airbags, antilock 4-wheel disc brakes, brake assist, antiskid system, emergency inside trunk release, air conditioning w/dual-zone automatic climate controls, interior air filter, power steering, tilt/telescope leather-wrapped steering wheel, cruise control, leather upholstery, 12-way power front bucket seats w/power lumbar adjustment, center console, cupholders, split folding rear seat, heated power mirrors w/passenger-side tilt-down back-up aid, power windows, power door locks, remote keyless entry, AM/FM radio w/6-disc CD changer in glovebox, digital clock, tachometer, trip computer, outside-temperature indicator, map lights, illuminated visor mirrors, rear defogger, variable-intermittent wipers w/heated washer nozzles, floormats, theft-deterrent system, front and rear fog lights, full-size spare tire, 225/55HR16 tires, alloy wheels.

4.2 sedan adds: 4.2-liter V8 335-horsepower engine, daytime running lights, power tilt/telescope steering wheel, memory system (driver seat, steering wheel, mirror), wood interior trim, automatic day/night outside and rearview mirrors, power sunroof, universal garage-door opener, compass, steering-linked adaptive bi-xenon headlights, 245/45HR17 tires.

2.7T allroad quattro adds to 3.2: 2.7-liter turbocharged V6 engine, 6-speed manual or 5-speed automatic transmission w/manual-shift capability, cloth upholstery, wood interior trim, AM/FM/cassette w/in-dash 6-disc CD changer, manual rear sunshade, cargo cover, rear wiper/washer, roof rails, height-adjustable suspension, 225/55HR17 tires. *Deletes:* brake assist, passenger-side tilt-down back-up aid, full-size spare tire.

4.2 allroad quattro adds: 4.2-liter V8 300-horsepower engine, 5-speed automatic transmission w/manual-shift capability, leather upholstery, power tilt/telescope steering wheel, memory system (driver seat, mirrors, steering wheel), universal garage-door opener, xenon headlights, 245/45WR18 tires.

OPTIONAL EQUIPMENT

Major Packages

	RETAIL PRICE	DEALER INVOICE
Premium Pkg., 3.2	$3000	$2730

Power sunroof, Bose sound system, wood interior trim, steering-linked adaptive bi-xenon headlights.

Convenience Pkg., 3.2	1000	910

Power-folding mirrors w/automatic day/night, memory system (driver seat, mirrors), automatic day/night rearview mirror, compass, universal garage-door opener, driver-information display.

OPTIONAL EQUIPMENT (cont.)

	RETAIL PRICE	DEALER INVOICE
Sport Pkg., 3.2	$1250	$1138
4.2 sedan	1500	1365
Front sport seats (4.2 sedan), sport suspension, 245/40R18 tires.		
Audio Pkg., 4.2 sedan	1300	1183
allroad	1100	1001
Satellite radio (requires monthly fee), Bose sound system.		
Premium Pkg., 2.7T allroad	3600	3276
Leather upholstery, power sunroof, driver-seat and mirror memory, steering-wheel radio controls, automatic day/night rearview and outside mirrors, compass, power-folding outside mirrors, universal garage-door opener, manual side sunshades, xenon headlights.		
Premium Pkg., 4.2 allroad	1400	1274
Power sunroof, automatic day/night rearview and outside mirrors, compass, power-folding outside mirrors.		
Warm Weather Pkg., 4.2 allroad	750	683
Solar sunroof, manual side sunshades. Requires Premium Pkg.		
Cold Weather Pkg., 4.2 sedan	1050	956
3.2	900	819
2.7T allroad	750	683
4.2 allroad	800	728
Heated front and rear seats, heated steering wheel (4.2 sedan, 4.2 allroad), ski sack, headlight washers (4.2 sedan).		
Safety		
Rear-obstacle-detection system	350	319
Tire-pressure monitor, 3.2, 4.2 sedan	250	228
allroad	390	355
Rear side airbags	350	319
Comfort & Convenience Features		
Navigation system, 3.2, 4.2 sedan	1500	1378
allroad	1350	1241
3.2 requires Convenience Pkg.		
Upgraded leather upholstery, 3.2	1000	910
Std. 4.2 sedan.		
Front sport seats, 3.2	500	445
Requires upgraded leather upholstery.		
Satellite radio, 3.2, 4.2 sedan	550	501
Requires monthly fee.		
Voice recognition, 3.2, 4.2 sedan	350	319
Remote keyless starting, 3.2, 4.2 sedan	750	683
Power rear sunshade, 3.2, 4.2 sedan	400	364
Includes manual side sunshades.		
Appearance & Special Purpose		
5-spoke alloy wheels, 2.7 allroad	950	865
4.2 allroad	NC	NC
Includes 225/55HR17 tires.		

 Specifications begin on page 547.

OPTIONAL EQUIPMENT (cont.)

	RETAIL PRICE	DEALER INVOICE
245/40HR17 tires, 3.2	$750	$683
245/40R18 tires, 3.2	1000	910
4.2 sedan	400	364

AUDI A8

CLASS: Premium large car
DRIVE WHEELS: All-wheel drive
BASE PRICE RANGE: $66,590-$69,900. Built in Germany.
ALSO CONSIDER: Lexus LS 430, Volkswagen Phaeton

Audi adds a shorter-wheelbase base model to its flagship A8 line for 2005. Priced below the A8 L, the A8 is shorter by 5.1 inches in wheelbase and in overall length, and gives up some standard equipment to the carryover L. The sole drivetrain for both models is a 330-hp 4.2-liter V8 mated to a 6-speed automatic transmission with manual shift gate and sport mode. Audi's quattro all-wheel drive is standard. Also standard is an air suspension with four driver-selectable settings: ride-oriented Comfort, self-adjusting Automatic, sporty Dynamic, and Lift for deep snow or unpaved surfaces. Front and rear side airbags, front knee airbags, and head-protecting curtain side airbags are standard. So are ABS, antiskid control, xenon headlights, and a navigation system. Among the options are heated front and rear seats and steering wheel, front-seat massagers, and 18- and 19-inch wheels (vs. standard 17s). Also available is satellite radio and adaptive cruise control designed to maintain a set distance from traffic ahead.

RATINGS	L w/18-inch wheels	L w/19-inch wheels
ACCELERATION	7	7
FUEL ECONOMY	4	4
RIDE QUALITY	8	7
STEERING/HANDLING	8	8
QUIETNESS	9	8
CONTROLS/MATERIALS	6	6
ROOM/COMFORT (FRONT)	10	10
ROOM/COMFORT (REAR)	10	10
CARGO ROOM	6	6

RATINGS (cont.)

	L w/18-inch wheels	L w/19-inch wheels
VALUE WITHIN CLASS	9	8

It centralizes too many accessory functions into a single console control. And the adjustable air suspension can't seem to deliver an optimal ride/handling balance. But overall, the A8 is a formidable rival to the BMW 7-Series and Mercedes-Benz S-Class. Audi trails those brands for prestige and resale value, but the A8 trumps its European rivals for interior decor, standard AWD, and base price. That qualifies it as a class Best Buy.

TOTAL	77	74

Average total for premium large cars: 68.7

ENGINES

	dohc V8
Size, liters/cu. in.	4.2/255
Horsepower @ rpm	330 @ 6500
Torque (lb-ft) @ rpm	317 @ 3500
Availability	S
EPA city/highway mpg	
6-speed automatic	17/24

PRICES

Audi A8	RETAIL PRICE	DEALER INVOICE
Base 4-door sedan	$66590	$62274
L 4-door sedan	69900	65352
Destination charge	720	720

STANDARD EQUIPMENT

Base: 4.2-liter V8 engine, 6-speed automatic transmission w/manual-shift capability, all-wheel drive, traction control, limited-slip front and rear differentials, dual front airbags, front and rear side airbags, curtain side airbags, front knee airbags, antilock 4-wheel disc brakes, antiskid system, tire-pressure monitor, emergency inside trunk release, daytime running lights, air conditioning w/dual-zone automatic climate controls, interior air filter, OnStar assistance system w/one-year service, power steering, power tilt/telescope leather-wrapped steering wheel w/radio controls, cruise control, leather upholstery, 16-way power front seats w/power lumbar adjustment and headrests, memory system (driver seat, mirrors, steering wheel, climate controls), center console, cupholders, wood interior trim, heated power mirrors w/automatic day/night and passenger-side tilt-down back-up aid, power windows, power door locks, remote keyless entry, power sunroof, Bose AM/FM radio, 6-disc CD changer, digital clock, tachometer, navigation system, trip computer, illuminated visor mirrors, automatic day/night rearview mirror, outside-temperature indicator, universal garage-door opener, rain-sensing variable-intermittent wipers w/heated nozzles, map lights, rear defogger, automatic headlights, floormats, theft-deterrent system, bi-xenon headlights w/washers, front and rear fog lights, adjustable air suspension, full-size spare tire, 235/55R17 tires, alloy wheels.

L adds: heated door locks, side sunshades, 5-inch-longer wheelbase.

 Specifications begin on page 547.

OPTIONAL EQUIPMENT

Major Packages

	RETAIL PRICE	DEALER INVOICE
Convenience Pkg.	$2000	$1780
Keyless starting, rear visor mirrors (L), manual side sunshades (Base), power rear sunshade, power trunk open/close.		
Cold Weather Pkg. I	1100	979
Heated front and rear seats, ski sack, heated steering wheel. NA w/wood/leather-wrapped steering wheel.		
Cold Weather Pkg. II	950	846
Heated front and rear seats, ski sack. Requires wood/leather-wrapped steering wheel.		

Safety

Front- and rear-obstacle-detection system	700	623
Dual-paned security glass	600	534

Comfort & Convenience Features

Rear air conditioning	600	534
Satellite radio	550	490
Requires monthly fee.		
Wood/leather-wrapped steering wheel	480	427
Includes wood shift knob.		
Ventilated/massaging front seats	1500	1335
Requires Cold Weather Pkg.		
Rear-seat power lumbar adjustment	350	312
Power door-close assist	450	405
Sunroof solar panel	650	579
Includes solar-powered fan.		
Adaptive cruise control	2100	1869

Appearance & Special Purpose

5-spoke alloy wheels	1150	1024
Includes 255/45HR18 tires.		
255/40YR19 tires	1900	1691

AUDI TT

CLASS: Premium sporty/performance car
DRIVE WHEELS: Front-wheel drive, all-wheel drive
BASE PRICE RANGE: $33,500-$43,150. Built in Hungary.
ALSO CONSIDER: BMW Z4, Honda S2000

These 4-seat hatchback coupes and 2-seat convertibles come in front- and all-wheel drive and with 4- and 6-cyl engines. Base TTs have front-wheel drive with traction control, a 180-hp turbocharged 4-cyl engine, and a 6-speed automatic transmission with steering-wheel buttons for manual shifting. The 225 models have Audi's quattro all-wheel drive, a 225-hp turbo four, and a 6-speed manual transmission. V6 versions have quattro, a 250-hp V6, and

Audi's Direct Shift Gearbox (DSG), essentially a clutchless manual transmission that can be set to shift like an automatic. All TTs include an antiskid system, front side airbags, and xenon headlamps. A power top with heated glass rear window is standard on 225 and V6 convertibles, optional for the base ragtop. Seventeen-inch wheels are standard; 225 and V6 models are available with 18s. Options include a navigation system.

RATINGS	Base conv	225-hp cpe	225-hp conv	V6 cpe
ACCELERATION	6	7	7	7
FUEL ECONOMY	6	6	6	5
RIDE QUALITY	4	3	3	3
STEERING/HANDLING	8	9	9	9
QUIETNESS	2	3	2	3
CONTROLS/MATERIALS	7	7	7	7
ROOM/COMFORT (FRONT)	4	4	4	4
ROOM/COMFORT (REAR)	0	1	0	1
CARGO ROOM	2	5	2	5
VALUE WITHIN CLASS	6	6	7	5

Any TT shines for solidity, interior dazzle, and road manners. Some rivals provide more power-per-dollar, but no sports car in the TT's price range offers the advantage of AWD. The DSG's compromised nature tarnishes the V6 just enough to make the 225 version the most-satisfying performance value in this line.

TOTAL	45	51	47	49

Average total for premium sporty/performance cars: 48.3

ENGINES	Turbocharged dohc I4	Turbocharged dohc I4	dohc V6
Size, liters/cu. in.	1.8/107	1.8/107	3.2/195
Horsepower @ rpm	180 @ 5500	225 @ 5900	250 @ 6300
Torque (lb-ft) @ rpm	173 @ 1950	207 @ 2200	236 @ 2800
Availability	S[1]	S[2]	S[3]
EPA city/highway mpg			
6-speed SMT			22/27
6-speed manual		20/28	
6-speed automatic	20/28[4]		

1. Base models. 2. 225-hp models. 3. V6 models. 4. Coupe, 21/29.

PRICES

Audi TT	RETAIL PRICE	DEALER INVOICE
Base 2-door hatchback	$33500	$30910
Base 2-door convertible	35500	32730
225-hp 2-door hatchback	36900	34100
225-hp 2-door convertible	39700	36648
V6 2-door hatchback	40150	37137
V6 2-door convertible	43150	39867
Destination charge	720	720

STANDARD EQUIPMENT

Base: 1.8-liter turbocharged 4-cylinder 180-horsepower engine, 6-speed automatic transmission w/manual-shift capability, traction control, limited-slip differential, dual front airbags, front side airbags, antilock 4-wheel disc brakes, antiskid system, roll bars (convertible), daytime running lights, air conditioning w/automatic climate control, interior air filter, power steering, tilt/telescope leather-wrapped steering wheel, cruise control, leather upholstery, height-adjustable front bucket seats, center console, cupholders, split folding rear seat (hatchback), aluminum interior trim, heated power mirrors, power windows, power door locks, remote keyless entry, AM/FM/CD player, digital clock, tachometer, trip computer, rear defogger, illuminated visor mirrors, map lights, variable-intermittent wipers, power-retractable windbreak (convertible), floormats, theft-deterrent system, rear spoiler, xenon headlights, headlight washers, 225/45ZR17 tires, fog lights, alloy wheels.

225 hp adds: 1.8-liter turbocharged 4-cylinder 225-horsepower engine, 6-speed manual transmission, all-wheel drive, power convertible top (convertible). *Deletes:* traction control.

V6 adds: 3.2-liter turbocharged V6 engine, 6-speed sequential-shift manual transmission (SMT).

OPTIONAL EQUIPMENT

Major Packages	RETAIL PRICE	DEALER INVOICE
Premium Pkg.	$700	$637
Heated front seats, universal garage-door opener.		
Comfort & Convenience Features		
Navigation system	1350	1241
Audio Pkg.	1200	1092
Bose premium sound system, 6-disc CD changer.		
Power convertible top, Base convertible	800	728
Baseball optic leather upholstery, convertible	1000	910
Alcantara steering wheel	300	273
Appearance & Special Purpose		
7-spoke alloy wheels, 225 hp, V6	800	728
Includes 225/40ZR18 tires.		
9-spoke alloy wheels, V6	1700	1547
Includes 225/40ZR18 tires.		

BMW 3-SERIES

CLASS: Premium compact car
DRIVE WHEELS: Rear-wheel drive, all-wheel drive
BASE PRICE RANGE: $29,300-$55,800. Built in Germany.
ALSO CONSIDER: Acura TL, Audi A4, Infiniti G35

Some previously optional features become standard for 2005 in BMW's most-popular lineup. Sedans and wagons wear an "i" suffix, coupes and convertibles a "Ci." All have an inline 6-cyl engine. The 325 models have a 2.5-liter, 330 models a 3.0, and the top-line M3 versions a high-power 3.2. The 325xi and 330xi have all-wheel drive. Other models have rear-wheel drive. The standard transmission is a 5-speed manual on 325s, a 6-speed manual on the others. A 5-speed automatic is optional on 325s and 330s. Previously optional on all models, a 6-speed sequential manual transmission is now offered only on M3s and rear-wheel-drive 330s. Essentially a clutchless manual operated via console lever or steering-wheel paddles, the sequential manual can also be set to shift like an automatic.

All 3-Series have antiskid/traction control and front torso side airbags. Rear side airbags are optional. All but convertibles have front head-protecting tubular side airbags. For 2005, the 325Ci convertible joins the 330Ci and M3 in having a standard power top with a heated glass rear window. Also for '05, sedans and coupes (except M3) get a standard sunroof, and coupes and convertibles join the M3 in getting a standard tire-pressure monitor. Bi-xenon headlights are optional for all 3-Series; on the 330Ci and 325Ci, the option includes steering-linked headlights. Run-flat tires are optional for 330s. An available Performance Package for 330s includes more power, 18-inch wheels in place of 17s, unique trim, and sport suspension and exhaust tuning. Available on all 3-Series models is BMW Assist emergency and concierge service.

RATINGS	325xi wgn, auto.	330Ci cpe, auto.	330i w/Sport Pkg., man.	330xi w/nav. sys., man.
ACCELERATION	6	7	7	7
FUEL ECONOMY	6	5	6	5
RIDE QUALITY	7	7	5	7
STEERING/HANDLING	8	8	9	8
QUIETNESS	6	6	5	6

Specifications begin on page 547.

RATINGS (cont.)

	325xi wgn, auto.	330Ci cpe, auto.	330i w/Sport Pkg., man.	330xi w/nav. sys., man.
CONTROLS/MATERIALS	7	7	7	5
ROOM/COMFORT (FRONT)	6	6	6	6
ROOM/COMFORT (REAR)	3	2	3	3
CARGO ROOM	6	2	2	2
VALUE WITHIN CLASS	7	7	8	7

A solid Recommended, the BMW 3-Series is the class choice for driving enthusiasts. Some competitors deliver more room, standard features, and even more power for less money. But none are more refined or dynamically capable overall. Resale values are strong, too.

TOTAL	62	57	58	56

Average total for premium compact cars: 57.5

ENGINES

	dohc I6	dohc I6	dohc I6
Size, liters/cu. in.	2.5/152	3.0/182	3.2/192
Horsepower @ rpm	184 @ 6000	225 @ 5900	333 @ 7900
Torque (lb-ft) @ rpm	175 @ 3500	214 @ 3500	262 @ 4900
Availability	S[1]	S[2]	S[3]
EPA city/highway mpg			
6-speed SMT		19/28	16/23
5-speed manual	20/29[4]		
6-speed manual		20/30	16/24
5-speed automatic	19/27[5]	19/27[6]	

1. 325i, 325Ci, 325xi. 2. 330i, 330Ci, 330xi; 235 hp, 222 lb-ft w/330i Perf. Pkg. 3. M3. 4. 19/27 w/AWD. 5. 19/26 w/AWD. 6. 18/25 w/AWD.

PRICES

BMW 3-Series

	RETAIL PRICE	DEALER INVOICE
325i 4-door sedan	$29300	$26825
AWD 325xi 4-door sedan	31050	28415
325i 4-door wagon	31200	28550
AWD 325xi 4-door wagon	32950	30145
325Ci 2-door coupe	31700	29005
325Ci 2-door convertible	39000	35650
330i 4-door sedan	35700	32645
AWD 330xi 4-door sedan	37450	34240
330Ci 2-door coupe	37300	34105
330Ci 2-door convertible	44600	40745
M3 2-door coupe	47300	43205
M3 2-door convertible	55800	50940
Destination charge	695	695

M3 adds $1000 Gas-Guzzler Tax. M3 convertible w/sequential transmission adds $1300 Gas-Guzzler Tax.

STANDARD EQUIPMENT

325i/325xi: 2.5-liter 6-cylinder engine, 5-speed manual transmission, traction control, dual front airbags, front side airbags, front side head-protection airbags, antiskid system, antilock 4-wheel disc brakes, brake assist, daytime running lights, air conditioning w/automatic climate control, interior air filter, power steering, tilt/telescope leather-wrapped steering wheel w/radio controls, cruise control, vinyl upholstery, front bucket seats, center console, cupholders, split folding rear seat (wagon), wood interior trim, heated power mirrors, power windows, power door locks, remote keyless entry, power sunroof, AM/FM/CD player, digital clock, tachometer, illuminated visor mirrors, map lights, cargo cover (wagon), rain-sensing variable-intermittent wipers, heated washer nozzles, rear defogger, rear wiper/washer (wagon), automatic headlights, theft-deterrent system, fog lights, roof rails (wagon), full-size spare tire (sedan), 205/55R16 tires, alloy wheels. **AWD** adds: all-wheel drive, hill descent control.

325Ci coupe adds: tire-pressure monitor, split folding rear seat, trip computer, sport suspension.

325Ci convertible adds: rollover-protection system, 10-way power front seats, passenger-side mirror tilt-down back-up aid, memory system (driver seat, mirrors), power convertible top. *Deletes:* front side head-protection airbags, split folding rear seat, power sunroof, sport suspension.

330i sedan/330xi sedan/330Ci coupe adds to 325i: 3.0-liter 225-horsepower 6-cylinder engine, 6-speed manual transmission, tire-pressure monitor (coupe), 8-way power front seats, memory system (driver seat, mirror), split folding rear seat (coupe), passenger-side mirror tilt-down back-up aid, Harman/Kardon sound system, trip computer, sport suspension, 205/50R17 tires. **AWD** adds: all-wheel drive, hill descent control.

330Ci convertible adds: rollover-protection system, tire-pressure monitor, leather upholstery, 10-way power front seats, automatic day/night rearview mirror, universal garage-door opener, power convertible top. *Deletes:* front side head-protection airbags, split folding rear seat, power sunroof, sport suspension.

M3 coupe adds to 330Ci coupe: 3.2-liter 6-cylinder engine, leather/cloth upholstery, aluminum interior trim, automatic day/night rearview mirror, outside-temperature display, heated door locks, visor mirrors, M sport suspension, 225/45ZR18 front tires, 255/40ZR18 rear tires, chrome alloy wheels. *Deletes:* 8-way power front seats, memory system (driver-seat, mirror), passenger-side mirror tilt-down back-up aid, wood interior trim, power sunroof, Harman/Kardon sound system, illuminated visor mirrors, full-size spare tire.

M3 convertible adds: rollover-protection system, leather upholstery, power front seats w/thigh-support adjustment, memory system (driver seat, mirrors), passenger-side mirror tilt-down back-up aid, power convertible top. *Deletes:* front side head-protection airbags.

OPTIONAL EQUIPMENT

Major Packages

	RETAIL PRICE	DEALER INVOICE
Premium Pkg., 325i, 325xi	$2300	$2095

8-way power front seats w/power lumbar adjustment, memory system (driver seat, mirror), BMW Assist system, passenger-side mirror tilt-down back-up aid, automatic day/night rearview mirror, trip computer.

 Specifications begin on page 547.

OPTIONAL EQUIPMENT (cont.)

	RETAIL PRICE	DEALER INVOICE
Premium Pkg., 325Ci coupe	$2000	$1820
8-way power front seats w/power lumbar adjustment, memory system (driver seat, mirror), BMW Assist system, passenger-side mirror tilt-down back-up aid, automatic day/night rearview mirror, universal garage-door opener.		
Premium Pkg., 325Ci convertible	1200	1090
Power lumbar adjustment, BMW Assist system, automatic day/night rearview mirror, universal garage-door opener.		
Premium Pkg., 330i, 330xi, 330Ci coupe	2200	2000
Leather upholstery, front-seat power lumbar adjustment, BMW Assist telematics system, automatic day/night rearview mirror. NA w/Performance Pkg.		
Premium Pkg., M3 coupe	3300	3005
Power sunroof, leather upholstery, 8-way power front seats w/memory, BMW Assist system.		
Sport Pkg., 325i	1400	1275
Sport steering wheel, 10-way power sport bucket seats w/adjustable thigh support, sport suspension, 225/45WR17 tires, special alloy wheels.		
Sport Pkg., 325xi	1100	1000
Sport steering wheel, 10-way power front sport seats w/adjustable thigh support, 205/50HR17 tires, special alloy wheels.		
Sport Pkg., 325Ci coupe	1000	910
12-way power front sport seats w/adjustable thigh support, memory system (driver seat, mirror), passenger-side mirror tilt-down back-up aid, 225/45WR17 tires, special alloy wheels.		
Sport Pkg., 325Ci convertible	1200	1090
10-way power sport bucket seats w/adjustable thigh support, sport suspension, 225/45WR17 tires, special alloy wheels. Requires leather upholstery.		
Sport Pkg., 330i, 330xi	1200	1090
Tire-pressure monitor (330xi), sport steering wheel, 8-way power front sport seats w/adjustable thigh support, memory system (driver seat, mirror), passenger-side mirror tilt-down back-up aid, aerodynamic pkg., sport suspension, 225/45ZR17 front tires and 245/40ZR17 rear tires (330i), 205/50R17 run-flat tires (330xi). NA w/Performance Pkg.		
Sport Pkg., 330Ci coupe	600	541
330Ci convertible	800	730
8-way power front sport seats w/adjustable thigh support, sport suspension (330Ci convertible), 225/45ZR17 front tires, 245/40ZR17 rear tires, special alloy wheels.		
Performance Pkg., 330i, 330Ci coupe	3900	3550
330Ci convertible	3600	3275
3.0-liter 235-horsepower 6-cylinder engine, leather/cloth upholstery (330i, 330Ci coupe), sport seats and steering wheel, aluminum interior trim, aerodynamics pkg., rear spoiler, unique exterior trim, M sport suspension, 225/40ZR18 front tires, 255/35ZR18 rear tires, special alloy wheels. NA w/6-speed sequential manual transmission.		

OPTIONAL EQUIPMENT (cont.)

	RETAIL PRICE	DEALER INVOICE
Club Sport Pkg., M3 coupe	$4000	NA
Direct steering ratio, cross-drilled compound brakes, alcantara steering wheel and handbrake, modified suspension 19-inch alloy wheels. Deletes cruise control.		
Cold Weather Pkg., 325i/325xi sedan, 330i, 330xi	1000	910
325i/325xi wagon, 325Ci, 330Ci, M3	750	685
Heated front seats, split folding rear seat w/armrest (sedan), ski sack, headlight washers.		
Powertrain		
5-speed automatic transmission w/manual-shift capability	1275	1210
NA M3.		
6-speed sequential manual transmission, 330	1500	1425
M3	2400	2185
M3 requires rear-obstacle-detection system. 330 requires Sport Pkg. NA AWD.		
Safety		
Rear side airbags	385	350
Rear-obstacle-detection system	350	320
Comfort & Convenience Features		
Navigation system	1800	1640
325i/325xi require Premium Pkg. or trip computer.		
BMW Assist system	750	685
Leather upholstery, 325, 330	1450	1320
M3 coupe	1100	1000
Std. 330Ci convertible, M3 convertible.		
Alcantara interior trim, M3 coupe	1000	910
Power front seats, 325i, 325xi, 325Ci, M3 coupe	995	905
Includes driver-seat memory. 325 includes mirror memory, passenger-side mirror tilt-down back-up aid.		
4-way lumbar support, M3 coupe	500	455
M3 convertible	400	365
Coupe includes adjustable seatback width. Coupe requires Premium Pkg. or power front seats.		
Heated front seats	500	455
Split folding rear seat w/ski sack, 325i/325xi sedan, 330i/330xi sedan	475	430
Harman/Kardon sound system, 325, M3	675	615
Trip computer, 325i, 325xi	300	275
Power sunroof, M3 coupe	1050	955
Power rear sunshade, sedan, coupe	400	365
Appearance & Special Purpose		
Removable hardtop, 325Ci/330Ci/M3 convertibles	2295	2090
Bi-xenon headlights, sedan, wagon, M3	700	635

OPTIONAL EQUIPMENT (cont.)

	RETAIL PRICE	DEALER INVOICE
Steering-linked adaptive bi-xenon headlights, 325/330 coupe/conv	$800	$730
Double-spoke alloy wheels, M3	1750	1595
Includes 225/40ZR19 front tires, 255/35ZR19 rear tires.		
Double-spoke alloy wheels, 330Ci	1000	910
Includes 225/40ZR18 front tires, 255/35ZR18 rear tires. Requires Sport Pkg.		
205/50R17 run-flat tires, 330	300	275
Includes tire-pressure monitor. Replaces full-size spare tire w/compact spare tire. NA w/Performance Pkg.		

BMW 5-SERIES

CLASS: Premium midsize car
DRIVE WHEELS: Rear-wheel drive
BASE PRICE RANGE: $41,300-$55,800. Built in Germany.
ALSO CONSIDER: Acura TL, Lexus LS 430, Mercedes-Benz E-Class

Minor equipment shuffling marks 2005 for BMW's 5-Series sedans. Three models are offered. The 525i has a 184-hp 2.5-liter inline 6-cyl engine, the 530i a 225-hp 3.0 inline 6. The 545i has a 325-hp 4.4-liter V8. For '05, the 545i joins the other two models in offering a standard 6-speed manual transmission. A 6-speed automatic is optional on all. Optional on the 530i and 545i is a 6-speed sequential manual transmission. SMT is essentially a clutchless manual operated via console lever or steering-wheel paddles; it can also be set to shift like an automatic.

Standard on all models are ABS, antiskid/traction control, front side airbags, and front and rear head-protecting tubular side airbags. Rear torso side airbags are optional. Also standard are BMW Assist emergency and concierge service and a tire-pressure monitor. All models have BMW's iDrive, which uses a console "joystick" knob to control entertainment, navigation, communication, and climate functions. The 525i has 16-inch wheels, the others 17s. Optional are a sport suspension teamed with run-flat tires, BMW's Active Roll Stabilization designed to counteract body lean, and BMW's Active Steering that electronically varies steering ratio and assist. Other options include head-up instrument display, satellite radio, and adaptive cruise control designed to maintain a set following distance. Also available are a navigation system, front and rear park assist, heated front and rear seats, and xenon headlights.

RATINGS	525i, auto.	530i, auto.	530i w/Sport Pkg., man.	545i w/Sport Pkg., auto.
ACCELERATION	6	6	6	8
FUEL ECONOMY	5	5	5	4
RIDE QUALITY	8	8	7	7
STEERING/HANDLING	8	8	9	9
QUIETNESS	8	8	7	7
CONTROLS/MATERIALS	4	4	4	4
ROOM/COMFORT (FRONT)	8	8	8	8
ROOM/COMFORT (REAR)	7	7	7	7
CARGO ROOM	3	3	3	3
VALUE WITHIN CLASS	6	6	6	6

The 5-Series bristles with technology, but not all of it is beneficial. Active Roll Stabilization is truly useful and helps BMW maintain the 5-Series' world-class handling without compromising its admirable ride quality. But Active Steering can be a love-hate affair, and iDrive can be downright confounding. Furthermore, 6-cyl models feel underpowered for this class, and no 5-Series is bargain priced.

TOTAL	63	63	62	63

Average total for premium midsize cars: 61.7

ENGINES

	dohc I6	dohc I6	dohc V8
Size, liters/cu. in.	2.5/152	3.0/182	4.4/268
Horsepower @ rpm	184 @ 6000	225 @ 5900	325 @ 6100
Torque (lb-ft) @ rpm	175 @ 3500	214 @ 3500	330 @ 3600
Availability	S[1]	S[2]	S[3]
EPA city/highway mpg			
6-speed SMT		19/28	17/24
6-speed manual	19/28	20/30	17/25
5-speed automatic			18/26
6-speed automatic	19/28	18/28	

1. 525i. 2. 530i. 3. 545i.

PRICES

BMW 5-Series	RETAIL PRICE	DEALER INVOICE
525i 4-door sedan, manual	$41300	$37745
530i 4-door sedan, manual	45400	41475
545i 4-door sedan, automatic	55800	50940
Destination charge	695	695

STANDARD EQUIPMENT

525i: 2.5-liter 6-cylinder engine, 6-speed manual transmission, traction control, dual front airbags, front side airbags, side head-protection airbags, antilock 4-wheel disc brakes, brake assist, antiskid system, tire-pressure

 Specifications begin on page 547.

monitor, daytime running lights, power steering, power tilt/telescope leather-wrapped steering wheel w/radio controls, cruise control, air conditioning w/dual-zone automatic climate controls, interior air filter, BMW Assist system, vinyl upholstery, 10-way power front seats, power front headrests, center console, cupholders, memory system (driver seat, steering wheel, mirrors), wood interior trim, heated power mirrors w/passenger-side tilt-down back-up aid, power windows, power door locks, remote keyless entry, power sunroof, AM/FM/CD player, digital clock, tachometer, outside-temperature display, trip computer, map lights, heated door lock, rain-sensing variable-intermittent wipers, rear defogger, illuminated visor mirrors, automatic headlights, theft-deterrent system, fog lights, 225/55VR16 tires, alloy wheels.

530i adds: 3.0-liter 6-cylinder engine, front-seat power lumbar adjustment, 225/50VR17 tires.

545i adds: 4.4-liter V8 engine, front- and rear-obstacle-detection system, leather upholstery, universal garage-door opener, steering-linked adaptive bi-xenon headlights.

OPTIONAL EQUIPMENT

Major Packages	RETAIL PRICE	DEALER INVOICE
Premium Pkg., 525	$2000	$1820
530	1800	1640
Leather upholstery, front-seat power lumbar adjustment (525), automatic day/night rearview and outside mirrors, universal garage-door opener, additional interior lights.		
Sport Pkg., 530, 545	3300	3005
525	3000	2730
Sport seats, satin chrome Shadowline exterior trim, active steering, Active Roll Stabilization, sport suspension, unique alloy wheels, 225/50R17 run-flat tires (525), 245/40WR18 run-flat tires (530, 545). 525, 530 require leather upholstery or Premium Pkg.		
Premium Sound Pkg	1800	1640
Upgraded sound system, AM/FM radio w/in-dash 6-disc CD changer.		
Cold Weather Pkg.	750	685
Heated front seats and steering wheel, heated headlight washers.		
Powertrain		
6-speed automatic transmission w/manual-shift capability, 525, 530	1275	1210
545	NC	NC
6-speed sequential-shift manual transmission (SMT), 530	1500	1425
545	NC	NC
Requires Sport Pkg.		
Safety		
Rear side airbags	385	350
Front- and rear-obstacle-detection system, 525, 530	700	635
Navigation system	1800	1640
Active steering	1250	1140

Comfort & Convenience Features	RETAIL PRICE	DEALER INVOICE
Active cruise control	$2200	$2000
Leather upholstery, 525, 530	1450	1320
525/530 w/ventilated seats	1850	1685
Upgraded leather upholstery, 545	1850	1685
Requires ventilated front seats		
Comfort 20-way power front seats, 530, 545	1200	1090
Includes active headrests, passenger-seat memory. 525, 530 require Premium Pkg. or leather upholstery.		
Split folding rear seat	475	430
Includes ski sack.		
Ventilated front seats	1025	935
Includes heated front seats. 525, 530 requires Premium Pkg. or leather upholstery.		
Heated rear seat	350	320
Requires Cold Weather Pkg. 525, 530 require leather upholstery or Premium Pkg.		
Satellite radio	595	540
NA w/navigation system.		
Head-up instrument display	1000	910
Requires navigation system.		
Power rear and manual rear-door sunshades	575	525
Appearance & Special Purpose		
Steering-linked adaptive bi-xenon headlights, 525, 530	800	730

BMW 6-SERIES

CLASS: Premium sporty/performance car
DRIVE WHEELS: Rear-wheel drive
BASE PRICE RANGE: $69,900-$76,900. Built in Germany.
ALSO CONSIDER: Cadillac XLR, Lexus SC 430, Mercedes-Benz CLK

A longer list of standard features marks 2005 for BMW's 4-seat coupe and convertible. Both 6-Series versions use a 325-hp V8 with a choice of three 6-speed transmissions: an automatic, a conventional manual, and BMW's sequential manual. The SMT is a clutchless manual operated via console lever or steering-wheel paddles; it can be set to shift like an automatic. ABS and antiskid/traction control are standard, as is BMW's Active Roll Stabilization to counteract body lean. Also standard is BMW's Dynamic Drive

 Specifications begin on page 547.

Control that firms suspension, quickens throttle response, and adjusts shift points on the automatic transmission and SMT. BMW's Active Steering option varies steering ratio and assist. Front torso side airbags and front knee airbags are standard; the coupe adds front head-protecting tubular side airbags. The convertible has a power soft top. Its heated glass rear window lowers for roof-up ventilation or raises to deflect top-down cabin drafts. Standard equipment includes leather and metal interior trim; navigation system; steering-linked headlights; and BMW's iDrive that uses a console "joystick" to adjust major climate, audio, and navigation functions. Newly standard is front and rear-obstacle detection. Optional is adaptive cruise control designed to maintain a set distance from traffic ahead. Other options include 19-inch wheels vs. standard 18s, and a head-up instrument display.

RATINGS	Coupe w/Sport Pkg., man.	Coupe w/Sport Pkg., SMT	Conv, man.	Conv, auto.
ACCELERATION	8	8	8	8
FUEL ECONOMY	4	4	4	4
RIDE QUALITY	5	5	6	6
STEERING/HANDLING	8	8	8	8
QUIETNESS	7	7	6	6
CONTROLS/MATERIALS	4	4	4	4
ROOM/COMFORT (FRONT)	8	8	8	8
ROOM/COMFORT (REAR)	2	2	2	2
CARGO ROOM	3	3	2	2
VALUE WITHIN CLASS	4	4	4	4

The 6-Series suffers all the typical coupe/convertible compromises, along with daunting prices and a firmer-than-necessary ride. That said, any version is a joy to drive: surprisingly fast, supremely capable, and very sophisticated.

TOTAL	53	53	52	52

Average total for premium sporty/performance cars: 48.3

ENGINES

	dohc V8
Size, liters/cu. in.	4.4/268
Horsepower @ rpm	325 @ 6100
Torque (lb-ft) @ rpm	330 @ 3600
Availability	S
EPA city/highway mpg	
6-speed SMT	17/24
6-speed manual	17/25
6-speed automatic	18/26

PRICES

BMW 6-Series	RETAIL PRICE	DEALER INVOICE
645Ci 2-door coupe	$69900	$63770
645Ci 2-door convertible	76900	70140
Destination charge	695	695

645Ci convertible w/6-speed sequential manual or transmission or standard 6-speed manual transmission adds $1300 Gas-Guzzler Tax.

STANDARD EQUIPMENT

645Ci: 4.4-liter V8 engine, 6-speed manual transmission, traction control, dual front airbags, front side airbags, front side head-protection airbags (coupe), rollover-protection system (convertible), front knee airbags, antilock 4-wheel disc brakes, brake assist, antiskid system, Active Roll Stabilization, front- and rear-obstacle-detection system, tire-pressure monitor, air conditioning w/dual-zone automatic climate controls, interior air filter, power steering, power tilt/telescope leather-wrapped steering wheel w/radio controls, cruise control, leather upholstery, 8-way power front seats w/lumbar adjustment, center console, cupholders, memory system (driver seat, mirrors, steering wheel), heated and automatic day/night power mirrors w/passenger-side tilt-down back-up aid, power windows, power door locks, remote keyless entry, power sunroof (coupe), retractable rear window (convertible), navigation system, AM/FM/CD player, tachometer, outside-temperature indicator, automatic day/night rearview mirror, universal garage-door opener, illuminated visor mirrors, rain-sensing variable-intermittent wipers, heated door lock, rear defogger, power convertible top, automatic headlights, floormats, theft-deterrent system, fog lights, steering-linked adaptive bi-xenon headlights w/washers, adjustable suspension, 245/45R18 run-flat tires, alloy wheels.

OPTIONAL EQUIPMENT

Major Packages	RETAIL PRICE	DEALER INVOICE
Sport Pkg.	$2800	$2550
Active steering, front sport seats w/thigh adjustment, 245/40WR19 front and 275/35WR19 rear run-flat tires, unique alloy wheels.		
Premium Sound Pkg.	1800	1640
Upgraded sound system, 6-disc CD changer.		
Cold Weather Pkg.	750	685
Heated front seats and steering wheel, ski sack.		
Powertrain		
6-speed sequential manual transmission	NC	NC
Requires Sport Pkg.		
6-speed automatic transmission w/manual-shift capability	NC	NC
Comfort & Convenience Features		
Adaptive cruise control	2200	2000
Active steering	1250	1140
Heated front seats	500	455
Satellite radio	595	540
Head-up instrument display	1000	910

2004 BMW 7-SERIES

CLASS: Premium large car
DRIVE WHEELS: Rear-wheel drive
BASE PRICE RANGE: $69,300-$117,200. Built in Germany.
ALSO CONSIDER: Audi A8 L, Lexus LS 430, Mercedes-Benz S-Class

Satellite radio is newly optional for 2004 in BMW's flagship sedans. The 7-Series models are called 745i, 745Li, and 760Li. The Li suffix denotes a 5.5-inch-longer wheelbase and body. The 745 models have a V8 engine, the 760Li a V12. All use a 6-speed automatic transmission with manual-shift control via steering-wheel buttons. Standard features include ABS, antiskid/traction control, and BMW's Active Roll Stabilization designed to counteract body lean. Standard on 760Li and optional on other 7s is an Adaptive Ride Package with automatically adjusting shock absorbers and rear self-leveling suspension. V8s come with 18-inch wheels, the 760Li and V8 Sport Package with 19s.

Front knee airbags, front torso side airbags, and front and rear head-protecting tubular side airbags are standard. Rear torso side airbags are optional. All 7s have BMW's iDrive, which controls the audio, navigation, phone, and climate functions via a console "joystick" knob and displays the settings on a dashboard screen. Conventional switches are also provided for basic audio and climate adjustments. BMW Assist emergency and concierge service is standard. Features standard on the 760Li and optional on other 7s include front- and rear-obstacle detection and ventilated front and rear seats.

RATINGS	745i	745i w/19-inch wheels	760Li
ACCELERATION	7	7	8
FUEL ECONOMY	4	4	2
RIDE QUALITY	9	8	8
STEERING/HANDLING	8	9	8
QUIETNESS	9	8	9
CONTROLS/MATERIALS	3	3	3
ROOM/COMFORT (FRONT)	10	10	10
ROOM/COMFORT (REAR)	9	9	10
CARGO ROOM	6	6	6
VALUE WITHIN CLASS	6	6	4

Smooth, powerful, athletic, the 7-Series has precious few dynamic flaws. Spacious and exceedingly comfortable, it's first-class travel by any standard. How well you adapt to iDrive and the other new-think controls depends on how comfortable you are with cutting-edge technology. We prefer simpler, time-proven systems.

TOTAL	71	70	68

Average total for premium large cars: 68.7

ENGINES

	dohc V8	dohc V12
Size, liters/cu. in.	4.4/268	6.0/366
Horsepower @ rpm	325 @ 6100	438 @ 6000
Torque (lb-ft) @ rpm	330 @ 3600	444 @ 3950
Availability	S[1]	S[2]
EPA city/highway mpg		
6-speed automatic	18/26	15/23

1. 745i, 745Li. 2. 760Li.

PRICES

BMW 7-Series	RETAIL PRICE	DEALER INVOICE
745i 4-door sedan	$69300	$63225
745Li 4-door sedan	73300	66685
760Li 4-door sedan	117200	106810
Destination charge	695	695

760Li adds $1300 Gas-Guzzler Tax

STANDARD EQUIPMENT

745: 4.4-liter V8 engine, 6-speed automatic transmission w/manual-shift capability, traction control, dual front airbags, front side airbags, front and rear side head-protection airbags, front knee airbags, front-seat active head restraints (745Li), antilock 4-wheel disc brakes, brake assist, antiskid system, Active Roll Stabilization, daytime running lights, emergency inside trunk release, power steering, power tilt/telescope leather-wrapped steering wheel w/radio controls, cruise control, air conditioning w/front and rear dual-zone automatic climate controls, interior air filter, navigation system, cellular telephone, BMW Assist system, memory system (steering wheel, driver seat, mirrors), leather upholstery, front bucket seats w/power headrests and lumbar adjustment, 12-way power driver seat (745i), 10-way power passenger seat (745i), 16-way power front comfort seats (745Li), center console, cupholders, wood interior trim, heated power mirrors w/automatic day/night and passenger-side tilt-down back-up aid, power windows, power door locks, remote keyless entry, power sunroof, rain-sensing variable-intermittent wipers w/deicer and heated washer jets, automatic day/night rearview mirror, map lights, illuminated visor mirrors, universal garage-door opener, AM/FM/CD player, digital clock, tachometer, trip computer, rear defogger, remote decklid release, automatic headlights, floormats, theft-deterrent system, xenon headlights, headlight washers, fog lights, 245/50VR18 tires, alloy wheels.

760 adds to 745: 6.0-liter V12 engine, front-seat active head restraints, front- and rear-obstacle-detection system, heated front and rear seats, 16-way power ventilated and massaging front seats, 10-way power-ventilated rear seats, trunk pass-through w/ski sack, power-closing doors and decklid, AM/FM radio w/in-dash 6-disc CD changer, upgraded sound system, power rear sunshade, rear side sunshades, electronic shock-absorber control, self-leveling rear suspension, 245/45YR19 front tires, 275/40YR19 rear tires.

Specifications begin on page 547.

OPTIONAL EQUIPMENT

Major Packages	RETAIL PRICE	DEALER INVOICE
Sport Pkg., 745i, 745Li	$3200	$2190
Sport seats and steering wheel, Shadowline exterior trim, color-keyed roof-rail trim (745Li), sport suspension, 245/45YR19 front and 275/40YR19 rear performance tires, unique alloy wheels.		
Luxury Seating Pkg., 745i	2350	2140
745Li	1450	1320
Heated front and rear seats, 16-way front ventilated and massaging comfort seats w/multiple backrest adjustments, front-seat active head restraints (745i). NA w/Cold Weather Pkg.		
Adaptive Ride Pkg., 745i, 745Li	1900	1730
Electronic shock-absorber control, self-leveling rear suspension.		
Convenience Pkg., 745i, 745Li	1000	910
Automatic soft-close doors, power trunk opening and closing.		
Cold Weather Pkg., 745i, 745Li	1100	1000
Heated front and rear seats, heated steering wheel, ski bag.		
Premium Sound Pkg., 745i, 745Li	1800	1640
In-dash 6-disc CD changer, upgraded sound system.		
Safety		
Rear side airbags	385	350
Front- and rear-obstacle-detection system, 745i, 745Li	700	635
Comfort & Convenience Features		
Active cruise control	2200	2000
Dual-zone rear air conditioning, 760	1800	1640
Front Comfort Seats, 745i	1400	1275
16-way ventilated comfort front seats w/multiple backrest adjustments, front passenger-seat memory, active head restraints.		
Ventilated comfort rear seats, 745Li	3500	3185
Satellite radio	595	540
Power rear sunshade, 745i, 745Li	750	685
Includes side window sunshades.		
Appearance & Special Purpose		
Steering-linked adaptive headlights	300	275
Star-spoke alloy wheels, 745i, 745Li	1300	1185
Includes 245/45YR19 front tires, 275/40YR19 rear tires.		
245/50VR18 run-flat tires	NC	NC

2004 BMW X3

CLASS: Compact sport-utility vehicle
DRIVE WHEELS: All-wheel drive
BASE PRICE RANGE: $30,300-$36,300. Built in Austria.
ALSO CONSIDER: Acura MDX, Cadillac SRX, Infiniti FX

BMW

BMW's new all-wheel-drive wagon is sportier but slightly smaller than most luxury SUVs. X3 slots below BMW's larger, costlier X5 SUV, but it has virtually the same passenger space, more cargo volume, and is some 600 lb lighter. It takes its inline 6-cyl powertrains from BMW's 3-Series cars. The X3 2.5i has a 184-hp 2.5-liter, the X3 3.0i a 225-hp 3.0. Both team with a 6-speed manual transmission or optional 5-speed automatic with manual shift gate. The X3 seats five and has a liftgate without separate-opening glass. Despite 8 inches of ground clearance, X3 is intended for only light-duty off-road work. It shares with X5 BMW's new xDrive AWD, designed in large part to enhance on-road handling. xDrive lacks low-range gearing, but hill descent control automatically limits steep downhill speeds to a crawl. ABS and antiskid/traction control are standard. So are front side airbags and head-protecting tubular side airbags; rear torso side airbags are optional. X3 comes with 17-inch wheels. A Sport Package option includes firmer suspension, 18-inch wheels with all-season tires, and sport front seats. Optional on the 3.0 are 18-inch wheels with summer performance treads. Leather upholstery is optional, as are dual sunroofs with sliding front panel and glass rear skylight. Other options include a navigation system, xenon headlamps, and front- and rear-obstacle detection.

RATINGS	2.5i w/Prem. Pkg., auto.	3.0i w/Prem. Pkg., auto.	3.0i w/Prem., Sport pkgs., nav. sys., man.	3.0i w/Prem., Sport pkgs., auto.
ACCELERATION	5	6	7	6
FUEL ECONOMY	5	4	4	4
RIDE QUALITY	5	5	3	3
STEERING/HANDLING	6	6	7	7
QUIETNESS	6	6	5	5
CONTROLS/MATERIALS	6	6	5	6
ROOM/COMFORT (FRONT)	7	7	7	7
ROOM/COMFORT (REAR)	5	5	5	5
CARGO ROOM	7	7	7	7
VALUE WITHIN CLASS	5	5	5	5

Base prices nudge X3 into luxury-SUV territory. Adding desirable options anchors it there: A 2.5i with automatic transmission and Premium Package lists for about $35,500, a loaded 3.0i approaches $48,000. Like BMW's 3-Series cars, the X3 gives up outright size to most like-priced competitors but delivers premium performance.

TOTAL	57	57	55	55

Average total for compact sport-utility vehicles: 49.0

ENGINES

	dohc I6	dohc I6
Size, liters/cu. in.	2.5/152	3.0/182
Horsepower @ rpm	184 @ 6000	225 @ 5900
Torque (lb-ft) @ rpm	175 @ 3500	214 @ 3500
Availability	S[1]	S[2]
EPA city/highway mpg		
6-speed manual	18/25	17/25
5-speed automatic	18/24	16/23

1. 2.5i. 2. 3.0i.

PRICES

BMW X3	RETAIL PRICE	DEALER INVOICE
2.5i 4-door wagon	$30300	$27735
3.0i 4-door wagon	36300	33195
Destination charge	695	695

STANDARD EQUIPMENT

2.5i: 2.5-liter 6-cylinder engine, 6-speed manual transmission, all-wheel drive, traction control, dual front airbags, front side airbags, side head-protection airbags, antilock 4-wheel disc brakes, brake assist, antiskid system, hill descent control, tire-pressure monitor, daytime running lights, air conditioning, power steering, tilt/telescope leather-wrapped steering wheel w/radio controls, vinyl upholstery, height-adjustable front bucket seats, cupholders, split folding rear seat, heated power mirrors, power windows, power door locks, remote keyless entry, AM/FM/CD player, tachometer, intermittent wipers, map lights, cargo cover, rear defogger, rear wiper/washer, theft-deterrent system, roof rails, rear spoiler, 235/55HR17 tires, alloy wheels.

3.0i adds: 3.0-liter 6-cylinder engine, automatic climate control, interior air filter, cruise control, 8-way power front seats, trip computer, rain-sensing wipers, illuminated visor mirrors, automatic headlights, fog lights.

OPTIONAL EQUIPMENT

Major Packages	RETAIL PRICE	DEALER INVOICE
Premium Pkg., 2.5i	$3800	$3460

Automatic climate control, interior air filter, BMW Assist telematics system, power Panorama sunroof, cruise control, 8-way power front seats, memory system, (driver seat, mirrors), automatic day/night rearview mirror, trip computer, wood interior trim, rain-sensing wipers, cargo nets, automatic headlights, fog lights.

Premium Pkg., 3.0i	3300	3005

Leather upholstery, front-seat lumbar adjustment, power Panorama sunroof, BMW Assist telematics system, wood interior trim, automatic day/night rearview mirror.

Sport Pkg.	1500	1365

Sport steering wheel, sport seats w/thigh-support adjustment, Shadowline exterior trim, sport suspension, 235/50HR18 tires, unique alloy wheels.

OPTIONAL EQUIPMENT (cont.)

	RETAIL PRICE	DEALER INVOICE
Lighting Pkg., 2.5i	$1100	$1000
Automatic xenon headlights, fog lights, rain-sensing wipers.		
Cold Weather Pkg.	750	685
Heated front seats, ski sack, headlight washers.		
Powertrain		
5-speed automatic transmission w/manual-shift capability	1275	1210
Safety		
Rear side airbags	385	350
Front- and rear-obstacle-detection system	700	635
Comfort & Convenience Features		
Power Panorama sunroof	1350	1230
Leather upholstery	1450	1320
8-way power front seats, 2.5i	995	905
Includes driver-seat and mirror memory.		
Heated steering wheel	150	135
2.5i requires Premium Pkg. or cruise control.		
Upgraded variable-assist power steering	250	230
Navigation system	1800	1640
2.5i requires Premium Pkg. or trip computer.		
BMW Assist telematics system	750	685
2.5i requires cruise control.		
Trip computer, 2.5i	300	275
Cruise control, 2.5i	475	430
Power-folding mirrors	250	230
Aluminum interior trim	NC	NC
Requires Premium Pkg.		
Upgraded sound system	675	615
Appearance & Special Purpose		
Fog lights, 2.5i	260	235
Rear privacy glass	350	320
235/50VR18 front tires and 255/45VR18 rear tires, 3.0i	500	455
Requires Sport Pkg.		

BMW X5

CLASS: Premium midsize sport-utility vehicle
DRIVE WHEELS: All-wheel drive
BASE PRICE RANGE: $41,700-$70,100. Built in USA.
ALSO CONSIDER: Acura MDX, Cadillac SRX, Lexus RX 330

Some optional features become standard for 2005 on BMW's American-built SUV. X5 comes in three models: the 3.0i with a 225-hp 6-cyl, the 4.4i with a 315-hp V8, and the 4.8is with a 355-hp V8. X5s have all-wheel drive without

 Specifications begin on page 547.

low-range gearing, plus ABS, antiskid/traction control, front torso side airbags, and front and rear head-protecting tubular side airbags. Rear torso side airbags are optional. The 3.0i comes with a 6-speed manual transmission or optional 5-speed automatic. V8s come with a 6-speed automatic. Automatics have a manual shift gate. The 3.0i comes with 17-inch wheels; 18s are available in its optional Sport Package. The 4.4i has standard 18s, with 19s available in tandem with its Sport Package. Both Sport Packages include firmer suspension tuning. The 4.8is comes with the Sport Package suspension and 20-inch wheels. Standard on V8s and optional on the 3.0i are automatic-leveling rear suspension and leather upholstery. Newly standard for 3.0i is automatic climate control. Newly standard for 4.4i is front- and rear-obstacle detection, which is optional on 3.0i. Xenon headlights standard on V8s and optional on the 3.0i are now steering linked. Other available features include adjustable ride-height suspension, heated rear seats, navigation system, and BMW Assist emergency and concierge system.

RATINGS	3.0i, auto.	4.4i	4.4i w/19-inch wheels, nav. sys.
ACCELERATION	5	7	7
FUEL ECONOMY	3	3	3
RIDE QUALITY	6	5	4
STEERING/HANDLING	6	7	7
QUIETNESS	6	5	4
CONTROLS/MATERIALS	7	7	5
ROOM/COMFORT (FRONT)	8	8	8
ROOM/COMFORT (REAR)	5	5	5
CARGO ROOM	7	7	7
VALUE WITHIN CLASS	4	5	3

Along with the Cadillac SRX, Infiniti FX, and more-expensive Porsche Cayenne, X5 is the premium midsize SUV of choice for sporty on-road driving. Absence of 3rd-row seating, modest rear-passenger room, and limited cargo volume make it, in effect, a high-riding compact-size AWD wagon, albeit one with BMW spirit. Prices are steep, but are partly offset by strong resale values.

TOTAL	57	59	53

Average total for premium midsize sport-utility vehicles: 59.6

ENGINES

	dohc I6	dohc V8	dohc V8
Size, liters/cu. in.	3.0/182	4.4/268	4.8/293
Horsepower @ rpm	225 @ 5900	315 @ 5400	355 @ 6200
Torque (lb-ft) @ rpm	214 @ 3500	324 @ 3600	360 @ 3400
Availability	S[1]	S[2]	S[3]
EPA city/highway mpg			
6-speed manual	15/21		
5-speed automatic	16/21		
6-speed automatic		16/22	16/21

1. 3.0i. 2. 4.4i. 3. 4.8is.

PRICES

BMW X5	RETAIL PRICE	DEALER INVOICE
3.0i 4-door wagon	$41700	$38105
4.4i 4-door wagon	52800	48210
4.8is 4-door wagon	70100	63950
Destination charge	695	695

STANDARD EQUIPMENT

3.0i: 3.0-liter 6-cylinder engine, 6-speed manual transmission, all-wheel drive, traction control, dual front airbags, front side airbags, side head-protection airbags, antilock 4-wheel disc brakes, brake assist, antiskid system, hill descent control, air conditioning w/dual-zone automatic climate controls, interior air filter, power steering, power tilt/telescope leather-wrapped steering wheel w/radio controls, cruise control, vinyl upholstery, 12-way power front bucket seats w/lumbar adjustment, memory system (driver seat, mirrors, steering wheel), center console, cupholders, split folding rear seat, wood interior trim, heated power mirrors w/passenger-side tilt-down back-up aid, power windows, power door locks, remote keyless entry, AM/FM/CD player, digital clock, map lights, rain-sensing variable-intermittent wipers w/heated washers, trip computer, outside-temperature indicator, illuminated visor mirrors, universal garage-door opener, rear defogger, intermittent rear wiper/washer, cargo cover, automatic headlights, theft-deterrent system, fog lights, roof rails, full-size spare, 235/65HR17 tires, alloy wheels.

4.4i adds: 4.4-liter V8 engine, 6-speed automatic transmission w/manual-shift capability, front- and rear-obstacle-detection system, rear climate controls, leather upholstery, steering-linked adaptive bi-xenon headlights w/washers, rear automatic-leveling suspension, 255/55HR18 tires.

4.8is adds: 4.8-liter V8 engine, heated front and rear seats, BMW Assist system, power sunroof, tilt-down back-up-aid passenger-side mirror, automatic day/night rearview mirror, compass, side sunshades, rear privacy glass, sport suspension w/adjustable ride height, 275/40R20 front tires, 315/35R20 rear tires. *Deletes:* full-size spare tire.

OPTIONAL EQUIPMENT

Major Packages	RETAIL PRICE	DEALER INVOICE
Premium Pkg., 3.0i	$3400	$3095

Leather upholstery, BMW Assist system, power-adjustable rear seatbacks, power sunroof, automatic climate control, upgraded trip computer, automatic headlights.

 Specifications begin on page 547.

OPTIONAL EQUIPMENT (cont.)

	RETAIL PRICE	DEALER INVOICE
Premium Pkg., 4.4i	$2500	$2275
Power sunroof, BMW Assist system, power-adjustable rear seatbacks, automatic day/night outside and rearview mirrors, compass, upgraded trip computer.		
Sport Pkg., 3.0i	2500	2275
4.4i	1600	1455
Sport seats, sport steering wheel, black headliner, light-colored wood interior trim (4.4i), titanium-colored grille insert, shadowline trim (4.4i), black-chrome exhaust tips, sport suspension, 255/55HR18 tires (3.0i), unique alloy wheels. 3.0i requires leather upholstery or Premium Pkg.		
Cold Weather Pkg., 3.0i, 4.4i	750	685
Heated front seats, ski sack, headlight washers.		
Rear Climate Pkg., 3.0i	600	545
4.4i	400	365
Rear climate controls (3.0i), side sunshades, rear privacy glass. 3.0i requires Premium Pkg.		
Powertrain		
5-speed automatic transmission w/manual-shift capability, 3.0i	1275	1210
Safety		
Rear side airbags	385	350
Front- and rear-obstacle-detection system, 3.0i	700	635
Comfort & Convenience Features		
Navigation system	1800	1640
Replaces CD player w/cassette player. 3.0i, 4.4i require Premium Pkg.		
BMW Assist system, 3.0i, 4.4i	750	685
Power sunroof, 3.0i, 4.4i	1350	1230
Premium sound system, 3.0i, 4.4i	1200	1090
Std. 4.8is.		
Heated steering wheel, 3.0i, 4.4i	150	135
Requires Cold Weather Pkg.		
Leather upholstery, 3.0i	1450	1320
Comfort seats, 4.4i	1200	1090
Std. 4.8is.		
Heated rear seats, 3.0i, 4.4i	350	320
Requires Cold Weather Pkg. 3.0i requires leather upholstery or Premium Pkg.		
Retractable load floor	380	345
Appearance & Special Purpose		
Steering-linked adaptive bi-xenon headlights, 3.0i	800	730
Rear automatic-leveling suspension, 3.0i	700	635
Adjustable ride-height suspension, 3.0i	1200	1090
4.4i	500	455
3.0i includes rear automatic-leveling suspension.		
Star-spoke alloy wheels, 4.4i	950	865
255/50YR19 front tires, 285/45YR19 rear tires. Requires Sport Pkg.		

BMW Z4

CLASS: Premium sporty/performance car
DRIVE WHEELS: Rear-wheel drive
BASE PRICE RANGE: $34,300-$41,300. Built in USA.
ALSO CONSIDER: Audi TT, Chrysler Crossfire, Porsche Boxster

BMW's 2-seat sports car adds standard features and deletes a transmission option on its base model for 2005. The Z4 is a convertible with a manual soft top or optional power soft top; both have a heated glass rear window. Two models are offered, both with an inline 6-cyl engine. The Z4 2.5i has a 184-hp 2.5-liter, the Z4 3.0i has a 225-hp 3.0. Manual transmission is standard, a 5-speed on the 2.5i, a 6-speed on the 3.0i. A 5-speed automatic with manual shift gate is optional on both. BMW's Sequential Manual Gearbox is optional on the 3.0i and no longer offered on the 2.5i. This 6-speed sequential manual transmission (SMT) has no clutch pedal, shifts via the gear lever or steering-wheel paddles, and can be set to shift like an automatic. All Z4s have run-flat tires, ABS, and an antiskid system. The 2.5i comes with 16-inch wheels, the 3.0i with 17s. An optional Sport Package includes a sport suspension and 17-inch wheels for the 2.5i, 18s for the 3.0i. It also adds Dynamic Driving Control in which a console button quickens throttle action and reduces power-steering assist. Leather upholstery is standard on the 3.0i, optional on the 2.5i. Newly standard for '05 are fog lamps and cruise control for the 2.5i, and automatic climate control for the 3.0. Heated seats, xenon headlights, a navigation system, and BMW Assist emergency and concierge service are optional. A removable hardtop and a wind deflector are dealer options.

RATINGS	2.5i w/Sport Pkg., man.	2.5i, auto.	3.0i, man.	3.0i w/Sport Pkg., auto.
ACCELERATION	7	6	8	8
FUEL ECONOMY	6	5	5	5
RIDE QUALITY	3	4	3	2
STEERING/HANDLING	9	9	10	10
QUIETNESS	3	3	3	3
CONTROLS/MATERIALS	7	7	7	7
ROOM/COMFORT (FRONT)	5	5	5	5

 Specifications begin on page 547.

RATINGS (cont.)

	2.5i w/Sport Pkg., man.	2.5i, auto.	3.0i, man.	3.0i w/Sport Pkg., auto.
ROOM/COMFORT (REAR)	0	0	0	0
CARGO ROOM	2	2	2	2
VALUE WITHIN CLASS	7	6	8	6

An excellent balance of performance, refinement, and driving excitement, any Z4 qualifies as a Recommended pick. Against prime competitors, the 2.5i costs as much as a Honda S2000, but is less powerful, while the 3.0i is a credible alternative to the comparably priced Porsche Boxster and Audi TT..

TOTAL	49	47	51	48

Average total for premium sporty/performance cars: 48.3

ENGINES

	dohc I6	dohc I6
Size, liters/cu. in.	2.5/152	3.0/182
Horsepower @ rpm	184 @ 5500	225 @ 5900
Torque (lb-ft) @ rpm	175 @ 3500	214 @ 3500
Availability	S[1]	S[2]
EPA city/highway mpg		
6-speed SMT		19/27
5-speed manual	20/28	
6-speed manual		21/29
5-speed automatic	21/28	20/29

1. 2.5i. 2. 3.0i.

PRICES

BMW Z4

	RETAIL PRICE	DEALER INVOICE
2.5i 2-door convertible	$34300	$31375
3.0i 2-door convertible	41300	37745
Destination charge	695	695

STANDARD EQUIPMENT

2.5I: 2.5-liter 6-cylinder engine, 5-speed manual transmission, traction control, dual front airbags, side airbags, active knee protection, antilock 4-wheel disc brakes, antiskid system, roll bars, tire-pressure monitor, air conditioning, interior air filter, power steering, tilt/telescope leather-wrapped steering wheel, cruise control, vinyl upholstery, height-adjustable bucket seats, cupholders, heated power mirrors, power windows, power door locks, brake assist, remote keyless entry, AM/FM/CD player, tachometer, outside-temperature indicator, rear defogger, rain-sensing variable-intermittent wipers w/heated washers, automatic headlights, theft-deterrent system, fog lights, 225/50R16 run-flat tires, alloy wheels.

3.0i adds: 3.0-liter 6-cylinder engine, 6-speed manual transmission, automatic climate control, leather upholstery, center console, aluminum interior trim, upgraded sound system, trip computer, map lights, 225/45R17 run-flat tires.

OPTIONAL EQUIPMENT

Major Packages	RETAIL PRICE	DEALER INVOICE
Premium Pkg., 2.5i	$3200	$2910
3.0i	2400	2185
Power convertible top, BMW Assist system, automatic climate control (2.5i), 8-way power seats, driver-seat memory, automatic day/night outside and rearview mirrors, trip computer (2.5i), interior storage nets.		
Sport Pkg., 2.5i	1300	1185
3.0i	1200	1090
Dynamic Driving Control console button, sport suspension, 225/45R17 run-flat tires (2.5i), 225/40R18 front and 235/45R18 rear run-flat tires (3.0i), unique alloy wheels.		
Powertrain		
5-speed automatic transmission w/manual-shift capability	1275	1210
6-speed sequential manual transmission, 3.0i	1500	1425
Requires Sport Pkg.		
Comfort & Convenience Features		
Navigation system	1800	1640
2.5i requires Premium Pkg. or trip computer.		
BMW Assist system	750	685
Leather upholstery, 2.5i	1150	1045
Includes aluminum interior trim, center console.		
Extended leather upholstery, 3.0i	1200	1090
Leather/cloth upholstery, 2.5i	850	775
Includes aluminum interior trim, center console.		
8-way power seats	995	905
Includes driver-seat memory.		
Heated seats	500	455
Sport seats	450	410
Requires Sport Pkg. 2.5 requires leather/cloth upholstery.		
Upgraded sound system, 2.5i	875	795
Trip computer, 2.5i	300	275
Power convertible top	750	685
Appearance & Special Purpose		
Bi-xenon headlights	700	635

BUICK LACROSSE

CLASS: Midsize car
DRIVE WHEELS: Front-wheel drive
BASE PRICE RANGE: $22,835-$28,335. Built in Canada.
ALSO CONSIDER: Honda Accord, Nissan Altima, Toyota Camry

Buick replaces its Century and Regal sedans for 2005 with a slightly larger version of their basic front-drive design. LaCrosse offers 5-place seating with front

Specifications begin on page 547.

buckets or 6-passenger seating with a flip-and-fold front center seat. It comes in three trim levels. CX and step-up CXL use GM's veteran overhead-valve 200-hp 3.8-liter V6. The top-line CXS gets 240 hp from GM's new double-overhead-cam 3.6 V6. It comes with a sportier suspension and 17-inch wheels vs. the others' 16s. All use a 4-speed automatic transmission. Every LaCrosse has 4-wheel disc brakes. ABS and traction control are standard on CXS, optional on the others. An antiskid system is an exclusive CXS option. Head-protecting curtain side airbags are optional on all; torso side airbags are unavailable. CXL and CXS have leather upholstery. Optional on CX and standard on the others are a tilt/telescope steering wheel, dual-zone automatic climate control, and a split folding rear seatback. Remote engine start and a sunroof are optional on all.

RATINGS	CXL w/6-passenger seating	CXS
ACCELERATION	5	6
FUEL ECONOMY	5	5
RIDE QUALITY	7	7
STEERING/HANDLING	5	7
QUIETNESS	7	7
CONTROLS/MATERIALS	8	8
ROOM/COMFORT (FRONT)	7	7
ROOM/COMFORT (REAR)	5	5
CARGO ROOM	5	5
VALUE WITHIN CLASS	6	7

LaCrosse is a significant improvement over the cars it replaces. The CX and CXL models are the traditional Buick: soft ride, soft handling, not much driving excitement. CXS's fine handling and modern V6 break the mold without sacrificing ride comfort, making it worth a look for anyone interested in a sporty family sedan.

TOTAL	60	64

Average total for midsize cars: 57.2

ENGINES	ohv V6	dohc V6
Size, liters/cu. in.	3.8/231	3.6/217
Horsepower @ rpm	200 @ 5200	240 @ 6000
Torque (lb-ft) @ rpm	230 @ 4000	230 @ 3200
Availability	S[1]	S[2]
EPA city/highway mpg		
4-speed automatic	20/29	19/28

1. CX, CXL. 2. CXS.

PRICES

Buick LaCrosse

	RETAIL PRICE	DEALER INVOICE
CX 4-door sedan	$22835	$20894
CXL 4-door sedan	25335	23182
CXS 4-door sedan	28335	25927
Destination charge	660	660

STANDARD EQUIPMENT

CX: 3.8-liter V6 engine, 4-speed automatic transmission, dual front airbags, 4-wheel disc brakes, daytime running lights, air conditioning, interior air filter, OnStar assistance system w/one-year service, power steering, tilt steering wheel, cruise control, front bucket seats, 6-way power driver seat, center console, cupholders, power mirrors, power windows, power door locks, remote keyless entry, AM/FM/CD player, digital clock, tachometer, intermittent wipers, map lights, visor mirrors, rear defogger, automatic headlights, floormats, theft-deterrent system, 225/60R16 tires, wheel covers.

CXL adds: dual-zone automatic climate controls, leather upholstery, driver-seat lumbar adjustment, split folding rear seat, tilt/telescope leather-wrapped steering wheel, illuminated visor mirrors, alloy wheels.

CXS adds: 3.6-liter V6 engine, traction control, antilock 4-wheel disc brakes, fog lights, Gran Touring Suspension, 225/55R17 tires.

OPTIONAL EQUIPMENT

Major Packages

	RETAIL PRICE	DEALER INVOICE
Silver Convenience Pkg., CX	$1150	$1024
Dual-zone automatic climate controls, remote engine start, tilt/telescope leather-wrapped steering wheel w/radio controls, personalization features, illuminated visor mirrors, driver information center.		
Gold Convenience Pkg., CXL, CXS	1150	1024
Rear-obstacle-detection system, steering-wheel radio controls, heated power mirrors, 6-way power passenger seat, automatic day/night rearview mirror, universal garage-door opener, interior-lighting switch.		
Chrome Appearance Pkg., CXL, CXS	295	263
Chrome exterior trim.		

Safety

	RETAIL PRICE	DEALER INVOICE
Curtain side airbags	395	352
Antilock brakes, CX, CXL	600	534
Includes traction control.		
Antiskid system, CXS	495	441

Comfort & Convenience Features

	RETAIL PRICE	DEALER INVOICE
Power sunroof	900	801
CX requires Silver Convenience Pkg.		
AM/FM/CD/MP3 player, CXL, CXS	545	485
Includes upgraded sound system.		
AM/FM radio w/in-dash 6-disc CD changer	695	619
Includes upgraded sound system.		

 Specifications begin on page 547.

OPTIONAL EQUIPMENT (cont.)

	RETAIL PRICE	DEALER INVOICE
Satellite radio	$325	$289
Requires monthly service fee after 3rd month.		
6-passenger seating, CX, CXL	195	174
6-way power passenger seat, CXL, CXS	350	312
Heated front seats, CXL, CXS	295	263
Split folding rear seat, CX	275	245
Driver information center, CX	195	173
Remote engine start	150	134
CX requires driver information center.		
Appearance & Special Purpose		
Rear spoiler	275	245
Alloy wheels, CX	350	312
Chrome alloy wheels, CXL, CXS	650	579

BUICK LESABRE

CLASS: Large car
DRIVE WHEELS: Front-wheel drive
BASE PRICE RANGE: $26,545-$32,205. Built in USA.
ALSO CONSIDER: Chrysler 300, Dodge Magnum, Toyota Avalon

OnStar assistance is standard on all LeSabres for 2005. Buick's best-selling car comes in Custom and Limited models and is among the few cars with a front bench seat for 6-passenger capacity. The only powertrain is a 205-hp 3.8-liter V6 and 4-speed automatic transmission. Antilock 4-wheel disc brakes are standard. Traction control, front side airbags, and leather upholstery are standard on the Limited, optional on Custom. Curtain side airbags are unavailable. An anit-skid system is an exclusive Limited option. A firmer Gran Touring suspension package is available for both. For '05, Custom joins Limited with standard OnStar assistance; service is free for the first year. Limited is newly available with a Celebration Edition package that includes 16-inch wheels vs. LeSabre's standard 15s, special body and interior trim, and outside mirrors with turn-signal lights. LeSabre shares a basic design with the Pontiac Bonneville.

RATINGS	Custom	Limited w/Gran Touring Pkg.
ACCELERATION	6	6
FUEL ECONOMY	4	4

RATINGS (cont.)	Custom	Limited w/Gran Touring Pkg.
RIDE QUALITY	7	5
STEERING/HANDLING	4	5
QUIETNESS	7	7
CONTROLS/MATERIALS	5	5
ROOM/COMFORT (FRONT)	7	7
ROOM/COMFORT (REAR)	5	5
CARGO ROOM	6	6
VALUE WITHIN CLASS	5	5

Desirable options add quickly to the bottom line, rear-seat accommodations are subpar, and interior furnishings are indifferent. But LeSabre earns our Recommendation in this class because it imparts a feeling of size and substance and offers a good helping of standard features at competitive—and frequently discounted—base prices.

TOTAL	**56**	**55**

Average total for large cars: 60.9

ENGINES

	ohv V6
Size, liters/cu. in.	3.8/231
Horsepower @ rpm	205 @ 5200
Torque (lb-ft) @ rpm	230 @ 4000
Availability	S
EPA city/highway mpg	
4-speed automatic	20/29

PRICES

Buick LeSabre	RETAIL PRICE	DEALER INVOICE
Custom 4-door sedan	$26545	$24288
Limited 4-door sedan	32205	29468
Destination charge	725	725

STANDARD EQUIPMENT

Custom: 3.8-liter V6 engine, 4-speed automatic transmission, dual front airbags, antilock 4-wheel disc brakes, emergency inside trunk release, daytime running lights, air conditioning, power steering, tilt steering wheel w/radio controls, cruise control, cloth upholstery, front split bench seat, 8-way power driver seat, cupholders, power mirrors, power windows, power door locks, remote keyless entry, OnStar assistance system w/one-year service, AM/FM/CD player, digital clock, variable-intermittent wipers, rear defogger, visor mirrors, automatic headlights, floormats, theft-deterrent system, automatic level control, 215/70R15 tires, wheel covers.

Limited adds: traction control, front side airbags, tire-pressure monitor, dual-zone automatic climate controls, leather upholstery, heated 8-way power front seats w/driver-side power lumbar adjustment, trunk pass-through, leather-wrapped steering wheel, heated power mirrors, AM/FM/cassette/CD player, trip computer, automatic day/night rearview mirror, compass, outside-

 Specifications begin on page 547.

temperature indicator, universal garage-door opener, illuminated visor mirrors, rain-sensing wipers, cornering lights, alloy wheels.

OPTIONAL EQUIPMENT

Major Packages

	RETAIL PRICE	DEALER INVOICE
Best Seller Pkg. 1SE, Custom	$1550	$1333

Traction control, upgraded sound system, automatic day/night rearview mirror, driver information center (including tire-pressure monitor and trip computer), illuminated visor mirrors, alarm, alloy wheels.

Celebration Edition Pkg. WH8, Limited	1950	1677
Manufacturer's Discount Price	*1200*	*1032*

Antiskid system, memory pkg. (driver seat, mirror, radio, air conditioning), head-up instrument display, special woodgrain interior trim, manual-folding mirrors w/turn signals, driver-side automatic day/night mirror, unique interior and exterior trim, cargo net, 225/60R16 tires, chrome alloy wheels.

Leather and Wheels Group, Custom	1835	1578
Manufacturer's Discount Price	*1085*	*933*

Leather upholstery, cargo net, 225/60R16 tires, chrome alloy wheels. Requires Pkg. 1SE.

Leather and Sound Group, Custom	1865	1604
Manufacturer's Discount Price	*1115*	*959*

Gran Touring Pkg. plus leather upholstery, AM/FM/cassette/CD player, satellite radio (requires monthly fee after 3rd month). Requires Pkg. 1SE.

Leather and Comfort Group, Custom	2120	1823
Manufacturer's Discount Price	*1370*	*1178*

Front side airbags, leather upholstery, heated front seats, 8-way power passenger seat, automatic day/night rearview mirror, compass, rain-sensing wipers. Requires Pkg. 1SE.

Wheel and Sound Pkg., Custom	525	452

AM/FM/cassette/CD player, 225/60R16 tires, machine-face alloy wheels.

Gran Touring Pkg.	395	340
Limited w/Celebration Edition	185	159

Performance axle ratio, leather-wrapped steering wheel (Custom), sport suspension, rear stabilizer bar, 225/60R16 tires. Custom requires Pkg. 1SE, AM/FM/cassette/CD player, machine-face alloy wheels.

Memory Pkg., Limited	190	163

Memory driver seat, mirrors, radio, air conditioning. Requires driver-side automatic day/night rearview mirror.

Safety

Front side airbags, Custom	350	301
Antiskid system, Limited	495	426

Comfort & Convenience Features

Power sunroof, Limited	1095	942
Leather upholstery, Custom	995	856

Requires Pkg. 1SE.

Heated front seats, Custom	295	254

Requires Pkg. 1SE, leather upholstery, power passenger seat.

OPTIONAL EQUIPMENT (cont.)

	RETAIL PRICE	DEALER INVOICE
Head-up instrument display, Limited	$325	$280
8-way power passenger seat, Custom	330	284
Requires Pkg. 1SE.		
AM/FM/cassette/CD player, Custom	150	129
Requires Pkg. 1SE.		
Satellite radio	325	280
Requires monthly fee after 3rd month. Custom requires Pkg. 1SE.		
Rain-sensing wipers, Custom	70	60
Requires Pkg. 1SE.		

Appearance & Special Purpose

Machine-face alloy wheels	375	323
Includes 225/60R16 tires. Custom requires Pkg. 1SE. Std. Gran Touring Pkg., Wheels and Sound Pkg.		

BUICK PARK AVENUE

CLASS: Large car
DRIVE WHEELS: Front-wheel drive
BASE PRICE RANGE: $35,555-$40,730. Built in USA.
ALSO CONSIDER: Chrysler 300, Toyota Avalon

Buick's flagship sedan gets revisions to grille and taillamps for 2005, and the base Park Avenue model gains the front-fender "portholes" previously reserved for the top-line Park Avenue Ultra. Both models have a 3.8-liter V6 and 4-speed automatic transmission. The base model has 205 hp, the Ultra is supercharged for 240 hp. ABS, self-leveling rear suspension, and leather upholstery are standard. So is a front bench seat for 6-passenger capacity; Ultra offers optional front buckets. Ultra has 17-inch wheels, the base model 16s. Also standard for Ultra and optional for the base model are a firmer Gran Touring suspension, OnStar assistance, traction and antiskid control, and a tire-pressure monitor. Optional rear-obstacle warning and a head-up instrument display are also available. Buick says 2005 is the final model year for Park Avenue's current design, which dates to 1997. It says the final 3000 Park Avenues will be Special Edition models with identifying logos, unique trim and wheels, and available black-and-platinum exterior.

 Specifications begin on page 547.

RATINGS

RATINGS	Base	Ultra
ACCELERATION	5	6
FUEL ECONOMY	5	4
RIDE QUALITY	7	8
STEERING/HANDLING	4	6
QUIETNESS	8	8
CONTROLS/MATERIALS	7	7
ROOM/COMFORT (FRONT)	7	8
ROOM/COMFORT (REAR)	6	6
CARGO ROOM	6	6
VALUE WITHIN CLASS	7	7

Park Avenue offers traditional American comfort and amenities at prices that undercut those of other premium large cars. For that, it earns Recommended status—with emphasis on the Ultra model as the better performer and the better value in this line. But don't pay full sticker for any Park Avenue. Continuing slow sales and end-of-line status mean attractive discounts and other incentives should be available.

TOTAL	**62**	**66**

Average total for large cars: 60.9

ENGINES

	ohv V6	Supercharged ohv V6
Size, liters/cu. in.	3.8/231	3.8/231
Horsepower @ rpm	205 @ 5200	240 @ 5200
Torque (lb-ft) @ rpm	230 @ 4000	280 @ 3600
Availability	S[1]	S[2]
EPA city/highway mpg		
4-speed automatic	20/29	18/28

1. Base. 2. Ultra.

PRICES

Buick Park Avenue	RETAIL PRICE	DEALER INVOICE
Base 4-door sedan	$35555	$32177
Ultra 4-door sedan	40730	36861
Destination charge	795	795

STANDARD EQUIPMENT

Base: 3.8-liter V6 engine, 4-speed automatic transmission, dual front airbags, front side airbags, antilock 4-wheel disc brakes, daytime running lights, air conditioning w/dual-zone automatic climate controls, power steering, tilt leather-wrapped steering wheel w/radio controls, cruise control, leather upholstery, front split bench seat, 10-way power front seats w/driver-seat lumbar adjustment, cupholders, power mirrors, power windows, power door locks, remote keyless entry, AM/FM/cassette, digital clock, tachometer, outside-temperature indicator, rear defogger, power remote decklid and fuel-door releases, map lights, illuminated visor mirrors, variable-intermittent wipers, automatic headlights, floormats, theft-deterrent system, cornering lights, automatic level-control suspension, 225/60R16 tires, alloy wheels.

Ultra adds: 3.8-liter V6 supercharged engine, traction control, antiskid system, tire-pressure monitor, OnStar assistance system w/one-year service, woodgrain/leather-wrapped steering wheel, heated front seats w/power lumbar adjustment, memory system (driver seat, mirrors, climate controls, radio), heated power mirrors w/turn-signal lights and passenger-side mirror tilt-down back-up aid, automatic day/night rearview and driver-side mirrors, compass, rain-sensing windshield wipers, AM/FM/cassette/CD player w/upgraded sound system, trip computer, universal garage-door opener, Gran Touring suspension, 235/55R17 tires, chrome alloy wheels.

OPTIONAL EQUIPMENT

Major Packages

	RETAIL PRICE	DEALER INVOICE
Option Pkg. 1SE, Base	$2140	$1840
Traction control, OnStar assistance system w/one-year service, AM/FM/cassette/CD player, heated front seats, memory system (driver seat, mirrors, climate controls, radio), driver information center (tire-pressure monitor, trip computer), rain-sensing wipers.		
Prestige Feature Pkg. PCR, Base	2150	1849
Manufacturer's Discount Price	*1400*	*1204*
Antiskid system, rear-obstacle-detection system, heated power mirrors w/turn-signal lights, automatic day/night driver-side and inside mirrors, compass, universal garage-door opener, head-up instrument display, chrome alloy wheels. Requires Option Pkg. 1SE.		
Gran Touring Pkg., Base	285	245
Gran Touring suspension, variable-assist power steering, 225/60R16 touring tires, unique alloy wheels. Requires Option Pkg. 1SE.		
Luxury Pkg. PCR, Ultra	1875	1613
Manufacturer's Discount Price	*875*	*753*
Power sunroof, front bucket seats, center console, rear air-conditioning vents, 12-disc CD changer.		
5-Passenger Seating Pkg., Ultra	185	159
Front bucket seats, center console, rear air-conditioning vents.		

Safety

Antiskid system, Base w/Pkg. 1SE	495	426
Rear-obstacle-detection system	295	254
Requires head-up display. Base requires Option Pkg. 1SE.		

Comfort & Convenience Features

12-disc CD changer	595	512
Base requires Option Pkg. 1SE, Concert Sound III speakers.		
Concert Sound III speakers, Base w/Pkg. 1SE	295	254
Power sunroof	1095	942
Base requires Option Pkg. 1SE, universal garage-door opener.		
Head-up display	325	280
Requires rear-obstacle-detection system. Base requires Option Pkg. 1SE, universal garage-door opener.		

 Specifications begin on page 547.

OPTIONAL EQUIPMENT (cont.)

	RETAIL PRICE	DEALER INVOICE
Universal garage-door opener, Base	$100	$86
Requires Option Group 1SE.		
Appearance & Special Purpose		
Chrome alloy wheels, Base	800	688
Requires Option Pkg. 1SE.		

BUICK RAINIER

CLASS: Premium midsize sport-utility vehicle
DRIVE WHEELS: Rear-wheel drive, all-wheel drive
BASE PRICE RANGE: $35,080-$36,905. Built in USA.
ALSO CONSIDER: Acura MDX, Volvo XC90

Curtain side airbags are newly optional on Buick's truck-based SUV for 2005. Rainier shares a basic design with the 5-passenger Chevrolet TrailBlazer, GMC Envoy, and Isuzu Ascender, but doesn't offer a stretched 7-seat model. It comes only in CXL trim with a standard 6-cyl engine or optional V8. A 4-speed automatic is the sole transmission. Rainier offers rear-wheel drive with traction control or all-wheel drive that lacks low-range gearing. Among standard features are ABS, load-leveling rear air suspension, 17-inch alloy wheels, leather upholstery, dual-zone climate control, and OnStar assistance. Other options include adjustable foot pedals, heated front seats, satellite radio, navigation system, and rear DVD entertainment.

RATINGS	CXL AWD, 6-cyl	CXL AWD, V8
ACCELERATION	6	7
FUEL ECONOMY	4	3
RIDE QUALITY	6	6
STEERING/HANDLING	4	4
QUIETNESS	6	7
CONTROLS/MATERIALS	7	7
ROOM/COMFORT (FRONT)	7	7
ROOM/COMFORT (REAR)	6	6
CARGO ROOM	8	8
VALUE WITHIN CLASS	4	4

RATINGS (cont.)

	CXL AWD, 6-cyl	CXL AWD, V8

Rainier is positioned as GM's most-luxurious midsize truck-type SUV, and it is the quietest and best-riding of the bunch. Still, Rainier costs more than its GM siblings and can't escape the faults common to their noncar-based design: indifferent handling and mediocre fuel economy.

TOTAL	**58**	**59**

Average total for premium midsize sport-utility vehicles: 59.6

ENGINES

	dohc I6	ohv V8
Size, liters/cu. in.	4.2/256	5.3/325
Horsepower @ rpm	275 @ 6000	290 @ 5200
Torque (lb-ft) @ rpm	275 @ 3600	330 @ 4000
Availability	S	O
EPA city/highway mpg		
4-speed automatic	15/21[1]	14/18[2]

1. 16/21 w/2WD. 2. 15/19 w/2WD.

PRICES

Buick Rainier

	RETAIL PRICE	DEALER INVOICE
2WD CXL 4-door wagon	$35080	$31747
AWD CXL 4-door wagon	36905	33399
Destination charge	685	685

STANDARD EQUIPMENT

CXL: 4.2-liter 6-cylinder engine, 4-speed automatic transmission, traction control, limited-slip differential, dual front airbags, antilock 4-wheel disc brakes, daytime running lights, air conditioning w/dual-zone automatic climate controls, OnStar assistance w/one-year service, power steering, tilt leather-wrapped steering wheel w/radio and climate controls, cruise control, leather upholstery, 8-way power front bucket seats w/driver-side lumbar adjustment, center console, cupholders, memory system (driver seat, mirrors), split folding rear seat, heated power mirrors w/turn signals, power windows, power door locks, remote keyless entry, AM/FM/cassette/CD player, rear radio controls, digital clock, trip computer, digital memo recorder, universal garage-door opener, illuminated visor mirrors, variable-intermittent wipers, rear defogger, rear wiper/washer, automatic headlights, floormats, theft-deterrent system, rear privacy glass, roof rails, fog lights, cornering lights, trailer-hitch platform, wiring harness, rear load-leveling air suspension, air inflator, full-size spare tire, 245/65R17 tires, alloy wheels. **AWD** adds: all-wheel drive. *Deletes:* traction control.

OPTIONAL EQUIPMENT

Major Packages

	RETAIL PRICE	DEALER INVOICE
V8 Power Play Pkg.	$1650	$1419
Manufacturer's Discount Price	*1150*	*989*

5.3-liter V8 engine, power-adjustable pedals.

OPTIONAL EQUIPMENT (cont.)

	RETAIL PRICE	DEALER INVOICE
Sun, Sound, and Entertainment Pkg.	$1865	$1603
Manufacturer's Discount Price	*1115*	*959*
Power sunroof, Bose AM/FM radio w/in-dash 6-disc CD changer.		
Sun, Sound, and Entertainment Pkg. w/satellite radio	1865	1604
Manufacturer's Discount Price	*865*	*744*
Satellite radio requires monthly fee after 3rd month.		
Luxury Pkg.	725	624
Manufacturer's Discount Price	*225*	*194*
Heated front seats, chrome side steps.		
Cargo Convenience Pkg.	150	129
Cargo cover, cargo mat and net.		
Safety		
Curtain side airbags	495	426
Comfort & Convenience Features		
Rear-seat DVD entertainment system	1295	1114
w/Sun, Sound Pkg.	495	425
NA w/power sunroof. Deletes Sun, Sound, and Entertainment Pkg. power sunroof.		
Navigation system	1995	1716
w/Sun, Sound Pkg.	1600	1376
Requires Bose sound system or Sun, Sound, and Entertainment Pkg. Replaces Sun, Sound, and Entertainment Pkg.'s 6-disc CD changer w/single-disc CD player.		
AM/FM/CD/MP3 player	135	116
AM/FM radio w/in-dash 6-disc CD changer	245	211
Bose sound system	495	426
Satellite radio	325	280
Requires monthly fee after 3rd month.		
Power sunroof	800	688
Power-adjustable pedals	150	129
Cargo organizer	165	142

BUICK RENDEZVOUS

CLASS: Midsize sport-utility vehicle
DRIVE WHEELS: Front-wheel drive, all-wheel drive
BASE PRICE RANGE: $26,585-$29,775. Built in Mexico.
ALSO CONSIDER: Ford Explorer, Honda Pilot, Toyota Highlander

Equipment revisions are the 2005 news for Buick's crossover SUV. Rendezvous shares a basic structure with the Pontiac Aztek, but is four inches longer to allow 3-row seating. Like Aztek, it's based on GM's front-wheel-drive minivan platform. CX, CXL, and top-line Ultra trim levels return. All are available with front-wheel drive with optional traction control or all-wheel drive without low-range gearing. Ultra was previously AWD only. CX and CXL versions come with a 185-hp 3.4-liter V6. The Ultra package includes a 245-hp 3.6 V6 that's optional for CXL. All have a 4-speed automatic transmission. For '05, standard 17-inch wheels

replace 16s on all but base CXs, which are slated to get 17s at midseason. ABS and front side airbags are optional for 2WD CX versions, standard otherwise. The CX and CXL packages include a standard 3-place 2nd-row split bench seat. Twin 2nd-row buckets and a 2-passenger 3rd-row seat are standard on Ultra and available with the other packages. Also standard for Ultra and available elsewhere are rear-obstacle detection, satellite radio, and head-up instrument display. Rear DVD entertainment is available except on CX. OnStar assistance is standard except on CX, where it's optional. Also for '05, the CXL package adds a wood/leather steering wheel and woodgrain interior trim, and a sunroof is newly available for CX versions. A touch-screen navigation/audio system is available for all.

RATINGS

	2WD CX	AWD CXL, 3.4 V6	AWD Ultra
ACCELERATION	4	4	5
FUEL ECONOMY	5	5	4
RIDE QUALITY	4	4	4
STEERING/HANDLING	3	4	4
QUIETNESS	5	5	6
CONTROLS/MATERIALS	6	6	6
ROOM/COMFORT (FRONT)	5	5	5
ROOM/COMFORT (REAR)	6	6	6
CARGO ROOM	9	9	9
VALUE WITHIN CLASS	3	3	4

Buick pitches Rendezvous as a lower-priced alternative to the Acura MDX and Lexus RX 330. Though the 3.6-liter V6 is a boon for refinement, Rendezvous lacks the performance and polish of other luxury SUVs or even of such popularly priced models as the Honda Pilot and Toyota Highlander.

TOTAL	50	51	53

Average total for midsize sport-utility vehicles: 54.7

ENGINES

	ohv V6	dohc V6
Size, liters/cu. in.	3.4/204	3.6/217
Horsepower @ rpm	185 @ 5200	242 @ 6000
Torque (lb-ft) @ rpm	210 @ 4000	232 @ 3500
Availability	S[1]	S[2]
EPA city/highway mpg		
4-speed automatic	18/24[3]	18/25[4]

1. CX, CXL. 2. Ultra; opt. CXL. 3. 19/26 w/2WD. 4. 18/27 w/2WD.

PRICES

Buick Rendezvous	RETAIL PRICE	DEALER INVOICE
2WD 4-door wagon	$26585	$24059
AWD 4-door wagon	29775	26946
Destination charge	685	685

All models require an Option Pkg.

STANDARD EQUIPMENT

2WD: 3.4-liter V6 engine, 4-speed automatic transmission, dual front airbags, 4-wheel disc brakes, daytime running lights, air conditioning, power steering, tilt leather-wrapped steering wheel, cruise control, cloth upholstery, front bucket seats w/lumbar adjustment, center console, cupholders, 2nd-row folding seat, power mirrors, power windows, power door locks, remote keyless entry, AM/FM/CD player, digital clock, illuminated driver-side visor mirror, passenger-side visor mirror, map lights, universal garage-door opener, variable-intermittent wipers, rear defogger, rear wiper/washer, automatic headlights, floormats, theft-deterrent system, fog lights, rear privacy glass, roof rails, 215/70R16 tires.

AWD adds: all-wheel drive, front side airbags, antilock 4-wheel disc brakes.

OPTIONAL EQUIPMENT

Major Packages	RETAIL PRICE	DEALER INVOICE
CX Option Pkg. 1SA	NC	NC
Standard equipment.		
CX Plus Option Pkg. 1SB	1860	1600
OnStar assistance system w/one-year service, rear-obstacle-detection system, tire-pressure monitor (AWD), dual-zone manual climate controls, driver information center (trip computer, compass), programmable door locks, rear storage system, cargo mat, theft-deterrent system w/alarm, 225/60R17 tires, alloy wheels.		
CXL Option Pkg. 1SC, 2WD	5330	4584
Manufacturer's Discount Price	*4330*	*3724*
AWD	4205	3616
Manufacturer's Discount Price	*3205*	*2756*
Traction control (2WD), antilock 4-wheel disc brakes (2WD), front side airbags (2WD), tire-pressure monitor, rear-obstacle-detection system, OnStar assistance system w/one-year service, dual-zone automatic climate controls, leather upholstery, 6-way power front seats, woodgrain interior trim, heated power mirrors, programmable door locks, AM/FM/cassette/CD player w/steering-wheel and rear-seat controls, driver information center (trip computer, compass), illuminated passenger-side visor mirror, rear storage system, theft-deterrent alarm, 225/60R17 tires, alloy wheels.		
CXL Plus Option Pkg. 1SD, 2WD	6590	5667
Manufacturer's Discount Price	*5590*	*4807*
AWD	5565	4700

OPTIONAL EQUIPMENT (cont.)

	RETAIL PRICE	DEALER INVOICE
Manufacturer's Discount Price	*$4565*	*$3840*
CXL Option Pkg. 1SC plus heated front seats, driver-seat and mirror memory, satellite radio, stowable 3rd-row seat. Deletes rear storage system.		
Ultra Option Pkg. 1SE, 2WD	10570	9090
Manufacturer's Discount Price	*9570*	*8230*
AWD	9445	8123
Manufacturer's Discount Price	*8445*	*7263*
3.6-liter V6 engine, traction control (2WD), front side airbags (2WD), antilock 4-wheel disc brakes (2WD), tire-pressure monitor, rear-obstacle-detection system, OnStar assistance system w/one-year service, dual-zone automatic climate controls, wood/leather-wrapped steering wheel, leather-suede upholstery, heated 6-way power front seats, memory system (driver seat, mirrors), 2nd-row captain chairs, 3rd-row stowable seat, wood interior trim, heated power mirrors, AM/FM radio w/in-dash 6-disc CD changer, satellite radio (requires monthly service fee after 3rd month), rear radio controls, head-up instrument display, automatic day/night rearview mirror, compass, trip computer, illuminated passenger-side visor mirror, woodgrain interior trim, 225/60R17 tires, alloy wheels.		
Sun and Satellite Pkg., w/CXL Pkg. 1SC	3120	2683
Manufacturer's Discount Price	*2620*	*2253*
w/CXL Pkg. 1SD	2795	2404
Manufacturer's Discount Price	*2295*	*1974*
w/Ultra Pkg.	2400	2064
Manufacturer's Discount Price	*1900*	*1634*
Power sunroof, navigation system, CD player, satellite radio. CXL deletes cassette player. Ultra deletes in-dash 6-disc CD changer. NA w/rear-seat DVD entertainment system, AM/FM radio w/in-dash 6-disc CD changer.		
Trailer Tow Pkg.	395	340
Heavy-duty engine cooling and alternator, air-inflator kit, load-leveling rear suspension, wiring harness. NA w/CX Option Pkg. 1SA.		

Powertrain

3.6-liter V6 engine	2025	1742
Requires CXL Pkg.		
Traction control, 2WD w/CX Pkg.	175	151
Includes tire-pressure monitor. Requires antilock brakes.		

Safety

Front side airbags, 2WD w/CX Pkg.	350	301
Requires antilock brakes.		
Antilock brakes, 2WD w/CX Pkg.	600	516

Comfort & Convenience Features

Rear-seat DVD entertainment system	1295	1114
Requires CXL or Ultra Pkg. NA w/power sunroof.		
Navigation system, w/CXL Pkg.	1995	1716
Ultra Pkg.	1600	1370

 Specifications begin on page 547.

OPTIONAL EQUIPMENT (cont.)

	RETAIL PRICE	DEALER INVOICE
Includes CD player. CXL deletes cassette player. Ultra deletes in-dash 6-disc CD changer. NA w/AM/FM radio w/in-dash 6-disc CD changer.		
AM/FM/cassette/CD player	$350	$301
Includes rear radio controls. Requires CX Plus Option Pkg. 1SB.		
AM/FM radio w/6-disc CD changer, w/CXL Pkg.	395	340
Satellite radio	325	280
Requires monthly service fee after 3rd month. NA w/CX Option Pkg. 1SA. Std. w/Ultra Pkg.		
Steering-wheel radio controls, w/CX Pkg.	125	108
Rear radio controls	105	90
Requires CX Plus Option Pkg. 1SB.		
Head-up instrument display, w/CXL Pkg.	350	301
Power sunroof	800	688
Heated front seats, w/CXL Pkg.	275	237
Requires driver-seat and mirror memory.		
6-way power driver seat	275	237
Requires CX Plus Option Pkg. 1SB.		
Driver-seat and mirror memory, w/CXL Pkg.	250	215
Requires heated front seats.		
Stowable 3rd-row seat	525	452
Deletes rear storage system and cargo mat. NA w/CX Option Pkg. 1SA. Std. w/Ultra Pkg.		
2nd-row captain chairs	395	340
Requires stowable 3rd-row seat. NA w/CX Option Pkg. 1SA. Std. w/Ultra Pkg.		
Leather upholstery	1280	1101
Includes 6-way power front seats. Requires CX Plus Option Pkg. 1SB. 2WD requires antilock brakes, front side airbags.		

Appearance & Special Purpose

Roof rack	175	151
NA w/CX Option Pkg. 1SA.		
Chrome alloy wheels	650	559
NA w/CX Pkg.		

BUICK TERRAZA

CLASS: Minivan
DRIVE WHEELS: Front-wheel drive, all-wheel drive
BASE PRICE RANGE: $28,110-$33,855. Built in USA.
ALSO CONSIDER: Chrysler Town & Country, Honda Odyssey, Toyota Sienna

Buick gets its first minivan as one of four new GM "crossover sport vans." Terraza shares its basic design with the 2005 Chevrolet Uplander, Pontiac Montana SV6, and Saturn Relay, all of which add an SUV-style nose to the 1997-2004 GM minivan design. Terraza is the costliest, most luxurious version and is the only one to come standard with automatic load-leveling rear suspension. Terraza offers

CX and uplevel CXL models in a single body length with dual sliding rear side doors. All Terrazas seat 7 via folding/removable 2nd-row bucket seats and a 50/50 fold-flat 3rd-row bench. The only powertrain is a 200-hp 3.5-liter V6 and 4-speed automatic transmission. There's a choice of front-wheel drive or all-wheel drive. Traction control is optional on CX, standard on CXL. GM's Stabilitrak antiskid/traction control is optional with front-drive. All models come with 4-wheel antilock disc brakes, 17-inch wheels, and OnStar assistance. Front side airbags providing head and torso protection are optional on CX and standard on CXL, but curtain side airbags aren't offered. Also standard are a CD/MP3 player, rear DVD entertainment, and a roof-rail system with optional snap-on storage modules. Rear-obstacle detection, rear air conditioning, and a rear cargo organizer are optional on CX, standard on CXL. CXL also adds leather seating surfaces. Among the options for both models are satellite radio and a remote starting system. Buick says a navigation system will be made available during the model year. This report is based on preview test drives.

RATINGS

	CXL	CXL w/AWD
ACCELERATION	3	3
FUEL ECONOMY	4	4
RIDE QUALITY	6	6
STEERING/HANDLING	4	5
QUIETNESS	7	7
CONTROLS/MATERIALS	7	7
ROOM/COMFORT (FRONT)	6	6
ROOM/COMFORT (REAR)	6	6
CARGO ROOM	9	9
VALUE WITHIN CLASS	5	5

A comfortable ride, available AWD, and standard rear DVD entertainment are Terraza's competitive advantages. The lack of side-curtain airbags, however, is a big minus for safety conscious buyers, and the rear seating rows and cargo area aren't as convenient or as roomy as the minivans from Chrysler, Honda, or Toyota. While Buick's first minivan is a competent entry, there is no compelling reason to chose it over our Recommended and Best Buy choices.

TOTAL	**57**	**58**

Average total for minivans: 58.0

 Specifications begin on page 547.

ENGINES

	ohv V6
Size, liters/cu. in.	3.5/213
Horsepower @ rpm	200 @ 5200
Torque (lb-ft) @ rpm	220 @ 4400
Availability	S
EPA city/highway mpg	
4-speed automatic	NA

PRICES

Buick Terraza	RETAIL PRICE	DEALER INVOICE
FWD CX 4-door van	$28110	$25440
AWD CX 4-door van	30990	28046
FWD CXL 4-door van	31170	28209
AWD CXL 4-door van	33855	30639
Destination charge	715	715

STANDARD EQUIPMENT

CX: 3.5-liter V6 engine, 4-speed automatic transmission, dual front airbags, antilock 4-wheel brakes, daytime running lights, air conditioning w/dual-zone manual climate controls and rear controls, OnStar assistance system w/one-year service, power steering, tilt leather-wrapped steering wheel, cruise control, leather/cloth upholstery, 7-passenger seating, quad bucket seats, 6-way power driver seat, 3rd-row split folding seat, wood interior trim, heated power mirrors, power windows, power door locks, remote keyless entry, power-sliding passenger-side door, AM/FM/CD/MP3 player, rear radio controls, digital clock, tachometer, compass, outside-temperature indicator, rear seat DVD entertainment system, universal garage-door opener, folding tray, illuminated visor mirrors, map lights, rear defogger, rear wiper, automatic headlights, floormats, theft-deterrent system, rear privacy glass, roof rails, air-inflation kit, load-leveling rear suspension, 225/60R17 tires, wheel covers. **AWD** adds: all-wheel drive, 225/60R17 tires, alloy wheels.

CXL adds: traction control, front side airbags, rear-obstacle-detection system, rear air conditioning, leather upholstery, 8-way power front seats, driver-seat memory, power sliding driver-side door, steering-wheel radio controls, cargo organizer, 255/60R17 tires, alloy wheels. **AWD** adds: all-wheel drive, 225/60R17 tires. *Deletes:* traction control.

OPTIONAL EQUIPMENT

Major Packages	RETAIL PRICE	DEALER INVOICE
Trailering Provisions Pkg.	$165	$147
Heavy-duty alternator and engine cooling, wiring harness.		
Powertrain		
Traction control, FWD CX	195	174
Safety		
Front side airbags, CX	350	312

OPTIONAL EQUIPMENT (cont.)

	RETAIL PRICE	DEALER INVOICE
Antiskid system, FWD	$450	$401
CX requires traction control.		
Comfort & Convenience Features		
Rear air conditioning, CX	475	422
Remote starting	165	156
Power-sliding passenger-side door, CX	545	485
Includes rear-obstacle-detection system.		
6-way power passenger seat, CX	275	245
Heated front seats, CXL	275	245
Navigation system, CXL	NA	NA
AM/FM radio w/in-dash 6-disc CD/MP3 changer	295	263
Satellite radio	325	289
Requires monthly fee after 3rd month.		
Cargo organizer, CX	285	254
Removable overhead consoles, CX	100	89
Two consoles, first-aid kit. Std. CXL.		
Appearance & Special Purpose		
Alloy wheels, FWD CX	325	289
Chrome alloy wheels, CXL	650	579

CADILLAC CTS

CLASS: Premium midsize car
DRIVE WHEELS: Rear-wheel drive
BASE PRICE RANGE: $31,850-$49,300. Built in USA.
ALSO CONSIDER: Acura TL, BMW 3-Series, Infiniti G35

Cadillac's smallest sedan offers V6 and V8 power. Base models have a 255-hp 3.6-liter V6. The high-performance CTS-V uses a 400-hp 5.7-liter V8. A 6-speed manual transmission is standard. Optional with the V6 is a 5-speed automatic with Sport and Winter modes but no manual shift gate. Cadillac says that, later in the 2005 model year, CTS will be available with a 210-hp 2.8-liter V6 to create a lower-cost entry-level model. Standard are antilock 4-wheel disc brakes, front side airbags, and head-protecting curtain side airbags. Also included are leather upholstery and OnStar assistance. Xenon headlamps and an antiskid

Specifications begin on page 547.

system are standard on the CTS-V and optional on V6 models. A Sport Package option upgrades V6s with speed-variable steering assist, larger brakes, rear load-leveling suspension, and 17-inch wheels vs. 16s. CTS-V features unique exterior and interior touches, sport suspension, and 18-inch wheels with run-flat tires. A navigation system with dashboard screen and voice activation is optional on V6 models. Satellite radio and a sunroof are available on all.

RATINGS	Base, 3.6 V6, auto.	Base w/Sport Pkg., 3.6 V6, auto.	CTS-V
ACCELERATION	7	7	8
FUEL ECONOMY	5	5	4
RIDE QUALITY	7	7	6
STEERING/HANDLING	7	7	8
QUIETNESS	7	6	5
CONTROLS/MATERIALS	7	7	7
ROOM/COMFORT (FRONT)	7	7	8
ROOM/COMFORT (REAR)	5	5	5
CARGO ROOM	5	5	5
VALUE WITHIN CLASS	9	8	5

Its bold styling may polarize, but the solid, sporty CTS is rewarding to drive, well-equipped, and a Best Buy value in its class. The 3.6 V6 has the response and refinement expected in a premium midsize sedan, while the rapid CTS-V costs much less than most V8 import rivals.

TOTAL	66	64	61

Average total for premium midsize cars: 61.7

ENGINES

	dohc V6	ohv V8
Size, liters/cu. in.	3.6/217	5.7/346
Horsepower @ rpm	255 @ 6200	400 @ 6000
Torque (lb-ft) @ rpm	252 @ 3200	395 @ 4800
Availability	S[1]	S[2]
EPA city/highway mpg		
6-speed manual	18/27	15/23
5-speed automatic	17/27	

1. Base. 2. CTS-V.

PRICES

Cadillac CTS	RETAIL PRICE	DEALER INVOICE
Base 4-door sedan	$31850	$29461
CTS-V 4-door sedan	49300	45603
Destination charge	695	695

2.8-liter model prices and equipment not available at time of publication. CTS-V adds $1300 Gas-Guzzler Tax.

STANDARD EQUIPMENT

Base: 3.6-liter V6 engine, 6-speed manual transmission, traction control, dual front airbags, front side airbags, curtain side airbags, antilock 4-wheel disc brakes, wiper-activated headlights, daytime running lights, air conditioning w/dual-zone automatic climate controls, OnStar assistance system w/one-year service, power steering, tilt leather-wrapped steering wheel w/radio and climate controls, cruise control, leather upholstery, front bucket seats, 8-way power driver seat, center console, cupholders, heated power mirrors, power windows, power door locks, remote keyless entry, AM/FM/CD player, analog clock, tachometer, automatic day/night rearview mirror, illuminated visor mirrors, rear defogger, variable-intermittent wipers, automatic headlights, floormats, theft-deterrent system, fog lights, 225/55HR16 tires, alloy wheels.

CTS-V adds: 5.7-liter V8 engine, upgraded brakes, antiskid system, tire-pressure monitor, navigation system, heated front seats w/power lumbar adjustment, 8-way power passenger seat, memory system (driver seat, mirrors), split folding rear seat, Bose AM/FM radio w/in-dash 6-disc CD changer, satellite radio, universal garage-door opener, xenon headlights w/washers, performance suspension, 245/45WR18 run-flat tires.

OPTIONAL EQUIPMENT

Major Packages

	RETAIL PRICE	DEALER INVOICE
Option Pkg. 1SC, Base	$8250	$7013
Luxury Pkg. and Sport Pkg. plus power sunroof, Bose AM/FM radio w/in-dash 6-disc CD changer, split folding rear seat, xenon headlights w/washers, polished alloy wheels.		
Luxury Pkg., Base	3165	2690
Base w/Sport Pkg.	2615	2223
Heated front seats, 8-way power passenger seat, driver-seat and mirror memory, wood/leather-wrapped steering wheel, universal garage-door opener, bright alloy wheels.		
Sport Pkg., Base	1875	1594
Base w/California Pkg.	1325	1126
Stabilitrak antiskid system, upgraded brake pads, variable-assist power steering, sport suspension, load-leveling rear suspension, 225/50WR17 tires, polished alloy wheels.		
California Pkg., Base	1820	1548
Manufacturer's Discount Price	*1270*	*1080*
5-speed automatic transmission, 8-way power passenger seat. Available only in California.		
Luxury California Pkg., Base	5965	5070
Manufacturer's Discount Price	*4965*	*4220*
Luxury Pkg. plus power sunroof, Bose AM/FM radio w/in-dash 6-disc CD changer, satellite radio (requires monthly service fee after 3rd month). Available only in California.		

Powertrain

5-speed automatic transmission, Base	1200	1020

Comfort & Convenience Features

Navigation system, Base	3125	2656
Base w/Pkg. 1SC	1850	1573
Includes Bose AM/FM radio w/in-dash 6-disc CD changer, satellite radio. Satellite radio requires monthly fee after 3rd month.		

 Specifications begin on page 547.

OPTIONAL EQUIPMENT (cont.)

	RETAIL PRICE	DEALER INVOICE
Bose AM/FM radio w/in-dash 6-disc CD changer, Base	$1275	$1084
Satellite radio, Base	325	276
Requires monthly fee after 3rd month.		
Power sunroof	1200	1020
Split folding rear seat, Base	450	382

Appearance & Special Purpose

Xenon headlights, Base	645	548
Includes headlight washers. Requires Sport Pkg.		

CADILLAC DEVILLE

CLASS: Premium large car
DRIVE WHEELS: Front-wheel drive
BASE PRICE RANGE: $45,695-$51,250. Built in USA.
ALSO CONSIDER: Lexus LS 430, Mercedes-Benz E-Class

Cadillac's largest car is also its only one with front-wheel drive. DeVille comes in three models, all with a 4.6-liter V8 and 4-speed automatic transmission. Base and DHS versions have a front bench seat and 275 hp. The sportier DTS has front bucket seats and 290 hp, down 10 from 2004. Traction control and ABS are standard for all. So are load-leveling rear suspension and front side airbags providing head and torso protection. Rear side airbags are optional. DTS includes an antiskid system that's available for other models. All DeVilles come with GM OnStar assistance and a tire-pressure monitor. DHS and DTS add heated/cooled front seats, heated steering wheel, and heated rear seats, all available for the base model. Linewide options include satellite radio, a navigation system with voice recognition and DVD playback with the transmission in Park, and Cadillac's Night Vision system, which uses infrared technology to detect heat-generating objects.

RATINGS	Base	DHS	DTS w/nav. sys.
ACCELERATION	7	7	7
FUEL ECONOMY	4	4	4
RIDE QUALITY	9	9	8
STEERING/HANDLING	6	6	7
QUIETNESS	8	8	8

RATINGS (cont.)	Base	DHS	DTS w/nav. sys.
CONTROLS/MATERIALS	7	7	6
ROOM/COMFORT (FRONT)	8	9	9
ROOM/COMFORT (REAR)	9	9	9
CARGO ROOM	6	6	6
VALUE WITHIN CLASS	6	7	7

Spacious and powerful, DeVille is the lowest-priced V8 sedan in the premium large-car class, and one of only two with front-wheel drive. Affluent younger buyers still favor imports, but a range of virtues qualify the big Cadillac as an alternative we Recommend.

TOTAL	70	72	71
Average total for premium large cars: 68.7			

ENGINES

	dohc V8	dohc V8
Size, liters/cu. in.	4.6/279	4.6/279
Horsepower @ rpm	275 @ 5600	290 @ 6000
Torque (lb-ft) @ rpm	300 @ 4000	295 @ 4400
Availability	S[1]	S[2]
EPA city/highway mpg		
4-speed automatic	18/27	18/27

1. Base, DHS. 2. DTS.

PRICES

Cadillac DeVille	RETAIL PRICE	DEALER INVOICE
Base 4-door sedan	$45695	$41811
DHS 4-door sedan	51250	46894
DTS 4-door sedan	51250	46894
Destination charge	795	795

STANDARD EQUIPMENT

Base: 4.6-liter V8 275-horsepower engine, 4-speed automatic transmission, traction control, dual front airbags, front side airbags, antilock 4-wheel disc brakes, tire-pressure monitor, wiper-activated headlights, daytime running lights, OnStar assistance system w/one-year service, air conditioning w/tri-zone automatic climate controls (including rear controls), interior air filter, power steering, tilt leather-wrapped steering wheel w/climate and radio controls, cruise control, leather upholstery, front split bench seat, 10-way power front seats, cupholders, trunk pass-through, heated power mirrors w/turn-signals, power windows, power door locks, remote keyless entry, AM/FM/CD player, digital clock, digital instruments, trip computer, illuminated front visor mirrors, variable-intermittent wipers, rear defogger, automatic day/night rearview mirror, compass, outside-temperature indicator, map lights, automatic headlights, automatic parking-brake release, floormats, theft-deterrent system, cornering lights, load-leveling suspension, 225/60SR16 tires, alloy wheels.

DHS adds: heated and cooled front seats, heated rear seats, front and rear power lumbar adjustment, front-seat lumbar massage, memory system (dri-

Specifications begin on page 547.

ver seat, mirrors, steering wheel), power tilt/telescope heated wood and leather-wrapped steering wheel, driver-side automatic day/night mirror, tilt-down back-up-aid mirrors, Bose AM/FM/cassette/CD player, analog instruments, tachometer, rear illuminated visor mirrors, rain-sensing wipers, power rear sunshade, chrome alloy wheels.

DTS adds: 4.6-liter V8 290-horsepower engine, antiskid system, front bucket seats, center console, tilt heated leather-wrapped steering wheel, fog lights, Continuously Variable Road Sensing Suspension, 235/55HR17 tires, alloy wheels. *Deletes:* memory system, power tilt/telescope wood and leather-wrapped steering wheel, rear-seat lumbar adjustment, driver-side automatic day/night mirror, tilt-down back-up-aid mirrors, rear illuminated visor mirrors, power rear-window sunshade, chrome alloy wheels.

OPTIONAL EQUIPMENT

Major Packages	RETAIL PRICE	DEALER INVOICE
Comfort and Convenience Pkg., Base	$1820	$1547
Heated and cooled front seats, heated rear seats, front-seat power lumbar adjustment, memory system (driver seat, mirrors, climate controls), heated steering wheel, driver-side automatic day/night mirror, tilt-down back-up-aid mirrors.		
Premium Pkg., Base	3315	2818
Power sunroof, satellite radio (requires monthly fee after 3rd month), 6-disc CD changer, cargo mat and net, chrome alloy wheels. Requires Comfort and Convenience Pkg.		
Premium Luxury Pkg., DTS	2080	1768
Rear side airbags, power tilt/telescope wood/leather-wrapped steering wheel, wood shift knob, memory system (seats, steering wheel, mirrors, climate controls), rear-obstacle-detection system, driver-side automatic day/night mirror, tilt-down back-up-aid mirrors, universal garage-door opener, cargo net, trunk mat.		
Safety and Security Pkg., Base, DHS	895	761
Antiskid system, rear-obstacle-detection system, universal garage-door opener. Base requires Comfort and Convenience Pkg.		
Safety		
Rear side airbags, Base, DHS	295	251
Night Vision	2250	1913
Includes head-up instrument display. Base includes rain-sensing wipers. Base requires Comfort and Convenience Pkg. DHS requires Safety and Security Pkg. DTS requires Premium Equipment Pkg.		
Comfort & Convenience Features		
Navigation system	1995	1696
Navigation system, DVD player, LCD screen, voice recognition. Requires 6-disc CD changer. Base requires Comfort and Convenience Pkg.		
Power sunroof	1550	1318
DHS deletes rear illuminated visor mirrors.		
AM/FM/cassette/CD player, Base	150	128

OPTIONAL EQUIPMENT (cont.)

	RETAIL PRICE	DEALER INVOICE
6-disc CD changer	$595	$506
Satellite radio	325	276
Requires monthly fee after 3rd month. Base requires Comfort and Convenience Pkg. DHS requires Safety and Security Pkg. DTS requires Premium Luxury Pkg.		
Digital instruments, DHS	150	128
Appearance & Special Purpose		
Chrome alloy wheels, Base, DTS	795	509
Base requires Comfort and Convenience Pkg.		

CADILLAC SRX

CLASS: Premium midsize sport-utility vehicle
DRIVE WHEELS: Rear-wheel drive, all-wheel drive
BASE PRICE RANGE: $38,340-$50,135. Built in USA.
ALSO CONSIDER: Acura MDX, Lexus RX, Volvo XC90

Cadillac's car-type SUV gets only detail changes for 2005. SRX seats up to seven and offers V6 and V8 engines. The only transmission is a 5-speed automatic with manual shift gate. Rear-wheel drive is standard, all-wheel drive optional. Intended for on-road use, the AWD system does not include low-range gearing. V6s come on 17-inch wheels and offer as options the 18s standard on V8s. Any SRX can be ordered with GM's Magnetic Ride Control suspension that automatically adjusts firmness based on road surface. Antilock 4-wheel disc brakes, traction control, and leather upholstery are standard. So are front side airbags and head-protecting curtain side airbags covering the front two seating rows. A split folding 2nd-row seat slides 4 inches fore/aft for extra leg room or cargo space. An available 3rd-row seat is power operated to fold flush with the cargo floor. It replaces an available compartmentalized storage bin. V8s include wood interior trim, heated front seats, and power-adjustable pedals; all are available for V6s. Also optional are rear DVD entertainment, Cadillac's UltraView sunroof with a 5.6-square-foot opening, and UltraViewPlus that adds a vented glass panel over the 3rd-row seat. For '05, the SRX gauge cluster adds chrome accents, a towing package

 Specifications begin on page 547.

is optional for V6 models as well as V8s, and rated towing capacity increases 1000 lb to 4250.

RATINGS

	V6 AWD	V8 2WD	V8 AWD
ACCELERATION	6	7	7
FUEL ECONOMY	4	4	4
RIDE QUALITY	7	7	7
STEERING/HANDLING	7	6	7
QUIETNESS	7	7	7
CONTROLS/MATERIALS	7	7	7
ROOM/COMFORT (FRONT)	7	7	7
ROOM/COMFORT (REAR)	7	7	7
CARGO ROOM	7	7	7
VALUE WITHIN CLASS	9	8	8

Against similarly priced premium midsize SUVs, SRX is competitive in performance, features, and accommodations, if not always in the quality of cabin appointments. But unless you off-road or tow heavy loads, the SRX's road manners and efficient packaging make it preferable to most truck-type rivals. Add AWD security, and it's a thoughtful alternative to a traditional luxury sedan. That's Best Buy material in this class.

TOTAL	68	67	68

Average total for premium midsize sport-utility vehicles: 59.6

ENGINES

	dohc V6	dohc V8
Size, liters/cu. in.	3.6/217	4.6/279
Horsepower @ rpm	255 @ 6500	320 @ 6400
Torque (lb-ft) @ rpm	254 @ 3200	315 @ 4400
Availability	S	O
EPA city/highway mpg		
5-speed automatic	16/22[1]	15/20[2]

1. 16/23 w/2WD. 2. 15/21 w/2WD.

PRICES

Cadillac SRX	RETAIL PRICE	DEALER INVOICE
V6 4-door wagon	$38340	$35465
V8 4-door wagon	50135	46375
Destination charge	695	695

STANDARD EQUIPMENT

V6: 3.6-liter V6 engine, 5-speed automatic transmission w/manual-shift capability, traction control, dual front airbags, front side airbags, front and 2nd-row curtain side airbags, antilock 4-wheel disc brakes, antiskid system, rear-obstacle-detection system, wiper-activated headlights, daytime running lights, air conditioning w/dual-zone automatic climate controls, OnStar assistance system w/one-year service, power steering, tilt leather-wrapped steering wheel w/radio and climate controls, cruise control, leather upholstery, front bucket seats, 8-way power driver seat, center console, cupholders, 2nd-row adjustable split folding seat, heated power mirrors, power windows, power door locks, remote keyless entry, AM/FM/CD player, digital clock, tachometer, variable-intermittent wipers, automatic day/night rearview mirror, compass, illuminated visor mirrors, cargo cover, rear defogger, intermittent rear wiper/washer, automatic headlights, floormats, theft-deterrent system, rear privacy glass, fog lights, roof rails, 235/65HR17 front tires, 255/60HR17 rear tires, alloy wheels.

V8 adds: 4.6-liter V8 engine, tire-pressure monitor, rear air conditioning, heated front seats, 8-way power passenger seat, power-adjustable pedals, memory system (driver seat, mirrors, pedals), wood/leather-wrapped steering wheel, wood interior trim, power sunroof, Bose AM/FM radio w/in-dash 6-disc CD changer, driver-side automatic day/night mirror, universal garage-door opener, rear storage system, roof rack, 235/60VR18 front tires, 255/55VR18 rear tires.

OPTIONAL EQUIPMENT

Major Packages	RETAIL PRICE	DEALER INVOICE
Luxury Option Pkg. 1SB, V6	$2640	$2244
Rear air conditioning, 8-way power passenger seat, memory system (driver seat, mirrors), wood/leather-wrapped steering wheel, wood interior trim, AM/FM radio w/in-dash 6-disc CD changer, driver-side automatic day/night mirror, universal garage-door opener, rear storage system.		
Luxury Performance Option Pkg. 1SC, V6	13660	11611
Luxury Option Pkg. 1SB plus all-wheel drive, tire-pressure monitor, power-adjustable pedals w/memory, heated front seats, 3rd-row power-stowable seat, Ultraview power sunroof, navigation system, rear-seat DVD entertainment system, Bose sound system, satellite radio (requires monthly fee after 3rd month), xenon headlights w/washers, Magnetic Ride Control Suspension, 235/60VR18 front tires, 255/VR18 rear tires. Deletes rear storage system.		
Luxury Performance Option Pkg. 1SC, V8	6920	5882
Navigation system, rear-seat DVD entertainment system, satellite radio (requires monthly fee after 3rd month), 3rd-row power-stowable seat, xenon headlights w/washers, trailering equipment (heavy-duty engine cooling, wiring harness), Magnetic Ride Control Suspension.		
Luxury Comfort Pkg., V6	995	846
Heated front seats, power-adjustable pedals, satellite radio (requires monthly fee after 3rd month).		
Luxury Utility Pkg., V6	2250	1913
All-wheel drive, tire-pressure monitor, power-stowable 3rd-row seat, Bose sound system. Requires Option Pkg. 1SB. Deletes rear storage system. Deletes rear storage system.		
Trailering Equipment Pkg.	250	213
Heavy-duty engine cooling, wiring harness.		
Powertrain		
All-wheel drive	1900	1615
V6 requires Luxury Option Pkg. 1SB.		

 Specifications begin on page 547.

Comfort & Convenience Features	RETAIL PRICE	DEALER INVOICE
UltraView power sunroof, V6	$1800	$1530
Includes power sunshades. V6 requires Luxury Option Pkg. 1SB. Std. V8.		
UltraView Plus power sunroof, V6 w/Pkg. 1SC, V8	450	383
V6 w/Pkg. 1SB and Luxury Utility Pkg.	2250	1913
Includes venting sunroof over 3rd-row seat, power sunshades.		
Navigation system, V6	1995	1696
Requires Luxury Option Pkg. 1SB., Luxury Utility Pkg.		
Satellite radio	325	276
Requires monthly fee after 3rd month. V6 requires Luxury Option Pkg. 1SB.		
3rd-row power-stowable seat, V8	1000	850
Deletes rear storage system.		
Power-adjustable pedals, V6	150	128
Includes memory. Requires Luxury Option Pkg. 1SB.		
Heated front seats, V6	450	383
Requires Luxury Option Pkg. 1SB.		
18-inch alloy wheels, V6	1000	850
Includes 235/60VR18 front tires, 255/55VR18 rear tires. Requires Luxury Option Pkg. 1SB.		

CADILLAC STS

CLASS: Premium midsize car
DRIVE WHEELS: Rear-wheel drive, all-wheel drive
BASE PRICE RANGE: $40,300-$46,800. Built in USA.
ALSO CONSIDER: Acura RL, BMW 5-Series, Mercedes-Benz E-Class

Cadillac launches a new midsize luxury sedan for 2005, replacing the front-wheel-drive Seville with the STS, which comes with either rear- or all-wheel drive. Basically a stretched version of Cadillac's premium midsize CTS sedan, STS is 4.7 inches shorter than Seville, but an inch taller and a sizable 4.2 inches longer in wheelbase. STS offers a 255-hp 3.6-liter V6 with rear-wheel drive or a 320-hp 4.6 V8 with rear-drive or AWD. The sole transmission is a 5-speed automatic with manual shift gate. Antilock 4-wheel disc brakes and antiskid/traction control are standard, as are front side airbags and head-protecting curtain side airbags. OnStar assistance is also included. Adaptive cruise control designed to maintain a set following distance is an option that can be teamed with a 4-color head-up instrument display. Also available are heated/cooled front seats, a touch-screen navigation system with voice recognition, and satellite radio. A $13,115 Preferred Equipment package includes performance tires and steering, and 18-inch alloy wheels vs. standard 17s. It also includes GM's Magnetic Ride Control with shock absorbers that automatically adjust firmness within Touring and Sport settings to match the road surface. Even more-aggressive 18-inch tires and upgraded brakes can be ordered in a Performance Handling package. This evaluation is based on preview test drives.

RATINGS	V6	V8	V8 w/AWD, 18-in. wheels
ACCELERATION	7	8	8
FUEL ECONOMY	5	5	5
RIDE QUALITY	8	8	6
STEERING/HANDLING	7	7	8
QUIETNESS	8	8	7
CONTROLS/MATERIALS	7	7	6
ROOM/COMFORT (FRONT)	7	7	7
ROOM/COMFORT (REAR)	5	5	5
CARGO ROOM	3	3	3
VALUE WITHIN CLASS	6	5	4

STS impresses with its dynamic capabilities, but disappoints with subpar rear-seat space and cargo room. Interior materials and assembly are not up to the best-in-class standard, either. We're disappointed that $62,500 is the price of admission for all-wheel drive, making this security feature an expensive proposition. Even without AWD, options can add quickly to the price, making an intelligently optioned, V6, rear-drive STS the best value in this line.

TOTAL	63	63	59

Average total for premium midsize cars: 61.7

ENGINES

	dohc V6	dohc V8
Size, liters/cu. in.	3.6/217	4.6/278
Horsepower @ rpm	255 @ 6500	320 @ 6400
Torque (lb-ft) @ rpm	252 @ 3200	315 @ 4400
Availability	S[1]	S[2]
EPA city/highway mpg		
5-speed automatic	NA	NA

1. V6. 2. V8.

PRICES

Cadillac STS

	RETAIL PRICE	DEALER INVOICE
V6 4-door sedan	$40300	$37278
V8 4-door sedan	46800	43290
Destination charge	695	695

V8 requires Preferred Equipment Group. V8 w/all-wheel drive adds $1000 Gas-Guzzler Tax.

 Specifications begin on page 547.

STANDARD EQUIPMENT

V6: 3.6-liter V6 engine, 5-speed automatic transmission w/manual-shift capability, traction control, dual front airbags, front side airbags, curtain side airbags, antilock 4-wheel disc brakes, brake assist, antiskid system, tire-pressure monitor, rear-obstacle-detection system, wiper-activated headlights, daytime running lights, air conditioning w/dual-zone automatic climate controls, power steering, power tilt/telescope leather-wrapped steering wheel w/radio and climate controls, cruise control, leather upholstery, front bucket seats, center console, cupholders, trunk pass-through, aluminum interior trim, heated power mirrors w/driver-side automatic day/night, power windows, power door locks, remote keyless entry, OnStar assistance system w/one-year service, Bose AM/FM/CD player, digital clock, tachometer, automatic day/night rearview mirror, compass, variable-intermittent wipers, illuminated visor mirrors, rear defogger, floormats, theft-deterrent system, fog lights, 235/50VR17 front tires, 255/45VR17 rear tires, alloy wheels.

V8 adds: 4.6-liter V8 engine, heated leather-wrapped steering wheel, heated front and rear seats, 8-way power front seats w/power lumbar adjustment, memory system (front seats, mirrors, steering wheel, radio, climate controls), wood interior trim, interior air filter, Bose AM/FM radio w/in-dash 6-disc CD changer, universal garage-door opener, 235/50SR17 tires, polished alloy wheels.

OPTIONAL EQUIPMENT

Major Packages	RETAIL PRICE	DEALER INVOICE
Preferred Equipment Group 1SB, V6	$2390	$2032
Heated 8-way power front seats, interior air filter, Bose AM/FM radio w/in-dash 6-disc CD changer, memory system (front seats, mirrors, steering wheel, radio, climate controls), rain-sensing wipers.		
Preferred Equipment Group 1SC, V6	8595	7376
Preferred Equipment Group 1SB plus limited-slip differential, upgraded tire-pressure monitor, power sunroof, navigation system, in-dash 6-disc CD/DVD changer, satellite radio (requires monthly fee after 3rd month), heated/cooled front seats, heated rear seats, wood interior trim, wood/leather-wrapped steering wheel, universal garage-door opener, trunk convenience pkg., rear spoiler, performance steering and brakes, polished alloy wheels.		
Premium Upgrade Pkg., V6	730	621
Satellite radio (requires monthly fee after 3rd month), wood interior trim, trunk convenience pkg. Requires Preferred Equipment Group 1SB.		
Preferred Equipment Group 1SE, V8	2845	2418
Standard equipment.		
Preferred Equipment Group 1SF, V8	11065	9405
Limited-slip differential, upgraded tire-pressure monitor, navigation system, in-dash 6-disc CD/DVD changer, power sunroof, heated/cooled front seats, heated wood/leather-wrapped steering wheel, rain-sensing wipers, rear spoiler, automatic headlight dimming, xenon headlights w/washers, Magnetic Ride Control Suspension, 235/50VR17 front tires, 255/45VR17 rear tires.		

OPTIONAL EQUIPMENT (cont.)

	RETAIL PRICE	DEALER INVOICE
Preferred Equipment Group 1SG, V8	$13115	$11148
Preferred Equipment Group 1SF plus upgraded leather upholstery, performance steering and brakes, additional engine cooling, power-steering-fluid cooling, 235/50WR18 front tires, 255/45WR18 rear tires, unique alloy wheels.		
Performance Handling Pkg., V8	795	676
Performance brakes, 235/45ZR18 front tires, 255/45ZR18 rear tires. Requires Preferred Equipment Group 1SG. NA w/all-wheel drive.		

Powertrain

All-wheel drive, V8	1900	1615
Requires Preferred Equipment Group 1SG.		

Comfort & Convenience Features

Power sunroof	1200	1020
V6 requires Preferred Equipment Group 1SB.		
Upgraded leather upholstery, V8 w/1SF	1200	1020
Adaptive cruise control, V8	2300	1955
Requires Preferred Equipment Group 1SF or 1SG. Includes head-up instrument display when ordered w/Preferred Equipment Group 1SG.		

CADILLAC XLR

CLASS: Premium sporty/performance car
DRIVE WHEELS: Rear-wheel drive
BASE PRICE: $75,835. Built in USA.
ALSO CONSIDER: Lexus SC 430, Mercedes-Benz SL-Class

Cadillac's 2-seat convertible is unchanged for 2005, except for paint and interior-trim colors. The XLR's chassis, structure, and composite-plastic body panels are similar to the Chevrolet Corvette's, but XLR has unique styling, a power-retactable hardtop, and different suspension tuning. Its V8, a 320-hp version of Cadillac's 4.6-liter Northstar, is also different. The sole transmission is a 5-speed automatic with manual shift gate. An antiskid/traction-control system is standard, as is GM's Magnetic Ride Control, which automatically adjusts suspension firmness based on the road surface. Tires are 18-inch run-flats; no spare is provided. XLR comes with heated/cooled leather seats, wood interior trim, and side airbags covering head and torso.

 Specifications begin on page 547.

A 7-inch dashboard screen displays navigation and audio functions and plays video DVDs with the transmission in Park. Also standard are adaptive cruise control designed to maintain a set following distance and Cadillac's Keyless Access that allows starting the engine and operating the locks without removing the keyfob from pocket or purse. Satellite radio is the only option.

RATINGS

	Base
ACCELERATION	8
FUEL ECONOMY	4
RIDE QUALITY	6
STEERING/HANDLING	8
QUIETNESS	6
CONTROLS/MATERIALS	7
ROOM/COMFORT (FRONT)	7
ROOM/COMFORT (REAR)	0
CARGO ROOM	2
VALUE WITHIN CLASS	5

Priced between the less-expensive Lexus SC430 and costlier Mercedes-Benz SL and Jaguar XK rivals, XLR need make no apology for features and performance. Cadillac's challenge is to convince well-heeled shoppers that it's in the same league as those prestige brands.

TOTAL	53

Average total for premium sporty/performance cars: 48.3

ENGINES

	dohc V8
Size, liters/cu. in.	4.6/279
Horsepower @ rpm	320 @ 6400
Torque (lb-ft) @ rpm	310 @ 4400
Availability	S
EPA city/highway mpg	
5-speed automatic	17/25

PRICES

Cadillac XLR	RETAIL PRICE	DEALER INVOICE
Base 2-door convertible	$75835	$70147
Destination charge	815	815

STANDARD EQUIPMENT

Base: 4.6-liter V8 engine, 5-speed automatic transmission w/manual-shift capability, traction control, dual front airbags, side airbags, antilock 4-wheel disc brakes, antiskid system, tire-pressure monitor, rear-obstacle-detection system, daytime running lights, air conditioning w/dual-zone automatic climate controls, interior air filter, OnStar assistance system w/one-year service, navigation system w/voice recognition, power steering, power tilt/telescope wood/leather-wrapped steering wheel w/radio controls, adaptive cruise control, leather upholstery, heated/cooled bucket seats, 8-way power front seats w/lumbar adjustment, memory system (driver seat, mirrors, steering wheel, radio, climate controls), center console, cupholders, wood interior trim, heated power mirrors w/tilt-down back-up aid and driver-side automatic day/night, power windows, power door locks, remote keyless entry, keyless access, Bose AM/FM radio w/in-dash 6-disc CD/DVD changer, digital clock, tachometer, head-up instrument display, automatic day/night rearview mirror, universal garage-door opener, illuminated visor mirrors, rain-sensing variable-intermittent wipers, map lights, rear defogger, power-retractable hardtop, automatic parking-brake release, automatic headlights, floormats, theft-deterrent system, bi-xenon headlights, fog lights, cornering lights, automatic suspension control, 235/50WR18 run-flat tires, alloy wheels.

OPTIONAL EQUIPMENT	RETAIL PRICE	DEALER INVOICE
Satellite radio	$325	$276
Requires monthly fee after 3rd month.		

CHEVROLET ASTRO

CLASS: Minivan
DRIVE WHEELS: Rear-wheel drive, all-wheel drive
BASE PRICE RANGE: $22,800-$26,300. Built in USA.
ALSO CONSIDER: Dodge Caravan, Honda Odyssey, Toyota Sienna

No news is the only news for Astro and GMC's near-identical Safari, which GM says will be dropped after model year 2005. America's only truck-type minivans, they share a basic design dating from the late 1980s. Astro comes in a single body length with right-side sliding door, a 4.3-liter V6, and automatic transmission. It's available with rear-wheel drive or all-wheel drive and seating for up to eight. Full-height rear cargo doors are standard; Dutch doors with separate-opening upper glass are optional. Astro is also sold as a 2-seat Cargo Van. Antilock 4-wheel disc brakes are standard. Traction control and side airbags are unavailable.

RATINGS	2WD LS	AWD LS
ACCELERATION	4	4
FUEL ECONOMY	3	3

RATINGS (cont.)	2WD LS	AWD LS
RIDE QUALITY	3	3
STEERING/HANDLING	3	3
QUIETNESS	3	3
CONTROLS/MATERIALS	6	6
ROOM/COMFORT (FRONT)	4	4
ROOM/COMFORT (REAR)	6	6
CARGO ROOM	10	10
VALUE WITHIN CLASS	3	3

These old-timers are best purchased for cargo hauling and light-duty towing. A front-drive minivan is the better choice for passenger use. Look for larger-than-usual discounts in Astro/Safari's final season.

TOTAL	45	45

Average total for minivans: 58.0

ENGINES

	ohv V6
Size, liters/cu. in.	4.3/262
Horsepower @ rpm	190 @ 4400
Torque (lb-ft) @ rpm	250 @ 2800
Availability	S
EPA city/highway mpg	
4-speed automatic	16/20[1]

1. 14/17 w/AWD.

PRICES

Chevrolet Astro	RETAIL PRICE	DEALER INVOICE
2WD 3-door Cargo van	$22800	$20634
AWD 3-door Cargo van	25300	22897
2WD 3-door Passenger van	24300	21992
AWD 3-door Passenger van	26300	23802
Destination charge	740	740

STANDARD EQUIPMENT

Cargo: 4.3-liter V6 engine, 4-speed automatic transmission, dual front airbags, antilock 4-wheel disc brakes, daytime running lights, front air conditioning, power steering, vinyl upholstery, front bucket seats, cupholders, black rubber floor covering, variable-intermittent wipers, AM/FM radio, digital clock, automatic headlights, theft-deterrent system, 215/70R16 tires. **AWD** models add: all-wheel drive.

Passenger adds: tilt steering wheel, cruise control, cloth upholstery, 8-passenger seating w/front bucket seats and two 3-passenger rear bench seats, power mirrors, power windows, power door locks, visor mirrors, map lights, carpeting, floormats, rear privacy glass, 6-wire trailer harness. **AWD** models add: all-wheel drive.

OPTIONAL EQUIPMENT

Major Packages

	RETAIL PRICE	DEALER INVOICE
LS Preferred Equipment Group 1SC, Passenger	$1245	$1071
Remote keyless entry, AM/FM/CD player, chrome grille, bodyside cladding, alloy wheels.		
LS Preferred Equipment Group 1SD, Passenger	3495	3006
LS Preferred Equipment Group 1SC plus rear air conditioning, rear heater, 6-way power driver seat, AM/FM/cassette/CD player, overhead console, compass, outside-temperature indicator, illuminated visor mirrors, rear defogger, rear Dutch doors, roof rack.		
LT Preferred Equipment Group 1SE, Passenger	5145	4425
LS Preferred Equipment Group plus leather-wrapped steering wheel, upgraded upholstery, rear radio controls, headphone jacks, universal garage-door opener, bodyside stripes.		
Trailering Special Equipment	265	228
Platform trailer hitch, 8-lead wiring harness.		

Powertrain

Limited-slip rear differential	280	241

Comfort & Convenience Features

Rear air conditioning, Passenger	525	452
Rear heater	240	206
Dutch doors, Passenger	460	396
Includes rear defogger.		
Leather upholstery, Passenger	950	817
Requires Preferred Equipment Group 1SE.		
2nd-row bucket seats, Passenger	NC	NC
Requires Preferred Equipment 1SE.		
Remote keyless entry	170	146
Cargo requires ZQ2 Convenience Group.		
AM/FM/CD player	205	176
Cargo requires ZQ2 Convenience Group.		
AM/FM/cassette/CD player, Passenger	100	86
Requires Preferred Equipment Group 1SC.		
Rear radio controls, Passenger	125	108
Includes headphone jacks. Requires Preferred Equipment Group 1SD.		
Overhead console, Passenger	225	194
Includes compass, outside-temperature indicator, storage. Requires Preferred Equipment Group 1SC, illuminated visor mirrors.		
Illuminated visor mirrors, Passenger	100	86
Requires overhead console.		

Appearance & Special Purpose

Running boards, Passenger	400	344
Requires Preferred Equipment Group.		
Roof rack, Passenger	130	112

CHEVROLET AVEO

CLASS: Compact car
DRIVE WHEELS: Front-wheel drive
BASE PRICE RANGE: $9,455-$12,795. Built in South Korea.
ALSO CONSIDER: Ford Focus, Hyundai Elantra, Kia Spectra

Chevrolet's entry-level car is among the smallest, least-expensive cars sold in the U.S. Aveo comes as a 4-dr hatchback and as a slightly longer sedan. Both use a 103-hp 4-cyl engine with manual or optional automatic transmissions. Trim levels ascend from Special Value Model (SVM), to LS, to LT. All come with tilt steering wheel, height-adjustable driver seat, and split folding rear seat. None offers side airbags. Optional ABS and standard air conditioning are exclusive to LS and LT. Alloy wheels and power windows/locks/heated mirrors are also standard for LTs, which is the only model to offer a sunroof. For '05, SVM and LS models get restyled wheel covers, and all Aveos add black roof-pillar trim. Aveo is built in South Korea by GM Daewoo Automotive Technologies, a General Motors-run remnant of bankrupt Daewoo Motors, which originated Aveo's design.

RATINGS	LS sdn, man.	LS hatch, auto.
ACCELERATION	3	2
FUEL ECONOMY	8	7
RIDE QUALITY	5	5
STEERING/HANDLING	4	4
QUIETNESS	4	4
CONTROLS/MATERIALS	4	4
ROOM/COMFORT (FRONT)	5	5
ROOM/COMFORT (REAR)	3	3
CARGO ROOM	2	6
VALUE WITHIN CLASS	3	3

The surprisingly refined and likable Aveo stacks up well against other budget wheels like Hyundai Accent and Kia Rio. An unproven track record is a minus. Shoppers considering any of these should check out larger, more-established rivals, if budget permits.

TOTAL	41	43

Average total for compact cars: 48.4

ENGINES

	dohc I4
Size, liters/cu. in.	1.6/98
Horsepower @ rpm	103 @ 6000
Torque (lb-ft) @ rpm	107 @ 3600
Availability	S
EPA city/highway mpg	
5-speed manual	27/35
4-speed automatic	26/34

PRICES

Chevrolet Aveo	RETAIL PRICE	DEALER INVOICE
SVM 4-door sedan	$9455	$8935
SVM 4-door hatchback	9455	8935
LS 4-door sedan	11300	10566
LS 4-door hatchback	11300	10566
LT 4-door sedan	12570	11753
LT 4-door hatchback	12795	11964
Destination charge	540	540

STANDARD EQUIPMENT

SVM: 1.6-liter 4-cylinder engine, 5-speed manual transmission, dual front airbags, daytime running lights, emergency inside trunk release (sedan), power steering, tilt steering wheel, cloth upholstery, front bucket seats, height-adjustable driver seat, center console, cupholders, split folding rear seat, AM/FM radio, digital clock, tachometer, variable-intermittent wipers, visor mirrors, cargo cover (hatchback), rear defogger, rear wiper/washer (hatchback), 185/60R14 tires, wheel covers.

LS adds: air conditioning, interior air filter, floormats.

LT adds: heated power mirrors, power windows, power door locks, remote keyless entry, AM/FM/CD/MP3 player, rear spoiler (hatchback), alloy wheels.

OPTIONAL EQUIPMENT

Powertrain	RETAIL PRICE	DEALER INVOICE
4-speed automatic transmission, LS, LT	$850	$765
Safety		
Antilock brakes, LS, LT	400	360
Comfort & Convenience Features		
Power sunroof, LT	725	653
AM/FM/CD/MP3 player, LS	300	270
Premium speakers, LT	250	225
Appearance & Special Purpose		
Alloy wheels, LS	375	338

CHEVROLET BLAZER

CLASS: Midsize sport-utility vehicle
DRIVE WHEELS: Rear-wheel drive, 4-wheel drive
BASE PRICE RANGE: $21,165-$24,165. Built in USA.
ALSO CONSIDER: Ford Explorer, Toyota 4Runner

Chevy consigns 4-dr Blazers to the fleet market for 2005, leaving retail buyers with an unchanged 2-dr model. This SUV uses an 11-year-old truck-based design and seats four. It has a 4.3-liter V6, manual and automatic transmissions, and standard antilock 4-wheel disc brakes. Front side airbags are unavailable. Blazer is offered with rear-wheel drive or one of two 4WD setups with low-range gearing: optional all-surface Autotrac or basic 4WD that should not be left engaged on dry pavement. An off-road-oriented ZR2 package features a high-riding suspension, larger tires, fortified chassis components, skid plates, tubular side steps, and front brush guard.

RATINGS

	2WD Base, auto.
ACCELERATION	5
FUEL ECONOMY	4
RIDE QUALITY	3
STEERING/HANDLING	2
QUIETNESS	3
CONTROLS/MATERIALS	5
ROOM/COMFORT (FRONT)	4
ROOM/COMFORT (REAR)	2
CARGO ROOM	7
VALUE WITHIN CLASS	2

Blazer is capable and usually carries deep discounts, but that's not enough to offset an indifferent ride, mediocre fit/finish, and the limitations of an elderly 2-dr design. ZR2 appeals to a small, select audience.

TOTAL	37

Average total for midsize sport-utility vehicles: 54.7

ENGINES

	ohv V6
Size, liters/cu. in.	4.3/262
Horsepower @ rpm	190 @ 4400
Torque (lb-ft) @ rpm	250 @ 2800
Availability	S
EPA city/highway mpg	
5-speed manual	15/20[1]
4-speed automatic	15/19[2]

1. 15/21 w/2WD. 2. 17/23 w/2WD.

PRICES

Chevrolet Blazer

	RETAIL PRICE	DEALER INVOICE
2WD Base 2-door wagon	$21165	$19154
4WD Base 2-door wagon	24165	21869
Destination charge	685	685

STANDARD EQUIPMENT

Base: 4.3-liter V6 engine, 5-speed manual transmission, dual front airbags, antilock 4-wheel disc brakes, daytime running lights, power steering, air conditioning, cloth upholstery, front bucket seats, center console, split front bench seat, cupholders, split folding rear seat, AM/FM/CD player, digital clock, tachometer, automatic headlights, variable-intermittent wipers, theft-deterrent system, tailgate, rear privacy glass, 235/70R15 tires, alloy wheels.
4WD adds: 4-wheel drive, 2-speed transfer case.

OPTIONAL EQUIPMENT

Major Packages

	RETAIL PRICE	DEALER INVOICE
1SB Preferred Equipment Group, 2WD	$1150	$989
Manufacturer's Discount Price	*150*	*129*
4WD	1190	1023
Manufacturer's Discount Price	*190*	*163*
Tilt leather-wrapped steering wheel, cruise control, floor-mounted shifter (w/automatic transmission), heated power mirrors, power windows and door locks, remote keyless entry, passenger-side visor mirror, floormats, roof rack, front tow hooks (4WD).		
1SC Preferred Equipment Group, 2WD	2305	1982
Manufacturer's Discount Price	*1305*	*1122*
4WD	2345	2017
Manufacturer's Discount Price	*1345*	*1157*
1SB Preferred Equipment Group plus 6-way power driver seat, passenger-seat walk-in device, overhead console, compass, outside-temperature indicator, illuminated visor mirrors, power liftgate release, rear defogger, rear wiper/washer, theft-deterrent alarm, rear deep-tinted glass.		
ZR2 Wide Stance Performance Pkg., 2WD	2500	2150
Manufacturer's Discount Price, 2WD w/1SB or 1SC Group	*1500*	*1290*

OPTIONAL EQUIPMENT (cont.)

	RETAIL PRICE	DEALER INVOICE
4WD	$2000	$1720
Manufacturer's Discount Price, 4WD w/1SB or 1SC Group	*1000*	*860*
Heavy-duty wide-stance chassis, heavy-duty suspension, raised ride height, Bilstein shock absorbers, skid plates, heavy-duty differential gears and axles, floormats, brush guard (2WD), side steps (2WD), fender flares, rear-mounted full-size spare tire, 265/75R15 on/off-road tires. Requires limited-slip differential. 2WD requires Trailering Special Equipment.		
ZM8 Rear Convenience Group	325	280
Power liftgate release, rear defogger, rear wiper/washer. Requires 1SB Preferred Equipment Group.		
Trailering Special Equipment	210	181
Includes platform hitch, 8-wire harness. 2WD models require ZR2 Wide Stance Performance Pkg. or automatic transmission.		
Powertrain		
4-speed automatic transmission	1000	860
Limited-slip rear differential	270	232
Autotrac 4WD transfer case, 4WD	225	194
Requires automatic transmission.		
Comfort & Convenience Features		
Power sunroof	800	688
Manufacturer's Discount Price, ordered w/AM/FM radio w/in-dash 6-disc CD changer (credit)	*(200)*	*(172)*
Requires Preferred Equipment Group.		
Deluxe overhead console	330	284
Includes universal garage-door opener, trip computer, automatic day/night rearview and driver-side mirrors, compass. Requires 1SC Preferred Equipment Group.		
AM/FM/cassette/CD player	100	86
Requires Preferred Equipment Group.		
AM/FM radio w/in-dash 6-disc CD changer	395	340
Requires Preferred Equipment Group.		
Rear defogger	125	108
Appearance & Special Purpose		
Fog lights	115	99
Requires Preferred Equipment Group.		
Roof rack	150	129

CHEVROLET CAVALIER

CLASS: Compact car
DRIVE WHEELS: Front-wheel drive
BASE PRICE RANGE: $10,325-$17,710. Built in USA.
ALSO CONSIDER: Ford Focus, Honda Civic, Toyota Corolla

CHEVROLET

Cavalier is unchanged for a brief 2005 finale. The new Cobalt is scheduled to take over by midmodel year. Cavalier offers coupes and sedans and comes in four trim levels: 1SV, base, LS, and top-line LS Sport. All use a 4-cyl engine with manual transmission or optional automatic except the price-leader 1SV coupe, which is manual only and offers no options. ABS is available for base models, standard on LS and LS Sport. Available front side airbags provide torso and head protection. Other options include OnStar assistance for LS and LS Sport, satellite radio, and a CD player that reads MP3 discs. LS Sports wear lower-body flares and a rear spoiler. They also come with a firmer suspension and 16-inch alloy wheels that are included in a base-model Sport Appearance package. Pontiac's Sunfire shares Cavalier's basic design, but doesn't offer sedans.

RATINGS	LS sdn, auto.	LS Sport cpe, man.
ACCELERATION	4	5
FUEL ECONOMY	5	6
RIDE QUALITY	4	3
STEERING/HANDLING	5	6
QUIETNESS	3	3
CONTROLS/MATERIALS	4	4
ROOM/COMFORT (FRONT)	3	3
ROOM/COMFORT (REAR)	3	2
CARGO ROOM	3	3
VALUE WITHIN CLASS	4	3

Cavalier and Sunfire are low-priced cars that are often discounted. But with a decade-old design, they feel ancient next to newer competitors and badly trail most for refinement, workmanship, and space efficiency. Sunfire emphasizes "expressive" styling, but does not offer the sedan body style most small-car buyers prefer.

TOTAL	38	38

Average total for compact cars: 48.4

ENGINES	dohc I4
Size, liters/cu. in.	2.2/134
Horsepower @ rpm	140 @ 5600
Torque (lb-ft) @ rpm	150 @ 4000
Availability	S
EPA city/highway mpg	
5-speed manual	26/37
4-speed automatic	24/34

Specifications begin on page 547.

PRICES

Chevrolet Cavalier

	RETAIL PRICE	DEALER INVOICE
1SV 2-door coupe	$10325	$9757
Base 2-door coupe	14410	13473
Base 4-door sedan	14610	13660
LS 2-door coupe	16090	15044
LS 4-door sedan	16290	15231
LS Sport 2-door coupe	17510	16372
LS Sport 4-door sedan	17710	16559
Destination charge	565	565

STANDARD EQUIPMENT

Base: 2.2-liter 4-cylinder engine, 5-speed manual transmission, dual front airbags, daytime running lights, air conditioning, power steering, cloth upholstery, front bucket seats, center console, cupholders, split folding rear seat w/trunk pass-through, AM/FM radio, digital clock, tachometer, rear defogger, power remote decklid release, theft-deterrent system, 195/70R14 tires, wheel covers.

1SV adds: AM/FM/CD player.

LS adds: antilock brakes, cruise control, tilt steering wheel, power mirrors, power windows, power door locks, remote keyless entry, map lights, variable-intermittent wipers, visor mirrors, floormats, 195/65R15 tires.

LS Sport adds: rear spoiler, fog lights, sport suspension, 205/55R16 tires, chrome alloy wheels.

OPTIONAL EQUIPMENT

Major Packages

	RETAIL PRICE	DEALER INVOICE
1SB Option Pkg., Base coupe	$365	$329
Base sedan	350	315

Tilt steering wheel, AM/FM/CD player, intermittent wipers, easy-entry front-passenger seat (coupe), visor mirrors, additional cupholder, floormats, bodyside moldings, front mudguards.

Sport Appearance Pkg., Base	600	540

Rear spoiler, sport suspension, 205/55R16 tires, alloy wheels. Requires 1SB Option Pkg.

Powertrain

4-speed automatic transmission	850	765

LS, LS Sport include traction control. Base includes traction control when ordered w/antilock brakes. Base requires 1SB Option Pkg. NA 1SV.

Safety

Front side airbags	395	356

Base requires 1SB Option Pkg. NA 1SV.

Antilock brakes, Base	400	360

Requires 1SB Option Pkg.

Comfort & Convenience Features

	RETAIL PRICE	DEALER INVOICE
OnStar assistance system, LS, LS Sport	$695	$626
LS/LS Sport w/front side airbags	430	387
Includes one-year service.		
Power sunroof, coupe	725	653
Base requires 1SB Option Pkg. NA 1SV.		
Cruise control, Base	275	248
Requires 1SB Option Pkg.		
Remote keyless entry, Base coupe	370	333
Base sedan	410	369
Includes power door locks, theft-deterrent system w/alarm. Requires 1SB Option Pkg.		
AM/FM/cassette/CD/MP3 player, Base	295	266
LS, LS Sport	150	135
Base includes premium speakers. Base requires 1SB Option Pkg.		
Satellite radio	325	293
Requires monthly service fee after 3rd month. Base requires 1SB Option Pkg. NA 1SV.		
Premium speakers, Base	150	135
Requires 1SB Option Pkg. Std. LS, LS Sport.		

Appearance & Special Purpose

	RETAIL PRICE	DEALER INVOICE
Rear spoiler, Base, LS	275	248
Base requires 1SB Option Pkg.		
Alloy wheels, LS	375	338
LS Sport (credit)	*(200)*	*(180)*

CHEVROLET COBALT

CLASS: Compact car
DRIVE WHEELS: Front-wheel drive
BASE PRICE RANGE: $13,625-$21,430. Built in USA.
ALSO CONSIDER: Ford Focus, Honda Civic, Toyota Corolla

Colbalt begins replacing Cavalier for 2005 as Chevrolet's first new compact design in 10 years. Larger and costlier than Chevy's Korean-built Aveo, Cobalt offers sedans and coupes sharing a platform with the Saturn Ion, though coupes don't have Saturn's rear access doors. Sedans come in base, LS, and LT trim; coupes offer base, LS, and SS Supercharged versions. All use 4-cyl

 Specifications begin on page 547.

engines. Base and LS models use Ion's 140-hp 2.2-liter. A 170-hp 2.4-liter will power SS coupes and sedans, which Chevy says will bow by mid 2005 as early '06 models. The SS Supercharged coupe features a supercharged 2.0-liter with 205 hp. It comes only with a 5-speed manual transmission. LT comes standard with a 4-speed automatic, which is optional on base and LS. Base and LS also have standard 15-inch wheels, the LT sedan 16s. SS models will have 17-inchers, and 18s are standard on the Supercharged SS. All Cobalts come with air conditioning, tilt steering wheel, CD player, and 60/40 split folding rear seat. Antilock brakes are optional on base models, standard elsewhere. Traction control is standard on LT and SS Supercharged models, available on base and LS. Other options include head-protecting curtain side airbags with front side airbags, sunroof, OnStar assistance, satellite radio, and CD/MP3 player. We have not yet tested the Cobalt.

ENGINES

	dohc I4	Supercharged dohc I4
Size, liters/cu. in.	2.2/134	2.0/122
Horsepower @ rpm	140 @ 5600	205 @ 5600
Torque (lb-ft) @ rpm	150 @ 4000	200 @ 4400
Availability	S[1]	S[2]
EPA city/highway mpg		
5-speed manual	25/34	23/29
4-speed automatic	24/32	

1. Base, LS, LT. 2. SS Supercharged.

PRICES

Chevrolet Cobalt

	RETAIL PRICE	DEALER INVOICE
Base 2-door coupe	$13625	$12739
Base 4-door sedan	13625	12739
LS 2-door coupe	15920	14885
LS 4-door sedan	15920	14885
LT 4-door sedan	18195	17012
SS Supercharged 2-door coupe	21430	20037
Destination charge	565	565

SS prices and equipment not available at time of publication.

STANDARD EQUIPMENT

Base: 2.2-liter 4-cylinder engine, 5-speed manual transmission, dual front airbags, daytime running lights, air conditioning, power steering, tilt steering wheel, cloth upholstery, front bucket seats, height-adjustable driver seat, center console, cupholders, split folding rear seat w/trunk pass-through, AM/FM/CD player, digital clock, tachometer, outside-temperature indicator, intermittent wipers, passenger-side visor mirror, rear defogger, automatic headlights, 195/60R15 tires, wheel covers.

LS adds: antilock brakes, cruise control, driver-seat lumbar adjustment, power mirrors, power windows, power door locks, remote keyless entry, map lights, driver-side visor mirror, floormats, alloy wheels.

LT adds: 4-speed automatic transmission, traction control, leather upholstery, heated front seats, leather-wrapped steering wheel w/radio controls, Pioneer sound system, 205/55R16 tires.

SS Supercharged adds: 2.0-liter supercharged 4-cylinder engine, 5-speed manual transmission, antilock 4-wheel disc brakes, leather upholstery, Pioneer AM/FM/CD/MP3 player, fog lights, rear spoiler, performance suspension, 215/45R18 tires. *Deletes:* heated front seats.

OPTIONAL EQUIPMENT

Major Packages	RETAIL PRICE	DEALER INVOICE
Sport Option Pkg., LS	$595	$536
Leather-wrapped steering wheel w/radio controls, fog lights, rear spoiler, 205/55R16 tires, machine-faced alloy wheels.		
Powertrain		
4-speed automatic transmission, Base, LS	850	765
LS includes traction control.		
Safety		
Curtain side airbags	395	356
Includes front side airbags. Base requires antilock brakes.		
Antilock brakes, Base	400	360
Includes traction control when ordered w/4-speed automatic transmission.		
Comfort & Convenience Features		
OnStar assistance system	695	626
Includes one-year service. Requires curtain side airbags. NA Base.		
Power sunroof, LS, LT, SS Supercharged	725	653
Leather upholstery, LS	695	626
Upgraded sound system, Base	185	167
AM/FM/CD/MP3 player, LS, LT	150	135
Includes premium speakers.		
Premium speakers, LS	150	135
Satellite radio	325	293
Requires monthly fee after 3rd month. Base coupe requires upgraded sound system. NA Base sedan.		
Remote keyless entry, Base sedan	410	369
Base coupe	370	333
Includes power door locks.		
Cruise control, Base	275	248
Appearance & Special Purpose		
Rear spoiler, Base, LS, LT	275	248

CHEVROLET CORVETTE

CLASS: Premium sporty/performance car
DRIVE WHEELS: Rear-wheel drive
BASE PRICE RANGE: $43,445-$51,445. Built in USA.
ALSO CONSIDER: Chrysler Crossfire, Porsche Boxster

 Specifications begin on page 547.

Chevrolet revamps its 2-seat sports car for 2005 with revised styling, more power, and new features. Dubbed the C6 to denote Corvette's 6th design generation since 1953, the '05 comes as a hatchback coupe with lift-off roof panel or as a convertible with a fabric soft top and heated glass rear window. A power top is newly available. A high-performance Z06 model is absent for '05, but is expected to return for '06.

Wheelbase grows by 1.2 inches vs. the 1997-2004 C5, but overall length shrinks 5 inches. Fiberglass body panels again clothe a metal structure. The sole engine is a 6.0-liter V8 with 400 hp and 400 lb-ft of torque, up 50 hp and 40 lb-ft from the C5's 5.7-liter V8. Transmission choices remain a 6-speed manual or 4-speed automatic. Also continued are antilock 4-wheel disc brakes, antiskid/traction control, and two suspension options. GM's Magnetic Selective Ride Control automatically adjusts firmness to match road surfaces within driver-selectable Tour and Sport modes. A Z51 package has a firmer nonadjustable suspension, larger brakes, and, with automatic transmission, acceleration-enhancing gearing. Standard run-flat tires return, but wheels grow an inch in diameter to 18 front, 19 rear. Front side airbags are standard on the convertible, optional on the coupe. Xenon headlamps are newly standard, as is keyless access that operates ignition and locks without removing keyfob from pocket or purse. New options include OnStar assistance, navigation system, and satellite radio. Heated seats and a head-up display that projects gauge readouts onto the windshield are optional. This evaluation is based on preview test drives.

RATINGS	Coupe, auto.	Coupe w/Z51, man.	Conv w/nav. sys., Mag. susp., man.	Conv w/Z51, man.
ACCELERATION	10	10	10	10
FUEL ECONOMY	5	5	5	5
RIDE QUALITY	4	3	4	4
STEERING/HANDLING	10	10	10	10
QUIETNESS	3	3	2	2
CONTROLS/MATERIALS	7	7	6	7
ROOM/COMFORT (FRONT)	5	5	5	5
ROOM/COMFORT (REAR)	0	0	0	0
CARGO ROOM	6	6	2	2
VALUE WITHIN CLASS	10	10	10	10

Corvette delivers thrilling acceleration, handling, and braking, is relatively comfortable in everyday driving, and costs tens of thousands less than rivals

RATINGS (cont.)	Coupe, auto.	Coupe w/Z51, man.	Conv w/nav. sys., Mag. susp., man.	Conv w/Z51, man.
with similar performance. If you like your sports cars bold and brawny, there's no better high-performance value and no stronger Best Buy in this class.				
TOTAL	**60**	**59**	**54**	**55**
Average total for premium sporty/performance cars: 48.3				

ENGINES

	ohv V8
Size, liters/cu. in.	6.0/364
Horsepower @ rpm	400 @ 6000
Torque (lb-ft) @ rpm	400 @ 4400
Availability	S
EPA city/highway mpg	
6-speed manual	19/28
4-speed automatic	18/25

PRICES

Chevrolet Corvette	RETAIL PRICE	DEALER INVOICE
Base 2-door hatchback	$43445	$38014
Base 2-door convertible	51445	45014
Destination charge	800	800

STANDARD EQUIPMENT

Base: 6.0-liter V8 engine, 6-speed manual transmission, limited-slip differential, traction control, dual front airbags, front side airbags (convertible), antilock 4-wheel disc brakes, antiskid system, tire-pressure monitor, daytime running lights, air conditioning w/dual-zone automatic climate controls, interior air filter, power steering, tilt leather-wrapped steering wheel, cruise control, leather upholstery, 6-way power driver seat, 6-way power passenger seat (convertible), center console, cupholders, heated power mirrors, power windows, remote keyless entry, keyless access, AM/FM/CD/MP3 player, digital clock, tachometer, outside-temperature indicator, intermittent wipers, map lights, illuminated visor mirrors, rear defogger, automatic headlights, floormats, theft-deterrent system, bi-xenon headlights, fog lights, body-colored removable roof panel (hatchback), manually folding convertible top (convertible), run-flat tires (245/40ZR18 front, 285/35ZR19 rear), alloy wheels.

OPTIONAL EQUIPMENT

Major Packages	RETAIL PRICE	DEALER INVOICE
Preferred Equipment Group 1SA, hatchback	$1405	$1208
Front side airbags, perforated leather upholstery, 6-way power passenger seat, cargo net and cover.		
Preferred Equipment Group 1SB, hatchback	4360	3750
convertible	2955	2541
Preferred Equipment Group 1SA (hatchback) plus manual-tilt/power-telescope steering wheel, memory system (driver seat, mirrors, steering		

 Specifications begin on page 547.

OPTIONAL EQUIPMENT (cont.)	RETAIL PRICE	DEALER INVOICE
wheel, climate controls, radio), heated seats, Bose AM/FM radio w/in-dash 6-disc CD/MP3 changer, head-up instrument display, automatic day/night driver-side and rearview mirrors, universal garage-door opener.		
Z51 Performance Handling Pkg.	$1495	$1286
Performance axle ratio (w/automatic transmission), power-steering-fluid cooler, engine- and transmission-oil cooler, larger brakes, firmer suspension.		
Magnetic Selective Ride Control Suspension	1695	1458
Adjustable ride-control suspension. NA w/Z51 Performance Handling Pkg.		
Powertrain		
4-speed automatic transmission	NC	NC
Comfort & Convenience Features		
Navigation system	1400	1204
Includes voice recognition. Substitutes Bose AM/FM/CD/MP3 player for in-dash 6-disc CD/MP3 player. Requires Preferred Equipment Group 1SB.		
OnStar assistance system	695	598
Includes one-year service.		
Satellite radio	395	280
Requires Preferred Equipment Pkg. 1SB, monthly service fee after 3rd month.		
Power convertible top, convertible	1995	1716
Requires Preferred Equipment Group 1SB.		
Appearance & Special Purpose		
Corvette Museum Delivery	490	421
Includes tour of Corvette factory and museum, delivery of car in museum w/broadcast on Internet, plaque, door badges, one-year Corvette Museum membership. In addition to normal delivery charge.		
Transparent roof panel, hatchback	750	645
Dual roof panels, hatchback	1400	1204
Standard removable roof panel and transparent roof panel.		
Polished alloy wheels	1295	1114

CHEVROLET EQUINOX

CLASS: Midsize sport-utility vehicle
DRIVE WHEELS: Front-wheel drive, all-wheel drive
BASE PRICE RANGE: $21,095-$24,335. Built in Canada.
ALSO CONSIDER: Honda Pilot, Nissan Murano, Toyota Highlander

Equinox debuts for 2005 as a smaller, less-expensive midsize-SUV companion to Chevrolet's TrailBlazer. It shares its car-type platform with the Vue from GM's Saturn division, but has a longer wheelbase and body, and has steel body panels in place of Vue's plastic. Equinox seats five; no 3rd-row seat is offered. The rear seat slides fore and aft 8 inches to maximize passenger or cargo space. The one-piece rear hatch does not include separate-opening glass. Equinox comes in LS and uplevel LT trim, both with front-wheel drive

or all-wheel drive without low-range gearing. A 185-hp V6 and 5-speed automatic transmission make up the sole powertrain. Traction control is standard on the 2WD LT, optional as part of the ABS option on the 2WD LS. ABS is standard on all but the 2WD LS. Head-protecting curtain side airbags are optional. Available features include leather upholstery, heated front seats, satellite radio, OnStar assistance, and 17-inch wheels in place of standard 16s.

RATINGS	2WD LS	2WD LT w/17-inch wheels	AWD LT w/17-inch wheels
ACCELERATION	5	5	5
FUEL ECONOMY	5	5	5
RIDE QUALITY	6	6	6
STEERING/HANDLING	3	4	4
QUIETNESS	5	5	5
CONTROLS/MATERIALS	6	6	6
ROOM/COMFORT (FRONT)	6	6	6
ROOM/COMFORT (REAR)	7	7	7
CARGO ROOM	7	7	7
VALUE WITHIN CLASS	5	6	6

Its sloppy steering and handling make it feel like a large, cumbersome SUV, and Equinox lacks the mechanical finesse of competitors such as the Toyota Highlander or Honda Pilot. But it has a carlike ride, plenty of utility, and prices that undercut those of most midsize rivals.

TOTAL	55	57	57

Average total for midsize sport-utility vehicles: 54.7

ENGINES

	ohv V6
Size, liters/cu. in.	3.4/204
Horsepower @ rpm	185 @ 5200
Torque (lb-ft) @ rpm	210 @ 3800
Availability	S

EPA city/highway mpg

5-speed automatic	19/25

 Specifications begin on page 547.

PRICES

Chevrolet Equinox

	RETAIL PRICE	DEALER INVOICE
2WD LS 4-door wagon	$21095	$19450
AWD LS 4-door wagon	23070	21271
2WD LT 4-door wagon	22810	21031
AWD LT 4-door wagon	24335	22529
Destination charge	565	565

STANDARD EQUIPMENT

LS: 3.4-liter V6 engine, 5-speed automatic transmission, dual front airbags, daytime running lights, air conditioning, power steering, tilt steering wheel, cloth upholstery, front bucket seats w/height-adjustable driver seat, fold-flat passenger seat, center console, cupholders, adjustable split folding rear seat, power mirrors, power windows, power door locks, remote keyless entry, AM/FM/CD player, digital clock, tachometer, intermittent wipers, visor mirrors, cargo cover, rear defogger, intermittent rear wiper/washer, automatic headlights, theft-deterrent system, roof rails, rear spoiler, 235/65R16 tires, wheel covers. **AWD** adds: all-wheel drive, antilock brakes.

LT adds: traction control, antilock brakes, cruise control, map lights, floormats, fog lights, rear privacy glass, roof rack, alloy wheels. **AWD** adds: all-wheel drive. *Deletes:* traction control.

OPTIONAL EQUIPMENT

Major Packages

	RETAIL PRICE	DEALER INVOICE
Preferred Equipment Group 1SB, LS *Cruise control, floormats, rear privacy glass, roof rack.*	$535	$482
Preferred Equipment Group 1SD, LT *Leather-wrapped steering wheel, 6-way power driver seat, automatic day/night rearview mirror.*	550	495
Preferred Equipment Group 1SE, LT *Preferred Equipment Group 1SD plus leather upholstery, heated front seats, power sunroof, OnStar assistance system w/one-year service, AM/FM radio w/in-dash 6-disc CD changer, steering-wheel radio controls, 235/60R17 tires, machine-finished alloy wheels.*	3745	3371
Trailering Equipment *Receiver hitch, 4-wire connector.*	350	315

Safety

Curtain side airbags	395	356
Antilock brakes, 2WD LS *Includes traction control.*	400	360

Comfort & Convenience Features

OnStar assistance system, LT	1045	941
LT w/1SD *Includes one-year service, steering-wheel radio controls.*	820	738
Leather upholstery, LT *Requires Preferred Equipment Group 1SD.*	545	491

OPTIONAL EQUIPMENT (cont.)

	RETAIL PRICE	DEALER INVOICE
Heated front seats, LT	$250	$225
Requires Preferred Equipment Group 1SD., leather upholstery.		
AM/FM/CD/MP3 player	135	122
LT w/1SE (credit)	*(260)*	*(234)*
AM/FM radio w/in-dash 6-disc CD changer	395	356
Upgraded sound system, LT	295	266
Requires optional radio.		
Satellite radio, LT	335	302
Requires monthly service fee after 3rd month.		
Power sunroof, LT	595	535
Automatic day/night rearview mirror	175	158

Appearance & Special Purpose

Fog lights, LS	230	207
Includes color-keyed bumpers.		
Alloy wheels, LS	375	338
Machine-finished alloy wheels, LT	295	266
Includes 235/60R17 tires.		

CHEVROLET IMPALA

CLASS: Large car
DRIVE WHEELS: Front-wheel drive
BASE PRICE RANGE: $22,220-$28,425. Built in Canada.
ALSO CONSIDER: Chrysler 300, Toyota Avalon

Standard OnStar assistance tops the short list of 2005 additions to Chevrolet's largest sedan. Impala offers base, uplevel LS, and sporty SS models, all with V6 engines. The base uses a 180-hp 3.4-liter, the LS a 200-hp 3.8, the SS a supercharged 240-hp 3.8. All come with automatic transmission, 4-wheel disc brakes, and now OnStar. LS and SS have ABS, traction control, and a tire-inflation monitor, all optional for the base. The SS also includes 17-inch wheels vs. other models' 16s; it offers chrome-finished 17s as a new option. Also new for SS are minor trim changes outside and different front headrests. SS and LS have front bucket seats and carry five passengers, though LS now offers a front bench seat for 6-passenger capacity. The base has a front bench or optional buckets. A side airbag for the driver is optional, but no front-passenger side airbag is available. Satellite radio is optional across the board. Impala shares its basic underskin design and running gear with Chevy's Monte Carlo coupe.

 Specifications begin on page 547.

RATINGS

RATINGS	Base	LS	SS
ACCELERATION	5	6	7
FUEL ECONOMY	5	5	4
RIDE QUALITY	6	6	5
STEERING/HANDLING	5	6	7
QUIETNESS	6	6	6
CONTROLS/MATERIALS	5	5	5
ROOM/COMFORT (FRONT)	7	7	7
ROOM/COMFORT (REAR)	5	5	5
CARGO ROOM	6	6	6
VALUE WITHIN CLASS	6	6	6

Impala isn't as refined as the class-leading Honda Accord and Toyota Camry, and it lags most rivals in available safety features and rear-seat comfort. It earns our Recommendation in this class, however, by fulfilling its mission as an affordable and relatively roomy sedan that's competent in most driving conditions.

TOTAL	56	58	58

Average total for large cars: 60.9

ENGINES

ENGINES	ohv V6	ohv V6	Supercharged ohv V6
Size, liters/cu. in.	3.4/204	3.8/231	3.8/231
Horsepower @ rpm	180 @ 5200	200 @ 5200	240 @ 5200
Torque (lb-ft) @ rpm	200 @ 4000	225 @ 4000	280 @ 3600
Availability	S[1]	S[2]	S[3]
EPA city/highway mpg			
4-speed automatic	21/32	20/30	18/28

1. Base. 2. LS. 3. SS.

PRICES

Chevrolet Impala	RETAIL PRICE	DEALER INVOICE
Base 4-door sedan	$22220	$20331
LS 4-door sedan	25330	23177
SS 4-door sedan	28425	26009
Destination charge	660	660

STANDARD EQUIPMENT

Base: 3.4-liter V6 engine, 4-speed automatic transmission, dual front airbags, 4-wheel disc brakes, daytime running lights, emergency inside trunk release, air conditioning w/manual dual-zone climate controls, interior air filter, OnStar assistance system w/one-year service, power steering, tilt steering wheel, cloth upholstery, front split bench seat, cupholders, power mirrors, power windows, power door locks, remote keyless entry, AM/FM/cassette, digital clock, rear defogger, variable-intermittent wipers, map lights, visor mirrors, automatic headlights, theft-deterrent system, 225/60R16 tires, wheel covers.

LS adds: 3.8-liter V6 engine, traction control, antilock 4-wheel disc brakes, tire-pressure monitor, cruise control, leather-wrapped steering wheel, front bucket seats, 6-way power driver seat w/lumbar adjustment, center console, split folding rear seat, tachometer, illuminated visor mirrors, rear spoiler, fog lights, Sport Touring Suspension, alloy wheels.

SS adds: 3.8-liter supercharged V6 engine, leather upholstery, AM/FM/CD player, floormats, Performance Suspension, 235/55WR17 tires.

OPTIONAL EQUIPMENT

Major Packages

	RETAIL PRICE	DEALER INVOICE
1SB Preferred Equipment Group, Base	$1195	$1064
Manufacturer's Discount Price	*695*	*619*

Cruise control, 6-way power driver seat, AM/FM/CD player, illuminated visor mirrors, cargo net, floormats.

1SB Preferred Equipment Group, LS	1075	957
Manufacturer's Discount Price	*575*	*512*

Steering-wheel radio controls, AM/FM/CD player, heated power mirrors, automatic day/night rearview mirror, trip computer, compass, outside-temperature indicator, universal garage-door opener, cargo net, floormats, alarm.

1SB Preferred Equipment Group, SS	1095	975
Manufacturer's Discount Price	*595*	*530*

Heated front seats, 6-way power passenger seat, steering-wheel radio controls, heated power mirrors, automatic day/night rearview mirror, trip computer, compass, outside-temperature indicator, universal garage-door opener, cargo net.

Sport Appearance Pkg. PCH, Base	625	556
Manufacturer's Discount Price	*375*	*333*

Rear spoiler, bodyside moldings, alloy wheels. Manufacturer's Discount Price not available when ordered w/1SB Preferred Equipment Group.

Sport Appearance Pkg. WBP, LS	1495	1331
Manufacturer's Discount Price	*995*	*886*

Leather upholstery, oil-pressure gauge, voltmeter, unique interior and exterior trim, floormats, special alloy wheels.

Comfort Seating Pkg., LS	445	396

Heated front seats, 6-way power passenger seat. Requires 1SB Preferred Equipment Group, leather upholstery.

Safety

Driver-side front side airbag	350	312

Base requires 1SB Preferred Equipment Group, sport cloth upholstery or bucket seats.

Antilock brakes, Base	600	534

Includes traction control, tire-pressure monitor.

Comfort & Convenience Features

Power sunroof	900	801

Base requires 1SB Preferred Equipment Group.

Bucket seats, Base	460	409

Includes upgraded upholstery, center console, split folding rear seat. Requires Preferred Equipment Group 1SB.

OPTIONAL EQUIPMENT (cont.)

	RETAIL PRICE	DEALER INVOICE
Front split bench seat, LS	NC	NC
Requires leather upholstery.		
Sport cloth upholstery, Base	410	365
Upgraded upholstery, split folding rear seat. Requires 1SB Preferred Equipment Group		
Leather upholstery, LS	625	556
6-way power driver seat, Base	325	289
AM/FM/CD player, Base, LS	345	307
Includes premium speakers.		
AM/FM/cassette/CD player, Base, LS	445	396
Base/LS w/1SB Group, SS	100	89
Includes premium speakers.		
Satellite radio	325	289
Requires monthly fee after 3rd month.		
Appearance & Special Purpose		
Alloy wheels, Base	350	312
Requires 1SB Preferred Equipment Group.		
Chrome alloy wheels, SS	795	708

CHEVROLET MALIBU

CLASS: Midsize car
DRIVE WHEELS: Front-wheel drive
BASE PRICE RANGE: $19,085-$24,495. Built in USA.
ALSO CONSIDER: Honda Accord, Nissan Altima, Toyota Camry

This midsize car comes as a 4-dr sedan and as a 4-dr hatchback called the Maxx. The Maxx has a 6-inch-longer wheelbase than the sedan, but is not as long overall. Both share some underskin structure with the Pontiac G6 and the premium-compact 9-3 models from GM's Saab brand. Malibu sedans and hatchbacks feature LS and LT models with a 200-hp V6. The sedan adds an entry-level base model with a 145-hp 4-cyl engine. A 4-speed automatic is the only transmission. ABS bundled with traction control is optional for the base sedan, standard on other Malibus. Maxx and LT sedan models have 4-wheel disc brakes. Head-protecting curtain side airbags are standard for LTs, optional on other models; for 2005, they include front side torso airbags.

All models come with a power height adjustment for the drivers seat, tilt/telescope steering column, and power windows/locks/mirrors. Among options are power-adjustable brake and accelerator pedals, OnStar assistance, satellite radio, and heated cloth front seats. Also available is a remote starter that turns on the engine via the keyfob up to 200 ft away. Both body styles have a fold-flat front-passenger seat and split folding rear seatbacks. The Maxx's rear seat also reclines and slides fore and aft to favor cargo space or rear leg room. Also standard for Maxx are a glass skylight over the rear seat, a rigid cargo cover/tailgate table and, for '05, a rear wiper on LT versions. Rear DVD entertainment is an exclusive Maxx option.

RATINGS

	Base	LT sdn	LT Maxx
ACCELERATION	4	6	6
FUEL ECONOMY	6	6	6
RIDE QUALITY	6	6	7
STEERING/HANDLING	6	6	6
QUIETNESS	6	7	7
CONTROLS/MATERIALS	7	7	7
ROOM/COMFORT (FRONT)	7	7	7
ROOM/COMFORT (REAR)	5	5	7
CARGO ROOM	4	4	7
VALUE WITHIN CLASS	6	7	8

Chevrolet aims Malibu at Honda Accord and Toyota Camry buyers. While the sedan is a bit smaller than those rivals, the versatile Maxx offers more rear seat room than either. Malibu's 4-cyl engine disappoints, but the V6 versions combine good pep with competent road manners and an impressive list of available features at reasonable prices.

	Base	LT sdn	LT Maxx
TOTAL	57	61	68

Average total for midsize cars: 57.2

ENGINES

	dohc I4	ohv V6
Size, liters/cu. in.	2.2/134	3.5/213
Horsepower @ rpm	145 @ 5600	200 @ 5400
Torque (lb-ft) @ rpm	155 @ 4000	220 @ 3200
Availability	S[1]	S[2]
EPA city/highway mpg		
4-speed automatic	24/34	23/32[3]

1. Base. 2. LS, LT. 3. Maxx, 22/30 mpg.

PRICES

Chevrolet Malibu	RETAIL PRICE	DEALER INVOICE
Base 4-door sedan	$19085	$17463
LS 4-door sedan	21150	19352
LS Maxx 4-door hatchback	21350	19535
LT 4-door sedan	23945	21910
LT Maxx 4-door hatchback	24495	22413
Destination charge	625	625

 Specifications begin on page 547.

STANDARD EQUIPMENT

Base: 2.2-liter 4-cylinder engine, 4-speed automatic transmission, dual front airbags, daytime running lights, air conditioning, power steering, tilt/telescope steering wheel, cloth upholstery, front bucket seats, power height-adjustable driver seat, fold-flat passenger seat, center console, cupholders, split folding rear seat, power mirrors, power windows, power door locks, AM/FM/CD player, digital clock, tachometer, outside-temperature indicator, variable-intermittent wipers, visor mirrors, rear defogger, automatic headlights, theft-deterrent system, 205/65R15 tires, wheel covers.

LS adds: 3.5-liter V6 engine, traction control, antilock brakes, cruise control, power-adjustable pedals, driver-seat lumbar adjustment, remote keyless entry, illuminated driver-side visor mirror, alloy wheels.

LS Maxx adds: antilock 4-wheel disc brakes, adjustable rear seat, glass roof panel, cargo cover, 215/60R16 tires.

LT adds to LS: front side airbags, curtain side airbags, antilock 4-wheel disc brakes, automatic climate control, remote starter, leather upholstery, heated front seats, 6-way power driver seat, leather-wrapped steering wheel w/radio controls, heated power mirrors, illuminated passenger-side visor mirror, floormats, rear spoiler, fog lights, 215/60R16 tires.

LT Maxx adds: adjustable rear seat, rear radio controls, glass roof panel, cargo cover, rear wiper.

OPTIONAL EQUIPMENT

Major Packages

	RETAIL PRICE	DEALER INVOICE
Preferred Equipment Group 1SB, Base	$835	$752
Cruise control, power-adjustable pedals, remote keyless entry, driver-seat lumbar adjustment, seatback map pockets, upgraded sound system, cargo nets, floormats.		
Preferred Equipment Group 1SC, Base	1295	1166
Preferred Equipment Group 1SB plus bodyside moldings, alloy wheels.		
Preferred Equipment Group 1SB, LS	1095	986
LS Maxx	1270	1143
Front side airbags, curtain side airbags, remote starter, 6-way power driver seat, satellite radio (requires monthly fee after 3rd month), rear radio controls (Maxx), floormats.		
Preferred Equipment Group 1SB, LT, LT Maxx	1230	1107
Power sunroof, satellite radio (requires monthly fee after 3rd month), automatic day/night rearview mirror, universal garage-door opener.		

Safety

Curtain side airbags, Base, LS, LS Maxx	690	621
Includes front side airbags.		
Antilock brakes, Base	400	360
Includes traction control.		

Comfort & Convenience Features

OnStar assistance system	695	625
Includes one-year service. LS, LS Maxx require Preferred Equipment Group 1SB. NA Base.		

OPTIONAL EQUIPMENT (cont.)

	RETAIL PRICE	DEALER INVOICE
Power sunroof	$725	$653
LS, LS Maxx require Preferred Equipment Group 1SB. NA Base.		
Heated front seats, Base, LS, LS Maxx	275	428
Requires Preferred Equipment Group.		
Remote starter, Base, LS, LS Maxx	150	135
Base requires cruise control.		
Upgraded sound system, Base	125	113
AM/FM radio w/in-dash 6-disc CD changer	300	270
Base requires Preferred Equipment Group.		
Satellite radio	325	293
Requires monthly service fee after 3rd month. Base requires Preferred Equipment Group or upgraded sound system.		
Rear-seat entertainment system, LS Maxx, LT Maxx	995	896
Includes DVD/CD player, headphones. LS requires Preferred Equipment Group 1SB.		
Cruise control, Base	425	383
Includes remote keyless entry.		

CHEVROLET MONTE CARLO

CLASS: Midsize car
DRIVE WHEELS: Front-wheel drive
BASE PRICE RANGE: $22,150-$28,225. Built in Canada.
ALSO CONSIDER: Honda Accord coupe, Toyota Solara coupe

Standard OnStar assistance is the main 2005 change for the coupe cousins of Chevrolet's Impala sedans. Monte Carlo returns in base LS and top-line Supercharged SS models; in between, 2004's semisporty SS package is renamed LT. The LS comes with a 180-hp V6, the LT a 200-hp V6. The Supercharged SS has 240 hp, firm suspension, 17-inch wheels vs. the other models' 16s, specific trim, plus chrome wheels as a new option. OnStar joins other linewide standard features, including front bucket seats, 4-speed automatic transmission, and 4-wheel disc brakes. ABS, traction control, and tire-pressure monitor are standard for LT and Supercharged SS, available for LS as a package. A driver-protecting side airbag is optional for LT and SS, but no front-passenger side airbag is offered. Satellite radio is optional.

Specifications begin on page 547.

RATINGS

RATINGS	LS	LT	Supercharged SS
ACCELERATION	5	6	7
FUEL ECONOMY	5	5	5
RIDE QUALITY	6	6	5
STEERING/HANDLING	5	6	7
QUIETNESS	6	6	6
CONTROLS/MATERIALS	6	6	6
ROOM/COMFORT (FRONT)	6	6	6
ROOM/COMFORT (REAR)	3	3	3
CARGO ROOM	4	4	4
VALUE WITHIN CLASS	4	4	4

Monte Carlo beats most similarly priced coupes for size and power, but trails Japanese-brand 2-dr models such as the Honda Accord and Toyota Solara for refinement, safety features, and resale value.

TOTAL	50	52	53

Average total for midsize cars: 57.2

ENGINES

ENGINES	ohv V6	ohv V6	Supercharged ohv V6
Size, liters/cu. in.	3.4/204	3.8/231	3.8/231
Horsepower @ rpm	180 @ 5200	200 @ 5200	240 @ 5200
Torque (lb-ft) @ rpm	205 @ 4000	225 @ 4000	280 @ 3600
Availability	S[1]	S[2]	S[3]
EPA city/highway mpg			
4-speed automatic	21/32	20/30	18/28

1. LS. 2. LT. 3. Supercharged SS.

PRICES

Chevrolet Monte Carlo

Chevrolet Monte Carlo	RETAIL PRICE	DEALER INVOICE
LS 2-door coupe	$22150	$20267
SS 2-door coupe	24560	22472
Supercharged SS 2-door coupe	28225	25826
Destination charge	660	660

STANDARD EQUIPMENT

LS: 3.4-liter V6 engine, 4-speed automatic transmission, dual front airbags, 4-wheel disc brakes, daytime running lights, emergency inside trunk release, air conditioning w/dual-zone manual climate controls, interior air filter, OnStar assistance system w/one-year service, power steering, tilt steering wheel, cloth upholstery, front bucket seats, center console, cupholders, split folding rear seat, power mirrors, power windows, power door locks, remote keyless entry, AM/FM/cassette, digital clock, tachometer, visor mirrors, map lights, variable-intermittent wipers, rear defogger, automatic headlights, theft-deterrent system, 225/60R16 tires, wheel covers.

LT adds: 3.8-liter V6 engine, traction control, antilock 4-wheel disc brakes, tire-inflation monitor, driver-seat lumbar adjustment, cruise control, leather-wrapped steering wheel w/radio controls, illuminated visor mirrors, fog lights, Sport Suspension, 225/60SR16 performance tires, alloy wheels.

Supercharged SS adds: 3.8-liter supercharged V6 engine, AM/FM/CD player, floormats, rear spoiler, Performance Suspension, 235/55WR17 tires.

OPTIONAL EQUIPMENT

Major Packages

	RETAIL PRICE	DEALER INVOICE
1SB Preferred Equipment Group, LS	$1490	$1326
Manufacturer's Discount Price	*990*	*881*
Cruise control, 6-way power driver seat, AM/FM/CD player, illuminated visor mirrors, cargo net, floormats, alloy wheels.		
1SB Preferred Equipment Group, LT	1165	1037
Manufacturer's Discount Price	*665*	*592*
Heated power mirrors, 6-way power driver seat, AM/FM/CD player, automatic day/night rearview mirror, outside-temperature indicator, compass, trip computer, universal garage-door opener, cargo net, floormats.		
1SB Preferred Equipment Group, SS	1810	1611
Manufacturer's Discount Price	*1060*	*943*
Heated power mirrors, leather upholstery, heated 6-way power front seats, automatic day/night rearview mirror, outside-temperature indicator, compass, trip computer, universal garage-door opener, cargo net.		
Seating Comfort Pkg., LT	445	396
Heated front seats, 6-way power passenger seat. Requires 1SB Preferred Equipment Group, leather upholstery.		
Sport Appearance Pkg., LS, LT	500	445
Manufacturer's Discount Price (credit)	*(250)*	*(223)*
Rear spoiler, special alloy wheels. LS requires 1SB Preferred Equipment Group.		
Winner's Circle Appearance Pkg., LS, LT	650	579
Manufacturer's Discount Price (credit)	*(100)*	*(89)*
Rear spoiler, bodyside graphics, special alloy wheels. LS requires 1SB Preferred equipment Pkg.		

Safety

Antilock brakes, LS	600	534
Includes traction control, tire-inflation monitor.		
Driver-side front side airbag, LT, SS	350	312
LT requires leather upholstery. SS requires 1SB Preferred Equipment Group.		

Comfort & Convenience Features

AM/FM/CD player, LS, LT	345	307
Includes premium speakers.		
AM/FM/cassette/CD player, LS, LT	445	396
LS/LT w/1SB, SS	100	89
Includes premium speakers.		
Satellite radio	325	289
Requires monthly fee after 3rd month.		
Steering-wheel radio controls, LS	195	174
Includes leather-wrapped steering wheel. Requires 1SB Preferred Equipment Group.		

OPTIONAL EQUIPMENT (cont.)

	RETAIL PRICE	DEALER INVOICE
Leather upholstery, LS, LT	$625	$556
Requires power driver seat.		
6-way power driver seat	325	289
Power sunroof	900	801
LS requires 1SB Preferred Equipment Group or illuminated visor mirrors.		
Illuminated visor mirrors, LS	95	85
Requires power sunroof.		

Appearance & Special Purpose

Alloy wheels, LS	350	312
Chrome alloy wheels, SS	795	708

CHEVROLET SSR

CLASS: Premium sporty/performance car
DRIVE WHEELS: Rear-wheel drive
BASE PRICE: $42,430. Built in USA.
ALSO CONSIDER: Chevrolet Corvette, Chrysler Crossfire convertible, Ford Mustang

A big power boost and first-time availability of a manual transmission highlight 2005 changes for this limited-edition convertible pickup. SSR retains a retro-styled body-on-frame design with seating for two and a power-retractable metal top. But the '05 exchanges a 300-hp 5.3-liter V8 for a 390-hp 6.0 V8. The '05 also gets a 6-speed manual transmission as an option to a 4-speed automatic. SSR continues with standard antilock 4-wheel disc brakes, traction control, 19-inch front wheels, and 20-inch rears. Also included is a rigid tonneau covering a cargo bed of about 5x3 ft. Among new options are a cockpit wind blocker and auxiliary-gauge package. The base CD stereo can now play MP3s. Torso side airbags are standard, head-protecting curtain side airbags are unavailable.

RATINGS

	Base	6-sp man.
ACCELERATION	8	8
FUEL ECONOMY	3	3
RIDE QUALITY	4	4
STEERING/HANDLING	6	6

RATINGS (cont.)	Base	6-sp man.
QUIETNESS	3	3
CONTROLS/MATERIALS	4	4
ROOM/COMFORT (FRONT)	5	5
ROOM/COMFORT (REAR)	0	0
CARGO ROOM	1	1
VALUE WITHIN CLASS	3	3

SSR is far from refined and has indifferent handling, though its covered bed offers a measure of utility not found in other 2-seat convertibles. It's really all about style, and SSR's brawny new V8 gives it the horsepower to match its street-rod image.

TOTAL	37	37

Average total for sporty/performance cars: 48.5

ENGINES

	ohv V8
Size, liters/cu. in.	6.0/364
Horsepower @ rpm	390 @ 5400
Torque (lb-ft) @ rpm	405 @ 4400
Availability	S
EPA city/highway mpg	
6-speed manual	NA
4-speed automatic	NA

PRICES

Chevrolet SSR	RETAIL PRICE	DEALER INVOICE
Base regular cab convertible pickup	$42430	$39672
Destination charge	625	625

STANDARD EQUIPMENT

Base: 6.0-liter V8 engine, 4-speed automatic transmission, traction control, limited-slip differential, dual front airbags, side airbags, antilock 4-wheel brakes, daytime running lights, air conditioning, power steering, leather-wrapped steering wheel w/radio controls, cruise control, leather upholstery, front bucket seats, 6-way power driver seat, 2-way power passenger seat, center console, cupholders, heated power mirrors, power windows, power door locks, remote keyless entry, AM/FM/CD/MP3 player, digital clock, tachometer, trip computer, map lights, intermittent wipers, rear defogger, power-retractable hardtop, automatic headlights, floormats, theft-deterrent system, rigid tonneau cover, bedliner, fog lights, trailer hitch, wiring harness, 255/45R19 front tires, 295/40R20 rear tires, alloy wheels.

OPTIONAL EQUIPMENT

Major Packages	RETAIL PRICE	DEALER INVOICE
Preferred Equipment Group 1SB	$1900	$1691

Heated front seats, driver-seat and mirror memory, Bose AM/FM radio w/in-dash 6-disc CD changer, driver-side and rearview automatic day/night mirrors, universal garage-door opener, chrome engine cover insert.

OPTIONAL EQUIPMENT (cont.)

	RETAIL PRICE	DEALER INVOICE
Cargo Compartment Trim Pkg.	$895	$797
Tonneau cover inner trim, bed-track covers, wood rub strips, light.		
Color-Keyed Accent Pkg.	640	550
Color-keyed engine cover insert and bed strips, voltmeter, delivered-torque gauge, outside-temperature indicator. Requires Cargo Compartment Trim Pkg.		
Color-Keyed Accent Pkg. w/Running Boards	1400	1204
Requires Cargo Compartment Trim Pkg.		
Cargo Netting Pkg.	220	190
Crossbar, cargo net, tie-down rings.		
Towing Pkg.	235	202
Hitch insert.		
Powertrain		
6-speed manual transmission	815	725
Comfort & Convenience Features		
Auxiliary gauge pkg.	400	344
Voltmeter, delivered-torque gauge, outside-temperature indicator		
Appearance & Special Purpose		
Running boards	745	641
Wind blocker	350	301
Side saddle storage	400	344
Chrome alloy wheels	1500	1335

CHEVROLET TRAILBLAZER

CLASS: Midsize sport-utility vehicle
DRIVE WHEELS: Rear-wheel drive, 4-wheel drive
BASE PRICE RANGE: $27,720-$34,270. Built in USA.
ALSO CONSIDER: Ford Explorer, Honda Pilot, Toyota Highlander

A revised V8, minor trim changes, and available head-protecting curtain side airbags mark Chevrolet's 2005 midsize SUVs. TrailBlazer is the top-selling version of a GM design shared with the Buick Rainier, GMC Envoy, and Isuzu Ascender. TrailBlazer, Envoy, and Ascender offer 5-passenger and extended-length 7-seat models; Rainier is a 5-seater only. The Envoy XUV is an extended-length 5-seater with a sliding cargo roof.

Regular and extended EXT TrailBlazers come in LS and uplevel LT trim. All include antilock 4-wheel disc brakes, 4-speed automatic transmission, and inline 6-cyl engine. EXTs offer an optional V8, now with GM's Displacement on Demand feature, which automatically deactivates four cylinders to save fuel. A computer reactivates the four cylinders as needed for full power. All models offer rear-wheel drive with available traction control or GM's all-surface Autotrac 4WD with low-range gearing. Seventeen-inch wheels are standard on all but the regular-length LS, which gets 16s.

The newly optional curtain side airbags cover the 1st and 2nd seating rows—and replace last year's available seat-mounted front side airbags. Also optional: rear DVD entertainment, OnStar assistance, and a radio/navigation system with control touch screen in the audio faceplate.

RATINGS

	4WD LT	4WD LT EXT, 6-cyl	4WD LT EXT, V8
ACCELERATION	6	5	6
FUEL ECONOMY	4	3	3
RIDE QUALITY	5	6	6
STEERING/HANDLING	3	3	3
QUIETNESS	4	4	4
CONTROLS/MATERIALS	6	6	6
ROOM/COMFORT (FRONT)	7	7	7
ROOM/COMFORT (REAR)	6	7	7
CARGO ROOM	8	9	9
VALUE WITHIN CLASS	6	6	6

TrailBlazers are the most affordable of GM's midsize SUVs and match most rivals for pace and space. The new curtain side airbags correct a competitive deficit. But the Displacement on Demand V8, while a nice idea, won't work the economy wonders many SUV buyers are hoping for. We prefer Envoy among GM's truck-type midsize SUVs as the best blend of performance, quality, and dollar value.

TOTAL	55	56	57

Average total for midsize sport-utility vehicles: 54.7

ENGINES

	dohc I6	ohv V8
Size, liters/cu. in.	4.2/256	5.3/325
Horsepower @ rpm	275 @ 6000	290 @ 5200
Torque (lb-ft) @ rpm	275 @ 3600	330 @ 4000
Availability	S	O[1]
EPA city/highway mpg		
4-speed automatic	15/21[2]	15/18[3]

1. EXT models. 2. 16/21 w/2WD. 3. 16/19 w/2WD.

PRICES

Chevrolet TrailBlazer

	RETAIL PRICE	DEALER INVOICE
2WD LS regular length 4-door wagon	$27720	$25087
4WD LS regular length 4-door wagon	29970	27123

 Specifications begin on page 547.

PRICES (cont.)

	RETAIL PRICE	DEALER INVOICE
2WD LS EXT extended length 4-door wagon	$29840	$27005
4WD LS EXT extended length 4-door wagon	32090	29041
2WD LT regular length 4-door wagon	30370	27485
4WD LT regular length 4-door wagon	32620	29521
2WD LT EXT extended length 4-door wagon	32020	28978
4WD LT EXT extended length 4-door wagon	34270	31014
Destination charge	685	685

STANDARD EQUIPMENT

LS: 4.2-liter 6-cylinder engine, 4-speed automatic transmission, dual front airbags, antilock 4-wheel disc brakes, daytime running lights, air conditioning w/dual-zone manual controls, rear climate controls (EXT), power steering, tilt steering wheel, cloth upholstery, front bucket seats w/lumbar adjustment, center console, cupholders, 2nd-row split folding seat, 3rd-row split folding seat (EXT), power windows, power door locks, AM/FM/CD player, digital clock, tachometer, variable-intermittent wipers, power rear-window release, rear intermittent wiper/washer, visor mirrors, map lights, automatic headlights, theft-deterrent system, rear privacy glass (EXT), fog lights (EXT), rear liftgate, roof rails, trailer-hitch platform, full-size spare tire, 235/75R16 tires (regular), 245/65R17 on/off-road tires (EXT), alloy wheels. **4WD** adds: 4-wheel drive, 2-speed transfer case, front tow hooks (EXT).

LT adds: 8-way power driver seat, heated power mirrors, power rear quarter windows (EXT), remote keyless entry, compass, outside-temperature indicator, universal garage-door opener, illuminated visor mirrors, rear defogger, floormats, rear privacy glass, roof rack, fog lights, 245/65R17 on/off-road tires. **4WD** adds: 4-wheel drive, 2-speed transfer case, front tow hooks.

OPTIONAL EQUIPMENT

Major Packages

	RETAIL PRICE	DEALER INVOICE
Preferred Equipment Group 1SB, 2WD LS regular	$1185	$1019
2WD LS EXT	1035	890
4WD LS regular	1225	1054
4WD LS EXT	1075	925

Heated power mirrors, remote keyless entry, rear defogger, floormats, rear privacy glass (regular length), roof rack, alarm, bodyside moldings, front tow hooks (4WD), 7-lead trailer harness.

Preferred Equipment Group 1SE, LT	1180	1014

Leather upholstery, 8-way power passenger seat, leather-wrapped steering wheel.

LT Pkg. 1 PDF, LT regular	680	585
LT regular w/1SE	625	538
LT EXT	640	550
LT EXT w/1SE	585	503

Dual-zone automatic climate controls, steering-wheel w/radio and climate controls, rear radio controls, trip computer, driver information center, automatic day/night rearview mirror, cargo mat (regular).

OPTIONAL EQUIPMENT (cont.)

	RETAIL PRICE	DEALER INVOICE
Luxury Pkg., LT regular	$1805	$1553
Manufacturer's Discount Price	*1055*	*908*
LT EXT	1765	1532
Manufacturer's Discount Price	*1015*	*873*
Includes Preferred Equipment Group 1SE and LT Pkg. 1.		
LT Pkg. 2 YC6, LT	915	786
Heated front seats, driver-seat memory, power-adjustable pedals, heated power mirrors w/turn signals, AM/FM/cassette/CD player. Requires Luxury Pkg. or Preferred Equipment Group 1SE and LT Pkg. 1.		
OnStar Plus Pkg	970	834
Manufacturer's Discount Price	*70*	*60*
OnStar assistance system w/one-year service, cruise control.		
V8 Power Play Pkg., EXT	1770	1522
Manufacturer's Discount Price	*1270*	*1092*
5.3-liter V8 engine w/cylinder deactivation, limited-slip differential.		
Sun, Sound, and Entertainment Pkg., LS	2165	1862
Manufacturer's Discount Price	*1165*	*1002*
LT	2015	1733
Manufacturer's Discount Price	*1015*	*873*
LT w/LT Pkg. 2	1865	1604
Manufacturer's Discount Price	*865*	*744*
Power sunroof, Bose AM/FM radio w/in-dash 6-disc CD changer, satellite radio. LS requires Preferred Equipment Group 1SB.		

Powertrain

Traction control, 2WD	195	168
Requires limited-slip rear differential.		
Limited-slip rear differential	270	232

Safety

Front and 2nd-row curtain side airbags	495	426

Comfort & Convenience Features

Navigation system, LT	1995	1716
LT w/ Sun, Sound, Entertainment Pkg.	1600	1376
Requires Bose sound system or Sun, Sound, and Entertainment Pkg.		
Rear-seat DVD entertainment system	1295	1114
ordered w/Sun, Sound, Entertainment Pkg.	495	426
LS requires Preferred Equipment Group 1SB. NA w/power sunroof. Deletes power sunroof when ordered w/Sun, Sound, and Entertainment Pkg.		
Power sunroof, LS	950	817
LT	800	688
LS requires Preferred Equipment Group 1SB.		
AM/FM/CD/MP3 player	135	116
LS requires Preferred Equipment Group 1SB.		
AM/FM/cassette/CD player	150	129

OPTIONAL EQUIPMENT (cont.)	RETAIL PRICE	DEALER INVOICE
AM/FM radio w/in-dash 6-disc CD changer	$395	$340
LT w/LT Pkg. 2	245	211
LS requires Preferred Equipment Group 1SB.		
Bose sound system	495	426
LS requires Preferred Equipment Group 1SB.		
Satellite radio	325	280
Requires monthly fee after 3rd-month.		
Rear defogger, LS	200	172
Rain-sensing wipers, LT	70	60
Requires LT Pkg. 2.		
8-way power driver seat, LS	300	258
Requires Preferred Equipment Group 1SB.		
Power-adjustable pedals, LT	150	129
Power rear quarter windows, LS EXT	280	241
LS EXT w/sunroof	130	112
Requires Preferred Equipment Group 1SB.		
Cargo-management system, LS/LT regular	165	142
LS requires Preferred Equipment Group 1SB.		
Cargo cover, LS/LT regular	70	60
LS requires Preferred Equipment Group 1SB.		
Appearance & Special Purpose		
Side steps	375	323
Skid plates, 4WD	130	112
Bright alloy wheels, LS EXT, LT	150	129

CHEVROLET UPLANDER

CLASS: Minivan
DRIVE WHEELS: Front-wheel drive, all-wheel drive
BASE PRICE RANGE: $23,635-$31,385. Built in USA.
ALSO CONSIDER: Dodge Caravan, Honda Odyssey, Toyota Sienna

Chevrolet's minivan is now what GM calls a "crossover sport van." Uplander uses the extended-length body from Chevy's 1997-2004 Venture minivan, but a new SUV-flavored nose adds slightly to length, wheelbase, and height. It retains a 4-speed automatic transmission, but replaces Venture's 185-hp 3.4-liter V6 with a 200-hp 3.5 V6.

Uplander offers front-wheel drive with base, LS, and uplevel LT trim; it is also available with GM's Versatrak all-wheel drive. GM's Stabilitrak antiskid/traction control is optional on front-drive LT models. All models have antilock 4-wheel disc brakes. Front side airbags with head and torso protection are optional, but full-length curtain side airbags are not available. Every Uplander comes with OnStar assistance, air conditioning, power windows and locks, CD/MP3 player, and rear DVD entertainment. Also standard are 2nd-row bucket seats, 17-inch wheels, sliding rear side doors, and 3-row seating for seven. Power sliding doors are available. The 3rd-row seat is a 50/50 split bench that folds flat above the cargo floor. All 2nd- and 3rd-row seats can be removed. A standard roof-rail system offers optional snap-on storage modules. A remote starting system that operates from the keyfob is also available. Full pricing and equipment were unavailable in time for this report, but Chevrolet announced a base price of $23,635, plus a $715 destination charge. Uplander shares its basic design with the 2005 Pontiac Montana SV6, Buick Terraza, and Saturn Relay. We have not yet tested an Uplander, but performance and accommodations should be similar to those reported in our evaluation of the Relay.

ENGINES

	ohv V6
Size, liters/cu. in.	3.5/213
Horsepower @ rpm	200 @ 5200
Torque (lb-ft) @ rpm	220 @ 4400
Availability	S
EPA city/highway mpg	
4-speed automatic	NA

PRICES

Chevrolet Uplander	RETAIL PRICE	DEALER INVOICE
FWD Base 4-door van	$23635	$21390
FWD LS 4-door van	26240	23747
FWD LT 4-door van	28670	25946
AWD LT 4-door van	31385	28403
Destination charge	715	715

STANDARD EQUIPMENT

Base: 3.5-liter V6 engine, 4-speed automatic transmission, dual front airbags, antilock 4-wheel disc brakes, daytime running lights, front air conditioning, power steering, tilt steering wheel, cloth upholstery, 7-passenger seating, quad bucket seats, 3rd-row split folding seat, cupholders, power mirrors, power front windows, power door locks, OnStar assistance system w/one-year service, AM/FM/CD/MP3 CD player, digital clock, tachometer, rear-seat DVD entertainment system, intermittent wipers, visor mirrors, automatic headlights, theft-deterrent system, 255/60R17 tires, wheel covers.

 Specifications begin on page 547.

LS adds: front side airbags, integrated child seat, rear air conditioning and heater w/rear controls, cruise control, heated power mirrors, power rear quarter windows, remote keyless entry, illuminated visor mirrors, rear defogger, intermittent rear wiper/washer, floormats, rear privacy glass.

LT adds: 6-way power driver seat, 2nd-row captain chairs, leather-wrapped steering wheel w/radio controls, power sliding passenger-side rear door, roof rails, alloy wheels. *Deletes:* integrated child seat. **AWD** adds: all-wheel drive, air-inflator kit, load-leveling rear suspension, 225/60R17 tires.

OPTIONAL EQUIPMENT

Major Packages	RETAIL PRICE	DEALER INVOICE
Climate Pkg., Base	$580	$516
Heated power mirrors, rear defogger, intermittent rear wiper/washer, rear privacy glass.		
Easy Order Pkg., LS	1230	1095
Power sliding passenger-side door, 6-way power driver seat, roof rails, alloy wheels.		
Convenience Pkg., LS, LT	545	485
Rear-obstacle-detection system, power sliding driver-side door. LS requires Easy Order Pkg.		
Security Pkg., LS, LT	170	165
Universal garage-door opener, alarm.		
Premium Seating Pkg., LT	1350	1202
Leather upholstery, heated front seats, power passenger seat.		
Storage and Organizer Pkg., LS	345	307
Removable overhead storage consoles, 2nd-row center console, first-aid kit, cargo net.		
Sport Suspension Pkg., LS, FWD LT	455	405
Air-inflator kit, sport suspension w/automatic load leveling, 225/60R17 tires. LS requires Easy Order Pkg., alloy wheels.		
Trailering Provisions Pkg., LS, LT	165	142
Includes heavy-duty cooling, wiring harness. LS, 2WD LT require Sport Suspension Pkg.		
Safety		
Front side airbags, Base	350	312
Antiskid system, FWD LT	450	401
Includes traction control. Requires Sport Suspension Pkg.		
Comfort & Convenience Features		
Rear air conditioning, Base	475	423
Includes rear heater, rear controls.		
Remote starting, LS, LT	175	156
Remote keyless entry, Base	175	156
6-way power driver seat, LS	275	245
4-passenger seating, Base, LS (credit)	*(230)*	*(205)*
FWD LT (credit)	*(905)*	*(805)*
Deletes 3rd-row split folding seat. LT adds integrated child seat. NA w/Premium Seating Pkg.		

OPTIONAL EQUIPMENT (cont.)

	RETAIL PRICE	DEALER INVOICE
Deluxe entertainment system, LS	$250	$223
Rear radio controls, headphone jacks, wireless headphones, additional auxiliary power outlet. Std. LT.		
AM/FM radio w/in-dash 6-disc CD/MP3 changer, LS, LT..	620	552
Includes satellite radio. Satellite radio requires monthly fee after 3rd month.		
Satellite radio, LS, LT	325	290
Requires monthly fee after 3rd month.		
Cruise control, Base	250	223
Appearance & Special Purpose		
Roof rails, LS	180	160
Rear spoiler, LS	250	223
Requires roof rails.		
Alloy wheels, LS	325	289

CHRYSLER 300

CLASS: Large car
DRIVE WHEELS: Rear-wheel drive, all-wheel drive
BASE PRICE RANGE: $23,295-$34,195. Built in Canada.
ALSO CONSIDER: Buick Park Avenue, Toyota Avalon

Chrysler christens a fresh flagship for 2005, switching from a front-wheel-drive V6 sedan to one that offers both rear-drive and all-wheel drive, plus a V8. The luxury-oriented 300 shares its platform with the sporty new Dodge Magnum wagon. Three models are offered: base with a 190-hp V6; Touring with a 250-hp V6; and the high-performance 300C, with a 340-hp V8 bearing Chrysler's Hemi badge. The V8 features Chrysler's Multi-Displacement System, which deactivates four cylinders in idle and cruise conditions to save fuel. AWD is available on Touring and 300C models. Rear-drive V6 models have a 4-speed automatic transmission. AWD and V8 versions use a 5-speed automatic with manual shift gate. Four-wheel disc brakes are standard. ABS and antiskid/traction control are optional on the base 300 and standard on Touring and 300C. Tilt/telescope steering wheel and power driver seat are also standard. The 300C has 18-inch wheels, the others 17s. Available features include curtain side airbags, adjustable pedals, satellite radio, and Chrysler's UConnect, which uses the audio system as a hands-free, wireless link to cell phones. This evaluation is based on preview test drives.

RATINGS

RATINGS	Base	Touring	300C w/nav. sys.
ACCELERATION	3	5	7
FUEL ECONOMY	5	5	4
RIDE QUALITY	7	7	7
STEERING/HANDLING	6	6	7
QUIETNESS	6	6	6
CONTROLS/MATERIALS	8	8	7
ROOM/COMFORT (FRONT)	7	7	7
ROOM/COMFORT (REAR)	7	7	7
CARGO ROOM	4	4	4
VALUE WITHIN CLASS	6	10	9

Acceleration with the 2.7 V6 is weak, but the boldly styled new 300 is otherwise an Best Buy combination of performance, roominess, and value. It's a worthy rival for a variety of family cars and sporty sedans.

TOTAL	59	65	65

Average total for large cars: 60.9

ENGINES

	dohc V6	sohc V6	ohv V8
Size, liters/cu. in.	2.7/167	3.5/215	5.7/345
Horsepower @ rpm	190 @ 6400	250 @ 6400	340 @ 5000
Torque (lb-ft) @ rpm	190 @ 4000	250 @ 3800	390 @ 4000
Availability	S[1]	S[2]	S[3]
EPA city/highway mpg			
4-speed automatic	21/28	19/27[4]	
5-speed automatic			17/25[5]

1. 300. 2. 300 Touring, Limited. 3. 300C. 4. 18/24 w/AWD. 5. 17/23 w/AWD.

PRICES

Chrysler 300	RETAIL PRICE	DEALER INVOICE
2WD Base 4-door sedan	$23295	$21806
2WD Touring 4-door sedan	27095	25226
AWD Touring 4-door sedan	29370	27273
2WD 300C 4-door sedan	32870	30423
AWD 300C 4-door sedan	34195	31616
Destination charge	625	625

STANDARD EQUIPMENT

Base: 2.7-liter V6 engine, 4-speed automatic transmission, dual front airbags, 4-wheel disc brakes, emergency inside trunk release, air conditioning, power steering, tilt/telescope steering wheel, cruise control, cloth upholstery, front bucket seats, 8-way power driver seat, center console, cupholders, split folding rear seat, power mirrors, power windows, power door locks, remote keyless entry, AM/FM/CD player, analog clock, tachometer, visor mirrors, map lights, variable-intermittent wipers, rear defogger, 215/65R17 tires, wheel covers.

Touring adds: 3.5-liter V6 engine, traction control, antilock 4-wheel disc brakes, brake assist, antiskid system, leather upholstery, heated power mirrors, fog lights, alloy wheels. **AWD** adds: all-wheel drive, 5-speed automatic transmission w/manual-shift capability, 225/60R18 tires.

300C adds: 5.7-liter V8 engine w/cylinder deactivation, 5-speed automatic transmission w/manual-shift capability, power tilt/telescope steering wheel w/radio controls, dual-zone automatic climate controls, heated front seats, power passenger seat, memory system (driver seat, mirrors), Boston Acoustics sound system, tilt-down back-up-aid mirrors w/driver-side automatic day/night, trip computer, automatic day/night rearview mirror, compass, outside-temperature indicator, universal garage-door opener, rain-sensing wipers, automatic headlights, touring suspension, 225/60R18 tires, chrome alloy wheels. **AWD** adds: all-wheel drive, alloy wheels. *Deletes:* chrome alloy wheels.

OPTIONAL EQUIPMENT

Major Packages

	RETAIL PRICE	DEALER INVOICE
Limited Quick Order Pkg. 26/27K, 2WD Touring	$2810	$2585
AWD Touring	1845	1697

Dual-zone automatic climate controls, heated front seats, 8-way power passenger seat, steering-wheel radio controls, trip computer, automatic day/night rearview mirror, compass, outside-temperature indicator, vehicle information center, universal garage-door opener, one-touch up/down power windows, cargo net, automatic headlights, alarm, chrome alloy wheels (2WD).

Luxury Group, Touring	2390	2199

Power sunroof, Boston Acoustics AM/FM/cassette w/in-dash 6-disc CD/MP3 changer, wood interior trim, wood/leather-wrapped steering wheel. Requires Limited Quick Order Pkg. 26/27K.

Signature Series Pkg., 2WD Touring	2185	2010

Leather upholstery, navigation system, power sunroof, Boston Acoustics AM/FM radio w/in-dash 6-disc CD changer, satellite radio.

Navigation and Sound Group I, Touring	2440	2245
Touring w/Luxury Group	1495	1375

Navigation system, Boston Acoustics AM/FM radio w/in-dash 6-disc CD changer. Requires Limited Quick Order Pkg. 26/27K.

Navigation and Sound Group II, 300C	2130	1960

Navigation system, upgraded Boston Acoustics sound system, AM/FM radio w/in-dash 6-disc CD changer.

Sound Group, Base, Touring	995	915
Touring w/Limited Pkg.	945	869

Boston Acoustics AM/FM/cassette w/in-dash 6-disc CD/MP3 changer.

Sound Group II, 300C	635	584

AM/FM/cassette w/in-dash 6-disc CD/MP3 changer, upgraded Boston Acoustics sound system.

Protection Group, Base, Touring	590	543
300C	840	773

Curtain side airbags, rear-obstacle-detection system (300C), interior air filter, 215/65R17 self-sealing tires (Base, Touring), 225/60R18 self-sealing tires (300C).

OPTIONAL EQUIPMENT (cont.)

	RETAIL PRICE	DEALER INVOICE
Comfort Convenience Group, Touring	$700	$644
Heated front seats, 8-way power passenger seat.		
Electronic Stability Program, Base	1025	943
Traction control, antilock 4-wheel disc brakes, brake assist, antiskid system.		
Safety		
Antilock 4-wheel disc brakes, Base	775	713
Includes traction control.		
Comfort & Convenience Features		
Navigation system, Touring, 300C	1895	1743
Touring w/Luxury or Sound Group	1495	1375
Includes AM/FM radio w/in-dash 6-disc CD changer. Requires Limited Quick Order Pkg. 26/27K.		
Power sunroof, 300C	950	874
Power-adjustable pedals, Base, Touring	125	115
300C	175	161
300C includes memory.		
AM/FM radio w/in-dash 6-disc CD/MP3 changer, Base	400	368
Satellite radio	195	179
Includes one-year service.		
UConnect, Base, Touring	360	331
Touring w/Limited Pkg., 300C	275	253
Hands-free cellular telephone link.		
Appearance & Special Purpose		
Xenon headlights, 300C	695	639
Includes headlight washers.		

CHRYSLER CROSSFIRE

CLASS: Premium sporty/performance car
DRIVE WHEELS: Rear-wheel drive
BASE PRICE RANGE: $29,045-$49,120. Built in Germany.
ALSO CONSIDER: BMW Z4, Chevrolet Corvette, Nissan 350Z

CHRYSLER

This 2-seater blends American styling with engineering from Chrysler's parent-company Mercedes-Benz. Crossfire is assembled in Germany and based largely on Mercedes' 1998-2004 SLK sports car. It comes as a hatchback coupe and as a convertible with a power soft top, heated glass rear window, and hard tonneau. Both body styles offer base, Limited, and SRT-6 models. All have a Mercedes V6. Base and Limited have 215 hp. SRT-6 is supercharged for 330 hp. Base and Limited come with a 6-speed manual transmission. A 5-speed automatic with manual shift gate is standard on the SRT-6 and optional on the others. SRT-6s also have a sport suspension and unique interior and exterior trim. ABS, antiskid/traction control, and torso side airbags are standard on all Crossfires. Curtain side airbags are unavailable. Wheels are 18-inch diameter in front, 19 in back. "Summer" tires are standard, all-season tires optional. A plug-in air compressor and a can of tire sealant are provided instead of a spare tire. SRT-6 has a stationary rear spoiler. On the others, a rear spoiler powers up and down depending on road speed or can be left deployed. Limited and SRT-6 come with leather upholstery and are available with a navigation system.

RATINGS	Limited hatch, man.	Limited hatch w/all-season tires, auto.	Limited conv w/all-season tires, man.
ACCELERATION	7	7	7
FUEL ECONOMY	5	5	5
RIDE QUALITY	3	4	6
STEERING/HANDLING	8	8	8
QUIETNESS	4	4	3
CONTROLS/MATERIALS	6	6	6
ROOM/COMFORT (FRONT)	5	5	5
ROOM/COMFORT (REAR)	0	0	0
CARGO ROOM	2	2	1
VALUE WITHIN CLASS	5	5	7

SRT-6 versions look to be narrowly focussed high-performance machines, while the other Crossfires are best considered high-style sporty cruisers. Our Recommended pick here really applies to the convertible, by far the more appealing of the two body styles. It deliverers open-air fun with more refinement and comfort than any similarly priced 2-seat droptop.

TOTAL	45	46	48

Average total for premium sporty/performance cars: 48.3

ENGINES	sohc V6	Supercharged sohc V6
Size, liters/cu. in.	3.2/195	3.2/195
Horsepower @ rpm	215 @ 5700	330 @ 6100
Torque (lb-ft) @ rpm	229 @ 3000	310 @ 3500
Availability	S[1]	S[2]
EPA city/highway mpg		
6-speed manual	17/25	
5-speed automatic	21/28	17/22

1. Base, Limited. 2. SRT-6.

 Specifications begin on page 547.

PRICES

Chrysler Crossfire

	RETAIL PRICE	DEALER INVOICE
Base 2-door hatchback	$29045	$27041
Base 2-door convertible	34085	31577
Limited 2-door hatchback	33745	31271
Limited 2-door convertible	38045	35141
SRT-6 2-door hatchback	44820	41673
SRT-6 2-door convertible	49120	45543
Destination charge	875	875

STANDARD EQUIPMENT

Base: 3.2-liter V6 engine, 6-speed manual transmission, traction control, dual front airbags, side airbags, antilock 4-wheel disc brakes, brake assist, antiskid system, power steering, air conditioning w/dual-zone climate controls, telescope leather-wrapped steering wheel, cruise control, cloth upholstery, bucket seats, height-adjustable driver seat, center console, cupholder, AM/FM/CD player, tachometer, power mirrors, power windows, power door locks, remote keyless entry, intermittent wipers, visor mirrors, rear defogger, power convertible top, automatic-off headlights, theft-deterrent system, rear spoiler, 225/40ZR18 front tires, 255/35ZR19 rear tires, alloy wheels.

Limited adds: tire-pressure monitor, leather upholstery, heated seats, 8-way power driver seat, 4-way power passenger seat, heated power mirrors, Infinity sound system, interior air filter, universal garage-door opener, fog lights.

SRT-6 adds: 3.2-liter supercharged V6 engine, 5-speed automatic transmission w/manual-shift capability, leather/alcantara upholstery, performance suspension.

OPTIONAL EQUIPMENT

	RETAIL PRICE	DEALER INVOICE
Powertrain		
5-speed automatic transmission w/manual-shift capability	$1075	$989
Comfort & Convenience Features		
Navigation system, Limited, SRT-6	1200	1104
Two-tone interior, Limited	250	230
Appearance & Special Purpose		
All-season tires *225/40ZR18 front, 255/35ZR19 rear.*	185	170

CHRYSLER PACIFICA

CLASS: Midsize sport-utility vehicle
DRIVE WHEELS: Front-wheel drive, all-wheel drive
BASE PRICE RANGE: $24,315-$36,315. Built in Canada.
ALSO CONSIDER: Ford Freestyle, Honda Pilot, Toyota Highlander

Chrysler creates a three-model lineup for the 2005 edition of its crossover

wagon, adding a lower-priced version and an uplevel luxury edition. Pacifica aims to blend traits of cars, SUVs, and minivans, and offers front- or all-wheel drive. The '05 line launched in April 2004 with the Touring edition, essentially a carryover of the 2004 standard-trim Pacifica; it's the middle version in the new three-model strategy. Added later were base and top-line Limited models.

Base comes with a 2nd-row bench seat for 5-passenger capacity. Touring and Limited have two 2nd-row buckets and a 3rd-row 2-passenger bench for 6-passenger capacity. Base versions are not available with such features as leather upholstery, power liftgate, sunroof, traction control, or rear DVD entertainment that are standard or optional on other models. Base models with front-wheel drive have a 215-hp 3.8-liter V6. AWD base versions share a 250-hp 3.5 V6 with all other Pacificas. A 4-speed automatic with manual shift gate is the only transmission. Antilock 4-wheel disc brakes are standard. Base and Touring have 17-inch wheels; Limiteds come with 19s that are optional for Touring. Pacifica's 2nd- and 3rd-row seats fold but don't remove. Chrysler lists maximum cargo volume of 92.2 cu ft for the 5-seat model, 79.5 for the others. A driver-side knee airbag is standard. Head-protecting curtain side airbags that cover all seating rows are standard on Limited, optional on base and Touring. No antiskid system is offered. The Limited comes only with AWD and has unique trim inside and out.

RATINGS	2WD Touring w/leather	AWD Touring	AWD Touring w/nav. sys.
ACCELERATION	4	4	4
FUEL ECONOMY	4	4	4
RIDE QUALITY	6	6	6
STEERING/HANDLING	5	5	5
QUIETNESS	6	6	6
CONTROLS/MATERIALS	7	7	6
ROOM/COMFORT (FRONT)	8	8	8
ROOM/COMFORT (REAR)	7	7	7
CARGO ROOM	8	8	8
VALUE WITHIN CLASS	4	5	4

Pacifica feels smaller inside than its generous exterior dimensions suggest, and it drives like a heavy minivan. Sales have been slower than expected. Chrysler hopes the new base model lures value-conscious shoppers, while the Limited attracts the upscale audience Pacifica aimed for in the first place.

TOTAL	59	60	58

Average total for midsize sport-utility vehicles: 54.7

 Specifications begin on page 547.

ENGINES

	ohv V6	sohc V6
Size, liters/cu. in.	3.8/231	3.5/215
Horsepower @ rpm	215 @ 5000	250 @ 6400
Torque (lb-ft) @ rpm	245 @ 4000	250 @ 3950
Availability	S[1]	S[2]
EPA city/highway mpg		
4-speed automatic	18/25	17/22

1. Base 2WD. 2. Base AWD, Touring, Limited.

PRICES

Chrysler Pacifica	RETAIL PRICE	DEALER INVOICE
2WD Base 4-door wagon	$24315	$22405
AWD Base 4-door wagon	27295	25113
2WD Touring 4-door wagon	27845	25602
AWD Touring 4-door wagon	30645	28094
AWD Limited 4-door wagon	36315	33140
Destination charge	680	680

STANDARD EQUIPMENT

Base: 3.8-liter V6 engine, 4-speed automatic transmission w/manual-shift capability, dual front airbags, driver-side knee airbag, antilock 4-wheel disc brakes, air conditioning w/dual-zone manual controls, interior air filter, power steering, tilt leather-wrapped steering wheel w/radio controls, cruise control, cloth upholstery, front bucket seats, 8-way power driver seat, 4-way power passenger seat, center console, cupholders, 2nd-row split folding seat, heated power mirrors, power windows, power door locks, remote keyless entry, Infinity AM/FM/CD player, digital clock, visor mirrors, map lights, variable-intermittent wipers, rear defogger, rear wiper/washer, automatic-off headlights, floormats, theft-deterrent system, rear privacy glass, roof rails, load-leveling rear suspension, 235/65R17 tires, wheel covers. **AWD** adds: all-wheel drive, 3.5-liter V6 250-horsepower engine, alloy wheels.

Touring adds: 3.5-liter V6 engine, dual-zone automatic climate controls, 10-way power driver seat, 2nd-row bucket seats, 3rd-row split folding seat, analog clock, tachometer, universal garage-door opener, illuminated visor mirrors, alloy wheels. **AWD** adds: all-wheel drive, leather upholstery.

Limited adds: all-wheel drive, curtain side airbags, rear-obstacle-detection system, tire-pressure monitor, leather upholstery, heated front and 2nd-row seats, power-adjustable pedals, memory system (driver seat, mirrors, pedals), wood/leather-wrapped steering wheel, power sunroof, Infinity AM/FM/cassette w/in-dash 6-disc CD changer, automatic day/night rearview and driver-side mirrors, power liftgate, cargo cover, fog lights, roof rack, performance suspension, 235/55HR19 tires, chrome alloy wheels.

OPTIONAL EQUIPMENT

Major Packages	RETAIL PRICE	DEALER INVOICE
Quick Order Pkg. 26T, 2WD Touring	$1895	$1668

Leather upholstery, AM/FM/cassette w/in-dash 6-disc CD/DVD changer, power liftgate, fog lights.

OPTIONAL EQUIPMENT (cont.)

	RETAIL PRICE	DEALER INVOICE
Quick Order Pkg. 26U, AWD Touring	$2280	$2006
Curtain side airbags, heated front and 2nd-row seats, power-adjustable pedals, AM/FM/cassette w/in-dash 6-disc CD/DVD changer, memory system (driver seat, mirrors, pedals), power-folding mirrors w/automatic day/night, power liftgate, automatic day/night rearview mirror, automatic headlights, fog lights.		
Comfort and Convenience Group, Touring	695	612
Heated front and 2nd-row seats, power-adjustable pedals. 2WD requires Quick Order Pkg.		
Cargo Convenience Group, Base, Touring	335	295
Cargo cover, cargo net, roof rails.		

Powertrain

Traction control, 2WD Touring	175	154

Safety

Curtain side airbags, Base, Touring	595	524
Rear-obstacle-detection system, Touring	285	251
Touring w/Comfort and Convenience Group	275	242
Tire-pressure monitor, Touring	70	62

Comfort & Convenience Features

Navigation system, Touring, Limited	1695	1492
Touring requires Quick Order Pkg.		
Rear-seat DVD entertainment system, Touring, Limited	990	871
Touring requires 6-disc CD/DVD changer and power liftgate or Quick Order Pkg.		
Upgraded Infinity sound system, Touring, Limited	700	616
Touring requires Quick Order Pkg.		
In-dash 6-disc CD/DVD changer, Base, Touring	555	488
AM/FM/cassette/CD player, Base, Touring	150	132
UConnect, 2WD Touring	360	317
AWD Touring, Limited	275	242
Hands-free cellular telephone link. Includes automatic day/night rearview mirror. Requires Bluetooth-equipped cellular telephone. Touring requires Quick Order Pkg.		
Heated Seat Group, Touring	550	484
Heated front and 2nd-row seats. 2WD requires Quick Order Pkg.		
Power sunroof, Touring	895	788
Power liftgate, Touring	400	352

Appearance & Special Purpose

Laminated side glass, Touring, Limited	300	264
Touring requires Quick Order Pkg.		
Xenon headlights, Touring, Limited	550	484
Touring requires Quick Order Pkg.		
Alloy wheels, 2WD Base	400	352
Chrome alloy wheels, Touring	750	660
19-inch chrome alloy wheels, Touring	1225	1078
Includes tire-pressure monitor, 235/55HR19 tires. Requires Quick Order Pkg.		

 Specifications begin on page 547.

CHRYSLER PT CRUISER

CLASS: Compact car
DRIVE WHEELS: Front-wheel drive
BASE PRICE RANGE: $13,405-$27,830. Built in Mexico.
ALSO CONSIDER: Pontiac Vibe, Toyota Matrix

Chrysler cuts prices on several PT Cruiser models for 2005, partly by making some previously standard equipment optional. Reductions range from $4190 on the Limited model to $2555 on the GT wagon, while a revised base version shaves $4085 from its 2004 counterpart.

PT Crusier comes as a 5-passenger 4-dr hatchback wagon and as a 4-seat 2-dr convertible with a power folding soft top. Both body styles offer base, Touring, and GT trim levels. The wagon also slots a Limited model below the GT. All have a 2.4-liter 4-cyl engine. Base, Touring, and Limited models have a 150-hp version. Touring and Limited are available with a 180-hp turbo variant. The GT has a 220-hp turbo. The 180-hp variant is available only with automatic transmission. The others come with manual or automatic. The GT's automatic is Chrysler's AutoStick with a manual shiftgate. Antilock 4-wheel disc brakes and traction control are standard on GT, optional on the Touring convertible and Limited wagon. ABS without traction control is optional on other models. GTs have a sport suspension and 17-inch wheels. The base wagon has 15-inch wheels, the other models have 16s. Front side airbags are standard on Limited and GT, optional elsewhere. Head-protecting curtain side airbags are unavailable. Options include satellite radio and Chrysler's UConnect, which uses the audio system as a hands-free wireless link to cell phones.

Among equipment revisions, the '05 price cuts make air conditioning optional instead of standard on the base wagon. Same goes for leather/suede upholstery, sunroof, and chrome alloy wheels on the Limited. The base wagon no longer has a folding front-passenger seat, but all wagons retain a rear seat that stows or removes for extra cargo room. The GT wagon sacrifices no standard equipment to its price cut.

RATINGS	Limited, man.	Limited, auto.	GT wgn, auto.	Touring conv, turbo
ACCELERATION	5	4	7	6
FUEL ECONOMY	5	5	5	5
RIDE QUALITY	6	6	5	6

RATINGS (cont.)	Limited, man.	Limited, auto.	GT wgn, auto.	Touring conv, turbo
STEERING/HANDLING	6	6	7	6
QUIETNESS	5	5	4	4
CONTROLS/MATERIALS	6	6	6	6
ROOM/COMFORT (FRONT)	7	7	7	6
ROOM/COMFORT (REAR)	6	6	6	5
CARGO ROOM	7	7	7	2
VALUE WITHIN CLASS	9	9	9	8

Despite mediocre acceleration in nonturbo versions, PT Cruiser is roomy, comfortable, adaptable, and fun. It's quite affordable, too, and softening demand has lowered prices further. Best of all, some of the standard equipment sacrificed in the 2005 price cuts can be made up with reasonably priced options. For example, the Limited was reduced by $4190, but restoring its former standard features costs only $1700 for Quick Order Group 2CK.

TOTAL	62	61	63	54

Average total for compact cars: 48.4

ENGINES

	dohc I4	Turbocharged dohc I4	Turbocharged dohc I4
Size, liters/cu. in.	2.4/148	2.4/148	2.4/148
Horsepower @ rpm	150 @ 5100	180 @ 5200	220 @ 5100
Torque (lb-ft) @ rpm	165 @ 4000	210 @ 2800	245 @ 2800
Availability	S[1]	O[2]	S[3]
EPA city/highway mpg			
5-speed manual	22/29		21/27
4-speed automatic	21/26	19/25	19/25

1. Base, Touring, Limited. 2. Touring, Limited. 3. GT.

PRICES

Chrysler PT Cruiser	RETAIL PRICE	DEALER INVOICE
Base 4-door wagon	$13405	$12699
Base 2-door convertible	19405	18622
Touring 4-door wagon	15405	14519
Touring 2-door convertible	23075	21573
Limited 4-door wagon	17405	16339
GT 4-door wagon	22905	21344
GT 2-door convertible	27830	25900
Destination charge	590	590

STANDARD EQUIPMENT

Base wagon: 2.4-liter 4-cylinder engine, 5-speed manual transmission, dual front airbags, power steering, tilt steering wheel, cloth upholstery, front bucket seats, center console, cupholders, split folding rear seat, power windows, AM/FM/cassette, digital clock, tachometer, variable-intermittent wipers, visor mirrors, rear defogger, rear wiper/washer, theft-deterrent system, 195/65R15 tires, wheel covers.

Touring wagon adds: air conditioning, fold-flat passenger seat, power mirrors, power door locks, remote keyless entry, AM/FM/CD player, floormats.

 Specifications begin on page 547.

Limited adds: front side airbags, cruise control, driver-seat power height adjuster and lumbar adjustment, leather-wrapped steering wheel, AM/FM/cassette/CD player, compass, outside-temperature indicator, universal garage-door opener, illuminated visor mirrors, rear privacy glass, fog lights, Touring Suspension, 205/55TR16 tires, alloy wheels.

GT wagon adds: 2.4-liter turbocharged 220-horsepower 4-cylinder engine, traction control, antilock 4-wheel disc brakes, leather upholstery, power sunroof, rear spoiler, Sport Suspension, 205/50HR17 tires, chrome alloy wheels.

Base convertible adds to Base wagon: air conditioning, power mirrors, power door locks, remote keyless entry, illuminated visor mirrors, compass, outside-temperature indicator, map lights, power convertible top, Touring Suspension. *Deletes:* rear wiper/washer.

Touring convertible adds: cruise control, AM/FM/CD player, floormats, fog lights, 205/55TR16 tires, alloy wheels.

GT convertible adds: 2.4-liter turbocharged 220-horsepower 4-cylinder engine, traction control, front side airbags, antilock 4-wheel disc brakes, leather upholstery, driver-seat power height adjuster and lumbar adjustment, leather-wrapped steering wheel, AM/FM/cassette/CD player, universal garage-door opener, Sport Suspension, 205/50HR17 tires.

OPTIONAL EQUIPMENT

Major Packages

	RETAIL PRICE	DEALER INVOICE
Quick Order Group 2CK, Limited	$1855	$1707
Leather/suede upholstery, power sunroof, additional chrome exterior trim, chrome alloy wheels.		
Signature Series Pkg., Limited	3085	2838
2.4-liter turbocharged 180-horsepower 4-cylinder engine, leather upholstery, power sunroof, navigation system, satellite radio (requires monthly fee), chrome interior and exterior trim, chrome alloy wheels. Deletes cassette player.		
Light Group, Touring wagon	350	322
Illuminated visor mirrors, map and console lights, additional auxiliary power outlets, overhead console, compass, outside-temperature indicator.		
Moonroof Group, Touring wagon	1100	1012
Light Group plus power sunroof.		
Chrome Accents Group, Limited	1220	1122
Limited w/2CK Group	210	193
GT wagon	400	368
Chrome exterior and interior trim, chrome alloy wheels (Limited).		

Powertrain

	RETAIL PRICE	DEALER INVOICE
2.4-liter turbocharged 180-horsepower 4-cylinder engine,		
Limited	1175	1081
Touring convertible	1280	1178
Requires 4-speed automatic transmission.		
4-speed automatic transmission, Base wagon, Touring,		
Limited	825	759
GT	550	506
GT includes manual-shift capability.		

Safety

	RETAIL PRICE	DEALER INVOICE
Front side airbags, Base wagon, Touring	$390	$359
Antilock brakes, Base wagon, Touring, Limited	595	547
NA w/2.4-liter turbocharged 4-cylinder engine, Quick Order Group 2CK.		
Antilock 4-wheel disc brakes, Touring convertible, Limited	825	795
Includes traction control. Requires 2.4-liter turbocharged 4-cylinder engine.		

Comfort & Convenience Features

	RETAIL PRICE	DEALER INVOICE
Air conditioning, Base wagon	1000	920
Requires 4-speed automatic transmission.		
Power sunroof, Limited	750	690
Navigation system, Touring convertible	1200	1104
Limited, GT	1100	1012
AM/FM/CD player, Base wagon	125	115
AM/FM/cassette/CD player, Touring	150	138
Infinity sound system, Touring/GT convertible	565	520
AM/FM radio w/in-dash 6-disc CD changer, Touring	300	276
Limited, GT	200	184
Satellite radio, Touring, Limited, GT	195	179
Includes one-year service. Touring requires front side airbags. NA convertibles.		
UConnect, Limited, GT wagon	360	331
Hands-free cellular telephone link. Includes automatic day/night rearview mirror.		
Leather upholstery, Touring convertible	1175	1081
Includes front side airbags, driver-seat power height adjuster, leather-wrapped steering wheel.		
Driver-seat power height adjuster, Touring	100	92
Heated front seats, Touring convertible, Limited, GT	250	230
Touring requires leather upholstery, Limited requires Quick Order Group 2CK.		
Cruise control, Touring wagon	250	230
Universal garage-door opener, Touring convertible	90	83

Appearance & Special Purpose

	RETAIL PRICE	DEALER INVOICE
Woodgrain Exterior Accents Group, Limited	895	823
Woodgrain exterior trim.		
Rear privacy glass, Touring wagon	275	253
Rear spoiler, Limited	150	138
Chrome alloy wheels, Touring convertible, Limited, GT convertible	700	644
Touring requires 2.4-liter turbocharged 4-cylinder engine.		

 Specifications begin on page 547.

CHRYSLER SEBRING

CLASS: Midsize car
DRIVE WHEELS: Front-wheel drive
BASE PRICE RANGE: $19,350-$31,020. Built in USA.
ALSO CONSIDER: Honda Accord, Toyota Camry and Solara

Chrysler's midsize line consists of sedans, convertibles, and coupes. The sedan and convertible share a Chrysler underskin design and use Chrysler powertrains. The coupe takes its platform and powertrains from Mitsubishi's Eclipse. The convertible body style is exclusive to the Sebring line, but sedans and coupes have Dodge Stratus counterparts.

All Sebrings offer 4- and 6-cyl engines. A 4-speed automatic is the only transmission. Chrysler's AutoStick automatic with manual shift gate is available on top-line coupes and convertibles. Head-protecting curtain side airbags are optional on sedans, unavailable on the other body styles. Front torso side airbags are optional for coupes. The convertible has no side airbags. ABS and traction control are standard on the Limited convertible and optional on all other Sebrings except the base coupe.

RATINGS	Base sdn, V6	Limited cpe, V6 auto.	Limited conv
ACCELERATION	5	5	5
FUEL ECONOMY	6	5	5
RIDE QUALITY	6	5	6
STEERING/HANDLING	6	6	6
QUIETNESS	5	5	4
CONTROLS/MATERIALS	6	6	6
ROOM/COMFORT (FRONT)	6	4	5
ROOM/COMFORT (REAR)	4	2	3
CARGO ROOM	5	5	2
VALUE WITHIN CLASS	5	3	5

Sebrings lack the polish of some import-brand rivals, but prices are competitive and sedans and convertibles have reasonably comfortable interiors. The standout here is the roomy, stylish ragtop.

TOTAL	54	46	47

Average total for midsize cars: 57.2

ENGINES

	sohc I4	dohc I4	dohc V6	sohc V6
Size, liters/cu. in.	2.4/143	2.4/148	2.7/167	3.0/181
Horsepower @ rpm	142 @ 5500	150 @ 5500	200 @ 5800	198 @ 5500
Torque (lb-ft) @ rpm	155 @ 4000	160 @ 4200	190 @ 4850	205 @ 4500
Availability	S[1]	S[2]	S[3]	S[4]
EPA city/highway mpg				
4-speed automatic	21/28	22/30	21/28	20/28

1. Base Coupe. 2. Base sedan and convertible. 3. Touring and Limited sedan; GTC, Touring and Limited convertible; optional base convertible. 4. Limited coupe.

PRICES

Chrysler Sebring	RETAIL PRICE	DEALER INVOICE
Base 4-door sedan	$19350	$17980
Touring 4-door sedan	20070	18628
Limited 4-door sedan	22360	20689
Base 2-door coupe	22145	20536
Limited 2-door coupe	24520	22673
Base 2-door convertible	25410	23564
GTC 2-door convertible	26885	24892
Touring 2-door convertible	28210	26084
Limited 2-door convertible	31020	28613
Destination charge	625	625

STANDARD EQUIPMENT

Base sedan: 2.4-liter 4-cylinder 150-horsepower engine, 4-speed automatic transmission, dual front airbags, emergency inside trunk release, air conditioning, power steering, tilt steering wheel, cloth upholstery, front bucket seats w/driver-seat lumbar adjustment, center console, cupholders, split folding rear seat, power mirrors, power windows, power door locks, AM/FM/cassette, tachometer, rear defogger, variable-intermittent wipers, visor mirrors, floormats, 205/65R15 tires, wheel covers.

Touring sedan adds: 2.7-liter V6 engine, cruise control, remote keyless entry, AM/FM/CD player, automatic-off headlights, theft-deterrent system, touring suspension, 205/60R16 tires, alloy wheels.

Limited sedan adds: leather upholstery, 8-way power driver seat, leather-wrapped steering wheel w/radio controls, trip computer, illuminated visor mirrors, map lights, fog lights, chrome alloy wheels.

Base coupe adds to Base sedan: 2.4-liter 4-cylinder 142-horsepower engine, cruise control, height-adjustable driver seat, remote keyless entry, AM/FM radio w/in-dash 4-disc CD changer, illuminated visor mirrors, map lights, theft-deterrent system, fog lights, 205/60HR16 tires. *Deletes:* split folding rear seat, emergency inside trunk release.

Limited coupe adds: 3.0-liter V6 engine, 4-wheel disc brakes, leather-wrapped steering wheel w/radio controls, Infinity sound system, 215/50R17 tires, alloy wheels.

 Specifications begin on page 547.

Base convertible adds to Base sedan: cruise control, AM/FM/CD player, remote keyless entry, illuminated visor mirrors, map lights, power vinyl convertible top, automatic-off headlights. *Deletes:* split folding rear seat.

GTC convertible adds: 2.7-liter V6 engine, 4-wheel disc brakes, vinyl upholstery, rear spoiler, sport suspension, 205/60R16 tires, alloy wheels.

Touring convertible adds: leather-wrapped steering wheel w/radio controls, leather upholstery, 6-way power driver seat, trip computer, theft-deterrent system, fog lights, touring suspension. *Deletes:* rear spoiler.

Limited convertible adds: traction control, antilock 4-wheel disc brakes, Infinity sound system, automatic day/night rearview mirror, power cloth convertible top, chrome alloy wheels.

OPTIONAL EQUIPMENT

Major Packages

	RETAIL PRICE	DEALER INVOICE
Signature Series Pkg., Base/Touring sedan	$1345	$1237
Leather upholstery, 8-way power driver seat, leather-wrapped steering wheel w/radio controls, power sunroof, illuminated visor mirrors, map lights.		
Signature Series Pkg., Touring convertible	2055	1891
Navigation system, Infinity AM/FM radio w/in-dash 6-disc CD changer, unique interior trim, cloth convertible top, bright exhaust tip, chrome alloy wheels.		
Quick Order Group 24/25W, Base sedan	1000	920
Manufacturer's Discount Price	*NC*	*NC*
Cruise control, remote keyless entry, AM/FM/CD player, automatic-off headlights, theft-deterrent system, 205/60TR16 tires, alloy wheels.		
Luxury Group, Limited sedan	580	534
Automatic climate control, upgraded sound system, automatic headlights.		
Luxury Group, Touring convertible	875	805
Manufacturer's Discount Price	*705*	*649*
Limited convertible	800	736
Manufacturer's Discount Price	*630*	*580*
Automatic climate controls, Infinity sound system, AM/FM/cassette w/in-dash 6-disc CD changer (Limited), automatic headlights		
Touring Group, Base coupe	565	520
Universal-garage door opener, 6-way power driver seat, automatic day/night rearview mirror, outside-temperature indicator, compass.		
Leather Interior Group, Limited coupe	1310	1205
Leather upholstery, 6-way power driver seat, universal garage-door opener, automatic day/night rearview mirror, compass, outside-temperature indicator.		
Protection Group, sedan	995	915
Traction control, curtain side airbags, antilock 4-wheel disc brakes.		
Electronics Convenience Group, Touring convertible, Limited sedan	575	529
Heated front seats, automatic central locking, universal garage-door opener, automatic day/night rearview mirror, additional auxiliary power outlet, alarm.		

OPTIONAL EQUIPMENT (cont.)

	RETAIL PRICE	DEALER INVOICE
Electronics Convenience Group,		
Limited convertible	$875	$805
Autostick manual-shift capability, heated front seats, universal garage-door opener, full-size spare tire.		
Travel Convenience Group,		
Base sedan, Touring sedan	355	327
Trip computer, automatic day/night rearview mirror, illuminated visor mirrors, map lights, premium headliner.		
Security Group, GTC	195	179
Theft-deterrent system w/alarm, automatic door locks.		

Powertrain

2.7-liter dohc V6 engine, Base convertible	850	782
Includes 4-wheel disc brakes, touring suspension.		
Autostick manual-shift capability, Limited coupe	165	152

Safety

Front side airbags, coupe	390	359
Antilock brakes, Limited coupe,		
Base/GTC/Touring convertible	740	681
Includes traction control, 4-wheel disc brakes.		

Comfort & Convenience Features

Navigation system,		
Touring convertible, Limited sedan/convertible	1725	1587
Limited Convertible w/Luxury Group	1325	1219
Includes in-dash 6-disc CD changer.		
Power sunroof, Touring sedan	860	791
Touring sedan w/Travel Convenience,		
Limited sedan, coupe	750	690
Touring sedan includes illuminated visor mirrors, map lights. Touring sedan requires 8-way power driver seat		
AM/FM/cassette/CD player,		
Base/Touring sedan, Base conv	100	92
Base coupe	145	133
Infinity AM/FM/cassette/CD player, Limited coupe	125	115
AM/FM/cassette w/in-dash 6-disc CD changer,		
Limited sedan, GTC, Touring convertible	400	368
Infinity sound system, GTC	475	437
8-way power driver seat, Base/Touring sedan	380	350
6-way power driver seat, Base convertible, GTC	350	322
Wood interior trim, Limited sedan	200	184
Limited convertible	300	276

Appearance & Special Purpose

Alloy wheels, Base coupe	390	359
Alloy wheels, Base convertible	425	391
Chrome alloy wheels, Limited coupe	750	690

 Specifications begin on page 547.

CHRYSLER TOWN & COUNTRY

CLASS: Minivan
DRIVE WHEELS: Front-wheel drive
BASE PRICE RANGE: $20,520-$35,260. Built in Canada, USA.
ALSO CONSIDER: Dodge Caravan, Honda Odyssey, Toyota Sienna

Chrysler updates its minivans for 2005, adding available curtain side airbags and fold-away 2nd- and 3rd-row seats, but dropping all-wheel drive. Town & Country is an upscale version of the Dodge Caravan. It comes in regular- and extended-length models, both with 7-passenger seating. Base regular-length and LX extended-length models have a 3.3-liter V6. Touring and Limited extended models have a 3.8 V6. All have automatic transmission. Traction control is available on extendeds. ABS is standard on extendeds, optional on regulars. Newly standard on all is a driver-side knee airbag. Newly available are head-protecting curtain side airbags that cover all three seating rows; they replace front side airbags and are standard on the top-line Limited model, optional on other Town & Countrys. A tire-pressure monitor is standard on Touring and Limited.

Exclusive to extendeds are Chrysler's Stow 'n Go 2nd- and 3rd-row seats that fold into wells in the floor. When the seats are raised, the wells provide covered storage bins. Other available features include power sliding side doors, power liftgate, power-adjustable pedals, rear DVD entertainment, and navigation system. Newly available are rear-obstacle detection; Chrysler's UConnect, which uses the audio system as a hands-free wireless link to cell phones; and ceiling tracks that allow moving and removing such items as storage bins, a CD holder, and a first-aid kit.

RATINGS	Base	Touring
ACCELERATION	4	5
FUEL ECONOMY	4	4
RIDE QUALITY	6	7
STEERING/HANDLING	5	5
QUIETNESS	6	6
CONTROLS/MATERIALS	7	7
ROOM/COMFORT (FRONT)	7	7
ROOM/COMFORT (REAR)	6	7

RATINGS (cont.)

	Base	Touring
CARGO ROOM	9	10
VALUE WITHIN CLASS	7	9

Outstanding seating versatility and such safety features as curtain side airbags help Town & Country sustain its place among our Best Buy minivans. Comfort and luxury touches add to its appeal. The main differences between Town & Country and its Dodge Caravan sibling are the grille appearance and what prestige may be associated with the Chrysler badge. Both are fine performers, with Caravan's lower sticker prices balanced by Town & Country's slightly higher resale value.

	Base	Touring
TOTAL	61	67

Average total for minivans: 58.0

ENGINES

	ohv V6	ohv V6
Size, liters/cu. in.	3.3/202	3.8/231
Horsepower @ rpm	180 @ 5000	207 @ 5000
Torque (lb-ft) @ rpm	210 @ 4000	238 @ 4000
Availability	S[1]	S[2]
EPA city/highway mpg		
4-speed automatic	19/26	18/25

1. Base, LX. 2. Touring, Limited.

PRICES

Chrysler Town & Country	RETAIL PRICE	DEALER INVOICE
Base regular length 4-door van	$20520	$18878
LX extended length 4-door van	24960	23044
Touring extended length 4-door van	27260	25091
Limited extended length 4-door van	35260	32211
Destination charge: Base	665	665
Destination charge: LX, Touring, Limited	680	680

STANDARD EQUIPMENT

Base: 3.3-liter V6 engine, 4-speed automatic transmission, dual front airbags, driver-side knee airbag, 4-wheel disc brakes, front air conditioning, power steering, tilt steering wheel, cruise control, cloth upholstery, front bucket seats, center console, cupholders, 2nd-row bench seat, 3rd-row folding bench seat, power mirrors, power windows, power door locks, remote keyless entry, AM/FM/CD player, digital clock, tachometer, variable-intermittent wipers, map lights, visor mirrors, rear defogger, intermittent rear wiper/washer, automatic-off headlights, floormats, rear privacy glass, 215/70R15 tires, wheel covers.

LX adds: antilock 4-wheel disc brakes, 2nd-row stowable bucket seats, 3rd-row stowable split folding bench seat, heated power mirrors, illuminated visor mirrors.

Touring adds: 3.8-liter V6 engine, traction control, tire-pressure monitor, tri-zone manual climate controls (including rear controls), rear air conditioning

 Specifications begin on page 547.

and heater, leather-wrapped steering wheel w/radio controls, 8-way power driver seat, power sliding rear doors, power liftgate, AM/FM/cassette/CD player, trip computer, universal garage-door opener, roof rack, 215/65R16 tires, alloy wheels.

Limited adds: curtain side airbags, rear-obstacle-detection system, tri-zone automatic climate controls (including rear controls), interior air filter, leather upholstery, 4-way power passenger seat, heated front seats, power-adjustable pedals, memory system (driver seat, mirrors, pedals, radio), navigation system, Infinity AM/FM radio w/in-dash 6-disc CD/DVD changer, removable center console, automatic day/night driver-side and rearview mirrors, automatic headlights, fog lights, chrome alloy wheels.

OPTIONAL EQUIPMENT

Major Packages

	RETAIL PRICE	DEALER INVOICE
Popular Equipment Group I, Base	$990	$871
Dual-zone manual climate controls, overhead console, trip computer, AM/FM/cassette/CD player, heated power mirrors, universal garage-door opener, illuminated visor mirrors, additional interior lights, roof rack.		
Popular Equipment Group II, LX	1475	1298
Tri-zone manual climate controls (including rear controls), rear air conditioning and heater, heavy-duty alternator, overhead console, trip computer, AM/FM/cassette/CD player, universal garage-door opener, additional interior lights, roof rack.		
Leather Interior Group, Touring	2100	1848
Leather upholstery, heated front seats, power passenger seat, tri-zone automatic climate control (including rear controls), overhead console, upgraded trip computer.		
Luxury Group, Touring	2215	1949
Rear-obstacle-detection system, power-adjustable pedals, Infinity sound system, automatic day/night driver-side and rearview mirrors, removable center console, electroluminescent instrument cluster, overhead rail system, automatic headlights, theft-deterrent system w/alarm, lower bodyside cladding, fog lights. Requires Leather Interior Group.		
Trailer Tow Prep Group, LX	665	585
LX w/Popular Equipment Group, Touring, Limited	600	528
Heavy-duty engine cooling, heavy-duty alternator and battery, trailer-wiring harness, load-leveling height-control suspension.		

Safety

Antilock brakes, Base	565	497
Curtain side airbags, Base, Touring	595	524
LX	1385	1219
Base requires passenger-side power sliding rear door. LX includes power sliding rear doors. LX requires Popular Equipment Group II.		

Comfort & Convenience Features

Rear-seat DVD entertainment system, Base	950	836
Base w/Popular Equipment Group	900	792

OPTIONAL EQUIPMENT (cont.)

	RETAIL PRICE	DEALER INVOICE
Touring	$1150	$1072
Touring w/Luxury Group, Limited	990	871
Touring requires AM/FM radio w/in-dash 6-disc DVD/CD changer. Base NA w/curtain side airbags.		
AM/FM radio w/in-dash 6-disc CD changer, Base	350	308
Base w/DVD system	300	264
Base w/Popular Equipment Group and DVD system, Touring	200	176
AM/FM radio w/in-dash 6-disc DVD/CD changer, Touring	555	488
Requires rear-seat DVD entertainment system.		
Satellite radio	195	172
Includes one-year service.		
UConnect, Base, LX, Touring	360	317
Touring w/Luxury Group, Limited	275	242
Hands-free cellular telephone link. Base includes automatic day/night rearview mirror, automatic headlights.		
Power sunroof, Touring	895	788
Touring w/Luxury Group or DVD system	735	647
Limited	250	219
NA w/curtain side airbags. Deletes Limited std. curtain side airbags.		
CYG 7-passenger seating, Base	945	832
Quad bucket seats, 3rd-row split folding bench seat.		
CYR 7-passenger seating, Base	225	198
Front bucket seats, 2nd-row bench seat w/dual integrated child seats, 3rd-row bench seat.		
Power-adjustable pedals	195	172
Std. Limited.		
8-way power driver seat, Base	425	374
LX	370	326
LX requires Popular Equipment Group II.		
Passenger-side power sliding rear door, Base	760	669
Base w/Popular Equipment Group	400	352
Requires Popular Equipment Group I.		
Removable center console, Base, Touring	195	172

Appearance & Special Purpose

	RETAIL PRICE	DEALER INVOICE
Roof rack, LX	250	220
Alloy wheels, Base	535	471
Includes 215/65R16 tires.		

DODGE CARAVAN

CLASS: Minivan
DRIVE WHEELS: Front-wheel drive
BASE PRICE RANGE: $18,330-$26,505. Built in Canada, USA.
ALSO CONSIDER: Honda Odyssey, Toyota Sienna

 Specifications begin on page 547.

First-time availability of curtain side airbags and fold-away 2nd- and 3rd-row seats highlight 2005 changes to Dodge's popular minivan. Caravan is built from the same design as Chrysler's Town & Country. It comes in a regular- or extended-length body styles and in SE and SXT trim. All have 7-passenger seating. The regular-length SE has a 2.4-liter 4-cyl engine. Regular-length SXT and Grand SE have a 3.3-liter V6. Grand SXT gets a 3.8-liter V6. All come with automatic transmission. Traction control is standard on Grand SXT, but all-wheel drive is no longer offered. ABS is standard on Grands, optional on SXT regular. Newly standard on all is a driver-knee airbag. Newly available are head-protecting curtain side airbags that cover all three seating rows; they replace front side airbags. Also available is a tire-inflation monitor.

Standard on the Grand SXT and optional on the Grand SE are Dodge's "Stow 'n Go" 2nd- and 3rd-row seats that fold into floor wells. With the seats raised, the wells provide covered storage space. Other available features include power sliding side doors, power liftgate, power-adjustable pedals, rear DVD entertainment, and navigation system. Newly available are Chrysler's UConnect, which uses the audio system as a hands-free wireless link to cell phones, and ceiling tracks that allow moving and removing such items as storage bins, a CD holder, and a first-aid kit.

RATINGS	SE	Grand SE	Grand SXT
ACCELERATION	2	4	5
FUEL ECONOMY	5	4	5
RIDE QUALITY	6	7	7
STEERING/HANDLING	4	5	5
QUIETNESS	5	6	6
CONTROLS/MATERIALS	7	7	7
ROOM/COMFORT (FRONT)	7	7	7
ROOM/COMFORT (REAR)	6	8	7
CARGO ROOM	9	10	10
VALUE WITHIN CLASS	7	9	10

The 2005 updates keep these Dodge and related Chrysler minivans among the minivan leaders for available convenience and safety features. Toyota's Sienna and Honda's Odyssey are their only real rivals for all-around appeal, and, in many respects, Grand Caravan blends Sienna's comfort-oriented approach with Odyssey's performance slant to create a tempting Best Buy mix of its own.

TOTAL	58	67	69

Average total for minivans: 58.0

ENGINES

	dohc I4	ohv V6	ohv V6
Size, liters/cu. in.	2.4/148	3.3/202	3.8/231
Horsepower @ rpm	150 @ 5200	180 @ 5000	207 @ 5000
Torque (lb-ft) @ rpm	165 @ 4000	210 @ 4000	238 @ 4000
Availability	S[1]	S[2]	S[3]
EPA city/highway mpg			
4-speed automatic	20/26	19/26	18/25

1. SE. 2. SXT, Grand SE. 3. Grand SXT.

PRICES

Dodge Caravan

	RETAIL PRICE	DEALER INVOICE
SE regular length 4-door van	$18330	$17295
SXT regular length 4-door van	21820	20035
Grand SE 4-door van	21505	20240
Grand SXT 4-door van	26505	24259
Destination charge: SE regular length, SXT regular length	665	665
Destination charge: Grand SE, Grand SXT	680	680

STANDARD EQUIPMENT

SE regular length: 2.4-liter 4-cylinder engine, 4-speed automatic transmission, dual front airbags, driver-side knee airbag, front air conditioning, power steering, cloth upholstery, front bucket seats, center console, 2nd- and 3rd-row bench seats, AM/FM/CD player, digital clock, variable-intermittent wipers, visor mirrors, intermittent rear wiper/washer, 215/70R15 tires, wheel covers.

SXT regular length adds: 3.3-liter V6 engine, tilt steering wheel, cruise control, dual-zone manual climate controls, 2nd-row bucket seats, heated power mirrors, power windows, power door locks, remote keyless entry, AM/FM/cassette/CD player, rear defogger, floormats, automatic-off headlights, theft-deterrent system, rear privacy glass, 215/65R16 tires, alloy wheels.

Grand SE adds to SE regular length: 3.3-liter V6 engine, antilock brakes, tilt steering wheel, cruise control, rear defogger.

Grand SXT adds to SXT regular length: 3.8-liter V6 engine, traction control, antilock 4-wheel disc brakes, tri-zone manual climate controls (including rear controls), rear air conditioning and heater, leather-wrapped steering wheel w/radio controls, 8-way power driver seat, 2nd-row stowable bucket seats, 3rd-row stowable split folding seat, power sliding rear doors, tachometer, trip computer, compass, outside-temperature indicator, universal garage-door opener, illuminated visor mirrors, roof rack, fog lights.

OPTIONAL EQUIPMENT

Major Packages

	RETAIL PRICE	DEALER INVOICE
Popular Equipment Group, SE regular length	$1130	$994
Manufacturer's Discount Price	*730*	*642*

Tilt steering wheel, cruise control, power windows and door locks.

 Specifications begin on page 547.

OPTIONAL EQUIPMENT (cont.)

	RETAIL PRICE	DEALER INVOICE
SE Plus Quick Order Pkg. 28G, Grand SE	$2995	$2636
Antilock 4-wheel disc brakes, 2nd-row stowable bucket seats, 3rd-row stowable split folding seat, heated power mirrors, power windows and door locks, remote keyless entry, tachometer, deluxe insulation group, cargo nets, automatic-off headlights, theft-deterrent system, rear privacy glass, roof rack, upgraded payload rating.		
Popular Equipment Group I, Grand SE	2000	1760
Tri-zone manual climate controls, rear air conditioning and heater, heated power mirrors, power windows and door locks, illuminated visor mirrors, tachometer, deluxe insulation group, rear privacy glass.		
Popular Equipment Group II, Grand SE	1465	1289
Tri-zone manual climate controls, rear air conditioning and heater, AM/FM/cassette/CD player, overhead console, trip computer, illuminated visor mirrors, universal garage-door opener, roof rack. Requires SE Plus Quick Order Pkg.		
Popular Equipment Group, SXT reg. length	1400	1232
Eight-way power driver seat, overhead console, trip computer, universal garage-door opener, illuminated visor mirrors, additional interior lighting, roof rack.		
Leather Interior Group, Grand SXT	2930	2578
Leather upholstery, heated power front seats, driver-seat lumbar adjustment, tri-zone automatic climate controls, interior air filter, Infinity sound system, removable center console, vehicle information center, overhead console, trip computer.		
Premium Group, Grand SXT	1795	1580
Grand SXT w/sunroof	1635	1439
Grand SXT w/Leather Group	1020	898
Grand SXT w/Leather Group and sunroof	860	757
Tri-zone automatic climate controls, interior air filter, power-adjustable pedals, power liftgate, overhead console and rail system (NA w/power sunroof), trip computer, vehicle information center, theft-deterrent system w/alarm, touring suspension.		
Entertainment Group, SXT reg. length	900	792
Grand SE	950	836
Rear-seat DVD entertainment system. NA w/curtain side airbags.		
Trailer Tow Prep Group, Grand SE	665	585
Grand SE w/Popular Equipment Group II, Grand SXT	600	528
Heavy-duty engine and transmission cooling, heavy-duty alternator and battery, load-leveling height-control suspension, trailer-wiring harness.		

Safety

	RETAIL PRICE	DEALER INVOICE
Antilock brakes, SXT reg. length	565	497
Curtain side airbags	595	524
Grand SE w/SE Plus Pkg.	1385	1219
SE requires Popular Equipment Group. SXT regular length requires power sliding passenger-side door. Grand SXT requires power liftgate. NA w/rear-seat DVD entertainment system, power sunroof.		

OPTIONAL EQUIPMENT (cont.)

	RETAIL PRICE	DEALER INVOICE
Tire-pressure monitor, Grand SXT	$70	$62

Comfort & Convenience Features

	RETAIL PRICE	DEALER INVOICE
Power sunroof,		
Grand SXT	895	788
Grand SXT w/Premium Group or DVD system	770	678
Navigation system, Grand SXT	1430	1258
Rear-seat DVD entertainment system,		
Grand SXT	1150	1012
Grand SXT w/Premium Group	990	871
SE	900	792
Requires 6-disc CD/DVD player.		
AM/FM/cassette/CD player, SE	150	132
SE w/DVD system	100	88
AM/FM radio w/in-dash 6-disc CD changer, SXT	200	176
6-disc CD/DVD changer, SXT	555	488
Satellite radio	195	172
Includes one-year service.		
UConnect	360	317
Hands-free cellular telephone link. Includes automatic day/night rearview mirror. SE requires SE Plus Quick Order Pkg. NA SE regular length.		
8-way power driver seat, Grand SE	370	326
Requires SE Plus Quick Order Pkg.		
Power-adjustable pedals	195	172
CYG 7-passenger seating, Grand SE	945	832
Quad bucket seats, 3rd-row split folding bench seat.		
CYL 7-passenger seating,		
SXT regular length	325	286
SXT regular length w/Popular Equipment Group	125	110
Quad bucket seats w/integrated child seat, 3rd-row 3-passenger split folding bench seat.		
CYR 7-passenger seating, SE	225	198
Front bucket seats, 2nd-row 2-passenger bench seat w/dual integrated child seats, 3rd-row 3-passenger bench seat.		
Rear defogger, SE regular length	195	172
Remote keyless entry, SE	300	264
Includes automatic-off headlights. Requires Popular Equipment Group.		
Power sliding passenger-side rear door,		
SXT regular length	400	352
Requires Popular Equipment Group.		
Power liftgate, Grand SXT	400	352
Removable console, SXT	195	172

Appearance & Special Purpose

	RETAIL PRICE	DEALER INVOICE
Roof rack, SE	250	220
Rear privacy glass, SE reg. length	450	396
Requires rear defogger.		

DODGE DURANGO

CLASS: Midsize sport-utility vehicle
DRIVE WHEELS: Rear-wheel drive, all-wheel drive
BASE PRICE RANGE: $26,735-$35,590. Built in USA.
ALSO CONSIDER: Ford Explorer, Honda Pilot, Toyota Highlander

An outdoor-enthusiast option package and a navigation system highlight 2005 additions to Dodge's midsize SUV. Durango comes as an ST model with two rows of seats for 5-passenger capacity, and as SLT and Limited models that seat seven on three rows. It offers rear-wheel drive and two all-wheel-drive systems, one with low-range gearing. Three engines are available: a 210-hp V6, a 230-hp 4.7 V8, and Chrysler's 335-hp 5.7-liter Hemi V8. V6 models come with a 4-speed automatic transmission; V8s have a 5-speed automatic with tow/haul mode. Antilock 4-wheel disc brakes are standard. Traction control is optional, but no antiskid system is offered. Also optional are head-protecting curtain side airbags that cover all three seating rows. Torso side airbags are unavailable. Durango's liftgate does not have separate-opening glass and is unavailable with power assist. The 3rd-row seat drops flat to the floor and is available in a split folding design. Leather upholstery is standard on Limited, optional on SLT. Other available features include adjustable brake and accelerator pedals, rear DVD entertainment, satellite radio, sunroof, and Chrysler's UConnect, which uses the audio system as a hands-free, wireless link to cell phones. Added for SLT models in '05 is the Adventurer package, which includes a rubber cargo-area liner with built-in cargo organizer, special roof rack, and unique trim. The navigation system is a new Limited-model option. And heated front seats are now available on SLT as well as Limited.

RATINGS	2WD ST, 3.7	AWD SLT, 4.7	AWD Limited, 5.7
ACCELERATION	1	3	5
FUEL ECONOMY	3	2	2
RIDE QUALITY	6	6	6
STEERING/HANDLING	3	3	3
QUIETNESS	5	5	5
CONTROLS/MATERIALS	7	7	7
ROOM/COMFORT (FRONT)	7	7	7
ROOM/COMFORT (REAR)	7	7	7

RATINGS (cont.)	2WD ST, 3.7	AWD SLT, 4.7	AWD Limited, 5.7
CARGO ROOM	9	9	9
VALUE WITHIN CLASS	4	7	8

Durango accelerates and rides like a good midsize SUV, but matches some large models for space and towing capacity. Unfortunately, it matches the big SUVs in poor fuel economy, too. Still, avoid the underpowered V6 in favor of a V8, preferably the 5.7-liter Hemi. Thus equipped, Durango is a Recommended pick with an array of talents.

TOTAL	52	56	59

Average total for midsize sport-utility vehicles: 54.7

ENGINES

	sohc V6	sohc V8	ohv V8
Size, liters/cu. in.	3.7/225	4.7/287	5.7/345
Horsepower @ rpm	210 @ 5200	230 @ 4600	335 @ 5200
Torque (lb-ft) @ rpm	235 @ 4000	290 @ 3600	370 @ 4200
Availability	S[1]	S[2]	O[3]
EPA city/highway mpg			
4-speed automatic	16/21		
5-speed automatic		14/18[4]	13/18[4]

1. 2WD ST, 2WD SLT. 2. AWD ST, AWD SLT, Limited; optional 2WD ST, 2WD SLT. 3. SLT, Limited. 4. 14/19 w/2WD.

PRICES

Dodge Durango	RETAIL PRICE	DEALER INVOICE
2WD ST 4-door wagon	$26735	$24474
AWD ST 4-door wagon	29715	27161
2WD SLT 4-door wagon	29150	26624
AWD SLT 4-door wagon	32130	29311
2WD Limited 4-door wagon	33300	30317
AWD Limited 4-door wagon	35590	32390
Destination charge	645	645

STANDARD EQUIPMENT

ST: 3.7-liter V6 engine, 4-speed automatic transmission, dual front airbags, antilock 4-wheel disc brakes, air conditioning, power steering, cruise control, tilt steering wheel, cloth upholstery, front bucket seats, center console, cupholders, 2nd-row split folding seat, power mirrors, power windows, power door locks, remote keyless entry, AM/FM/CD player, digital clock, tachometer, passenger-side visor mirror, variable-intermittent wipers, map lights, rear defogger, intermittent rear wiper/washer, floormats, rear privacy glass, full-size spare, 245/70R17 on/off-road tires. **AWD** adds: all-wheel drive, 4.7-liter V8 engine, 5-speed automatic transmission.

SLT adds: rear air conditioning and heater, 8-way power driver seat, 3rd-row folding bench seat, roof rails, fog lights. **AWD** adds: all-wheel drive, 4.7-liter V8 engine, 5-speed automatic transmission.

Limited adds: 4.7-liter V8 engine, 5-speed automatic transmission, automatic climate control, leather upholstery, 8-way power passenger seat, power-

 Specifications begin on page 547.

adjustable pedals, memory system (driver seat, mirrors, pedals), leather-wrapped steering wheel w/radio controls, AM/FM radio w/in-dash 6-disc CD/MP3 changer, heated power mirrors w/driver-side automatic day/night, universal garage-door opener, illuminated visor mirrors, automatic day/night rearview mirror, map lights, automatic headlights, alloy wheels. **AWD** adds: all-wheel drive, 265/65R17 on/off-road tires.

OPTIONAL EQUIPMENT

Major Packages

	RETAIL PRICE	DEALER INVOICE
24/26B Quick Order Pkg., 2WD ST	$910	$783
AM/FM radio w/in-dash 6-disc CD/MP3 changer, running boards, roof rails, bodyside moldings.		
26/28F Adventurer Quick Order Pkg., SLT	1360	1170
Rear cargo organizer, rubber floormats and cargo mat, roof rack, tubular side steps, unique exterior trim, alloy wheels. 2WD requires optional engine.		
26/28G Quick Order Pkg., SLT	1715	1475
AM/FM radio w/in-dash 6-disc CD/MP3 changer, upgraded sound system, overhead console, illuminated visor mirrors, universal garage-door opener, map lights, automatic headlights, cargo net, alarm, alloy wheels. 2WD requires optional engine.		
Travel Convenience Group, Limited	1990	1711
Curtain side airbags, navigation system, AM/FM radio w/in-dash 6-disc CD/MP3 changer.		
Family Value Group, SLT	1720	1479
Leather upholstery, 3rd-row split folding seat, rear-seat DVD entertainment system, running boards. Requires 26/28G Quick Order Pkg. 2WD requires optional engine.		
Sun, Safe, and Sound Group, SLT	1265	1088
Curtain side airbags, power sunroof, leather-wrapped steering wheel w/radio controls, satellite radio w/one-year service, subwoofer. Requires 26/28G Quick Order Pkg. 2WD requires optional engine.		
Interior Convenience Group, SLT	560	482
Overhead console, illuminated visor mirrors, universal garage-door opener, map lights, cargo net, automatic headlights.		
Light-Duty Trailer Tow Group AHT, 2WD ST/SLT	345	297
Heated power mirrors, 7-wire harness, hitch receiver. NA w/V8 engine.		
Trailer Tow Group AHC, ST, SLT	525	452
Limited	455	391
Heated power mirrors, heavy-duty service group, heavy-duty cooling and battery, 7-wire harness, Class IV hitch receiver. 2WD ST/SLT require optional engine.		

Powertrain

4.7-liter V8 engine, 2WD ST/SLT	785	675
Requires 5-speed automatic transmission.		
5.7-liter V8 engine, 2WD SLT	1780	1531
AWD SLT, Limited	995	856
2WD SLT requires 5-speed automatic transmission.		

OPTIONAL EQUIPMENT (cont.)

	RETAIL PRICE	DEALER INVOICE
5-speed automatic transmission, 2WD ST/SLT	$75	$65
Requires V8 engine. AWD requires 2-speed transfer case.		
Traction control, 2WD	200	172
AWD	300	258
2-speed transfer case, AWD SLT/Limited	195	168

Safety

Curtain side airbags	495	426

Comfort & Convenience Features

Rear-seat DVD entertainment system, SLT, Limited	1200	1037
SLT requires 26/28G Quick Order Pkg. 2WD SLT requires optional engine.		
Navigation system, Limited	1595	1372
Power sunroof, SLT, Limited	850	731
SLT requires Interior Convenience Group.		
Power-adjustable pedals, SLT	120	103
Leather upholstery, SLT	875	753
Includes 3rd-row split folding seat.		
Heated front seats, SLT, Limited	250	215
3rd-row split folding seat, SLT, Limited	150	129
AM/FM radio w/in-dash 6-disc CD/MP3 changer, ST, SLT	300	258
Subwoofer, SLT	225	194
Includes leather-wrapped steering wheel w/radio controls.		
Satellite radio, SLT, Limited	195	168
Includes one-year service. Requires subwoofer or 8-speaker sound system.		
UConnect, SLT	360	310
Limited	275	237
Hands-free cellular telephone link.		

Appearance & Special Purpose

Running boards, SLT	395	340
Limited	445	383
Alloy wheels, ST, SLT	280	241
Chrome alloy wheels, Limited	700	602

DODGE MAGNUM

CLASS: Large car
DRIVE WHEELS: Rear-wheel drive, all-wheel drive
BASE PRICE RANGE: $21,870-$31,370. Built in Canada.
ALSO CONSIDER: Chrysler 300, Ford Freestyle

Dodge redesigns its large car for 2005, switching from a V6 sedan with front-wheel drive to a wagon that offers rear- or all-wheel drive and a V8. Magnum replaces the Intrepid and shares a platform with Chrysler's 300 sedan. It has a rear liftgate without separate-opening glass. Three models are

offered. SE versions use a 190-hp 2.7-liter V6 or optional 250-hp 3.5 V6. SXT models come with the 3.5. RT models have a 340-hp 5.7-liter V8 Chrysler calls the Hemi. The V8 features Chrysler's Multi-Displacement System, which deactivates four cylinders in idle and cruise conditions to save fuel. AWD is standard on the SXT, optional on the RT. The SE has a 4-speed automatic transmission, the other models get a 5-speed automatic with manual shift gate. Four-wheel disc brakes are standard. Optional on SE and standard on the others are ABS and antiskid/traction control. Optional on all is a Protection Group that includes front side airbags and front and rear head-protecting curtain side airbags. SEs have 17-inch wheels, SXT and the RT 18s. RTs add a firmer suspension. Optional on all is rear load-leveling suspension. Magnum standard featurs include split folding rear seatbacks and tilt/telescope steering wheel. Available are adjustable pedals, satellite radio, and Chrysler's UConnect, which uses the audio system as a hands-free, wireless link to cell phones.

RATINGS

	SE, 2.7 V6	SE, 3.5 V6	RT w/nav. sys.
ACCELERATION	2	4	7
FUEL ECONOMY	5	5	4
RIDE QUALITY	7	7	6
STEERING/HANDLING	6	6	7
QUIETNESS	6	6	6
CONTROLS/MATERIALS	7	7	6
ROOM/COMFORT (FRONT)	7	7	7
ROOM/COMFORT (REAR)	7	7	7
CARGO ROOM	7	7	7
VALUE WITHIN CLASS	6	10	9

This Best Buy pick proves aggressive styling and functionality are not mutually exclusive. The 2.7 V6 can't move this large wagon with enough verve, but a Magnum with the 3.5 V6 or Hemi V8 is a fine performer. And its cargo versatility, passenger room, available AWD, and solid construction inside and out make it an outstanding value for the money.

TOTAL	60	66	66

Average total for large cars: 60.9

ENGINES

	dohc V6	sohc V6	ohv V8
Size, liters/cu. in.	2.7/167	3.5/215	5.7/345
Horsepower @ rpm	190 @ 6400	250 @ 6400	340 @ 5000
Torque (lb-ft) @ rpm	190 @ 4000	250 @ 3800	390 @ 4000
Availability	S[1]	S[2]	S[3]
EPA city/highway mpg			
4-speed automatic	21/28	19/27	
5-speed automatic		NA	17/25

1. SE. 2. SXT, optional SE. 3. RT.

PRICES

Dodge Magnum

	RETAIL PRICE	DEALER INVOICE
2WD SE 4-door wagon	$21870	$20353
AWD SXT 4-door wagon	27900	25780
2WD RT 4-door wagon	29370	27103
AWD RT 4-door wagon	31370	28903
Destination charge	625	625

STANDARD EQUIPMENT

SE: 2.7-liter V6 engine, 4-speed automatic transmission, dual front airbags, 4-wheel disc brakes, air conditioning, power steering, tilt/telescope steering wheel, cruise control, cloth upholstery, front bucket seats, center console, cupholders, split folding rear seat, power mirrors, power windows, power door locks, remote entry system, AM/FM/CD player, digital clock, tachometer, passenger-side visor mirror, map lights, variable-intermittent wipers, rear defogger, rear wiper/washer, floormats, theft-deterrent system, 215/65R17 tires, wheel covers.

SXT adds: 3.5-liter V6 engine, all-wheel drive, 5-speed automatic transmission w/manual-shift capability, traction control, antilock 4-wheel disc brakes, brake assist, antiskid system, 8-way power driver seat, illuminated visor mirrors, cargo cover, rear privacy glass, 225/60R18 tires, polished alloy wheels.

RT adds to SE: 5.7-liter V8 engine w/cylinder deactivation, 5-speed automatic transmission w/manual-shift capability, traction control, antilock 4-wheel disc brakes, brake assist, antiskid system, leather upholstery, 8-way power driver seat, leather-wrapped steering wheel, heated power mirrors, Boston Acoustics sound system, illuminated visor mirrors, cargo cover, rear privacy glass, fog lights, touring suspension, 225/60R18 tires, polished alloy wheels.

AWD adds: all-wheel drive.

OPTIONAL EQUIPMENT

Major Packages

	RETAIL PRICE	DEALER INVOICE
SXT Quick Order Pkg., SE	$2500	$2300

Traction control, antilock brakes, brake assist, antiskid system, 8-way power driver seat, illuminated visor mirrors, cargo cover, cargo net, rear privacy glass, heavy-duty alternator and engine cooling, alloy wheels. Requires 3.5-liter V6 engine.

 Specifications begin on page 547.

OPTIONAL EQUIPMENT (cont.)

	RETAIL PRICE	DEALER INVOICE
Electronic Stability Program, SE	$1025	$943
Traction control, antilock 4-wheel disc brakes, brake assist, antiskid system.		
Protection Group	590	543
Front side airbags, curtain side airbags, interior air filter, all-season self-sealing tires. SE requires SXT Quick Order Pkg.		
Comfort Seating Group, SE, SXT	1440	1325
Leather upholstery, heated front seats, power passenger seat, power-adjustable pedals, leather-wrapped steering wheel and shift knob. SE requires SXT Quick Order Pkg.		
Convenience Group I, SE	505	465
Power-adjustable pedals, 8-way power driver seat. NA w/SXT Quick Order Pkg.		
Convenience Group II, RT	925	851
Automatic climate control, power-adjustable pedals, heated front seats, power passenger seat.		
Electronics Convenience Group, RT	630	580
Steering-wheel radio controls, universal garage-door opener, compass, outside-temperature indicator, trip computer, vehicle information center, theft-deterrent system w/alarm.		
Cargo Convenience Group, SE	485	446
SE w/SXT Pkg., SXT, RT	410	377
Cargo cover, cargo organizer, cargo nets, roof rack.		
Trailer Tow Pkg., RT	350	322
Heavy-duty engine cooling, load-leveling and height-control suspension.		

Powertrain

3.5-liter V6 engine, SE	1000	920
Requires SXT Quick Order Pkg.		

Safety

Curtain side airbags, SE	390	359
Antilock disc brakes, SE	775	713
Includes traction control.		

Comfort & Convenience Features

Navigation system, RT	1895	1743
Includes AM/FM 6-disc CD/MP3 changer.		
Power sunroof	895	823
SE requires SXT Quick Order Pkg.		
Leather upholstery, SE, SXT	715	658
Includes leather-wrapped steering wheel and shift knob. SE requires SXT Quick Order Pkg.		
Power-adjustable pedals, SE, SXT	125	115
SE requires SXT Quick Order Pkg.		
AM/FM 6-disc CD/MP3 changer	400	368
SE requires SXT Quick Order Pkg.		
Boston Acoustics sound system, SE, SXT	595	547
SE requires SXT Quick Order Pkg.		

OPTIONAL EQUIPMENT (cont.)

	RETAIL PRICE	DEALER INVOICE
Satellite radio	$195	$179
SE requires SXT Quick Order Pkg. Includes one-year service.		
UConnect	360	331
Hands-free cellular telephone link.		
Appearance & Special Purpose		
Load-leveling and height-control suspension, SE, SXT	290	267
SE requires SXT Quick Order Pkg.		

DODGE NEON

CLASS: Compact car
DRIVE WHEELS: Front-wheel drive
BASE PRICE RANGE: $13,615-$20,650. Built in USA.
ALSO CONSIDER: Ford Focus, Honda Civic, Kia Spectra

Dodge's smallest car loses one of its sporty models for 2005. Neon comes in SE, SXT, and high-performance SRT-4 models; dropped for '05 is the sporty R/T. All have a 4-cyl engine. SE and SXT have a 2.0 with 132 hp. The SRT-4 has a turbocharged 2.4 with 230 hp, along with a limited-slip differential. SRT-4 comes only with manual transmission. SE and SXT offer manual or optional automatic. Antilock 4-wheel disc brakes are standard on SRT-4, optional on the others. Traction control is not available. Front side airbags are optional. The SE has 14-inch steel wheels. The SXT has 15-inch alloys, the SRT-4 17s. SRT-4 gets specially tuned sport suspension and brakes, sport seats, a 160-mph speedometer, and racing-inspired polished-metal pedals. It also includes special body trim, including a hood scoop and rear spoiler.

RATINGS	SE, auto.	SRT-4
ACCELERATION	4	8
FUEL ECONOMY	6	6
RIDE QUALITY	4	4
STEERING/HANDLING	6	8
QUIETNESS	4	2
CONTROLS/MATERIALS	6	6
ROOM/COMFORT (FRONT)	4	4
ROOM/COMFORT (REAR)	4	4

 Specifications begin on page 547.

RATINGS (cont.)	SE, auto.	SRT-4
CARGO ROOM	3	3
VALUE WITHIN CLASS	5	6

Pressured by newer, more-polished rivals such as the Ford Focus and Honda Civic, Neon fights back with high-value models and the sporty SRT-4. Still, it needs frequent factory incentives and/or dealer discounts to keep sales steady, so don't buy without taking advantage of these deals.

TOTAL	46	51

Average total for compact cars: 48.4

ENGINES

	sohc I4	Turbocharged dohc I4
Size, liters/cu. in.	2.0/122	2.4/148
Horsepower @ rpm	132 @ 5600	230 @ 5300
Torque (lb-ft) @ rpm	130 @ 4600	250 @ 2200
Availability	S[1]	S[2]
EPA city/highway mpg		
5-speed manual	27/33	22/30
4-speed automatic	24/31	

1. SE, SXT. 2. SRT-4.

PRICES

Dodge Neon	RETAIL PRICE	DEALER INVOICE
SE 4-door sedan	$13615	$12750
SXT 4-door sedan	15925	14852
SRT-4 4-door sedan	20650	19152
Destination charge	545	545

STANDARD EQUIPMENT

SE: 2.0-liter 4-cylinder engine, 5-speed manual transmission, dual front airbags, emergency inside trunk release, power steering, tilt steering wheel, cloth upholstery, front bucket seats, center console, cupholders, AM/FM/cassette, variable-intermittent wipers, visor mirrors, rear defogger, theft-deterrent system, 175/70R14 tires, wheel covers.

SXT adds: air conditioning, power mirrors, power front windows, power door locks, remote keyless entry, AM/FM/CD player, tachometer, map lights, floormats, 185/60R15 tires, alloy wheels.

SRT-4 adds: 2.4-liter turbocharged 4-cylinder engine, limited-slip differential, antilock 4-wheel disc brakes, leather-wrapped steering wheel, rear spoiler, fog lights, high-performance suspension, 205/50YR17 tires.

OPTIONAL EQUIPMENT

Major Packages	RETAIL PRICE	DEALER INVOICE
Quick Order Pkg. 21/24J, SXT (credit)	*($940)*	*($865)*
Standard equipment.		
Antilock Brake Group, SE	695	639

OPTIONAL EQUIPMENT (cont.)

	RETAIL PRICE	DEALER INVOICE
SXT	$595	$547
Antilock 4-wheel disc brakes, tachometer (SE).		
Special Edition Group, SXT	945	869
AM/FM/cassette w/in-dash 6-disc CD changer, upgraded sound system, chrome alloy wheels.		
Sport Appearance Group, SXT	150	138
Color-keyed instrument panel, fog lights. Requires rear spoiler.		

Powertrain

4-speed automatic transmission, SE, SXT	825	759

Safety

Front side airbags	390	359

Comfort & Convenience Features

Air conditioning, SE	1000	920
Power sunroof, SXT, SRT-4	695	639
Cruise control, SE, SXT	250	230
AM/FM/CD player, SE	175	161
AM/FM/cassette w/in-dash 6-disc CD changer, SXT	350	322
Upgraded sound system, SXT	495	455
SRT-4	795	731
SRT-4 includes in-dash 6-disc CD changer.		
Upgraded mirror, SXT	120	110
Includes compass, outside-temperature indicator, map lights.		

Appearance & Special Purpose

Rear spoiler, SXT	100	92
Chrome alloy wheels, SXT	700	644

DODGE STRATUS

CLASS: Midsize car
DRIVE WHEELS: Front-wheel drive
BASE PRICE RANGE: $20,025-$22,870. Built in USA.
ALSO CONSIDER: Honda Accord, Nissan Altima, Toyota Camry

Dodge's Stratus has a divided parentage: Sedans have a Chrysler-based design shared with the Chrysler Sebring sedan, while Stratus coupes have a Mitsubishi-based design shared with the Chrysler Sebring coupe.

Sedans come in SXT and sporty R/T models. A 2.4-liter 4-cyl engine is standard in the SXT. A 2.7-liter V6 is standard in the R/T and optional in the SXT. Both have a 4-speed automatic transmission; the R/T's includes a manual shift gate. R/T also has antilock 4-wheel disc brakes and traction control, which are optional on SXT sedans. Head-protecting curtain side airbags are optional; no torso side airbags are offered in sedans.

Coupes use powertrains and platforms from Mitsubishi's Eclipse. They come in 2.4-liter 4-cyl SXT and 3.0-liter V6 R/T models, both with manual or automatic transmission. The R/T's automatic is available with a manual shift gate. R/T comes with 4-wheel disc brakes and offers optional ABS; neither are available on the SXT coupe. Front torso side airbags are optional on both coupes.

RATINGS

RATINGS	SXT cpe, auto.	R/T cpe, man.	SXT sdn, 4-cyl	R/T sdn, V6
ACCELERATION	4	6	4	6
FUEL ECONOMY	5	5	5	5
RIDE QUALITY	5	4	6	4
STEERING/HANDLING	6	7	6	7
QUIETNESS	5	5	6	6
CONTROLS/MATERIALS	6	6	6	6
ROOM/COMFORT (FRONT)	4	4	6	6
ROOM/COMFORT (REAR)	2	2	4	4
CARGO ROOM	5	5	5	5
VALUE WITHIN CLASS	4	4	6	6

Stratus sedans and coupes fulfill their particular missions. Sedans represent the better value and, in V6 guise at least, do credible duty as sporty-feeling family cars. What all these Dodges lack is the mechanical refinement and design polish of the top import-brand rivals.

TOTAL	46	48	54	55

Average total for midsize cars: 57.2

ENGINES

ENGINES	sohc I4	dohc I4	dohc V6	sohc V6
Size, liters/cu. in.	2.4/143	2.4/148	2.7/167	3.0/181
Horsepower @ rpm	147 @ 5500	150 @ 5500	200 @ 5900	200 @ 5500
Torque (lb-ft) @ rpm	158 @ 4000	160 @ 4200	192 @ 4300	205 @ 4500
Availability	S[1]	S[2]	S[3]	S[4]
EPA city/highway mpg				
5-speed manual	22/29		20/27	20/29
4-speed automatic	21/28	22/30	20/27	20/28

1. SXT coupe; 142 hp and 155 lb-ft w/automatic trans. 2. SXT sedan. 3. R/T sedan. 4. R/T coupe.

PRICES

Dodge Stratus

Dodge Stratus	RETAIL PRICE	DEALER INVOICE
SXT 2-door coupe	$20025	$18543
R/T 2-door coupe	22870	21103
SXT 4-door sedan	20145	18666
R/T 4-door sedan	21625	19998
Destination charge	625	625

SXT requires Quick Order Pkg.

STANDARD EQUIPMENT

SXT coupe: 2.4-liter 4-cylinder 147-horsepower engine, 5-speed manual transmission, dual front airbags, air conditioning, power steering, tilt steering wheel, cruise control, cloth upholstery, front bucket seats, height-adjustable driver seat, center console, cupholders, power mirrors, power windows, power door locks, AM/FM radio w/in-dash 4-disc CD changer, digital clock, tachometer, variable-intermittent wipers, rear defogger, visor mirrors, map lights, floormats, theft-deterrent system, 205/60HR16 tires, alloy wheels.

R/T coupe adds: 3.0-liter V6 engine, 4-wheel disc brakes, leather-wrapped steering wheel w/radio controls, remote keyless entry, Infinity sound system, illuminated visor mirrors, fog lights, rear spoiler, sport suspension, 215/50HR17 tires.

SXT sedan adds to SXT coupe: 2.4-liter 4-cylinder 150-horsepower engine, 4-speed automatic transmission, emergency inside trunk release, split folding rear seat, remote keyless entry, AM/FM/CD player, automatic-off headlights, 205/60TR16 tires.

R/T sedan adds: 2.7-liter V6 engine, 4-speed automatic transmission w/manual-shift capability, traction control, antilock 4-wheel disc brakes, illuminated visor mirrors, trip computer, rear spoiler, fog lights, performance suspension, 215/50VR17 tires.

OPTIONAL EQUIPMENT

Major Packages

Major Packages	RETAIL PRICE	DEALER INVOICE
SXT Quick Order Pkg. 21/22Y, SXT coupe	$880	$810
Manufacturer's Discount Price	*350*	*322*
Remote keyless entry, alarm, rear spoiler, alloy wheels.		
SXT Quick Order Pkg. 24Y, SXT sedan (credit)	*(1000)*	*(920)*
Standard equipment.		
Special Edition Group, SXT coupe	995	915
Leather upholstery, 6-way power driver seat, leather-wrapped steering wheel and shift knob, power sunroof, unique interior trim, additional map lights.		
Special Edition Group, SXT sedan	875	805
Leather-wrapped steering wheel w/radio controls, AM/FM/cassette w/in-dash 6-disc CD changer, graphite instrument panel bezel, fog lights, rear spoiler, chrome alloy wheels.		

 Specifications begin on page 547.

OPTIONAL EQUIPMENT (cont.)	RETAIL PRICE	DEALER INVOICE
Leather Interior Group, R/T coupe	$1255	$1155
Leather upholstery, 6-way power driver seat, universal garage-door opener, automatic day/night rearview mirror, outside-temperature indicator, compass.		
Convenience Group, R/T sedan	325	299
Universal garage-door opener, automatic day/night rearview mirror, central-locking system, alarm.		
Travel Convenience Group, SXT	355	327
Trip computer, illuminated visor mirrors, automatic day/night rearview mirror, rear assist handles.		
Powertrain		
2.7-liter V6 engine, SXT sedan	850	782
Includes upgraded suspension.		
4-speed automatic transmission, SXT coupe, R/T coupe	825	759
Autostick manual-shift capability, R/T coupe	165	152
Requires 4-speed automatic transmission.		
Safety		
Front side airbags, coupes	390	359
Curtain side airbags, sedans	390	359
Antilock 4-wheel disc brakes,		
R/T coupe w/manual	565	520
SXT sedan, R/T coupe w/automatic	740	681
Includes traction control w/automatic transmission. Std. R/T sedan.		
Comfort & Convenience Features		
Leather upholstery, R/T sedan	695	639
Includes leather-wrapped steering wheel w/radio controls. Requires 8-way power driver seat.		
6-way power driver seat, SXT coupe	245	225
8-way power driver seat, sedans	380	350
Power sunroof, SXT sedan	805	741
SXT sedan w/Travel Convenience, R/T sedan, coupes	695	639
SXT sedan includes illuminated visor mirrors, additional map lights. Sedans require 8-way power driver seat. R/T coupe requires Leather Interior Group.		
AM/FM/cassette/CD player,		
SXT sedan	100	92
R/T coupe	125	115
AM/FM/cassette w/in-dash 6-disc CD changer, R/T sedan	400	368
Appearance & Special Purpose		
Chrome alloy wheels, R/T coupe	750	690

Prices accurate at publication.

DODGE VIPER

CLASS: Premium sporty/performance car
DRIVE WHEELS: Rear-wheel drive
BASE PRICE: $81,495. Built in USA.
ALSO CONSIDER: Acura NSX, Chevrolet Corvette, Porsche 911

Viper is a convertible with a manual folding top and heated glass rear window. The only engine is a 500-hp 8.3-liter V10. The sole transmission is a 6-speed manual. ABS is standard. Tires are run-flats on 18-inch front wheels and 19-inch rears. Side airbags and antiskid or traction-control systems are unavailable. Standard features include leather-and-faux-suede seats, tilt steering column, power-adjustable pedals, and xenon high- and low-beam headlamps. In its only change for 2005, Viper gets two new colors: yellow, and, due later in the year, Copperhead Orange.

RATINGS

	SRT-10
ACCELERATION	10
FUEL ECONOMY	2
RIDE QUALITY	2
STEERING/HANDLING	10
QUIETNESS	2
CONTROLS/MATERIALS	5
ROOM/COMFORT (FRONT)	2
ROOM/COMFORT (REAR)	0
CARGO ROOM	2
VALUE WITHIN CLASS	3

Viper is an emotional statement that makes little sense as daily transportation. A Chevrolet Corvette or base Porsche 911 mimic its usable street performance at lower cost and with more refinement. But it hard to top a Viper for overall shock value.

TOTAL	38

Average total for premium sporty/performance cars: 48.3

Specifications begin on page 547.

ENGINES

	ohv V10
Size, liters/cu. in.	8.3/505
Horsepower @ rpm	500 @ 5600
Torque (lb-ft) @ rpm	525 @ 4200
Availability	S
EPA city/highway mpg	
6-speed manual	12/21

PRICES

Dodge Viper	RETAIL PRICE	DEALER INVOICE
SRT-10 2-door convertible	$81495	$74236
Destination charge	800	800

Add $3000 Gas-Guzzler Tax.

STANDARD EQUIPMENT

SRT-10: 8.3-liter V10 engine, 6-speed manual transmission, limited-slip differential, dual front airbags, antilock 4-wheel disc brakes, emergency inside trunk release, tire-pressure monitor, air conditioning, power steering, tilt leather-wrapped steering wheel, power-adjustable pedals, leather/faux-suede upholstery, front bucket seats, center console, power mirrors, power windows, power door locks, remote keyless entry, AM/FM radio w/in-dash 6-disc CD changer, digital clock, tachometer, rear defogger, variable-intermittent wipers, theft-deterrent system, xenon headlights, fog lights, manual folding soft top, run-flat tires (275/35ZR18 front, 345/30ZR19 rear), alloy wheels.

FORD CROWN VICTORIA

CLASS: Large car
DRIVE WHEELS: Rear-wheel drive
BASE PRICE RANGE: $24,085-$30,165. Built in Canada.
ALSO CONSIDER: Chrysler 300, Toyota Avalon

Ford's large, rear-wheel-drive V8 sedan shares its design with Mercury's Grand Marquis. Crown Vic offers standard, LX, and LX Sport models. Standard and LX have a front bench seat; the LX Sport has buckets with a center console. Automatic transmission is standard. The sole engine is a 4.6-liter V8 with 224 hp in base form, 239 in the LX Sport or with the optional Handling and Performance Package. ABS is standard; front side airbags are optional on LX and LX Sport, traction control is optional on all.

RATINGS

	LX w/Handling and Perf. Pkg.
ACCELERATION	5
FUEL ECONOMY	4
RIDE QUALITY	7
STEERING/HANDLING	6
QUIETNESS	7
CONTROLS/MATERIALS	4
ROOM/COMFORT (FRONT)	7
ROOM/COMFORT (REAR)	6
CARGO ROOM	6
VALUE WITHIN CLASS	5

Rear-drive traditionalists are well-served by the Crown Victoria and Grand Marquis. But these sedans still don't feel or act as lively and efficient as more-modern designs such as the Chrysler 300.

TOTAL	57

Average total for large cars: 60.9

ENGINES

	sohc V8	sohc V8
Size, liters/cu. in.	4.6/281	4.6/281
Horsepower @ rpm	224 @ 4800	239 @ 4900
Torque (lb-ft) @ rpm	275 @ 4000	287 @ 4100
Availability	S[1]	S[2]
EPA city/highway mpg		
4-speed automatic	17/25	17/25

1. Standard and LX. 2. LX Sport, LX w/Handling and Perf. Pkg.

PRICES

Ford Crown Victoria	RETAIL PRICE	DEALER INVOICE
Standard 4-door sedan	$24085	$22554
LX 4-door sedan	27220	24893
LX Sport 4-door sedan	30165	27544
Destination charge	725	725

STANDARD EQUIPMENT

Standard: 4.6-liter V8 224-horsepower engine, 4-speed automatic transmission, dual front airbags, antilock 4-wheel disc brakes, emergency inside trunk release, air conditioning, power steering, tilt steering wheel, cruise control, cloth upholstery, front split bench seat, 8-way power driver seat, cupholders, column shifter, AM/FM/cassette, digital clock, power mirrors, power windows, power door locks, map lights, variable-intermittent wipers, rear defogger, automatic headlights, floormats, theft-deterrent system, 225/60R16 tires, wheel covers.

 Specifications begin on page 547.

LX adds: remote keyless entry, AM/FM/CD player, overhead console, compass, alloy wheels.

LX Sport adds: 4.6-liter V8 239-horsepower engine, performance axle ratio, automatic climate control, leather upholstery, front bucket seats w/power lumbar adjustment, 8-way power passenger seat, center console w/floor shifter, leather-wrapped steering wheel w/radio and climate controls, automatic day/night rearview mirror, performance suspension, rear air suspension, full-size spare tire, 235/55HR17 tires.

OPTIONAL EQUIPMENT

Major Packages	RETAIL PRICE	DEALER INVOICE
Premier Group, LX	$1205	$1072
Automatic climate control, power passenger seat, leather-wrapped steering wheel w/radio and climate controls, AM/FM/cassette/CD player, automatic day/night rearview mirror.		
Handling and Performance Pkg., LX	615	547
Includes 239-horsepower engine, dual exhaust, performance springs, shocks, and stabilizer bars, rear air suspension, performance axle ratio, 225/60TR16 touring tires, unique alloy wheels.		
Powertrain		
Traction control	175	156
Safety		
Front side airbags, LX, LX Sport	300	267
Comfort & Convenience Features		
Power sunroof, LX, LX Sport	1025	913
LX requires Premier Group.		
Power-adjustable pedals	120	107
Remote keyless entry, Standard	255	227
Leather upholstery, LX	795	708
Requires Premier Group.		
AM/FM/cassette/CD player, Standard, LX	185	165
6-disc CD changer, LX, LX Sport	165	147
Electronic instruments, LX	235	209
Digital instruments, trip computer.		
Trunk storage unit, LX, LX Sport	190	169
Laminated side windows, LX, LX Sport	295	263

FORD ESCAPE

CLASS: Compact sport-utility vehicle
DRIVE WHEELS: Front-wheel drive, all-wheel drive
BASE PRICE RANGE: $19,405-$28,005. Built in USA.
ALSO CONSIDER: Honda CR-V, Jeep Liberty, Subaru Forester

The introduction of a gas/electric hybrid version tops 2005 changes to Ford's smallest SUV. Escape also gets a larger base engine, freshened styling, and

added safety features. This 5-passenger, 4-dr wagon has a rear liftgate with separate-opening glass. Replacing a 127-hp 2.0-liter 4-cyl as the base engine is a 153-hp 2.3. It's available with manual transmission or, new for '05, optional automatic. The Hybrid has a 4-cyl gas engine assisted by an electric motor for a combined 155 hp. The electric motor helps save fuel by powering the Hybrid at low speeds and assisting the gas engine during acceleration. There's no plug-in charging; the system recharges the motor's batteries when coasting or decelerating. The Hybrid uses a continuously variable transmission (CVT) that functions like an automatic but has a near-infinite number of ratios. A 200-hp V6 with automatic transmission is also available. All models offer front-wheel drive or all-wheel drive; the AWD system does not include low-range gearing. For '05, Escape's automatic-transmission shift lever is mounted on the floor console rather than the steering column. ABS, previously optional, is standard. Newly optional are head-protecting curtain side airbags for both seating rows. They're designed to deploy in side impacts and rollovers. Escape also gets revised front and rear styling, and Ford says it has more sound insulation. Mazda's Tribute and the new 2005 Mercury Mariner are similar to Escape, but don't offer a hybrid version.

RATINGS	2WD XLS	2WD XLT Sport	AWD XLT Sport	AWD Hybrid
ACCELERATION	2	5	5	4
FUEL ECONOMY	5	5	5	8
RIDE QUALITY	4	4	4	4
STEERING/HANDLING	4	4	5	5
QUIETNESS	4	4	4	4
CONTROLS/MATERIALS	5	5	5	5
ROOM/COMFORT (FRONT)	6	6	6	6
ROOM/COMFORT (REAR)	5	5	5	5
CARGO ROOM	7	7	7	7
VALUE WITHIN CLASS	7	9	10	8

By any name, these Best Buy compact SUVs are solid, spacious, and pleasant to drive. Competitive pricing makes them high-value alternatives to some larger truck-based SUVs that use more gas and don't have significantly more interior space. The Escape Hybrid is America's only compact SUV hybrid, and it adds fuel savings to Escape's other attributes. Though its base prices are relatively

 Specifications begin on page 547.

RATINGS (cont.)

	2WD XLS	2WD XLT Sport	AWD XLT Sport	AWD Hybrid

steep, its doesn't compromise performance, and the initial cost can be offset some by the one-time federal tax deduction for hybrid-vehicle purchases.

	2WD XLS	2WD XLT Sport	AWD XLT Sport	AWD Hybrid
TOTAL	**49**	**54**	**56**	**56**

Average total for compact sport-utility vehicles: 49.0

ENGINES

	dohc I4	dohc I4/electric	dohc V6
Size, liters/cu. in.	2.3/138	2.3/138	3.0/182
Horsepower @ rpm	153 @ 5800	133 @ 6000	200 @ 6000
Torque (lb-ft) @ rpm	152 @ 4250	129 @ 4500	196 @ 4850
Availability	S	S[1]	O
EPA city/highway mpg			
5-speed manual	NA		
4-speed automatic	NA		18/23
CVT automatic		NA	

1. Gas engine; 155 hp in combination with electric motor.

PRICES

Ford Escape	RETAIL PRICE	DEALER INVOICE
2WD XLS Value 4-door wagon	$19405	$18038
AWD XLS Value 4-door wagon	21115	19631
2WD XLS 4-door wagon	19705	18311
AWD XLS 4-door wagon	21455	19904
2WD XLT 4-cylinder 4-door wagon	22455	20814
AWD XLT 4-cylinder 4-door wagon	24205	22406
2WD XLT V6 4-door wagon	23205	21496
AWD XLT V6 4-door wagon	24955	23089
2WD XLT Sport 4-door wagon	24105	22315
AWD XLT Sport 4-door wagon	25855	23908
2WD Limited 4-door wagon	24805	22952
AWD Limited 4-door wagon	26555	24545
2WD Hybrid 4-door wagon	26380	24385
AWD Hybrid 4-door wagon	28005	25864
Destination charge	590	590

STANDARD EQUIPMENT

XLS Value: 2.3-liter 4-cylinder engine, 5-speed manual transmission, dual front airbags, antilock brakes, air conditioning, power steering, tilt steering wheel, cloth upholstery, front bucket seats, console, cupholders, split folding rear seat, power mirrors, power windows, power door locks, remote keyless entry, AM/FM/CD player, digital clock, tachometer, map lights, visor mirrors, variable-intermittent wipers, rear defogger, rear wiper/washer, theft-deterrent system, roof rails, 225/75R15 tires. **AWD** adds: all-wheel drive, antilock 4-wheel disc brakes.

XLS adds: 4-speed automatic transmission. **AWD** adds: all-wheel drive, antilock 4-wheel disc brakes.

XLT adds: 2.3-liter 4-cylinder engine or 3.0-liter V6 engine, cruise control, 6-way power driver seat, AM/FM radio w/in-dash 6-disc CD changer, floormats, rear privacy glass, roof rack, fog lights, 235/70R16 tires, alloy wheels. **AWD** adds: all-wheel drive, antilock 4-wheel disc brakes, 235/70R16 white-letter tires.

XLT Sport adds: 3.0-liter V6 engine, side steps, 235/70R16 white-letter tires, bright alloy wheels. **AWD** adds: all-wheel drive, antilock 4-wheel disc brakes.

Limited adds to XLT: leather upholstery, leather-wrapped steering wheel, automatic day/night rearview mirror, illuminated visor mirrors, cargo cover, automatic headlights, bright alloy wheels. **AWD** adds: all-wheel drive, antilock 4-wheel disc brakes, 235/70R16 white-letter tires.

Hybrid adds to XLT: 2.3-liter 4-cylinder engine, electric drive motor, continuously variable automatic transmission (CVT), antilock 4-wheel disc brakes, brake assist. **AWD** adds: all-wheel drive.

OPTIONAL EQUIPMENT

Major Packages

	RETAIL PRICE	DEALER INVOICE
Hybrid Energy Audiophile and Navigation System, Hybrid	$1850	$1666
Navigation system, upgraded sound system, energy-flow graphic and fuel-economy display. Relocates CD changer from dash to under passenger seat.		
Convenience Group, XLS Value, XLS	325	293
Cruise control, floormats, perimeter alarm system.		
Safety Pkg.	595	536
Curtain side airbags w/rollover sensor, front side airbags.		
Leather Comfort Group, XLT, XLT Sport, Hybrid	575	517
Leather upholstery, leather-wrapped steering wheel.		
No Boundaries Pkg., XLT V6	1055	950
Class II Trailer Towing Pkg. plus unique roof rack, step bars, wheel-lip moldings, 235/70R16 all-terrain white-letter tires, painted alloy wheels. NA w/power sunroof.		
Luxury Comfort Pkg., Limited	1095	986
Rear-obstacle-detection system, heated front seats and mirrors, Mach sound system.		
Cargo Convenience Group	125	113
Cargo cover, storage bin.		
Appearance Pkg., Hybrid	625	563
Bodyside cladding, body-colored door handles and liftgate molding.		
Class II Trailer Towing Pkg., XLT V6, XLT Sport, Limited	350	316
Trailer hitch, 4-wire harness, oil cooler.		

Comfort & Convenience Features

	RETAIL PRICE	DEALER INVOICE
Power sunroof, XLT, XLT Sport, Limited	585	527
AM/FM/cassette/CD player, XLT, XLT Sport	NC	NC
Mach sound system, XLT, XLT Sport, Limited, Hybrid	565	509
AC power outlet, Hybrid	110	99

Appearance & Special Purpose	RETAIL PRICE	DEALER INVOICE
Roof rack, XLS Value, XLS	$40	$36
Side step bars, XLS Value, XLS, XLT	325	293
XLS Value, XLS require alloy wheels.		
Alloy wheels, XLS Value, XLS	375	337

FORD EXPLORER

CLASS: Midsize sport-utility vehicle
DRIVE WHEELS: Rear-wheel drive, 4-wheel drive
BASE PRICE RANGE: $26,770-$37,530. Built in USA.
ALSO CONSIDER: Dodge Durango, Honda Pilot, Toyota 4Runner

A standard antiskid system and the loss of AWD availability mark 2005 for America's best-selling SUV. Explorer is available with a 3rd-row seat for 7-passenger capacity and comes with a V6 or V8 engine and a 5-speed automatic transmission. Available with either engine is rear-wheel drive or Ford's ControlTrac 4WD that can be left engaged on dry pavement and has low-range gearing. All-wheel drive is no longer available. Explorer is among the few midsize SUVs with independent rear suspension. ABS is standard. Newly standard on all Explorers is Ford's AdvanceTrac antiskid system with Roll Stability Control. Roll Stability Control is designed to detect an impending tip and activate the antiskid system to reduce the chances of a rollover. Torso side airbags are unavailable, but the optional head-protecting curtain side airbags cover the 1st and 2nd seating rows and are designed to deploy in side impacts and rollovers. Other available features include 2nd-row bucket seats, rear DVD entertainment, tire-pressure monitor, rear-obstacle detection, and power-adjustable pedals. The Lincoln Aviator also shares the basic Explorer/Mountaineer design. The off-road-oriented NBX model has been dropped.

RATINGS

RATINGS	XLT 4WD, V6	Limited 4WD, V8
ACCELERATION	4	5
FUEL ECONOMY	4	3
RIDE QUALITY	4	4
STEERING/HANDLING	4	4
QUIETNESS	4	5
CONTROLS/MATERIALS	7	7
ROOM/COMFORT (FRONT)	7	8
ROOM/COMFORT (REAR)	7	7
CARGO ROOM	8	8
VALUE WITHIN CLASS	8	7

Explorer is a more-than-competent overall performer with an unmatched array of useful features: available V8 power, 7-passenger seating, adjustable pedals, curtain airbags, DVD entertainment, rear-obstacle detection, and standard antiskid system. Mountaineer's higher sticker price brings more-expressive styling but, in all, Explorer is the better value and a solid Recommended pick.

TOTAL	57	58

Average total for midsize sport-utility vehicles: 54.7

ENGINES

	sohc V6	sohc V8
Size, liters/cu. in.	4.0/245	4.6/281
Horsepower @ rpm	210 @ 5100	239 @ 4000
Torque (lb-ft) @ rpm	254 @ 3700	282 @ 4000
Availability	S[1]	S[2]
EPA city/highway mpg		
5-speed automatic	15/21	15/19[3]

1. V6 models. 2. V8 models. 3. 15/20 w/2WD.

PRICES

Ford Explorer

	RETAIL PRICE	DEALER INVOICE
2WD XLS V6 4-door wagon	$26770	$24330
4WD XLS V6 4-door wagon	29235	26524
2WD XLS Sport V6 4-door wagon	28185	25590
4WD XLS Sport V6 4-door wagon	30415	27574
2WD XLT V6 4-door wagon	29575	26827
2WD XLT V8 4-door wagon	30375	27539
4WD XLT V6 4-door wagon	31800	28807
4WD XLT V8 4-door wagon	32600	29519
2WD XLT Sport V6 4-door wagon	30930	28033
2WD XLT Sport V8 4-door wagon	31730	28745
4WD XLT Sport V6 4-door wagon	33155	30009
4WD XLT Sport V8 4-door wagon	33955	30721
2WD Eddie Bauer V6 4-door wagon	33630	30436
2WD Eddie Bauer V8 4-door wagon	34430	31148

 Specifications begin on page 547.

Ford Explorer

	RETAIL PRICE	DEALER INVOICE
4WD Eddie Bauer V6 4-door wagon	$35855	$32416
4WD Eddie Bauer V8 4-door wagon	36655	33128
2WD Limited V6 4-door wagon	34505	31214
2WD Limited V8 4-door wagon	35305	31926
4WD Limited V6 4-door wagon	36730	33195
4WD Limited V8 4-door wagon	37530	33907
Destination charge	645	645

STANDARD EQUIPMENT

XLS: 4.0-liter V6 engine, 5-speed automatic transmission, dual front airbags, antilock 4-wheel disc brakes, antiskid system, roll stability control, air conditioning, power steering, tilt steering wheel, cruise control, cloth upholstery, front bucket seats, center console, cupholders, split folding rear seat, power mirrors, power windows, power door locks, remote keyless entry, AM/FM/CD player, digital clock, tachometer, variable-intermittent wipers, rear defogger, intermittent rear wiper/washer, visor mirrors, map lights, cargo-management system, theft-deterrent system, rear liftgate, rear privacy glass, roof rails, Class II trailer-hitch receiver, 4-pin connector, full-size spare tire, 235/70R16 tires. **4WD** adds: 4-wheel drive, 2-speed transfer case.

XLS Sport adds: tire-pressure monitor, floormats, step bars, 235/70R16 white-letter tires, alloy wheels. **4WD** adds: 4-wheel drive, 2-speed transfer case.

XLT adds to XLS: 4.0-liter V6 or 4.6-liter V8 engine, tire-pressure monitor, leather-wrapped steering wheel, front bucket seats w/lumbar adjustment, 6-way power driver seat, overhead console, outside-temperature indicator, compass, illuminated visor mirrors, floormats, fog lights, alloy wheels. **4WD** adds: 4-wheel drive, 2-speed transfer case.

XLT Sport adds: keypad entry, automatic day/night rearview mirror, automatic headlights, step bars, 245/65R17 all-terrain white-letter tires, machined alloy wheels. **4WD** adds: 4-wheel drive, 2-speed transfer case.

Eddie Bauer/Limited adds to XLT: leather upholstery, heated front seats, driver-seat memory, 6-way power passenger seat, steering-wheel radio and climate controls, dual-zone automatic climate controls, heated power mirrors, keypad entry, Audiophile AM/FM radio w/in-dash 6-disc CD changer, automatic day/night rearview mirror, automatic headlights, 2-tone paint (Eddie Bauer), monotone paint (Limited), running boards, 245/65R17 all-terrain white-letter tires, chrome alloy wheels (Limited). **4WD** adds: 4-wheel drive, 2-speed transfer case.

OPTIONAL EQUIPMENT

Major Packages

	RETAIL PRICE	DEALER INVOICE
Convenience Group, XLT	$250	$213
Keypad entry, automatic day/night rearview mirror, automatic headlights.		
Appearance Pkg., XLT	695	591
Unique interior trim, side steps, silver-painted roof rails and wheels.		
Class III/IV Trailer Towing Prep Pkg	150	128
Special axle ratio, Class III hitch, 7-wire harness, 7- to 4-pin adapter. NA XLS, XLS Sport.		

Safety

	RETAIL PRICE	DEALER INVOICE
Front and 2nd-row curtain side airbags	$560	$476
Rear-obstacle-detection system, XLT, XLT Sport, Eddie Bauer, Limited	255	217

Comfort & Convenience Features

Rear-seat DVD entertainment system	1295	1101
Requires power sunroof and curtain side airbags or rear air conditioning and heater. XLT requires Convenience Group. NA XLS, XLS Sport.		
Rear air conditioning and heater, XLT, XLT Sport, Eddie Bauer, Limited	650	553
Power sunroof, XLT, XLT Sport, Eddie Bauer, Limited	850	723
Power-adjustable pedals, XLT, XLT Sport	120	102
Eddie Bauer, Limited	350	298
Eddie Bauer, Limited include memory, universal garage-door opener.		
AM/FM/cassette/CD player, XLT, XLT Sport	150	128
Eddie Bauer, Limited	NC	NC
AM/FM radio w/in-dash 6-disc CD changer, XLT, XLT Sport	510	433
Leather upholstery, XLT, XLT Sport	695	591
Includes 6-way power passenger seat.		
Folding 3rd-row seat, XLT, XLT Sport, Eddie Bauer, Limited	745	633
Includes 40/20/40 split folding 2nd-row seat.		
Quad captain chairs, Eddie Bauer, Limited	745	676
Requires folding 3rd-row seat.		

Appearance & Special Purpose

Running boards, XLT	450	383
Chrome side steps, Limited	150	128

FORD EXPLORER SPORT TRAC

CLASS: Midsize sport-utility vehicle
DRIVE WHEELS: Rear-wheel drive, 4-wheel drive
BASE PRICE RANGE: $23,820-$31,090. Built in USA.
ALSO CONSIDER: Dodge Dakota Quad Cab, Toyota Tacoma Double Cab

 Specifications begin on page 547.

The Sport Trac crew-cab returns for 2005 vitually unchanged. Sport Trac plays a dual role, combining a 4-dr, 5-seat SUV cabin with a 4-ft-long pick-up-truck bed. Based on the 1995-2001 Explorer design, Sport Trac has a V6 engine and 5-speed automatic transmission. It's available with rear-wheel drive or Ford's ControlTrac 4WD that can be left engaged on dry pavement and includes low-range gearing. ABS is standard. Head-protecting curtain side airbags are optional. Also available are leather upholstery, heated front seats, and a sunroof.

RATINGS

	4WD XLT Premium
ACCELERATION	5
FUEL ECONOMY	4
RIDE QUALITY	4
STEERING/HANDLING	3
QUIETNESS	3
CONTROLS/MATERIALS	6
ROOM/COMFORT (FRONT)	6
ROOM/COMFORT (REAR)	6
CARGO ROOM	6
VALUE WITHIN CLASS	5

Compared to crew-cab pickup trucks, the novel Sport Trac offers more passenger space but a smaller cargo bed. If that combination suits you, it's a good choice as a multipurpose vehicle.

TOTAL	48

Average total for midsize sport-utility vehicles: 54.7

ENGINES

	sohc V6
Size, liters/cu. in.	4.0/245
Horsepower @ rpm	205 @ 5500
Torque (lb-ft) @ rpm	242 @ 3000
Availability	S
EPA city/highway mpg	
5-speed automatic	15/20[1]

1. 16/20 w/2WD.

PRICES

Ford Explorer Sport Trac

	RETAIL PRICE	DEALER INVOICE
2WD XLS 4-door crew cab	$23820	$21625
2WD XLT 4-door crew cab	25060	22729
2WD XLT Premium 4-door crew cab	27465	24869
2WD Adrenalin 4-door crew cab	28260	25577
4WD XLS 4-door crew cab	26590	24090
4WD XLT 4-door crew cab	27890	25247
4WD XLT Premium 4-door crew cab	30235	27334
4WD Adrenalin 4-door crew cab	31090	28095
Destination charge	645	645

STANDARD EQUIPMENT

XLS: 4.0-liter V6 engine, 5-speed automatic transmission, dual front airbags, antilock 4-wheel disc brakes, air conditioning, power steering, cloth upholstery, front bucket seats, center console, cupholders, split folding rear seat, power windows, power door locks, front-hinged rear doors, AM/FM/CD/MP3 player, digital clock, tachometer, map light, variable-intermittent wipers, cargo-box light, visor mirrors, theft-deterrent system, rear privacy glass, rear cargo box, roof rails, 4-wire trailering harness, full-size spare tire, 235/70R16 tires, alloy wheels. **4WD** models add: 4-wheel drive, 2-speed transfer-case.

XLT adds: tilt leather-wrapped steering wheel, cruise control, power mirrors, remote keyless entry, keypad entry, floormats. **4WD** adds: 4-wheel drive, 2-speed transfer case, 235/70R16 white-letter tires.

XLT Premium adds: 8-way power driver seat w/power lumbar adjustment, rear climate and radio controls, overhead console, automatic day/night rearview mirror, outside-temperature indicator, compass, automatic headlights, fog lights, side steps, 255/70R16 all-terrain white-letter tires, bright alloy wheels. **4WD** adds: 4-wheel drive, 2-speed transfer case, front tow hooks.

Adrenalin adds: Pioneer AM/FM radio w/in-dash 6-disc CD/MP3 changer, chrome alloy wheels. **4WD** adds: 4-wheel drive, 2-speed transfer case, front tow hooks.

OPTIONAL EQUIPMENT

Major Packages	RETAIL PRICE	DEALER INVOICE
Comfort Group, XLT	$1230	$1046
8-way power driver seat w/power lumbar adjustment, overhead console, automatic day/night rearview mirror, outside-temperature indicator, compass, rear radio and climate controls, automatic headlights.		
Leather Seat Group, XLT Premium, Adrenalin	795	676
Leather upholstery, heated front seats, 8-way power passenger seat.		
Premium Sport Group, 2WD XLT	700	595
4WD XLT	730	621
Side step bars, fog lights, front tow hooks (4WD), 255/70R16 all-terrain white-letter tires, bright cast alloy wheels.		
Powertrain		
Limited-slip differential	355	302
Safety		
Curtain side airbags	560	476
Comfort & Convenience Features		
Power sunroof, XLT Premium, Adrenalin	800	680
AM/FM/cassette/CD player, XLT, XLT Premium	150	128
Pioneer AM/FM radio, XLT, XLT Premium	510	433
Includes in-dash 6-disc CD changer.		
Appearance & Special Purpose		
Bed extender	195	166
Hard tonneau cover	590	502

 Specifications begin on page 547.

FORD FIVE HUNDRED

CLASS: Large car
DRIVE WHEELS: Front-wheel drive, all-wheel drive
BASE PRICE RANGE: \$22,145-\$27,845. Built in USA.
ALSO CONSIDER: Chrysler 300, Dodge Magnum, Toyota Avalon

A new generation of Ford cars debuts for 2005 with the Five Hundred, a 4-dr sedan with slightly elevated seating and available all-wheel drive. Based on a platform developed by Ford subsidiary Volvo, Five Hundred's exterior dimensions slot it between the Chrysler 300 and Ford's own Crown Victoria. Borrowing an SUV cue, it accommodates five passengers on seats Ford says are mounted about 4 inches higher than in other sedans. SE, SEL, and Limited models are offered, all with a 203-hp 3.0-liter V6 and front-wheel drive or AWD. Front-drive SEs and every AWD version use a continuously variable automatic transmission. A CVT provides variable drive ratios vs. a conventional automatic's preset ratios. Front-drive SEL and Limited versions get a 6-speed automatic transmission. Antilock 4-wheel disc brakes and traction control are standard. No antiskid system is available. SE and SEL have 17-inch wheels, Limited has 18s. Front torso side airbags and head-protecting curtain side airbags are optional; the curtain airbags are designed to deploy in rollovers as well as in side collisions. Standard equipment includes a power driver seat and split folding rear seatbacks; SEL and Limiteds add a folding front-passenger seat. Leather upholstery is standard on Limited, optional on SEL. Other options include a sunroof and rear-obstacle detection. The Five Hundred shares its basic design and powertrains with the new Mercury Montego sedan and with Ford's new Freestyle crossover SUV. This evaluation is based on preview test drives.

RATINGS	FWD SE	FWD SEL	AWD Limited
ACCELERATION	6	5	6
FUEL ECONOMY	5	5	5
RIDE QUALITY	7	7	7
STEERING/HANDLING	6	6	6
QUIETNESS	7	7	7
CONTROLS/MATERIALS	7	7	7
ROOM/COMFORT (FRONT)	9	9	9

RATINGS (cont.)	FWD SE	FWD SEL	AWD Limited
ROOM/COMFORT (REAR)	8	8	8
CARGO ROOM	6	6	6
VALUE WITHIN CLASS	7	7	7

The Five Hundred and Montego impress for passenger and cargo space, take-charge driving position, and great visibility. They're also on par with most rivals for acceleration and road manners, and available all-wheel drive is a class plus. The transmissions have their quirks—especially the CVT—but Ford trusts they'll be accepted by consumers and prove to be reliable.

TOTAL	68	67	68

Average total for large cars: 60.9

ENGINES

	dohc V6
Size, liters/cu. in.	3.0/182
Horsepower @ rpm	203 @ 5750
Torque (lb-ft) @ rpm	207 @ 4500
Availability	S
EPA city/highway mpg	
6-speed automatic	21/29[1]
CVT automatic	20/27[2]

1. FWD SEL and Limited. 2. FWD SE and all AWD models; 19/26 w/AWD.

PRICES

Ford Five Hundred	RETAIL PRICE	DEALER INVOICE
FWD SE 4-door sedan	$22145	$20300
AWD SE 4-door sedan	23845	21830
FWD SEL 4-door sedan	24145	22100
AWD SEL 4-door sedan	25845	23630
FWD Limited 4-door sedan	26145	23900
AWD Limited 4-door sedan	27845	25430
Destination charge	650	650

STANDARD EQUIPMENT

SE: 3.0-liter V6 engine, continuously variable automatic transmission (CVT), traction control, dual front airbags, antilock 4-wheel disc brakes, air conditioning, power steering, tilt steering wheel, cruise control, cloth upholstery, front bucket seats, 6-way power driver seat, center console, cupholders, split folding rear seat, power mirrors, power windows, power door locks, remote keyless entry, keypad entry, AM/FM/CD player, digital clock, tachometer, map lights, intermittent wipers, illuminated visor mirrors, rear defogger, floormats, theft-deterrent system, 215/60R17 tires, alloy wheels. **AWD** adds: all-wheel drive.

SEL adds: 6-speed automatic transmission, dual-zone automatic climate controls, leather-wrapped steering wheel w/radio controls, 8-way power driver seat, 2-way power fold-flat passenger seat, heated power mirrors, AM/FM radio w/in-dash 6-disc CD/MP3 changer, trip computer, automatic day/night

 Specifications begin on page 547.

rearview mirror, compass, outside-temperature indicator, automatic headlights, fog lights. **AWD** adds: all-wheel drive, continuously variable automatic transmission (CVT).

Limited adds: leather upholstery, heated front seats, 4-way power passenger seat, memory system (driver seat, mirrors), upgraded sound system, analog clock, 225/55R18 tires. **AWD** adds: all-wheel drive, continuously variable automatic transmission (CVT).

OPTIONAL EQUIPMENT

Major Packages	RETAIL PRICE	DEALER INVOICE
Safety and Security Pkg., SE	$795	$708
Front side airbags, curtain side airbags w/rollover sensor, heated power mirrors, perimeter lighting, alarm.		
Safety Pkg., SEL, Limited	595	530
Front side airbags, curtain side airbags w/rollover sensor.		
Safety		
Rear-obstacle-detection system, SEL, Limited	250	223
Comfort & Convenience Features		
Power sunroof, SEL, Limited	895	797
Leather upholstery, SEL	895	797
Power-adjustable pedals w/memory, Limited	175	156
Universal garage-door opener, Limited	115	102

FORD FOCUS

CLASS: Compact car
DRIVE WHEELS: Front-wheel drive
BASE PRICE RANGE: $13,090-$17,990. Built in USA.
ALSO CONSIDER: Honda Civic, Hyundai Elantra, Mazda 3

Ford's smallest car is revamped for 2005, getting more power and revised styling inside and out. Focus comes as a 2-dr hatchback called the ZX3, and with four doors as the ZX4 sedan, ZX5 hatchback, and ZXW wagon. All have a 2.0-liter 4-cyl except the ZX4 ST version of the sedan, which has a 2.3-liter 4-cyl. The 2.3-liter has 151 hp vs. 145 for 2004. The others have 136 hp, up from 110 or 130, depending on model. The ZX4 ST replaces the sporty SVT hatchbacks and comes with sport suspension, 4-wheel disc brakes, and mandatory manual transmission. The 2.0-liter engine offers manual or automatic transmission. Wheel diameters are 16 inches for SES and ZX4 ST models, 15 elsewhere. ABS is standard on ZX4 ST, optional otherwise. ZX4 ST also comes with traction control, which is optional on SE and SES trim levels. Head-and-torso front side airbags are optional on all models. Available features include sunroof, leather upholstery, and heated front seats. Standard on all are a height-adjustable driver seat and split folding rear seatbacks.

RATINGS

	ZX3 SES, auto.	ZX5 SES, man.	ZX4 ST, man.
ACCELERATION	3	4	5
FUEL ECONOMY	6	6	6
RIDE QUALITY	6	6	6
STEERING/HANDLING	6	6	7
QUIETNESS	4	4	4
CONTROLS/MATERIALS	6	6	6
ROOM/COMFORT (FRONT)	5	5	5
ROOM/COMFORT (REAR)	3	4	4
CARGO ROOM	6	6	3
VALUE WITHIN CLASS	8	8	8

Focus is fun to drive, especially in enthusiast-oriented ST trim. Though it's not as refined as a Volkswagen Jetta or as outright sporty as a Mazda 3, Focus measures up well overall, and is very competitively priced. An array of body styles and useful options enhance its appeal.

TOTAL	53	55	54

Average total for compact cars: 48.4

ENGINES

	dohc I4	dohc I4
Size, liters/cu. in.	2.0/121	2.3/138
Horsepower @ rpm	136 @ 6000	151 @ 5750
Torque (lb-ft) @ rpm	133 @ 4500	154 @ 4250
Availability	S[1]	S[2]
EPA city/highway mpg		
5-speed manual	26/35	22/31
4-speed automatic	26/32	

1. All except ZX4 ST. 2. ZX4 ST.

PRICES

Ford Focus

	RETAIL PRICE	DEALER INVOICE
ZX3 S 2-door hatchback	$13090	$12278
ZX4 S 4-door sedan	13690	12830
ZX5 S 4-door hatchback	14390	13474
ZX3 SE 2-door hatchback	14590	13658
ZX4 SE 4-door sedan	15190	14210
ZX5 SE 4-door hatchback	15890	14854
ZXW SE 4-door wagon	16890	15774

PRICES (cont.)

	RETAIL PRICE	DEALER INVOICE
ZX3 SES 2-door hatchback	$15690	$14670
ZX4 SES 4-door sedan	16290	15222
ZX5 SES 4-door hatchback	16990	15866
ZXW SES 4-door wagon	17990	16786
ZX4 ST 4-door sedan	17790	16602
Destination charge	545	545

STANDARD EQUIPMENT

ZX3/4/5 S: 2.0-liter 4-cylinder engine, 5-speed manual transmission, dual front airbags, power steering, cloth upholstery, front bucket seats, height-adjustable driver seat, center console, cupholders, split folding rear seat, AM/FM/CD player, digital clock, visor mirrors, rear defogger, intermittent wipers, rear wiper/washer (hatchback), front floormats, theft-deterrent system, 195/60R15 tires, wheel covers.

ZX3/4/5, ZXW SE adds: air conditioning, power mirrors, power windows, power door locks, remote entry system, AM/FM/CD/MP3 player, variable-intermittent wipers, map lights, rear wiper/washer (wagon), rear floormats, roof rails (wagon).

ZX3/4/5, ZXW SES adds: tilt/telescope leather-wrapped steering wheel w/radio controls, cruise control, AM/FM radio w/in-dash 6-disc CD/MP3 player, tachometer, rear spoiler (sedan, 4-door hatchback), fog lights, 205/50R16 tires, alloy wheels.

ZX4 ST adds: 2.3-liter 4-cylinder engine, traction control, antilock 4-wheel disc brakes, heated power mirrors, sport suspension.

OPTIONAL EQUIPMENT

Major Packages

	RETAIL PRICE	DEALER INVOICE
Convenience Group, SE	$525	$468
Tilt/telescope steering wheel w/radio controls, cruise control.		
Weather Pkg., SES	175	156
Heated front seats and mirrors.		
Sport Group, SE	475	423
Leather-wrapped steering wheel, tachometer, fog lights, alloy wheels.		

Powertrain

4-speed automatic transmission, ZX3/ZX4 S, SE, SES	815	725
Traction control, SE, SES	115	102
SE includes tachometer. Requires antilock brakes.		

Safety

Antilock brakes	400	356
Std. ST.		
Front side airbags	350	312

Comfort & Convenience Features

Air conditioning, S	910	810

OPTIONAL EQUIPMENT (cont.)

	RETAIL PRICE	DEALER INVOICE
Power sunroof, SE, SES, ST	$625	$557
Leather upholstery, SES, ST	695	619
Heated front seats, ST	115	102
AM/FM radio w/in-dash 6-disc CD/MP3 changer, SE	340	302
Audiophile Pkg., SE	795	708
SES, ST	455	405
AM/FM radio w/in-dash 6-disc CD/MP3 changer, upgraded sound system.		
Cargo cover, hatchback, wagon	65	58

FORD FREESTAR

CLASS: Minivan
DRIVE WHEELS: Front-wheel drive
BASE PRICE RANGE: $21,610-$32,710. Built in Canada.
ALSO CONSIDER: Dodge Caravan, Honda Odyssey, Toyota Sienna

Ford carries its minivan into 2005 virtually unchanged after a 2004 revamp that saw the Windstar name dropped in favor of Freestar. Mercury has a version called Monterey. Freestar comes in a single body length that's similar in size to such rivals as the Toyota Sienna and Dodge Grand Caravan. Freestar comes in S, SE, SES, SEL, and Limited trim levels. All have 7-passenger capacity and include 2md-row 2-passenger bench seat or two bucket seats. The 3rd-row bench folds into the floor. The 3rd-row bench also flips for rear-facing "tailgate" seating under the open liftgate. Power operation is available for the sliding side doors. S, SE, and SES models have a 193-hp 3.9-liter V6. SEL and Limited models use a 201-hp 4.2-liter V6. A 4-speed automatic is the sole transmission. All-wheel drive is not offered, but antiskid control is available. Antilock 4-wheel disc brakes are standard. Head-protecting curtain side airbags that cover all three seating rows are optional; they are designed to deploy in a side impact or when sensors detect an impending rollover. Self-sealing tires are available on all but the base S model. Rear DVD entertainment is optional. Options include a rear cargo organizer and 17-inch alloy wheels vs. standard 16s. Freestar is also available in two-seat Cargo trim.

 Specifications begin on page 547.

RATINGS

	SEL
ACCELERATION	5
FUEL ECONOMY	4
RIDE QUALITY	5
STEERING/HANDLING	4
QUIETNESS	5
CONTROLS/MATERIALS	6
ROOM/COMFORT (FRONT)	7
ROOM/COMFORT (REAR)	7
CARGO ROOM	9
VALUE WITHIN CLASS	5

Freestar and Monterey can't match such rivals as the Honda Odyssey or Dodge Caravan for driving enjoyment, or Toyota Sienna for refinement. On the upside, these Ford and Mercury minivans boast some laudable safety and convenience features, base prices are competitive, and discounts should be available.

TOTAL	57

Average total for minivans: 58.0

ENGINES

	ohv V6	ohv V6
Size, liters/cu. in.	3.9/232	4.2/256
Horsepower @ rpm	193 @ 4500	201 @ 4250
Torque (lb-ft) @ rpm	240 @ 3750	263 @ 3650
Availability	S[1]	S[2]
EPA city/highway mpg		
4-speed automatic	17/23	16/23

1. S, SE, SES. 2. SEL, Limited.

PRICES

Ford Freestar	RETAIL PRICE	DEALER INVOICE
Cargo 4-door van	$21610	$19673
S 4-door van	23910	22198
SE 4-door van	26510	24034
SES 4-door van	28010	25369
SEL 4-door van	29010	26259
Limited 4-door van	32710	29552
Destination charge	685	685

STANDARD EQUIPMENT

Cargo: 3.9-liter V6 engine, 4-speed automatic transmission, dual front airbags, antilock 4-wheel disc brakes, front air conditioning, power steering, tilt steering wheel, cloth upholstery, front bucket seats, cupholders, power mirrors, power windows, power door locks, remote keyless entry, AM/FM radio, digital clock, tachometer, intermittent wipers, visor mirrors, rear defogger, intermittent rear wiper/washer, floormats, theft-deterrent system, 235/60R16 tires, wheel covers.

S adds: tire-pressure monitor, 7-passenger seating, 2nd-row bench seat, 3rd-row stowable bench seat, 225/60R16 tires.

SE adds: cruise control, AM/FM/CD player, map lights, rear privacy glass, roof rails.

SES adds: rear air conditioning, tri-zone manual climate controls (including rear controls), 6-way power driver seat, conversation mirror, 235/60R16 tires, alloy wheels.

SEL adds: 4.2-liter V6 engine, leather-wrapped steering wheel w/radio controls, 2nd-row captain chairs, keypad entry, illuminated visor mirrors, compass, outside-temperature indicator, automatic headlights, cornering lights.

Limited adds: leather upholstery, power-adjustable pedals, tri-zone automatic climate controls (including rear controls), heated power mirrors w/turn signals, power sliding rear doors, rear radio controls, trip computer, analog clock.

OPTIONAL EQUIPMENT

Major Packages	RETAIL PRICE	DEALER INVOICE
Value Group, Cargo	$690	$587
Cruise control, rear privacy glass.		
Electronics Group, SE, SES	290	247
Overhead console, automatic day/night rearview mirror, compass, outside-temperature indicator, automatic headlights. SE requires rear air conditioning.		
Value Group I, SES	245	208
Power-adjustable pedals, perimeter alarm.		
Value Group II, SEL	750	638
Power-adjustable pedals, heated power mirrors w/turn signals, puddle lights, automatic day/night rearview mirror, trip computer, perimeter alarm.		
Value Group III, Limited	280	238
Universal garage-door opener, automatic day/night rearview mirror, perimeter alarm.		
Active Safety Pkg. I, Cargo, SE, SES	730	621
Manufacturer's Discount Price	*395*	*336*
Traction control, brake assist, antiskid system.		
Active Safety Pkg. II, SEL, Limited	975	829
Manufacturer's Discount Price	*750*	*637*
Active Safety Pkg. I plus rear-obstacle-detection system.		
Class II Trailer Towing Pkg.	335	285
Trailer-tow wiring, heavy-duty cooling and battery. NA Cargo, S.		
Safety		
Curtain side airbags	695	591
Includes front side airbags. S, SE require rear air conditioning. NA Cargo.		
Comfort & Convenience Features		
Rear air conditioning w/tri-zone manual controls, S, SE	675	574
Rear-seat DVD entertainment system, SE, SES, SEL, Limited	1395	1186

OPTIONAL EQUIPMENT (cont.)	RETAIL PRICE	DEALER INVOICE
Floor console, SE, SES, SEL, Limited	$150	$128
Leather upholstery, SEL	890	757
Heated front seats, Limited	245	208
6-way power driver seat, SE	325	277
6-way power passenger seat, SEL, Limited	305	259
SEL requires leather upholstery.		
2nd-row captain chairs, SE, SES	795	676
Memory Pkg., Limited	425	362
Memory system (driver seat, mirrors, pedals). Requires Active Safety Pkg. II, curtain side airbags.		
AM/FM/cassette/CD player, Cargo	345	293
SE, SES, SEL, Limited	105	89
SE, SES include rear controls.		
AM/FM radio w/in-dash 6-disc CD changer, SEL, Limited	255	217
Power sliding rear doors, SEL	900	765
Power liftgate, SEL, Limited	400	340
SEL requires power sliding rear doors.		
Cargo-management system	125	107
NA Cargo.		
Appearance & Special Purpose		
Rear spoiler, SES	290	247
Rear privacy glass, S	415	352
Self-sealing tires, SE, SES, SEL, Limited	280	238
17-inch alloy wheels, SES, SEL, Limited	245	208
Includes 235/55R17 tires.		

FORD FREESTYLE

CLASS: Midsize sport-utility vehicle
DRIVE WHEELS: Front-wheel drive, all-wheel drive
BASE PRICE RANGE: $24,945-$30,245. Built in USA.
ALSO CONSIDER: Chrysler Pacifica, Honda Pilot, Toyota Highlander

Ford launches its first crossover SUV for 2005, a wagon that seats up to seven and uses an unconventional automatic transmission. Freestyle blends carlike attributes—it shares its underskin design with Ford's new Five Hundred sedan—and SUV cues—it has 3-row seating and available all-wheel drive. SE, SEL, and Limited trim levels are offered, each with front-wheel drive or optional AWD. The AWD system does not include low-range gearing and is not intended for off-road use. The sole powertrain is a 203-hp 3.0-liter V6 linked to a continuously variable automatic transmission. A CVT provides variable drive ratios vs. a conventional automatic's preset ratios. Antilock 4-wheel disc brakes and traction control are standard. No antiskid system is available. SE and SEL come with 17-inch wheels, the Limited with 18s. An option package groups front torso side aribags and head-protecting curtain side airbags. The curtain airbags cover all three seating rows and are designed to deploy in rollovers as well as in side collisions. Standard seating is for six and includes a folding front-passenger seat, 2nd-row buckets, and a 50/50 split folding third row. An available 60/40 split folding 2nd-row bench increases capacity to seven. The 3rd-row seats fold flush with the floor. Options include power-adjustable pedals, rear DVD entertainment, sunroof, and rear-obstacle detection. The top-line Limited model comes with leather upholstery, rear center console, and 2nd-row buckets that slide fore and aft to adjust leg room. Freestyle shares its basic design and powertrains with the Five Hundred as well as Mercury's new Montego sedan. All are based on a platform developed by Volvo, which is owned by Ford. This evaluation is based on preview test drives.

RATINGS

	2WD SE	AWD SEL	AWD Limited
ACCELERATION	5	5	5
FUEL ECONOMY	6	6	6
RIDE QUALITY	6	6	6
STEERING/HANDLING	5	5	5
QUIETNESS	6	6	6
CONTROLS/MATERIALS	6	6	6
ROOM/COMFORT (FRONT)	8	8	8
ROOM/COMFORT (REAR)	8	8	8
CARGO ROOM	8	8	8
VALUE WITHIN CLASS	6	6	6

Among midsize SUVs, Freestyle excels in its ability to accommodate passengers and cargo, and its road manners are competitive with those of most rivals. But some drivers might wish for more power—particularly when carrying a full load—and Ford is staking much on the acceptance and reliability of Freestyle's CVT transmission.

TOTAL	64	64	64

Average total for midsize sport-utility vehicles: 54.7

ENGINES

	dohc V6
Size, liters/cu. in.	3.0/182
Horsepower @ rpm	203 @ 5750
Torque (lb-ft) @ rpm	207 @ 4500
Availability	S
EPA city/highway mpg	
CVT automatic	19/24[1]

1. 20/27 w/2WD.

 Specifications begin on page 547.

PRICES

Ford Freestyle

	RETAIL PRICE	DEALER INVOICE
2WD SE 4-door wagon	$24945	$22870
AWD SE 4-door wagon	26645	24400
2WD SEL 4-door wagon	26345	24130
AWD SEL 4-door wagon	28045	25660
2WD Limited 4-door wagon	28545	26110
AWD Limited 4-door wagon	30245	27640
Destination charge	650	650

STANDARD EQUIPMENT

SE: 3.0-liter V6 engine, continuously variable automatic transmission (CVT), traction control, dual front airbags, antilock 4-wheel disc brakes, front air conditioning, power steering, tilt steering wheel, cloth upholstery, front bucket seats, 6-way power driver seat, center console, cupholders, fold-flat passenger seat, 2nd-row bucket seats, 3rd-row stowable bench seat, power mirrors, power windows, power door locks, remote keyless entry, keypad entry, AM/FM/CD player, digital clock, tachometer, illuminated visor mirrors, intermittent wipers, conversation mirror, map lights, rear defogger, floormats, theft-deterrent system, rear privacy glass, roof rack, 215/65R17 tires, alloy wheels. **AWD** adds: all-wheel drive.

SEL adds: leather-wrapped steering wheel w/radio controls, heated power mirrors, AM/FM radio w/in-dash 6-disc CD/MP3 changer, trip computer, automatic day/night rearview mirror, compass, outside-temperature indicator, automatic headlights. **AWD** adds: all-wheel drive.

Limited adds: dual-zone automatic climate controls, leather upholstery, heated front seats, 8-way power driver seat, 4-way power passenger seat, memory system (driver seat, mirrors), 2nd-row adjustable bucket seats, 2nd-row center console, 3rd-row stowable split seat, fog lights, 225/60R18 tires. **AWD** adds: all-wheel drive.

OPTIONAL EQUIPMENT

Major Packages

	RETAIL PRICE	DEALER INVOICE
Safety and Security pkg., SE	$795	$708
SEL, Limited	695	619
Front side airbags, curtain side airbags w/rollover sensor, heated power mirrors (SE), alarm.		
Convenience Group, SE	295	263
Dual-zone automatic climate controls, automatic headlights.		
Comfort Pkg., SEL	495	441
Dual-zone automatic climate controls, 8-way power driver seat, 4-way power passenger seat, outside-temperature indicator.		

Safety

Rear-obstacle-detection system, SEL, Limited	250	223

Comfort & Convenience Features

	RETAIL PRICE	DEALER INVOICE
Rear air conditioning	$595	$530
SE requires Convenience Group. SEL requires Comfort Pkg.		
Power sunroof, SEL, Limited	895	797
Leather upholstery, SEL	795	708
Power-adjustable pedals w/memory, Limited	175	156
2nd-row 3-passener split folding seat, SEL, Limited	NC	NC
3rd-row stowable split seat, SEL	115	102
2nd-row center console, SE, SEL	95	85
Rear-seat DVD entertainment system, SEL, Limited	995	886
Universal garage-door opener, Limited	115	102

FORD MUSTANG

CLASS: Sporty/performance car
DRIVE WHEELS: Rear-wheel drive
BASE PRICE RANGE: $18,785-$25,705. Built in USA.
ALSO CONSIDER: Nissan 350Z, Pontiac GTO, Scion tC

Mustang is redesigned for 2005, getting more power, new features, and interior and exterior styling inspired by 1960s versions of America's original ponycar. Launched as a coupe, with a convertible due later in the model year, Mustang gains some 6 inches in wheelbase and overall length vs. the 1999-2004 generation, and is about 100 lb heavier. The underbody structure replaces one that dated from 1979, though Mustang retains a solid rear axle rather than adopting independent rear suspension. Base V6 and GT V8 models return in Deluxe and Premium trim. Base versions use a 210-hp 4.0-liter V6. It supplants a 193-hp 3.8 V6. GTs retain a 4.6-liter V8, but with 300 hp vs. the outgoing GT's 260. A 5-speed manual remains the standard transmission. The optional automatic has five speeds vs. the previous four. All Mustangs have 4-wheel disc brakes. ABS and traction control are standard on GTs, optional on base models. No antiskid system is available. Base versions have 16-inch wheels, GTs 17s. Among options new to Mustang are front side airbags that cover torso and head, and an Interior Upgrade Package, which includes a dashboard button to change instrument lighting from green to one of 125 other hues. All Mustangs come with air conditioning and CD player. Coupes have 50/50 split folding rear seatbacks. Leather upholstery is standard on the GT Premium, optional on other models. GTs include grille-mounted fog lamps and a rear spoiler. This evaluation is based on preview test drives.

RATINGS	Base coupe w/ABS, auto.	GT Premium coupe, man.
ACCELERATION	6	8
FUEL ECONOMY	5	4
RIDE QUALITY	4	4
STEERING/HANDLING	6	8
QUIETNESS	5	4
CONTROLS/MATERIALS	4	4
ROOM/COMFORT (FRONT)	6	6
ROOM/COMFORT (REAR)	2	2
CARGO ROOM	2	2
VALUE WITHIN CLASS	4	7

Most rivals have interior appointments that shame those found here. And the Acura RSX and Scion tC trump the base Mustang for fun-to-drive character in the $20,000-range. Pontiac's GTO is the Mustang GT's chief rear-drive V8-coupe rival. The larger, costlier GTO is more powerful, but the V8 Mustang gives up little to any car in its blend of usable high performance and muscle-car excitement.

TOTAL	44	49

Average total for sporty/performance cars: 48.5

ENGINES

	sohc V6	sohc V8
Size, liters/cu. in.	4.0/245	4.6/281
Horsepower @ rpm	210 @ 5250	300 @ 5750
Torque (lb-ft) @ rpm	240 @ 3500	320 @ 4500
Availability	S[1]	S[2]
EPA city/highway mpg		
5-speed manual	19/28	17/25
5-speed automatic	19/25	18/23

1. Base models. 2. GT models.

PRICES

Ford Mustang	RETAIL PRICE	DEALER INVOICE
Base Deluxe 2-door coupe	$18785	$17262
Base Deluxe 2-door convertible	NA	NA
Base Premium 2-door coupe	19370	17788
Base Premium 2-door convertible	NA	NA
GT Deluxe 2-door coupe	24370	22288
GT Deluxe 2-door convertible	NA	NA
GT Premium 2-door coupe	25705	23489
GT Premium 2-door convertible	NA	NA
Destination charge	625	625

STANDARD EQUIPMENT

Base Deluxe: 4.0-liter V6 engine, 5-speed manual transmission, dual front airbags, 4-wheel disc brakes, air conditioning, power steering, tilt steering wheel, cruise control, cloth upholstery, front bucket seats, height-adjustable driver seat, center console, cupholders, split folding rear seat (coupe), power mirrors, power windows, power door locks, remote keyless entry, AM/FM/CD player, digital clock, tachometer, variable-intermittent wipers, rear defogger, floormats, theft-deterrent system, 215/65R16 tires, alloy wheels.

Base Premium adds: 6-way power driver seat w/lumbar adjustment, upgraded sound system, AM/FM radio w/in-dash 6-disc CD/MP3 changer, bright alloy wheels.

GT Deluxe adds to Base Deluxe: 4.6-liter V8 engine, traction control, antilock 4-wheel disc brakes, 6-way power driver seat w/lumbar adjustment, leather-wrapped steering wheel, rear spoiler, fog lights, 235/55ZR17 tires.

GT Premium adds: leather upholstery, upgraded sound system, AM/FM radio w/in-dash 6-disc CD/MP3 changer.

OPTIONAL EQUIPMENT

Major Packages	RETAIL PRICE	DEALER INVOICE
Sport Appearance Pkg., Base	$295	$263
Rear spoiler, body stripes.		
Interior Upgraded Pkg.	450	401
Aluminum interior trim, leather-wrapped steering wheel (Base), changeable instrument-lighting color, unique interior trim.		
Interior Color Accent Pkg	175	156
Red and grey interior-color combination. Requires Interior Upgrade Pkg. Base, GT Deluxe require leather upholstery.		
Powertrain		
5-speed automatic transmission	995	886
Safety		
Front side airbags	370	329
Requires Interior Upgrade Pkg.		
Antilock brakes, Base	775	690
Includes traction control.		
Comfort & Convenience Features		
Leather upholstery, Base, GT Deluxe	695	619
6-way power driver seat, Base Deluxe	365	325
AM/FM radio w/in-dash 6-disc CD/MP3 changer, Base Deluxe, GT Deluxe	665	592
Includes upgraded sound system.		
Upgraded sound system, Base Premium, GT Premium	1295	1153
GT Deluxe	1770	1575
Includes additional speakers. GT Deluxe includes AM/FM radio w/in-dash 6-disc CD/MP3 changer.		
Appearance & Special Purpose		
Bright alloy wheels, GT	195	174
Base Deluxe	150	134

FORD TAURUS

CLASS: Midsize car
DRIVE WHEELS: Front-wheel drive
BASE PRICE RANGE: $20,485-$23,345. Built in USA.
ALSO CONSIDER: Honda Accord, Nissan Altima, Toyota Camry

Due to be dropped from the Ford lineup during the model year, Taurus sedans and wagons soldier on with fewer trim levels for 2005. Taurus comes in SE and SEL model groupings; LX and SES versions have been dropped. All have automatic transmission and a 3.0-liter V6. The engine makes 153 hp in standard form; a 201-hp dohc version is optional on SEL. Antilock brakes are available. Wagons have rear disc brakes vs. drums for sedans. Depending on model, Taurus sedans offer a 3-passenger front bench seat for 6-passenger capacity or two front buckets for 5-passenger capacity. Wagons do the same, but also offer a standard 2-passenger rear-facing 3rd-row seat for up to 8-passenger capacity. Traction control and head-and-torso front side airbags are available. Mercury sells a retrimmed Taurus as the Sable.

RATINGS	SE sdn	SEL sdn, dohc V6	SEL wgn, dohc V6
ACCELERATION	4	5	5
FUEL ECONOMY	5	5	5
RIDE QUALITY	5	5	5
STEERING/HANDLING	6	6	6
QUIETNESS	5	5	5
CONTROLS/MATERIALS	6	6	6
ROOM/COMFORT (FRONT)	6	6	6
ROOM/COMFORT (REAR)	6	6	6
CARGO ROOM	5	5	8
VALUE WITHIN CLASS	4	4	5

Taurus and Sable deliver capable road manners, comfortable accommodations, commendable cargo room, and plenty of safety features at a competitive price. But ride comfort is a sore point, and build quality and refinement trail standards set by midsize sales leaders Honda Accord and Toyota Camry.

TOTAL	52	53	57

Average total for midsize cars: 57.2

ENGINES

	ohv V6	dohc V6
Size, liters/cu. in.	3.0/182	3.0/181
Horsepower @ rpm	153 @ 5800	201 @ 5500
Torque (lb-ft) @ rpm	186 @ 3250	207 @ 4500
Availability	S	O[1]
EPA city/highway mpg		
4-speed automatic	19/26	20/27

1. SEL.

PRICES

Ford Taurus	RETAIL PRICE	DEALER INVOICE
SE 4-door sedan	$20485	$18772
SE 4-door wagon	22355	20455
SEL 4-door sedan	22395	20491
SEL 4-door wagon	23345	21345
Destination charge	660	660

STANDARD EQUIPMENT

SE: 3.0-liter V6 153-horsepower engine, 4-speed automatic transmission, dual front airbags, 4-wheel disc brakes (wagon), emergency inside trunk release (sedan), air conditioning, power steering, tilt steering wheel, cruise control, cloth upholstery, 6-passenger seating, front split bench seat w/flip-fold center console, column shift, cupholders, 2nd-row split folding seat (wagon), 3rd-row rear-facing seat (wagon), power mirrors, power windows, power door locks, remote keyless entry, AM/FM/cassette, power antenna (wagon), digital clock, tachometer, trip computer (wagon), variable-intermittent wipers, visor mirrors, map lights, cargo cover (wagon), rear defogger, rear wiper/washer (wagon), floormats, theft-deterrent system, 215/60R16 tires, wheel covers.

SEL adds: 5-passenger seating, front bucket seats (sedan), 6-way power driver seat w/lumbar adjustment, center console w/floor shift (sedan), split folding rear seat, keypad entry, AM/FM/CD player, trip computer, automatic day/night rearview mirror, universal garage-door opener, illuminated visor mirrors, alloy wheels.

OPTIONAL EQUIPMENT

Major Packages	RETAIL PRICE	DEALER INVOICE
Preferred Equipment Group 90A, SE sedan	$1185	$1055
SE wagon	580	516
6-way power driver seat w/lumbar adjustment, split folding rear seat (sedan), rear spoiler (sedan), alloy wheels.		
Preferred Equipment Group 96P, SEL sedan	2120	1887
SEL wagon	1365	1215
Leather upholstery, power passenger seat, automatic climate control, AM/FM/cassette w/in-dash 6-disc CD changer, automatic headlights, rear spoiler (sedan).		

 Specifications begin on page 547.

OPTIONAL EQUIPMENT (cont.)

	RETAIL PRICE	DEALER INVOICE
Safety and Security Pkg.	$1165	$1037
Manufacturer's Discount Price	*995*	*886*
Traction control, front side airbags, antilock brakes.		
Powertrain		
3.0-liter V6 201-horsepower engine, SEL	1050	935
Traction control	175	156
Requires antilock brakes.		
Safety		
Front side airbags	390	347
Antilock brakes	600	534
Comfort & Convenience Features		
Leather upholstery, SE sedan	1035	921
wagons, SE sedan w/Group 90A	895	797
SE sedan includes split folding rear seat. SE, SEL wagon require 5-passenger seating.		
2-tone leather upholstery, SE sedan	1175	1046
SE sedan w/Group 90A, SEL sedan	945	841
SE sedan includes split folding rear seat. SE requires 5-passenger seating.		
5-passenger seating, SE	125	112
SEL wagon	NC	NC
Front bucket seats, center console, floor shift.		
AM/FM/CD player, SE	150	134
AM/FM/cassette and 6-disc CD changer, SEL	350	312
Mach Premium Sound, SEL	345	307
Requires Preferred Equipment Group 96P or AM/FM/cassette w/in-dash 6-disc CD changer.		
Power sunroof	895	797
Appearance & Special Purpose		
Alloy wheels, SE	420	374

FORD THUNDERBIRD

CLASS: Premium sporty/performance car
DRIVE WHEELS: Rear-wheel drive
BASE PRICE RANGE: $37,605-$38,650. Built in USA.
ALSO CONSIDER: Chrysler Crossfire, Mercedes-Benz SLK

Ford's 2-seat convertible gets no changes of note for 2005. Thunderbird comes with a power-folding soft top with heated glass rear window or a removable hardtop with trademark porthole windows. The only powertrain is a 280-hp V8 with 5-speed automatic transmission; optional is a manual-shift feature for the automatic. Antilock 4-wheel disc brakes, traction control, and head-and-torso side airbags are standard. Available features include heated seats and chrome wheels.

RATINGS

	Premium
ACCELERATION	7
FUEL ECONOMY	5
RIDE QUALITY	5
STEERING/HANDLING	7
QUIETNESS	4
CONTROLS/MATERIALS	6
ROOM/COMFORT (FRONT)	6
ROOM/COMFORT (REAR)	0
CARGO ROOM	2
VALUE WITHIN CLASS	3

Ford aims Thunderbird at "relaxed sportiness," and pretty much hits the mark. It is not as mechanically refined as it should be, and interior materials don't impress. But Thunderbird is more practical than a genuine sports car. And as a near-luxury 2-passenger V8 convertible, it's in a class by itself. Demand has cooled, so don't buy without a discount.

TOTAL	45

Average total for premium sporty/performance cars: 48.3

ENGINES

	dohc V8
Size, liters/cu. in.	3.9/240
Horsepower @ rpm	280 @ 6000
Torque (lb-ft) @ rpm	286 @ 4000
Availability	S
EPA city/highway mpg	
5-speed automatic	17/23

PRICES

Ford Thunderbird	RETAIL PRICE	DEALER INVOICE
Deluxe 2-door convertible	$37605	$34484
Premium 2-door convertible	38650	35426
Destination charge	605	605

STANDARD EQUIPMENT

Deluxe: 3.9-liter V8 engine, 5-speed automatic transmission, traction control, dual front airbags, side airbags, antilock 4-wheel disc brakes, emergency

 Specifications begin on page 547.

inside trunk release, air conditioning w/dual-zone automatic climate controls, power steering, power tilt/telescope leather-wrapped steering wheel w/radio controls, cruise control, leather upholstery, bucket seats, 6-way power driver seat w/lumbar adjustment, 2-way power passenger seat, center console, cupholders, power mirrors, power windows, power door locks, remote keyless entry, AM/FM radio w/in-dash 6-disc CD changer, digital clock, tachometer, power convertible top, variable-intermittent wipers, universal garage-door opener, rear defogger, visor mirrors, automatic headlights, floormats, theft-deterrent system, 235/50VR17 tires, alloy wheels.

Premium adds: heated seats, chrome alloy wheels.

OPTIONAL EQUIPMENT

Major Packages	RETAIL PRICE	DEALER INVOICE
Light Sand Appearance Pkg., Premium	$1000	$890
Unique interior trim, cream-colored gauges.		
Partial Interior Color Accent Pkg., Premium	595	530
Exterior-color steering wheel, shifter trim, and seat insert.		
Full Interior Color Accent Pkg., Premium	800	712
Exterior-color dashboard, console, door, steering wheel, shifter trim and seat insert.		
Black Accent Pkg.	295	263
Black steering wheel and shifter trim.		
Powertrain		
Manual-shift capability	130	116
Appearance & Special Purpose		
Removable hardtop, Premium	2500	2225

GMC ENVOY

CLASS: Midsize sport-utility vehicle
DRIVE WHEELS: Rear-wheel drive, 4-wheel drive
BASE PRICE RANGE: $29,750-$37,840. Built in USA.
ALSO CONSIDER: Dodge Durango, Ford Explorer, Honda Pilot

Envoy starts 2005 with newly available curtain side airbags and a cylinder-deactivation feature for its V8. Due later in the model year are posh Denali and XL Denali models. This midsize SUV shares a basic GM design with the Buick Rainier, Chevrolet TrailBlazer, and Isuzu Ascender. Envoy offers 5-passenger and extended-length 7-passenger XL wagons in SLE and upscale SLT trim. The Envoy-exclusive XUV is a special 5-passenger extended with a power sliding rear roof section, plus a "midgate" that can be dropped with the rear seat to extend the cargo area. The midgate includes a power-down glass divider window. XUV also has a swing-open/drop-down tailgate with power window vs. other models' liftgate with separate-opening glass.

A 4.2-liter inline 6-cyl engine is standard except for Denalis. Denalis will come with a 5.3 V8 that's optional for XUV and the Envoy XL. GMC says the V8 will no longer be available in Envoy XLs when the Denalis debut at midyear. New for the V8 is GM's Displacement on Demand system. It's designed to automatically shut down four cylinders in gentle driving to save fuel; the cylinders reactivate when more power is needed. All Envoys come with antilock 4-wheel disc brakes, 17-inch alloy wheels, and 4-speed automatic transmission. They also offer rear-wheel drive with available traction control or GM's all-surface Autotrac 4WD with low-range gearing. Head-protecting curtain side airbags that cover the first and second seating rows are optional.

Envoy Denalis stand apart with a chrome grille, specific front/rear fascias, and body-color running boards. They also include leather upholstery, heated power front seats, unique interior trim, and extra sound insulation. A CD/MP3 player is newly available for all Envoys. Other options include a rear load-leveling air-spring suspension, power-adjustable pedals, rear DVD entertainment, satellite radio, and a stereo/navigation system with control touch screen. This evaluation covers Envoy and Ascender.

RATINGS	4WD SLT	4WD SLT w/air susp.	4WD XL SLT, 6-cyl	4WD XUV w/air susp., V8
ACCELERATION	6	6	5	6
FUEL ECONOMY	4	4	3	3
RIDE QUALITY	5	6	6	6
STEERING/HANDLING	3	4	3	4
QUIETNESS	4	4	4	4
CONTROLS/MATERIALS	7	7	7	7
ROOM/COMFORT (FRONT)	7	7	7	7
ROOM/COMFORT (REAR)	6	6	7	7
CARGO ROOM	8	8	9	8
VALUE WITHIN CLASS	6	7	6	6

We judge Envoy the best choice among GM-built midsize SUVs. It has a pleasing enough interior. And its good ride/handling mix with the optional rear air suspension is shared only with Buick Rainier, among this GM family. Truck-tough engineering is a plus for towing, and Envoy XUV offers unique utility. Still, car-type SUVs remain more sensible for most everyday users. Ascender shares the virtues of comparably outfitted Envoys, but suffers from a thinner dealer network and potentially lower resale value.

TOTAL	56	59	57	58

Average total for midsize sport-utility vehicles: 54.7

 Specifications begin on page 547.

ENGINES

	dohc I6	ohv V8
Size, liters/cu. in.	4.2/256	5.3/325
Horsepower @ rpm	275 @ 6000	290 @ 5200
Torque (lb-ft) @ rpm	275 @ 3600	325 @ 4000
Availability	S	O[1]
EPA city/highway mpg		
4-speed automatic	15/21[2]	15/18[3]

1. XL, XUV; std. Denalis. 2. 16/21 w/2WD; 15/19 XL and XUV w/2WD or 4WD. 3. 16/19 w/2WD.

PRICES

GMC Envoy	RETAIL PRICE	DEALER INVOICE
2WD SLE regular length 4-door wagon	$29750	$26924
4WD SLE regular length 4-door wagon	32000	28960
2WD XL SLE extended length 4-door wagon	31420	28435
4WD XL SLE extended length 4-door wagon	33670	30471
2WD XUV SLE extended length 4-door wagon	31505	28512
4WD XUV SLE extended length 4-door wagon	33755	30548
2WD SLT regular length 4-door wagon	33885	30666
4WD SLT regular length 4-door wagon	36135	32702
2WD XL SLT extended length 4-door wagon	35535	32159
4WD XL SLT extended length 4-door wagon	37785	34195
2WD XUV SLT extended length 4-door wagon	35590	32209
4WD XUV SLT extended length 4-door wagon	37840	34245
Destination charge	685	685

Denali and Denali XL prices and equipment not available at time of publication.

STANDARD EQUIPMENT

SLE: 4.2-liter 6-cylinder engine, 4-speed automatic transmission, dual front airbags, antilock 4-wheel disc brakes, daytime running lights, air conditioning w/dual-zone manual controls, rear climate controls (XL), power steering, tilt leather-wrapped steering wheel, cloth upholstery, front bucket seats w/driver-side lumbar adjustment, center console, cupholders, 2nd-row split folding seat, 3rd-row split folding seat (XL), heated power mirrors, power windows, power rear tailgate window (XUV), power door locks, remote keyless entry, power sliding rear roof (XUV), midgate w/power sliding window (XUV), AM/FM/CD player, digital clock, tachometer, variable-intermittent wipers, universal garage-door opener (XUV), map lights, cargo cover (XL), rear defogger, intermittent rear wiper/washer, automatic headlights, floormats, theft-deterrent system, rear liftgate (regular, XL), drop or swing tailgate (XUV), rear privacy glass, roof rails (regular, XL), fog lights, cornering lights, platform hitch, 7-wire trailer harness, full-size spare tire, 245/65R17 tires, alloy wheels. **4WD** adds: 4-wheel drive, 2-speed transfer case.

SLT adds: leather upholstery, heated front seats (XUV), 8-way power front seats, driver-seat and mirror memory, dual-zone automatic climate controls, steering-wheel radio and climate controls, rear radio controls, rear headphone jacks, mirror-mounted turn-signal lights, trip computer, illuminated visor mirrors, universal garage-door opener, outside-temperature indicator, automatic day/night rearview mirror, compass, cargo cover (regular, XL), roof rack (regular, XL). **4WD** adds: 4-wheel drive, 2-speed transfer case.

OPTIONAL EQUIPMENT

Major Packages

	RETAIL PRICE	DEALER INVOICE
Preferred Equipment Group 1SB, SLE regular	$970	$834
XL SLE	905	778
8-way power driver seat, overhead console, universal garage-door opener, illuminated visor mirrors, automatic day/night rearview mirror, compass, outside-temperature indicator, roof rack.		
Preferred Equipment Group 1SB, XUV SLE	565	486
8-way power driver seat, automatic day/night rearview mirror, compass, outside-temperature indicator, illuminated visor mirrors.		
Preferred Equipment Group 1SD, SLT regular, XL SLT	585	503
XUV SLT	295	254
Heated front seats (regular, XL), AM/FM/cassette/CD player, rain-sensing wipers, theft-deterrent system w/alarm (regular, XL), headlight washers. NA w/AM/FM/CD/MP3 player.		
Luxury Pkg., SLT regular, XL SLT	1080	928
Manufacturer's Discount Price	*330*	*284*
XUV SLT	790	679
Manufacturer's Discount Price	*40*	*34*
Preferred Equipment Pkg. 1SD plus Bose sound system.		
OnStar Plus Pkg	970	834
Manufacturer's Discount Price	*70*	*60*
OnStar assistance system w/one-year service, cruise control.		
Sun, Sound, and Entertainment Pkg., SLE, SLT	2015	1733
Manufacturer's Discount Price	*1015*	*873*
SLT w/1SD	1370	1178
Manufacturer's Discount Price	*370*	*318*
Power sunroof, Bose AM/FM radio w/in-dash 6-disc CD changer, satellite radio (requires monthly fee after 3rd month). SLE requires Preferred Equipment Group 1SB.		
V8 Power Play Pkg., XL, XUV	1770	1522
Manufacturer's Discount Price	*1270*	*1092*
5.3-liter V8 engine w/cylinder deactivation, limited-slip differential. SLE requires Preferred Equipment Group 1SB.		
Camping Pkg., XUV	250	215
Tent, air mattress.		

Powertrain

Traction control, 2WD	175	151
Requires limited-slip differential.		
Limited-slip rear differential	270	232
2WD SLE requires Preferred equipment Group 1SB or traction control.		

Safety

Front and 2nd-row curtain side airbags	495	426

Comfort & Convenience Features

	RETAIL PRICE	DEALER INVOICE
Navigation system, SLT	$1995	$1716
Requires Bose sound system.		
Power sunroof	800	688
SLE requires Preferred Equipment Group 1SB.		
Power rear-quarter windows, XL	130	112
Rear-seat DVD entertainment system	1295	1114
w/Sun, Sound, Entertainment	495	426
SLE requires Preferred Equipment Group 1SB. NA w/power sunroof.		
AM/FM/CD/MP3 player	135	116
AM/FM/cassette/CD player	150	129
AM/FM radio w/in-dash 6-disc CD changer	395	340
SLT w/1SD	245	211
SLE requires Preferred Equipment Group 1SB.		
Bose sound system	495	426
SLE requires Preferred equipment Group 1SB.		
Satellite radio	325	280
Requires monthly fee after 3rd month.		
8-way power passenger seat, SLE	275	237
Requires Preferred Equipment Group 1SB. NA XUV.		
Heated front seats, SLT regular, XL SLT	275	237
Power-adjustable pedals	150	129
Cargo cover, SLE regular	70	60
Requires Preferred Equipment Group 1SB.		
Cargo-management system, regular length	165	142

Appearance & Special Purpose

	RETAIL PRICE	DEALER INVOICE
Running boards	375	323
SLE requires Preferred Equipment Pkg. 1SB.		
Roof rack, SLE regular, XL SLE	45	39
XUV	185	159
Rear load-leveling suspension	375	323
Includes air inflator. SLE requires Preferred Equipment Group 1SB.		
Polished forged alloy wheels	495	426
Polished alloy wheels, XUV	395	340

GMC SAFARI

CLASS: Minivan
DRIVE WHEELS: Rear-wheel drive, all-wheel drive
BASE PRICE RANGE: $22,800-$26,300. Built in USA.
ALSO CONSIDER: Dodge Caravan, Honda Odyssey, Toyota Sienna

Safari and its Chevrolet Astro twin are unchanged for 2005. General Motors says this is their last model year. America's only truck-type minivans share a basic design dating from the late 1980s. Like Astro, Safari comes in a single body length with right-side sliding door, a 4.3-liter V6, and automatic transmission. It's available with rear-wheel drive or all-wheel drive and seating for

up to eight. Antilock 4-wheel disc brakes are standard. Traction control and side airbags are unavailable. Full-height rear cargo doors are standard, but Dutch doors with separate-opening upper glass are optional. Safari is also sold as a 2-seat Cargo Van. Safari's performance and accommodations mirror those of comparably equipped Astros.

RATINGS

	AWD w/SLE Pkg
ACCELERATION	4
FUEL ECONOMY	3
RIDE QUALITY	3
STEERING/HANDLING	3
QUIETNESS	3
CONTROLS/MATERIALS	6
ROOM/COMFORT (FRONT)	4
ROOM/COMFORT (REAR)	6
CARGO ROOM	10
VALUE WITHIN CLASS	3

If you need a minivan mainly for towing or hauling heavy loads, Astro and Safari fill the bill. Otherwise, most any front-drive model is a better choice.

TOTAL	45

Average total for minivans: 58.0

ENGINES

	ohv V6
Size, liters/cu. in.	4.3/262
Horsepower @ rpm	190 @ 4400
Torque (lb-ft) @ rpm	250 @ 2800
Availability	S
EPA city/highway mpg	
4-speed automatic	16/20[1]

1. 14/17 with AWD.

PRICES

GMC Safari	RETAIL PRICE	DEALER INVOICE
2WD Cargo 3-door van	$22800	$20634

 Specifications begin on page 547.

PRICES (cont.)

	RETAIL PRICE	DEALER INVOICE
AWD Cargo 3-door van	$25300	$22897
2WD Passenger 3-door van	24300	21992
AWD Passenger 3-door van	26300	23802
Destination charge	740	740

STANDARD EQUIPMENT

Cargo: 4.3-liter V6 engine, 4-speed automatic transmission, antilock 4-wheel disc brakes, dual front airbags, daytime running lights, power steering, front air conditioning, vinyl upholstery, front bucket seats, cupholders, AM/FM radio, digital clock, map lights, vinyl floor covering, intermittent wipers, automatic headlights, theft-deterrent system, rear panel doors, 215/70R16 tires. **AWD** adds: all-wheel drive.

Passenger adds: cloth upholstery, 8-passenger seating, front bucket seats, 2nd-row bench seat, 3rd-row bench seat, tilt steering wheel, cruise control, power mirrors, power windows, power door locks, carpeting, floormats, deep-tinted rear glass, 6-wire trailer harness. **AWD** adds: all-wheel drive.

OPTIONAL EQUIPMENT

Major Packages

	RETAIL PRICE	DEALER INVOICE
SLE Marketing Option Pkg. 1SC, Passenger	$1245	$1071
Remote keyless entry, AM/FM/CD player, bodyside cladding, chrome grille, alloy wheels.		
SLE Marketing Option Pkg. 1SD, Passenger	3495	3006
SLE Marketing Option Pkg. 1SC plus rear air conditioning, rear heater, 6-way power driver seat, AM/FM/cassette/CD player, illuminated visor mirrors, overhead console, compass, outside-temperature indicator, rear Dutch doors, rear defogger, roof rack.		
SLT Marketing Option Pkg. 1SE, Passenger	5145	4425
SLE Marketing Option Pkg. 1SD plus leather-wrapped steering wheel, upgraded cloth upholstery, universal garage-door opener, rear radio controls, additional cupholders, bodyside stripes.		
ZQ2 Convenience Pkg., Cargo	475	409
Power door locks, power windows.		
ZQ3 Convenience Pkg., Cargo	395	340
Tilt steering wheel, cruise control.		
Heavy-Duty Trailering Equipment	265	228
Platform hitch, 8-lead wiring harness.		

Powertrain

Limited-slip differential	280	241

Comfort & Convenience Features

Rear air conditioning, Passenger	525	452
Rear heater	240	206
Rear Dutch doors, Passenger	460	396
Includes rear defogger.		

OPTIONAL EQUIPMENT (cont.)

	RETAIL PRICE	DEALER INVOICE
7-passenger seating, Passenger	NC	NC
2nd-row bucket seats. Requires SLT Pkg. 1SE.		
Leather upholstery, Passenger	950	817
Requires SLT Pkg. 1SE.		
AM/FM/CD player	205	176
Cargo requires Convenience Pkg. ZQ2.		
AM/FM/cassette/CD player, Passenger	100	86
Requires SLE Pkg. 1SC.		
Rear headphone jacks/radio controls, Passenger	125	108
Requires SLE Pkg. 1SD.		
Overhead console, Passenger	225	194
Includes storage, compass, outside-temperature indicator. Requires SLE Pkg. 1SC, illuminated visor mirrors.		
Illuminated visor mirrors, Passenger	100	86
Requires SLE Pkg. 1SC., overhead console.		
Appearance & Special Purpose		
Running boards, Passenger	400	344
Requires option pkg. AWD w/Heavy-Duty Trailering Equipment requires 7-passenger seating.		
Roof rack, Passenger	130	112

HONDA ACCORD

CLASS: Midsize car
DRIVE WHEELS: Front-wheel drive
BASE PRICE RANGE: $16,195-$28,800. Built in USA.
ALSO CONSIDER: Chevrolet Malibu, Nissan Altima, Toyota Camry

A new gas/electric hybrid sedan and standard curtain side airbags for all models mark 2005 for this popular midsize car. Accord offers coupes and sedans in LX and EX trim, plus a price-leader DX sedan. All use a 160-hp 4-cyl engine. LX and EX models also offer a 240-hp V6. The 4-cyl teams with 5-speed manual transmission or optional 5-speed automatic. The automatic is standard on V6 models. The sporty EX V6 coupe also offers a 6-speed manual.

The Hybrid has 255 hp with a V6 assisted by an electric motor. The engine employs Honda's new Variable Cylinder Management that deactivates three cylinders when cruising or decelerating to save fuel. There's no plug-in charging, but the car can't be driven on electricity alone.

All Accords come with ABS. V6 models add traction control. Front torso side airbags and head-protecting curtain side airbags are standard. These safety features had been available only on select models. The manual-transmission V6 coupe has 17-inch wheels; other Accords have 16s or 15s. EX-L, EX V6, and Hybrid models come with leather upholstery, satellite radio, dual-zone automatic climate control, and heated front seats. Those models also offer a navigation system with voice control for some navigation, audio, and climate functions. The Hybrid has a unique grille, a decklid spoiler, special instrumentation, and electric power steering vs. hydraulic. It also includes Honda's new active-noise-control system, designed to electronically quell mechanical, road, and wind noise.

RATINGS	LX sdn, auto.	EX-L sdn w/nav. sys., auto.	EX V6 sdn, auto.	EX V6 cpe, 6-sp man.
ACCELERATION	5	5	7	7
FUEL ECONOMY	7	7	6	6
RIDE QUALITY	7	7	7	7
STEERING/HANDLING	6	7	7	7
QUIETNESS	7	7	7	7
CONTROLS/MATERIALS	10	9	10	10
ROOM/COMFORT (FRONT)	7	7	7	7
ROOM/COMFORT (REAR)	6	6	6	3
CARGO ROOM	4	4	4	3
VALUE WITHIN CLASS	10	9	10	7

Accord is a Best Buy blend of confident road manners, precision engineering, and enviable refinement. Add in Honda's sterling record for reliability and resale value, and it's no wonder Accord is so popular—and so seldom discounted. Official Accord Hybrid prices were not announced in time for this report, but Honda says it will list for about $30,000, with its sole option the navigation system, at $2000. That's pricey vs. its potential fuel savings, but a combination of short supply and steep gas prices mean this appealing new model will likely command well over sticker for some time to come.

TOTAL	69	68	71	64

Average total for midsize cars: 57.2

ENGINES	dohc I4	sohc V6	sohc V6/electric
Size, liters/cu. in.	2.4/144	3.0/183	3.0/183
Horsepower @ rpm	160 @ 5500	240 @ 6250	255 @ 6000
Torque (lb-ft) @ rpm	161 @ 4500	212 @ 5000	232 @ 5000
Availability	S[1]	S[2]	S[3]
EPA city/highway mpg			
5-speed manual	26/34		
6-speed manual		20/30	
5-speed automatic	24/34	21/30	30/37

1. DX, LX, EX. 2. LX V6, EX V6. 3. Hybrid.

PRICES

Honda Accord

Honda Accord	RETAIL PRICE	DEALER INVOICE
DX 4-door sedan, manual	$16195	$14583
DX 4-door sedan, automatic	16995	15302
LX 2-door coupe, manual	19775	17800
LX 2-door coupe, automatic	20575	18519
LX 4-door sedan, manual	19675	17711
LX 4-door sedan, automatic	20475	18430
LX V6 2-door coupe, automatic	23900	21507
LX V6 4-door sedan, automatic	23800	21417
EX 2-door coupe, manual	22200	19980
EX 2-door coupe, automatic	23000	20699
EX 4-door sedan, manual	22100	19890
EX 4-door sedan, automatic	22900	20609
EX-L 2-door coupe, manual	23800	21417
EX-L 2-door coupe, automatic	24600	22135
EX-L 2-door coupe w/navigation system, manual	25800	23215
EX-L 2-door coupe w/navigation system, automatic	26600	29934
EX-L 4-door sedan, manual	23700	21328
EX-L 4-door sedan, automatic	24500	22047
EX-L 4-door sedan w/navigation system, manual	25700	23125
EX-L 4-door sedan w/navigation system, automatic	26500	23844
EX V6 2-door coupe, manual	26800	24113
EX V6 2-door coupe, automatic	26800	24113
EX V6 2-door coupe w/navigation system, manual	28800	25911
EX V6 2-door coupe w/navigation system, automatic	28800	25911
EX V6 4-door sedan, automatic	26700	24024
EX V6 4-door sedan w/navigation system, automatic	28700	25821
Destination charge	515	515

Hybrid prices and equipment not available at time of publication.

STANDARD EQUIPMENT

DX: 2.4-liter 4-cylinder engine, 5-speed manual or 5-speed automatic transmission, dual front airbags, front side airbags, curtain side airbags, antilock brakes, emergency inside trunk release, power steering, tilt/telescope steering wheel, cloth upholstery, front bucket seats, center console, cupholders, folding rear seat, power windows, AM/FM/CD player, digital clock, tachometer, intermittent wipers, rear defogger, visor mirrors, floormats, theft-deterrent system, 195/65R15 tires, wheel covers.

LX adds: automatic-off headlights, cruise control, air conditioning, interior air filter, power mirrors, power door locks, remote keyless entry, illuminated visor mirrors, manual driver-seat height adjustment, rear-seat trunk pass-through (sedan), split folding rear seat (coupe), variable-intermittent wipers, map lights, 205/65R15 tires.

LX V6 adds: 3.0-liter V6 engine, 5-speed automatic transmission, traction control, antilock 4-wheel disc brakes, 8-way power driver seat, AM/FM radio w/in-dash 6-disc CD changer, steering-wheel radio controls, 205/60R16 tires.

 Specifications begin on page 547.

EX adds to LX: antilock 4-wheel disc brakes, driver seat w/power height adjustment and adjustable lumbar support, power sunroof, AM/FM radio w/in-dash 6-disc CD changer, steering-wheel radio controls, alloy wheels.

EX-L adds: dual-zone automatic climate controls, leather upholstery, leather-wrapped steering wheel, heated front seats, 8-way power driver seat, satellite radio, outside-temperature indicator.

EX V6 adds: 3.0-liter V6 engine, 5-speed automatic transmission (sedan), 6-speed manual or 5-speed automatic transmission (coupe), traction control, 4-way power passenger seat, universal garage-door opener, 215/50R17 tires (manual).

Options are available as dealer-installed accessories.

HONDA CIVIC

CLASS: Compact car
DRIVE WHEELS: Front-wheel drive
BASE PRICE RANGE: $13,160-$20,800. Built in USA.
ALSO CONSIDER: Ford Focus, Mazda 3, Toyota Corolla

New top-line models join Honda's entry-level cars for 2005. Civic offers three body styles in a variety of trim levels. Notable models include a gas/electric Hybrid sedan and the a sporty Si 2-dr hatchback. All use a 4-cyl engine. Horsepower is 115 for DX, VP, and LX versions; 117 for the HX model; 127 for EX versions; and 160 for Si. The Hybrid has 93 hp. A battery pack and electric motor assist its gas engine; coasting or decelerating recharges the batteries, so there's no plugging-in. All Civics come with manual transmission, and all but DX and Si offer automatic. In the HX coupe and Hybrid, the automatic is a continuously variable transmission (CVT) that effectively provides near-infinite drive ratios. Front side airbags are standard for the Hybrid, optional on other Civics. ABS is standard for the EX, Hybrid, and Si models, but is unavailable otherwise. The Si includes a sport suspension and 16-inch wheels. Wheels are 15 inches for LX and EX models, 14s otherwise. The new top-line Civiic is the EX-based Special Edition coupe and sedan. They come with a rear spoiler, leather-wrapped steering wheel, and an in-dash CD changer that plays MP3 discs. The Hybrid includes automatic climate control, which is otherwise unavailable. It's also the only Civic without a split folding rear seatback. LX, EX, and Hybrid models have a height-adjustable driver seat.

RATINGS	HX cpe, CVT	LX sdn, auto.	EX sdn, auto.	Hybrid, CVT
ACCELERATION	4	4	4	2
FUEL ECONOMY	7	7	7	9
RIDE QUALITY	5	5	5	5
STEERING/HANDLING	5	6	6	5
QUIETNESS	5	5	5	5
CONTROLS/MATERIALS	6	6	6	7
ROOM/COMFORT (FRONT)	5	5	5	5
ROOM/COMFORT (REAR)	3	4	4	4
CARGO ROOM	3	3	3	3
VALUE WITHIN CLASS	7	10	10	8

Despite test-car glitches and worrisome non-ABS braking, Civic is a clear Best Buy. Most any model offers top-of-class comfort, refinement, and fuel thrift, plus Honda's strong resale and reliability record. The Si adds extra sportiness and utility to this appealing mix. The Hybrid sacrifices good acceleration for great fuel economy. Still, even with hybrid owners allowed a one-time federal tax deduction, it will take years to recoup in fuel savings the Civic Hybrid's higher initial cost. And unlike other Civics, it's in high enough demand to preclude discounts.

TOTAL	50	55	55	53

Average total for compact cars: 48.4

ENGINES	sohc I4/electric	sohc I4	sohc I4	dohc I4
Size, liters/cu. in.	1.3/80	1.7/102	1.7/102	2.0/122
Horsepower @ rpm	93 @ 5700	115 @ 6100	127 @ 6300	160 @ 6500
Torque (lb-ft) @ rpm	116 @ 1500	110 @ 4500	114 @ 4800	132 @ 5000
Availability	S[1]	S[2]	S[3]	S[4]
EPA city/highway mpg				
5-speed manual	46/51	32/38[5]	32/37	26/31
4-speed automatic		29/38	31/38	
CVT automatic	48/47	35/40		

1. Hybrid. With CVT, torque is 105 lb-ft @ 3000. 2. DX, VP, LX, HX. HX has 117 hp and is rated 36/44 mpg w/manual transmission. 3. EX. 4. Si. 5. 36/44 for HX.

PRICES

Honda Civic	RETAIL PRICE	DEALER INVOICE
DX 4-door sedan, manual	$13160	$12035
DX 4-door sedan w/side airbags, manual	13410	12263
VP 2-door coupe, manual	13560	12399
VP 2-door coupe, automatic	14360	13129
VP 2-door coupe w/side airbags, manual	13810	12627
VP 2-door coupe w/side airbags, automatic	14610	13357
VP 2-door sedan, automatic	14560	13312
VP 2-door sedan w/side airbags, automatic	14810	13540

Specifications begin on page 547.

PRICES (cont.)

	RETAIL PRICE	DEALER INVOICE
HX 2-door coupe, manual	$13860	$12673
HX 2-door coupe, CVT	14860	13585
HX 2-door coupe w/side airbags, manual	14110	12901
HX 2-door coupe w/side airbags, CVT	15110	13813
LX 2-door coupe, manual	15310	13996
LX 2-door coupe, automatic	16110	14726
LX 2-door coupe w/side airbags, manual	15560	14224
LX 2-door coupe w/side airbags, automatics	16360	14954
LX 4-door sedan, manual	15510	14178
LX 4-door sedan, automatic	16310	14908
LX 4-door sedan w/side airbags, manual	15760	14406
LX 4-door sedan w/side impact airbags, automatic	16560	15136
EX 2-door coupe, manual	17010	15547
EX 2-door coupe, automatic	17810	16276
EX 2-door coupe w/side airbags, manual	17260	15775
EX 2-door coupe w/side airbags, automatic	18060	16504
EX 4-door sedan, manual	17410	15911
EX 4-door sedan, automatic	18210	16641
EX 4-door sedan w/side impact airbags, manual	17660	16139
EX 4-door sedan w/side impact airbags, automatic	18460	16869
EX Special Edition 2-door coupe, manual	17460	16957
EX Special Edition 2-door coupe, automatic	18260	16687
EX Special Edition 4-door sedan, manual	17860	16322
EX Special Edition 4-door sedan, automatic	18660	17052
Si 2-door hatchback, manual	19220	17562
Si 2-door hatchback w/side airbags, manual	19470	17790
Hybrid 4-door sedan, manual	19800	18092
Hybrid 4-door sedan, CVT	20800	19004
Destination charge	515	515

STANDARD EQUIPMENT

DX: 1.7-liter 4-cylinder 115-horsepower engine, 5-speed manual transmission, dual front airbags, emergency inside trunk release, power steering, tilt steering wheel, cloth upholstery, front bucket seats, cupholders, split folding rear seat, AM/FM radio, digital clock, rear defogger, intermittent wipers, visor mirrors, theft-deterrent system, 185/70R14 tires, wheel covers.

HX adds: 1.7-liter 4-cylinder 117-horsepower engine, 5-speed manual or continuously variable automatic transmission (CVT), cruise control, power mirrors, power door locks, AM/FM/CD player, tachometer, alloy wheels.

VP adds to DX: 5-speed manual or 4-speed automatic transmission, air conditioning, interior air filter, center console, AM/FM/CD player.

LX adds: cruise control, height-adjustable driver seat, power mirrors, power windows, power door locks, remote keyless entry, tachometer, map lights, floormats, 195/60HR15 tires.

EX adds: 1.7-liter 4-cylinder 127-horsepower engine, antilock brakes, power sunroof, variable-intermittent wipers, alloy wheels.

EX Special Edition adds: leather-wrapped steering wheel, AM/FM radio w/in-dash 6-disc CD/MP3 changer, rear spoiler.

Si adds to EX: 2.0-liter 4-cylinder engine, antilock 4-wheel disc brakes, leather-wrapped steering wheel, cargo cover, rear wiper/washer, rear spoiler, sport suspension, 205/55VR16 tires. *Deletes:* height-adjustable driver seat.

Hybrid adds to LX: 1.3-liter 4-cylinder gasoline/electric motor, 5-speed manual or continuously variable automatic transmission (CVT), front side airbags, antilock brakes, automatic climate control, trip computer, variable-intermittent wipers, rear spoiler, 185/70SR14 tires, alloy wheels. *Deletes:* split folding rear seat.

Options are available as dealer-installed accessories.

HONDA CR-V

CLASS: Compact sport-utility vehicle
DRIVE WHEELS: Front-wheel drive, all-wheel drive
BASE PRICE RANGE: $19,995-$25,050. Built in Japan.
ALSO CONSIDER: Ford Escape, Mazda Tribute, Subaru Forester

CR-V gains more standard safety features for 2005, including curtain side airbags. Other additions include a leather-upholstered model and a new automatic transmission. Detail styling changes round out the revisions. This compact 5-passenger SUV offers LX, EX, and new SE models. LXs come with front- or all-wheel drive. The others have AWD. CR-V's AWD lacks low-range gearing. All models have a 4-cyl engine and manual or automatic transmission. The automatic for '05 is a 5-speed unit vs. a 4-speed. Four-wheel disc brakes continue as standard, and are joined for '05 by ABS, which had been standard only on the LX. All models also gain an antiskid system, which was previously unavailable. Front side airbags were an extra-cost feature but are standard for '05 and are joined by head-protecting curtain side airbags for both seating rows. Sixteen-inch wheels replace 15s for '05. The SE has standard leather upholstery and heated front seats. Both are new CR-V features, as are steering-wheel radio controls and an outside-temperature indicator for EX and SE models. All CR-Vs have a 60/40 split folding rear seat and a lift-out rear cargo floor that doubles as a picnic table.

RATINGS	2WD LX, auto.	AWD LX, man.	EX, auto.
ACCELERATION	4	5	4
FUEL ECONOMY	5	5	5

 Specifications begin on page 547.

RATINGS (cont.)	2WD LX, auto.	AWD LX, man.	EX, auto.
RIDE QUALITY	5	5	5
STEERING/HANDLING	5	5	5
QUIETNESS	4	4	4
CONTROLS/MATERIALS	6	6	6
ROOM/COMFORT (FRONT)	7	7	7
ROOM/COMFORT (REAR)	7	7	7
CARGO ROOM	7	7	7
VALUE WITHIN CLASS	10	10	10

Efficient and well-built, CR-V also appeals for relative comfort, refinement, and spaciousness. Some small SUVs offer more muscle, but none beats this Honda for thoughtful design, proven reliability, and resale value. The '05 addition of standard head-protecting curtain side airbags, ABS, and antiskid system only enhance its Best Buy credentials.

TOTAL	60	61	60

Average total for compact sport-utility vehicles: 49.0

ENGINES

	dohc I4
Size, liters/cu. in.	2.4/146
Horsepower @ rpm	160 @ 6000
Torque (lb-ft) @ rpm	162 @ 3600
Availability	S
EPA city/highway mpg	
5-speed manual	21/26
5-speed automatic	22/27

PRICES

Honda CR-V	RETAIL PRICE	DEALER INVOICE
2WD LX 4-door wagon, automatic	$19995	$18473
AWD LX 4-door wagon, automatic	21195	19580
AWD EX 4-door wagon, manual	22450	20738
AWD EX 4-door wagon, automatic	23350	21568
AWD SE 4-door wagon, automatic	25050	23136
Destination charge	515	515

STANDARD EQUIPMENT

LX: 2.4-liter 4-cylinder engine, 5-speed automatic transmission, dual front airbags, front side airbags, curtain side airbags, antilock 4-wheel disc brakes, antiskid system, air conditioning, interior air filter, power steering, tilt steering wheel, cruise control, cloth upholstery, front bucket seats w/driver-seat height adjustment, cupholders, split folding rear seat, power mirrors, power windows, power door locks, remote keyless entry, AM/FM/cassette/CD player, digital clock, tachometer, intermittent wipers, visor mirrors, map lights, lift-out folding picnic table, rear defogger, intermittent rear wiper/washer, floormats, theft-deterrent system, roof rails, outside-mounted full-size spare tire, 215/65R16 tires. **AWD** models add: all-wheel drive.

EX adds: 5-speed manual or 5-speed automatic transmission, all-wheel drive, power sunroof, AM/FM/cassette w/in-dash 6-disc CD changer, steering-wheel radio controls, outside-temperature indicator, rear privacy glass, alloy wheels.

SE adds: leather upholstery, heated front seats, leather-wrapped steering wheel, heated power mirrors.

Options are available as dealer-installed accessories.

HONDA ELEMENT

CLASS: Compact sport-utility vehicle
DRIVE WHEELS: Front-wheel drive, all-wheel drive
2004 BASE PRICE RANGE: $16,100-$21,350. Built in USA.
ALSO CONSIDER: Ford Escape, Honda CR-V, Subaru Forester

Standard front side airbags and optional satellite radio mark 2005 additions to this youth-oriented compact SUV. Element is based on Honda's CR-V wagon, but has unique styling with center-opening side doors and uses compositelike plastic for some body panels. Its rear-hinged back doors are shorter than the front doors and don't open or close independently of them. Element is taller, wider, and heavier than CR-V, and has an upper liftgate and drop-down tailgate vs. a swing-out cargo door. It comes in DX, LX, and top-trim EX models. All use CR-V's 4-cyl engine with manual or automatic transmission and either front-wheel drive or all-wheel drive without low-range gearing. Sixteen-inch wheels and 4-wheel disc brakes are standard; ABS is an EX exclusive. Elements seat four on front bucket seats and a split rear bench. The bench's 30-lb sections swing up to the sides or remove to expand cargo space. AWD models include a tilt/removable glass "skylight" over the cargo bay. All 2005 Elements come with front side airbags, previously an EX-only option, and offer satellite radio as a first-time extra. Also, the DX gains other models' standard CD audio, which adds MP3 playback. LXs now match EXs with standard cruise control and power mirrors. Exclusive EX standards include ABS, alloy wheels, and remote keyless entry. A new EX color scheme pairs silver paint with blue instead of black plastic body panels. Elements have water-resistant cloth upholstery and rubberlike floor covering. Air conditioning is standard for LX and EX, a dealer-installed option for the bare-bones DX.

 Specifications begin on page 547.

RATINGS

RATINGS	2WD DX, man.	2WD EX, auto.	AWD EX, auto.
ACCELERATION	5	3	3
FUEL ECONOMY	6	5	5
RIDE QUALITY	4	4	4
STEERING/HANDLING	5	5	5
QUIETNESS	4	4	4
CONTROLS/MATERIALS	6	6	6
ROOM/COMFORT (FRONT)	6	6	6
ROOM/COMFORT (REAR)	6	6	6
CARGO ROOM	7	7	7
VALUE WITHIN CLASS	7	8	8

Element isn't so much an SUV as a motorized gear tote for "active lifestyle" types. Though not designed for posh comfort or serious off-roading, we recommend it as a versatile, practical, and roomy little wagon with Honda's expected solid workmanship and thoughtful features. We also applaud the standard front side airbags, but adding curtain side airbags would be even better.

TOTAL	56	54	54

Average total for compact sport-utility vehicles: 49.0

ENGINES

	dohc I4
Size, liters/cu. in.	2.4/144
Horsepower @ rpm	160 @ 5500
Torque (lb-ft) @ rpm	161 @ 4500
Availability	S
EPA city/highway mpg	
5-speed manual	21/24[1]
4-speed automatic	21/24[2]

1. 21/26 w/2WD. 2. 22/26 w/2WD.

2005 prices unavailable at time of publication.

2004 PRICES

Honda Element	RETAIL PRICE	DEALER INVOICE
2WD DX 4-door wagon, manual	$16100	$14881
2WD DX 4-door wagon, automatic	16900	15619
AWD DX 4-door wagon, manual	17500	16172
AWD DX 4-door wagon, automatic	18300	16910
2WD LX 4-door wagon, manual	17100	15803
2WD LX 4-door wagon, automatic	17900	16541
AWD LX 4-door wagon, manual	18500	17094
AWD LX 4-door wagon, automatic	19300	17832
2WD EX 4-door wagon, manual	18900	17463
2WD EX 4-door wagon, automatic	19700	18201
2WD EX 4-door wagon w/side airbags, manual	19150	17694
2WD EX 4-door wagon w/side airbags, automatic	19950	18432

PRICES (cont.)

	RETAIL PRICE	DEALER INVOICE
AWD EX 4-door wagon, manual	$20300	$18755
AWD EX 4-door wagon, automatic	21100	19493
AWD EX 4-door wagon w/side airbags, manual	20550	18985
AWD EX 4-door wagon w/side airbags, automatic	21350	19723
Destination charge	490	490

STANDARD EQUIPMENT

DX: 2.4-liter 4-cylinder engine, 5-speed manual or 4-speed automatic transmission, dual front airbags, 4-wheel disc brakes, power steering, tilt steering wheel, cloth upholstery, center console, cupholders, front bucket seats w/height-adjustable driver seat, stowable split folding or flip-up rear seat, power windows, power door locks, tachometer, intermittent wipers, rear defogger, intermittent rear wiper/washer, theft-deterrent system, rear privacy glass, 215/70R16 tires. **AWD** adds: all-wheel drive, manual rear sunroof.

LX adds: air conditioning, interior air filter, AM/FM/CD player, digital clock. **AWD** adds: all-wheel drive, manual rear sunroof.

EX adds: antilock 4-wheel disc brakes, cruise control, power mirrors, remote keyless entry, map lights, visor mirrors, alloy wheels. **AWD** adds: all-wheel drive, manual rear sunroof.

Options are available as dealer-installed accessories.

HONDA INSIGHT

CLASS: Compact car
DRIVE WHEELS: Front-wheel drive
2004 BASE PRICE RANGE: $19,180-$21,380. Built in Japan.
ALSO CONSIDER: Honda Civic Hybrid, Toyota Echo and Prius

The first gasoline/electric hybrid on U.S. roads is unchanged for 2005. Insight is a 2-seat hatchback coupe with a 3-cyl gasoline engine assisted by a battery-powered electric motor for a combined 73 hp. Batteries recharge when coasting or decelerating, so there's no plugging-in. Aerodynamic styling and aluminum-intensive construction contribute to industry-leading EPA fuel-economy ratings. Insight offers manual transmission and an optional continuously variable automatic transmission (CVT). The CVT lacks conventional gears, using a belt-and-pulley system to vary drive ratios as needed, but has steering-wheel "D" and "S" buttons to select normal and higher-

 Specifications begin on page 547.

performance ranges. ABS is standard, but neither side nor curtain side airbags are offered. Air conditioning is optional on the base model, standard with CVT.

RATINGS

	Base w/air conditioning	CVT
ACCELERATION	2	2
FUEL ECONOMY	10	9
RIDE QUALITY	2	2
STEERING/HANDLING	4	4
QUIETNESS	3	4
CONTROLS/MATERIALS	5	5
ROOM/COMFORT (FRONT)	4	4
ROOM/COMFORT (REAR)	0	0
CARGO ROOM	2	2
VALUE WITHIN CLASS	2	3

Despite modest acceleration and a stiff ride, Insight is a useful city/suburban commuter, especially in CVT form, with a high-tech, environment-friendly appeal. But even with a one-time federal tax deduction for hybrid-vehicle buyers, Insight is costly for an economy car, and the payback in fuel savings will take years to recoup. Insight has its charms, but we'd opt for Honda's larger but similarly priced Civic Hybrid sedan or a Toyota Prius.

TOTAL	34	35

Average total for compact cars: 48.4

ENGINES

	sohc I3/electric
Size, liters/cu. in.	1.0/61
Horsepower @ rpm	73 @ 5700
Torque (lb-ft) @ rpm	79 @ 1500
Availability	S[1]
EPA city/highway mpg	
5-speed manual	60/66
CVT automatic	57/56

1. Torque is 89 lb-ft w/CVT.

2005 prices unavailable at time of publication.

2004 PRICES

Honda Insight	RETAIL PRICE	DEALER INVOICE
Base 2-door hatchback coupe	$19180	$17917
Base w/air conditioning 2-door hatchback coupe	20380	19036
CVT 2-door hatchback coupe	21380	19969
Destination charge	490	490

STANDARD EQUIPMENT

Base: 1.0-liter 3-cylinder gasoline engine/electric motor, 5-speed manual transmission, dual front airbags, antilock brakes, interior air filter, power steering, front bucket seats, cupholders, power mirrors, power windows, power door locks, remote keyless entry, AM/FM/CD player, digital clock, tachometer, trip computer, intermittent wipers, rear defogger, rear wiper/washer, map lights, driver-side visor mirror, remote fuel-door release, theft-deterrent system, 165/65R14 tires, alloy wheels.

Base w/air conditioning adds: air conditioning w/automatic climate control.

CVT adds: continuously variable automatic transmission.

Options are available as dealer-installed accessories.

HONDA ODYSSEY

CLASS: Minivan
DRIVE WHEELS: Front-wheel drive
BASE PRICE RANGE: $24,995-$38,295. Built in USA.
ALSO CONSIDER: Chrysler Town & Country, Mazda MPV, Toyota Sienna

---

Honda updates its minivan for 2005, revising the styling and adding a new model and additional safety features. Odyssey offers LX, EX, EX-L, and new Touring models. All have front-wheel drive, a 255-hp 3.5-liter V6 with 15 more hp than last year, and a 5-speed automatic transmission. EX-L and Touring feature Honda's Variable Cylinder Management system, which deactivates three cylinders when cruising or decelerating to save fuel. Safety features standard on all Odysseys include antilock 4-wheel disc brakes, traction control, and front side airbags. New for '05 are an antiskid system and curtain side airbags for all three seating rows. Exterior dimensions are unchanged but interior space grows an inch in width, two inches in length. Standard on all models are front and 2nd-row bucket seats and a fold-into-the floor 3rd-row seat, which is now split 60/40. New features include a storage compartment in the floor between the front seats, and side windows that power down into the sliding doors. EX models add a removable second-row jump seat for occasional 8-passenger seating, power sliding side doors, and a conversation mirror. EX-L and Touring versions add leather upholstery, tri-zone climate control, sunroof, and Honda's active noise-control system designed to electronically quell unwanted mechanical, road, and wind noise. Touring models have 17.5-inch wheels with run-flat tires, plus a tire-pressure monitor. Other Odysseys have 16-inch wheels and conventional tires. Tourings also get a 2nd-row floor console, power liftgate, front- and rear-obstacle detection,

Specifications begin on page 547.

power-adjustable pedals, and a 115-volt A/C power outlet. Available on EX-L and Touring are navigation and rear-entertainment systems. The navigation system has voice recognition, real-time traffic alerts, and comes with a rearview camera. This evaluation is based on preview test drives.

RATINGS

	EX	Touring w/nav. sys.
ACCELERATION	6	6
FUEL ECONOMY	4	4
RIDE QUALITY	7	6
STEERING/HANDLING	6	6
QUIETNESS	6	6
CONTROLS/MATERIALS	6	6
ROOM/COMFORT (FRONT)	8	8
ROOM/COMFORT (REAR)	8	8
CARGO ROOM	9	9
VALUE WITHIN CLASS	10	8

Odyssey's firm ride, relatively austere interior decor, and daunting array of buttons and switches may put off some mainstream minivan buyers. But this is a Best Buy benchmark for its near-perfect blend of carlike road manners and minivan room and versatility.

TOTAL	70	67

Average total for minivans: 58.0

ENGINES

	sohc V6	sohc V6
Size, liters/cu. in.	3.5/212	3.5/212
Horsepower @ rpm	255 @ 5750	255 @ 5750
Torque (lb-ft) @ rpm	250 @ 5000	250 @ 4500
Availability	S[1]	S[2]
EPA city/highway mpg		
5-speed automatic	19/25	20/28

1. LX, EX. 2. EX-L, Touring.

PRICES

Honda Odyssey	RETAIL PRICE	DEALER INVOICE
LX 4-door van	$24995	$22586
EX 4-door van	27995	25012
EX-L 4-door van	30295	27034
EX-L w/DVD 4-door van	31895	28472
EX-L w/DVD navigation 4-door van	34095	30449
Touring 4-door van	34495	30628
Touring w/DVD navigation 4-door van	38295	34043
Destination charge	515	515

STANDARD EQUIPMENT

LX: 3.5-liter V6 engine, 5-speed automatic transmission, traction control, dual front airbags, front side airbags, curtain side airbags, antilock 4-wheel disc brakes, brake assist, antiskid system, front and rear air conditioning w/rear controls, power steering, tilt steering wheel, cruise control, cloth upholstery, 7-passenger seating, front bucket seats, height-adjustable driver seat, cupholders, two 2nd-row bucket seats, removable center tray, 3rd-row stowable split bench seat, power mirrors, power windows, power door locks, remote keyless entry, AM/FM/CD player, digital clock, tachometer, variable-intermittent wipers, illuminated visor mirrors, map lights, rear defogger, rear wiper/washer, floormats, theft-deterrent system, rear privacy glass, 235/65R16 tires, wheel covers.

EX adds: front dual-zone automatic climate controls, interior air filter, 8-way power driver seat w/lumbar adjustment, 8-passenger seating, 2nd-row stowable seat, power sliding rear doors, heated power mirrors, AM/FM radio w/in-dash 6-disc CD changer, steering-wheel radio controls, universal garage-door opener, conversation mirror, automatic-off headlights, roof rails, alloy wheels.

EX-L adds: 3.5-liter V6 engine w/cylinder deactivation, leather upholstery, heated front seats, power sunroof, active noise reduction.

EX-L w/DVD adds: rear-seat DVD entertainment system.

EX-L w/DVD navigation adds: navigation system w/voice recognition, rearview camera, satellite radio.

Touring adds to EX-L: front- and rear-obstacle-detection system, tire-pressure monitor, rear automatic climate controls, driver-seat memory, power-adjustable pedals, 2nd-row removable center console, upgraded sound system, trip computer, compass, outside-temperature indicator, automatic day/night rearview mirror, 115-volt A/C power outlet, power liftgate, automatic headlights, run-flat tires, 17.5-inch alloy wheels.

Touring w/DVD navigation adds: navigation system w/voice recognition, rearview camera, satellite radio, rear-seat DVD entertainment system.

Options are available as dealer-installed accessories.

HONDA PILOT

CLASS: Midsize sport-utility vehicle
DRIVE WHEELS: All-wheel drive
BASE PRICE RANGE: $27,350-$34,120. Built in Canada.
ALSO CONSIDER: Ford Explorer, Nissan Murano, Toyota Highlander

Honda's midsize SUV adds power and features for 2005. Pilot shares a basic chassis and powertrain with the costlier MDX at Honda's upscale

Specifications begin on page 547.

Acura division, but it seats eight vs. seven, and has 8.8 cu ft more cargo volume than MDX. It also has a softer suspension and 16-inch wheels vs. 17s. Pilot offers three models: LX, upscale EX, and a top-line EX-L with leather upholstery. All have a V6 with 255 hp, an increase of 15 hp for '05. MDX tunes this same engine for 265 hp. Pilot's only transmission is a 5-speed automatic. All-wheel drive is standard. It lacks low-range gearing, but has a dashboard button for locking-in an even front/rear power split. All Pilots include antilock 4-wheel disc brakes and for '05 add a tire-pressure monitor. An antiskid system also is new as a standard feature exclusive to the EX-L. Front side airbags are standard, but unlike MDX, curtain side airbags are unavailable. Pilot has 60/40 split folding bench seats for the 2nd and 3rd rows, plus a one-piece liftgate with fixed glass. EX-L includes heated front seats and mirrors. Fuel-tank capacity increases to 20.4 gal from 19.2 for '05, EX and EX-L replace a single-CD player with an in-dash changer, and their standard remote-entry system dumps a separate keyfob for controls in the master key. Navigation system and rear DVD entertainment are exclusive EX-L options, but aren't available together.

RATINGS

	EX
ACCELERATION	6
FUEL ECONOMY	4
RIDE QUALITY	6
STEERING/HANDLING	5
QUIETNESS	6
CONTROLS/MATERIALS	7
ROOM/COMFORT (FRONT)	7
ROOM/COMFORT (REAR)	7
CARGO ROOM	8
VALUE WITHIN CLASS	10

Pilot is the Honda Accord of midsize SUVs—pleasant, practical, family friendly. Honda has little excuse for denying it such an important safety feature as curtain side airbags. But there's no question about this wagon's laudable balance of utlity and comfort, refinement and workmanship. Toss in Honda's strong reputation for reliability and resale value, and Pilot is a bonafide Best Buy.

TOTAL	66

Average total for midsize sport-utility vehicles: 54.7

ENGINES

	sohc V6
Size, liters/cu. in.	3.5/212
Horsepower @ rpm	255 @ 5600
Torque (lb-ft) @ rpm	250 @ 4500
Availability	S
EPA city/highway mpg	
5-speed automatic	17/22

PRICES

Honda Pilot	RETAIL PRICE	DEALER INVOICE
LX 4-door wagon	$27350	$24608
EX 4-door wagon	29920	26917
EX-L 4-door wagon	32120	28894
EX-L 4-door wagon w/DVD	33620	30242
EX-L 4-door wagon w/navigation system	34120	30691
Destination charge	515	515

STANDARD EQUIPMENT

LX: 3.5-liter V6 engine, 5-speed automatic transmission, all-wheel drive, dual front airbags, front side airbags, antilock 4-wheel disc brakes, tire-pressure monitor, front and rear air conditioning, interior air filter, power steering, tilt steering wheel, cruise control, cloth upholstery, front bucket seats, height-adjustable driver seat, cupholders, split folding 2nd- and 3rd-row seats, power mirrors, power windows, power door locks, remote keyless entry, AM/FM/CD player, digital clock, variable-intermittent wipers, illuminated visor mirrors, map lights, rear defogger, intermittent rear wiper/washer, floormats, theft-deterrent system, rear spoiler, 235/70R16 tires.

EX adds: automatic climate controls, 8-way power driver seat, AM/FM/cassette w/in-dash 6-disc CD changer, steering-wheel radio controls, universal garage-door opener, 2nd-row tray, automatic-off headlights, rear privacy glass, roof rails, alloy wheels.

EX-L adds: brake assist, antiskid system, leather upholstery, heated front seats, heated power mirrors, power sunroof.

EX-L w/DVD adds: rear-seat DVD entertainment system.

EX-L w/navigation system adds to EX-L: navigation system.

Options are available as dealer-installed accessories.

HONDA S2000

CLASS: Sporty/performance car
DRIVE WHEELS: Rear-wheel drive
BASE PRICE: $32,950. Built in Japan.
ALSO CONSIDER: BMW Z4, Nissan 350Z

Honda's sports car is unchanged for 2005. This 2-seat convertible has a power soft top and heated glass rear window. The only powertrain is a

 Specifications begin on page 547.

240-hp 4-cyl engine and 6-speed manual transmission. Antilock 4-wheel disc brakes, xenon headlamps, and leather upholstery are standard. S2000 comes with no suspension options and no factory alternatives to its 17-inch wheels. It includes a cockpit wind deflector.

RATINGS

	Base
ACCELERATION	8
FUEL ECONOMY	6
RIDE QUALITY	3
STEERING/HANDLING	10
QUIETNESS	2
CONTROLS/MATERIALS	6
ROOM/COMFORT (FRONT)	4
ROOM/COMFORT (REAR)	0
CARGO ROOM	2
VALUE WITHIN CLASS	7

The S2000 is pure sports-car fun and a solid Recommended pick. It's a bit stiff and noisy, and the Mazda Miata is a little more practical and a lot less costly. But the spicy S2000 runs with the Porsche Boxster and BMW Z4 3.0i for thousands less. And while the comparably priced Nissan 350Z convertible beats the S2000 for power, it can't match it for engineering precision.

TOTAL	48

Average total for sporty/performance cars: 48.5

ENGINES

	dohc I4
Size, liters/cu. in.	2.2/134
Horsepower @ rpm	240 @ 7800
Torque (lb-ft) @ rpm	162 @ 6500
Availability	S
EPA city/highway mpg	
6-speed manual	20/25

PRICES

Honda S2000

	RETAIL PRICE	DEALER INVOICE
Base 2-door convertible	$32950	$29640
Destination charge	515	515

STANDARD EQUIPMENT

Base: 2.2-liter 4-cylinder engine, 6-speed manual transmission, limited-slip differential, dual front airbags, antilock 4-wheel disc brakes, emergency inside trunk release, air conditioning, interior air filter, power steering, leather-wrapped steering wheel, cruise control, leather upholstery, bucket seats, center console, cupholders, power mirrors, power windows, power door locks, remote keyless entry, AM/FM/CD player, digital clock, tachometer, map lights, intermittent wipers, rear defogger, wind deflector, power convertible top, floormats, theft-deterrent system, xenon headlights, 215/45WR17 front tires, 245/40WR17 rear tires, alloy wheels.

Options are available as dealer-installed accessories.

HYUNDAI ACCENT

CLASS: Compact car
DRIVE WHEELS: Front-wheel drive
BASE PRICE RANGE: $9,999-$11,399. Built in South Korea.
ALSO CONSIDER: Ford Focus, Honda Civic, Toyota Corolla

Hyundai's smallest car gets available antilock brakes for 2005. Accent offers GLS and GT models. GLS is offered as a 2-dr hatchback and a 4-dr sedan. The GT is a hatchback. All use a 1.6-liter 4-cyl engine with either manual or automatic transmission. Front side airbags are standard. For '05, ABS is offered in a $1685 option package that also includes air conditioning, power windows and locks, and a CD player. This South Korean automaker's warranty is one of the industry's longest at 5-years/60,000-mi. bumper-to-bumper and 10/100,000 powertrain.

RATINGS	GLS hatch, man.	GLS sdn, auto.
ACCELERATION	3	2
FUEL ECONOMY	7	7
RIDE QUALITY	3	3
STEERING/HANDLING	4	4
QUIETNESS	3	3
CONTROLS/MATERIALS	5	5
ROOM/COMFORT (FRONT)	4	4
ROOM/COMFORT (REAR)	2	2
CARGO ROOM	5	2
VALUE WITHIN CLASS	2	3

Accent makes some sense as a budget-priced commuter car bolstered by a generous warranty. However, most rivals offer better performance and refinement for little more money. And Accent lags most competitors in resale value.

TOTAL	38	35

Average total for compact cars: 48.4

ENGINES	dohc I4
Size, liters/cu. in.	1.6/98
Horsepower @ rpm	104 @ 5800

 Specifications begin on page 547.

ENGINES (cont.)

	dohc I4
Torque (lb-ft) @ rpm	106 @ 3000
Availability	S
EPA city/highway mpg	
5-speed manual	29/33
4-speed automatic	26/35

PRICES

Hyundai Accent	RETAIL PRICE	DEALER INVOICE
GLS 2-door hatchback, manual	$9999	$9499
GLS 2-door hatchback, automatic	10799	10251
GLS 4-door sedan, manual	10499	9869
GLS 4-door sedan, automatic	11299	10621
GT 2-door hatchback, manual	10599	9963
GT 2-door hatchback, automatic	11399	10715
Destination charge	545	545

STANDARD EQUIPMENT

GLS: 1.6-liter 4-cylinder engine, 5-speed manual or 4-speed automatic transmission, dual front airbags, front side airbags, power steering, cloth upholstery, front bucket seats, height-adjustable driver seat, center console, cupholders, split folding rear seat, AM/FM/cassette, digital clock, tachometer, variable-intermittent wipers, rear defogger, rear wiper/washer (hatchback), cargo cover (hatchback), 175/70R13 tires, wheel covers.

GT adds: leather-wrapped steering wheel, fog lights, rear spoiler, sport suspension, 185/60HR14 tires, alloy wheels.

OPTIONAL EQUIPMENT

Major Packages	RETAIL PRICE	DEALER INVOICE
Accessory Group 2 *Air conditioning.*	$795	$748
Accessory Group 3 *Air conditioning, power mirrors, power windows and door locks, AM/FM/CD player.*	1290	1212
Accessory Group 4 *Accessory Group 3 plus antilock brakes.*	1685	1583

Postproduction options also available.

HYUNDAI ELANTRA

CLASS: Compact car
DRIVE WHEELS: Front-wheel drive
BASE PRICE RANGE: $13,299-$15,649. Built in South Korea.
ALSO CONSIDER: Ford Focus, Honda Civic, Toyota Corolla

Hyundai's best-selling car line adds a base-model hatchback for 2005. Elantra comes as a 4-dr sedan or 4-dr hatchback. For '05, GLS and sportier GT trim are offered for both body styles. All Elantras have a 2.0-liter 4-cyl engine and manual or optional automatic transmission. Front side airbags are standard. ABS with traction control is optional. Standard equipment includes air conditioning and power windows/locks/mirrors. GTs add a sport suspension, alloy wheels, and leather upholstery. The new GLS hatchback gets the GT's sport suspension. Hyundai's warranty is among the industry's longest: 5-years/60,000-mi. basic, 10/100,000 powertrain.

RATINGS	GLS, man.	GLS, auto.	GT hatch, man.
ACCELERATION	5	4	5
FUEL ECONOMY	7	7	7
RIDE QUALITY	6	6	5
STEERING/HANDLING	5	5	6
QUIETNESS	5	5	4
CONTROLS/MATERIALS	6	6	6
ROOM/COMFORT (FRONT)	5	5	5
ROOM/COMFORT (REAR)	4	4	4
CARGO ROOM	2	2	6
VALUE WITHIN CLASS	7	7	7

In features, comfort, and even road manners, Elantra is a budget alternative to the class-leading but costlier Honda Civic, Ford Focus, and Mazda 3. However, Elantra still trails top Japanese-brand rivals for resale value.

TOTAL	52	51	55

Average total for compact cars: 48.4

ENGINES	dohc I4
Size, liters/cu. in.	2.0/121
Horsepower @ rpm	138 @ 6000
Torque (lb-ft) @ rpm	136 @ 4500
Availability	S
EPA city/highway mpg	
5-speed manual	27/34
4-speed automatic	24/32

 Specifications begin on page 547.

PRICES

Hyundai Elantra

	RETAIL PRICE	DEALER INVOICE
GLS 4-door sedan, manual	$13299	$12302
GLS 4-door sedan, automatic	14099	13038
GLS 4-door hatchback, manual	13599	12579
GLS 4-door hatchback, automatic	14399	13315
GT 4-door sedan, manual	14849	13735
GT 4-door sedan, automatic	15649	14471
GT 4-door hatchback, manual	14849	13735
GT 4-door hatchback, automatic	15649	14471
Destination charge	545	545

STANDARD EQUIPMENT

GLS: 2.0-liter 4-cylinder engine, 5-speed manual or 4-speed automatic transmission, dual front airbags, front side airbags, 4-wheel disc brakes (hatchback), air conditioning, power steering, tilt steering wheel, cloth upholstery, front bucket seats w/driver-seat height adjustment, center console, cupholders, split folding rear seat, heated power mirrors, power windows, power door locks, remote keyless entry, AM/FM/cassette, digital clock, tachometer, visor mirrors, variable-intermittent wipers, rear defogger, rear wiper/washer (hatchback), map lights, sport suspension (hatchback) 195/60HR15 tires, wheel covers.

GT adds: 4-wheel disc brakes, leather-wrapped steering wheel, cruise control, leather upholstery, AM/FM/CD/MP3 player, trip computer, floormats, fog lights, rear spoiler, sport suspension, alloy wheels.

OPTIONAL EQUIPMENT

Major Packages

	RETAIL PRICE	DEALER INVOICE
Option Pkg. 2, GLS *Cruise control.*	$195	$164
Option Pkg. 3, GLS *Option Pkg. 2 plus AM/FM/CD player.*	545	456
Option Pkg. 4, GLS *Option Pkg. 3 plus traction control, antilock 4-wheel disc brakes.*	1140	1016
Option Pkg. 5, GLS *Power sunroof, cruise control, AM/FM/CD player.*	1295	1109
Option Pkg. 6, GLS *Traction control, antilock 4-wheel disc brakes, cruise control, AM/FM/CD player, power sunroof.*	1890	1669
Option Pkg. 7, GT *Power sunroof.*	750	653
Option Pkg. 8, GT *Traction control, antilock brakes, power sunroof.*	1345	1213

Appearance & Special Purpose

Rear spoiler, GLS	395	269

Postproduction options also available.

2004 HYUNDAI SANTA FE

CLASS: Compact sport-utility vehicle
DRIVE WHEELS: Front-wheel drive, all-wheel drive
BASE PRICE RANGE: $17,999-$25,499. Built in South Korea.
ALSO CONSIDER: Ford Escape, Honda CR-V, Subaru Forester

Hyundai's SUV is unchanged for 2004. The base Santa Fe has a 4-cyl engine and front-wheel drive. The GLS version comes with a 2.7-liter V6. A 3.5 V6 is optional on the GLS and standard on the LX model. V6 models offer front-wheel drive or all-wheel drive without low-range gearing. The 4-cyl comes with manual or automatic transmission, the V6s with automatic only: a 4-speed with the 2.7, a 5-speed with the 3.5. Santa Fe's automatic transmission includes a manual-shift feature. Traction control is standard on the GLS 3.5 and LX, optional on the GLS 2.7. ABS is standard on GLS 3.5 and LX, optional on other models. Front side airbags and 4-wheel disc brakes are standard on all models.

RATINGS	2WD GLS 2.7	AWD GLS 2.7	2WD LX	AWD LX
ACCELERATION	4	3	5	5
FUEL ECONOMY	5	5	4	4
RIDE QUALITY	4	4	4	4
STEERING/HANDLING	4	4	4	4
QUIETNESS	4	4	4	4
CONTROLS/MATERIALS	6	6	6	6
ROOM/COMFORT (FRONT)	6	6	6	6
ROOM/COMFORT (REAR)	5	5	5	5
CARGO ROOM	8	8	8	8
VALUE WITHIN CLASS	4	4	5	5

Santa Fe is underpowered except with the 3.5-liter engine—which we recommend—and all models need more suspension composure. But this high features-per-dollar SUV is no embarrassment to Hyundai. Still, this South Korean automaker has yet to establish a record for long-term reliability, a negative it attempts to overcome with a generous 5-year/60,000-mi. basic warranty and 10/100,000 powertrain coverage.

TOTAL	50	49	51	51

Average total for compact sport-utility vehicles: 49.0

 Specifications begin on page 547.

ENGINES

	dohc I4	dohc V6	dohc V6
Size, liters/cu. in.	2.4/143	2.7/162	3.5/212
Horsepower @ rpm	138 @ 5500	173 @ 6000	200 @ 5500
Torque (lb-ft) @ rpm	147 @ 3000	182 @ 4000	219 @ 3500
Availability	S[1]	S[2]	S[3]
EPA city/highway mpg			
5-speed manual	20/27		
4-speed automatic	20/27	18/24[4]	
5-speed automatic			17/21[5]

1. GL. 2. GLS 2.7. 3. GLS 3.5, LX. 4. 20/26 w/2WD. 5. 16/22 w/2WD.

PRICES

Hyundai Santa Fe	RETAIL PRICE	DEALER INVOICE
2WD Base 4-door wagon, manual	$17999	$16847
2WD Base 4-door wagon, automatic	18799	17596
2WD GLS 2.7 4-door wagon, automatic	20999	19611
AWD GLS 2.7 4-door wagon, automatic	22499	21012
2WD GLS 3.5 4-door wagon, automatic	21999	20545
AWD GLS 3.5 4-door wagon, automatic	23499	21946
2WD LX 4-door wagon, automatic	23999	22388
AWD LX 4-door wagon, automatic	25499	23788
Destination charge	590	590

STANDARD EQUIPMENT

Base: 2.4-liter 4-cylinder engine, 5-speed manual or 4-speed automatic transmission w/manual-shift capability, dual front airbags, front side airbags, 4-wheel disc brakes, air conditioning, power steering, tilt steering wheel, cloth upholstery, front bucket seats, driver-seat height adjustment, center console, cupholders, split folding rear seat, heated power mirrors, power windows, power door locks, AM/FM/CD player, digital clock, tachometer, variable-intermittent wipers, visor mirrors, map lights, rear defogger, remote fuel-door release, roof rails, full-size spare wheel, 225/70R16 tires, alloy wheels.

GLS 2.7 adds: 2.7-liter V6 engine, 4-speed automatic transmission w/manual-shift capability, leather-wrapped steering wheel, cruise control, remote keyless entry, Monsoon AM/FM/cassette/CD player, illuminated visor mirrors, rear wiper/washer, cargo cover, floormats, theft-deterrent system, fog lights. **AWD** adds: all-wheel drive.

GLS 3.5 adds: 3.5-liter V6 engine, 5-speed automatic transmission w/manual-shift capability, traction control, antilock 4-wheel disc brakes. **AWD** adds: all-wheel drive.

LX adds: automatic climate control, leather upholstery, heated front seats, AM/FM radio w/in-dash 6-disc CD changer, automatic day/night rearview mirror, universal garage-door opener. **AWD** adds: all-wheel drive.

OPTIONAL EQUIPMENT

Major Packages

	RETAIL PRICE	DEALER INVOICE
Option Pkg. 2, Base	$495	$464
Cruise control, remote keyless entry, rear wiper/washer, cargo cover and net, theft-deterrent system, first-aid kit.		
Option Pkg. 3, Base	990	928
Option Pkg. 2 plus antilock brakes.		
Option Pkg. 4, GLS 2.7	595	557
Traction control, antilock brakes.		
Option Pkg. 5, GLS, LX	595	526
Power sunroof.		
Option Pkg. 6, GLS 2.7	1190	1083
Traction control, antilock brakes, power sunroof.		
Option Pkg. 7, GLS	395	370
Monsoon AM/FM radio w/in-dash 6-disc CD changer.		
Option Pkg. 8, GLS 2.7	990	927
Traction control, antilock brakes, Monsoon AM/FM radio w/in-dash 6-disc CD changer.		
Option Pkg. 9, GLS	990	896
Power sunroof, Monsoon AM/FM radio w/in-dash 6-disc CD changer.		
Option Pkg. 10, GLS 2.7	1585	1453
Traction control, antilock brakes, power sunroof, Monsoon AM/FM radio w/in-dash 6-disc CD changer.		

Appearance & Special Purpose

	RETAIL PRICE	DEALER INVOICE
Running boards	495	440
Roof rack	180	110
Tow hitch, GLS, LX	350	260

Postproduction options also available.

HYUNDAI SONATA

CLASS: Midsize car
DRIVE WHEELS: Front-wheel drive
BASE PRICE RANGE: $15,999-$19,799. Built in South Korea.
ALSO CONSIDER: Chevrolet Malibu, Mazda 6, Nissan Altima

Heated front seats are newly available for Hyundai's midsize sedan. Sonata continues in GL, GLS, and LX trim and, for 2005, adds a GLS Special Value version that is the only model with heated front seats. GL models have a 138-hp 4-cly engine and a manual transmission or an automatic with manual shift gate. GL V6, GLS, and LX models have a 170-hp V6 and the automatic. Front side airbags are standard. All models have 4-wheel disc brakes. ABS is optional. Traction control is available on GLS versions and the LX. Also for '05, a universal garage-door opener is new and included on the GLS Special Value and LX. This South Korean automaker's basic warranty is among the industry's longest: 5-years/60,000-mi. bumper-to-bumper, 10/100,000 powertrain. Sonata shares its mechanical components with the Kia Optima.

RATINGS

	GL 4-cyl, man.	GLS, auto.
ACCELERATION	4	5
FUEL ECONOMY	6	6
RIDE QUALITY	7	7
STEERING/HANDLING	5	6
QUIETNESS	5	6
CONTROLS/MATERIALS	6	7
ROOM/COMFORT (FRONT)	7	7
ROOM/COMFORT (REAR)	4	4
CARGO ROOM	5	5
VALUE WITHIN CLASS	7	7

For equipment and comfort, Sonata and Optima are impressive values, with generous warranties to boot. They earn Recommended status as bargain-priced alternatives to the Toyota Camry, though resale values trail those of top Japanese competitors.

TOTAL	56	60
Average total for midsize cars: 57.2		

ENGINES

	dohc I4	dohc V6
Size, liters/cu. in.	2.4/146	2.7/162
Horsepower @ rpm	138 @ 5500	170 @ 6000
Torque (lb-ft) @ rpm	147 @ 3000	181 @ 4000
Availability	S[1]	S[2]
EPA city/highway mpg		
5-speed manual	22/30	
4-speed automatic	22/30	19/27

1. GL. 2. GLS, GLS Special Value, LX.

PRICES

Hyundai Sonata

	RETAIL PRICE	DEALER INVOICE
GL 4-cylinder 4-door sedan, manual	$15999	$14719
GL 4-cylinder 4-door sedan, automatic	16799	15471
GL V6 4-door sedan, automatic	17649	16237
GLS 4-door sedan, automatic	18799	17201
GLS Special Value 4-door sedan, automatic	18799	17201
LX 4-door sedan, automatic	19799	18017
Destination charge	595	595

STANDARD EQUIPMENT

GL 4-cylinder/V6: 2.4-liter 4-cylinder engine or 2.7-liter V6 engine, 5-speed manual or 4-speed automatic transmission w/manual-shift capability, dual front airbags, front side airbags, 4-wheel disc brakes, air conditioning, power steering, tilt steering wheel, leather-wrapped steering wheel (automatic), cruise control, cloth upholstery, front bucket seats w/driver-seat height and lumbar adjustment, center console, cupholders, split folding rear seat, power mirrors, power windows, power door locks, remote keyless entry, AM/FM/CD player, digital clock, tachometer, driver-side illuminated visor mirror, variable-intermittent wipers, rear defogger, floormats (V6), theft-deterrent system, fog lights, 205/65R15 tires, wheel covers.

GLS adds: 2.7-liter V6 engine, leather-wrapped steering wheel, heated power mirrors, AM/FM/cassette/CD player, power antenna, illuminated visor mirrors, map lights, floormats, 205/60HR16 tires, alloy wheels.

GLS Special Value adds: automatic climate control, heated front seats, automatic day/night rearview mirror, universal garage-door opener.

LX adds: leather upholstery, 8-way power driver seat. *Deletes:* heated front seats.

OPTIONAL EQUIPMENT

Major Packages

	RETAIL PRICE	DEALER INVOICE
Accessory Group 2, GL 4-cylinder manual, GLS, GLS Special Value, LX	$595	$571
Antilock brakes.		
Accessory Group 3	750	645
Power sunroof. NA GL 4-cylinder w/manual transmission.		
Accessory Group 4, GL 4-cylinder automatic, GL V6	1345	1216
Antilock brakes, power sunroof.		
Accessory Group 5, GLS, GLS Special Value, LX	1445	1299
Traction control, antilock brakes, power sunroof.		

Postproduction options also available.

2004 HYUNDAI TIBURON

CLASS: Sporty/performance car
DRIVE WHEELS: Front-wheel drive
BASE PRICE RANGE: $16,999-$20,497. Built in South Korea.
ALSO CONSIDER: Acura RSX, Mini Cooper, Scion tC

Hyundai's sporty hatchback coupe added a third trim level during the 2004 model year. Base and GT V6 models were joined by the GT Special Edition. Base Tiburons have a 2.0-liter 4-cyl engine. GTs get a 2.7-liter V6. A 5-speed manual transmission is standard and 4-speed automatic with manual shift gate is optional on base and GT V6 models. A 6-speed manual is standard on the GT Special Edition, optional on the GT V6. Base models use 16-inch wheels, GTs have 17s. All have standard 4-wheel disc brakes and front side airbags. ABS is standard on the GT Special Edition, optional on base and GT V6. Traction control is unavailable. The GT V6 offers optional leather upholstery. Hyundai's warranty is among the industry's longest: 5-years/60,000-mi. bumper-to-bumper, 10/100,000 powertrain.

RATINGS

	GT V6, 6-sp man.	GT V6, auto.
ACCELERATION	6	5
FUEL ECONOMY	5	5
RIDE QUALITY	3	3
STEERING/HANDLING	7	7
QUIETNESS	3	3
CONTROLS/MATERIALS	5	5
ROOM/COMFORT (FRONT)	4	4
ROOM/COMFORT (REAR)	1	1
CARGO ROOM	4	4
VALUE WITHIN CLASS	5	4

It's not that quick, refined, or practical, and depreciation is historically steep. But the Tiburon is a credible effort and fun to drive. Backed by a long warranty, and with a fully equipped GT V6 listing for around $20,000, it's a tempting choice for the budget-conscious sporty-compact crowd.

TOTAL	43	41

Average total for sporty/performance cars: 48.5

ENGINES

	dohc I4	dohc V6
Size, liters/cu. in.	2.0/121	2.7/162
Horsepower @ rpm	138 @ 6000	172 @ 6000
Torque (lb-ft) @ rpm	136 @ 4500	181 @ 4000
Availability	S[1]	S[2]
EPA city/highway mpg		
5-speed manual	24/30	19/26
6-speed manual		18/26
4-speed automatic	23/29	20/26

1. Base. 2. GT models.

PRICES

Hyundai Tiburon	RETAIL PRICE	DEALER INVOICE
Base 2-door hatchback, manual	$16999	$15469
Base 2-door hatchback, automatic	17899	16311
GT V6 2-door hatchback, 5-speed manual	18199	16561
GT V6 2-door hatchback, 6-speed manual	19149	17447

 Prices accurate at publication.

PRICES (cont.)

	RETAIL PRICE	DEALER INVOICE
GT V6 2-door hatchback, automatic	$19099	$17403
GT Special Edition 2-door hatchback, manual	20497	18699
GT Special Edition 2-door hatchback, automatic	20447	18652
Destination charge	540	540

GT V6 6-speed manual requires an Option Pkg.

STANDARD EQUIPMENT

Base: 2.0-liter 4-cylinder engine, 5-speed manual or 4-speed automatic transmission w/manual-shift capability, dual front airbags, front side airbags, 4-wheel disc brakes, air conditioning, power steering, tilt steering wheel, cruise control, cloth upholstery, front bucket seats, center console, cupholders, split folding rear seat, heated power mirrors, power windows, power door locks, remote keyless entry, AM/FM/CD player, digital clock, tachometer, rear defogger, visor mirrors, variable-intermittent wipers, map lights, remote fuel-door and decklid release, intermittent rear wiper/washer, floormats, theft-deterrent system, fog lights, rear spoiler, 205/55R16 tires, alloy wheels.

GT V6 adds: 2.7-liter V6 engine, 5-speed manual; 6-speed manual; or 4-speed automatic transmission w/manual-shift capability, aluminum pedals (6-speed), 215/45R17 tires.

GT Special Edition adds: 6-speed manual or 4-speed automatic transmission w/manual-shift capability, antilock 4-wheel disc brakes, power sunroof, Kenwood AM/FM/CD/MP3 player, rear wiper/washer, floormats.

OPTIONAL EQUIPMENT

Major Packages

	RETAIL PRICE	DEALER INVOICE
Option Pkg. 2, Base *Infinity AM/FM/cassette/CD player.*	$649	$574
Option Pkg. 3 *Power sunroof, Infinity AM/FM/cassette/CD player. NA GT 6-speed manual transmission, GT Special Edition.*	1349	1193
Option Pkg. 4, GT V6 *Option Pkg. 3 plus leather upholstery, leather-wrapped steering wheel and shift knob. NA GT 6-speed manual transmission.*	1949	1755
Option Pkg. 5, GT V6 *Option Pkg. 4 plus antilock brakes. NA GT 6-speed manual transmission.*	2448	2222
Option Pkg. 10, GT V6 6-speed manual *Infinity AM/FM/cassette/CD player, leather upholstery, leather-wrapped steering wheel and shift knob.*	1249	1136
Option Pkg. 11, GT V6 6-speed manual *Option Pkg. 10 plus antilock brakes, power sunroof.*	2448	2222

HYUNDAI TUCSON

CLASS: Compact sport-utility vehicle
DRIVE WHEELS: Front-wheel drive, all-wheel drive
BASE PRICE RANGE: $17,499-$22,749. Built in South Korea.
ALSO CONSIDER: Ford Escape, Honda CR-V, Subaru Forester

Hyundai unveils a new compact SUV for 2005. Tucson is built on a car-type platform similar to that used on Hyundai's larger, more-expensive Santa Fe SUV. Tucson offers 4- or 6-cyl engines and a choice of front- or all-wheel-drive. GL , GLS, and LX models are available. GLs come with a 140-hp 4-cyl with a 5-speed manual or 4-speed automatic transmissioon. GLSs and LXs come with a 173-hp V6 with automatic transmission only. All are available with front-wheel drive or AWD that lacks low-range gearing but has a driver switch that locks in a 50/50 front/rear torque split. ABS and traction control are standard on all models. So are front side airbags and head-protecting curtain side airbags. Leather upholstery and heated front seats are exclusive to LX models. A sunroof is available on GLS and LX. This evaluation is based on preview test drives.

RATINGS	2WD GLS	AWD GLS w/sunroof
ACCELERATION	3	3
FUEL ECONOMY	5	5
RIDE QUALITY	5	5
STEERING/HANDLING	4	4
QUIETNESS	3	3
CONTROLS/MATERIALS	6	6
ROOM/COMFORT (FRONT)	0	0
ROOM/COMFORT (REAR)	0	0
CARGO ROOM	0	0
VALUE WITHIN CLASS	0	0

An impressive list of standard equipment and attractive sticker prices are Tucson's draw.

TOTAL	26	26

Average total for compact sport-utility vehicles: 49.0

ENGINES

	dohc I4	dohc V6
Size, liters/cu. in.	2.0/120.5	2.7/162
Horsepower @ rpm	140 @ 6000	173 @ 6000
Torque (lb-ft) @ rpm	136 @ 4500	178 @ 4000
Availability	S[1]	S[2]
EPA city/highway mpg		
5-speed manual	21/26[1]	
4-speed automatic	22/27	19/24[2]

1. 22/27 w/2WD. 2. 20/26 w/2WD.

PRICES

Hyundai Tucson

	RETAIL PRICE	DEALER INVOICE
2WD GL 4-door wagon, manual	$17499	$16449
2WD GL 4-door wagon, automatic	18299	17201
AWD GL 4-door wagon, manual	18999	17859
2WD GLS 4-door wagon, automatic	19999	18759
AWD GLS 4-door wagon, automatic	21499	20166
2WD LX 4-door wagon, automatic	21249	19910
AWD LX 4-door wagon, automatic	22749	21316
Destination charge	595	595

STANDARD EQUIPMENT

GL: 2.0-liter 4-cylinder engine, 5-speed manual or 4-speed automatic transmission w/manual-shift capability, traction control, dual front airbags, front side airbags, curtain side airbags, antilock 4-wheel disc brakes, antiskid system, air conditioning, power steering, tilt steering wheel, cruise control, cloth upholstery, front bucket seats, center console, cupholders, split folding rear seat, heated power mirrors, power windows, power door locks, remote keyless entry, AM/FM/CD player, digital clock, tachometer, intermittent wipers, visor mirrors, map lights, cargo cover, rear defogger, rear wiper/washer, floormats, theft-deterrent system, rear privacy glass, roof rails, skid plates, 215/65R16 tires, alloy wheels. **AWD** adds: all-wheel drive.

GLS adds: 2.7-liter V6 engine, 4-speed automatic transmission w/manual-shift capability, height-adjustable driver seat, leather-wrapped steering wheel, AM/FM/cassette/CD/MP3 player, windshield wiper deicer, fog lights, 235/60R16 tires. **AWD** adds: all-wheel drive.

LX adds: leather upholstery, heated front seats, AM/FM/cassette w/in-dash 6-disc CD changer. **AWD** adds: all-wheel drive.

OPTIONAL EQUIPMENT

Major Packages

	RETAIL PRICE	DEALER INVOICE
Accessory Group 3, GLS, LX *Power sunroof.*	$750	$668
Accessory Group 4, GLS *Power sunroof, AM/FM/cassette w/in-dash 6-disc CD changer.*	1145	1020

 Specifications begin on page 547.

2004 HYUNDAI XG350

CLASS: Midsize car
DRIVE WHEELS: Front-wheel drive
BASE PRICE RANGE: $23,999-$25,599. Built in South Korea.
ALSO CONSIDER: Honda Accord, Nissan Altima, Toyota Camry

Hyundai's flagship sedan gets a mild facelift for 2004. The front-wheel-drive XG350 has a 3.5-liter V6 and a 5-speed automatic transmission with manual shift gate. Standard equipment includes front side airbags, antilock 4-wheel disc brakes, traction control, and leather upholstery. Exclusive to the L model are a sunroof and heated front seats with seat/mirror memory. Changes for '04 include revised front and rear styling and lighter-tone woodgrain interior trim. Hyundai's basic warranty is among the industry's longest: 5-years/60,000-mi. bumper-to-bumper, 10/100,000 powertrain.

RATINGS

	XG350L
ACCELERATION	5
FUEL ECONOMY	4
RIDE QUALITY	7
STEERING/HANDLING	6
QUIETNESS	7
CONTROLS/MATERIALS	7
ROOM/COMFORT (FRONT)	6
ROOM/COMFORT (REAR)	5
CARGO ROOM	4
VALUE WITHIN CLASS	5

The XG350 delivers perfectly adequate performance, comfort-oriented road manners, and good interior room. Yet it's not as solidly built as the leading midsize cars, specifically the Toyota Camry and Honda Accord, or as sporty as the Nissan Altima. Its real lure is a long warranty and lots of features for the money. Balancing that is XG350's unproven track record and lower resale value.

TOTAL	56

Average total for midsize cars: 57.2

ENGINES

	dohc V6
Size, liters/cu. in.	3.5/212
Horsepower @ rpm	194 @ 5500
Torque (lb-ft) @ rpm	216 @ 3500
Availability	S
EPA city/highway mpg	
5-speed automatic	17/26

PRICES

Hyundai XG350	RETAIL PRICE	DEALER INVOICE
Base 4-door sedan	$23999	$21465
L 4-door sedan	25599	22896
Destination charge	590	590

STANDARD EQUIPMENT

Base: 3.5-liter V6 engine, 5-speed automatic transmission w/manual-shift capability, traction control, dual front airbags, front side airbags, antilock 4-wheel disc brakes, air conditioning w/automatic climate control, power steering, tilt leather-wrapped steering wheel, cruise control, leather upholstery, front bucket seats, 8-way power driver seat, 4-way power passenger seat, center console, cupholders, split folding rear seat, heated power mirrors, power windows, power door locks, remote keyless entry, AM/FM/cassette/CD player, digital clock, tachometer, trip computer, automatic day/night rearview mirror, universal garage-door opener, illuminated visor mirrors, map lights, variable-intermittent wipers, rear defogger, remote fuel-door/decklid release, automatic headlights, theft-deterrent system, fog lights, full-size spare tire, 205/60HR16 tires, alloy wheels.

L adds: power sunroof, heated front seats, driver-seat and mirror memory, passenger-side tilt-down back-up-aid mirror, wood/leather-wrapped steering wheel.

OPTIONAL EQUIPMENT	RETAIL PRICE	DEALER INVOICE
Option Pkg. 2	$500	$447
8-disc CD changer.		

Postproduction options also available.

INFINITI FX

CLASS: Premium midsize sport-utility vehicle
DRIVE WHEELS: Rear-wheel drive, all-wheel drive
2004 BASE PRICE RANGE: $34,350-$44,375. Built in Japan.
ALSO CONSIDER: Acura MDX, Cadillac SRX, Lexus RX

Additional safety equipment tops the list of 2005 changes to Infiniti's crossover SUV. FX is a 5-seat wagon derived from Infiniti's G35 sedan. Two models are offered. The FX35 has a 280-hp V6 and rear-wheel drive or

all-wheel drive. The FX45 has a 315-hp V8 and AWD. Both have a 5-speed automatic transmission with manual shift gate. FX's AWD lacks low-range gearing and is not intended for off-roading. ABS, antiskid/traction control, front torso side airbags, head-protecting curtain side airbags, and xenon headlamps are standard. For '05 the curtain side airbags are designed to deploy if the system detects an impending rollover. Also new for 2005 is Nissan's Lane Departure Warning system that alerts the driver to unintentional movement from a designated traffic lane. FX35 comes with 18-inch wheels. A sport suspension with 20-inch wheels is standard for FX45, optional for FX35. Same goes for leather upholstery, heated front seats, power tilt/telescope steering wheel, and driver-seat memory. Rear DVD entertainment, sunroof, and roof rails are optional. So is a Technology Package with a navigation system, adaptive cruise control designed to maintain a set following distance, rearview camera, and tire-pressure monitor. The package also includes an "intelligent key" system that allows the driver to unlock the vehicle by pressing buttons on the doors and to start it without inserting the key into the ignition.

RATINGS	**AWD FX35**	**AWD FX35 w/Sport Pkg.**	**FX45 w/Tech Pkg.**
ACCELERATION	6	6	7
FUEL ECONOMY	4	4	3
RIDE QUALITY	4	3	3
STEERING/HANDLING	7	7	7
QUIETNESS	6	6	6
CONTROLS/MATERIALS	7	7	6
ROOM/COMFORT (FRONT)	8	8	8
ROOM/COMFORT (REAR)	7	7	7
CARGO ROOM	6	6	6
VALUE WITHIN CLASS	7	6	5

FX emphasizes sport over utility, probably too much so for some buyers. But otherworldly styling along with sporty road manners help it stand out among premium midsize SUVs. Infiniti's strong warranty and kid-gloves customer care are noteworthy, too.

TOTAL	**62**	**60**	**58**

Average total for premium midsize sport-utility vehicles: 59.6

ENGINES

	dohc V6	dohc V8
Size, liters/cu. in.	3.5/214	4.5/274
Horsepower @ rpm	280 @ 6200	315 @ 6400
Torque (lb-ft) @ rpm	270 @ 4800	329 @ 4000
Availability	S[1]	S[2]
EPA city/highway mpg		
5-speed automatic	16/22[3]	15/19

1. FX35. 2. FX45. 3. 17/23 w/2WD.

2005 prices unavailable at time of publication.

2004 PRICES

Infiniti FX	RETAIL PRICE	DEALER INVOICE
2WD FX35 4-door wagon	$34350	$31098
AWD FX35 4-door wagon	35850	32452
AWD FX45 4-door wagon	44375	40144
Destination charge	590	590

STANDARD EQUIPMENT

FX35: 3.5-liter V6 engine, 5-speed automatic transmission w/manual-shift capability, traction control, dual front airbags, front side airbags, curtain side airbags, front and rear active head restraints, antilock 4-wheel disc brakes, brake assist, antiskid system, air conditioning w/dual-zone climate controls, power steering, tilt/telescope leather-wrapped steering wheel, cruise control, cloth upholstery, 8-way power front bucket seats, center console, cupholders, split folding rear seat, power mirrors, power windows, power door locks, remote keyless entry, power rear liftgate, AM/FM/cassette w/in-dash 6-disc CD changer, analog clock, tachometer, trip computer, variable-intermittent wipers, automatic day/night rearview mirror, compass, illuminated visor mirrors, rear defogger, map lights, intermittent rear wiper, theft-deterrent system, rear privacy glass, rear spoiler, xenon headlights, 265/60VR18 tires, alloy wheels. **AWD** adds: all-wheel drive.

FX45 adds: 4.5-liter V8 engine, all-wheel drive, leather upholstery, heated front seats w/power lumbar adjustment, memory system (driver seat, mirrors, steering wheel), power tilt/telescope steering wheel, heated power mirrors, sport suspension, 265/50VR20 tires.

OPTIONAL EQUIPMENT

Major Packages	RETAIL PRICE	DEALER INVOICE
Touring Pkg., FX35	$2900	$2499
Leather upholstery, heated front seats, power tilt/telescope steering wheel, memory system (driver seat, mirrors, steering wheel), heated power mirrors, power sunroof, Bose sound system, universal garage-door opener, cargo net, automatic headlights, black roof rails.		
Premium Pkg., FX45	2500	2155
Power sunroof, Bose sound system, universal garage-door opener, cargo net, automatic headlights, polished alloy roof rails.		

 Specifications begin on page 547.

Major Packages

	RETAIL PRICE	DEALER INVOICE
Sport Pkg., FX35	$1500	$1293
Aluminum pedals, polished alloy roof rails, sport suspension, 265/50VR20 tires. Requires Touring Pkg.		
Technology Pkg.	4300	3705
Navigation system, rearview camera, adaptive cruise control, intelligent key unlocking and starting, tire-pressure monitor. FX35 requires Touring Pkg. FX45 requires Premium Pkg.		

Comfort & Convenience Features

Rear-seat DVD entertainment system	1600	1379
FX35 requires Touring Pkg., Sport Pkg., and Technology Pkg. FX45 requires Premium Pkg. and Technology Pkg.		
Satellite radio	400	345
Requires monthly fee. Includes 2 months of free service.		

Appearance & Special Purpose

Trailer hitch, AWD	600	506
Chrome alloy wheels	1600	840
FX35 requires Touring Pkg., Sport Pkg. FX45 requires Premium Pkg.		

INFINITI G35

CLASS: Premium midsize car
DRIVE WHEELS: Rear-wheel drive, all-wheel drive
2004 BASE PRICE RANGE: $27,950-$32,450. Built in Japan.
ALSO CONSIDER: Acura TL, BMW 3-Series, Cadillac CTS

More power and revised styling mark 2005 for Infiniti's least-expensive models. With automatic transmission, sedans gain 20 hp for '05, sharing the coupe's 280-hp V6. Manual-transmission models now have 298 hp, a gain of 18 for coupes, 38 for sedans. Both carry base and Leather model designations and come with rear-wheel drive. The AWD Leather sedan has all-wheel drive with Snow Mode that allows the driver to lock in a 50/50 front/rear torque split. Rear-drive G35s are available with a 6-speed manual transmission or 5-speed automatic with manual shift gate. AWD comes only with the automatic. Standard on all are antilock 4-wheel disc brakes, front side airbags, and head-protecting curtain side airbags; the coupe's curtain bags cover only the front seats. All sedans have standard 17-inch wheels. The Leather sedan includes such features as leather upholstery, Sport Tuned Suspension on cars equipped with manual transmission, and heated front seats. Manual-transmission sedans get a limited-slip differential. Leather sedans can be upgraded with wood interior trim, sunroof, and reclining rear seatbacks. The coupe's suspension is equivalent to the sedan's sport setup. Compared to automatic-transmission coupes, manual coupes have upgraded brakes and 18-inch wheels vs. 17s; the 18s are optional on automatics. Leather models are available with a navigation system and satellite radio. All but the base sedan have xenon headlamps. All G35s have a standard tire-pressure monitor.

RATINGS	Base sdn	Lthr. sdn w/Sport Susp., auto.	AWD Lthr. sdn w/Prem. Pkg.	Lthr. cpe, man.
ACCELERATION	7	7	7	8
FUEL ECONOMY	4	4	4	4
RIDE QUALITY	7	5	7	3
STEERING/HANDLING	7	8	7	8
QUIETNESS	7	6	7	3
CONTROLS/MATERIALS	7	7	7	7
ROOM/COMFORT (FRONT)	8	8	8	6
ROOM/COMFORT (REAR)	6	6	6	3
CARGO ROOM	4	4	4	2
VALUE WITHIN CLASS	8	7	8	5

Infiniti isn't as prestigious a brand as BMW, Lexus, or Mercedes, and doesn't quite match them or Audi for refinement or interior materials. But in performance, style, space, and available all-wheel drive, we recommend the G35 as a credible and less-expensive alternative to rival models from those automakers.

TOTAL	65	62	65	49

Average total for premium midsize cars: 61.7

ENGINES	dohc V6	dohc V6
Size, liters/cu. in.	3.5/214	3.5/214
Horsepower @ rpm	280 @ 6200	298 @ 6400
Torque (lb-ft) @ rpm	270 @ 4800	260 @ 4800
Availability	S[1]	S[2]
EPA city/highway mpg		
6-speed manual		NA
5-speed automatic	17/24	

1. Automatic-transmission models. 2. Manual-transmission models.

2005 prices unavailable at time of publication.

2004 PRICES

Infiniti G35	RETAIL PRICE	DEALER INVOICE
RWD Base 4-door sedan, automatic	$27950	$25607
RWD Leather 4-door sedan, manual	29850	27037
RWD Leather 4-door sedan, automatic	30100	27263

PRICES (cont.)

	RETAIL PRICE	DEALER INVOICE
AWD Leather 4-door sedan, automatic	$31900	$28887
RWD Base 2-door coupe, automatic	29250	26794
RWD Leather 2-door coupe, automatic	31550	28571
RWD Leather 2-door coupe, manual	32450	29384
Destination charge	590	590

STANDARD EQUIPMENT

Base sedan: 3.5-liter V6 260-horsepower engine, 5-speed automatic transmission w/manual-shift capability, traction control, dual front airbags, front side airbags, curtain side airbags, front-seat active head restraints, antilock 4-wheel disc brakes, brake assist, antiskid system, tire-pressure monitor, emergency inside trunk release, air conditioning w/automatic climate control, interior air filter, power steering, tilt leather-wrapped steering wheel, cruise control, cloth upholstery, front bucket seats, driver-seat lumbar adjustment, center console, cupholders, trunk pass-through, heated power mirrors, power windows, power door locks, remote keyless entry, AM/FM/cassette w/in-dash 6-disc CD changer, analog clock, tachometer, outside-temperature indicator, compass, visor mirrors, map lights, variable-intermittent wipers, rear defogger, remote decklid release, floormats, theft-deterrent system, 215/55VR17 tires, alloy wheels.

Leather sedan adds: leather upholstery, heated front seats, 8-way power driver seat, 4-way power passenger seat, steering-wheel radio controls, illuminated visor mirrors, xenon headlights. **AWD** adds: all-wheel drive.

Leather sedan w/manual transmission adds: 6-speed manual transmission, limited-slip differential, sport suspension, 215/55WR17 tires.

Base coupe adds to Base sedan: 3.5-liter V6 280-horsepower engine, front curtain side airbags, 6-way power driver seat, 2-way power passenger seat, folding rear seat, heated power mirrors, xenon headlights, sport suspension, 225/50VR17 front tires, 235/50VR17 rear tires. *Deletes:* rear curtain side airbags, trunk pass-through.

Leather coupe adds: leather upholstery, heated front seats, illuminated visor mirrors.

Leather coupe w/manual transmission adds: 6-speed manual transmission, limited-slip differential, upgraded brakes, 225/45WR18 front tires, 245/45WR18 rear tires.

OPTIONAL EQUIPMENT

Major Packages

	RETAIL PRICE	DEALER INVOICE
Premium Pkg., Leather sedan	$3200	$2757

Power sunroof, driver-seat memory, power passenger seat, reclining rear seats, dual-zone climate controls, rear vents, Bose sound system, automatic day/night rearview mirror, universal garage-door opener, all-window one-touch up/down, automatic headlights, full-size spare tire.

Premium Pkg., Leather coupe	2250	1939

Power sunroof, driver-seat memory, dual-zone climate controls, Bose sound system, automatic day/night rearview mirror, universal garage-door opener. NA Base coupe.

Major Packages

	RETAIL PRICE	DEALER INVOICE
Sport Tuned Suspension Pkg., 2WD Leather sedan	$425	$366
Additional titanium-tinted interior trim, sport suspension, 215/55WR17 tires.		
Performance Tire and Wheel Pkg., Coupe automatic	900	776
Additional titanium-tinted interior trim, limited-slip differential, 225/45WR18 front tires, 245/45WR18 rear tires, titanium-tinted alloy wheels. NA Base coupe.		
Aero Pkg.	550	471
Rear spoiler, underbody aerodynamic side fairings. Leather sedan requires power sunroof. Leather coupe requires Sport Tuned Suspension Pkg. NA Base.		

Comfort & Convenience Features

Navigation system	2000	1805
Includes trip computer. Requires Premium Pkg. NA Base.		
Power sunroof	1000	862
NA Base.		
Bose sound system	900	776
NA Base.		
Satellite radio	400	345
Requires monthly fee. NA Base.		
Wood Pkg., Leather sedan automatic	250	216
Wood interior trim, wood/leather shift knob. Requires Premium Pkg. NA w/Sport Tuned Suspension Pkg.		

Appearance & Special Purpose

Chrome alloy wheels, 2WD Leather sedan	1600	1138

INFINITI Q45

CLASS: Premium large car
DRIVE WHEELS: Rear-wheel drive
2004 BASE PRICE RANGE: \$52,400-\$61,600. Built in Japan.
ALSO CONSIDER: Lexus LS 430, Mercedes-Benz E-Class

The flagship of Nissan's luxury brand gets a mild facelift and some equipment revisions for 2005. The Q45 has a 340-hp V8 and a 5-speed automatic transmission with manual shift gate. Recalibrations to the transmission for '05 are intended to improve response and smoothness. ABS and antiskid/traction control are standard, as are front side airbags and head-protecting curtain side airbags. A dashboard screen shows audio, climate, and trip-computer functions; it also serves as the display for the available navigation system and, when the transmission is in Reverse, a rearview camera. Q45 has voice control for audio, climate, and navigation functions. Luxury and uplevel Premium models are offered. The adjustable suspension previously exclusive to the Premium is also standard on the Luxury for '05. The Luxury model has 17-inch wheels, the Premium 18s. The Premium comes with heated and cooled front seats and reclining heated rear seats. And it includes the navigation system and radar cruise control designed to maintain a set following distance from other traffic. A Journey option for the Luxury adds the radar cruise control, navigation system, and run-flat tires. Satellite radio is optional for both models.

RATINGS

	Luxury	Premium
ACCELERATION	7	7
FUEL ECONOMY	4	4
RIDE QUALITY	8	8
STEERING/HANDLING	8	8
QUIETNESS	9	8
CONTROLS/MATERIALS	8	7
ROOM/COMFORT (FRONT)	8	8
ROOM/COMFORT (REAR)	7	8
CARGO ROOM	3	3
VALUE WITHIN CLASS	5	5

Slow sales are evidence that Q45 tends to be overlooked among premium large cars. It's competitive with the class leaders in terms of power, features, and build quality. But it can't quite stay with them for unqualified comfort and control on the road. And Infiniti, despite an enviable record of reliability and customer service, trails BMW, Mercedes, and Lexus in the prestige sweepstakes.

	Luxury	Premium
TOTAL	67	66

Average total for premium large cars: 68.7

ENGINES

	dohc V8
Size, liters/cu. in.	4.5/274
Horsepower @ rpm	340 @ 6400
Torque (lb-ft) @ rpm	333 @ 4000
Availability	S
EPA city/highway mpg	
5-speed automatic	17/23

2005 prices unavailable at time of publication.

2004 PRICES

Infiniti Q45	RETAIL PRICE	DEALER INVOICE
Luxury 4-door sedan	$52400	$47386
Premium 4-door sedan	61600	55688
Destination charge	590	590

STANDARD EQUIPMENT

Luxury: 4.5-liter V8 engine, 5-speed automatic transmission w/manual-shift capability, traction control, dual front airbags, front side airbags, curtain side airbags, front-seat active head restraints, antilock 4-wheel brakes, brake assist, antiskid system, tire-pressure monitor, emergency inside trunk release, air conditioning w/dual-zone automatic climate controls, interior air filter, power steering, power tilt/telescope wood/leather-wrapped steering wheel w/radio controls, cruise control, leather upholstery, heated front bucket seats, 10-way power driver seat w/power lumbar adjustment, 8-way power passenger seat, center console, cupholders, memory system (driver seat, mirrors, steering wheel), wood interior trim, heated power mirrors w/turn signals, driver-side automatic day/night and passenger-side tilt-down back-up-aid mirrors, power windows, power door locks, remote keyless entry, power sunroof, Bose AM/FM w/in-dash 6-disc CD changer, analog clock, tachometer, rearview monitor, trip computer, outside-temperature indicator, voice-recognition system for radio and climate controls, rear defogger, automatic day/night rearview mirror, compass, universal garage-door opener, illuminated visor mirrors, map lights, variable-intermittent wipers, power decklid closer, automatic headlights, floormats, theft-deterrent system, xenon headlights, 225/55VR17 tires, full-size spare tire, alloy wheels.

Premium adds: intelligent cruise control, navigation system, climate-controlled front seats, heated and power-reclining rear seats, rear climate and radio controls, power rear sunshade, manual rear side sunshades, power decklid opener and closer, computer-controlled and driver-adjustable rear suspension, 245/45VR18 tires.

OPTIONAL EQUIPMENT

Major Packages	RETAIL PRICE	DEALER INVOICE
Journey Pkg., Luxury	$3600	$3102
Intelligent cruise control, navigation system, larger LCD screen, power rear sunshade, manual rear side sunshades.		
Comfort & Convenience Features		
Satellite radio	400	345
Appearance & Special Purpose		
Run-flat tires, Luxury	400	345
Replaces full-size spare tire w/compact spare tire.		
Chrome alloy wheels	1600	840

ISUZU ASCENDER

CLASS: Midsize sport-utility vehicle
DRIVE WHEELS: Rear-wheel drive, 4-wheel drive
BASE PRICE RANGE: $28,569-$31,398. Built in USA.
ALSO CONSIDER: Ford Explorer, Honda Pilot, Toyota Highlander

Ascender is Isuzu's sole offering for 2005. Shedding the Axiom and Rodeo

 Specifications begin on page 547.

SUVs from its lineup, the ailing Japanese brand soldiers on with a single model based on General Motors' midsize truck-type SUV family. Ascender is closely related to the GMC Envoy. It comes in a regular-length version with 2-row, 5-passenger seating, and in extended-length form with 3-row, 7-passenger seating. Extendeds offer 6-cyl or V8 power, regulars only the 6-cyl. Both come with a 4-speed automatic transmission. For '05 the V8 comes with GM's Displacement on Demand feature, which automatically deactivates four cylinders to save fuel. A computer reactivates the four cylinders as needed for full power. Ascender is available with rear-wheel drive or 4WD that can be left engaged on dry pavement and includes low-range gearing. Antilock 4-wheel disc brakes are standard. Newly standard for '05 are head-protecting curtain side airbags that cover the 1st and 2nd seating rows; they replace last year's available seat-mounted front side airbags. OnStar assistance and power-adjustable pedals are optional; traction control is available with 2WD. Ascender comes with Isuzu's 3-year/50,000-mile bumper-to-bumper warranty and 7-year/75,000-mile powertrain warranty vs. GM's 3-year/36,000-mile coverage. Maximum towing capacity is 7200 lb.

RATINGS	4WD S, 6-cyl	2WD S EXT, 6-cyl	4WD S EXT, V8
ACCELERATION	6	5	6
FUEL ECONOMY	4	3	3
RIDE QUALITY	5	6	6
STEERING/HANDLING	3	3	3
QUIETNESS	4	4	4
CONTROLS/MATERIALS	7	7	7
ROOM/COMFORT (FRONT)	7	7	7
ROOM/COMFORT (REAR)	6	7	7
CARGO ROOM	8	9	9
VALUE WITHIN CLASS	5	5	5

Though Ascender matches most rivals for pace and space, Isuzu's longer warranty doesn't fully compensate for a spotty dealer network. Additionally, Isusu's financial woes put the company's future in doubt. Shoppers considering Ascender would do well to consider the similar GMC Envoy instead.

TOTAL	55	56	57

Average total for midsize sport-utility vehicles: 54.7

ENGINES

	dohc I6	ohv V8
Size, liters/cu. in.	4.2/256	5.3/327
Horsepower @ rpm	275 @ 6000	300 @ 5200
Torque (lb-ft) @ rpm	275 @ 3600	330 @ 4000
Availability	S	O
EPA city/highway mpg		
4-speed automatic	15/20[1]	14/19[2]

1. 15/19 w/2WD. 2. 15/20 w/2WD.

PRICES

Isuzu Ascender	RETAIL PRICE	DEALER INVOICE
2WD S 4-door wagon	$28569	$26855
4WD S 4-door wagon	31398	29514
Destination charge	685	685

STANDARD EQUIPMENT

2WD S: 4.2-liter 6-cylinder engine, 4-speed automatic transmission, dual front airbags, antilock 4-wheel disc brakes, daytime running lights, air conditioning w/dual-zone manual climate controls and rear controls, power steering, tilt steering wheel, cruise control, cloth upholstery, front bucket seats, center console, cupholders, 2nd-row split folding seat, 3rd-row split folding seat, power windows, power door locks, AM/FM/CD player, digital clock, tachometer, map lights, universal garage-door opener, variable-intermittent wipers, visor mirrors, rear defogger, rear intermittent wiper/washer, automatic headlights, theft-deterrent system, rear privacy glass, fog lights, roof rails, platform hitch, 7-wire trailer harness, full-size spare tire, 245/65R17 on/off-road tires, alloy wheels.

4WD S adds: 4-wheel drive, 2-speed transfer case, 8-way power driver seat w/lumbar adjustment, heated power mirrors, remote keyless entry, illuminated visor mirrors, floormats.

OPTIONAL EQUIPMENT

Major Packages	RETAIL PRICE	DEALER INVOICE
P10 Preferred Equipment Pkg., 2WD S	$1036	$980
Manufacturer's Discount Price	*829*	*779*
Heated power mirrors, 8-way power driver seat w/lumbar adjustment, remote keyless entry, illuminated visor mirrors, floormats, alarm. Std. 4WD S.		
K5/K51 LS Pkg., 2WD S	3443	3237
Manufacturer's Discount Price	*2699*	*2537*
4WD S	3267	3072
Manufacturer's Discount Price	*2599*	*2443*
Traction control (2WD), limited-slip differential, dual-zone automatic climate controls, power sunroof, 8-way power passenger seat, AM/FM radio w/in-dash 6-disc CD changer, leather-wrapped steering wheel w/radio controls, rear radio controls, automatic day/night rearview mirror, compass, driver information center, roof rack, machine-finished alloy wheels. 2WD S requires P10 Preferred Equipment Group.		

 Specifications begin on page 547.

OPTIONAL EQUIPMENT (cont.)

	RETAIL PRICE	DEALER INVOICE
K10 Limited Pkg.	$3591	$3396
Manufacturer's Discount Price	*2589*	*2433*

Special axle ratio, leather upholstery, heated front seats, 8-way power passenger seat, power-adjustable pedals, driver-seat and mirror memory, OnStar assistance system w/one-year service, Bose sound system, power rear quarter windows, rain-sensing wipers, mirror-mounted turn signals, running boards, color-keyed bumpers, skid plates (4WD). Requires K5/K51 LS Pkg., 5.3-liter V8 engine. 2WD S requires P10 Preferred Equipment Pkg.

Leather Pkg.	1299	1221

Leather upholstery. Requires K5/K51 LS. 2WD S requires P10 Preferred Equipment Pkg. NA w/5.3-liter V8 engine.

Powertrain

5.3-liter V8 engine w/cylinder deactivation	1499	1409

Requires K5/K51 LS Pkg. or K10 Limited Pkg. 2WD requires P10 Preferred Equipment Pkg.

Safety

Front and 2nd-row curtain side airbags	499	469

2WD S requires P10 Preferred Equipment Pkg.

Comfort & Convenience Features

OnStar assistance system	615	579

Includes one-year service.

JAGUAR S-TYPE

CLASS: Premium midsize car
DRIVE WHEELS: Rear-wheel drive
BASE PRICE RANGE: $44,230-$58,330. Built in England.
ALSO CONSIDER: Acura RL, Mercedes-Benz E-Class

Revisions to styling, instrumentation, and cabin trim mark the 2005 S-Type. Occupying the middle of Jaguar's sedan range in size and price, the S-Type comes in three models: the 235-hp V6 3.0, the 294-hp V8 4.2, and the high-performance supercharged 390-hp V8 R. All have a 6-speed automatic transmission; the 3.0 no longer offers a 5-speed manual. Standard are antilock 4-wheel disc brakes, antiskid/traction control, front side airbags, and head-protecting curtain side airbags. For '05, all get a freshened front end and revised main gauges. The 3.0 model trades its 16-inch wheels for the 4.2's 17-inch size, and both models are available with a taut-suspension Sport Package. That option for '05 replaces its 17-inch wheels with the 18s. The 18s also are now a stand-alone option for the 3.0 and 4.2. Newly available with the Sport Package and on the R is aluminum interior trim to replace wood. Also new is a luxuy VDP Edition Package for the 4.2 with upgrades to the standard leather and wood interior decor among its features. The R continues with its exclusive mesh grille, seats, and interior trim, and comes with the xenon headlamps that are optional for other S-Types. Power-adjustable pedals are standard on V8s, optional for the 3.0. Other options include a navigation system; voice activation for some audio, phone, and climate functions; and Adaptive Cruise Control designed to maintain a set following distance. The British-built S-Type shares its basic underskin design with the Lincoln LS from Jaguar's parent-company Ford.

RATINGS	**3.0 w/Sport Pkg.**	**4.2**	**4.2 w/Sport Pkg.**	**R w/nav. sys.**
ACCELERATION	6	7	7	8
FUEL ECONOMY	5	5	5	4
RIDE QUALITY	7	8	7	6
STEERING/HANDLING	7	7	7	8
QUIETNESS	6	7	6	6
CONTROLS/MATERIALS	7	7	7	4
ROOM/COMFORT (FRONT)	6	6	6	6
ROOM/COMFORT (REAR)	4	4	4	4
CARGO ROOM	3	3	3	3
VALUE WITHIN CLASS	5	5	5	3

The best value here is a base-suspension 4.2 model, but all these Jaguars are a pleasure to drive, with appointments and features worthy of the class. On the downside, prices are steep, and resale values pale vs. BMW, Lexus, and Mercedes-Benz rivals.

TOTAL	**56**	**59**	**57**	**52**

Average total for premium midsize cars: 61.7

ENGINES	**dohc V6**	**dohc V8**	**Supercharged dohc V8**
Size, liters/cu. in.	3.0/181	4.2/256	4.2/256
Horsepower @ rpm	235 @ 6800	294 @ 6000	390 @ 6100
Torque (lb-ft) @ rpm	216 @ 4100	303 @ 4100	399 @ 3500
Availability	S[1]	S[2]	S[3]
EPA city/highway mpg			
6-speed automatic	18/26	18/28	17/24

1. 3.0 model. 2. 4.2 model. 3. R model.

 Specifications begin on page 547.

PRICES

Jaguar S-Type	RETAIL PRICE	DEALER INVOICE
3.0 4-door sedan	$44230	$40250
4.2 4-door sedan	51330	46711
R 4-door sedan	58330	53081
Destination charge	665	665

R base price includes $1000 Gas-Guzzler Tax.

STANDARD EQUIPMENT

3.0: 3.0-liter V6 engine, 6-speed automatic transmission, traction control, dual front airbags, front side airbags, curtain side airbags, antilock 4-wheel disc brakes, antiskid system, rear-obstacle-detection system, emergency inside trunk release, air conditioning w/dual-zone automatic climate controls, interior air filter, power steering, power tilt/telescope wood/leather-wrapped steering wheel, cruise control, leather upholstery, front bucket seats, 8-way power driver seat, 6-way power passenger seat, center console, cupholders, split folding rear seat, wood interior trim, heated power mirrors, power windows, power door locks, remote keyless entry, AM/FM/CD player, digital clock, tachometer, trip computer, outside-temperature indicator, illuminated visor mirrors, rear defogger, heated variable-intermittent wipers, automatic headlights, floormats, theft-deterrent system, fog lights, 235/50R17 tires, alloy wheels.

4.2 adds: 4.2-liter V8 engine, power sunroof, memory system (driver seat, mirrors, steering wheel, pedals), power-adjustable pedals, Alpine sound system, 6-disc CD changer, automatic day/night rearview and outside mirrors, compass, universal garage-door opener, rain-sensing wipers.

R adds: 4.2-liter supercharged V8 engine, heated front seats, 16-way power driver seat, 12-way power passenger seat, trunk pass-through, steering-wheel radio controls, xenon headlights, rear spoiler, sport suspension, computer-controlled shock absorbers, 245/40ZR18 front tires, 275/35ZR18 rear tires. *Deletes:* split folding rear seat.

OPTIONAL EQUIPMENT

Major Packages	RETAIL PRICE	DEALER INVOICE
Sport Pkg., 3.0, 4.2	$1200	$1020
Leather-wrapped steering wheel, sport bucket seats, unique interior and exterior trim, upgraded brakes, sport suspension, 245/40ZR18 tires, special alloy wheels.		
Aluminum Sport Pkg., 3.0, 4.2	1700	1445
Sport Pkg. plus aluminum interior trim.		
Premium Pkg., 3.0	1600	1360
Power-adjustable pedals, memory system (driver seat, mirrors, steering wheel, pedals), front-seat lumbar adjustment, automatic day/night rearview and outside mirrors, universal garage-door opener, rain-sensing wipers.		
VDP Edition Pkg., 4.2	3300	2805
Heated front seats, 16-way power driver seat, 12-way power passenger seat, overhead console, power rear sunshade, voice-activated telephone prewiring, upgraded leather upholstery and wood interior trim, xenon headlights, unique alloy wheels.		

Safety

	RETAIL PRICE	DEALER INVOICE
Front-obstacle-detection system	$250	$213

Comfort & Convenience Features

Navigation system	2300	1955
Adaptive cruise control	2200	1870
Power sunroof, 3.0	1100	935
Alpine sound system, 3.0 *Includes 6-disc CD changer.*	1600	1360
Heated front seats, 3.0, 4.2	500	425
Two-tone interior trim, R	1000	850
Aluminum interior trim, R	500	425

Appearance & Special Purpose

Xenon headlights, 3.0, 4.2	675	574
245/40ZR18 tires, 3.0, 4.2	800	680

JAGUAR X-TYPE

CLASS: Premium compact car
DRIVE WHEELS: All-wheel drive
BASE PRICE RANGE: $30,330-$36,330. Built in England.
ALSO CONSIDER: Acura TL, Audi A4, BMW 3-Series

Jaguar's smallest, least-expensive line gains a luxury VDP Edition package and a wagon for 2005. X-Type offers three models; all have all-wheel drive and a V6 engine. The 2.5 model has a 192-hp 2.5-liter. The 3.0 and Sportwagon models have a 227-hp 3.0. Sedans are available with manual or automatic transmission. Sportwagon is automatic only. Antilock 4-wheel disc brakes, front side airbags, and head-protecting curtain side airbags are standard. Also standard is leather-and-wood interior trim. The 2.5 comes with 16-inch wheels, the 3.0 and Sportwagon with 17s. A Sport Package option for the 3.0 adds a sport suspension with 18-inch wheels, antiskid system, xenon headlights, aggressive aero body trim, and unique interior trim. The antiskid system is optional on the 3.0 and Sportwagon. The VDP Edition Package adds Alpine sound system, heated front seats, upgraded leather upholstery, and burled walnut trim to the 3.0. Heated front seats are optional on all models. Navigation and rear-obstacle-detection systems are available. Dealer-installed voice activation for some audio, climate, and navigation functions is also available.

 Specifications begin on page 547.

RATINGS

	2.5, man.	3.0 w/nav. sys., auto.
ACCELERATION	5	6
FUEL ECONOMY	5	5
RIDE QUALITY	7	6
STEERING/HANDLING	7	7
QUIETNESS	6	7
CONTROLS/MATERIALS	6	6
ROOM/COMFORT (FRONT)	6	6
ROOM/COMFORT (REAR)	4	4
CARGO ROOM	4	4
VALUE WITHIN CLASS	2	3

The X-Type is an acceptable blend of performance and luxury, and it comes with the all-weather capability of AWD. It offers Jaguar cachet, but top rivals offer better all-around cars.

TOTAL	52	54

Average total for premium compact cars: 57.5

ENGINES

	dohc V6	dohc V6
Size, liters/cu. in.	2.5/152	3.0/181
Horsepower @ rpm	192 @ 6800	227 @ 6800
Torque (lb-ft) @ rpm	178 @ 3000	206 @ 3000
Availability	S[1]	S[2]
EPA city/highway mpg		
5-speed manual	19/28	18/28
5-speed automatic	18/26	18/25

1. 2.5. 2. 3.0, Sportwagon models.

PRICES

Jaguar X-Type	RETAIL PRICE	DEALER INVOICE
2.5 4-door sedan	$30330	$27601
3.0 4-door sedan	34330	31241
Sportwagon 4-door wagon	36330	33060
Destination charge	665	665

STANDARD EQUIPMENT

2.5: 2.5-liter V6 engine, 5-speed manual transmission, all-wheel drive, dual front airbags, front side airbags, curtain side airbags, antilock 4-wheel disc brakes, tachometer, air conditioning w/automatic climate control, interior air filter, power steering, tilt/telescope leather-wrapped steering wheel w/radio controls, cruise control, leather upholstery, front bucket seats, 8-way power driver seat w/lumbar adjustment, 2-way power passenger seat, center console, cupholders, wood interior trim, heated power mirrors, power windows, power door locks, remote keyless entry, AM/FM/CD player, digital clock, tachometer, outside-temperature indicator, rear defogger, variable-intermittent wipers w/heated washers, illuminated visor mirrors, floormats, theft-deterrent system, front and rear fog lights, 205/55HR16 tires, alloy wheels.

3.0/Sportwagon adds: 3.0-liter V6 engine, 5-speed automatic transmission, wood/leather-wrapped steering wheel, power sunroof, split folding rear seat, automatic day/night rearview mirror (sedan), cargo cover (wagon), automatic headlights (sedan), roof rails (wagon), 225/45ZR17 tires.

OPTIONAL EQUIPMENT

Major Packages

	RETAIL PRICE	DEALER INVOICE
Moonroof and Seat Pkg., 2.5	$1750	$1488
Power sunroof, split folding rear seat.		
Premium Pkg., 3.0 sedan	1150	978
Driver-seat and mirror memory, 8-way power passenger seat w/lumbar adjustment, universal garage-door opener, trip computer, rain-sensing wipers.		
Sport Pkg., 3.0 sedan	2950	2508
Antiskid system, sport seats, leather-wrapped steering wheel, Alpine sound system, rear spoiler, body-colored exterior trim and body cladding, sport suspension, 225/40ZR18 tires, unique alloy wheels.		
VDP Edition, 3.0 sedan	3750	3188
Premium Pkg. plus rear-obstacle-detection system, upgraded leather upholstery and wood interior trim, heated front seats, Alpine sound system, 6-disc CD changer, chrome outside mirrors, unique alloy wheels.		

Powertrain

5-speed automatic transmission, 2.5	1250	1063
5-speed manual transmission, 3.0 sedan	NC	NC

Safety

Antiskid system, 3.0 sedan	525	446
Rear-obstacle-detection system, 3.0 sedan, Sportwagon	325	276

Comfort & Convenience Features

Navigation system, 3.0 sedan, Sportwagon	2300	1955
Alpine sound system, 3.0 sedan	1475	1254
Includes 6-disc CD changer.		
Heated front seats	500	425
Carbon-fiber/alcantara interior trim, 3.0 sedan	450	383
Requires X2 Sport Pkg.		

Appearance & Special Purpose

Xenon headlights, 3.0 sedan	675	574
Includes automatic headlight leveling.		
Aguila alloy wheels, 3.0 sedan	NC	NC
Includes 225/45HR17 tires. Requires Sport Pkg.		
Melbourne alloy wheels, 3.0 sedan	3000	2550
Requires Sport Pkg.		

JAGUAR XJ SERIES

CLASS: Premium large car
DRIVE WHEELS: Rear-wheel drive
BASE PRICE RANGE: $60,830-$89,330. Built in England.
ALSO CONSIDER: Lexus LS 430, Volkswagen Phaeton

Jaguar gives its flagship more rear-seat room with an available stretched body style for 2005. Base XJ8 and performance XJR models continue on a 119-inch wheelbase. XJ8 L, Vanden Plas, and the new Super V8 use a 124-inch chassis. All models use a 4.2-liter V8. The XJ8, XJ8 L, and Vanden Plas have 294 hp. The supercharged XJR and Super V8 have 390. A 6-speed automatic is the only transmission. ABS and antiskid/traction control are standard, as are head-protecting curtain side airbags and front-side airbags. All models also have a self-leveling air suspension with automatic-adjusting shock absorbers. For '05, the XJ8 exchanges 17-inch wheels for the 18s used on the XJ8 L and Vanden Plas; XJR and Super V8 have 19s. The XJR also has a firmer suspension than other models and unique cosmetic touches. Vanden Plas and Super V8 versions have a more luxurious interior, including wooden fold-down trays for rear-seat passengers. A rear-seat entertainment system with a video screen in the back of each front headrest is standard on Super V8 and available on all other models except XJ8. Available features include adaptive cruise control designed to maintain a set following distance, 4-zone automatic climate control, heated front and rear seats, and a navigation system with available voice activation.

RATINGS	XJ8	XJ8 w/nav. sys.	XJR	XJ8 Vanden Plas
ACCELERATION	7	7	8	7
FUEL ECONOMY	4	4	4	4
RIDE QUALITY	9	9	8	9
STEERING/HANDLING	7	7	8	7
QUIETNESS	9	9	8	9
CONTROLS/MATERIALS	7	6	7	7
ROOM/COMFORT (FRONT)	7	7	7	7
ROOM/COMFORT (REAR)	8	8	8	9
CARGO ROOM	4	4	4	4
VALUE WITHIN CLASS	6	5	4	4

Ford owns Jaguar, and the British marque's special character feels watered

RATINGS (cont.)	XJ8	XJ8 w/nav. sys.	XJR	XJ8 Vanden Plas

down in the XJ. Still, this is a solid enough luxury sedan, and tends to undercut most rivals on price. The XJ8 versions are the best value within the XJ lineup. While the XJR is fun to drive, it isn't as satisfying as its high-performance competition. XJ8 L, Vanden Plas, and Super V8 add limousinelike rear-seat room without penalizing performance.

	XJ8	XJ8 w/nav. sys.	XJR	XJ8 Vanden Plas
TOTAL	68	66	66	67

Average total for premium large cars: 68.7

ENGINES

	dohc V8	Supercharged dohc V8
Size, liters/cu. in.	4.2/256	4.2/256
Horsepower @ rpm	294 @ 6000	390 @ 6100
Torque (lb-ft) @ rpm	303 @ 4100	399 @ 3500
Availability	S[1]	S[2]
EPA city/highway mpg		
6-speed automatic	18/28	17/24

1. XJ8, XJ8L, Vanden Plas. 2. XJR, Super V8.

PRICES

Jaguar XJ Series

	RETAIL PRICE	DEALER INVOICE
XJ8 4-door sedan	$60830	$55356
XJ8 L 4-door sedan	62830	57176
Vanden Plas 4-door sedan	70330	64001
XJR 4-door sedan	75330	68551
Super V8 4-door sedan	89330	81291
Destination charge	665	665

STANDARD EQUIPMENT

XJ8: L adds: 5-inch-longer wheelbase, 4.2-liter V8 engine, 6-speed automatic transmission, traction control, dual front airbags, front side airbags, curtain side airbags, antilock 4-wheel disc brakes, brake assist, antiskid system, rear-obstacle-detection system, emergency inside trunk release, air conditioning w/dual-zone automatic climate controls, interior air filter, power steering, power tilt/telescope wood/leather-wrapped steering wheel w/radio controls, cruise control, leather upholstery, front bucket seats, 12-way power driver seat, 8-way power passenger seat, power-adjustable pedals, memory system (driver seat, mirrors, steering wheel, pedals), center console, cupholders, wood interior trim, heated power mirrors w/automatic day/night, power windows, power door locks, remote keyless entry, power sunroof, AM/FM/CD player, analog clock, tachometer, trip computer, automatic day/night rearview mirror, compass, outside-temperature indicator, illuminated visor mirrors, universal garage-door opener, map lights, rain-sensing variable-intermittent wipers, rear defogger, automatic headlights, floormats, theft-deterrent system, front and rear fog lights, computer-controlled self-leveling suspension, full-size spare tire, 235/50R18 tires, alloy wheels.

 Specifications begin on page 547.

XJ8 L adds: 5-inch-longer wheelbase.

Vanden Plas adds to XJ8 L: heated front and rear seats, heated steering wheel, 16-way power front seats, Alpine sound system, 6-disc CD changer, rear-seat fold-down trays, power rear sunshade, lamb's-wool floormats.

XJR adds: 4.2-liter supercharged V8 engine, upgraded brakes, adaptive cruise control, xenon headlights, sport suspension, 255/40ZR19 tires. *Deletes:* 5-inch-longer wheelbase, rear-seat fold-down trays, lamb's-wool floormats.

Super V8 adds: front-obstacle-detection system, 4-zone automatic climate controls, navigation system, rear-seat DVD entertainment system, adjustable rear seat, rear control for front-passenger seat, rear-seat fold-down trays, manual side sunshades, heated washer jets, lamb's-wool floormats, 5-inch-longer wheelbase. *Deletes:* sport suspension.

OPTIONAL EQUIPMENT

	RETAIL PRICE	DEALER INVOICE
Major Packages		
Multimedia Pkg., XJ8 L	$2950	$2508
Vanden Plas, XJR	2650	2253
DVD player, two rear video screens, 16-way power front seats (XJ8 L).		
Warm Climate Pkg., XJ8 L	1750	1488
Vanden Plas, XJR	1300	1105
4-zone automatic climate controls (including rear controls), power rear sunshade (XJ8 L), manual side sunshades.		
Safety		
Front-obstacle-detection system, XJ8 L, Vanden Plas, XJR	250	213
Comfort & Convenience Features		
Navigation system, XJ8, XJ8 L, Vanden Plas, XJR	2300	1955
Premium sound system, XJ8, XJ8 L	1600	1360
Alpine sound system, 6-disc CD changer.		
Adaptive cruise control, XJ8, XJ8 L, Vanden Plas	2200	1870
Heated front and rear seats, XJ8, XJ8 L	950	808
Heated steering wheel, XJ8, XJ8 L	400	340
Requires heated front and rear seats.		
Heated windshield	300	255
Power rear seats, Vanden Plas	1750	1488
Includes power headrests and adjustable backrests w/4-way lumbar adjustment. Requires Multimedia Pkg.		
Appearance & Special Purpose		
Xenon headlights, XJ8, XJ8 L, Vanden Plas	675	574
19-inch alloy wheels, XJ8, XJ8 L, Vanden Plas	1200	1020
19-inch chrome alloy wheels, XJ8, XJ8L, Vanden Plas, Super V8	2600	2210
20-inch modular alloy wheels, XJR	4500	3825

JAGUAR XK SERIES

CLASS: Premium sporty/performance car
DRIVE WHEELS: Rear-wheel drive
BASE PRICE RANGE: $69,830-$86,330. Built in England.
ALSO CONSIDER: Lexus SC 430, Mercedes-Benz SL-Class

Appearance changes to the grille, wheels, and tailpipes mark the 2005 alterations to Jaguar's sportiest cars. XKs come as coupes and convertibles in XK8 and XKR trim. All use a 4.2-liter V8. It has 294 hp in the XK8, 390 hp in the supercharged XKR. A 6-speed automatic is the only transmission. Front side airbags, rear-obstacle warning, antiskid/traction control, and ABS are standard. XKRs have Brembo-brand brakes. All XKs come with 18-inch wheels. XK8s offer optional 19s; 20s are available for XKRs. XKRs have a mesh grille, louvered hood, rear spoiler, and computer-controlled shock absorbers. Standard on XKR and optional on XK8 are a navigation system and self-leveling xenon headlamps. Jaguar's Adaptive Cruise Control, designed to maintain a set following distance, is optional on both models.

RATINGS	XK8 cpe	XK8 conv	XKR cpe
ACCELERATION	7	7	8
FUEL ECONOMY	5	5	4
RIDE QUALITY	7	7	6
STEERING/HANDLING	7	7	8
QUIETNESS	6	4	5
CONTROLS/MATERIALS	5	5	5
ROOM/COMFORT (FRONT)	4	4	4
ROOM/COMFORT (REAR)	1	1	1
CARGO ROOM	2	2	2
VALUE WITHIN CLASS	2	2	2

Without a retractable hardtop, XK convertibles lose out to the newer Lexus SC 430, Mercedes-Benz SL, and Cadillac XLR for solid-roof security and insulation. Interior room is tight and prices are steep. Still, XKs shine for silky performance in an elegant package with Jaguar's unique charm.

TOTAL	46	44	45

Average total for premium sporty/performance cars: 48.3

 Specifications begin on page 547.

ENGINES

	dohc V8	Supercharged dohc V8
Size, liters/cu. in.	4.2/256	4.2/256
Horsepower @ rpm	294 @ 6000	390 @ 6000
Torque (lb-ft) @ rpm	303 @ 4100	399 @ 3500
Availability	S[1]	S[2]
EPA city/highway mpg		
6-speed automatic	18/26	16/23

1. XK8. 2. XKR.

PRICES

Jaguar XK Series

	RETAIL PRICE	DEALER INVOICE
XK8 2-door coupe	$69830	$63546
XK8 2-door convertible	74830	68096
XKR 2-door coupe	81330	74011
XKR 2-door convertible	86330	78561
Destination charge	665	665

XKR requires $1000 Gas-Guzzler Tax.

STANDARD EQUIPMENT

XK8: 4.2-liter V8 engine, 6-speed automatic transmission, traction control, dual front airbags, front side airbags, antilock 4-wheel disc brakes, brake assist, antiskid system, rear-obstacle-detection system, emergency inside trunk release, air conditioning w/automatic climate control, power steering, power tilt/telescope wood/leather-wrapped steering wheel w/radio controls, cruise control, leather upholstery, heated 12-way power front bucket seats w/power lumbar support, memory system (driver seat, steering wheel, mirrors), center console, cupholders, wood interior trim, heated power mirrors, power windows, power door locks, remote keyless entry, power top (convertible), Alpine AM/FM/cassette, 6-disc CD changer, analog clock, tachometer, trip computer, universal garage-door opener, illuminated visor mirrors, automatic day/night rearview mirror, compass, outside-temperature indicator, rear defogger, rain-sensing variable-intermittent windshield wipers, map lights, automatic headlights, floormats, theft-deterrent system, front and rear fog lights, 245/45ZR18 front tires, 255/45ZR18 rear tires, alloy wheels.

XKR adds: 4.2-liter supercharged V8 engine, upgraded brakes, navigation system, rear spoiler, xenon headlights, sport suspension, computer-controlled shock absorbers.

OPTIONAL EQUIPMENT

Major Packages

	RETAIL PRICE	DEALER INVOICE
Handling Pkg., XKR	$3000	$2550

Cross-drilled brakes, revised suspension and steering. Requires 20-inch alloy wheels.

Comfort & Convenience Features

Navigation system, XK8	2400	2040

OPTIONAL EQUIPMENT (cont.)

	RETAIL PRICE	DEALER INVOICE
Adaptive cruise control	$2200	$1870
Recaro sport seats, XKR	2000	1700

Appearance & Special Purpose

	RETAIL PRICE	DEALER INVOICE
Xenon headlights, XK8	675	574
19-inch Atlas alloy wheels, XK8	1200	1020
Includes 245/40ZR19 front tires, 255/40ZR19 rear tires.		
20-inch alloy wheels, XKR	6000	5100
Includes 255/35ZR20 front tires, 285/30ZR20 rear tires.		

JEEP GRAND CHEROKEE

CLASS: Midsize sport-utility vehicle
DRIVE WHEELS: Rear-wheel drive, all-wheel drive
BASE PRICE RANGE: $26,130-$34,045. Built in USA.
ALSO CONSIDER: Ford Explorer, Honda Pilot, Toyota Highlander and 4Runner

Grand Cherokee is redesigned for 2005, gaining size, power, and features. It's longer than the 1999-2004 version by 3.5 inches in wheelbase and five inches overall, but interior dimensions change little. Laredo and upscale Limited models are offered. Both seat five; no 3rd-row seat is available. Laredos swap a 195-hp 4.0-liter inline 6-cyl engine for a 210-hp 3.7-liter V6. Optional for Laredo, standard on Limited, is a 230-hp 4.7-liter V8. Optional for Limited is parent-company Chrysler's 325-hp 5.7-liter Hemi V8. The 5.7 has Chrysler's Multi-Displacement System, which deactivates four cylinders under idle and cruise conditions to save fuel. Grand Cherokee's sole transmission is a 5-speed automatic with manual shift gate; V8s include a tow-haul mode. V6 and 4.7-liter V8 models offer rear- or all-wheel drive. The 5.7 V8 comes only with AWD. Each V8 uses its own AWD setup, but both include low-range gearing. Low-range gearing is unavailable for the AWD V6. Maximum towing capacity with the 5.7 V8 is 7200 lb. All Grand Cherokees have antilock 4-wheel disc brakes, 17-inch wheels, and a rear liftgate with separate-opening glass. An antiskid system is available on AWD versions. Optional on all are curtain side airbags providing head and torso protection for both seating rows. AWD V8s offer optional front and rear limited-slip differentials and, later in the year, are scheduled to get Jeep's new Dynamic Handling System, designed to

 Specifications begin on page 547.

reduce body lean in fast turns. Other new options include rear-obstacle detection, satellite radio, DVD rear entertainment, and Chrysler's UConnect, which uses the audio system as a hands-free, wireless link to cell phones. Also available are navigation system, power-adjustable pedals, heated front seats, tire-pressure monitor, and an off-road package with tow hooks and chassis skid plates. This evaluation is based on preview drives.

RATINGS	2WD Laredo, V6	AWD Laredo, 4.7 V8	AWD Limited w/nav. sys., 5.7 V8
ACCELERATION	4	5	6
FUEL ECONOMY	4	3	3
RIDE QUALITY	6	6	6
STEERING/HANDLING	4	4	4
QUIETNESS	5	6	6
CONTROLS/MATERIALS	6	6	5
ROOM/COMFORT (FRONT)	7	7	7
ROOM/COMFORT (REAR)	5	5	5
CARGO ROOM	7	7	7
VALUE WITHIN CLASS	5	7	6

The new Grand Cherokee improves on the old within the realm of Jeep family values. It's most improved for solidity, ride comfort, road manners, and ergonomics, with the muscular Hemi V8 a new emotional draw. It's most let down by a tepid V6, mediocre cabin decor, subpar cargo space—and the lack of 3-row seating, a deal-breaker for many buyers. Even so, Jeep's new flagship has a lot to like and is competitively priced.

TOTAL	53	56	55

Average total for midsize sport-utility vehicles: 54.7

ENGINES

	sohc V6	sohc V8	ohv V8
Size, liters/cu. in.	3.7/226	4.7/287	5.7/345
Horsepower @ rpm	210 @ 5200	230 @ 4700	325 @ 5100
Torque (lb-ft) @ rpm	235 @ 4000	290 @ 3700	370 @ 3500
Availability	S[1]	S[2]	O[3]
EPA city/highway mpg			
5-speed automatic	17/21[4]	15/21	14/21

1. Laredo. 2. Limited; optional Laredo. 3. Limited. 4. 17/22 w/2WD.

PRICES

Jeep Grand Cherokee	RETAIL PRICE	DEALER INVOICE
2WD Laredo 4-door wagon	$26130	$24036
AWD Laredo 4-door wagon	28100	25824
2WD Limited 4-door wagon	31455	28775
AWD Limited 4-door wagon	34045	31115
Destination charge	645	645

STANDARD EQUIPMENT

Laredo: 3.7-liter V6 engine, 5-speed automatic transmission w/manual-shift capability, dual front airbags, antilock 4-wheel disc brakes, air conditioning, power steering, tilt steering wheel, cruise control, cloth upholstery, front bucket seats, 8-way power driver seat, center console, cupholders, split folding rear seat, power mirrors, power windows, power door locks, remote keyless entry, AM/FM/CD player, digital clock, tachometer, trip computer, variable-intermittent wipers, visor mirrors, rear defogger, rear wiper/washer, floormats, rear privacy glass, roof rails, rear spoiler, full-size spare tire, 235/65R17 tires, alloy wheels. **AWD** adds: all-wheel drive, front and rear traction control.

Limited adds: 4.7-liter V8 engine, front and rear traction control, dual-zone automatic climate controls, leather upholstery, memory system (driver seat, mirrors, pedals), power-adjustable pedals, 4-way power passenger seat, leather-wrapped steering wheel w/radio controls, heated power mirrors, Boston Acoustics AM/FM radio w/in-dash 6-disc CD/MP3 changer, illuminated visor mirrors, automatic day/night rearview mirror, universal garage-door opener, rain-sensing wipers, cargo cover, automatic headlights, theft-deterrent system, roof rack, fog lights. **AWD** adds: all-wheel drive, 2-speed transfer case, front and rear traction control.

OPTIONAL EQUIPMENT

Major Packages	RETAIL PRICE	DEALER INVOICE
Quick Order Pkg. 26/28F, Laredo	$1580	$1390
Heated power mirrors, 4-way power passenger seat, upgraded sound system, additional auxiliary power outlet, illuminated visor mirrors, universal garage-door opener, automatic day/night rearview mirror, automatic headlights, theft-deterrent system w/alarm, fog lights.		
Quick Order Pkg. 26/28X, Laredo	3355	2952
Quick Order Pkg. 26/28F plus leather upholstery, leather-wrapped steering w/radio controls, power sunroof, cargo cover, roof rack.		
Quick Order Pkg. 25/28K, 2WD Limited	1425	1254
AWD Limited	1925	1694
Power sunroof, antiskid system (AWD), heated front seats, UConnect hands-free cellular telephone link, automatic-dimming headlights, 235/65R17 performance tires (AWD).		
Popular Equipment Group, AWD Limited w/4.7-liter V8	1190	1047
Off-Road Group and Trailer Tow Group IV plus front and rear limited-slip differentials. Requires Quick Order Pkg. 25/28K.		
Off-Road Group, AWD	420	370
Skid plates, tow hooks, 245/65R17 all-terrain white-letter tires. Laredo requires 4.7-liter V8 engine. NA w/Quick Order Pkg. 25/28K.		
Cargo Convenience Group, Laredo	125	110
Cargo cover, roof rack.		
Trailer Tow Group, Laredo	180	158
Class II trailer hitch receiver, wiring harness. NA w/4.7-liter V8 engine.		
Trailer Tow Group IV	255	224
Class IV receiver hitch, 7-wire harness w/4-pin adaptor.		
Powertrain		
4.7-liter V8 engine, 2WD Laredo	720	634
AWD Laredo	1340	1179
AWD includes Quadra-Trac II 2-speed transfer case.		

OPTIONAL EQUIPMENT (cont.)

	RETAIL PRICE	DEALER INVOICE
5.7-liter Hemi V8 engine w/cylinder deactivation, AWD Limited	$1245	$1096
Includes Quadra-Drive II 2-speed transfer case, front and rear limited-slip differentials, antiskid system.		
Limited-slip differential, 2WD	345	304
Laredo requires Quick Order Pkg.		

Safety

Curtain side airbags	490	431
Antiskid system, AWD	500	440
Tire-pressure monitor, Limited	85	75
Rear-obstacle-detection system, Limited	255	244

Comfort & Convenience Features

Navigation system, Laredo	1500	1320
Limited	1200	1056
Laredo includes 6-disc CD/MP3 changer. Laredo requires Quick Order Pkg. 26/28X. Limited requires Quick Order Pkg. 25/28K.		
Power sunroof	800	704
Laredo requires Quick Order Pkg. 26/28F.		
Electronic Infotainment System Group	1200	1056
Rear-seat DVD entertainment system. Laredo requires Quick Order Pkg. 26/28X and AM/FM radio w/in-dash 6-disc CD/MP3 changer or navigation system.		
AM/FM radio w/in-dash 6-disc CD/MP3 changer, Laredo	300	264
Requires Quick Order Pkg.		
Satellite radio	195	172
Laredo requires Quick Order Pkg.		
UConnect, Laredo	275	242
Hands-free cellular telephone link. Requires Quick Order Pkg. 26/28X.		
Heated front seats	250	220
Laredo requires Quick Order Pkg. 26/28X, power-adjustable pedals.		
Power-adjustable pedals, Laredo	120	106
Requires Quick Order Pkg.		
Chrome alloy wheels, Limited	820	722

JEEP LIBERTY

CLASS: Compact sport-utility vehicle
DRIVE WHEELS: Rear-wheel drive, 4-wheel drive
BASE PRICE RANGE: $19,190-$25,035. Built in USA.
ALSO CONSIDER: Ford Escape, Honda CR-V, Mazda Tribute

An available turbocharged diesel engine and two new transmissions highlight 2005 additions to Jeep's 4-dr compact SUV. Liberty is a 5-seat wagon with a swing-open tailgate and exterior spare tire. The base Sport model comes with a 150-hp 4-cyl engine. A 210-hp V6 is optional for the Sport,

standard on Limited and Renegade models. The new turbodiesel, a 160-hp 4-cyl is optional for Sport and Limited. The 4-cyl gas engine teams only with manual transmission, now a 6-speed in place of a 5-speed. The V6 offers the 6-speed manual or optional 4-speed automatic. The turbodiesel comes only with a 5-speed automatic, also new to Liberty. All models offer rear-wheel drive or a choice of two 4WD systems, both with low-range gearing. Jeep's Command-Trac 4WD should not be left engaged on dry pavement. Selec-Trac 4WD can be left engaged on dry pavement. Liberty's 5000-lb towing capacity is tops among compact SUVs. Four-wheel disc brakes are standard. ABS and head-protecting curtain side airbags are optional. All models get a modest styling update for '05, with Renegades gaining a flatter hood, taller grille, fender flares and other specific touches. Sports and Renegades have 16-inch wheels, Limiteds have 17s. All have a 65/35 split folding rear seat. Leather upholstery, heated front seats, and a sunroof are available. New options include satellite radio, navigation system, and Chrysler's UConnect, which uses the audio system as a hands-free, wireless link to cell phones.

RATINGS	4WD Sport, V6 auto.	4WD Limited, V6 auto.
ACCELERATION	4	4
FUEL ECONOMY	4	4
RIDE QUALITY	4	4
STEERING/HANDLING	4	4
QUIETNESS	4	4
CONTROLS/MATERIALS	6	6
ROOM/COMFORT (FRONT)	6	6
ROOM/COMFORT (REAR)	4	4
CARGO ROOM	7	7
VALUE WITHIN CLASS	8	7

Liberty is capable, solid, and competitively priced. Its on-road behavior is less carlike than that of its top competitors. But, being a Jeep, it has much better off-road ability than most. We recommend it for its range of attributes.

TOTAL	51	50

Average total for compact sport-utility vehicles: 49.0

 Specifications begin on page 547.

ENGINES

	dohc I4	sohc V6	Turbodiesel dohc I4
Size, liters/cu. in.	2.4/148	3.7/225	2.8/171
Horsepower @ rpm	150 @ 5200	210 @ 5200	160 @ 3800
Torque (lb-ft) @ rpm	165 @ 4000	235 @ 4000	295 @ 1800
Availability	S[1]	S[2]	O[3]
EPA city/highway mpg			
6-speed manual	20/24	16/22	
4-speed automatic		17/21	
5-speed automatic			21/27

1. Sport. 2. Renegade and Limited; optional Sport. 3. Sport and Limited.

PRICES

Jeep Liberty

	RETAIL PRICE	DEALER INVOICE
2WD Sport 4-door wagon	$19190	$18043
4WD Sport 4-door wagon	20700	19437
2WD Renegade 4-door wagon	21975	20577
4WD Renegade 4-door wagon	23485	21971
2WD Limited Edition 4-door wagon	23525	21988
4WD Limited Edition 4-door wagon	25035	23382
Destination charge	610	610

Diesel engine price not available at time of publication.

STANDARD EQUIPMENT

Sport: 2.4-liter 4-cylinder engine, 6-speed manual transmission, dual front airbags, 4-wheel disc brakes, air conditioning, power steering, tilt steering wheel, cloth upholstery, front bucket seats, center console, cupholders, split folding rear seat, AM/FM/CD player, digital clock, tachometer, variable-intermittent wipers, rear defogger, rear wiper/washer, automatic-off headlights, theft-deterrent system, roof rails, outside-mounted full-size spare tire, 225/75R16 all-terrain white-letter tires. **4WD** adds: 4-wheel drive, 2-speed transfer case.

Renegade adds: 3.7-liter V6 engine, leather-wrapped steering wheel, cruise control, power mirrors, power windows, power door locks, remote keyless entry, illuminated visor mirrors, map lights, floormats, fog lights, roof rack, rear privacy glass, front tow hooks, alloy wheels. **4WD** adds: 4-wheel drive, 2-speed transfer case.

Limited Edition adds: 4-speed automatic transmission, 6-way power driver seat, cargo cover, 235/65VR17 tires. *Deletes:* front tow hooks. **4WD** adds: 4-wheel drive, 2-speed transfer case.

OPTIONAL EQUIPMENT

Major Packages

	RETAIL PRICE	DEALER INVOICE
26/28B Quick Order Pkg., Sport	$45	$41
Illuminated visor mirrors, map lights, cargo light, rear auxiliary power outlet, cargo net.		
28C Quick Order Pkg., Sport	795	716
26/28B Quick Order Pkg. plus leather-wrapped steering wheel, cruise control, rear privacy glass, fog lights, alloy wheels. Requires 3.7-liter V6 engine, 4-speed automatic transmission.		

OPTIONAL EQUIPMENT (cont.)

	RETAIL PRICE	DEALER INVOICE
26/28D Quick Order Pkg., 2WD Renegade	$600	$540
4WD Renegade	750	675
6-way power driver seat, roof-mounted light bar, taillight guards, skid plates (4WD).		
28G Quick Order Pkg., 2WD Limited	1175	1058
4WD Limited	1570	1413
Leather upholstery, 6-way power passenger seat, Infinity AM/FM radio w/in-dash 6-disc CD changer, steering-wheel radio controls, mini overhead console, universal garage-door opener, trip computer, vehicle information center, heated power mirrors, automatic day/night rearview mirror, Selec-Trac 4-wheel drive (4WD).		
Luxury Group, Renegade	1245	1121
Leather upholstery, 6-way power passenger seat, heated power mirrors, mini overhead console, universal garage-door opener, trip computer, vehicle information center. Requires 26/28D Quick Order Pkg.		
Security Group, Sport, Renegade	175	158
Cargo cover, theft-deterrent system w/alarm. Sport requires 26/28B Quick Order Pkg. and rear privacy glass or 28C Quick Order Pkg. Renegade requires 26/28D Quick Order Pkg.		
Off-Road Group, 4WD Sport	760	684
4WD Renegade	660	594
4WD Renegade w/26/28D Pkg	610	549
Limited-slip rear differential, heavy-duty engine cooling, tow hooks (Sport), skid plates, 235/70R16 all-terrain tires. Sport requires 26/28C Quick Order Pkg., 3.7-liter engine.		
Trailer Tow Group, Renegade w/manual transmission	245	221
Sport, Renegade w/automatic trans., Limited	365	329
Heavy-duty engine cooling, 7-wire trailer harness, Class III hitch receiver. Sport requires 28C Quick Order Pkg., 3.7-liter engine, 4-speed automatic transmission.		

Powertrain

3.7-liter V6 engine, Sport	850	765
4-speed automatic transmission, Sport, Renegade	825	743
Sport requires 3.7-liter engine.		
Selec-Trac 4-wheel drive, 4WD	395	356
Sport requires 28C Quick Order Pkg. Renegade requires 26/28D Quick Order Pkg.		
Limited-slip rear differential	285	257
Sport requires 28C Quick Order Pkg.		

Safety

Curtain side airbags	490	441
Antilock brakes	600	540
Sport requires a Quick Order Pkg.		
Tire-pressure monitor, Renegade, Limited	75	68
Renegade requires 26/28D Quick Order Pkg., Luxury Group. Limited requires Quick Order Pkg. 28G or mini overhead console.		

 Specifications begin on page 547.

Comfort & Convenience Features	RETAIL PRICE	DEALER INVOICE
Air conditioning, Sport	$850	$765
Power sunroof	700	630
Sport requires Quick Order Pkg.		
Navigation system, Renegade, Limited	1500	1350
Limited w/26G Pkg.	1200	1080
Replaces in-dash 6-disc CD changer of Limited 26G Quick Order Pkg. w/single-disc CD player.		
AM/FM radio w/in-dash 6-disc CD changer	300	270
Sport requires Quick Order Pkg.		
Infinity speakers	475	428
Includes steering-wheel radio controls. Requires AM/FM radio w/in-dash 6-disc CD changer or navigation system. Sport requires Quick Order Pkg., cruise control.		
Satellite radio	195	176
Includes one-year service. Sport requires Quick Order Pkg.		
UConnect, Renegade, Limited	275	245
Hands-free cellular telephone link. Requires Quick Order Pkg. Renegade requires Luxury Group.		
Cruise control, Sport	300	270
Includes leather-wrapped steering wheel. Requires 26/28B Quick Order Pkg.		
Heated front seats, Renegade, Limited	250	225
Renegade requires 26/26D Quick Order Pkg., Luxury Group, light bar delete. Limited requires 28G Quick Order Pkg.		
Mini overhead console, Renegade, Limited	400	360
Includes universal garage-door opener, trip computer, vehicle information center.		
Cargo organizer, Sport, Renegade	250	225
Sport/Renegade w/Security Group, Limited	175	158
Appearance & Special Purpose		
Fog lights, Sport	120	108
Requires 26/28B Quick Order Pkg.		
Light bar delete, Renegade (credit)	*(120)*	*(108)*
Requires 26/28D Quick Order Pkg.		
Rear privacy glass, Sport	270	243
Alloy wheels, Sport	310	279
Requires 26/28B Quick Order Pkg.		
Chrome alloy wheels, Limited	720	738

JEEP WRANGLER

CLASS: Compact sport-utility vehicle
DRIVE WHEELS: 4-wheel drive
BASE PRICE RANGE: $17,900-$28,215. Built in USA.
ALSO CONSIDER: Honda CR-V, Subaru Forester, Toyota RAV4

Availability of a 6-speed manual transmission marks 2005 for Jeep's tradition-bound compact SUV. Wrangler comes in regular-length SE, X, Sport, and Rubicon models. The extended-length Unlimited rides a 10-inch-longer wheelbase and is 15 inches longer overall. Due later in the model year is a Rubicon version. Unlimited's additional length adds 1.4 inches of rear leg room and more cargo volume behind the rear seat. Wranglers are available with a soft top and plastic side windows or with an extra-cost hardtop with glass windows; Unlimited's soft top features a fold-back forward section for a sunroof effect. The SE has a 147-hp 4-cyl engine. All other Wranglers have a 190-hp inline 6-cyl. A 6-speed manual transmission replaces a 5-speed and is standard on all models. A 4-speed automatic is optional with the 6-cyl. All Wranglers have 4WD that must be disengaged on dry pavement but includes low-range gearing. Four-wheel disc brakes are standard or optional on all but the SE and X. ABS is available only on the Sport. Front side and curtain side airbags aren't offered. A 30-inch tire package is standard on Unlimiteds, optional on Sport. Rubicon and UNlimited Rubicon are intended for severe off-road use.

RATINGS	SE, man.	Sport, man.	Rubicon w/hardtop, auto.	Unlimited, auto.
ACCELERATION	3	4	4	4
FUEL ECONOMY	4	3	2	3
RIDE QUALITY	3	2	2	3
STEERING/HANDLING	3	3	2	3
QUIETNESS	1	1	2	2
CONTROLS/MATERIALS	4	4	4	4
ROOM/COMFORT (FRONT)	4	4	4	4
ROOM/COMFORT (REAR)	2	2	2	3
CARGO ROOM	6	6	6	7
VALUE WITHIN CLASS	3	3	2	2

Wrangler is an uncomfortable, unrefined throwback. But few vehicles have more personality or better off-road ability. All versions have strong resale value, but prices are relatively steep. The Sport quickly tops $24,000. Unlimited starts at about that. Positioned just above the 4-cyl SE, the X delivers 6-cyl power for reasonable cost. Unlimiteds add cargo space and slightly better on-road feel.

TOTAL	33	32	30	35

Average total for compact sport-utility vehicles: 49.0

 Specifications begin on page 547.

ENGINES

	dohc I4	ohv I6
Size, liters/cu. in.	2.4/148	4.0/242
Horsepower @ rpm	147 @ 5200	190 @ 4600
Torque (lb-ft) @ rpm	165 @ 4000	235 @ 3200
Availability	S[1]	S[2]
EPA city/highway mpg		
6-speed manual	18/20	16/20
4-speed automatic		16/20

1. SE. 2. All except SE.

PRICES

Jeep Wrangler	RETAIL PRICE	DEALER INVOICE
SE 2-door convertible	$17900	$16659
X 2-door convertible	20210	18886
Sport 2-door convertible	22990	20956
Unlimited 2-door convertible	23745	21743
Rubicon 2-door convertible	27215	24716
Unlimited Rubicon 2-door convertible	28215	25721
Destination charge	610	610

STANDARD EQUIPMENT

SE: 2.4-liter 4-cylinder engine, 6-speed manual transmission, 4-wheel drive, 2-speed transfer case, dual front airbags, roll bar, power steering, tilt steering wheel, vinyl upholstery, front bucket seats, mini floor console, cupholder, folding rear seat, AM/FM/CD player, digital clock, tachometer, variable-intermittent wipers, carpeting, skid plates, outside-mounted full-size spare tire, P215/75R15 all-terrain tires.

X adds: 4.0-liter 6-cylinder engine, cloth upholstery.

Sport adds: air conditioning, full metal doors w/roll-up windows, full-length center console, upgraded sound system, deep-tinted rear windows, fog lights, front and rear tow hooks, 225/75R15 all-terrain white-letter tires.

Unlimited adds: Trac-Loc axle, Dana 44 rear axle, 4-wheel disc brakes, 10-inch-longer wheelbase, 30x9.5R15 all-terrain white-letter tires, alloy wheels. *Deletes:* upgraded sound system, deep-tinted rear windows.

Rubicon/Unlimited Rubicon adds to Sport: front and rear heavy-duty locking differentials, 4-wheel disc brakes, 10-inch-longer wheelbase (Unlimited Rubicon), off-road suspension, LT245/75R16 on/off-road tires, alloy wheels.

OPTIONAL EQUIPMENT

Major Packages	RETAIL PRICE	DEALER INVOICE
Willys Edition Group, X	$1490	$1311

Camouflage cloth upholstery, full-metal doors w/roll-up windows, upgraded sound system, deep-tinted rear windows, diamond plate sill guards, front and rear tow hooks, styled steel wheels. NA w/hardtop, Ecco Tire and Wheel Group.

OPTIONAL EQUIPMENT (cont.)

	RETAIL PRICE	DEALER INVOICE
Premium Quick Order Pkg. 24/25H, Unlimited	$1670	$1470
Leather-wrapped steering wheel, cruise control, upgraded cloth upholstery, automatic day/night rearview mirror, compass, outside-temperature indicator, upgraded sound system, front floormats, theft-deterrent system, unique interior and exterior trim.		
Brake and Traction Group, Sport	435	383
Trac-Loc axle, special axle ratio, 4-wheel disc brakes. Requires Tire and Wheel Group AAS.		
Tire and Wheel Group AAS, Sport	670	590
Five alloy wheels, heavy-duty shock absorbers and rear axle, Dana 44 rear axle, 30x9.5R15 all-terrain white-letter tires.		
Ecco Tire and Wheel Group, X	575	506
P225/75R15 all-terrain white-letter tires, alloy wheels.		
Chrome Tubular Group	NA	NA
Chrome tubular side steps and bumpers. NA Rubicon, Unlimited Rubicon.		
Security Group	295	260
Automatic day/night rearview mirror, compass, outside-temperature indicator, theft-deterrent system. NA SE, X.		

Powertrain

	RETAIL PRICE	DEALER INVOICE
4.0-liter 6-cylinder engine, SE	1280	1126
4-speed automatic transmission	825	726
SE requires 4.0-liter 6-cylinder engine.		
Trac-Loc axle, X, Sport	285	251
Sport requires antilock brakes.		
Dana 44 rear axle, Sport	310	273

Safety

	RETAIL PRICE	DEALER INVOICE
Antilock brakes, Sport	600	528
Requires Tire and Wheel Group AAS. NA w/Brake and Traction Group.		

Comfort & Convenience Features

	RETAIL PRICE	DEALER INVOICE
Hardtop, X	1160	1021
Sport, Unlimited, Rubicon, Unlimited Rubicon	795	700
Includes full metal doors with roll-up windows (X), rear wiper/washer, deep-tinted glass, rear defogger.		
Soft top and hardtop, Sport, Rubicon	1435	1263
NA Unlimited Rubicon.		
Full metal doors w/roll-up windows, SE	125	110
Air conditioning, SE, X	895	788
Leather-wrapped steering wheel	300	264
Includes cruise control. NA SE.		
Premium Audio Group, X, Unlimited	595	524
X w/Willys Group	300	264
AM/FM radio w/6-disc CD changer, upgraded sound system.		

Appearance & Special Purpose	RETAIL PRICE	DEALER INVOICE
Upgraded sound system, X, Unlimited	$295	$260
Includes 7 speakers, tweeter, subwoofer. Std. Sport, Rubicon.		
Add-A-Trunk lockable storage, Sport, Rubicon	125	110
NA Unlimited Rubicon.		
Deep-tinted rear windows, X	240	211
Side steps, Sport, Unlimited	150	132

2004 KIA AMANTI

CLASS: Large car
DRIVE WHEELS: Front-wheel drive
BASE PRICE: $24,995. Built in South Korea.
ALSO CONSIDER: Chevrolet Impala, Chrysler 300, Toyota Avalon

Kia's first midsize sedan shares its engine with corporate-parent Hyundai's XG350, but uses different architecture, with a 2-inch-longer wheelbase, 4-inch-longer body, and some 350 lb more curb weight. It uses a V6 and 5-speed automatic transmission with manual shift gate. Antilock 4-wheel disc brakes, front and rear side airbags, and head-protecting curtain side airbags are standard. So are dual-zone climate control, CD/cassette audio, keyless entry, and power front seats. Options include antiskid/traction control, leather upholstery, heated front seats, in-dash CD changer, and driver-seat memory system. Kia shares Hyundai's warranty coverage of 5-years/50,000-mi. basic, 10/100,000 powertrain, 5/unlimited roadside assistance.

RATINGS	Base w/ESP, Leather, Convenience Pkgs.
ACCELERATION	5
FUEL ECONOMY	4
RIDE QUALITY	6
STEERING/HANDLING	4
QUIETNESS	8
CONTROLS/MATERIALS	8
ROOM/COMFORT (FRONT)	7
ROOM/COMFORT (REAR)	6
CARGO ROOM	4

RATINGS (cont.)

	Base w/ESP, Leather, Convenience Pkgs.
VALUE WITHIN CLASS	5

Amanti's soft, floaty ride, quiet cabin, and noseplow in turns recall American sedans of years ago. For some buyers, that throwback flavor is a virtue, for others a curse. There's no debate about the car's high level of features per dollar, which helps its perceived value.

TOTAL	57

Average total for large cars: 60.9

ENGINES

	dohc V6
Size, liters/cu. in.	3.5/212
Horsepower @ rpm	200 @ 5500
Torque (lb-ft) @ rpm	220 @ 3500
Availability	S
EPA city/highway mpg	
5-speed automatic	17/25

PRICES

Kia Amanti

	RETAIL PRICE	DEALER INVOICE
Base 4-door sedan	$24995	$22655
Destination charge	540	540

STANDARD EQUIPMENT

Base: 3.5-liter V6 engine, 5-speed automatic transmission w/manual-shift capability, dual front airbags, front and rear side airbags, curtain side airbags, antilock 4-wheel disc brakes, air conditioning w/dual-zone automatic climate controls, power steering, tilt leather-wrapped steering wheel w/radio controls, cruise control, cloth upholstery, 8-way power driver seat w/lumbar adjustment, 4-way power passenger seat, center console, cupholders, trunk pass-through, heated power mirrors, power windows, power door locks, remote keyless entry, AM/FM/cassette/CD player, analog clock, tachometer, trip computer, illuminated visor mirrors, map lights, automatic headlights, floormats, theft-deterrent system, fog lights, full-size spare tire, 225/60R16 tires, alloy wheels.

OPTIONAL EQUIPMENT

Major Packages

	RETAIL PRICE	DEALER INVOICE
Leather Pkg.	$1805	$1611
Leather upholstery, memory system (driver seat, mirrors), Infinity AM/FM/cassette w/in-dash 6-disc CD changer, trip computer.		
Convenience Pkg.	900	803
Power sunroof, heated front seats, universal garage-door opener, automatic day/night rearview mirror. Requires Leather Pkg.		
Electronic Stability Pkg.	550	491
Traction control, antiskid system, brake assist. Requires Leather Pkg., Convenience Pkg.		

 Specifications begin on page 547.

2004 KIA OPTIMA

CLASS: Midsize car
DRIVE WHEELS: Front-wheel drive
BASE PRICE RANGE: $15,500-$19,495. Built in South Korea.
ALSO CONSIDER: Chevrolt Malibu, Honda Accord, Nissan Altima

Larger-diameter wheels for V6 models and a new grille design highlight 2004 changes to Kia's compact sedan. Optima is based on the Hyundai Sonata produced by Kia's corporate parent. Sharing Sonata's 4-cyl and V6 engines, Optima comes in LX and EX models; EX replaces SE for '04. With the 4-cyl, manual transmission is standard and an automatic with manual-shift feature is optional. The V6 comes with automatic only. Front side airbags are standard. All Optimas have 4-wheel disc brakes, but ABS is optional only with the V6. For '04, V6 models get 16-inch wheels to replace 15s; the 4-cyl models retain 15s. Optima does not offer Sonata's available traction control. Optima's performance and accommodations mirror those of like-equipped Sonatas.

RATINGS

	EX V6
ACCELERATION	5
FUEL ECONOMY	6
RIDE QUALITY	7
STEERING/HANDLING	6
QUIETNESS	6
CONTROLS/MATERIALS	7
ROOM/COMFORT (FRONT)	7
ROOM/COMFORT (REAR)	4
CARGO ROOM	5
VALUE WITHIN CLASS	6

In equipment and comfort, Optima and Sonata are impressive values for the money. Those attributes, combined with generous warranties, have fueled a sales increase and earned them our Recommended nod. What's can't yet be determined is whether the low resale values associated with Kia also will being to climb.

TOTAL	59

Average total for midsize cars: 57.2

ENGINES

	dohc I4	dohc V6
Size, liters/cu. in.	2.4/144	2.7/163
Horsepower @ rpm	138 @ 6000	170 @ 6000
Torque (lb-ft) @ rpm	159 @ 4500	181 @ 4000
Availability	S[1]	S[2]
EPA city/highway mpg		
5-speed manual	23/30	
4-speed automatic	22/30	20/27

1. LX, EX. 2. LX V6, EX V6.

PRICES

Kia Optima	RETAIL PRICE	DEALER INVOICE
LX 4-cylinder 4-door sedan, manual	$15500	$14370
LX 4-cylinder 4-door sedan, automatic	16420	15220
LX V6 4-door sedan, automatic	17895	16310
EX 4-cylinder 4-door sedan, automatic	18095	16630
EX V6 4-door sedan, automatic	19495	17755
Destination charge	540	540

STANDARD EQUIPMENT

LX 4-cylinder: 2.4-liter 4-cylinder engine, 5-speed manual or 4-speed automatic transmission w/manual-shift capability, dual front airbags, front side airbags, 4-wheel disc brakes, emergency inside trunk release, air conditioning, power steering, tilt steering wheel, cruise control, cloth upholstery, front bucket seats w/driver-seat height and lumbar adjustment, center console, cupholders, split folding rear seat, power mirrors, power windows, power door locks, AM/FM/CD player, digital clock, tachometer, illuminated visor mirrors, rear defogger, variable-intermittent wipers, map lights, 205/60HR15 tires, wheel covers.

LX V6 adds: 2.7-liter V6 engine, 4-speed automatic transmission w/manual-shift capability, 205/55R16 tires, alloy wheels.

EX 4-cylinder adds to LX 4-cylinder: 4-speed automatic transmission w/manual-shift capability, automatic climate control, leather-wrapped steering wheel, 8-way power driver seat, heated power mirrors, remote keyless entry, power sunroof, Infinity AM/FM/cassette/CD player, automatic day/night rearview mirror, universal garage-door opener, automatic headlights, fog lights, alloy wheels.

EX V6 adds: 2.7-liter V6 engine, 205/55R16 tires.

OPTIONAL EQUIPMENT

Major Packages	RETAIL PRICE	DEALER INVOICE
Leather Pkg., EX	$1095	$950

Leather upholstery, 4-way power passenger seat, wood/leather-wrapped steering wheel.

Safety		
Antilock brakes, LX V6, EX V6	795	691

Specifications begin on page 547.

Comfort & Convenience Features

	RETAIL PRICE	DEALER INVOICE
Infinity AM/FM/cassette/CD player, LX	$595	$517
CD changer	375	288
LX requires Infinity AM/FM/cassette/CD player.		

Appearance & Special Purpose

Rear spoiler	220	169

KIA RIO

CLASS: Compact car
DRIVE WHEELS: Front-wheel drive
BASE PRICE RANGE: $9,740-$12,390. Built in South Korea.
ALSO CONSIDER: Ford Focus, Honda Civic, Kia Spectra

Standard alloy wheels for the wagon version is the 2004 headline for Kia's entry-level compact line. Among the least-expensive cars on the market, Rio comes as a sedan and as a wagon. Kia calls the wagon the Cinco. Both have a 4-cyl engine. Manual transmission is standard, automatic optional. ABS, air conditioning, power windows, and power door locks are optional. Side airbags are unavailable. Power steering, tilt steering wheel, and a CD player are optional on the sedan and standard on the Cinco. Kia is owned by Hyundai and both South Korean automakers share warranty coverage: 5-years/60,000-mi. basic, 10/100,000 powertrain, 5-years/unlimited roadside assistance.

RATINGS

	Base sdn, man.
ACCELERATION	3
FUEL ECONOMY	6
RIDE QUALITY	4
STEERING/HANDLING	4
QUIETNESS	4
CONTROLS/MATERIALS	5
ROOM/COMFORT (FRONT)	3
ROOM/COMFORT (REAR)	2

RATINGS (cont.)

	Base sdn, man.
CARGO ROOM	2
VALUE WITHIN CLASS	2

Rio is outclassed by most rivals. It may have lower base prices, but a few options negate the advantage, and Rio's more generous warranty is more than offset by Kia's mediocre reliability record. For superior all-around "cheap wheels," we recommend a Ford Focus or, if your budget allows, a Honda Civic.

TOTAL	35

Average total for compact cars: 48.4

ENGINES

	dohc I4
Size, liters/cu. in.	1.6/97
Horsepower @ rpm	104 @ 5800
Torque (lb-ft) @ rpm	104 @ 4700
Availability	S
EPA city/highway mpg	
5-speed manual	26/33
4-speed automatic	25/32

PRICES

Kia Rio

	RETAIL PRICE	DEALER INVOICE
Base 4-door sedan, manual	$9740	$9355
Base 4-door sedan, automatic	10615	10190
Cinco 4-door wagon, manual	11365	10895
Cinco 4-door wagon, automatic	12390	11715
Destination charge	540	540

STANDARD EQUIPMENT

Base: 1.6-liter 4-cylinder engine, 5-speed manual or 4-speed automatic transmission, dual front airbags, emergency inside trunk release, manual steering, cloth upholstery, front bucket seats w/height-adjustable driver seat, center console, cupholders, rear defogger, variable-intermittent wipers, automatic-off headlights, 175/65R14 tires, wheel covers.

Cinco adds: power steering, tilt steering wheel, split folding rear seat, AM/FM/CD player, digital clock, tachometer, visor mirrors, map lights, rear wiper/washer, alloy wheels.

OPTIONAL EQUIPMENT

Major Packages

	RETAIL PRICE	DEALER INVOICE
Upgrade Pkg., Base	$525	$475
Power steering, tilt steering wheel, tachometer, map lights, visor mirrors, bodyside moldings.		
Power Pkg.	335	299
Power windows and door locks.		

Safety	RETAIL PRICE	DEALER INVOICE
Antilock brakes	$400	$357
Comfort & Convenience Features		
Air conditioning	800	715
AM/FM/CD player, Base	425	379
Appearance & Special Purpose		
Rear spoiler, Base	300	231
Cinco	100	89

2004 KIA SEDONA

CLASS: Minivan
DRIVE WHEELS: Front-wheel drive
BASE PRICE RANGE: $19,975-$22,085. Built in South Korea.
ALSO CONSIDER: Chevrolet Uplander, Dodge Caravan, Honda Odyssey,

A new grille is the only 2004 change of note for this South Korean automaker's minivan. Sedona has standard V6 power, 7-passenger seating, and comes in a single body length, which is about 2 inches longer than a regular-length Dodge Caravan. LX and uplevel EX models are offered. Both use a 3.5-liter V6 teamed with a 5-speed automatic transmission. Dual sliding rear side doors are standard, but power doors and side airbags are unavailable. ABS is optional. The LX's 2nd-row seat is a bench; the EX has buckets. Leather upholstery and a power sunroof are optional on EX. For '04, LX models get a standard center tray table that was previously standard on EX and optional on LX. Kia is owned by Hyundai and duplicates Hyundai's warranty: 5-years/60,000-mi. bumper-to-bumper, 10/100,000 powertrain, and 5-years/unlimited roadside assistance.

RATINGS

	EX w/ABS
ACCELERATION	3
FUEL ECONOMY	4
RIDE QUALITY	6
STEERING/HANDLING	3

RATINGS (cont.)

	EX w/ABS
QUIETNESS	6
CONTROLS/MATERIALS	8
ROOM/COMFORT (FRONT)	8
ROOM/COMFORT (REAR)	7
CARGO ROOM	9
VALUE WITHIN CLASS	6

Korean automakers stake their fortunes on delivering more features per dollar than class competitors. On that score, Sedona trumps most rivals. Additionally, Kia says its comprehensive warranty is the No. 1 reason buyers purchase its vehicles. However, Kia's resale values are among the industry's lowest.

TOTAL	60

Average total for minivans: 58.0

ENGINES

	dohc V6
Size, liters/cu. in.	3.5/213
Horsepower @ rpm	195 @ 5500
Torque (lb-ft) @ rpm	218 @ 3500
Availability	S
EPA city/highway mpg	
5-speed automatic	16/22

PRICES

Kia Sedona	RETAIL PRICE	DEALER INVOICE
LX 4-door van	$19975	$18760
EX 4-door van	22085	20305
Destination charge	640	640

STANDARD EQUIPMENT

LX: 3.5-liter V6 engine, 5-speed automatic transmission, dual front airbags, front and rear air conditioning w/rear controls, power steering, tilt steering wheel, cruise control, cloth upholstery, 7-passenger seating, front bucket seats w/driver-seat height adjustment, center console w/extendable table, cupholders, 2nd-row bench seat, 3rd-row split folding seat, power mirrors, power front windows, power door locks, AM/FM/CD player, digital clock, tachometer, variable-intermittent wipers w/deicer, map lights, visor mirrors, rear defogger, intermittent rear wiper/washer, remote fuel-door release, floormats, rear privacy glass, full-size spare tire, 215/70R15 tires, wheel covers.

EX adds: 8-way power driver seat w/power lumbar support, 4-way power passenger seat, 2nd-row bucket seats, leather-wrapped steering wheel, heated power mirrors, power rear quarter windows, remote keyless entry, AM/FM/cassette/CD player, illuminated visor mirrors, trip computer, universal garage-door opener, automatic headlights, roof rack, fog lights, alloy wheels.

 Specifications begin on page 547.

OPTIONAL EQUIPMENT

Safety	RETAIL PRICE	DEALER INVOICE
Antilock brakes	$595	$531
Comfort & Convenience Features		
Leather upholstery, EX	850	759
Power sunroof, EX	700	625
Appearance & Special Purpose		
Roof rack, LX	200	154
Rear spoiler	200	154
Tow hitch	350	269

2004 KIA SORENTO

CLASS: Midsize sport-utility vehicle
DRIVE WHEELS: Rear-wheel drive, 4-wheel drive
BASE PRICE RANGE: $18,995-$24,850. Built in South Korea.
ALSO CONSIDER: Ford Explorer, Honda Pilot, Toyota Highlander

Manual transmission and a Sport Package are newly available for Sorento for 2004. This 5-passenger wagon has the size, power, and body-on-frame construction typical of midsize SUVs, but is priced to compete with less-expensive compact SUVs. The sole engine is a 192-hp 3.5-liter V6. A 4-speed automatic transmission is joined for '04 by an available 5-speed manual. Rear-wheel drive and two 4WD systems are available. Both 4WD systems have a limited-slip rear axle and low-range gearing, but the Torque-On-Demand setup included in the optional Luxury Package can be left engaged on dry pavement. LX and EX trim levels are offered. Head-protecting curtain side airbags are standard. ABS is optional. All Sorentos have 16-inch wheels, a liftgate with a separate-opening window, and a full-size spare tire. Air conditioning; power windows, locks, and mirrors; cruise control; CD player; and 60/40 split folding rear seatback are standard. For '04, LX models offer a Sport Package with the new manual transmission, side steps, alloy wheels, keyless entry, and a roof rack. Kia is owned by Hyundai. Both South Korean companies share warranty coverage of 5-years/60,000-mi. bumper-to-bumper, 10/100,000 powertrain, and 5/unlimited roadside assistance.

RATINGS

	2WD LX, auto.	4WD EX w/Lux. Pkg., auto.
ACCELERATION	5	5
FUEL ECONOMY	4	4
RIDE QUALITY	4	4
STEERING/HANDLING	3	3
QUIETNESS	4	4
CONTROLS/MATERIALS	5	6
ROOM/COMFORT (FRONT)	7	7
ROOM/COMFORT (REAR)	6	6
CARGO ROOM	7	7
VALUE WITHIN CLASS	4	5

Sorento is priced like a compact SUV yet acts like a midsize, and impresses for interior decor and features per dollar. As for long-term value, Sorento is backed by Kia's generous warranty, but Kias have suffered from poor resale values.

TOTAL	49	51

Average total for midsize sport-utility vehicles: 54.7

ENGINES

	dohc V6
Size, liters/cu. in.	3.5/213
Horsepower @ rpm	192 @ 5500
Torque (lb-ft) @ rpm	217 @ 3000
Availability	S
EPA city/highway mpg	
5-speed manual	15/19[1]
4-speed automatic	15/20[1]

1. 16/19 w/2WD.

PRICES

Kia Sorento

	RETAIL PRICE	DEALER INVOICE
2WD LX 4-door wagon, manual	$18995	$17990
2WD LX 4-door wagon, automatic	20750	19625
4WD LX 4-door wagon, manual	20800	19660
4WD LX 4-door wagon, automatic	22650	21380
2WD EX 4-door wagon, automatic	23050	21385
4WD EX 4-door wagon, automatic	24850	23050
Destination charge	640	640

STANDARD EQUIPMENT

LX: 3.5-liter V6 engine, 5-speed manual or 4-speed automatic transmission, dual front airbags, curtain side airbags, 4-wheel disc brakes, power steering, tilt steering wheel, cruise control, air conditioning, cloth upholstery, front bucket seats w/driver-seat height and lumbar adjustment, center console, cupholders, split folding rear seat, heated power mirrors, power windows, power door locks, AM/FM/CD player, digital clock, tachometer, variable-intermittent wipers w/deicer, illuminated visor mirrors, map lights, cargo cover, rear defogger, intermittent rear wiper/washer, remote tailgate release, auto-

 Specifications begin on page 547.

matic-off headlights, rear privacy glass, roof rack (automatic), skid plates, front and rear tow hooks, trailer-wiring harness, full-size spare tire, 245/70HR16 tires, alloy wheels (automatic). **4WD** adds: 4-wheel drive, 2-speed transfer case, limited-slip differential.

EX adds: 4-speed automatic transmission, leather-wrapped steering wheel, 8-way power driver seat, remote keyless entry, power sunroof, AM/FM/cassette/CD player, automatic day/night rearview mirror, compass, outside-temperature indicator, altimeter, barometer, universal garage-door opener, floormats, roof rack, fog lights, alloy wheels. **4WD** adds: 4-wheel drive, 2-speed transfer case, limited-slip differential.

OPTIONAL EQUIPMENT

Major Packages	RETAIL PRICE	DEALER INVOICE
Sport Pkg., LX manual	$1200	$1070
Remote keyless entry, leather-wrapped steering wheel, side steps, roof rack, fog lights, alloy wheels.		
Leather Pkg., EX	900	804
Leather upholstery, heated front seats.		
Luxury Pkg., 2WD EX	1500	1340
4WD EX	2000	1785
Leather Pkg. plus automatic climate control, AM/FM radio w/in-dash 6-disc CD changer, Torque-On-Demand, full-time 4-wheel drive (4WD), automatic headlights, chrome exterior trim.		
Safety		
Antilock brakes	595	531
Appearance & Special Purpose		
Side steps	345	265
Rear spoiler, EX	200	154
Tow hitch	340	265
Load-leveling rear suspension, EX	510	455

KIA SPECTRA

CLASS: Compact car
DRIVE WHEELS: Front-wheel drive
BASE PRICE RANGE: $12,620-$15,970. Built in South Korea.
ALSO CONSIDER: Ford Focus, Honda Civic, Toyota Corolla

Spectra is the larger of Kia's two compact cars and is among the least-expensive vehicles with standard head-protecting curtain side airbags. Spectra slots above Kia's entry-level Rio and is based on the Elantra from Kia's corporate parent, Hyundai. It comes as a sedan and as a 4-dr wagon called the Spectra5. The only engine is Elantra's 138-hp 2.0-liter 4-cyl. Manual transmission is standard, automatic is optional. Sedans offer LX, EX, and SX models. Spectra5 comes in a single trim, and is positioned as a sporty model with a firmer suspension and different interior details. All Spectras have front side airbags, curtain side airbags, and 4-wheel disc brakes. ABS is unavailable on LX models but is optional on other Spectras. Tilt steering wheel, height-adjustable driver seat, and CD audio are standard on all. SX, EX, and Spectra5 add air conditioning, remote keyless entry, and power windows/locks/heated mirrors. Kia shares Hyundai's warranty of 5-years/60,000-mi. basic, 10/100,000 powertrain, and 5/unlimited roadside assistance.

RATINGS

RATINGS	LX sdn, auto.	EX sdn, man.
ACCELERATION	4	5
FUEL ECONOMY	6	7
RIDE QUALITY	6	6
STEERING/HANDLING	5	5
QUIETNESS	5	5
CONTROLS/MATERIALS	6	6
ROOM/COMFORT (FRONT)	5	5
ROOM/COMFORT (REAR)	4	4
CARGO ROOM	2	2
VALUE WITHIN CLASS	7	7

The sedans are far from sporty feeling, but Spectra is solidly class competitive for comfort, room, and features. Kudos to Kia for including the safety bonus of front side airbags and curtain side airbags among the many standard features. Kia quality is improving, though it still trails the Japanese leaders, as do resale values. The generous warranty compensates some. Overall, Spectra deserves a look if your budget is tight.

TOTAL	50	52

Average total for compact cars: 48.4

ENGINES

	dohc I4
Size, liters/cu. in.	2.0/121
Horsepower @ rpm	138 @ 6000
Torque (lb-ft) @ rpm	136 @ 4500
Availability	S
EPA city/highway mpg	
5-speed manual	25/32
4-speed automatic	25/34

PRICES

Kia Spectra	RETAIL PRICE	DEALER INVOICE
LX 4-door sedan, manual	$12620	$11925
LX 4-door sedan, automatic	13595	12815

 Specifications begin on page 547.

PRICES (cont.)

	RETAIL PRICE	DEALER INVOICE
EX 4-door sedan, manual	$13750	$12870
EX 4-door sedan, automatic	14725	13745
SX 4-door sedan, manual	14995	14045
SX 4-door sedan, automatic	15970	14955
Spectra5 4-door wagon, manual	14995	14045
Spectra5 4-door wagon, automatic	15970	14955
Destination charge	540	540

STANDARD EQUIPMENT

LX: 2.0-liter 4-cylinder engine, 5-speed manual or 4-speed automatic transmission, dual front airbags, front side airbags, curtain side airbags, 4-wheel disc brakes, emergency inside trunk release, power steering, tilt steering wheel, cloth upholstery, front bucket seats, height-adjustable driver seat, center console, cupholders, split folding rear seat, AM/FM/CD player, digital clock, tachometer, map lights, visor mirrors, variable-intermittent wipers, rear defogger, automatic-off headlights, 195/60R15 tires, wheel covers.

EX adds: air conditioning, heated power mirrors, power windows, power door locks, remote keyless entry, fog lights.

SX/Spectra5 adds: leather-wrapped steering wheel, rear wiper/washer (Spectra5), rear spoiler, sport suspension (Spectra5), 205/50R16 tires, alloy wheels.

OPTIONAL EQUIPMENT

Safety	RETAIL PRICE	DEALER INVOICE
Antilock brakes, EX, SX, Spectra5	$400	$360
Comfort & Convenience Features		
Air conditioning, LX	960	860
Power sunroof, EX, SX, Spectra5	700	625
Cruise control, EX, SX, Spectra5	250	225
Appearance & Special Purpose		
Alloy wheels, EX	360	320

LAND ROVER FREELANDER

CLASS: Compact sport-utility vehicle
DRIVE WHEELS: All-wheel drive
BASE PRICE: $26,830. Built in England.
ALSO CONSIDER: Ford Escape, Honda CR-V, Mazda Tribute

An abbreviated lineup marks 2005 for Land Rover's entry-level model. Freelander comes as a 4-dr wagon called the SE and a 2-dr semiconvertible called the SE3. Exterior dimensions are shared, but the SE3 features removable roof panels over the front seats and a removable hardtop over the rear-seat/cargo area. Both models have a 174-hp V6, 5-speed automatic trans-

mission with manual shift gate, ABS, and all-wheel drive. SE models have 16-inch wheels; SE3 17s. All models have AWD that lacks low-range gearing, but includes traction control and Land Rover's Hill Descent Control. Also shared is a swing-out cargo door with a power up/down rear window. Side airbags are unavailable. Largely replacing last year's top-line HSE model is a $3000 Premium Package available on the SE. It includes leather upholstery, a harman/kardon 6-disc CD sound system, 18-inch wheels, a cargo cover, and illuminated vanity mirrors.

RATINGS	SE3	SE w/Prem. Pkg.
ACCELERATION	3	3
FUEL ECONOMY	4	4
RIDE QUALITY	5	5
STEERING/HANDLING	5	5
QUIETNESS	5	5
CONTROLS/MATERIALS	4	4
ROOM/COMFORT (FRONT)	5	6
ROOM/COMFORT (REAR)	4	5
CARGO ROOM	5	5
VALUE WITHIN CLASS	2	3

Fault Freelander for premium pricing, prosaic interior decor, and awkward details like the debatable design of the rear-seat releases. For SE3, add poor rear visibility and entry/exit. Credit Freelander for being solid, comfortable, and competent. Overall, its key asset is whatever cachet the Land Rover image carries.

TOTAL	42	45

Average total for compact sport-utility vehicles: 49.0

ENGINES	dohc V6
Size, liters/cu. in.	2.5/152
Horsepower @ rpm	174 @ 6250
Torque (lb-ft) @ rpm	177 @ 4000
Availability	S
EPA city/highway mpg	
5-speed automatic	17/21

 Specifications begin on page 547.

PRICES

Land Rover Freelander	RETAIL PRICE	DEALER INVOICE
SE 4-door wagon	$26830	$24415
SE3 2-door wagon	26830	24415
Destination charge	665	665

STANDARD EQUIPMENT

SE: 2.5-liter V6 engine, 5-speed automatic transmission w/manual-shift capability, all-wheel drive, traction control, dual front airbags, antilock brakes, hill descent control, air conditioning, power steering, tilt leather-wrapped steering wheel, cruise control, alcantara/leather upholstery, front bucket seats w/driver-seat lumbar adjustment, center console, cupholders, split folding rear seat, heated power mirrors, power windows, power rear window, power door locks, remote keyless entry, power sunroof, AM/FM/CD player, digital clock, tachometer, variable-intermittent wipers, heated windshield, rear defogger, rear wiper/washer, theft-deterrent system, roof rails, rear privacy glass, front and rear fog lights, 215/65HR16 tires, alloy wheels.

SE3 adds: cloth upholstery, Harman/Kardon AM/FM radio w/in-dash 6-disc CD changer, steering-wheel radio controls, removable front roof panels, removable rear hardtop, full-size spare tire, 225/55R17 tires. *Deletes:* power sunroof.

OPTIONAL EQUIPMENT

Major Packages	RETAIL PRICE	DEALER INVOICE
Premium Pkg.	$3000	$2730

Leather upholstery, Harman/Kardon AM/FM radio w/in-dash 6-disc CD changer, steering-wheel radio controls, illuminated visor mirrors, cargo cover, 235/50R18 tires.

Comfort & Convenience Features		
Heated front seats, SE	300	276
235/50R18 tires, SE3	750	683

LAND ROVER LR3

CLASS: Premium midsize sport-utility vehicle
DRIVE WHEELS: All-wheel drive
BASE PRICE RANGE: $44,330-$49,330. Built in England.
ALSO CONSIDER: Acura MDX, Cadillac SRX, Lexus RX 330

LAND ROVER

Land Rover's best-selling model is redesigned for 2005, getting a new name, new styling, and more power. Replacing the 1994-2004 Discovery is the LR3, which is nearly 14 inches longer in wheelbase, 5.7 inches longer overall, and some 850 lb heavier. Cargo volume increases by 27 cu ft, but passenger space is little-changed. LR3 retains the Discovery's raised rear roof section, but the spare tire now mounts inside, and a glass liftgate with drop-down tailgate replaces a swing-out cargo door. Seating for five is standard and increases to seven with optional 3rd-row seating. The 2nd-row seat is a bench split 65/35 on 5-passenger models, 40/20/40 on 7-seaters. Front torso and head-protecting curtain side airbags are standard for LR3. The curtain airbags cover the first two rows on 5-passenger models, all rows on 7-seat versions.

Replacing Discovery's 217-hp V8 is a 300-hp V8. A 6-speed automatic transmission with manual shift gate replaces a 4-speed automatic. All-wheel drive with low-range gearing is standard and includes a locking center differential for severe off-road conditions; a locking rear differential is available. Also standard are antilock 4-wheel disc brakes, antiskid/traction control, and hill descent control. New is Land Rover's Active Roll Mitigation. Active Roll Mitigation is designed to detect an impending tip and activate the antiskid system to reduce the chances of a roll.

SE and HSE models are offered. The HSE has 19-inch wheels vs. SE's 18s, plus additional standard equipment and unique trim.

Replacing the Discovery's solid axles and metal springs, LR3 has an independent air-spring suspension with four available ride heights and automatic load leveling.

In addition, LR3 introduces Land Rover's Terrain Response system as standard. Twisting a dial changes suspension and powertrain electronic calibrations to accomodate normal driving, slippery pavement, mud, sand, and low-speed off-roading. This evaluation is based on preview test drives.

RATINGS	SE	HSE w/Rear Seat Pkg.
ACCELERATION	6	6
FUEL ECONOMY	3	3
RIDE QUALITY	6	6
STEERING/HANDLING	4	4
QUIETNESS	7	7
CONTROLS/MATERIALS	6	5
ROOM/COMFORT (FRONT)	7	7
ROOM/COMFORT (REAR)	7	7
CARGO ROOM	8	8
VALUE WITHIN CLASS	5	5

LR3 offers a great balance of passenger and cargo room, on-road comfort, and off-road prowess but suffers from difficult-to-decipher interior controls and poor fuel economy. It is a credible effort by Land Rover to garner some coveted premium midsize SUV market share, but we are wary of Land Rover's traditionally poor resale values and spotty reliability record.

TOTAL	59	58

Average total for premium midsize sport-utility vehicles: 59.6

 Specifications begin on page 547.

ENGINES

	dohc V8
Size, liters/cu. in.	4.4/268
Horsepower @ rpm	300 @ 5500
Torque (lb-ft) @ rpm	315 @ 4000
Availability	S
EPA city/highway mpg	
6-speed automatic	14/18[1]

1. Land Rover estimates.

PRICES

Land Rover LR3	RETAIL PRICE	DEALER INVOICE
SE 4-door wagon	$44330	$40340
HSE 4-door wagon	49330	44890
Destination charge	665	665

STANDARD EQUIPMENT

SE: 4.4-liter V8 engine, 6-speed automatic transmission w/manual-shift capability, all-wheel drive, 2-speed transfer case, 4-wheel traction control, locking center differential, dual front airbags, front side airbags, front and 2nd-row curtain side airbags, antilock 4-wheel disc brakes, brake assist, antiskid system, roll-stability control, hill descent control, air conditioning w/dual-zone automatic climate controls, power steering, tilt leather-wrapped steering wheel w/radio controls, cruise control, leather/alcantara upholstery, front bucket seats, 8-way power driver seat, 6-way power passenger seat, center console, cupholders, 2nd-row split folding seat, heated power mirrors w/passenger-side tilt-down back-up aid, power windows, power door locks, remote keyless entry, power sunroof, Harman/Kardon AM/FM radio w/in-dash 6-disc CD changer, digital clock, tachometer, outside-temperature indicator, variable-intermittent wipers, cargo cover, rear defogger, rear wiper/washer, height-adjustable and load-leveling air suspension, theft-deterrent system, rear privacy glass, rear fog light, 255/60HR18 tires, alloy wheels.

HSE adds: rear-obstacle-detection system, memory system (driver seat, mirrors), navigation system, upgraded sound system, automatic day/night rearview mirror, universal garage-door opener, automatic headlights, rain-sensing wipers, bi-xenon headlights, fog lights, 255/55HR19 tires.

OPTIONAL EQUIPMENT

Major Packages	RETAIL PRICE	DEALER INVOICE
Convenience Pkg.	$175	$159
35/30/35 split folding 2nd-row seat, additional front cupholder, cargo net.		
Rear Seat Pkg.	1250	1138
Convenience Pkg. plus 3rd-row curtain side airbags, 3rd-row split folding seat, rear map lights and auxiliary power outlet.		
Cold Climate Pkg.	1050	956
Heated front and 2nd-row seats, heated windshield, heated washer jets.		

OPTIONAL EQUIPMENT (cont.)

	RETAIL PRICE	DEALER INVOICE
Lighting Pkg., SE	$1050	$956
Bi-xenon headlights w/washers, universal garage-door opener, automatic day/night rearview mirror, rain-sensing wipers, front fog lights.		
Heavy-Duty Pkg.	625	569
Active-locking rear differential, full-size spare tire w/alloy wheel.		
Tow Pkg.	500	455
Class III hitch receiver, remote rear height adjuster.		
Safety		
Rear-obstacle-detection system, SE	350	319
Comfort & Convenience Features		
Navigation system, SE	2650	2412
Automatic rear climate control	950	865
Includes additional rear vents.		

LEXUS ES 330

CLASS: Premium midsize car
DRIVE WHEELS: Front-wheel drive
BASE PRICE: $31,975. Built in Japan.
ALSO CONSIDER: Acura TL, Audi A4, Infiniti G35

Lexus' best-selling car gets minor styling changes and several first-time features for 2005. The ES 330 comes with a 3.3-liter V6, 5-speed automatic transmission, and antilock 4-wheel disc brakes. Also standard are front torso side airbags and head-protecting curtain side airbags. Antiskid/traction control is available, as is Lexus' Adaptive Variable Suspension with driver-selectable shock-absorber settings. Sixteen-inch wheels are standard, but 17s are a new option, as are heated/cooled front seats. Newly standard for '05 is a memory system for both power front seats, not just the driver seat, plus power door mirrors that automatically tilt down on selecting Reverse. The extra-cost navigation system gets more-detailed screen graphics and a larger DVD database. It also now offers optional voice control, activated by steering-wheel buttons, for its navigation, audio, and climate functions. And the audio system is now preconfigured to accept dealer-activated satellite radio service. Returning options include power-adjustable pedals, premium Mark

 Specifications begin on page 547.

Levinson audio, CD changer, power rear sunshade, and xenon headlamps packaged with rain-sensing windshield wipers. The ES shares its basic design with the Camry from Lexus-parent Toyota.

RATINGS	Base w/adaptive susp., 17-inch wheels	Base w/nav. sys., adaptive susp.
ACCELERATION	6	6
FUEL ECONOMY	5	5
RIDE QUALITY	7	7
STEERING/HANDLING	6	6
QUIETNESS	7	8
CONTROLS/MATERIALS	7	7
ROOM/COMFORT (FRONT)	8	8
ROOM/COMFORT (REAR)	6	6
CARGO ROOM	4	4
VALUE WITHIN CLASS	8	8

Though no excitement machine, the ES 330 is very civilized, solidly built, and nicely appointed. The Adaptive Variable Suspension is a needless extra; we recommend the optional antiskid system for about the same money. Otherwise, this is an easy Recommended pick for comfort, refinement, and amenities. Note that a Camry XLE V6 delivers most of the ES's polish at a lower price, but doesn't include the longer warranty coverage or red-carpet customer treatment you get with the step up to Lexus.

TOTAL	64	65

Average total for premium midsize cars: 61.7

ENGINES

	dohc V6
Size, liters/cu. in.	3.3/202
Horsepower @ rpm	225 @ 5600
Torque (lb-ft) @ rpm	240 @ 3600
Availability	S
EPA city/highway mpg	
5-speed automatic	20/29

PRICES

Lexus ES 330	RETAIL PRICE	DEALER INVOICE
Base 4-door sedan	$31975	$28350
Destination charge	625	625

STANDARD EQUIPMENT

Base: 3.3-liter V6 engine, 5-speed automatic transmission, dual front airbags, front side airbags, curtain side airbags, antilock 4-wheel disc brakes, daytime running lights, air conditioning w/dual-zone automatic climate controls, interior air filter, power steering, tilt leather-wrapped steering wheel w/radio controls, cruise control, leather upholstery, front bucket seats, 10-way power driver seat, 8-way power passenger seat, memory system (front seats, mirrors), center console, cupholders, wood interior trim, heated power mirrors w/automatic day/night and passenger-side tilt-down back-up aid, power windows, power door locks, remote keyless entry, power sunroof, AM/FM/cassette/CD player, digital clock, tachometer, automatic day/night rearview mirror, universal garage-door opener, illuminated visor mirrors, trip computer, compass, outside-temperature indicator, map lights, variable-intermittent wipers, rear defogger, automatic headlights, floormats, theft-deterrent system, fog lights, full-size spare tire, 215/60VR16 tires, alloy wheels.

OPTIONAL EQUIPMENT

Major Packages	RETAIL PRICE	DEALER INVOICE
Navigation System Pkg.	$2200	$1843
Navigation system, in-dash 6-disc CD changer, voice-activated controls.		
Navigation System/Mark Levinson Audio Pkg.	3100	2518
Navigation System Pkg. plus Mark Levinson sound system.		
Safety		
Antiskid system	640	512
Includes traction control, brake assist.		
Comfort & Convenience Features		
Heated/cooled front seats	640	512
Power-adjustable pedals	140	112
Includes memory.		
In-dash 6-disc CD changer	550	440
Wood/leather-wrapped steering wheel	330	264
Power rear sunshade	210	168
Appearance & Special Purpose		
Xenon headlights	640	512
Includes rain-sensing wipers.		
Adaptive Variable Suspension	620	496
Requires antiskid system, xenon headlights.		
Chrome alloy wheels	1780	890
Includes 215/55VR17 tires.		

Postproduction options also available.

LEXUS GS

CLASS: Premium midsize car
DRIVE WHEELS: Rear-wheel drive, all-wheel drive
2004 BASE PRICE RANGE: $38,875-$47,975. Built in Japan.
ALSO CONSIDER: Cadillac CTS, Mercedes-Benz E-Class

Lexus' midrange sedans are little-changed for 2005. New-design '06 models are expected by summer '05. The GS 300 uses a 3.0-liter inline 6-cyl engine, the GS 430 a 4.3 V8. Both include 5-speed automatic transmission, antiskid/traction-control system, antilock 4-wheel disc brakes, front side airbags, sunroof, and in-dash CD changer. GS 430 has leather upholstery, memory driver seat, and heated front seats, all available for the 300. A navigation system is available for both models.

 Specifications begin on page 547.

RATINGS	GS 300	GS 430 w/nav. sys., 17-inch wheels
ACCELERATION	6	7
FUEL ECONOMY	4	4
RIDE QUALITY	9	8
STEERING/HANDLING	7	7
QUIETNESS	8	7
CONTROLS/MATERIALS	8	6
ROOM/COMFORT (FRONT)	7	7
ROOM/COMFORT (REAR)	5	5
CARGO ROOM	4	4
VALUE WITHIN CLASS	6	5

Neither GS is a sports-sedan all-star, but they do have a smooth ride, plentiful features, and quality workmanship. They also stack up well for value against direct price rivals. The GS 300 is the smarter buy, giving up little to its costlier V8 sibling.

TOTAL	64	60

Average total for premium midsize cars: 61.7

ENGINES	dohc I6	dohc V8
Size, liters/cu. in.	3.0/183	4.3/262
Horsepower @ rpm	220 @ 5800	300 @ 5600
Torque (lb-ft) @ rpm	220 @ 3800	325 @ 3400
Availability	S[1]	S[2]
EPA city/highway mpg		
5-speed automatic	18/25	18/23

1. GS 300. 2. GS 430.

2005 prices unavailable at time of publication.

2004 PRICES

Lexus GS	RETAIL PRICE	DEALER INVOICE
GS 300 4-door sedan	$38875	$34208
GS 430 4-door sedan	47975	41736
Destination charge	625	625

STANDARD EQUIPMENT

GS 300: 3.0-liter 6-cylinder engine, 5-speed automatic transmission w/manual-shift capability, traction control, dual front airbags, front side airbags, front curtain side airbags, antilock 4-wheel disc brakes, antiskid system, emergency inside trunk release, daytime running lights, air conditioning w/automatic dual-zone climate controls, interior air filter, power steering, power tilt/telescope leather-wrapped steering wheel, cruise control, cloth upholstery, 10-way power front bucket seats w/power lumbar adjustment, center console, cupholders, wood interior trim, heated power mirrors w/automatic day/night, power windows, power door locks, remote keyless entry, power sunroof, AM/FM/cassette w/in-dash 6-disc CD changer, digital clock, tachometer, automatic day/night rearview mirror, compass, variable-intermittent wipers, rear defogger, outside-temperature indicator, illuminated visor mirrors, universal garage-door opener, remote fuel-door and trunk releases, map lights, automatic headlights, floormats, theft-deterrent system, fog lights, full-size spare tire, 225/55VR16 tires, alloy wheels.

GS 430 adds: 4.3-liter V8 engine, leather upholstery, heated front seats, memory system (driver seat, steering wheel, mirrors), high-intensity-discharge headlights.

OPTIONAL EQUIPMENT

Major Packages	RETAIL PRICE	DEALER INVOICE
Leather Trim Pkg., GS 300	$1660	$1494
Leather upholstery, memory system (driver seat, steering wheel, mirrors).		
Navigation/Mark Levinson Radio System Pkg., GS 300	4910	4419
GS 430	3250	2925
Leather Trim Pkg. (GS 300), navigation system, Mark Levinson Radio System.		
Comfort & Convenience Features		
Navigation system	2000	1800
Mark Levinson Radio System	1250	1125
Heated front seats, GS 300	440	396
Requires Leather Trim Pkg. or Navigation/Mark Levinson Radio System Pkg.		
Wood/leather-wrapped steering wheel, GS 430	300	240
Appearance & Special Purpose		
High-intensity-discharge headlights, GS 300	515	464
Rear spoiler	440	352
235/45ZR17 tires, GS 430	215	172
Chrome alloy wheels	1700	850

Postproduction options also available.

2004 LEXUS GX 470

CLASS: Premium midsize sport-utility vehicle
DRIVE WHEELS: All-wheel drive
BASE PRICE: $45,375. Built in Japan.
ALSO CONSIDER: Acura MDX, Cadillac SRX

 Specifications begin on page 547.

Based on parent-company Toyota's 4Runner, GX 470 gained several new features during the 2004 model year. GX 470 comes with a V8 engine, 5-speed automatic transmission, and all-wheel drive with low-range gearing. ABS and antiskid/traction control are standard, along with a tire-pressure monitor added midyear. A roll-detection sensor for the head-protecting 1st- and 2nd-row curtain side airbags was added midyear. Front torso side airbags are standard. So is a hill ascent/descent control designed to maintain a slow, steady speed on steep grades. The suspension offers height adjustment, rear self-leveling suspension, and automatic shock-absorber control with four driver-selectable modes. Another midyear addition was Lexus' Kinetic Dynamic Suspension option. It uses sensor-activated electrohydraulic couplings that temporarily "release" the antiroll bars as needed to improve comfort and stability on rough surfaces. Continuing options include a navigation system, rear DVD entertainment, and a 3rd-row bench seat for up to 8-passenger capacity. As of midyear, the navigation screen serves a camera that displays a rear view when Reverse is selected. Sunroof and lighted running boards are standard. The GX has a swing-open tailgate with fixed glass vs. 4Runner's liftgate with power window. Also included: leather upholstery, heated front seats, automatic climate control, in-dash CD changer, and driver-seat memory.

RATINGS	Base w/nav. sys.
ACCELERATION	6
FUEL ECONOMY	4
RIDE QUALITY	4
STEERING/HANDLING	4
QUIETNESS	6
CONTROLS/MATERIALS	7
ROOM/COMFORT (FRONT)	8
ROOM/COMFORT (REAR)	7
CARGO ROOM	8
VALUE WITHIN CLASS	6

GX 470 is roomier than the Infiniti FX or BMW's X5, though not as sporty, and it's more modern than the Mercedes-Benz M-Class, though no larger inside. The quality and red-carpet dealer service associated with the Lexus brand help this embellished 4Runner compete in the luxury-SUV field. But car-type rivals, such as the Acura MDX and Lexus' own RX 330, are more-sensible choices overall.

TOTAL	60

Average total for premium midsize sport-utility vehicles: 59.6

ENGINES

	dohc V8
Size, liters/cu. in.	4.7/285
Horsepower @ rpm	235 @ 4800
Torque (lb-ft) @ rpm	320 @ 3400
Availability	S
EPA city/highway mpg	
5-speed automatic	15/19

PRICES

Lexus GX 470	RETAIL PRICE	DEALER INVOICE
Base 4-door wagon	$45375	$39474
Destination charge	625	625

STANDARD EQUIPMENT

Base: 4.7-liter V8 engine, 5-speed automatic transmission, all-wheel drive, 2-speed transfer case, traction control, limited-slip differential, dual front airbags, front side airbags, front and 2nd-row curtain side airbags w/rollover-detection sensor, antilock 4-wheel disc brakes, brake assist, antiskid system, hill ascent/descent control, tire-pressure monitor, daytime running lights, front air conditioning w/dual-zone automatic climate controls, cruise control, power steering, power tilt/telescope wood/leather-wrapped steering wheel w/radio controls, leather upholstery, heated front bucket seats, 10-way power driver seat, 4-way power passenger seat, center console, cupholders, memory system (driver seat, mirrors, steering wheel), split folding rear seat, wood interior trim, heated power mirrors, power windows, power door locks, remote keyless entry, power sunroof, AM/FM/cassette w/in-dash 6-disc CD changer, rear radio controls, digital clock, tachometer, trip computer, rain-sensing wipers, automatic day/night rearview mirror, universal garage-door opener, illuminated visor mirrors, cargo cover, rear defogger, variable-intermittent rear wiper/washer, automatic headlights, floormats, roof rack, theft-deterrent system, fog lights, rear privacy glass, running boards, height-adjustable suspension w/adjustable shock absorbers and rear load-leveling suspension, full-size spare tire, 265/65HR17 tires, alloy wheels.

OPTIONAL EQUIPMENT

Major Packages	RETAIL PRICE	DEALER INVOICE
Navigation/Audio Pkg	$3050	$2471
Navigation system, Mark Levinson sound system, rearview camera. Moves in-dash CD changer to glovebox.		
Comfort & Convenience Features		
Lexus Link	1215	1015
Telematics system. Includes one-year service.		
Rear-seat DVD entertainment system	1560	1248
3rd-row split folding seat	2030	1624
Includes rear air conditioning.		
Tow-hitch receiver	420	300
Kinetic Dynamic Suspension	1750	1400

 Specifications begin on page 547.

LEXUS IS 300

CLASS: Premium compact car
DRIVE WHEELS: Rear-wheel drive
2004 BASE PRICE RANGE: $29,435-$30,805. Built in Japan.
ALSO CONSIDER: Acura TL, BMW 3-Series, Infiniti G35

The sporty compacts at Toyota's luxury division come as the IS 300 sedan and SportCross wagon. Both use an inline 6-cyl engine and 5-speed automatic transmission. The sedan is also available with 5-speed manual; so equipped, it includes a firmer suspension. The SportCross has a slightly different front-end look, fold-down front-passenger seat, and split folding rear seat. All IS 300s have front side airbags and head-protecting curtain side airbags, antilock 4-wheel disc brakes with full-power assist, traction control, 17-inch wheels, and performance tires. The wagon has wider tires at the rear. All-season tires on 16-inch wheels are a no-charge option. An antiskid system is available with automatic transmission. Also optional are navigation system, power moonroof, heated front seats with driver-seat memory, and leather upholstery. A limited-slip differential is no longer available, the sole 2005 change for this line.

RATINGS	Base sdn, man.	Base sdn w/leather, man.	Base sdn, auto.	SportCross w/nav. sys.
ACCELERATION	6	6	6	6
FUEL ECONOMY	5	5	5	5
RIDE QUALITY	6	6	6	6
STEERING/HANDLING	7	7	7	7
QUIETNESS	6	6	6	6
CONTROLS/MATERIALS	6	6	6	5
ROOM/COMFORT (FRONT)	6	6	6	6
ROOM/COMFORT (REAR)	4	4	4	4
CARGO ROOM	2	2	2	6
VALUE WITHIN CLASS	5	5	4	6

Rival BMW 3-Series and Audi A4 models have "built for the autobahn" cachet and more ultimate dynamic ability. But IS 300s offer sporty driving fun Lexus style, and that's no bad thing.

TOTAL	53	53	52	57

Average total for premium compact cars: 57.5

ENGINES

	dohc I6
Size, liters/cu. in.	3.0/183
Horsepower @ rpm	215 @ 5800
Torque (lb-ft) @ rpm	218 @ 3800
Availability	S
EPA city/highway mpg	
5-speed manual	18/25
5-speed automatic	18/24

2005 prices unavailable at time of publication.

2004 PRICES

Lexus IS 300	RETAIL PRICE	DEALER INVOICE
Base 4-door sedan, manual	$29435	$25901
Base 4-door sedan, automatic	30805	27108
SportCross 4-door wagon, automatic	30805	27108
Destination charge	545	545

STANDARD EQUIPMENT

Base: 3.0-liter 6-cylinder engine, 5-speed manual or 5-speed automatic transmission w/manual-shift capability, traction control, dual front airbags, front side airbags, front curtain side airbags, antilock 4-wheel disc brakes, brake assist, daytime running lights, emergency inside trunk release, air conditioning w/automatic climate control, interior air filter, power steering, tilt leather-wrapped steering wheel, cruise control, cloth upholstery, front bucket seats, center console, cupholders, trunk pass-through, heated power mirrors w/driver-side automatic day/night, power windows, power door locks, remote keyless entry, AM/FM radio w/in-dash 6-disc CD changer, digital clock, tachometer, automatic day/night rearview mirror, compass, rear defogger, map lights, variable-intermittent wipers, visor mirrors, remote decklid release, automatic headlights, floormats, theft-deterrent system, high-intensity-discharge headlights, fog lights, sport suspension (manual), 215/45ZR17 tires, alloy wheels.

SportCross adds: 5-speed automatic transmission w/manual-shift capability, fold-down front-passenger seat, split folding rear seat, cargo cover, rear wiper/washer, rear spoiler, 215/45ZR17 front tires, 225/45ZR17 rear tires. *Deletes:* emergency inside trunk release, trunk pass-through.

OPTIONAL EQUIPMENT

Major Packages	RETAIL PRICE	DEALER INVOICE
Leather Pkg., Base	$2465	$1971
SportCross	2505	2004
Leather upholstery, 8-way power front seats, driver-seat memory, universal garage-door opener.		
Leather and Alcantara Pkg., Base	2065	1652
SportCross	2105	1684
Leather and alcantara upholstery, 8-way power front seats, driver-seat memory, universal garage-door opener.		

 Specifications begin on page 547.

OPTIONAL EQUIPMENT (cont.)

	RETAIL PRICE	DEALER INVOICE
Power and Leather Pkg., Base	$1465	$1318
SportCross	1505	1354
Leather Pkg. plus power sunroof.		
Power and Alcantara Pkg., Base	1065	958
SportCross	1105	994
Leather and Alcantara Pkg. plus power sunroof.		
SportDesign Edition, Base	1715	1543
Leather Pkg. plus power sunroof, unique interior and exterior trim, Euro-Tuned Suspension (manual).		
Powertrain		
Limited-slip differential	390	312
Safety		
Antiskid system, Base w/automatic, SportCross	350	280
Includes limited-slip differential.		
Comfort & Convenience Features		
Navigation system	2000	1700
Power sunroof	500	400
Heated front seats	440	352
Requires a Leather or Leather and Alcantara Pkg.		
Appearance & Special Purpose		
Rear spoiler, Base	440	352
205/55VR16 all-season tires	NC	NC
NA w/polished alloy wheels.		
215/45ZR17 all-season tires, Base	NC	NC
Polished alloy wheels	400	320

Postproduction options also available.

LEXUS LS 430

CLASS: Premium large car
DRIVE WHEELS: Rear-wheel drive
BASE PRICE: $55,675. Built in Japan.
ALSO CONSIDER: Audi A8, Mercedes-Benz S-Class, Volkswagen Phaeton

LEXUS

An assistance and concierge service is no longer available on Lexus' flagship sedan for 2005. The LS 430 has a 290-hp V8 and a 6-speed automatic transmission with manual shift gate. Antiskid/traction control, antilock 4-wheel disc brakes, tire-pressure monitor, and steering-linked headlights are standard. A firmer Euro-Tuned Suspension option substitutes 18-inch wheels for the standard 17s, and for '05 switches from performance tires to all-season treads. Head-protecting curtain side airbags are standard, as are torso side airbags and knee airbags for driver and front passenger. Gone is the optional Lexus Link service, which provided assistance through the OnStar network. Continuing option groups start with a Premium Package including front/rear-obstacle detection, heated rear seats, and heated/cooled front seats. The Modern Luxury Package includes a navigation system with a rearview camera that displays on the navigation screen when backing up. To that, the Custom group adds power door closers and adaptive cruise control designed to maintain a set following distance. The top-line Ultra Luxury Package includes self-adjusting air suspension, rear air conditioning, massaging rear seats, and other features. Available with the Custom or Ultra options is Lexus' Pre-Collision Safety System, which uses a grille-mounted radar sensor to "anticipate" a crash and automatically tighten seatbelts and readies full braking power. Also optional is Lexus' SmartAccess keyless entry/starting system with pocket transmitter. Satellite radio is a dealer-installed extra.

RATINGS	Base	Base w/Euro suspension	Base w/Ultra Lux. Pkg.
ACCELERATION	7	7	7
FUEL ECONOMY	5	5	5
RIDE QUALITY	9	8	9
STEERING/HANDLING	6	7	6
QUIETNESS	10	9	10
CONTROLS/MATERIALS	7	7	6
ROOM/COMFORT (FRONT)	10	10	10
ROOM/COMFORT (REAR)	9	9	10
CARGO ROOM	6	6	6
VALUE WITHIN CLASS	10	10	9

The LS 430 is priced at about the midpoint among premium large cars, but matches any of them for expected standard features and optional gadgets. It's less sporty than its German rivals, but this Lexus is an unsurpassed Best Buy blend of comfort, refinement, workmanship, and resale value.

TOTAL	79	78	78

Average total for premium large cars: 68.7

ENGINES	dohc V8
Size, liters/cu. in.	4.3/262
Horsepower @ rpm	290 @ 5600
Torque (lb-ft) @ rpm	320 @ 3400
Availability	S
EPA city/highway mpg	
6-speed automatic	18/25

Specifications begin on page 547.

PRICES

Lexus LS 430

	RETAIL PRICE	DEALER INVOICE
Base 4-door sedan	$55675	$48435
Destination charge	625	625

STANDARD EQUIPMENT

Base: 4.3-liter V8 engine, 6-speed automatic transmission w/manual-shift capability, traction control, dual front airbags, front side airbags, curtain side airbags, front knee airbags, antilock 4-wheel disc brakes, brake assist, anti-skid system, tire-pressure monitor, emergency inside trunk release, daytime running lights, power steering, power tilt/telescope wood/leather-wrapped steering wheel w/radio controls, cruise control, air conditioning w/dual-zone automatic climate controls, interior air filter, leather upholstery, front bucket seats, 14-way power driver seat, 10-way power passenger seat, front power headrests and lumbar adjustment, memory system (driver seat, headrest, steering wheel, mirrors), center console, cupholders, wood interior trim, heated power mirrors w/automatic day/night and passenger-side tilt-down back-up aid, power windows, power door locks, remote keyless entry, power sunroof, AM/FM/cassette w/in-dash 6-disc CD changer, digital clock, tachometer, trip computer, automatic day/night rearview mirror, compass, outside-temperature indicator, illuminated visor mirrors, universal garage-door opener, map lights, rain-sensing variable-intermittent wipers, power rear sunshade, rear defogger, automatic headlights, floormats, theft-deterrent system, steering-linked adaptive xenon headlights, fog lights, full-size spare tire, 225/55HR17 tires, alloy wheels.

OPTIONAL EQUIPMENT

Major Packages

	RETAIL PRICE	DEALER INVOICE
Premium Pkg.	$1390	$1112
Front- and rear-obstacle-detection system, heated/cooled front seats, heated rear seats.		
Modern Luxury Pkg.	4980	4040
Premium Pkg. plus navigation system w/voice activation, hands-free cellular telephone link, rearview camera, Mark Levinson sound system.		
Custom Luxury Pkg.	5935	4804
Modern Luxury Pkg. plus adaptive cruise control, power door closers, headlight washers. Requires Comfort Leather or Semi Anilin Leather Interior Upgrade Pkg.		
Custom Luxury Pkg. w/Pre-Collision Safety System	8185	6604
Custom Luxury Pkg. plus precollision-tightening front seatbelts and preparation of brake assist. Requires Comfort Leather or Semi Anilin Leather Interior Upgrade Pkg.		
Ultra Luxury Pkg.	11320	9112
Front- and rear-obstacle-detection system, navigation system w/voice activation, hands-free cellular telephone link, rearview camera, Mark Levinson sound system, adaptive cruise control, hands-free cellular telephone link, keyless entry and starting system, power door closers, heated/cooled front		

OPTIONAL EQUIPMENT (cont.)

	RETAIL PRICE	DEALER INVOICE
and rear seats, power rear seats w/memory and massage, rear air conditioning w/rear controls, cooler box in rear armrest, rear radio controls, rear side-window sunshades, laminated side windows, headlight washers, self-adjusting air suspension. Requires Comfort Leather or Semi Anilin Leather Interior Upgrade Pkg.		
Ultra Luxury Pkg. w/Pre-Collision Safety System	$13570	$10912
Ultra Luxury Pkg. plus precollision-tightening front seatbelts and preparation of brake assist. Requires Comfort Leather or Semi Anilin Leather Interior Upgrade Pkg.		
Comfort Leather/Semi Anilin Leather Interior Upgrade Pkg.,		
w/comfort leather	1460	1168
w/semi anilin leather	2100	1680
Comfort or semi anilin leather interior trim. Requires Custom Luxury Pkg. or Ultra Luxury Pkg.		

Comfort & Convenience Features

Keyless entry and starting system	1000	800

Appearance & Special Purpose

Sport Pkg.	220	176
Euro-Tuned Suspension, 245/45R18 tires.		
Sport Pkg. w/chrome alloy wheels	1920	960
Chrome alloy wheels	1700	850

Postproduction options also available.

LEXUS RX 330

CLASS: Premium midsize sport-utility vehicle
DRIVE WHEELS: Front-wheel drive, all-wheel drive
BASE PRICE RANGE: $35,775-$37,175. Built in Canada.
ALSO CONSIDER: Acura MDX, Cadillac SRX, Infiniti FX

A power liftgate is standard instead of optional for 2005 on Lexus' best-selling vehicle, which is to add a gas/electric hybrid version midyear. The RX 330 is the upscale cousin of the Toyota Highlander from Lexus's parent company. Both employ the platform used by the Lexus ES 330 and Toyota Camry sedans. The RX has a 230-hp V6 and a 5-speed automatic transmission. It offers front-wheel drive or all-wheel drive without low-range gearing.

Specifications begin on page 547.

Antiskid/traction control and antilock 4-wheel disc brakes are standard. Unlike Highlander, RX doesn't offer 3rd-row seating. But it does come with head-protecting curtain side airbags that are optional for the Toyota. Added for '05 are sensors designed to detect a rollover and trigger the curtain airbags. Front side airbags and a driver-knee airbag also are standard. So are a 40/20/40 split rear seat with slide and recline adjustments, tire-pressure monitor, and 17-inch wheels. Optional are 18-inch wheels, xenon headlamps, self-leveling air suspension with driver-selectable height settings, and adaptive cruise control designed to maintain a set following distance. Also available: power tilt/telescope steering column, rear DVD entertainment, rearview camera, voice-control navigation, and Lexus Link assistance through OnStar. Steering-linked headlights are available, as is a multipanel sunroof with a larger opening than the regular sunroof. Also for 2005, the power front-passenger seat goes from 4-way to 8-way, and a wireless connection to cell phones is now included with navigation, which is revised with new graphics and a more-detailed database. Called the RX 400h, the hybrid version will combine a 3.3-liter gas V6 and a battery-powered electric motor for a total of 270 hp. It uses a continuously variable automatic transmission (CVT) and will offer 2WD and AWD. As with Toyota's small Prius hybrid sedan, the 400h can be driven on electricity, the gas engine, or both. Pricing won't be announced before the early calendar-2005 sales start.

RATINGS

	2WD Base	AWD w/nav. sys., air susp.
ACCELERATION	5	5
FUEL ECONOMY	5	5
RIDE QUALITY	7	7
STEERING/HANDLING	5	5
QUIETNESS	7	7
CONTROLS/MATERIALS	9	8
ROOM/COMFORT (FRONT)	8	8
ROOM/COMFORT (REAR)	7	7
CARGO ROOM	7	7
VALUE WITHIN CLASS	10	10

The pioneer "crossover" now has many imitators, but none offer a more-appealing blend of comfort, refinement, luxury, and build quality. Consider, too, Lexus's strong resale values and kid-gloves customer service. Prices soar with options, some of which you can easily do without. Even with that, the RX is an impressive Best Buy.

TOTAL	70	69

Average total for premium midsize sport-utility vehicles: 59.6

ENGINES

	dohc V6
Size, liters/cu. in.	3.3/201
Horsepower @ rpm	230 @ 5600
Torque (lb-ft) @ rpm	242 @ 3600
Availability	S
EPA city/highway mpg	
5-speed automatic	18/24[1]

1. 20/26 w/2WD.

2005 prices unavailable at time of publication.

2004 PRICES

Lexus RX 330

	RETAIL PRICE	DEALER INVOICE
2WD Base 4-door wagon	$35275	$31216
AWD Base 4-door wagon	36675	32455
Destination charge	625	625

STANDARD EQUIPMENT

Base: 3.3-liter V6 engine, 5-speed automatic transmission, traction control, dual front airbags, front side airbags, curtain side airbags, driver-side knee airbag, antilock 4-wheel disc brakes, brake assist, antiskid system, tire-pressure monitor, daytime running lights, air conditioning w/dual-zone automatic climate controls, power steering, tilt leather-wrapped steering wheel w/radio controls, cruise control, cloth upholstery, front bucket seats, 8-way power driver seat w/power lumbar adjustment, 4-way power passenger seat, center console, cupholders, adjustible split folding rear seat, wood interior trim, heated power mirrors w/automatic day/night, power windows, power door locks, remote keyless entry, AM/FM/cassette/CD player, digital clock, tachometer, universal garage-door opener, automatic day/night rearview mirror, outside-temperature indicator, variable-intermittent wipers, illuminated visor mirrors, map lights, cargo cover, rear defogger, intermittent rear wiper/washer, automatic headlights, floormats, theft-deterrent system, rear privacy glass, fog lights, rear spoiler, full-size spare tire, 225/65SR17 tires, alloy wheels. **AWD** adds: all-wheel drive.

OPTIONAL EQUIPMENT

Major Packages

	RETAIL PRICE	DEALER INVOICE
Premium Pkg.	$2145	$1716
Leather upholstery, power tilt/telescope steering wheel, memory system (driver seat, mirrors, steering wheel), power sunroof, compass, roof rack.		
Premium Plus Pkg.	3440	2752
Premium Pkg. plus wood/leather-wrapped steering wheel, power liftgate, xenon headlights.		
Performance Pkg.	5455	4364
Premium Pkg. plus manual-shift capability for automatic transmission, power liftgate, rain-sensing wipers, steering-linked adaptive xenon headlights, rear self-leveling and height-adjustable air suspension, 235/55HR18 tires, unique alloy wheels.		
Navigation System/Radio System Pkg.	6770	5471
Premium Plus Pkg. plus navigation system, rearview camera, Mark Levinson sound system.		
Multipanel Moon Roof Pkg.	4220	3376
Multipanel sunroof, leather upholstery, power tilt/telescope wood/leather-wrapped steering wheel, memory system (driver seat, mirrors, steering wheel), power liftgate. NA w/roof rack.		
Towing Pkg.	160	128
Transmission-oil cooler, heavy-duty radiator, wiring harness.		

 Specifications begin on page 547.

Comfort & Convenience Features

	RETAIL PRICE	DEALER INVOICE
Lexus Link assistance system	$1215	$1015
Includes one-year service.		
Navigation system	2350	1980
Includes rearview camera.		
Rear-seat entertainment system	1840	1416
DVD player, wireless headphones, remote control.		
Adaptive cruise control	600	480
Power liftgate	400	320
Heated front seats	540	432
Includes heated headlight washers.		
Adjustable heated front seats	665	532
Includes heated headlight washers, rain-sensing wipers.		

Appearance & Special Purpose

	RETAIL PRICE	DEALER INVOICE
Roof rack	220	176
Xenon headlights	515	412
235/55HR18 tires	215	172

LEXUS SC 430

CLASS: Premium sporty/performance car
DRIVE WHEELS: Rear-wheel drive
2004 BASE PRICE: $62,875. Built in Japan.
ALSO CONSIDER: Cadillac XLR, Mercedes-Benz SL 500

Lexus' upper-crust convertible loses its Lexus Link assistance system, but otherwise sees only detail changes for 2005. The SC 430 features a power-retractable metal roof and a small rear seat intended for occasional use, mainly by kids. Its 4.3-liter V8 and 5-speed automatic transmission come from Lexus' flagship LS 430 sedan. Standard are front side airbags, ABS, antiskid/traction-control system, tire-pressure monitor, 18-inch wheels, leather/wood cabin trim, navigation system, and premium Mark Levinson audio. Options include rear spoiler, and run-flat tires. The optional run-flats switch from performance to all-season treads. For 2005, the SC 430 gets revised shock absorbers and a navigation system with more-detailed screen graphics and a larger DVD database.

RATINGS

	Base	Base w/run-flat tires
ACCELERATION	7	7
FUEL ECONOMY	4	4
RIDE QUALITY	6	4
STEERING/HANDLING	8	7
QUIETNESS	7	6
CONTROLS/MATERIALS	7	7
ROOM/COMFORT (FRONT)	7	7
ROOM/COMFORT (REAR)	1	1
CARGO ROOM	2	2
VALUE WITHIN CLASS	5	4

SC 430 is a posh, pleasant, semisporting convertible with the extra security and convenience of a power metal roof, plus Lexus' highly rated customer service, workmanship, and reliability. It isn't cheap, but some rivals with similar power and features cost more.

TOTAL	54	49

Average total for premium sporty/performance cars: 48.3

ENGINES

	dohc V8
Size, liters/cu. in.	4.3/262
Horsepower @ rpm	300 @ 5600
Torque (lb-ft) @ rpm	325 @ 3400
Availability	S
EPA city/highway mpg	
5-speed automatic	18/23

2005 prices unavailable at time of publication.

2004 PRICES

Lexus SC 430	RETAIL PRICE	DEALER INVOICE
Base 2-door convertible	$62875	$54699
Destination charge	625	625

STANDARD EQUIPMENT

Base: 4.3-liter V8 engine, 5-speed automatic transmission, traction control, dual front airbags, front side airbags, antilock 4-wheel disc brakes, brake assist, antiskid system, tire-pressure monitor, daytime running lights, air conditioning w/automatic climate control, interior air filter, power steering, power tilt/telescope wood/leather-wrapped steering wheel w/radio controls, cruise control, leather upholstery, heated 10-way power front seats w/power lumbar adjustment, memory system (front seats, steering wheel, mirrors), center console, cupholders, wood interior trim, heated power mirrors w/automatic day/night, power windows, power door locks, remote keyless entry, Mark Levinson AM/FM radio w/in-dash 6-disc CD changer, digital clock, tachometer, navigation system, power-retractable steel hardtop, rear defogger, automatic day/night rearview mirror, outside-temperature indicator, uni-

 Specifications begin on page 547.

versal garage-door opener, variable-intermittent wipers, remote fuel-door/decklid release, automatic headlights, floormats, theft-deterrent system, wind deflector, xenon headlights, fog lights, 245/40ZR18 tires, alloy wheels.

OPTIONAL EQUIPMENT

Major Packages	RETAIL PRICE	DEALER INVOICE
Pebble Beach Special Edition	$2000	$1660

Unique interior and exterior trim, special wood interior trim, golf bag, rear spoiler, run-flat tires.

Comfort & Convenience Features

Lexus Link	1215	1015

Telematics system. Includes one-year service.

Appearance & Special Purpose

Rear spoiler	440	352
Run-flat tires	400	320

LINCOLN AVIATOR

CLASS: Premium midsize sport-utility vehicle
DRIVE WHEELS: Rear-wheel drive, all-wheel drive
BASE PRICE RANGE: $40,615-$43,565. Built in USA.
ALSO CONSIDER: Acura MDX, Cadillac SRX, Lexus RX 330

Lincoln's luxury version of the Ford Explorer/Mercury Mountaineer gets standard Roll Stability Control for 2005. Aviator differs from Explorer and Mountaineer in styling, engine power, suspension tuning, and cabin decor. Aviator uses a 302-hp version of the 239-hp V8 that's optional in the Ford and Mercury. It has a 5-speed automatic transmission and offers rear-wheel drive or all-wheel drive without low-range gearing. Newly standard for '05, the anti-skid/traction-control system includeds Ford's Roll Stability Control, which is designed to detect an impending tip and activate the antiskid system to reduce chances of a rollover. A folding 3rd-row bench seat is standard, and a 3-passenger 2nd-row bench seat is available in place of buckets for up to 7-passenger capacity. Standard head-protecting curtain side airbags serve the 1st and 2nd seating rows. Power-adjustable pedals, rear-obstacle detection, and dual-zone climate system with rear controls are also standard. Options include a sunroof, navigation system, and rear DVD entertainment.

RATINGS

	AWD Luxury
ACCELERATION	5
FUEL ECONOMY	2
RIDE QUALITY	5
STEERING/HANDLING	5
QUIETNESS	6
CONTROLS/MATERIALS	6
ROOM/COMFORT (FRONT)	8
ROOM/COMFORT (REAR)	7
CARGO ROOM	8
VALUE WITHIN CLASS	5

Aviator is more than competent, has V8 muscle, and offers an array of features at a relatively reasonable price that should benefit from steep discounts. Still, top rivals beat it for quality of interior materials, overall refinement, and prestige.

TOTAL	57

Average total for premium midsize sport-utility vehicles: 59.6

ENGINES

	dohc V8
Size, liters/cu. in.	4.6/281
Horsepower @ rpm	302 @ 5750
Torque (lb-ft) @ rpm	300 @ 3250
Availability	S
EPA city/highway mpg	
5-speed automatic	13/17[1]

1. 13/18 w/2WD.

PRICES

Lincoln Aviator	RETAIL PRICE	DEALER INVOICE
2WD Luxury 4-door wagon	$40615	$37253
AWD Luxury 4-door wagon	43565	39908
Destination charge	740	740

STANDARD EQUIPMENT

Luxury: 4.6-liter V8 engine, 5-speed automatic transmission, traction control, dual front airbags, front and 2nd-row curtain side airbags, antilock 4-wheel disc brakes, brake assist, antiskid system, roll stability control, rear-obstacle-detection system, tire-pressure monitor, air conditioning w/dual-zone automatic climate controls, rear climate controls, power steering, tilt wood/leather-wrapped steering wheel w/radio controls, cruise control, leather upholstery, 8-way power front bucket seats w/power lumbar adjustment, power-adjustable pedals, memory system (driver seat, mirrors, pedals), front center console, cupholders, 2nd-row stowable bucket seats w/center console, 3rd-row stowable bench seat, wood interior trim, heated power mirrors w/turn-

 Specifications begin on page 547.

signals, power windows, power door locks, remote keyless entry, keypad entry, AM/FM/cassette/CD player, analog clock, tachometer, automatic day/night rearview mirror, compass, outside-temperature indicator, universal garage-door opener, illuminated visor mirrors, variable-intermittent wipers, map lights, rear defogger, intermittent rear wiper/washer, automatic headlights, floormats, theft-deterrent system, fog lights, rear privacy glass, running boards, roof rails, Class II trailer hitch, wiring harness, full-size spare tire, 245/65HR17 tires, alloy wheels. **AWD** adds: all-wheel drive.

OPTIONAL EQUIPMENT

Major Packages

	RETAIL PRICE	DEALER INVOICE
Elite Pkg., 2WD	$9505	$8269
Manufacturer's Discount Price	*8000*	*6960*
AWD	9800	8526
Manufacturer's Discount Price	*8300*	*7221*
Navigation system, heated/cooled front seats, rear-seat DVD entertainment system, power sunroof, xenon headlights, roof rack, Class III trailer tow equipment (AWD), chrome alloy wheels.		
Luxury Enhancement Moonroof Pkg.	4600	4002
Manufacturer's Discount Price	*3600*	*3132*
Power sunroof, heated/cooled front seats, AM/FM radio w/in-dash 6-disc CD changer, roof rack, chrome alloy wheels.		
Luxury Enhancement RSES Pkg.	4420	3845
Manufacturer's Discount Price	*3600*	*3132*
Rear-seat DVD entertainment system, heated/cooled front seats, AM/FM radio w/in-dash 6-disc CD changer, roof rack, chrome alloy wheels.		
Jet Black Pkg.	NA	NA
Monochromatic exterior, rear spoiler, chrome exhaust tip, chrome alloy wheels.		

Comfort & Convenience Features

Navigation system	2995	2606
Includes in-dash 6-disc CD changer. Requires a Luxury Enhancement Pkg.		
Rear-seat DVD entertainment system	1415	1231
Heated/cooled front seats	895	779
Power sunroof	1595	1388
AM/FM radio w/in-dash 6-disc CD changer	895	799
2nd-row split bench seat	NC	NC

Appearance & Special Purpose

Xenon headlights	495	431
Chrome alloy wheels	595	518

LINCOLN LS

CLASS: Premium midsize car
DRIVE WHEELS: Rear-wheel drive
BASE PRICE RANGE: $32,330-$43,280. Built in USA.
ALSO CONSIDER: Acura TL, BMW 3-Series, Infiniti G35

Lincoln LS shares a platform with the British-built S-Type from Ford subsidiary Jaguar, but differs in styling and equipment. A 232-hp Ford V6 and a 280-hp Jaguar-designed V8 are the engine choices. Both use a 5-speed automatic transmission. V6s come with 16-inch wheels, V8s with 17s and a sport suspension. Front side airbags, ABS, and traction control are standard. Head-protecting curtain side airbags are optional, as is an antiskid system. Also optional are heated rear seats, navigation system, and xenon headlights. Power-adjustable pedals are optional. Heated and cooled front seats are available on all but the base V6 model. Satellite radio is a dealer-installed option. Available for V8 Sport is the LSE Appearance Package that includes unique front and rear styling, chrome wheels, spoiler, and interior cues.

RATINGS

	V6 Premium	V8 Ultimate w/nav. sys.
ACCELERATION	5	7
FUEL ECONOMY	5	4
RIDE QUALITY	7	7
STEERING/HANDLING	6	7
QUIETNESS	7	7
CONTROLS/MATERIALS	7	6
ROOM/COMFORT (FRONT)	7	7
ROOM/COMFORT (REAR)	6	6
CARGO ROOM	3	3
VALUE WITHIN CLASS	3	4

LS offers a reasonable array of features, capable road manners, and the least-expensive V8 in the premium midsize class. But sales are slow, reflecting its unexceptional interior decor and relative lack of cachet compared to like-priced rivals.

TOTAL	56	58

Average total for premium midsize cars: 61.7

ENGINES

	dohc V6	dohc V8
Size, liters/cu. in.	3.0/181	3.9/240
Horsepower @ rpm	232 @ 6750	280 @ 6000
Torque (lb-ft) @ rpm	220 @ 4500	286 @ 4000
Availability	S[1]	S[2]
EPA city/highway mpg		
5-speed automatic	20/27	17/24

1. Luxury, Appearance, Premium. 2. Sport, Ultimate.

 Specifications begin on page 547.

PRICES

Lincoln LS

	RETAIL PRICE	DEALER INVOICE
V6 Luxury 4-door sedan	$32330	$29707
V6 Appearance 4-door sedan	36050	33055
V6 Premium 4-door sedan	36680	33622
V8 Sport 4-door sedan	39880	36502
V8 Ultimate Sport 4-door sedan	43280	39562
Destination charge	635	635

V6 Appearance requires Appearance Discount Pkg.

STANDARD EQUIPMENT

V6 Luxury: 3.0-liter V6 engine, 5-speed automatic transmission, traction control, dual front airbags, front side airbags, antilock 4-wheel disc brakes, brake assist, emergency inside trunk release, air conditioning w/dual-zone automatic climate controls, interior air filter, power steering, power tilt/telescope leather-wrapped steering wheel w/radio controls, cruise control, leather upholstery, front bucket seats, 8-way power driver seat, 6-way power passenger seat, center console, cupholders, split folding rear seat, heated power mirrors, power windows, power door locks, remote keyless entry, AM/FM/cassette/CD player, tachometer, map lights, illuminated visor mirrors, rear defogger, variable-intermittent wipers w/deicer, automatic headlights, floormats, theft-deterrent system, fog lights, 225/55VR16 tires, alloy wheels.

V6 Appearance adds: front-seat power lumbar adjustment, memory system (driver seat, steering wheel, mirrors), automatic day/night rearview and driver-side mirrors, compass, Audiophile AM/FM radio w/in-dash 6-disc CD changer, universal garage-door opener, polished alloy wheels.

V6 Premium adds: wood interior trim, wood/leather-wrapped steering wheel, alloy wheels. *Deletes:* polished alloy wheels.

V8 Sport adds: 3.9-liter V8 engine, manual-shift capability, leather-wrapped steering wheel, aluminum interior trim, sport suspension, 235/50VR17 tires. *Deletes:* wood/leather-wrapped steering wheel, wood interior trim.

V8 Ultimate adds: antiskid system, front-seat heating and cooling, power sunroof, wood interior trim, chrome alloy wheels.

OPTIONAL EQUIPMENT

Major Packages

	RETAIL PRICE	DEALER INVOICE
Appearance Discount Pkg., Appearance (credit)	*($885)*	*($770)*
Standard equipment.		
LSE Appearance Pkg., Sport	3395	2954
Unique interior and exterior trim, rear spoiler, chrome alloy wheels.		

Safety

	RETAIL PRICE	DEALER INVOICE
Curtain side airbags	545	474
Antiskid system, Luxury, Appearance, Premium, Sport	775	675
Rear-obstacle-detection system	295	257

Comfort & Convenience Features

	RETAIL PRICE	DEALER INVOICE
Navigation system, Appearance, Premium, Sport, Ultimate	$2995	$2606
Includes THX sound system. Requires dealer accessory kit.		
Power sunroof, Appearance, Premium, Sport	1275	1110
Front-seat heating and cooling, Appearance, Premium, Sport	595	518
Heated rear seats, Premium, Sport, Ultimate	405	352
Power-adjustable pedals, Luxury	125	109
Appearance, Premium, Sport, Ultimate	195	170
Appearance, Premium, Sport, Ultimate include memory.		
Wood interior trim, Sport	495	431

Appearance & Special Purpose

	RETAIL PRICE	DEALER INVOICE
Xenon headlights, Appearance, Premium, Sport, Ultimate	595	518
Chrome alloy wheels, Premium	695	605

LINCOLN TOWN CAR

CLASS: Premium large car
DRIVE WHEELS: Rear-wheel drive
BASE PRICE RANGE: $41,675-$50,120. Built in USA.
ALSO CONSIDER: Cadillac DeVille, Lexus LS 430

Revised trim levels mark 2005 for the lone American-brand rear-wheel-drive premium large sedan. Lincoln Town Car ascends through three trim levels: Signature, Signature Limited, and the limousinelike Signature L, which adds six inches to the wheelbase to create more rear leg room. Ultimate and Ultimate L models are gone. All have a 4.6-liter V8 and a 4-speed automatic transmission. ABS, traction control, and front side airbags are standard, but no antiskid system is offered. Rear airbags or curtain side airbags are unavailable. Other standard features include power-adjustable pedals, dual-zone climate control, front bench seat, and leather upholstery. Xenon headlamps and a navigation system are optional; satellite radio is a dealer-installed option.

RATINGS	Signature L
ACCELERATION	4
FUEL ECONOMY	4

 Specifications begin on page 547.

RATINGS (cont.)

	Signature L
RIDE QUALITY	8
STEERING/HANDLING	4
QUIETNESS	8
CONTROLS/MATERIALS	7
ROOM/COMFORT (FRONT)	7
ROOM/COMFORT (REAR)	9
CARGO ROOM	6
VALUE WITHIN CLASS	4

Town Car shines for traditional American-style luxury, space, and isolation. Though not nimble, it also has a welcome measure of dynamic confidence and ride control. Cadillac's DeVille still has an edge with its more-modern engineering, but the Town Car is a thoughtful take on a time-honored formula.

TOTAL	61

Average total for premium large cars: 68.7

ENGINES

	sohc V8
Size, liters/cu. in.	4.6/281
Horsepower @ rpm	239 @ 4900
Torque (lb-ft) @ rpm	287 @ 4100
Availability	S
EPA city/highway mpg	
4-speed automatic	17/25

PRICES

Lincoln Town Car	RETAIL PRICE	DEALER INVOICE
Signature 4-door sedan	$41675	$38198
Signature Limited 4-door sedan	44515	40753
Signature L 4-door sedan	50120	45798
Destination charge	795	795

STANDARD EQUIPMENT

Signature: 4.6-liter V8 engine, 4-speed automatic transmission, traction control, dual front airbags, front side airbags, antilock 4-wheel disc brakes, rear-obstacle-detection system, daytime running lights, air conditioning w/dual-zone automatic climate controls, power steering, tilt leather-wrapped steering wheel w/radio and climate controls, cruise control, leather upholstery, dual 8-way power front split bench seat w/power recliners and lumbar support, power-adjustable pedals, cupholders, heated power mirrors w/driver-side automatic day/night, power windows, power door locks, remote keyless entry, keypad entry, rear defogger, AM/FM/cassette/CD player, analog clock, universal garage-door opener, automatic day/night rearview mirror, compass, outside-temperature indicator, power decklid pull-down, variable-intermittent wipers, illuminated visor mirrors, map lights, automatic headlights, automatic parking-brake release, floormats, theft-deterrent system, cornering lights, 225/60R17 tires, alloy wheels.

Signature Limited adds: memory system (driver seat, mirrors, pedals), heated front seats, wood/leather-wrapped steering wheel, upgraded sound system, power decklid open and pull-down.

Signature L adds: 6-inch-longer wheelbase, 6-disc CD changer, rear radio and climate controls, rear controls for front-passenger seat, heated rear seats.

OPTIONAL EQUIPMENT

Major Packages	RETAIL PRICE	DEALER INVOICE
Limited Edition, Signature Limited	$1595	$1388
2-tone leather upholstery, special floormats, chrome alloy wheels.		
Comfort & Convenience Features		
Navigation system, Signature Limited	3600	3132
Signature L	2995	2606
Includes in-dash 6-disc CD changer, voice recognition.		
Power sunroof, Signature Limited	1595	1388
Manufacturer's Discount Price, ordered w/6-disc CD changer	*990*	*862*
6-disc CD changer, Signature Limited	605	526
Trunk organizer, Signature Limited, Signature L	195	170
Appearance & Special Purpose		
Xenon headlights, Signature Limited, Signature L	495	431
Chrome alloy wheels, Signature Limited, Signature L	895	779

MAZDA 3

CLASS: Compact car
DRIVE WHEELS: Front-wheel drive
BASE PRICE RANGE: $13,680-$17,105. Built in Japan.
ALSO CONSIDER: Ford Focus, Honda Civic, Kia Spectra

Mazda's compact comes in 4-dr sedan and hatchback body styles. The sedan is available in base "i" and uplevel "s" trim. The hatchback is offered only as an s model. Two 4-cyl engines are available: a 148-hp 2.0-liter for i models, a 160-hp 2.3 for s versions. With either engine, a 5-speed manual transmission is standard; a 4-speed automatic with manual shift gate is optional. The i model has 15-inch wheels or optional 16s. The s sedan comes with 16s; 17s are included in its Sport Package option. The hatchback uses 17s. Front side airbags, head-protecting curtain side airbags, and ABS are grouped in an option package for every Mazda 3. Options exclusive to s versions are leather upholstery, navigation system, and a package that includes a tire-pressure monitor and xenon headlights. Air conditioning is optional on the i model, standard on s versions.

RATINGS	i w/16-inch wheels, man.	i w/16-inch wheels, auto.	s sdn w/Sport Package, auto.	s hatch, man.
ACCELERATION	5	4	5	5
FUEL ECONOMY	6	6	6	6
RIDE QUALITY	5	5	5	5
STEERING/HANDLING	6	6	7	7
QUIETNESS	4	4	5	4
CONTROLS/MATERIALS	7	7	7	7
ROOM/COMFORT (FRONT)	5	5	5	5
ROOM/COMFORT (REAR)	4	4	4	4
CARGO ROOM	2	2	2	6
VALUE WITHIN CLASS	9	9	9	10

With its solid build, pleasant interior, and sporty character, the Mazda 3 is a strong competitor. It's more fun than comparable Honda Civic and Toyota Corolla models, rivaling the Jetta, Golf, and Ford Focus for driving dynamics. Add in competitive pricing, and the 3 is a worthy Best Buy.

TOTAL	53	52	55	59

Average total for compact cars: 48.4

ENGINES

	dohc I4	dohc I4
Size, liters/cu. in.	2.0/122	2.3/138
Horsepower @ rpm	148 @ 6500	160 @ 6500
Torque (lb-ft) @ rpm	135 @ 4500	150 @ 4500
Availability	S[1]	S[2]
EPA city/highway mpg		
5-speed manual	28/35	25/32
4-speed automatic	26/34	24/29

1. i model. 2. s model.

PRICES

Mazda 3	RETAIL PRICE	DEALER INVOICE
i 4-door sedan	$13680	$12801
s 4-door sedan	16615	15337
s 4-door hatchback	17105	15994
Destination charge	545	545

STANDARD EQUIPMENT

i: 2.0-liter 4-cylinder engine, 5-speed manual transmission, dual front airbags, 4-wheel disc brakes, emergency inside trunk release, power steering, tilt/telescope steering wheel w/radio controls, cloth upholstery, front bucket seats, center console, cupholders, split folding rear seat, AM/FM/CD player, digital clock, tachometer, map lights, intermittent wipers, visor mirrors, rear defogger, floormats, theft-deterrent system, 195/65HR15 tires, wheel covers.

s sedan adds: 2.3-liter 4-cylinder engine, air conditioning, leather-wrapped steering wheel, cruise control, height-adjustable driver seat w/lumbar adjustment, power mirrors, power windows, power door locks, remote keyless entry, fog lights, 205/55HR16 tires, alloy wheels.

s hatchback adds: cargo cover, intermittent rear wiper, rear spoiler, 205/50VR17 tires. *Deletes:* emergency inside trunk release.

OPTIONAL EQUIPMENT

Major Packages

	RETAIL PRICE	DEALER INVOICE
ABS/SAB/SAC Pkg.	$800	$688
Antilock brakes w/electronic brake-force distribution, front side airbags, curtain side airbags. i requires Power and Alloy Wheel Pkg., air conditioning.		
Moonroof and 6-CD Pkg.	890	765
Power sunroof, in-dash 6-disc CD changer. i requires Power and Alloy Wheel Pkg., air conditioning.		
Power and Alloy Wheel Pkg., i	1400	1204
Cruise control, power mirrors and windows, power door locks, remote keyless entry, height-adjustable driver seat w/lumbar adjustment, illuminated entry, 205/55HR16 tires, alloy wheels. Requires air conditioning.		
Appearance Pkg. 2, i	840	672
Body cladding.		
Appearance Pkg. 3, i	1070	856
Body cladding, fog lights.		
Sport Pkg., s sedan	490	421
Side sill extensions, 205/50VR17 tires.		
Xenon and TPMS Pkg., s	700	602
Xenon headlights, tire-pressure monitor. Requires ABS/SAB/SAC Pkg. Sedan requires Sport Pkg.		

Powertrain

4-speed automatic transmission w/manual-shift capability	900	810
i requires air conditioning.		

Comfort & Convenience Features

Air conditioning, i	850	731
Navigation system, s	1750	1505
Requires ABS/SAB/SAC Pkg., Xenon and TPMS Pkg. Sedan requires Sport Pkg.		
AM/FM/MP3 player	325	260
AM/FM radio w/in-dash 6-disc CD changer	500	400
Leather upholstery, s	590	507
Sedan requires Sport Pkg.		

 Specifications begin on page 547.

Appearance & Special Purpose	RETAIL PRICE	DEALER INVOICE
Fog lights, i	$275	$220
Rear spoiler, sedan	300	240
Alloy wheels, i	400	344
Requires air conditioning.		

MAZDA 6

CLASS: Midsize car
DRIVE WHEELS: Front-wheel drive
BASE PRICE RANGE: \$18,995-\$26,795. Built in USA.
ALSO CONSIDER: Chevrolet Malibu, Honda Accord, Nissan Altima

Standard ABS for all models and an available 6-speed automatic transmission are key 2005 changes for the Mazda 6. Four-door sedan, wagon, and hatchback body styles are offered in base, Sport, and Grand Touring equipment levels. The "i" designation denotes a 160-hp 4-cyl engine and is limited to sedans and hatchbacks. Uplevel "s" versions use a 220-hp V6 and come in all three body types. Both engines come with a 5-speed manual transmission. The i models are available with a 4-speed automatic. For '05, s versions exchange an available 5-speed automatic for a 6-speed, making this one of the few cars in its price range to offer that feature. Both automatics have a manual shift gate. Standard on all Mazda 6s are antilock 4-wheel disc brakes; the ABS feature had been optional on base-level versions. Traction control is also standard on all models for '05; it had been optional on i versions. Base-trim i and s models have 16-inch wheels, all others have 17s. Front torso side airbags and head-protecting curtain side airbags for both seating rows are optional on the base i sedan and standard on other 6s. All models have a tilt/telescope steering wheel and split folding rear seatbacks. Leather upholstery and heated front seats are standard on Grand Touring models, optional on Sports. A sunroof is standard on Grand Touring versions, optional on other 6s.

RATINGS	Base i sdn, auto.	i Sport hatch, man.	s Sport sdn, man.	Base s wgn, man.
ACCELERATION	4	5	6	6
FUEL ECONOMY	6	6	5	5
RIDE QUALITY	6	6	6	6
STEERING/HANDLING	6	7	7	7
QUIETNESS	6	6	6	6
CONTROLS/MATERIALS	7	7	7	7

RATINGS (cont.)	Base i sdn, auto.	i Sport hatch, man.	s Sport sdn, man.	Base s wgn, man.
ROOM/COMFORT (FRONT)	6	6	6	6
ROOM/COMFORT (REAR)	5	5	5	5
CARGO ROOM	4	7	4	7
VALUE WITHIN CLASS	8	8	8	8

In terms of overall refinement and interior materials, the Mazda 6 is a shade off the pace set by the Honda Accord and Toyota Camry in this class. But despite tepid 4-cyl acceleration with automatic transmission, it's a match for any rival in terms of driving satisfaction. It's roomy, pricing and equipment levels are competitive, and the wagon and hatchback have little class competition. This is a solid Recommended choice.

TOTAL	58	63	60	63

Average total for midsize cars: 57.2

ENGINES

	dohc I4	dohc V6
Size, liters/cu. in.	2.3/138	3.0/181
Horsepower @ rpm	160 @ 6000	220 @ 6300
Torque (lb-ft) @ rpm	155 @ 4000	192 @ 5000
Availability	S[1]	S[2]
EPA city/highway mpg		
5-speed manual	23/31	19/26
4-speed automatic	23/28	
6-speed automatic		20/27

1. i models. 2. s models.

PRICES

Mazda 6

	RETAIL PRICE	DEALER INVOICE
i Base 4-door sedan	$18995	$17530
i Sport 4-door sedan	21495	19830
i Sport 4-door hatchback	22025	20318
i Grand Touring 4-door sedan	24195	22314
s Base 4-door wagon	22895	21118
s Sport 4-door sedan	23295	21486
s Sport 4-door hatchback	23995	22131
s Sport 4-door wagon	24025	22158
s Grand Touring 4-door sedan	26125	24091
s Grand Touring 4-door wagon	26795	24707
Destination charge	545	545

STANDARD EQUIPMENT

i Base: 2.3-liter 4-cylinder engine, 5-speed manual transmission, traction control, dual front airbags, antilock 4-wheel disc brakes, emergency inside trunk release, air conditioning, interior air filter, power steering, tilt/telescope leather-wrapped steering wheel w/radio controls, cruise control, cloth upholstery, front bucket seats w/driver-seat height adjustment, center console, cupholders, split folding rear seat, power mirrors, power windows, power door locks, remote keyless entry, AM/FM/CD player, digital clock, tachometer, outside-temperature indicator, illuminated visor mirrors, variable-intermittent wipers, map lights, rear defogger, automatic-off headlights, floormats, theft-deterrent system, 205/60VR16 tires, wheel covers.

i Sport adds: front side airbags, curtain side airbags, 8-way power driver seat w/lumbar adjustment, cargo cover (hatchback, wagon), rear wiper/washer (hatchback, wagon), rear spoiler, fog lights, 215/50VR17 tires, alloy wheels.

i Grand Touring adds: 4-speed automatic transmission w/manual-shift capability, leather upholstery, heated front seats, heated power mirrors, power sunroof, Bose AM/FM radio w/in-dash 6-disc CD changer. *Deletes:* rear spoiler, fog lights.

s Base adds to i Base: 3.0-liter V6 engine, front side airbags, curtain side airbags, automatic climate control, cargo cover (hatchback, wagon), rear wiper/washer (hatchback, wagon), 215/50VR17 tires, alloy wheels.

s Sport adds: 8-way power driver seat w/lumbar adjustment, rear spoiler, fog lights.

s Grand Touring adds: 6-speed automatic transmission w/manual-shift capability, leather upholstery, heated front seats, heated power mirrors, power sunroof, Bose AM/FM radio w/in-dash 6-disc CD changer. *Deletes:* rear spoiler, fog lights.

OPTIONAL EQUIPMENT

Major Packages	RETAIL PRICE	DEALER INVOICE
Convenience Pkg., i Base	$975	$780
8-way power driver seat, alarm, 215/50VR17 tires, alloy wheels.		
Bose Audio and Moonroof Pkg., Base, Sport	1335	1068
Bose AM/FM radio w/in-dash 6-disc CD changer, power sunroof.		
Leather Pkg., Sport	1240	992
Leather upholstery, heated front seats and mirrors.		
Appearance Pkg., i Base, Grand Touring sedan	800	640
Aerodynamic body cladding, exhaust tips.		
Grand Touring Appearance Pkg., Grand Touring sedan	710	568
Fog lights, sport bumpers and side sills, dual oval exhaust tips. NA w/Appearance Pkg.		
Powertrain		
4-speed automatic transmission w/manual-shift capability, i Base, i Sport	850	740
6-speed automatic transmission w/manual-shift capability, s Base, s Sport	900	827
Safety		
Front side airbags, i Base	450	360
Includes curtain side airbags.		
Comfort & Convenience Features		
Automatic day/night rearview mirror	250	200
Includes compass, universal garage-door opener.		

OPTIONAL EQUIPMENT (cont.)

	RETAIL PRICE	DEALER INVOICE
Cassette player	$200	$160
AM/FM radio w/in-dash 6-disc CD changer, Base, Sport	500	400
Cargo organizer	150	125
Appearance & Special Purpose		
Roof rails, wagon	300	240
Fog lights, Base, Grand Touring	250	200
Rear lip spoiler, Base/Grand Touring sedan	420	336
Base/Grand Touring wagon	300	240
Rear wing spoiler, Base/Grand Touring sedan	300	240

MAZDA MIATA

CLASS: Sporty/performance car
DRIVE WHEELS: Rear-wheel drive
BASE PRICE RANGE: $22,098-$26,580. Built in Japan.
ALSO CONSIDER: Honda S2000, Mini Cooper, Nissan 350Z

Mazda's 2-seat sports car has a standard manual-folding soft top with a heated glass rear window. A removable hardtop is optional. Miata's lineup starts with the base and upscale LS, both with a 142-hp 4-cyl teamed with standard 5-speed manual transmission or optional 4-speed automatic. A 6-speed manual is optional on LS. The MazdaSpeed Miata has a turbocharged 178-hp engine, 6-speed manual transmission, sport suspension, and 17-inch wheels in place of 16s. New for 2005 is the MazdaSpeed Grand Touring, which adds leather upholstery. ABS is unavailable on base, optional on LS, and standard on MazdaSpeed models. Sport-suspension packages are available for base and LS models, as are appearance packages with rear mud guards and unique lower-body sills.

RATINGS	Base, man.	Base, auto.	LS, 6-sp man.
ACCELERATION	6	5	6
FUEL ECONOMY	7	7	7
RIDE QUALITY	3	3	3
STEERING/HANDLING	9	9	9
QUIETNESS	2	2	2
CONTROLS/MATERIALS	8	8	8

RATINGS (cont.)

	Base, man.	Base, auto.	LS, 6-sp man.
ROOM/COMFORT (FRONT)	4	4	4
ROOM/COMFORT (REAR)	0	0	0
CARGO ROOM	1	1	1
VALUE WITHIN CLASS	10	9	9

Mazda's spritely roadster defends front-engine sports-car tradition and earns a Best Buy rating in the process. Miata offers a measure of usable cargo room, impressive fuel economy, and is sensibly priced. Though less powerful than entries from the likes of Nissan, Honda, and BMW, Miata offers just as much driving joy and a reputation for trouble-free ownership.

	Base, man.	Base, auto.	LS, 6-sp man.
TOTAL	50	48	49

Average total for sporty/performance cars: 48.5

ENGINES

	dohc I4	Turbocharged dohc I4
Size, liters/cu. in.	1.8/112	1.8/112
Horsepower @ rpm	142 @ 7000	178 @ 6000
Torque (lb-ft) @ rpm	125 @ 5500	166 @ 4500
Availability	S[1]	S[2]
EPA city/highway mpg		
5-speed manual	23/28	
6-speed manual	23/28	20/26
4-speed automatic	22/28	

1. Base, LS. 2. MazdaSpeed.

PRICES

Mazda Miata	RETAIL PRICE	DEALER INVOICE
Base 2-door convertible	$22098	$20398
LS 2-door convertible	24903	22982
MazdaSpeed 2-door convertible	25780	23791
MazdaSpeed Grand Touring 2-door convertible	26580	24528
Destination charge	545	545

STANDARD EQUIPMENT

Base: 1.8-liter 4-cylinder engine, 5-speed manual transmission, dual front airbags, 4-wheel disc brakes, emergency inside trunk release, air conditioning, power steering, leather-wrapped steering wheel, cloth upholstery, bucket seats, center console, cupholders, power mirrors, power windows, AM/FM/CD player, power antenna, digital clock, tachometer, intermittent wipers, map lights, rear defogger, visor mirrors, floormats, theft-deterrent system, windblock panel, fog lights, 205/45WR16 tires, alloy wheels.

LS adds: limited-slip differential, cruise control, leather upholstery, power door locks, remote keyless entry, Bose sound system.

MazdaSpeed adds: 1.8-liter turbocharged 4-cylinder engine, 6-speed manual transmission, antilock 4-wheel disc brakes, Bose AM/FM radio w/in-dash 6-disc CD changer, rear spoiler, sport suspension, 205/40WR17 tires. *Deletes:* leather upholstery.

MazdaSpeed Grand Touring adds: leather upholstery.

OPTIONAL EQUIPMENT

Major Packages	RETAIL PRICE	DEALER INVOICE
Convenience Pkg., Base	$895	$752
Cruise control, power door locks, remote keyless entry, upgraded sound system. NA w/Suspension Pkg.		
Suspension Pkg., Base	800	672
LS	395	332
Sport suspension w/Bilstein shock absorbers, limited-slip differential (Base). LS requires 6-speed manual transmission. NA w/automatic transmission, detachable hardtop. NA Base w/Convenience Package.		
2AP Appearance Pkg., Base, LS	450	360
Small side sills, small rear mud guards.		
1AP Appearance Pkg., Base, LS	800	644
Front air dam, large side sills, small rear mud guards.		
Powertrain		
6-speed manual transmission, LS	650	565
4-speed automatic transmission, Base, LS	800	695
LS requires antilock brakes. LS deletes limited-slip differential.		
Safety		
Antilock brakes, LS	550	468
Comfort & Convenience Features		
AM/FM/cassette/CD player, Base, LS	200	160
In-dash 6-disc CD changer, Base, LS	500	400
Automatic day/night rearview mirror, Base, LS	230	185
Includes compass.		
Appearance & Special Purpose		
Detachable hardtop	1500	1215
Rear spoiler, Base, LS	295	236

MAZDA MPV

CLASS: Minivan
DRIVE WHEELS: Front-wheel drive
BASE PRICE RANGE: $22,940-$28,505. Built in Japan.
ALSO CONSIDER: Dodge Caravan, Honda Odyssey, Toyota Sienna

Available in one body length, MPV is among the smallest minivans. It uses a 200-hp V6 engine and 5-speed automatic transmission. ABS is standard. Two models are offered: LX with 16-inch alloy wheels, and top-shelf ES with 17s. Front side airbags and traction control are optional on LX, standard on ES. For 2005, rear air conditioning moves from standard on LX to optional; it remains standard on ES. MPVs seat seven. The 2nd-row bucket seats can slide together to create a 2-passenger bench. The 3-passenger 3rd-row bench folds into the floor. Dual sliding side doors are standard and have roll-down power windows. Power-operated side doors are available.

RATINGS

	LX	ES
ACCELERATION	4	4
FUEL ECONOMY	5	5
RIDE QUALITY	5	6
STEERING/HANDLING	5	6
QUIETNESS	5	5
CONTROLS/MATERIALS	5	5
ROOM/COMFORT (FRONT)	7	7
ROOM/COMFORT (REAR)	6	6
CARGO ROOM	9	9
VALUE WITHIN CLASS	7	8

MPV feels well-built and does an admirable job of people and parcel packaging. It's among the best-handling minivans, and while the V6 isn't a paragon of power or smoothness, it is more than adequate. MPV earns a Recommended rating and merits consideration if sheer interior expanse isn't a priority.

	LX	ES
TOTAL	**58**	**61**

Average total for minivans: 58.0

ENGINES

	dohc V6
Size, liters/cu. in.	3.0/181
Horsepower @ rpm	200 @ 6200
Torque (lb-ft) @ rpm	200 @ 3000
Availability	S
EPA city/highway mpg	
5-speed automatic	18/25

PRICES

Mazda MPV	RETAIL PRICE	DEALER INVOICE
LX 4-door van	$22940	$21209
ES 4-door van	28505	26341
Destination charge	545	545

STANDARD EQUIPMENT

LX: 3.0-liter V6 engine, 5-speed automatic transmission, dual front airbags, antilock 4-wheel disc brakes, front air conditioning, interior air filter, power steering, tilt steering wheel w/radio controls, cruise control, cloth upholstery, 7-passenger seating, front bucket seats, center console, cupholders, 2nd-row bucket seats, 3rd-row stowable bench seat, side table, power mirrors, power windows, power door locks, remote keyless entry, AM/FM/CD player, digital clock, tachometer, map lights, illuminated visor mirrors, variable-intermittent wipers, rear defogger, rear intermittent wiper/washer, 215/60HR16 tires, alloy wheels.

ES adds: traction control, front side airbags, rear air conditioning w/rear controls, leather upholstery, 8-way power driver seat, leather-wrapped steering wheel, AM/FM radio w/in-dash 6-disc CD changer, power sliding rear doors, floormats, rear privacy glass, fog lights, 215/60HR17 tires.

OPTIONAL EQUIPMENT

Major Packages

	RETAIL PRICE	DEALER INVOICE
LX Plus Pkg., LX	$1505	$1294
Rear air conditioning w/rear controls, floormats, cargo mat, fog lights, rear privacy glass, bodyside moldings.		
Traction and Airbag Pkg., LX	400	344
Traction control, front side airbags. Requires LX Plus Pkg.		
All Sport Pkg., LX	975	839
Leather-wrapped steering wheel, 8-way power driver seat, AM/FM radio w/in-dash 6-disc CD changer, automatic day/night rearview mirror, compass, outside-temperature indicator, universal garage-door opener, rear spoiler, 215/60HR17 tires. Requires LX Plus Pkg., Traction and Airbag Pkg. NA w/4-Seasons/Towing Pkg., power sliding doors, power sunroof.		
4-Seasons/Towing Pkg.	425	366
Rear heater, heated mirrors, heavy-duty wiper motor, larger washer tank, transmission-oil cooler, heavy-duty battery and radiator. LX requires LX Plus Pkg.		

Comfort & Convenience Features

Power sunroof	900	744
LX requires LX Plus Pkg., power sliding rear doors.		
Power sliding rear doors, LX	800	688
Requires LX Plus Pkg.		
Rear-seat DVD entertainment system	1200	960
AM/FM/cassette/CD player	200	160
Automatic day/night rearview mirror	230	184
Includes compass, outside-temperature indicator.		
Cargo organizer	145	116

Appearance & Special Purpose

Rear spoiler	190	163
Roof rack	250	215
Trailer-hitch receiver	450	360
Includes wiring harness.		

 Specifications begin on page 547.

MAZDA RX-8

CLASS: Sporty/performance car
DRIVE WHEELS: Rear-wheel drive
BASE PRICE RANGE: $25,375-$26,875. Built in Japan.
ALSO CONSIDER: Acura RSX, Mini Cooper, Nissan 350Z

Mazda's rotary-engine-powered sporty car is a 4-passenger 4 dr with rear-hinged rear doors that do not open or close independently of the fronts. Conventional engines use pistons that move up and down in cylinders. A rotary has triangular rotors that spin inside oval housings. The RX-8's displaces 1.3-liters and has 197 hp when teamed with a 4-speed automatic transmission, 238 hp when linked with a 6-speed manual. The automatic includes a manual-shift mode using steering-wheel paddles or floor lever. Manual-transmission RX-8s have 18-inch wheels, stiffer sport suspension, and a limited-slip differential. A Sport Package option for automatics replaces their 16-inch wheels with 18s and adds the stiffer suspension. ABS, front side airbags, and head-protecting curtain side airbags are standard.

RATINGS	Base w/Sport Pkg., auto.	Base w/Grand Touring Pkg., man.
ACCELERATION	6	7
FUEL ECONOMY	4	4
RIDE QUALITY	5	5
STEERING/HANDLING	9	9
QUIETNESS	4	4
CONTROLS/MATERIALS	8	8
ROOM/COMFORT (FRONT)	5	5
ROOM/COMFORT (REAR)	2	2
CARGO ROOM	2	2
VALUE WITHIN CLASS	6	6

The rewardingly agile, solidly built RX-8 has less straightline performance than other similarly priced sports cars. However, it does offer the convenience of four seats and rear doors, making it more practical for everyday use than most competitors. It even qualifies as a rear-wheel-drive alternative to front-wheel-drive sporty coupes such as the Mini Cooper and Acura RSX.

TOTAL	51	52

Average total for sporty/performance cars: 48.5

ENGINES

	Rotary	Rotary
Size, liters/cu. in.	1.3/80	1.3/80
Horsepower @ rpm	197 @ 7200	238 @ 8500
Torque (lb-ft) @ rpm	164 @ 5600	159 @ 5000
Availability	S[1]	S[2]
EPA city/highway mpg		
6-speed manual		18/24
4-speed automatic	18/25	

1. Automatic transmission. 2. Manual transmission.

PRICES

Mazda RX-8	RETAIL PRICE	DEALER INVOICE
Base 4-door coupe, automatic	$25375	$23460
Base 4-door coupe, manual	26875	24844
Destination charge	545	545

STANDARD EQUIPMENT

Base automatic: 1.3-liter 197-horsepower rotary engine, 4-speed automatic transmission w/manual-shift capability, dual front airbags, front side airbags, curtain side airbags, antilock 4-wheel disc brakes, tire-pressure monitor, emergency inside trunk release, air conditioning, power steering, tilt leather-wrapped steering wheel w/radio controls, cruise control, cloth upholstery, front and rear bucket seats, center console, cupholders, trunk pass-through, power mirrors, power windows, power door locks, remote keyless entry, AM/FM/CD player, digital clock, tachometer, outside-temperature indicator, variable-intermittent wipers, illuminated visor mirrors, rear defogger, floormats, 225/55R16 tires, alloy wheels.

Base manual adds: 1.3-liter 238-horsepower rotary engine, 6-speed manual transmission, limited-slip differential, sport suspension, 225/45ZR18 tires.

OPTIONAL EQUIPMENT

Major Packages	RETAIL PRICE	DEALER INVOICE
Sport Pkg., automatic	$2000	$1721
Traction control, antiskid system, limited-slip differential, fog lights, xenon headlights, upgraded brakes, sport suspension, 225/45ZR18 tires.		
Touring Pkg., automatic	3775	3248
Sport Pkg. plus power sunroof, Bose sound system, automatic day/night rearview mirror, universal garage-door opener.		
Grand Touring Pkg., automatic	4950	4258
Touring Pkg. plus leather upholstery, 8-way power driver seat w/lumbar adjustment, heated front seats and mirrors.		
Sport Pkg., manual	1300	1118
Traction control, antiskid system, xenon headlights, fog lights.		
Touring Pkg., manual	2975	2559
Sport Pkg. plus power sunroof, Bose sound system, automatic day/night rearview mirror, universal garage-door opener.		

 Specifications begin on page 547.

OPTIONAL EQUIPMENT (cont.)

	RETAIL PRICE	DEALER INVOICE
Grand Touring Pkg., manual	$4250	$3656
Touring Pkg. plus leather upholstery, 8-way power driver seat w/lumbar adjustment, heated front seats and mirrors.		
Appearance Pkg.	970	775
Body cladding.		
Comfort & Convenience Features		
Navigation system	2000	1721
AM/FM radio w/in-dash 6-disc CD changer	500	400
AM/FM/cassette	200	160
Appearance & Special Purpose		
Rear spoiler	355	285
Limited-use spare tire	395	320

MAZDA TRIBUTE

CLASS: Compact sport-utility vehicle
DRIVE WHEELS: Front-wheel drive, all-wheel drive
BASE PRICE RANGE: $19,630-$24,390. Built in USA.
ALSO CONSIDER: Honda CR-V, Jeep Liberty, Subaru Forester

Mazda's compact SUV gets a larger base engine and added safety features for 2005. Tribute shares its car-type design with Ford's Escape, but does not offer Escape's available gas/electric hybrid powertrain. Tribute comes in models labeled i and s. It offers front-wheel drive or all-wheel drive that does not have low-range gearing. Standard on i models is a new 4-cyl engine, a 153-hp 2.3-liter in place of a 130-hp 2.0. Standard on s models is a 200-hp V6. A manual transmission is available in the 2WD i. All other models have automatic. ABS, previously optional, is standard for '05. Newly optional for s models are head-protecting curtain side airbags that cover both seating rows. Continuing as standard are CD audio, 16-inch alloy wheels, 60/40 split folding rear seatbacks, and a rear liftgate with separate hatch window. Available features include heated front seats, leather upholstery, sunroof, and rear DVD entertainment. Tribute's performance and accommodations mirror those of comparably equipped Escapes.

RATINGS

	AWD s model
ACCELERATION	5
FUEL ECONOMY	5
RIDE QUALITY	4
STEERING/HANDLING	5
QUIETNESS	4
CONTROLS/MATERIALS	5
ROOM/COMFORT (FRONT)	6
ROOM/COMFORT (REAR)	5
CARGO ROOM	7
VALUE WITHIN CLASS	10

Tribute and the related Escape are solid, spacious, and rewarding to drive. They cost in the mid-$20,000 range, well-equipped, making them Best Buy alternatives to some truck-based SUVs that may be larger on the outside, but use more gas and don't have significantly more interior space.

TOTAL	56

Average total for compact sport-utility vehicles: 49.0

ENGINES

	dohc I4	dohc V6
Size, liters/cu. in.	2.3/138	3.0/181
Horsepower @ rpm	153 @ 5800	200 @ 6000
Torque (lb-ft) @ rpm	152 @ 4250	193 @ 4850
Availability	S[1]	S[2]
EPA city/highway mpg		
5-speed manual	22/26[3]	
4-speed automatic	19/22[4]	18/22[5]

1. i models. 2. s models. 3. 24/29 w/2WD. 4. 22/25 w/2WD. 5. 20/25 w/2WD.

PRICES

Mazda Tribute	RETAIL PRICE	DEALER INVOICE
2WD i 4-door wagon, manual	$19630	$18352
2WD i 4-door wagon, automatic	20235	18916
AWD i 4-door wagon, manual	21330	19937
AWD i 4-door wagon, automatic	21735	20315
2WD s 4-door wagon, automatic	22890	21392
AWD s 4-door wagon, automatic	24390	22791
Destination charge	590	590

STANDARD EQUIPMENT

i: 2.3-liter 4-cylinder engine, 5-speed manual or 4-speed automatic transmission, dual front airbags, antilock brakes, air conditioning, power steering, tilt steering wheel, cloth upholstery, front bucket seats, center console, cupholders, split folding rear seat, power mirrors, power windows, power door locks, remote keyless entry, AM/FM/CD player, digital clock, tachometer, variable-intermittent wipers, visor mirrors, rear defogger, intermittent rear wiper/washer, map lights, automatic-off headlights, floormats, theft-

 Specifications begin on page 547.

deterrent system, rear privacy glass, roof rack, 235/70TR16 tires, alloy wheels. **AWD** adds: all-wheel drive.

s adds: 3.0-liter V6 engine, 4-speed automatic transmission, antilock 4-wheel disc brakes, cruise control, height-adjustable driver seat w/lumbar adjustment, illuminated visor mirrors, fog lights. **AWD** adds: all-wheel drive.

OPTIONAL EQUIPMENT

Major Packages

	RETAIL PRICE	DEALER INVOICE
Pkg. 1, s	$1380	$1201
Power sunroof, overhead console, 6-way power driver seat, AM/FM radio w/in-dash 6-disc CD changer, upgraded sound system, cargo cover. NA w/rear-seat DVD entertainment system.		
Pkg. 2, s	1645	1431
Leather upholstery, 6-way power driver seat, leather-wrapped steering wheel, woodgrain instrument panel, dual overhead consoles, AM/FM radio w/in-dash 6-disc CD changer, upgraded sound system, cargo cover.		
Pkg. 3, s	2495	2171
Pkg. 1 plus leather upholstery, leather-wrapped steering wheel, heated front seats and mirrors, woodgrain instrument panel. NA w/rear-seat DVD entertainment system.		
Tow Pkg., s	350	305
Trailer hitch, Class II trailer tow prep, trailer-wiring harness.		

Safety

Curtain side airbags, s	315	274

Comfort & Convenience Features

Rear-seat DVD entertainment system	1200	960
Cassette player	200	160
In-dash 6-disc CD changer	500	400
Cargo tray and organizer	150	120

Appearance & Special Purpose

Rear spoiler	275	220
Tubular side steps	400	320
Alarm system	115	90

MERCEDES-BENZ C-CLASS

CLASS: Premium compact car
DRIVE WHEELS: Rear-wheel drive, all-wheel drive
BASE PRICE RANGE: $25,850-$53,900. Built in Germany.
ALSO CONSIDER: Acura TL, Audi A4, BMW 3-Series

Revised styling and introduction of a V8 high-performance model highlight 2005 changes to Mercedes-Benz' least-expensive cars. The C-Class offers three body styles: sedan, wagon, and 2-dr hatchback coupe. Mercedes divides the line into Sport and Luxury versions. C230s have a 189-hp supercharged 4-cyl engine; they come in Sport Coupe and Sport Sedan trim. C240s

have a 168-hp V6; they come as Luxury sedans and wagons. C320s have a 215-hp V6; they come as a Sport coupe and sedan, and as a Luxury sedan. The new high-performance C55 AMG sedan has a 362-hp V8. It replaces the 349-hp V6 C32 AMG sedan and has front-end styling distinct from other models'. C230 Sport and C320 Sport models are available with a 6-speed manual transmission or the 5-speed automatic that's standard on the other models. Rear-wheel drive is standard. The C240 sedan and wagon and C320 sedan are available with Mercedes' 4Matic all-wheel drive. For '05, Luxury sedans and wagons get new-style wheels and adopt body trim used on the 2004 Sport versions. Sport sedans adopt body trim used on the C32 AMG. Sport coupes get a perforated grille. All have revised headlamps and taillamps and a redesigned dashboard. Interior trim—wood on Luxury versions, aluminum on Sports—is also revised. The C55 and Sports come with sport-tuned suspension. The C55 has 18-inch wheels, the Sports 17s; other models have 16s. Every C-Class has ABS, antiskid/traction control, front/rear side airbags, and head-protecting curtain side airbags. Options include a navigation system and bi-xenon headlamps. Coupes are available with Mercedes' large Panorama sunroof that teams with a fixed-glass panel over the rear seat; each has a power sunshade.

RATINGS	C240 Lux. sdn, auto.	C320 Lux. sdn w/nav. sys., auto.	C320 4Matic Lux. sdn	C320 Sport cpe, auto.
ACCELERATION	4	6	6	7
FUEL ECONOMY	5	5	5	4
RIDE QUALITY	7	7	7	7
STEERING/HANDLING	6	7	7	7
QUIETNESS	7	7	7	7
CONTROLS/MATERIALS	7	6	7	7
ROOM/COMFORT (FRONT)	6	6	6	6
ROOM/COMFORT (REAR)	4	4	4	3
CARGO ROOM	3	3	3	6
VALUE WITHIN CLASS	4	6	6	5

We're sad to see the versatile C320 wagon shelved, a move that leaves the C320 sedan as the best overall value in this line. It's a desirable premium compact in its own right, and vies with the best in class for driving composure, features, and long-term value. The 4Matic C240s and C320s impress with all-season security. C-Class coupes are less accommodating than the sedans, and lack the performance or styling to score with enthusiast buyers.

TOTAL	53	57	58	59

Average total for premium compact cars: 57.5

 Specifications begin on page 547.

ENGINES

	Supercharged dohc I4	sohc V6	sohc V6	sohc V8
Size, liters/cu. in.	1.8/110	2.6/159	3.2/195	5.4/332
Horsepower @ rpm	189 @ 5800	168 @ 5700	215 @ 5700	362 @ 5750
Torque (lb-ft) @ rpm	192 @ 3500	177 @ 4700	221 @ 3000	376 @ 4000
Availability	S[1]	S[2]	S[3]	S[4]
EPA city/highway mpg				
6-speed manual	22/30		19/26	
5-speed automatic	23/30	20/25[5]	20/26[6]	16/22

1. C230. 2. C240. 3. C320. 4. C55 AMG. 5. 19/25 w/4Matic AWD. 6. 19/27 w/4Matic AWD.

PRICES

Mercedes-Benz C-Class

	RETAIL PRICE	DEALER INVOICE
C230 Sport Coupe 2-door hatchback, manual	$25850	$24040
C230 Sport Sedan 4-door sedan, manual	29250	27203
C240 Luxury Sedan 4-door sedan, automatic	32650	30365
C240 4Matic AWD Luxury Sedan 4-door sedan, auto.	33850	31481
C240 Luxury Wagon 4-door wagon, automatic	34150	31760
C240 4Matic AWD Luxury Wagon 4-door wagon, auto.	35350	32876
C320 Sport Coupe 2-door hatchback, manual	28250	26273
C320 Sport Sedan 4-door sedan, manual	37350	34736
C320 Luxury Sedan 4-door sedan, automatic	37950	35294
C320 4Matic AWD Luxury Sedan 4-door sedan, auto.	39150	36410
C55 4-door sedan, automatic	53900	50127
Destination charge	720	720

C55 adds $1300 Gas-Guzzler tax.

STANDARD EQUIPMENT

C230/C320 Sport Coupe: 1.8-liter 4-cylinder supercharged engine (C230), 3.2-liter V6 engine (C320), 6-speed manual transmission, traction control, dual front airbags w/automatic child-seat recognition system, front and rear side airbags, curtain side airbags, antilock 4-wheel disc brakes, brake assist, antiskid system, daytime running lights, emergency inside trunk release, power steering, tilt/telescope leather-wrapped steering wheel w/radio and additional controls, cruise control, air conditioning w/dual-zone automatic climate controls, interior air filter, cloth upholstery, height-adjustable front bucket seats, center console, cupholders, split folding rear seat, aluminum interior trim, heated power mirrors w/turn signals, power windows, power door locks, remote keyless entry, AM/FM/weatherband/CD player, digital clock, tachometer, trip computer, map lights, rear defogger, cargo cover, heated intermittent wipers, visor mirrors, automatic headlights, floormats, theft-deterrent system, front and rear fog lights, sport suspension, 225/45ZR17 front tires, 225/45ZR17 rear tires (C230), 245/40ZR17 rear tires (C320), alloy wheels.

C230 Sport Sedan adds: cloth/leather upholstery, front-seat power height adjustment and reclining, illuminated visor mirrors, 225/45ZR17 front tires, 245/40ZR17 rear tires. *Deletes:* split folding rear seat, cargo cover.

C240 adds: 2.6-liter V6 engine, 5-speed automatic transmission w/manual-shift capability, wood interior trim, split folding rear seat (wagon), cargo cover (wagon), heated intermittent rear wiper/washer (wagon), roof rails (wagon), 205/55HR16 tires. *Deletes:* sport suspension. **AWD** adds: all-wheel drive, heated front seats.

C320 sedan adds: 3.2-liter V6 engine, 6-speed manual transmission (Sport), power tilt/telescope steering wheel, 10-way power front seats, memory system (driver seat, mirrors, steering wheel), aluminum interior trim (Sport), Harman/Kardon sound system, sport suspension (Sport), 225/45ZR17 front and 245/40ZR17 rear tires (Sport). **AWD** adds: all-wheel drive, heated front seats.

C55 adds: 5.4-liter V8 engine, 5-speed automatic transmission w/manual-shift capability, upgraded brakes, TeleAid assistance system, leather upholstery, heated front seats, split folding rear seat, power sunroof, automatic day/night driver-side and rearview mirrors, performance suspension, 225/40ZR18 rear tires, 245/35ZR18 rear tires.

OPTIONAL EQUIPMENT

Major Packages	RETAIL PRICE	DEALER INVOICE
Entertainment Pkg., C230, C240, C320 Sport Coupe	$970	$903
Harman/Kardon sound system, 6-disc CD changer.		
Sunroof Pkg., coupe	1390	1293
wagon	1660	1544
sedan	1790	1665
Power Panorama sunroof (coupe), power sunroof (sedan, wagon), rain-sensing wipers, universal garage-door opener, automatic day/night driver-side and rearview mirrors, power rear sunshade (sedan). NA C55.		
Premium Pkg., C55	NA	NA
6-disc CD changer, rain-sensing wipers, power rear sunshade.		

Powertrain

5-speed automatic transmission w/manual-shift capability, C230/C320 Sport	1390	1293

Comfort & Convenience Features

TeleAid assistance system	820	763
Std. C55.		
COMAND navigation system	2210	2056
Full leather upholstery	1500	1395
Std. C55.		
Power driver seat, C230, C240, C320 Sport Coupe	600	558
10-way power driver seat, power tilt/telescope steering wheel, driver seat and mirror memory.		
Heated front seats	680	633
Std. AWD, C55.		
Multicontour driver seat, C240, C320 Luxury	240	224
Split folding rear seat, sedan	290	270
Std. C55.		
6-disc CD changer	420	391
NA C55.		

 Specifications begin on page 547.

OPTIONAL EQUIPMENT (cont.)

	RETAIL PRICE	DEALER INVOICE
Hands-free cellular telephone kit	$765	$712
Integrated cellular telephone. Does not include handset/cradle.		

Appearance & Special Purpose

Lighting Pkg	790	735
Bi-xenon headlights w/washers.		

MERCEDES-BENZ CLK

CLASS: Premium sporty/performance car
DRIVE WHEELS: Rear-wheel drive
2004 BASE PRICE RANGE: $44,350-$79,500. Built in Germany.
ALSO CONSIDER: Audi A4 Cabriolet, BMW 3-Series, Infiniti G35 coupe

A new automatic transmission highlights 2005 for these 2-dr 4-passenger coupes and convertibles. CLK coupes have "hardtop" styling with no middle roof posts. Convertibles have a power fabric top with heated glass rear window. They also have roll bars in the rear headrests designed to pop up if sensors detect an impending rollover. Both body styles are available as a CLK320 with a 215-hp V6, a CLK500 with a 302-hp V8, and a CLK55 with a 362-hp V8. CLK55s were developed by Mercedes' AMG performance arm. All use automatic transmission, a 7 speed in CLK500s for'05, a 5-speed in the others. Both transmissions have a manual shift gate. V8 models include manual-shift steering-wheel buttons. All CLKs come with ABS, antiskid/traction control, Mercedes' TeleAid assistance, and front and rear side airbags. The convertibles' front side airbags cover head and torso. Coupes have head-protecting curtain side airbags. CLK55s include sport suspension and, for '05, 18-inch wheels vs other models' 17s. All get a mild facelift and redesigned center console for '05. Also, CLK500s get AMG-style wheels and rear spoiler, plus digital automatic climate control. CLK320s add the features of 2004's $1080 Appearance Package. All versions offer Mercedes' COMAND video-screen control for audio and available navigation and phone systems. Other options include front/rear-obstacle detection and cruise control designed to maintain a set following distance. Mercedes' available Keyless Go system uses a pocket transmitter for keyless starting and door-lock operation. CLKs are prewired for dealer-installed satellite radio.

RATINGS	CLK320 cpe	CLK320 conv	CLK500 cpe	CLK55 cpe
ACCELERATION	6	6	8	9
FUEL ECONOMY	5	5	5	4
RIDE QUALITY	7	7	7	6
STEERING/HANDLING	7	7	7	8
QUIETNESS	7	6	7	6
CONTROLS/MATERIALS	6	6	6	6
ROOM/COMFORT (FRONT)	7	7	7	7
ROOM/COMFORT (REAR)	2	2	2	2
CARGO ROOM	3	2	3	3
VALUE WITHIN CLASS	7	7	6	4

Stylish, solid, and sporty, CLKs make sense for well-heeled buyers who value fashion over 4-dr utility. Performance that ranges from outstanding to outrageous, numerous safety features, and Mercedes' strong resale values help cinch a Recommended ribbon.

TOTAL	57	55	58	55

Average total for premium sporty/performance cars: 48.3

ENGINES

	sohc V6	sohc V8	sohc V8
Size, liters/cu. in.	3.2/195	5.0/303	5.4/332
Horsepower @ rpm	215 @ 5700	302 @ 5600	362 @ 5750
Torque (lb-ft) @ rpm	229 @ 3000	339 @ 2700	376 @ 4000
Availability	S[1]	S[2]	S[3]
EPA city/highway mpg			
7-speed automatic		17/25	
5-speed automatic	20/28		16/22

1. CLK320 models. 2. CLK500 models. 3. CLK55 AMG.

2005 Prices unavailable at time of publication

2004 PRICES

Mercedes-Benz CLK	RETAIL PRICE	DEALER INVOICE
CLK320 2-door coupe	$44350	$41246
CLK320 2-door convertible	51400	47802
CLK500 2-door coupe	52800	49104
CLK500 2-door convertible	59850	55661
CLK55 2-door coupe	69900	65007
CLK55 2-door convertible	79500	73935
Destination charge	720	720

CLK500 adds $1000 Gas-Guzzler Tax. CLK55 adds $1300 Gas-Guzzler Tax.

STANDARD EQUIPMENT

CLK320: 3.2-liter V6 engine, 5-speed automatic transmission w/manual-shift capability, traction control, dual front airbags w/automatic child-seat recognition system, front and rear side airbags, curtain side airbags (coupe), antilock 4-wheel disc brakes, brake assist, antiskid system, automatic roll bars (convertible), emergency inside trunk release, daytime running lights, air conditioning w/dual-

 Specifications begin on page 547.

zone automatic climate controls, interior air filter, TeleAid assistance system w/one-year service, power steering, power tilt/telescope leather-wrapped steering wheel w/radio controls, cruise control, leather upholstery, 10-way power front seats, memory system (driver seat, mirrors, steering wheel), center console, cupholder, split folding rear seat (coupe), wood interior trim, heated power mirrors w/driver-side automatic day/night and passenger-side tilt-down back-up aid, power windows, power door locks, remote keyless entry, power convertible top (convertible), Bose AM/FM/weatherband/cassette, digital clock, tachometer, trip computer, rain-sensing variable-intermittent wipers, illuminated visor mirrors, universal garage-door opener, automatic day/night rearview mirror, map lights, rear defogger, automatic headlights, floormats, theft-deterrent system, front and rear fog lights, 205/55HR16 front tires, 225/50HR16 rear tires, alloy wheels.

CLK500 adds: 5.0-liter V8 engine, 225/45ZR17 front tires, 245/40ZR17 rear tires.

CLK55 adds: 5.4-liter V8 engine, heated multicontour front seats, power sunroof, rear spoiler, sport suspension, polished alloy wheels. *Deletes:* wood interior trim.

OPTIONAL EQUIPMENT

Major Packages	RETAIL PRICE	DEALER INVOICE
Appearance Pkg., 320	$1080	$1004
Aluminum or standard burl walnut interior trim, aluminum pedals, chrome exhaust tips, 225/45ZR17 front tires, 245/40ZR17 rear tires, 5-spoke alloy wheels.		
Moon Roof Pkg., 320/500 coupe	1410	1311
Power sunroof, power rear sunshade.		
Comfort Pkg., 320, 500	1200	1116
Active-ventilated multicontour front seats.		
Lighting Pkg	975	907
Xenon headlights w/washers.		
designo Bronze/Espresso Edition, 320/500 coupe	6200	5766
320/500 convertible	6900	6417
55	6100	5673
Unique interior trim, special paint. Requires heated front seats.		
Safety		
Front- and rear-obstacle-detection system	1060	986
Comfort & Convenience Features		
COMAND System	2170	2018
Navigation system, CD player. Deletes cassette player.		
6-disc CD changer	410	381
Keyless Go	1040	967
Distronic adaptive cruise control	3010	2799
Active-ventilated front seats, 320, 500	910	846
55	675	628
Heated front seats, 320, 500	670	623
Wood/leather-wrapped steering wheel, 320, 500	510	474
Integrated cellular telephone	NA	NA
Voice-activated integrated cellular telephone	1995	1437
Power rear sunshade, 55	450	419

MERCEDES-BENZ E-CLASS

CLASS: Premium midsize car
DRIVE WHEELS: Rear-wheel drive, all-wheel drive
BASE PRICE RANGE: $48,500-$79,500. Built in Germany.
ALSO CONSIDER: Acura RL, Audi A6, Lexus ES 330

The E-Class line offers sedans and wagons with 6- and 8-cyl power and rear- or all-wheel drive. E320 models have a 221-hp V6, E500s a 302-hp V8; both are available in either body style. Offered as sedans only are the high-performance E55 with a 469-hp V8 and the E320 CDI with a 201-hp inline 6-cyl turbodiesel engine. Emissions regulations prevent the CDI's sale in California and four northeastern states. Mercedes' 4Matic all-wheel drive is standard on E500 wagons, optional on other models except the CDI and E55. All have automatic transmission with manual shift gate. It's a 7-speed in the rear-drive E500 sedan, a 5-speed in other models. The E55 adds manual-shift steering-wheel buttons. All models include ABS and antiskid/traction control. E55 and E500s have an air-spring suspension with driver-adjustable shock-absorber firmness. It's not available for E320s and the CDI. E55s come with 18-inch wheels, E500s 17s, the other models 16s. The 17s and 18s are optional on certain E320s and E500s.

Front and rear side airbags, head-protecting curtain side airbags, and Mercedes' TeleAid assistance are standard. Options include voice-activated cell phone and navigation, dealer-installed satellite radio, and Mercedes' Distronic cruise control designed to maintain a set following distance. Also available: steering-linked bi-xenon headlamps, heated/ventilated front seats, and massaging front seats. Mercedes' optional Keyless Go system uses a carry-along transmitter for unlocking and starting. Rear-obstacle detection is available for sedans. So is Mercedes' full-length Panorama glass sunroof with a power tilt/slide panel above the front seats. The E55 has exclusive trim and sport suspension, exhaust, and seats. E500s and V6 E320s offer an Appearance Package with body cladding and unique wood trim.

RATINGS	E320 sdn	E320 4Matic wgn w/Appr. Pkg.	E320 CDI	E500 sdn
ACCELERATION	6	5	6	8
FUEL ECONOMY	5	4	7	5
RIDE QUALITY	10	7	10	7
STEERING/HANDLING	7	7	7	7
QUIETNESS	8	7	7	8

 Specifications begin on page 547.

RATINGS (cont.)	E320 sdn	E320 4Matic wgn w/Appr. Pkg.	E320 CDI	E500 sdn
CONTROLS/MATERIALS	7	7	7	7
ROOM/COMFORT (FRONT)	8	8	8	8
ROOM/COMFORT (REAR)	6	6	6	6
CARGO ROOM	5	7	5	5
VALUE WITHIN CLASS	9	8	9	8

Contemporary and sophisticated, rock-solid and confident on the road, every E-Class brims with worthwhile features and Mercedes cachet. Prices are steep, and nonlinear throttle and brake response often annoy. But overall, these very appealing cars are solid Best Buys.

TOTAL	71	66	72	69

Average total for premium midsize cars: 61.7

ENGINES	sohc V6	Turbodiesel dohc I6	sohc V8	Supercharged sohc V8
Size, liters/cu. in.	3.2/195	3.2/197	5.0/303	5.4/332
Horsepower @ rpm	221 @ 5600	201 @ 4200	302 @ 5600	469 @ 6100
Torque (lb-ft) @ rpm	232 @ 3000	369 @ 1800	339 @ 2700	516 @ 2650
Availability	S[1]	S[2]	S[3]	S[4]
EPA city/highway mpg				
7-speed automatic			17/25	
5-speed automatic	20/28[5]	27/37	17/25[6]	14/21

1. E320. 2. E320 CDI 3. E500. 4. E55. 5. 19/25 sedan w/4Matic, 18/24 wagon w/4Matic. 6. 16/20 w/4Matic.

PRICES

Mercedes-Benz E-Class	RETAIL PRICE	DEALER INVOICE
E320 4-door sedan	$48500	$45105
E320 CDI 4-door sedan	49075	45640
AWD E320 4Matic 4-door sedan	51000	47430
E320 4-door wagon	50750	47198
AWD E320 4Matic 4-door wagon	53250	49523
E500 4-door sedan	56900	52917
AWD E500 4Matic 4-door sedan	59400	55242
AWD E500 4Matic 4-door wagon	60500	56265
E55 4-door sedan	79500	73935
Destination charge	720	720

AWD E500 adds $1300 Gas-Guzzler Tax. E55 adds $1700 Gas-Guzzler Tax. CDI not available in Calif., Mass., Maine, N.Y., Vt.

STANDARD EQUIPMENT

E320: 3.2-liter V6 engine, 3.2-liter turbodiesel 6-cylinder engine (CDI), 5-speed automatic transmission w/manual-shift capability, traction control, dual front airbags, front and rear side airbags, curtain side airbags, antilock 4-wheel disc brakes, brake assist, antiskid system, emergency inside trunk release, daytime running lights, TeleAid assistance system, air conditioning w/dual-zone automatic climate controls, interior air filter, power steering, power tilt/telescope leather-wrapped steering wheel w/radio controls, cruise control, vinyl/leather upholstery, 10-way power front bucket seats w/lumbar adjustment, center console, cupholders, memory system (front seats, mirrors, steering wheel), split folding rear seat (wagon), 3rd-row rear-facing folding seat (wagon), wood interior trim, heated power mirrors w/turn signals and driver-side automatic day/night, passenger-side mirror tilt-down back-up aid, power windows, power door locks, remote keyless entry, AM/FM/weatherband/CD player, analog clock, tachometer, trip computer, automatic day/night rearview mirror, outside-temperature indicator, illuminated visor mirrors, universal garage-door opener, rain-sensing variable-intermittent wipers w/heated nozzles, map lights, cargo cover (wagon), rear defogger, intermittent rear wiper/washer (wagon), automatic headlights, floormats, theft-deterrent system, roof rails (wagon), front and rear fog lights, rear air load-leveling suspension (wagon), 225/55HR16 tires, alloy wheels. **AWD** adds: all-wheel drive.

E500 adds: 5.0-liter V8 engine, 7-speed automatic transmission w/manual-shift capability, 4-zone automatic climate controls (including rear controls), leather upholstery, automatic and driver-adjustable air suspension w/level control, 245/45HR17 tires. **AWD** adds: all-wheel drive, 5-speed automatic transmission w/manual-shift capability.

E55 adds: 5.4-liter supercharged V8 engine, 5-speed automatic transmission w/manual-shift capability, power sunroof, heated multicontour front seats, Harmon/Kardon sound system, sport suspension, 245/40ZR18 front tires, 265/35ZR18 rear tires.

OPTIONAL EQUIPMENT

Major Packages

	RETAIL PRICE	DEALER INVOICE
Premium Pkg., E320/E500 sedan	$3950	$3674
wagon	3850	3581
Active-ventilated front seats w/automatic body-securing side bolsters and massaging seatbacks, power sunroof, navigation system, Harman/Kardon sound system, CD changer, power rear sunshade (sedan). Requires full leather upholstery.		
Entertainment Pkg., E320, E500	970	902
Harman/Kardon sound system, in-dash 6-disc CD changer.		
Heating Pkg., E320, E500	920	856
Heated seats and steering wheel.		
Lighting Pkg.	1200	1116
Steering-linked bi-xenon headlights w/washers.		
Rear Seat Pkg., E320/E500 sedan	540	502
Split folding rear seat, ski sack.		
Appearance Pkg., E320	3960	3683
E500	1440	1339
Unique wood interior trim, full-leather upholstery (E320), blue-tinted glass, steering-linked bi-xenon headlights w/washers, aerodynamic body cladding, 245/45HR17 tires. NA CDI.		
AMG Sport Pkg., E320/E500 sedan	4900	4557
AMG styling kit, 245/40ZR18 front tires, 265/35ZR18 rear tires, unique alloy wheels. NA AWD, CDI.		

 Specifications begin on page 547.

OPTIONAL EQUIPMENT (cont.)

	RETAIL PRICE	DEALER INVOICE
Moon Roof Pkg., E320/E500 sedan	$1550	$1442
wagon	1430	1330
Power sunroof, power rear sunshade (sedan), manual rear sunshades.		

Safety

Rear-obstacle-detection system, sedan	1080	1005
Tire-pressure monitor	400	372

Comfort & Convenience Features

Navigation system	1220	1135
Distronic adaptive cruise control, E55	3070	2855
Power Panorama sunroof, sedan	1560	1451
Full leather upholstery, E320	1500	1395
Heated front seats, E320, E500	680	632
Active-ventilated front seats, E320, E500	1250	1163
E55	660	614
Includes heated seats. E320 requires full leather upholstery.		
Drive Dynamic Seats	1180	1097
Automatic body-securing side bolsters and massaging seatbacks.		
Power rear-window sunshade, E55	460	428
Side sunshades, E55	340	316
In-dash 6-disc CD changer	420	391
Cellular telephone	925	860
Cellular telephone w/voice control	1450	1349
Wood/leather-wrapped steering wheel	520	484
Keyless Go	1060	986
Power trunk closer, sedan	500	465
Power liftgate, wagon	510	474

MERCEDES-BENZ M-CLASS

CLASS: Premium midsize sport-utility vehicle
DRIVE WHEELS: All-wheel drive
BASE PRICE RANGE: $37,950-$46,400. Built in USA.
ALSO CONSIDER: Acura MDX, Cadillac SRX, Lexus RX 330

MERCEDES-BENZ

The addition of a special-equipment trim package helps bring down the curtain on the 1998-2005 design generation of this American-built SUV. A redesigned M-Class is due for model year 2006. For '05, M-Class continues with the ML350, which has a 232-hp V6, and the ML500, which has a 288-hp V8. Both have all-wheel drive with low-range gearing. A 5-speed automatic with manual shift gate is the sole transmission. Antilock 4-wheel disc brakes, antiskid/traction control, and 17-inch alloy wheels are standard. So are front and rear torso side airbags and head-protecting curtain side airbags. Mercedes' TeleAid assistance system and dashboard screen for controlling audio and navigation systems are also included. A navigation system and leather upholstery are standard on the ML500, optional on the ML350. A 2-person 3rd-row seat is available for both. The new equipment option is called the Special Edition. Available on both models, it includes among its exclusive features unique wheels, a "power dome" hood, silver-painted grille, polished aluminum roof rails, darkened taillamps, sport seats, and special badging.

RATINGS

	ML350	ML500
ACCELERATION	5	7
FUEL ECONOMY	3	3
RIDE QUALITY	4	4
STEERING/HANDLING	4	4
QUIETNESS	5	5
CONTROLS/MATERIALS	5	5
ROOM/COMFORT (FRONT)	8	8
ROOM/COMFORT (REAR)	7	7
CARGO ROOM	8	8
VALUE WITHIN CLASS	6	5

Though our Also Consider picks hold an edge in carlike driving feel, the M-Class is one of the most competent and pleasant truck-type SUVs. Prices are in line with Mercedes' lofty image, but typically high resale values compensate some.

TOTAL	55	56

Average total for premium midsize sport-utility vehicles: 59.6

ENGINES

	sohc V6	sohc V8
Size, liters/cu. in.	3.7/227	5.0/303
Horsepower @ rpm	232 @ 5750	288 @ 5600
Torque (lb-ft) @ rpm	254 @ 3000	325 @ 2700
Availability	S[1]	S[2]
EPA city/highway mpg		
5-speed automatic	15/18	14/17

1. ML350. 2. ML500.

PRICES

Mercedes-Benz M-Class	RETAIL PRICE	DEALER INVOICE
ML350 4-door wagon	$37950	$35294
ML500 4-door wagon	46400	43152
Destination charge	720	720

STANDARD EQUIPMENT

ML350: 3.7-liter V6 engine, 5-speed automatic transmission w/manual-shift capability, all-wheel drive, 2-speed transfer case, traction control, dual front airbags w/automatic child-seat recognition system, front and rear side airbags, curtain side airbags, antiskid system, antilock 4-wheel disc brakes, brake assist, hill descent control, daytime running lights, air conditioning w/dual-zone automatic climate control and rear controls, interior air filter, TeleAid assistance system, power steering, tilt leather-wrapped steering wheel, cruise control, cloth upholstery, front bucket seats, center console, cupholders, split folding rear seat, wood interior trim, heated power mirrors, power front windows, power door locks, remote keyless entry, AM/FM/weatherband/cassette, digital clock, tachometer, outside-temperature indicator, universal garage-door opener, intermittent wipers, map lights, illuminated visor mirrors, cargo cover, rear defogger, intermittent rear wiper/washer, automatic headlights, floormats, theft-deterrent system, roof rails, front and rear fog lights, front and rear tow hooks, 255/60HR17 tires, alloy wheels.

ML500 adds: 5.0-liter V8 engine, leather upholstery, heated 8-way power front seats, automatic day/night driver-side and rearview mirrors, navigation system, trip computer, compass, rear privacy glass, 275/55VR17 tires.

OPTIONAL EQUIPMENT

Major Packages

	RETAIL PRICE	DEALER INVOICE
Trim Pkg., ML350	$1700	$1581
Leather upholstery, 8-way power front seats, additional wood interior trim, rear privacy glass. Requires Sunroof Pkg.		
Comfort Pkg., ML350	2975	2767
Trim Pkg. plus memory system (driver seat, mirrors), trip computer, compass, power-folding mirrors, automatic day/night outside mirrors w/tilt-down back-up aid, rain-sensing wipers, automatic day/night rearview mirror, under-passenger-seat storage box. Requires Sunroof Pkg.		
Comfort Pkg., ML500	800	744
Memory system (driver seat, mirrors), power-folding mirrors, tilt-down back-up aid, rain-sensing wipers, under-passenger-seat storage box. Requires Sunroof Pkg.		
Rear Seat Pkg., ML350 w/Trim Pkg., ML500	1200	1116
ML350	975	907
3rd-row split folding seat. Deletes cargo cover. Requires Sunroof Pkg.		
Appearance Pkg.	3350	3116
Bodyside cladding, color-keyed bumpers, 275/55VR17 tires, unique alloy wheels. Requires Sunroof Pkg.		
Special Edition Pkg., ML350	2200	2046
Leather upholstery, 8-way power front seats, unique front seats, additional wood interior trim, rear privacy glass, running boards, metallic paint, special hood and grille, unique exterior trim and alloy wheels. Requires Sunroof Pkg.		
Special Edition w/Comfort Pkg., ML350	3475	3232
Special Edition Pkg. plus Comfort Pkg.		

OPTIONAL EQUIPMENT (cont.)

	RETAIL PRICE	DEALER INVOICE
Special Edition Pkg., ML500	$1300	$1209
Memory system, (driver seat, mirrors), power-folding mirrors, tilt-down back-up aid, rain-sensing wipers, unique front seats, additional wood interior trim, rear privacy glass, running boards, metallic paint, special hood and grille, unique exterior trim and alloy wheels. Requires Sunroof Pkg.		
Sunroof Pkg.	1350	1256
Power sunroof, power rear quarter windows.		
Safety		
Rear-obstacle-detection system	1015	944
Comfort & Convenience Features		
Navigation system, ML350	995	925
Bose sound system	1250	1163
Includes 6-disc CD changer.		
Heated front seats, ML350	650	605
Requires Trim Pkg.		
Bi-xenon headlights	875	814
Includes headlight washers.		

MERCEDES-BENZ S-CLASS/CL-CLASS

CLASS: Premium large car
DRIVE WHEELS: Rear-wheel drive, all-wheel drive
2004 BASE PRICE RANGE: $73,600-$126,000. Built in Germany.
ALSO CONSIDER: Audi A8, BMW 7-Series, Lexus LS 430

All-wheel drive at no extra cost makes 2005 news for Mercedes' largest cars. S-Class sedans share basic engineering with CL-Class coupes. The S430 has a 275-hp V8, the S500 and CL500 a 302-hp V8. S55 and CL55 versions, tuned by Mercedes' AMG performance arm, have a supercharged 493-hp V8. The flagship S600 and CL600 use a 493-hp twin-turbocharged V12. The limited-edition CL65 AMG has a twin-turbo V12 with 604 hp. For 2005, the S430 and S500 offer Mercedes' 4Matic all-wheel drive as a no-

Specifications begin on page 547.

charge instead of extra-cost option. The CL500 and rear-drive S430/S500 have a 7-speed automatic transmission. Others use a 5-speed automatic. Both transmissions have a manual shift gate. All models come with anti-skid/traction control, ABS, front/rear torso side airbags, and head-protecting curtain side airbags. AMG models have aero body addenda and uprated brakes. The CL65 has 19-inch wheels vs. 18s for other AMGs and the V12s. Remaining models have 17s, with 18s optional.

Mercedes' Active Body Control, designed to minimize cornering lean, is available for S430 and S500, standard otherwise. All models include Mercedes' TeleAid assistance and COMAND video control for audio, navigation, and phone. Sedans add Mercedes' Pre-Safe system, designed to sense a crash and automatically tension seatbelts and adjust seat position to minimize possible injury. Options include Mercedes' Distronic cruise control, designed to automatically maintain a set following distance, and Mercedes' Keyless Go locking/engine-start system. All models are factory prewired for optional dealer-installed satellite radio.

RATINGS

RATINGS	S430	S430 w/4Matic	S500	CL500
ACCELERATION	7	7	7	7
FUEL ECONOMY	4	4	4	4
RIDE QUALITY	10	10	10	10
STEERING/HANDLING	7	7	7	9
QUIETNESS	10	10	10	9
CONTROLS/MATERIALS	5	5	5	5
ROOM/COMFORT (FRONT)	10	10	10	10
ROOM/COMFORT (REAR)	9	9	9	2
CARGO ROOM	4	4	4	2
VALUE WITHIN CLASS	5	6	6	4

Thumbs-up for no-cost AWD. Thumbs-down for faint signs of cost cutting and some fairly frivolous features. Still, these are among the world's very best premium large cars—as they should be at these prices—bolstered by Mercedes' pacesetting engineering and rock-solid resale values.

TOTAL	71	72	72	62

Average total for premium large cars: 68.7

ENGINES

ENGINES	sohc V8	sohc V8	Supercharged sohc V8	Turbocharged sohc V12
Size, liters/cu. in.	4.3/260	5.0/303	5.4/332	5.5/336
Horsepower @ rpm	275 @ 5750	302 @ 5500	493 @ 6100	493 @ 5000
Torque (lb-ft) @ rpm	295 @ 3000	339 @ 2700	516 @ 2750	590 @ 1800
Availability	S[1]	S[2]	S[3]	S[4]
EPA city/highway mpg				
7-speed automatic	18/26	16/24		
5-speed automatic	17/22	16/22	14/21	12/19

1. S430. 2. S500, CL500. 3. S55 AMG, CL55 AMG. 4. S600, CL600. CL65 AMG has 6.0-liter V12 w/604 hp, 738 lb-ft.

2005 prices unavailable at time of publication

PRICES

Mercedes-Benz S-Class/CL-Class

	RETAIL PRICE	DEALER INVOICE
S430 4-door sedan	$73600	$68448
AWD S430 4Matic 4-door sedan	76500	71145
S500 4-door sedan	82050	76307
AWD S500 4Matic 4-door sedan	84950	79004
S55 4-door sedan	109450	101789
S600 4-door sedan	122100	113553
CL500 2-door coupe	92800	86304
CL55 2-door coupe	117100	108903
CL600 2-door coupe	126000	117180
Destination charge	720	720

S430 AWD, S500, CL500, add $1000 Gas-Guzzler Tax. S500 AWD adds $1300 Gas-Guzzler Tax. S55, CL55 add $1700 Gas-Guzzler Tax. CL600 adds $2600 Gas-Guzzler Tax. S600 adds $3000 Gas-Guzzler Tax.

STANDARD EQUIPMENT

S430: 4.3-liter V8 engine, 7-speed automatic transmission w/manual-shift capability, traction control, dual front airbags w/automatic child-seat recognition system, front and rear side airbags, curtain side airbags, antiskid system, antilock 4-wheel disc brakes, brake assist, Pre-Safe precrash safety system, tire-pressure monitor, daytime running lights, emergency inside trunk release, air conditioning w/dual-zone automatic climate controls, interior air filter, TeleAid assistance system, navigation system, power steering, power tilt/telescope leather-wrapped steering wheel w/radio and climate controls, cruise control, leather upholstery, 14-way power front bucket seats w/adjustable lumbar support, memory system (front seats, outside and rearview mirrors, steering wheel), center console, cupholders, wood interior trim, heated power mirrors w/turn signals, driver-side automatic day/night and passenger-side tilt-down back-up-aid mirrors, power windows, power door locks, remote keyless entry, door and trunk closing assist, power sunroof, Bose AM/FM/CD player, digital clock, tachometer, trip computer, automatic day/night rearview mirror, outside-temperature indicator, universal garage-door opener, front and rear illuminated visor mirrors, rain-sensing intermittent wipers w/deicer, rear defogger, power rear sunshade, remote fuel-door and decklid release, map lights, automatic headlights, floormats, theft-deterrent system, front and rear fog lights, adjustable and self-leveling air suspension, 225/55HR17 tires, alloy wheels. **AWD** adds: all-wheel drive, 5-speed automatic transmission w/ manual-shift capability.

S500 adds: 5.0-liter V8 engine, upgraded leather upholstery, heated front seats, xenon headlights, headlight washers. **AWD** adds: all-wheel drive, 5-speed automatic transmission w/manual-shift capability.

CL500 adds: 6-disc CD changer, wood/leather-wrapped steering wheel, active suspension. *Deletes:* Pre-Safe, rear visor mirrors, air suspension.

S55/CL55 add to S500: 5.4-liter supercharged V8 engine, 5-speed automatic transmission w/manual-shift capability, 6-disc CD changer, multicontour and active-ventilated front seats w/automatic body-securing side bolsters, active suspension, 245/45YR18 front tires, 265/40YR18 rear tires. *Deletes:* rear visor mirrors (CL55), air suspension.

 Specifications begin on page 547.

S600/CL600 adds: 5.5-liter turbocharged V12 engine, rear-obstacle-detection system (S600), rear dual-zone automatic climate controls (S600), wood/leather-wrapped steering wheel, multicontour and active-ventilated front seats, power-adjustable heated rear seats w/lumbar adjustment (S600), additional leather interior trim, voice-activated cellular telephone, 245/45ZR18 tires, polished alloy wheels. *Deletes:* front-seat automatic body-securing side bolsters.

OPTIONAL EQUIPMENT

Major Packages	RETAIL PRICE	DEALER INVOICE
Appearance Pkg., S430, S500, CL500	$1500	$1395
S600, CL600	NC	NC
245/45ZR18 tires, light alloy wheels.		
Heating Pkg., S430	900	837
Heated front seats and steering wheel.		
Rear Seating Pkg., S430, S500	2800	2604
Active-ventilated power rear seats, dual-zone automatic rear climate controls.		
AMG Sport Pkg., S430, S500, S600, CL500, CL600	5210	4845
Aerodynamics pkg., 245/45ZR18 front tires and 265/40ZR18 rear tires (2WD), 245/45ZR18 tires (AWD).		
Safety		
Rear-obstacle-detection system	1060	986
Std. S600		
Comfort & Convenience Features		
Keyless Go	1040	967
Remote keyless entry and ignition-starting system.		
327 Comfort Pkg., S430	2090	1944
S500	1560	1451
Multicontour front seats w/pulsating air chambers, and active lumbar support, heated and active ventilated front seats.		
323/317 Comfort Pkg., S430	2590	2409
S500	2060	1916
CL500	1560	1451
327 Comfort Pkg. plus Drive Dynamic (automatic body-securing side bolsters) seats.		
Multicontour Drive Dynamic front seats, S600	1180	1097
Includes automatic body-securing side bolsters.		
Active ventilated rear seats, S55	1640	1525
S600	970	902
Includes heated rear seats. Requires power rear-seat adjusters or Four Place Seating Pkg.		
Power rear-seat adjusters, S55	1885	1753
Four Place Seating Pkg., S500, S55	6010	5589
S600	4120	3832
Includes rear bucket multicontour seats, power-reclining seatbacks, wood console. S55 requires heated rear seats.		

OPTIONAL EQUIPMENT (cont.)

	RETAIL PRICE	DEALER INVOICE
Heated front seats, S430	$670	$623
Heated rear seats, S430, S500, S55	670	623
S430 requires heated front seats. S55 requires Four Place Seating Pkg.		
Heated steering wheel, S430, S500, CL500, S600, CL600	410	381
Rear dual-zone climate controls, S55	1960	1823
Distronic cruise control	3010	2799
Rear side sunshades	330	307
Power trunk closer	480	446
Voice-activated cellular telephone, S430, S500, CL500, S55, CL55	1995	1437
6-disc CD changer, S430, S500	410	381
Appearance & Special Purpose		
Xenon headlights w/washers, S430	1210	1125
Active suspension, S430, S500	3090	2874
Special order charge	1150	1150
Fee for car ordered with one or more options requiring special order charge.		

MERCEDES-BENZ SL-CLASS

CLASS: Premium sporty/performance car
DRIVE WHEELS: Rear-wheel drive
BASE PRICE RANGE: $88,500-$125,950. Built in Germany.
ALSO CONSIDER: Cadillac XLR, Lexus SC 430

Mercedes' costliest convertible revises its navigation system and center console for 2005. These 2-seaters have a power-retractable metal hardtop. Four models are offered. The SL500 has a 302-hp 5.0-liter V8. The high-performance SL55 AMG has a 493-hp supercharged 5.4 V8. The SL600 uses a twin-turbo 5.5-liter V12 that's also rated at 493 hp, but at lower rpm and with more torque than the SL55's V8. New for '05 is the limited-production SL65 AMG with a 604-hp twin-turbo 6.0 V12, plus larger brakes and specific styling touches. The SL500 uses Mercedes' exclusive 7-speed automatic transmission. Other SLs uses a 5-speed automatic with manual-shift gate; the SL55's "SpeedShift" version includes performance programming and steering-wheel shift buttons. All have antiskid/traction control and Mercedes' ABC active suspension designed to reduce cornering lean. Also standard is "by-wire" ABS that can modulate brake pressure to each wheel. The SL65 comes on 19-inch wheels; others have 18s. All SLs include head/torso side airbags, driver-knee airbag, and a rollover bar that pops up if sensors detect an impending tip. Also standard are navigation and assistance systems, bi-xenon headlamps, and ventilated and massaging seats. Options include Mercedes' Distronic cruise control, designed to maintain a set following distance, and Mercedes' Keyless Go locking system with engine-start button. Voice control for audio, phone, and other functions is a dealer option, as is satellite radio. SL's revamped center console includes an updated version of Mercedes' COMAND video control for navigation, audio, and climate functions.

RATINGS

	SL500	SL600
ACCELERATION	7	10
FUEL ECONOMY	4	3
RIDE QUALITY	6	6
STEERING/HANDLING	8	8
QUIETNESS	6	6
CONTROLS/MATERIALS	7	7
ROOM/COMFORT (FRONT)	8	8
ROOM/COMFORT (REAR)	0	0
CARGO ROOM	2	2
VALUE WITHIN CLASS	6	6

SLs are intriguingly engineered, solidly built, impeccably finished, and a pleasure to drive. Their style and cachet should stay fresh for years, boosting long-term resale values and taking some sting out of startling sticker prices.

TOTAL	54	56

Average total for premium sporty/performance cars: 48.3

ENGINES

	sohc V8	Supercharged sohc V8	Turbocharged sohc V12	Turbocharged sohc V12
Size, liters/cu. in.	5.0/303	5.4/332	5.5/336	6.0/365
Horsepower @ rpm	302 @ 5600	493 @ 6100	493 @ 5000	604 @ 5500
Torque (lb-ft) @ rpm	339 @ 2700	516 @ 2750	590 @ 1800	738 @ 2000
Availability	S[1]	S[2]	S[3]	S[4]
EPA city/highway mpg				
7-speed automatic	16/23			
5-speed automatic		14/20	13/19	12/19

1. SL500. 2. SL55 AMG. 3. SL600. 4. SL65 AMG.

2005 prices unavailable at time of publication

PRICES

Mercedes-Benz SL-Class

	RETAIL PRICE	DEALER INVOICE
SL500 2-door convertible	$88500	$82305
SL55 2-door convertible	119750	111368

PRICES (cont.)

	RETAIL PRICE	DEALER INVOICE
SL600 2-door convertible	$125950	$117134
Destination charge	720	720

SL500 adds $1300 Gas-Guzzler Tax. SL55 adds $1700 Gas-Guzzler Tax. SL600 adds $2600 Gas-Guzzler Tax.

STANDARD EQUIPMENT

SL500: 5.0-liter V8 engine, 7-speed automatic transmission w/manual-shift capability, traction control, dual front airbags w/automatic child-seat recognition system, side airbags, driver-side knee airbag, antilock 4-wheel disc brakes, brake assist, antiskid system, pop-up roll bar, emergency inside trunk release, daytime running lights, air conditioning w/dual-zone automatic climate controls, interior air filter, navigation system, TeleAid assistance system, power steering, power tilt/telescope leather-wrapped steering wheel w/radio controls, cruise control, leather upholstery, heated 12-way power bucket seats w/lumbar adjustment, memory system (driver seat, outside and rearview mirrors, steering wheel), center console, cupholders, wood interior trim, heated power mirrors w/driver-side automatic day/night and passenger-side tilt-down back-up aid, power windows, power door locks, remote keyless entry, Bose AM/FM/weatherband/CD player, 6-disc CD changer, tachometer, trip computer, illuminated visor mirrors, rear defogger, automatic day/night rearview mirror, outside-temperature indicator, universal garage-door opener, rain-sensing variable-intermittent wipers, map lights, automatic headlights, power-retractable steel hardtop, power trunk closer, floormats, theft-deterrent system, xenon low-beam headlights, heated headlight washers, front and rear fog lights, active suspension, 255/40WR18 front tires, 285/35WR18 rear tires, alloy wheels.

SL55 adds: 5.4-liter supercharged V8 engine, 5-speed automatic transmission w/manual-shift capability, massaging-multicontour seats, sport active suspension, air-inflator, 255/40YR18 front tires, 285/35YR18 rear tires.

SL600 adds to SL500: 5.5-liter turbocharged V12 engine, 5-speed automatic transmission w/manual-shift capability, active-ventilated massaging-multicontour seats, wood/leather-wrapped steering wheel, voice-activated cellular telephone, 255/40YR18 front tires, 285/35YR18 rear tires.

OPTIONAL EQUIPMENT

Major Packages

	RETAIL PRICE	DEALER INVOICE
designo Espresso/Graphite/Silver Edition, SL500	$7650	NA
SL55, SL600	6850	NA
Unique interior and exterior trim. NA w/heated steering wheel.		
Comfort Pkg., SL500	1550	1442
Massaging-multicontour seats, active-ventilated seats.		
AMG Sport Pkg., SL500, SL600	5210	4845
Aerodynamics pkg., 255/40YR18 front tires, 285/35YR18 rear tires, unique alloy wheels.		
Trim Pkg., SL500	860	800
Wood/leather-wrapped steering wheel and shift knob.		

 Specifications begin on page 547.

Safety

	RETAIL PRICE	DEALER INVOICE
Parktronic rear-obstacle-detection system	$1060	$986
Tire-pressure monitor	650	605

Comfort & Convenience Features

Active-ventilated seats, SL55	1220	1135
Heated steering wheel, SL500, SL600	410	381
Wood/leather-wrapped steering wheel, SL500	840	782
Keyless Go	1040	967
Distronic cruise control	3010	2799
Voice-activated cellular telephone, SL500, SL55	1995	NA

Appearance & Special Purpose

Panorama glass roof	1840	1711
Xenon dual-beam headlights, SL500, SL55	750	698

MERCEDES-BENZ SLK-CLASS

CLASS: Premium sporty/performance car
DRIVE WHEELS: Rear-wheel drive
BASE PRICE: $45,500. Built in Germany.
ALSO CONSIDER: BMW Z4, Chevrolet Corvette

Redesigned for 2005, this 2-seat convertible gains new styling, features, and a new engine. It's slightly longer, wider, and heavier than its 1998-2004 predecessor, but retains a power-folding hardtop. Launched as the SLK350, it has a 3.5-liter V6 with 268 hp, 53 hp more than the previous 3.2 V6. Transmission choices are a 6-speed manual or 7-speed automatic with manual shift gate. Due later in the model year is a high-performance SLK55 AMG version with a 355-hp V8. The SLK350 comes with antilock 4-wheel disc brakes and anti-skid/traction control. Also standard are knee airbags and side airbags designed to protect both the thorax and head and to deploy in a side collision as well as in an impending rollover. Seventeen-inch wheels are standard. A sport-package option includes firmer suspension, lower-profile tires on different-style 17-inch wheels, lower-body aero trim, and steering-wheel shift buttons for the automatic transmission. Also optional is an industry-first feature Mercedes calls the Airscarf. It places a heater and fan within each seatback to deliver heated air through neck-level vents. This evaluation is based on preview test drives.

RATINGS

	Base, auto.	Base w/Sport Pkg., man.
ACCELERATION	7	8
FUEL ECONOMY	5	5
RIDE QUALITY	4	3
STEERING/HANDLING	8	9
QUIETNESS	4	3
CONTROLS/MATERIALS	7	7
ROOM/COMFORT (FRONT)	5	5
ROOM/COMFORT (REAR)	0	0
CARGO ROOM	2	2
VALUE WITHIN CLASS	6	6

It may not be the first nameplate mentioned when talk turns to sports cars, but the SLK350 makes accessible enough everyday performance to hold its own in pretty fast company. Of broader appeal is its blend of open-air excitement, hardtop security, solid engineering, and Mercedes prestige.

TOTAL	48	48

Average total for premium sporty/performance cars: 48.3

ENGINES

	dohc V6	sohc V8
Size, liters/cu. in.	3.5/213	5.4/332
Horsepower @ rpm	268 @ 6000	355 @ 3500
Torque (lb-ft) @ rpm	258 @ 2400	376 @ 5750
Availability	S[1]	S[2]
EPA city/highway mpg		
7-speed automatic	19/25	16/22
6-speed manual	18/25	

1. SLK350. 2. SLK55.

PRICES

Mercedes-Benz SLK-Class

	RETAIL PRICE	DEALER INVOICE
SLK350 2-door convertible	$45500	$42315
SLK55 2-door convertible	NA	NA
Destination charge	720	720

STANDARD EQUIPMENT

SLK350: 3.5-liter V6 engine, 6-speed manual transmission, traction control, dual front airbags w/automatic child-seat recognition system, side airbags, knee airbags, antilock 4-wheel disc brakes, brake assist, antiskid system, roll bars, daytime running lights, emergency inside trunk release, TeleAid assistance system, air conditioning w/dual-zone manual controls, power steering, tilt/telescope leather-wrapped steering wheel w/radio controls, cruise control, leather upholstery, bucket seats, center console, cupholders, aluminum interior trim, heated power mirrors, power windows, power door locks, remote keyless entry, AM/FM/CD player, digital clock, tachometer, map lights, visor mirrors, rear defogger, wind deflector, floormats, power-retractable steel hardtop, theft-deterrent system, front and rear fog lights, 225/45ZR17 front tires, 245/40ZR17 rear tires, alloy wheels.

 Specifications begin on page 547.

SLK55 adds: 5.4-liter V8 engine, 7-speed automatic transmission w/manual-shift capability, power tilt/telescope steering wheel, heated 8-way power seats, memory system (driver seat, steering wheel), automatic day/night rearview mirror, 18-inch wheels, rear spoiler, sport suspension.

OPTIONAL EQUIPMENT

Major Packages	RETAIL PRICE	DEALER INVOICE
Comfort Pkg., SLK350	$1125	$1046
8-way power seats, power tilt/telescope steering wheel, driver seat and steering-wheel memory.		
Premium Pkg., SLK350	1450	1349
SLK55	NA	NA
Automatic climate controls, variable-assist power steering, remote control roof, automatic day/night driver-side and rearview mirrors, universal garage-door opener, rain-sensing wipers.		
Entertainment Pkg.	1600	1488
Harman/Kardon sound system, 6-disc CD changer.		
Entertainment Pkg. w/Navigation System	2800	2604
Sport Pkg., SLK350	4000	3720
AMG aerodynamic enhancements, steering-wheel shift buttons (automatic transmission), sport suspension, special alloy wheels.		
Heating Pkg., SLK350	950	884
Heated seats, neck-level heating.		
Lighting Pkg	975	907
Bi-xenon headlights, headlight washers.		
Run-Flat Tire Pkg., SLK350	250	233
Run-flat tires, tire-pressure monitor.		
Interior trim Pkg., SLK350	700	651
Wood interior trim, wood/leather-wrapped steering wheel and shift knob.		
Powertrain		
7-speed automatic transmission w/manual-shift capability, SLK350	1390	1293
Comfort & Convenience Features		
Heated front seats, SLK350	680	632
Neck-level heating	NA	NA
6-disc CD changer	420	391
Appearance & Special Purpose		
Sport suspension, SLK350	200	186

MERCURY GRAND MARQUIS

CLASS: Large car
DRIVE WHEELS: Rear-wheel drive
BASE PRICE RANGE: $24,370-$30,725. Built in Canada.
ALSO CONSIDER: Chrysler 300, Dodge Magnum, Toyota Avalon

Mercury's rear-wheel-drive large sedan shares its design with Ford's Crown Victoria and is among the few traditional body-on-frame automobiles. Grand Marquis groups models under GS and LS labels. ABS is standard; traction control is standard on all but the base GS, where it's not available. Front side airbags are available on LS models. The only engine is a 4.6-liter V8 teamed with automatic transmission. An optional LS Handling Package includes dual exhausts for 239 hp vs. 224 standard. All models have a front bench seat. All but the base GS have standard power-adjustable pedals. The performance-oriented Marauder model was discontinued for 2005. Grand Marquis' performance and accommodations mirror those of similarly equipped Crown Victorias.

RATINGS

	LS Ultimate
ACCELERATION	5
FUEL ECONOMY	4
RIDE QUALITY	7
STEERING/HANDLING	5
QUIETNESS	7
CONTROLS/MATERIALS	4
ROOM/COMFORT (FRONT)	7
ROOM/COMFORT (REAR)	6
CARGO ROOM	6
VALUE WITHIN CLASS	5

These sedans ride and handle nicely, but don't feel or act as lively and efficient as more-modern designs such as the Chrysler 300.

TOTAL	56

Average total for large cars: 60.9

ENGINES

	sohc V8	sohc V8
Size, liters/cu. in.	4.6/281	4.6/281
Horsepower @ rpm	224 @ 4800	239 @ 4900
Torque (lb-ft) @ rpm	275 @ 4000	287 @ 4100
Availability	S	O[1]
EPA city/highway mpg		
4-speed automatic	17/25	17/25

1. LS.

Specifications begin on page 547.

PRICES

Mercury Grand Marquis

	RETAIL PRICE	DEALER INVOICE
GS 4-door sedan	$24370	$22850
GS Convenience 4-door sedan	25520	23909
LS Premium 4-door sedan	29425	26913
LS Ultimate 4-door sedan	30725	28083
Destination charge	725	725

STANDARD EQUIPMENT

GS: 4.6-liter V8 engine, 4-speed automatic transmission, dual front airbags, antilock 4-wheel disc brakes, emergency inside trunk release, air conditioning, power steering, tilt steering wheel, cruise control, cloth upholstery, front split bench seat, 8-way power driver seat w/power lumbar adjustment, cupholders, heated power mirrors, power windows, power door locks, AM/FM/CD player, digital clock, variable-intermittent wipers, rear defogger, passenger-side visor mirror, map lights, automatic parking-brake release, automatic headlights, floormats, theft-deterrent system, cornering lights, 225/60TR16 whitewall tires, wheel covers.

GS Convenience adds: traction control, power-adjustable pedals, remote keyless entry, keypad entry.

LS Premium adds: automatic climate control, leather-wrapped steering wheel, 8-way power passenger seat, heated power mirrors, universal garage-door opener, automatic day/night rearview mirror, compass, illuminated visor mirrors, alloy wheels.

LS Ultimate adds: wood/leather-wrapped steering wheel w/climate and radio controls, trip computer, AM/FM/cassette/CD player, rear load-leveling air suspension.

OPTIONAL EQUIPMENT

Major Packages

	RETAIL PRICE	DEALER INVOICE
Handling Pkg., LS Premium/Ultimate	$615	$547
4.6-liter 239-horsepower V8 engine, dual exhaust, handling suspension, rear load-leveling suspension, 225/60TR16 tires, unique alloy wheels.		
Enhanced Color Pkg., GS Convenience	1300	1157
Manufacturer's Discount Price	*995*	*886*
2-tone leather upholstery, bodyside stripes, unique exterior trim.		

Safety

Front side airbags, LS Premium/Ultimate	395	352

Comfort & Convenience Features

Leather upholstery, GS Convenience, LS Premium/Ultimate	995	886
Manufacturer's Discount Price, LS Premium/Ultimate	*NC*	*NC*
Heated front seats, LS Premium/Ultimate	295	263
Requires front side airbags, leather upholstery.		
Power sunroof, LS Premium/Ultimate	1025	915

OPTIONAL EQUIPMENT (cont.)

	RETAIL PRICE	DEALER INVOICE
AM/FM/cassette/CD player, GS Convenience, LS Premium...	$185	$165
6-disc CD changer, LS Premium/Ultimate	395	352
Trunk organizer	200	178
NA GS.		

Appearance & Special Purpose

Laminated side-window glass, LS Premium/Ultimate	295	263
Chrome alloy wheels, LS Premium/Ultimate	695	619

MERCURY MARINER

CLASS: Compact sport-utility vehicle
DRIVE WHEELS: Front-wheel drive, all-wheel drive
BASE PRICE RANGE: $21,405-$26,405. Built in USA.
ALSO CONSIDER: BMW X3, Honda CR-V, Subaru Forester

Mariner is Mercury's first compact SUV, a gilded version of the Ford Escape and Mazda Tribute. All are Ford-built, car-type 5-passenger wagons. Mariner differs in styling and interior-trim elements. It offers the same 4-cyl and V6 engines, but not a gas/electric hybrid model like Escape. A 4-speed automatic is the sole transmission. Mariner comes in Convenience, Luxury, and Premier trim. All offer front-wheel drive or an all-wheel-drive system that lacks low-range gearing. ABS is standard. V6 AWD models get 4-wheel disc brakes vs. the others' disc/drum setup. Head-protecting curtain side airbags are optional; they're designed to deploy when sensors detect an impending rollover, as well as in side impacts. Also optional is rear-obstacle detection, a feature unavailable on the Ford and Mazda. Mariner performance and accommodations mirror those of comparably equipped Escapes and Tributes. This evaluation is based on preview test drives.

RATINGS	Premier	AWD Premier
ACCELERATION	5	5
FUEL ECONOMY	5	5
RIDE QUALITY	4	4
STEERING/HANDLING	5	5
QUIETNESS	5	5

 Specifications begin on page 547.

RATINGS (cont.)

	Premier	AWD Premier
CONTROLS/MATERIALS	6	6
ROOM/COMFORT (FRONT)	6	6
ROOM/COMFORT (REAR)	5	5
CARGO ROOM	7	7
VALUE WITHIN CLASS	8	9
TOTAL	56	57

Average total for compact sport-utility vehicles: 49.0

ENGINES

	dohc I4	dohc V6
Size, liters/cu. in.	2.3/138	3.0/181
Horsepower @ rpm	153 @ 5800	200 @ 6000
Torque (lb-ft) @ rpm	152 @ 4250	193 @ 4850
Availability	S[1]	S[2]
EPA city/highway mpg		
4-speed automatic	20/23[3]	18/23[4]

1. Convenience. 2. Luxury, Premier. 3. 22/26 w/2WD. 4. 20/25 w/2WD.

PRICES

Mercury Mariner	RETAIL PRICE	DEALER INVOICE
2WD Convenience 4-door wagon	$21405	$19858
AWD Convenience 4-door wagon	23155	21451
2WD Luxury 4-door wagon	22905	21223
AWD Luxury 4-door wagon	24655	22816
2WD Premiere 4-door wagon	24655	22816
AWD Premiere 4-door wagon	26405	24408
Destination charge	590	590

STANDARD EQUIPMENT

Convenience: 2.3-liter 4-cylinder engine, 4-speed automatic transmission, dual front airbags, antilock brakes, brake assist, air conditioning, tilt leather-wrapped steering wheel, cruise control, cloth upholstery, front bucket seats, center console, cupholders, split folding rear seat, power mirrors, power windows, power door locks, remote keyless entry, keypad entry, AM/FM/CD player, digital clock, tachometer, variable-intermittent wipers, visor mirrors, map lights, rear defogger, rear wiper/washer, floormats, theft-deterrent system, fog lights, 235/70TR16 tires, alloy wheels. **AWD** adds: all-wheel drive.

Luxury adds: 3.0-liter V6 engine, rear privacy glass. **AWD** adds: all-wheel drive, antilock 4-wheel disc brakes.

Premiere adds: leather/suede upholstery, heated front seats, 6-way power driver seat, heated power mirrors, Mach AM/FM radio w/in-dash 6-disc CD changer, trip computer, automatic day/night rearview mirror, compass, illuminated visor mirrors, automatic headlights. **AWD** adds: all-wheel drive, antilock 4-wheel disc brakes.

OPTIONAL EQUIPMENT

Major Packages	RETAIL PRICE	DEALER INVOICE
Dynamic Side Impact Airbag Pkg.	$595	$536
Front side airbags, curtain side airbags.		
Comfort Pkg., Luxury	500	450
Automatic day/night rearview mirror, compass, illuminated visor mirrors, message center, overhead console, automatic headlights. Requires Dynamic Side Impact Airbag Pkg.		
Enhancement Pkg., Luxury	595	536
6-way power driver seat, AM/FM radio w/in-dash 6-disc CD changer, alarm.		
Rear Cargo Convenience Pkg	135	121
Cargo-management system, cargo cover.		
Class II Trailer Tow Pkg., Luxury, Premiere	350	316
Trailer-hitch receiver, wiring harness.		
Safety		
Rear-obstacle-detection system, Premiere	255	230
Comfort & Convenience Features		
Power sunroof, Luxury, Premiere	895	806
Includes roof rack.		
Leather upholstery, Luxury	1050	946
Includes heated front seats. Requires Enhancement Pkg.		
Appearance & Special Purpose		
Rear privacy glass, Convenience	275	247
Roof rack	160	144
Running boards	325	293

MERCURY MONTEGO

CLASS: Large car
DRIVE WHEELS: Front-wheel drive, all-wheel drive
BASE PRICE RANGE: $24,345-$28,245. Built in USA.
ALSO CONSIDER: Buick LaCrosse, Chrysler 300, Toyota Avalon

 Specifications begin on page 547.

This upscale version of the new Ford Five Hundred is the first Mercury car in over a decade offering all-wheel drive. Montego comes in Luxury and Premier models with a 203-hp 3.0-liter V6. Both offer front-wheel drive with 6-speed automatic transmission or AWD with a continuously variable automatic transmission. The CVT provides variable drive ratios vs. the conventional automatic's fixed-ratio gears. Both transmissions are new to Ford Motor Company. All Montegos have antilock 4-wheel disc brakes and traction control, but no antiskid system is available. Luxury models come on 17-inch wheels, Premiers on 18s. An optional Safety Package bundles front torso side airbags with head-protecting curtain side airbags designed to deploy in rollovers as well as in side impacts. The Montego and Five Hundred share a platform originated by Ford-owned Volvo, plus a five-passenger design with seats mounted about 4 inches higher than in other cars. A power driver seat, fold-flat front-passenger seat, and split folding rear seatbacks are standard. Leather upholstery and power-adjustable pedals are standard on Premier, optional on Luxury. All models come with xenon headlamps and LED taillamps. Options include sunroof and rear-obstacle detection. Montego performance and accommodations mirror those of comparably equipped Five Hundreds. This evaluation is based on preview test drives.

RATINGS

	Premier	AWD Premier
ACCELERATION	6	6
FUEL ECONOMY	5	5
RIDE QUALITY	7	7
STEERING/HANDLING	6	6
QUIETNESS	7	7
CONTROLS/MATERIALS	7	7
ROOM/COMFORT (FRONT)	9	9
ROOM/COMFORT (REAR)	8	8
CARGO ROOM	6	6
VALUE WITHIN CLASS	7	7
TOTAL	68	68

Average total for large cars: 60.9

ENGINES

	dohc V6
Size, liters/cu. in.	3.0/182
Horsepower @ rpm	203 @ 5750
Torque (lb-ft) @ rpm	207 @ 4500
Availability	S
EPA city/highway mpg	
6-speed automatic	21/29
CVT automatic	20/27[1]

1. 19/26 w/AWD.

PRICES

Mercury Montego	RETAIL PRICE	DEALER INVOICE
FWD Luxury 4-door sedan	$24345	$22320
AWD Luxury 4-door sedan	26045	23850

PRICES (cont.)

	RETAIL PRICE	DEALER INVOICE
FWD Premier 4-door sedan	$26545	$24300
AWD Premier 4-door sedan	28245	25830
Destination charge	650	650

STANDARD EQUIPMENT

Luxury: 3.0-liter V6 engine, 6-speed automatic transmission, traction control, dual front airbags, antilock 4-wheel disc brakes, air conditioning w/dual-zone automatic climate controls, power steering, tilt leather-wrapped steering wheel w/radio controls, cruise control, cloth upholstery, front bucket seats, 6-way power driver seat w/lumbar adjustment, center console, cupholders, fold-flat passenger seat, split folding rear seat, heated power mirrors, power windows, power door locks, remote keyless entry, keypad entry, AM/FM/CD player, analog clock, tachometer, trip computer, compass, intermittent wipers, automatic day/night rearview mirror, map lights, rear defogger. *Deletes:* automatic headlights, floormats, theft-deterrent system, xenon headlights, fog lights, 215/60R17 tires, alloy wheels. **AWD** adds: all-wheel drive, continuously variable automatic transmission (CVT).

Premier adds: rear-obstacle-detection system, leather upholstery, heated front seats, 8-way power driver seat, 4-way power passenger seat, power-adjustable pedals, memory system (driver seat, mirrors, pedals), AM/FM radio w/in-dash 6-disc CD/MP3 changer, universal garage-door opener, outside-temperature indicator, 225/55R18 tires. **AWD** adds: all-wheel drive, continuously variable automatic transmission (CVT).

OPTIONAL EQUIPMENT

Major Packages

	RETAIL PRICE	DEALER INVOICE
Comfort Pkg., Luxury	$795	$708
8-way power driver seat w/power recline, 2-way power passenger seat, AM/FM radio w/in-dash 6-disc CD/MP3 changer.		
Safety Pkg.	595	530
Front side airbags, curtain side airbags w/rollover sensor.		

Safety

Rear-obstacle-detection system, Luxury	250	223

Comfort & Convenience Features

Power sunroof	895	797
Leather upholstery, Luxury	250	223

MERCURY MONTEREY

CLASS: Minivan
DRIVE WHEELS: Front-wheel drive
BASE PRICE RANGE: $29,010-$34,910. Built in Canada.
ALSO CONSIDER: Chrysler Town & Country, Honda Odyssey, Toyota Sienna

 Specifications begin on page 547.

Mercury's Monterey minivan shares its design with Ford's Freestar. Monterey comes in a single body length that matches in size the extended-length versions of rival minivans. Convenience, Luxury, and Premier trim levels are offered. All have 7-passenger capacity. Two 2nd-row bucket seats are standard; they flip and fold forward. The 3rd-row bench folds into the floor. The 3rd-row bench also flips backward for rear-facing seating under the open liftgate when the vehicle is parked. Power operation for the sliding side doors is available. A power liftgate is standard on Premier, unavailable elsewhere. All Montereys have a 201-hp 4.2-liter V6 and 4-speed automatic transmission. All-wheel drive is not offered, but traction control and an antiskid system are available on Luxury and Premier. Antilock 4-wheel disc brakes and front and rear park assist are standard. Front side airbags and head-protecting curtain side airbags that cover all three seating rows are standard on all but Convenience, where they are unavailable. Power-adjustable pedals, rear DVD entertainment, heated and cooled front seats, and self-sealing tires are also available. Monterey's performance and accommodations mirror those of similarly equipped Freestars.

RATINGS

	Luxury
ACCELERATION	5
FUEL ECONOMY	4
RIDE QUALITY	5
STEERING/HANDLING	4
QUIETNESS	5
CONTROLS/MATERIALS	6
ROOM/COMFORT (FRONT)	7
ROOM/COMFORT (REAR)	7
CARGO ROOM	9
VALUE WITHIN CLASS	5

Monterey can't match such rivals as Honda Odyssey or Dodge Caravan for driving enjoyment, or Toyota Sienna for refinement. On the upside, these revamped Mercury minivans boast some laudable safety and convenience features, base prices are competitive, and discounts should be available.

TOTAL	57

Average total for minivans: 58.0

ENGINES

	ohv V6
Size, liters/cu. in.	4.2/256
Horsepower @ rpm	201 @ 4250
Torque (lb-ft) @ rpm	263 @ 3500
Availability	S
EPA city/highway mpg	
4-speed automatic	16/23

PRICES

Mercury Monterey	RETAIL PRICE	DEALER INVOICE
Convenience 4-door van	$29010	$26324
Luxury 4-door van	33610	29528
Premier 4-door van	34910	31575
Destination charge	685	685

STANDARD EQUIPMENT

Convenience: 4.2-liter V6 engine, 4-speed automatic transmission, dual front airbags, antilock 4-wheel disc brakes, tire-pressure monitor, front- and rear-obstacle-detection system, air conditioning w/dual-zone manual climate controls, rear climate controls, power steering, tilt steering wheel, cruise control, cloth upholstery, 7-passenger seating, front bucket seats, 6-way power driver seat w/lumbar adjustment, cupholders, 2nd-row bucket seats, 3rd-row stowable bench seat, power mirrors, power windows, power door locks, remote keyless entry, AM/FM/CD player, analog clock, tachometer, compass, outside-temperature indicator, variable-intermittent wipers, visor mirrors, map lights, conversation mirror, rear defogger, intermittent rear wiper, floormats, theft-deterrent system, rear privacy glass, fog lights, 235/60R16 tires, alloy wheels.

Luxury adds: front side airbags, curtain side airbags, leather upholstery, heated front seats, center console, power-adjustable pedals, memory system (driver seat, mirrors, pedals), leather-wrapped steering wheel w/radio controls, power sliding rear doors, keypad entry, heated power mirrors w/turn signals, AM/FM radio w/in-dash 6-disc CD changer, rear radio controls, illuminated visor mirrors, automatic headlights, roof rails.

Premier adds: dual-zone automatic climate controls w/manual rear controls, heated/cooled front seats, 6-way power passenger seat, automatic day/night rearview mirror, universal garage-door opener, power liftgate, cargo-management system.

OPTIONAL EQUIPMENT

Major Packages	RETAIL PRICE	DEALER INVOICE
AdvanceTrac Stability Control System, Luxury, Premier	$730	$621
Manufacturer's Discount Price	*395*	*336*
Traction control, brake assist, antiskid system.		
Comfort Pkg., Luxury	690	588
Manufacturer's Discount Price	*500*	*425*
Dual-zone automatic climate controls w/manual rear controls, 6-way power passenger seat, automatic day/night rearview mirror, universal garage-door opener.		

OPTIONAL EQUIPMENT (cont.)

	RETAIL PRICE	DEALER INVOICE
Class II Trailer Tow Prep Pkg.	$335	$285
Trailer-tow wiring, self-sealing tires.		
Comfort & Convenience Features		
Rear-seat DVD entertainment system, Luxury, Premier	1395	1186
Deletes rear climate controls. Luxury requires Comfort Pkg.		
AM/FM/cassette/CD player, Convenience	105	89
Power liftgate, Luxury	400	340
Cargo-management system, Convenience, Luxury	125	107
Appearance & Special Purpose		
Rear spoiler, Luxury, Premier	290	247

MERCURY MOUNTAINEER

CLASS: Midsize sport-utility vehicle
DRIVE WHEELS: Rear-wheel drive, all-wheel drive
BASE PRICE RANGE: $29,525-$38,370. Built in USA.
ALSO CONSIDER: GMC Envoy, Honda Pilot

A standard antiskid system highlights the new year for Mountaineer. Mercury's version of the Ford Explorer and Lincoln Aviator comes in Convenience, Luxury, and Premier trim. All have three rows of seats for 7-passenger capacity. The 3rd row can be deleted for credit, and 2nd-row bucket seats are now optional on Luxury and Premier. All offer a V6 or V8 engine and rear-wheel drive or all-wheel drive without low-range gearing. A 5-speed automatic transmission and antilock 4-wheel disc brakes are standard. Newly standard on all Mountaineers is Ford's AdvanceTrac antiskid system with Roll Stability Control. Roll Stability Control is designed to detect an impending tip and activate the antiskid system to reduce the chances of a rollover. Torso side airbags are not offered, but head-protecting curtain side airbags that cover the 1st and 2nd seating rows are standard on Premier, optional on other models. Power-adjustable pedals are optional. A rear-obstacle-warning system is standard on Premier and optional on other Mountaineers. A rear DVD entertainment system is optional on Luxury and Premier. A tire-pressure monitor is standard on all models. Mountaineer's performance and accommodations mirror those of like-equipped Explorers.

RATINGS

	AWD Convenience V6	AWD Luxury V8
ACCELERATION	4	5
FUEL ECONOMY	4	3
RIDE QUALITY	4	4
STEERING/HANDLING	4	4
QUIETNESS	4	5
CONTROLS/MATERIALS	7	7
ROOM/COMFORT (FRONT)	7	8
ROOM/COMFORT (REAR)	7	7
CARGO ROOM	8	8
VALUE WITHIN CLASS	6	5

Mountaineer offers more-expressive styling and more standard features than its Ford Explorer cousin, while slotting in below Lincoln's new Aviator in price and power. Basically, it fills a niche for domestic-SUV buyers who want to combine Mercury's take on individualistic design with such useful features as 7-passenger seating, adjustable pedals, curtain airbags, rear obstacle detection and standard antiskid system.

TOTAL	**55**	**56**

Average total for midsize sport-utility vehicles: 54.7

ENGINES

	sohc V6	sohc V8
Size, liters/cu. in.	4.0/245	4.6/281
Horsepower @ rpm	210 @ 5100	239 @ 4000
Torque (lb-ft) @ rpm	254 @ 3700	282 @ 4000
Availability	S[1]	S[2]
EPA city/highway mpg		
5-speed automatic	15/20[3]	14/19[4]

1. V6 models. 2. V8 models. 3. 15/21 w/2WD. 4. 15/20 w/2WD.

PRICES

Mercury Mountaineer	RETAIL PRICE	DEALER INVOICE
2WD Convenience V6 4-door wagon	$29525	$26818
2WD Convenience V8 4-door wagon	30830	27979
AWD Convenience V6 4-door wagon	32030	29047
AWD Convenience V8 4-door wagon	32860	29786
2WD Luxury V6 4-door wagon	33440	30301
2WD Luxury V8 4-door wagon	34270	31040
AWD Luxury V6 4-door wagon	35470	32108
AWD Luxury V8 4-door wagon	36300	32847
2WD Premier V6 4-door wagon	35510	32144
2WD Premier V8 4-door wagon	36340	32822
AWD Premier V6 4-door wagon	37540	33950
AWD Premier V8 4-door wagon	38370	34689
Destination charge	645	645

Luxury, Premier require Discount Pkg.

 Specifications begin on page 547.

STANDARD EQUIPMENT

Convenience: 4.0-liter V6 engine or 4.6-liter V8 engine, 5-speed automatic transmission, dual front airbags, antilock 4-wheel disc brakes, antiskid system, roll stability control, tire-pressure monitor, front air conditioning, power steering, tilt leather-wrapped steering wheel, cruise control, cloth upholstery, front bucket seats, 6-way power driver seat w/manual lumbar adjustment, center console, cupholders, 2nd-row split bench seat, 3rd-row stowable bench seat, power mirrors, power windows, power door locks, remote keyless entry, keypad entry, AM/FM/CD player, digital clock, tachometer, compass, outside-temperature indicator, variable-intermittent wipers, illuminated visor mirrors, map lights, cargo-management system, rear defogger, intermittent rear wiper/washer, automatic headlights, floormats, theft-deterrent system, rear privacy glass, rear liftgate, roof rails, fog lights, front tow hooks, trailer hitch, full-size spare tire, 235/70R16 tires, alloy wheels. **AWD** adds: all-wheel drive.

Luxury adds: leather upholstery, heated front seats, 8-way power driver seat w/power lumbar adjustment, 6-way power passenger seat, dual-zone automatic climate controls, steering-wheel radio and climate controls, heated power mirrors, automatic day/night rearview mirror, running boards, 245/65R17 all-terrain tires. **AWD** adds: all-wheel drive.

Premier adds: front and 2nd-row curtain side airbags, rear-obstacle-detection system, power sunroof, AM/FM radio w/in-dash 6-disc CD changer, trip computer, universal garage-door opener. **AWD** adds: all-wheel drive.

OPTIONAL EQUIPMENT

Major Packages	RETAIL PRICE	DEALER INVOICE
50L/50P Discount Pkg., Luxury, Premier (credit)	*($695)*	*($619)*
Standard equipment.		
Designer Series Pkg., Convenience	995	846
Leather/suede upholstery, chrome alloy wheels.		
Security Group, Convenience, Luxury	795	676
Front and 2nd-row curtain side airbags, rear-obstacle-detection system.		
Trailer Towing Pkg.	150	128
Special axle ratio, Class III/IV trailer hitch, 7/4-pin trailer connector.		
Comfort & Convenience Features		
Rear-seat DVD entertainment system, Luxury, Premier	1295	1101
Luxury requires power sunroof and rear air conditioning or Security Group.		
AM/FM radio w/in-dash 6-disc CD changer, Luxury	510	433
Rear air conditioning	650	553
Includes rear controls, rear heater. Rear controls deleted w/power sunroof or rear-seat entertainment system.		
Power sunroof, Convenience, Luxury	850	723
Universal garage-door opener, Luxury	150	128
Power-adjustable pedals, Luxury, Premier	225	192
Convenience	120	102
Luxury, Premier include memory.		

OPTIONAL EQUIPMENT (cont.)

	RETAIL PRICE	DEALER INVOICE
Leather upholstery, Convenience	$695	$591
2nd-row bucket seats, Luxury, Premier	490	417
Includes center console.		
3rd-row seat delete (credit)	*(375)*	*(319)*
Includes cargo cover. NA w/rear air conditioning, 2nd-row bucket seats.		

Appearance & Special Purpose

	RETAIL PRICE	DEALER INVOICE
Running boards, Convenience	450	383
Roof rack	60	51

MERCURY SABLE

CLASS: Midsize car
DRIVE WHEELS: Front-wheel drive
BASE PRICE RANGE: $20,855-$25,130. Built in USA.
ALSO CONSIDER: Honda Accord, Nissan Altima, Toyota Camry

Due to be dropped from the Mercury lineup during the model year, Sable sedans and wagons roll into 2005 virtually unchanged. GS and LS models are offered. GS versions have a standard front bench seat for 6-passenger capacity. Front bucket seats are standard on the LS and optional on GS. Both use a 3.0-liter V6 engine: a 153-hp version in GS, a 201-hp dohc variant for LS. A 4-speed automatic is the sole transmission. Antilock brakes are optional on GS, standard on LS; wagons include rear disc brakes instead of drums. An available package bundles traction control with front side airbags. Sable shares its design with the Ford Taurus, and its performance and accommodations mirror those of like-equipped Taurus models.

RATINGS	GS wgn	LS sdn
ACCELERATION	4	5
FUEL ECONOMY	5	5
RIDE QUALITY	5	5
STEERING/HANDLING	6	6
QUIETNESS	5	5
CONTROLS/MATERIALS	6	6
ROOM/COMFORT (FRONT)	6	6

 Specifications begin on page 547.

RATINGS (cont.)

	GS wgn	LS sdn
ROOM/COMFORT (REAR)	6	6
CARGO ROOM	8	5
VALUE WITHIN CLASS	5	4

Like its Taurus cousin, Sable delivers good acceleration, capable road manners, commendable passenger and cargo room, and plenty of safety features at competitive prices. Ride comfort and build quality fall short of standards set by midsize sales leaders Honda Accord and Toyota Camry, though. And Sable costs slightly more than corresponding Taurus models with negligible differences in equipment.

TOTAL	56	53

Average total for midsize cars: 57.2

ENGINES

	ohv V6	dohc V6
Size, liters/cu. in.	3.0/182	3.0/181
Horsepower @ rpm	153 @ 5800	201 @ 5500
Torque (lb-ft) @ rpm	186 @ 3250	207 @ 4500
Availability	S[1]	S[2]
EPA city/highway mpg		
4-speed automatic	19/26	20/27[3]

1. GS. 2. LS. 3. 19/26 wagon.

PRICES

Mercury Sable	RETAIL PRICE	DEALER INVOICE
GS 4-door sedan	$20855	$19120
LS 4-door sedan	23820	21788
LS 4-door wagon	25130	22967
Destination charge	670	670

STANDARD EQUIPMENT

GS: 3.0-liter V6 153-horsepower engine, 4-speed automatic transmission, dual front airbags, emergency inside trunk release, air conditioning, interior air filter, power steering, tilt steering wheel, cruise control, cloth upholstery, 6-passenger seating, split front bench seat, column shifter, cupholders, split folding rear seat, power mirrors, power windows, power door locks, remote keyless entry, AM/FM/cassette, digital clock, tachometer, variable-intermittent wipers, rear defogger, visor mirrors, map lights, floormats, theft-deterrent system, 215/60R16 tires, wheel covers.

LS adds: 3.0-liter V6 201-horsepower engine, antilock brakes (sedan), antilock 4-wheel disc brakes (wagon), wood/leather-wrapped steering wheel, 5-passenger seating w/front bucket seats, 6-way power driver seat w/lumbar adjustment, center console, floor shifter, AM/FM/CD player, power antenna (wagon), heated power mirrors, keypad entry, automatic day/night rearview mirror, compass, illuminated visor mirrors, rear wiper/washer (wagon), fog lights, roof rack (wagon), alloy wheels.

OPTIONAL EQUIPMENT

Major Packages

	RETAIL PRICE	DEALER INVOICE
Secure Group	$595	$530
Traction control, front side airbags. Requires antilock brakes.		
Wagon Group, LS wagon	350	312
Rear-facing 3rd-row seat, cargo cover.		
Premium Pkg., LS	1315	1170
Manufacturer's Discount Price	*420*	*373*
Leather upholstery, automatic climate control, AM/FM/cassette, automatic headlights.		
Platinum Feature Vehicle Pkg., LS Premium sedan	795	708
Two-tone leather upholstery, unique interior and exterior trim, rear spoiler, badging. NA w/6-passenger seating, power passenger seat.		
Monochrome Wagon Pkg., LS wagon	400	356
Color-keyed grille and bodyside moldings, unique alloy wheels. Requires Premium Pkg.		

Safety

	RETAIL PRICE	DEALER INVOICE
Antilock brakes, GS	600	534

Comfort & Convenience Features

	RETAIL PRICE	DEALER INVOICE
5-passenger seating, GS	150	134
Includes center console, floor shift.		
6-passenger seating, LS	NC	NC
Leather upholstery	895	797
GS requires 5-passenger seating. NA w/6-passenger seating.		
6-way power driver seat, GS	395	352
Requires leather upholstery.		
Power passenger seat, LS	395	352
Requires leather upholstery. NA w/ Premium Pkg., Platinum Feature Vehicle Pkg.		
Power sunroof, LS	995	886
Manufacturer's Discount Price	*NC*	*NC*
Manufacturer's discount price available only in California, Hawaii, New York City, Boston, Philadelphia, Pittsburgh, and Washington, D.C.		
AM/FM/CD player, GS	140	124
Mach AM/FM/cassette	695	620
Includes in-dash 6-disc CD changer.		
Universal garage-door opener, LS	115	102

Appearance & Special Purpose

	RETAIL PRICE	DEALER INVOICE
Rear spoiler, LS sedan	295	263
Alloy wheels, GS	495	441
Chrome alloy wheels, LS	395	352

 Specifications begin on page 547.

MINI COOPER

CLASS: Sporty/performance car
DRIVE WHEELS: Front-wheel drive
BASE PRICE RANGE: $16,449-$24,400. Built in England.
ALSO CONSIDER: Acura RSX, Scion tC, Volkswagen New Beetle

A convertible body style joins Mini Cooper's 2-dr hatchback for 2005. The convertible has a power top with heated glass rear window and, like the hatchback, seats four. All Mini Coopers have a 1.6-liter 4-cyl engine and come in base and sportier S trim. Base versions have 115 hp. S models are supercharged and have 168 hp, up 5 from 2004. Manual transmission is standard—a 5-speed for base models, a 6-speed for the S. A continuously variable automatic transmission (CVT) is optional on both. All Minis have antilock 4-wheel disc brakes. Hatchbacks come with front torso side airbags and front and rear head-protecting side curtain airbags. Convertibles get front side airbags that protect the head and torso. S models have a functional hood scoop and sport suspension with 16-inch wheels vs. base versions' 15s. Optional Sport Packages include an anti-skid system and increase wheel size to 17 inches on the S, 16 on the base. Convertibles come with rear-obstacle detection and a "sunroof" mode that opens the top above the front seats only. For '05, all Minis get appearance revisions to headlights, taillights, and grille. Options include xenon headlamps and a navigation system—both unusual in this price range. Also available for hatchbacks are dealer-applied Union Jack, American-flag, and checkerboard roof graphics. Mini is owned by BMW, and Coopers are sold at most major-market BMW dealers.

RATINGS	Base hatch, man.	Base hatch w/Sport Pkg., man.	S hatch w/Sport Pkg., man.	S conv, man.
ACCELERATION	4	4	6	6
FUEL ECONOMY	7	7	6	6
RIDE QUALITY	3	2	1	3
STEERING/HANDLING	8	9	10	9
QUIETNESS	4	3	3	2
CONTROLS/MATERIALS	5	5	5	5
ROOM/COMFORT (FRONT)	6	6	6	5
ROOM/COMFORT (REAR)	2	2	2	2
CARGO ROOM	6	6	6	1

RATINGS (cont.)

	Base hatch, man.	Base hatch w/Sport Pkg., man.	S hatch w/Sport Pkg., man.	S conv, man.
VALUE WITHIN CLASS	7	6	7	6

Minis may look like "economy" cars, but they're actually rewarding-to-drive machines. The base model has no surplus of power, and any model's driving dynamics are compromised by a harsh ride on imperfect pavement. But these hatchbacks and convertibles are reasonably priced, brim with character, and are available with a dizzying array of personalizing accessories. The convertible adds open-air fun, but loses the every day utility of an open hatch area. All in all, we Recommend them.

TOTAL	52	50	52	45

Average total for sporty/performance cars: 48.5

ENGINES

	dohc I4	Supercharged dohc I4
Size, liters/cu. in.	1.6/98	1.6/98
Horsepower @ rpm	115 @ 6000	163 @ 6000
Torque (lb-ft) @ rpm	110 @ 4500	155 @ 4000
Availability	S[1]	S[2]
EPA city/highway mpg		
5-speed manual	28/37	
6-speed manual		25/34
CVT automatic	25/32	NA

1. Cooper. 2. Cooper S.

PRICES

Mini Cooper	RETAIL PRICE	DEALER INVOICE
Base 2-door hatchback	$16449	$14887
Base 2-door convertible	20950	18937
S 2-door hatchback	19899	17992
S 2-door convertible	24400	22042
Destination charge	550	550

STANDARD EQUIPMENT

Base: 1.6-liter 4-cylinder engine, 5-speed manual transmission, dual front airbags, front side airbags, side head-protection airbags (hatchback), antilock 4-wheel disc brakes, rear-obstacle-detection system (convertible), tire-pressure monitor, roll bars (convertible), air conditioning, interior air filter, power steering, tilt leather-wrapped steering wheel, vinyl upholstery, height-adjustable front bucket seats, center console, cupholders, split folding rear seat, power mirrors, power windows, power door locks, remote keyless entry, AM/FM/CD player, digital clock, tachometer, outside-temperature indicator, variable-intermittent wipers, illuminated visor mirrors, map lights, power convertible top (convertible), rear defogger, rear wiper, theft-deterrent system, rear fog light, 175/65HR15 tires, alloy wheels.

S adds: 1.6-liter 4-cylinder supercharged engine, 6-speed manual transmission, traction control, antiskid system, sport seats, rear spoiler (hatchback), sport suspension, 195/55VR16 run-flat tires.

 Specifications begin on page 547.

OPTIONAL EQUIPMENT

Major Packages

	RETAIL PRICE	DEALER INVOICE
Premium Pkg.	$1350	$1215
Automatic climate control, cruise control, steering-wheel radio controls, Harman/Kardon sound system (convertible), power sunroof (hatchback), chrome interior trim (convertible), trip computer.		
Sport Pkg., Base	1350	1215
Antiskid system, sport seats, front fog lights, rear spoiler (hatchback), 195/55R16 run-flat tires.		
Sport Pkg., S	1350	1215
Antiskid system, xenon headlights, headlight washers, front fog lights, hood stripes, 205/45R17 run-flat tires.		
Comfort Pkg.	NA	NA
Universal garage-door opener, automatic day/night rearview mirror, automatic headlights.		
Cold Weather Pkg.	300	270
Heated front seats, heated washer jets, heated mirrors.		

Powertrain

Continuously variable automatic transmission (CVT), Base	1300	1170
S	NA	NA
Limited-slip differential	NA	NA

Safety

Antiskid system	500	450
Includes traction control.		
Rear-obstacle-detection system, hatchback	350	315

Comfort & Convenience Features

Navigation system	1700	1530
Includes trip computer.		
Trip computer	200	180
Harman/Kardon sound system	550	495
Satellite radio	499	NA
Requires monthly fee.		
Power sunroof, hatchback	850	765
Cruise control	250	225
Includes steering-wheel radio controls.		
Cloth/leather upholstery	800	712
Leather upholstery	1300	1170

Appearance & Special Purpose

Rear spoiler, Base hatchback	150	135
Xenon headlights w/washers	550	495
Front fog lights	140	125
Sport suspension, Base	500	450

MITSUBISHI ECLIPSE

CLASS: Sporty/performance car
DRIVE WHEELS: Front-wheel drive
BASE PRICE RANGE: $19,449-$30,699. Built in USA.
ALSO CONSIDER: Acura RSX, Volkswagen New Beetle

Eclipse hatchback coupes and Spyder convertibles return for 2005 in GS, GT, and GTS. The price-leader RS coupe is dropped. GS trim has a 147-hp 4-cyl engine. GT coupes have a 200-hp V6. GT Spyders and both GTS models have a 210-hp V6. All offer manual transmission or an optional automatic with manual shift gate. Spyders include a power top with heated glass window. Every Eclipse comes with air conditioning, CD stereo, power windows/locks, and alloy wheels—17-inchers on GT/GTS, 16s on GS. Front side airbags and ABS are standard for GTS, unavailable otherwise. Available for GS is a Remix package with 16-inch SXC-brand alloy wheels and top-stitched charcoal leather on front seats, steering wheel, and shift knob.

RATINGS	GS, man.	GT, man.	GT, auto.	GT Spyder, auto.
ACCELERATION	4	6	5	5
FUEL ECONOMY	6	6	5	5
RIDE QUALITY	4	3	3	3
STEERING/HANDLING	7	8	8	7
QUIETNESS	3	3	3	2
CONTROLS/MATERIALS	5	5	5	5
ROOM/COMFORT (FRONT)	4	4	4	4
ROOM/COMFORT (REAR)	1	1	1	1
CARGO ROOM	5	5	5	1
VALUE WITHIN CLASS	4	5	4	4

An available V6 and a relatively pliant suspension help Eclipse feel a bit more mature than the Acura RSX and Toyota Celica, but those rivals are better built, more fun to drive, and hold their value far better.

TOTAL	43	46	43	37

Average total for sporty/performance cars: 48.5

 Specifications begin on page 547.

ENGINES

	sohc I4	sohc V6	sohc V6
Size, liters/cu. in.	2.4/143	3.0/181	3.0/181
Horsepower @ rpm	147 @ 5500	200 @ 5500	210 @ 5750
Torque (lb-ft) @ rpm	158 @ 4000	205 @ 4000	205 @ 3750
Availability	S[1]	S[2]	S[3]
EPA city/highway mpg			
5-speed manual	23/31	21/28	21/27
4-speed automatic	20/26	20/29	20/28

1. GS; 142 hp w/auto. trans. 2. GT hatchback. 3. GT conv, GTS.

PRICES

Mitsubishi Eclipse

	RETAIL PRICE	DEALER INVOICE
GS 2-door hatchback, manual	$19449	$18371
GS 2-door hatchback, automatic	20449	19315
GS Spyder 2-door convertible, manual	24899	23543
GS Spyder 2-door convertible, automatic	25899	24488
GT 2-door hatchback, manual	22899	21629
GT 2-door hatchback, automatic	23899	22573
GT Spyder 2-door convertible, manual	27099	25621
GT Spyder 2-door convertible, automatic	28099	26565
GTS 2-door hatchback, manual	24649	23282
GTS 2-door hatchback, automatic	25849	24416
GTS Spyder 2-door convertible, manual	29499	27888
GTS Spyder 2-door convertible, automatic	30699	29022
Destination charge	595	595

STANDARD EQUIPMENT

GS adds: 2.4-liter 4-cylinder engine, 5-speed manual or 4-speed automatic transmission w/manual-shift capability, dual front airbags, air conditioning, power steering, tilt leather-wrapped steering wheel, cruise control, cloth upholstery, front bucket seats, height-adjustable driver seat, center console, cupholders, split folding rear seat (hatchback), power mirrors, power windows, power door locks, remote keyless entry, AM/FM/CD player, Infinity sound system (convertible), steering-wheel radio controls (convertible), digital clock, tachometer, variable-intermittent wipers, illuminated visor mirrors, map lights, rear defogger, power convertible top (convertible), automatic-off headlights, floormats, theft-deterrent system, fog lights (convertible), rear spoiler, 205/55HR16 tires, alloy wheels.

GT adds: 3.0-liter V6 (200-horsepower hatchback, 210-horsepower convertible) engine, 4-wheel disc brakes, power sunroof (hatchback), Infinity sound system, steering-wheel radio controls, sport suspension, fog lights, 215/50VR17 tires, polished alloy wheels.

GTS adds: 3.0-liter V6 210-horsepower engine, front side airbags, antilock 4-wheel disc brakes, leather upholstery, 6-way power driver seat, Infinity AM/FM radio w/in-dash 6-disc CD changer, rear wiper/washer (hatchback).

OPTIONAL EQUIPMENT

Major Packages

	RETAIL PRICE	DEALER INVOICE
Remix Special Edition, GS hatchback	$1800	$1566
GS convertible	700	609

Leather upholstery, power sunroof (hatchback), Infinity AM/FM radio w/in-dash 6-disc CD changer, unique interior trim, chrome exhaust tip, unique alloy wheels.

Powertrain

Traction control	NA	NA

MITSUBISHI ENDEAVOR

CLASS: Midsize sport-utility vehicle
DRIVE WHEELS: Front-wheel drive, all-wheel drive
2004 BASE PRICE RANGE: $24,999-$32,799. Built in USA.
ALSO CONSIDER: Ford Explorer, Honda Pilot, Toyota Highlander

This car-type midsize SUV is little-changed for 2005. Endeavor comes in LS, XLS, and top-line Limited models. All have a 225-hp 3.8-liter V6 and a 4-speed automatic transmission with manual shift gate. All offer front-wheel drive or all-wheel drive that lacks low-range gearing and is not intended for severe off-roading. A liftgate with separate-opening glass is included. So are 60/40 split folding rear seat, 17-inch alloy wheels, tire-pressure monitor, and 4-wheel disc brakes. ABS is optional for the 2WD LS, standard elsewhere. Traction control is included on XLS and Limited 2WDs, and is optional for the 2WD LS. Limited AWDs offer an optional antiskid system. For 2005, LS models join other Endeavors with standard front side airbags. Curtain side airbags are unavailable. Rear DVD entertainment is available for all XLS and Limited models. New for '05 is an XLS appearance package with fender flares and rear mudguards. Limiteds also offer these items in packages that include a cargo tray and cargo net, plus a trailer hitch on the AWD model.

RATINGS	2WD XLS	AWD Limited
ACCELERATION	5	5
FUEL ECONOMY	5	4

RATINGS (cont.)	2WD XLS	AWD Limited
RIDE QUALITY	6	6
STEERING/HANDLING	5	5
QUIETNESS	5	5
CONTROLS/MATERIALS	6	7
ROOM/COMFORT (FRONT)	7	7
ROOM/COMFORT (REAR)	7	7
CARGO ROOM	8	8
VALUE WITHIN CLASS	5	5

Despite bold styling, pleasant driving manners and a roomy interior, Endeavor trails the likes of the Nissan Murano, Honda Pilot, and Toyota Highlander. Granted, it's discounted far more than most class rivals, but that's because of Mitsubishi's troubled image, lower-rung customer-satisfaction scores, and mediocre resale values.

TOTAL	59	59

Average total for midsize sport-utility vehicles: 54.7

ENGINES

	sohc V6
Size, liters/cu. in.	3.8/234
Horsepower @ rpm	215 @ 5000
Torque (lb-ft) @ rpm	255 @ 3750
Availability	S
EPA city/highway mpg	
4-speed automatic	17/21[1]

1. 17/23 w/ 2WD.

2005 prices unavailable at time of publication.

2004 PRICES

Mitsubishi Endeavor	RETAIL PRICE	DEALER INVOICE
2WD LS 4-door wagon	$24999	$23485
AWD LS 4-door wagon	27299	25646
2WD XLS 4-door wagon	28399	26679
AWD XLS 4-door wagon	29899	28089
2WD Limited 4-door wagon	31299	29404
AWD Limited 4-door wagon	32799	30813
Destination charge	595	595

STANDARD EQUIPMENT

LS: 3.8-liter V6 engine, 4-speed automatic transmission w/manual-shift capability, dual front airbags, 4-wheel disc brakes, tire-pressure monitor, daytime running lights, air conditioning, power steering, tilt steering wheel, cruise control, cloth upholstery, front bucket seats, height-adjustable driver seat, center console, cupholders, split folding rear seat, power mirrors, power windows, power door locks, remote keyless entry, AM/FM/CD player, tachometer, visor mirrors, map lights, intermittent wipers, rear defogger, intermittent rear wiper/washer, automatic-off headlights, floormats, theft-deterrent system, rear privacy glass, roof rails, 235/65R17 tires, alloy wheels. **AWD** adds: all-wheel drive, antilock 4-wheel disc brakes, full-size spare tire.

XLS adds: traction control, front side airbags, antilock 4-wheel disc brakes, leather-wrapped steering wheel, Infinity AM/FM radio w/in-dash 6-disc CD changer, outside-temperature indicator, compass, cargo cover, roof rack, full-size spare tire. **AWD** adds: all-wheel drive. *Deletes:* traction control.

Limited adds: automatic climate control, leather upholstery, heated front seats, heated power mirrors, power sunroof, fog lights. **AWD** adds: all-wheel drive. *Deletes:* traction control.

OPTIONAL EQUIPMENT

	RETAIL PRICE	DEALER INVOICE
Major Packages		
Cold Zone Pkg., AWD XLS	$300	$262
Heated front seats, heated power mirrors.		
Towing Prep Pkg., 2WD LS	300	262
Transmission cooler, trailer-hitch wiring, full-size spare tire. Std. all models except 2WD LS.		
Powertrain		
Traction control, 2WD LS	100	87
Requires antilock brakes.		
Safety		
Antiskid system, AWD Limited	998	868
Includes traction control.		
Antilock brakes, 2WD LS	500	436
Comfort & Convenience Features		
Rear-seat DVD entertainment system, XLS, Limited	1200	1047
Limited requires power sunroof delete.		
Power sunroof delete, Limited (credit)	*(900)*	*(785)*
Power sunroof, XLS	900	785

MITSUBISHI GALANT

CLASS: Midsize car
DRIVE WHEELS: Front-wheel drive
BASE PRICE RANGE: $18,699-$26,299. Built in USA.
ALSO CONSIDER: Honda Accord, Nissan Altima, Toyota Camry

Front side airbags are standard on all Galants for 2005, not just the most-expensive model. Mitsubishi's midsize sedan offers 4-cyl DE and ES models and V6 LS and sporty GTS versions. The only transmission is a 4-speed automatic; V6 models add a manual shift gate. All come with 4-wheel disc brakes, keyless entry, and power windows/locks/mirrors. Head-protecting curtain side airbags remain unavailable. ABS is standard on V6 models, optional for the ES. GTS features sport-tuned suspension, specific grille, rear spoiler, leather upholstery, and sunroof. It also has 17-inch alloy wheels vs. other models' steel 16s. In other '05 changes, the LS joins GTS with a standard

power driver seat; 16-inch alloy wheels are now available for ES; and a new Sport Package dresses up ES and LS with a bright exhaust tip and rear spoiler. Galant lends its platform to Mitsubishi's Endeavor midsize SUV.

RATINGS

	ES	LS	GTS
ACCELERATION	5	7	7
FUEL ECONOMY	6	5	5
RIDE QUALITY	6	6	5
STEERING/HANDLING	6	6	7
QUIETNESS	7	7	6
CONTROLS/MATERIALS	7	7	7
ROOM/COMFORT (FRONT)	7	7	7
ROOM/COMFORT (REAR)	5	5	5
CARGO ROOM	3	3	3
VALUE WITHIN CLASS	5	6	5

Galant matches class-favorites Honda Accord and Toyota Camry for roominess and holds its own in acceleration and handling. But it lags in refinement, ride comfort and workmanship, and the Mitsubishi brand's weak resale-value record offsets typically lower transaction prices. Still, Galant is worth a look, especially if you're on a budget.

TOTAL	57	59	57

Average total for midsize cars: 57.2

ENGINES

	sohc I4	sohc V6
Size, liters/cu. in.	2.4/145	3.8/234
Horsepower @ rpm	160 @ 5500	230 @ 5250
Torque (lb-ft) @ rpm	157 @ 4000	250 @ 4000
Availability	S[1]	S[2]
EPA city/highway mpg		
4-speed automatic	23/30	19/27[3]

1. DE, ES. 155 hp and 155 lb-ft in Calif. 2. LS, GTS. 3. 18/26 w/GTS.

PRICES

Mitsubishi Galant	RETAIL PRICE	DEALER INVOICE
DE 4-door sedan	$18699	$17786
ES 4-door sedan	19599	18453

PRICES (cont.)

	RETAIL PRICE	DEALER INVOICE
LS 4-door sedan	$22299	$20983
GTS 4-door sedan	26299	24746
Destination charge	595	595

STANDARD EQUIPMENT

DE: 2.4-liter 4-cylinder engine, 4-speed automatic transmission, dual front airbags, front side airbags, 4-wheel disc brakes, emergency inside trunk release, daytime running lights, air conditioning, power steering, tilt steering wheel, cloth upholstery, front bucket seats, height-adjustable driver seat, center console, cupholders, trunk pass-through, power mirrors, power windows, power door locks, remote keyless entry, AM/FM/CD player, digital clock, tachometer, rear defogger, variable-intermittent wipers, map lights, automatic-off headlights, floormats, theft-deterrent system, 215/60HR16 tires, wheel covers.

ES adds: cruise control, upgraded sound system.

LS adds: 3.8-liter V6 engine, 4-speed automatic transmission w/manual-shift capability, traction control, antilock 4-wheel disc brakes, 8-way power driver seat.

GTS adds: automatic climate control, leather upholstery, heated front seats, leather-wrapped steering wheel w/radio controls, heated power mirrors, power sunroof, Infinity AM/FM radio w/in-dash 6-disc CD changer, illuminated visor mirrors, compass, outside-temperature indicator, fog lights, rear spoiler, sport suspension, 215/55VR17 tires, alloy wheels.

OPTIONAL EQUIPMENT

Major Packages

	RETAIL PRICE	DEALER INVOICE
Diamond Pkg., ES, LS	$1262	$1100
Leather-wrapped steering wheel w/radio controls, Infinity AM/FM radio w/in-dash 6-disc CD changer, dual-integrated antenna, special interior trim, alloy wheels. Requires Sunroof Pkg. and Sport Pkg. or Leather Plus Pkg.		
Sunroof Pkg., ES, LS	800	698
Power sunroof, overhead console, illuminated visor mirrors. Requires Diamond Pkg. LS requires Leather Plus Pkg.		
Leather Plus Pkg., ES	1485	1296
LS	1185	1033
Leather upholstery, heated front seats, 8-way power driver seat (ES), heated power mirrors. Requires Diamond Pkg., antilock brakes. LS requires Sport Pkg.		
Sport Pkg., ES, LS	363	315
Rear spoiler, chrome exhaust tip. Requires Diamond Pkg. LS requires Leather Plus Pkg.		

Safety

Antilock brakes, ES	500	435

Appearance & Special Purpose

Alloy wheels, ES	300	262

MITSUBISHI LANCER

CLASS: Compact car
DRIVE WHEELS: Front-wheel drive, all-wheel drive
BASE PRICE RANGE: $13,999-$19,099. Built in Japan.
ALSO CONSIDER: Ford Focus, Honda Civic, Toyota Corolla

A smaller lineup and an additional high-performance model top the 2005 updates to Mitsubishi's smallest cars. All Lancers are sedans and use 4-cyl engines. Wagon versions have been dropped for '05. A 120-hp 2.0-liter powers the two least-expensive models: the ES and O-Z Rally. Last year's LS versions have been dropped. A 162-hp 2.4 powers the Ralliart models, and all these Lancers have front-wheel drive. The high-performance Evolution models, RS, VIII, and new MR have all-wheel drive and a turbocharged 2.0-liter. For '05, all Evos have 276 hp, up 5.

Automatic transmission is available for the ES, O-Z , and Ralliart models. All others have a 5-speed manual transmission except the Evolution MR, which has a 6-speed.

ABS is included on Ralliarts and Evos, not available on other Lancers. Front side airbags are available for O-Z and Ralliart models. The O-Z includes 15-inch O-Z Racing-brand alloy wheels, aero body add-ons, and metal-look interior accents. Ralliarts feature 16-inch alloys, sport-tuned suspension, Evo-style front seats and unique trim. Evolutions have 17-inch alloys, plus cosmetics and suspension tuning inspired by rallye-racing Evos. For 2005, the original Evo is redubbed Evolution VIII. The new MR adds xenon headlights and pares performance-sapping pounds with an aluminum roof panel and lightweight BBS-brand forged-alloy wheels. The RS has less equipment and a lower price vs. the Evo VIII and saves weight with thinner body sheetmetal and rear glass. All Evos have a limited-slip front differential and a new center differential with electronic instead of mechanical control, changes Mitsubishi says improve AWD responsiveness.

RATINGS	ES, man.	ES, auto.	Ralliart, man.	Evolution VIII
ACCELERATION	4	3	6	8
FUEL ECONOMY	7	7	6	5
RIDE QUALITY	5	5	4	2
STEERING/HANDLING	5	6	7	9
QUIETNESS	5	5	5	2
CONTROLS/MATERIALS	6	6	6	6
ROOM/COMFORT (FRONT)	5	5	6	6

RATINGS (cont.)	ES, man.	ES, auto.	Ralliart, man.	Evolution VIII
ROOM/COMFORT (REAR)	4	4	4	4
CARGO ROOM	2	2	7	2
VALUE WITHIN CLASS	4	5	5	3

Lancer is ordinary in ES and O-Z form, but the Ralliart models are worth a look. Still, no mainstream Lancer is a class star, and resale values are generally subpar. Evolutions are pricey, but deliver fast, rowdy fun.

TOTAL	47	48	56	47

Average total for compact cars: 48.4

ENGINES	sohc I4	sohc I4	Turbocharged dohc I4
Size, liters/cu. in.	2.0/122	2.4/145	2.0/122
Horsepower @ rpm	120 @ 5500	162 @ 5750	276 @ 6500
Torque (lb-ft) @ rpm	130 @ 4250	162 @ 4000	286 @ 3500
Availability	S[1]	S[2]	S[3]
EPA city/highway mpg			
5-speed manual	26/33	23/29	19/26
6-speed manual			19/26
4-speed automatic	24/31	22/28	

1. ES, LS sedan, O-Z Rally. 2. LS wagon, Ralliart models. 3. Evolution models.

PRICES

Mitsubishi Lancer	RETAIL PRICE	DEALER INVOICE
ES 4-door sedan, manual	$13999	$13315
ES 4-door sedan, automatic	14899	14171
O-Z Rally 4-door sedan, manual	16399	15599
O-Z Rally 4-door sedan, automatic	17299	16455
Ralliart 4-door sedan, manual	18199	17301
Ralliart 4-door sedan, automatic	19099	18156
Evolution RS 4-door sedan	27629	26012
Evolution VIII 4-door sedan	30499	28714
Evolution MR Edition 4-door sedan	34199	32198
Destination charge	575	575

STANDARD EQUIPMENT

ES: 2.0-liter 4-cylinder engine, 5-speed manual or 4-speed automatic transmission, dual front airbags, air conditioning, power steering, tilt steering wheel, cloth upholstery, front bucket seats, height-adjustable driver seat, center console, cupholders, power mirrors, power windows, power door locks, AM/FM/CD player, digital clock, tachometer, intermittent wipers, rear defogger, visor mirrors, automatic-off headlights, 185/65R14 tires, wheel covers.

O-Z Rally adds: cruise control, split folding rear seat, remote keyless entry, variable-intermittent wipers, floormats, rear spoiler, 195/60HR15 tires, alloy wheels.

Ralliart adds: 2.4-liter 4-cylinder engine, antilock 4-wheel disc brakes, fog lights, sport suspension, 205/50R16 tires.

 Specifications begin on page 547.

Evolution RS adds to ES: 2.0-liter turbocharged 4-cylinder engine, all-wheel drive, limited-slip differential, antilock 4-wheel disc brakes, tilt/telescope leather-wrapped steering wheel, floormats, performance suspension, 235/45WR17 tires, alloy wheels. *Deletes:* height-adjustable driver seat, power windows, power door locks, AM/FM/CD player, visor mirrors, automatic-off headlights.

Evolution VIII adds: power windows, power door locks, remote keyless entry, AM/FM/CD player, visor mirrors, intermittent rear wiper/washer, rear spoiler.

Evolution MR Edition adds: 6-speed manual transmission, fog lights, xenon headlights, MR Edition Suspension.

OPTIONAL EQUIPMENT

Major Packages

	RETAIL PRICE	DEALER INVOICE
ES Convenience Pkg., ES	$800	$704
Cruise control, remote keyless entry, split folding rear seat w/armrest, additional cupholders, variable-intermittent wipers, floormats, color-keyed door handles.		
Sun, Sound, and Airbag Pkg., O-Z Rally, Ralliart	1500	1320
Front side airbags, power sunroof, Infinity sound system. Requires Rally Pkg.		
Rally Pkg., O-Z Rally, Ralliart	131	114
Cargo net, scuff plate, chrome exhaust tip. Requires Sun, Sound, and Airbag Pkg.		
Sun, Sound, and Leather Pkg., Evolution VIII	3120	2727
Leather upholstery, power sunroof, Infinity sound system, fog lights, xenon headlights.		

Comfort & Convenience Features

Leather upholstery, Evolution VIII	NA	NA

MITSUBISHI MONTERO

CLASS: Midsize sport-utility vehicle
DRIVE WHEELS: 4-wheel drive
2004 BASE PRICE: $34,999. Built in Japan.
ALSO CONSIDER: Dodge Durango, Ford Explorer, Honda Pilot

MITSUBISHI

Mitsubishi's largest SUV exchanges standard 16-inch-diameter wheels for 17s in its only change for 2005. Montero comes in a single Limited trim level. It has a 215-hp 3.8-liter V6 and a 5-speed automatic transmission with manual shift gate. Standard is Mitsubishi's ActiveTrac 4WD, which can be left engaged on dry pavement and includes low-range gearing. Also included are ABS, antiskid/traction control, tire-pressure monitor, and front side airbags; curtain side airbags are unavailable. Montero has a right-hinged cargo door instead of a liftgate or tailgate. It seats seven via a 3rd-row bench that removes or folds flush with the cargo floor. Rear air conditioning and power sunroof are among other standards. Rear DVD entertainment is the only factory option.

RATINGS

	Limited
ACCELERATION	4
FUEL ECONOMY	3
RIDE QUALITY	5
STEERING/HANDLING	3
QUIETNESS	5
CONTROLS/MATERIALS	6
ROOM/COMFORT (FRONT)	7
ROOM/COMFORT (REAR)	6
CARGO ROOM	8
VALUE WITHIN CLASS	3

This SUV offers solid build, three-row seating, versatile 4WD and a standard antiskid/traction-control system. But the lack of curtain side airbags betrays an aging design. So do mediocre performance and trucky ride and handling. Poor fuel economy and the Mitsubishi brand's weak resale values round out Montero's list of demerits.

TOTAL	50

Average total for midsize sport-utility vehicles: 54.7

ENGINES

	sohc V6
Size, liters/cu. in.	3.8/234
Horsepower @ rpm	215 @ 5500
Torque (lb-ft) @ rpm	248 @ 3250
Availability	S
EPA city/highway mpg	
5-speed automatic	15/19

2005 prices unavailable at time of publication.

2004 PRICES

Mitsubishi Montero	RETAIL PRICE	DEALER INVOICE
Limited 4-door wagon	$34999	$32880
Destination charge	625	625

STANDARD EQUIPMENT

Limited: 3.8-liter V6 engine, 5-speed automatic transmission w/manual-shift capability, 4-wheel drive, 2-speed transfer case, traction control, dual front

 Specifications begin on page 547.

airbags, front side airbags, antilock 4-wheel disc brakes, antiskid system, tire-pressure monitor, front and rear air conditioning w/automatic climate control, power steering, tilt wood/leather-wrapped steering wheel, cruise control, leather upholstery, heated front bucket seats, 10-way power driver seat, 8-way power passenger seat, center console, cupholders, 2nd-row split folding seat, 3rd-row stowable seat, heated power mirrors, power windows, power door locks, remote keyless entry, power sunroof, Infinity AM/FM/CD player w/in-dash 6-disc CD changer, power antenna, digital clock, tachometer, compass, outside-temperature indicator, trip computer, variable-intermittent wipers, rear defogger, intermittent rear wiper/washer, illuminated visor mirrors, map lights, cargo cover, remote fuel-door release, automatic-off headlights, floormats, theft-deterrent system, roof rails, fog lights, rear privacy glass, running boards, front and rear tow hooks, skid plates, full-size spare tire, 265/70R16 tires, alloy wheels.

OPTIONAL EQUIPMENT

Comfort & Convenience Features	RETAIL PRICE	DEALER INVOICE
Rear-seat DVD entertainment system	$1500	$1308
Requires power sunroof delete.		
Power sunroof delete (credit)	*(1050)*	*(916)*
Deletes power sunroof, deletes in-dash 6-disc CD changer. Requires rear-seat DVD entertainment system.		

MITSUBISHI OUTLANDER

CLASS: Compact sport-utility vehicle
DRIVE WHEELS: Front-wheel drive, all-wheel drive
2004 BASE PRICE RANGE: $18,449-$22,349. Built in Japan.
ALSO CONSIDER: Ford Escape, Honda CR-V, Subaru Forester

Mitsubishi's least-expensive SUV adds new top-shelf models, standard 4-wheel disc brakes, and available manual transmission for 2005. This compact wagon is based on Mitsubishi's Lancer car platform and offers front-wheel drive or all-wheel drive. Joining LS and uplevel XLS models for '05 is the Limited version with unique trim touches inside and out. All Outlanders seat five and share a 160-hp 4-cyl engine. Their AWD lacks low-range gearing and is not designed for severe off-roading. A 5-speed manual transmission is now standard for the LS model. Optional for LS and standard on the others is a 4-speed automatic transmission with manual shift gate. The

4-wheel disc brakes replace rear drums for '05 and include larger front discs. ABS and front side airbags are optional for XLS and Limited; head-protecting curtain side airbags are not offered. Also for '05, rear-end styling is slightly revised and XLS joins the new Limited with standard 17-inch alloy wheels vs. steel 16s on other models. XLS also gets black fender flares. Limited adds body-color fender flares, leather upholstery, heated front seats, and a premium audio system with in-dash CD/MP3 changer; the last is available for XLS. All models come with air conditioning, CD audio, cruise control, power windows/locks/mirrors, and 60/40 split folding rear seat,

RATINGS	2WD LS, auto.	AWD LS, auto.	2WD XLS	AWD XLS
ACCELERATION	4	3	4	3
FUEL ECONOMY	6	6	6	6
RIDE QUALITY	6	6	6	6
STEERING/HANDLING	5	5	5	5
QUIETNESS	4	4	4	4
CONTROLS/MATERIALS	5	5	5	5
ROOM/COMFORT (FRONT)	5	5	5	5
ROOM/COMFORT (REAR)	4	4	4	4
CARGO ROOM	7	7	7	7
VALUE WITHIN CLASS	3	4	3	4

Though pleasantly carlike in many respects, Outlander isn't a class standout, let down mainly by a coarse, relatively weak engine. Also, Mitsubishi doesn't match most other import brands on workmanship and resale values. But that usually means deeper discounts, so Outlander is worth considering if you're on a tight budget.

TOTAL	49	49	49	49

Average total for compact sport-utility vehicles: 49.0

ENGINES

	sohc I4
Size, liters/cu. in.	2.4/143
Horsepower @ rpm	160 @ 5750
Torque (lb-ft) @ rpm	162 @ 4000
Availability	S
EPA city/highway mpg	
4-speed automatic	20/26[1]

1. 21/27 w/2WD.

2005 prices unavailable at time of publication.

2004 PRICES

Mitsubishi Outlander	RETAIL PRICE	DEALER INVOICE
2WD LS 4-door wagon	$18449	$17332
AWD LS 4-door wagon	20249	19022
2WD XLS 4-door wagon	19949	18741
AWD XLS 4-door wagon	22349	20993
Destination charge	595	595

 Specifications begin on page 547.

STANDARD EQUIPMENT

LS: 2.4-liter 4-cylinder engine, 4-speed automatic transmission w/manual-shift capability, dual front airbags, air conditioning, power steering, tilt steering wheel, cruise control, cloth upholstery, front bucket seat w/height-adjustable driver seat, center console, cupholders, split folding rear seat, power mirrors, power windows, power door locks, AM/FM/CD player, analog clock, tachometer, variable-intermittent wipers, map lights, visor mirrors, rear defogger, intermittent rear wiper/washer, automatic-off headlights, theft-deterrent system, 225/60R16 tires, wheel covers. **AWD** adds: all-wheel drive, remote keyless entry, cargo cover, floormats, roof rails.

XLS adds: leather-wrapped steering wheel, remote keyless entry, cargo cover, floormats, rear privacy glass, fog lights, roof rails, rear spoiler, alloy wheels. **AWD** adds: all-wheel drive, power sunroof, Infinity sound system.

OPTIONAL EQUIPMENT

Major Packages	RETAIL PRICE	DEALER INVOICE
Convenience Pkg., 2WD LS	$550	$479
Remote keyless entry, cargo cover, floormats, roof rails.		
Appearance Pkg., LS	500	435
Rear privacy glass, alloy wheels. 2WD LS requires Convenience Pkg.		
Sun and Sound Pkg., 2WD XLS	1150	1000
Power sunroof, Infinity sound system.		
Luxury Pkg., XLS	1450	1262
Leather upholstery, heated front seats, front side airbags, heated mirrors, automatic day/night rearview mirror. Requires antilock brakes. 2WD XLS requires Sun and Sound Pkg.		
Security Pkg., XLS	990	862
Front side airbags, antilock brakes, heated front seats.		
Safety		
Antilock brakes, XLS	500	435
Requires Luxury Pkg. 2WD XLS requires Sun and Sound Pkg.		

NISSAN 350Z

CLASS: Sporty/performance car
DRIVE WHEELS: Rear-wheel drive
BASE PRICE RANGE: $26,500-$37,450. Built in Japan.
ALSO CONSIDER: Honda S2000, Mini Cooper, Pontiac GTO

Addition of a tire-pressure monitor as standard equipment is among the few 2005 changes to Nissan's 2-seat sports. The 350Z is available as a hatchback coupe and a convertible. The coupe comes in base, Enthusiast, Performance, Touring, and Track models. Nissan calls the convertible the Z Roadster and offers it in Enthusiast and Touring trim. All use a 287-hp V6. A 6-speed manual transmission is standard. A 5-speed automatic with manual shift gate is available for Enthusiast and Touring models. Convertibles have a power cloth top with heated glass rear window, a rigid tonneau, and a cockpit wind deflector. Added midyear

was a 35th Anniversary Edition with 300 hp, and unique wheels and badges. All Zs have identical suspension settings and ABS. Traction control is standard on all but the base model. An antiskid system is exclusive to Performance, Track, and manual-transmission Touring coupes. Those models also come with 18-inch wheels. The 18s are optional on convertibles, which, like base and Enthusiast coupes, come with 17s. Torso front side airbags are standard on the Touring convertible, optional otherwise. Head-protecting curtain side airbags are available for coupes. Touring models are available with a navigation system. Track coupes have Brembo-brand brakes with gold-colored accents. Besides the tire-pressure monitor, all Zs now come with manual driver-seat height adjustment and heated door mirrors.

RATINGS	Enthusiast cpe, man.	Touring conv, man.	Touring cpe, auto.	Track, man.
ACCELERATION	8	8	8	8
FUEL ECONOMY	5	5	5	5
RIDE QUALITY	3	3	3	1
STEERING/HANDLING	9	9	9	9
QUIETNESS	2	2	2	1
CONTROLS/MATERIALS	5	5	5	5
ROOM/COMFORT (FRONT)	6	6	6	6
ROOM/COMFORT (REAR)	0	0	0	0
CARGO ROOM	2	1	2	2
VALUE WITHIN CLASS	8	8	8	6

High noise levels and a rough ride are tradeoffs for the 350Z's outstanding smooth-road handling. And cost-conscious pricing dictates cut-rate interior decor. But these coupes and convertibles deliver serious performance and high style at a relative bargain price. They make our Recommended list.

TOTAL	48	47	48	43

Average total for sporty/performance cars: 48.5

ENGINES

	dohc V6
Size, liters/cu. in.	3.5/214
Horsepower @ rpm	287 @ 6200
Torque (lb-ft) @ rpm	274 @ 4800
Availability	S
EPA city/highway mpg	
6-speed manual	20/26
5-speed automatic	19/26

 Specifications begin on page 547.

PRICES

Nissan 350Z

	RETAIL PRICE	DEALER INVOICE
Base 2-door hatchback coupe, manual	$26500	$24786
Enthusiast 2-door hatchback coupe, manual	28450	26311
Enthusiast 2-door hatchback coupe, automatic	29450	27236
Enthusiast Roadster 2-door convertible, manual	34050	31490
Enthusiast Roadster 2-door convertible, automatic	35050	32415
Performance 2-door hatchback coupe, manual	30650	28346
Touring 2-door hatchback coupe, manual	33400	30540
Touring 2-door hatchback coupe, automatic	31800	29409
Touring Roadster 2-door convertible, manual	36450	33710
Touring Roadster 2-door convertible, automatic	37450	34634
Track 2-door hatchback coupe, manual	34300	31363
Destination charge	560	560

STANDARD EQUIPMENT

Base: 3.5-liter V6 engine, 6-speed manual transmission, dual front airbags, antilock 4-wheel disc brakes, brake assist, tire-pressure monitor, air conditioning w/automatic climate control, power steering, tilt leather-wrapped steering wheel, cloth upholstery, bucket seats, height-adjustable driver seat, center console, cupholders, heated power mirrors, power windows, power door locks, remote keyless entry, AM/FM/CD player, digital clock, tachometer, trip computer, outside-temperature indicator, variable-intermittent wipers, illuminated visor mirrors, rear defogger, intermittent rear wiper, theft-deterrent system, 225/50WR17 front tires, 235/50WR17 rear tires, alloy wheels.

Enthusiast adds: 6-speed manual or 5-speed automatic transmission w/manual-shift capability, limited-slip differential, traction control, cruise control, power seats (Roadster), automatic day/night rearview mirror, universal garage-door opener, power convertible top (Roadster), wind deflector (Roadster), xenon headlights.

Touring adds: side airbags (Roadster), leather upholstery, heated power seats, Bose AM/FM/cassette w/in-dash 6-disc CD changer.

Touring coupe manual adds: antiskid system, 225/45WR18 front tires, 245/45WR18 rear tires.

Performance adds to Enthusiast: 6-speed manual transmission, antiskid system, 225/45WR18 front tires, 245/45WR18 rear tires.

Track adds: upgraded brakes, rear spoiler.

OPTIONAL EQUIPMENT

Major Packages

	RETAIL PRICE	DEALER INVOICE
Aerodynamics Pkg.	$530	$408
Front and rear spoilers. NA Roadsters, Track.		

Safety

Side airbags, Enthusiast Roadster	250	217
Side airbags and curtain side airbags, coupe	620	538

Comfort & Convenience Features

	RETAIL PRICE	DEALER INVOICE
Navigation system, Touring	$2000	$1735
Satellite radio, Touring coupe	400	324
Requires monthly fee.		
Ventilated-net seat inserts, Touring Roadster	NC	NC

Appearance & Special Purpose

225/45WR18 front tires and 245/45WR18 rear tires, Roadster	1200	1041
Chrome alloy wheels, Performance, Touring coupe manual	1660	1178

Postproduction options also available.

NISSAN ALTIMA

CLASS: Midsize car
DRIVE WHEELS: Front-wheel drive
BASE PRICE RANGE: $17,200-$29,200. Built in USA.
ALSO CONSIDER: Chevrolet Malibu, Honda Accord, Toyota Camry

A sporty new top-line model joins the 2005 roster of Nissan's top-selling vehicle. Altima shares a basic design with Nissan's Maxima, but costs less and offers 4-cyl as well as V6 power. Altima comes in 2.5 and 2.5 S models with a 175-hp 4-cyl engine. The 3.5 SE and 3.5 SL versions have a 250-hp V6. The sporty new SE-R model has a 260-hp V6. Manual and optional automatic transmissions are offered, but V6s now use a 5-speed automatic vs. 4-cyl models' 4-speed. And the SE-R's manual is a 6-speed vs. the other models' 5-speed. All Altimas have 4-wheel disc brakes. ABS is standard on 3.5 SL and SE-R and on automatic-transmission 3.5 SEs; it's optional on the other models except base 2.5. The SE-R comes with 18-inch wheels vs. 17s for 3.5 SE, and 16s on other Altimas. Front torso side airbags and head-protecting curtain side airbags are available except on the base 2.5. Traction control is optional for automatic-transmission V6 models and the manual-transmission SE-R. All models get revised interior trim for '05, and a navigation system joins the options list. Other available features include: xenon headlights, leather upholstery, and heated seats. The SE-R includes the xenons plus firmer suspension; high-speed tires, larger front brakes; and unique nose, tail, and lower-body styling. It also comes with two-tone leather-trimmed seats and extra gauges.

 Specifications begin on page 547.

RATINGS

RATINGS	2.5 S, man.	2.5 S, auto.	3.5 SE, man.	3.5 SE, auto.
ACCELERATION	5	5	7	7
FUEL ECONOMY	6	5	5	5
RIDE QUALITY	6	6	6	6
STEERING/HANDLING	6	6	6	6
QUIETNESS	6	6	6	6
CONTROLS/MATERIALS	7	7	7	7
ROOM/COMFORT (FRONT)	7	7	7	7
ROOM/COMFORT (REAR)	6	6	6	6
CARGO ROOM	4	4	4	4
VALUE WITHIN CLASS	8	8	8	8

It's made important advances in the grade of its interior materials, but Altima still lags Camry and Accord in overall refinement and assembly quality. It earns Recommended status based on a strong features-per-dollar showing and a spunky demeanor—though torque steer makes V6s a bit too spunky at times. The 4-cyl models easily satisfy most needs.

TOTAL	61	60	62	62

Average total for midsize cars: 57.2

ENGINES

	dohc I4	dohc V6	dohc V6
Size, liters/cu. in.	2.5/152	3.5/214	3.5/214
Horsepower @ rpm	175 @ 6000	250 @ 5800	260 @ 5800
Torque (lb-ft) @ rpm	180 @ 4000	249 @ 4400	251 @ 4400
Availability	S[1]	S[2]	S[3]
EPA city/highway mpg			
5-speed manual	24/31	21/27	
6-speed manual			21/27
4-speed automatic	23/29		
5-speed automatic		20/30	20/30

1. 2.5, 2.5 S. 2. 3.5 SE, 3.5 SL. 3. SE-R.

PRICES

Nissan Altima	RETAIL PRICE	DEALER INVOICE
2.5 4-door sedan, manual	$17200	$16805
2.5 S 4-door sedan, manual	19050	17818
2.5 S 4-door sedan, automatic	19550	18824
3.5 SE 4-door sedan, manual	23100	21364
3.5 SE 4-door sedan, automatic	23750	21965
3.5 SL 4-door sedan, automatic	26900	24878
SE-R 4-door sedan, manual	29200	27005
SE-R 4-door sedan, automatic	29200	27005
Destination charge	560	560

STANDARD EQUIPMENT

2.5: 2.5-liter 4-cylinder engine, 5-speed manual transmission, dual front airbags, 4-wheel disc brakes, emergency inside trunk release, power steering, tilt/telescope steering wheel, cloth upholstery, front bucket seats, center console, cupholders, split folding rear seat, power windows, power door locks, tachometer, variable-intermittent wipers, rear defogger, visor mirrors, map light, theft-deterrent system, 215/60R16 tires, wheel covers.

2.5 S adds: 5-speed manual or 4-speed automatic transmission, air conditioning, interior air filter, cruise control, height-adjustable driver seat, power mirrors, remote keyless entry, AM/FM/CD player.

3.5 SE adds: 3.5-liter V6 250-horsepower engine, 5-speed manual or 5-speed automatic transmission w/manual-shift capability, antilock 4-wheel disc brakes (automatic), 8-way power driver seat w/lumbar adjustment, leather-wrapped steering wheel w/radio controls, trip computer, outside-temperature indicator, illuminated visor mirrors, automatic headlights, fog lights, performance suspension, 215/55VR17 tires (manual), 215/55HR17 tires (automatic), alloy wheels.

3.5 SL adds: 5-speed automatic transmission w/manual-shift capability, antilock 4-wheel disc brakes, automatic climate control, leather upholstery, heated front seats, heated power mirrors, power sunroof, Bose AM/FM radio w/in-dash 6-disc CD changer, automatic day/night inside mirror, universal garage-door opener, xenon headlights, 215/60R16 tires. *Deletes:* performance suspension.

SE-R adds: 3.5-liter V6 260-horsepower engine, 6-speed manual or 5-speed automatic transmission w/manual-shift capability, rear spoiler, SE-R performance suspension, 225/45YR18 tires.

OPTIONAL EQUIPMENT

Major Packages

	RETAIL PRICE	DEALER INVOICE
Convenience Pkg., 2.5 S	$1680	$1457
Leather-wrapped steering wheel w/radio controls, 8-way power driver seat, upgraded sound system, trip computer, illuminated visor mirrors, cargo net, automatic headlights, theft-deterrent system w/alarm, alloy wheels.		
SL Pkg., 2.5 S automatic	3850	3501
Convenience Pkg. plus automatic climate control, leather upholstery, heated front seats and mirrors, Bose AM/FM radio w/in-dash 6-disc CD changer, automatic day/night rearview mirror, universal garage-door opener, chrome accents.		
Convenience Plus Pkg., 2.5 S	2500	2168
Convenience Pkg. plus power sunroof.		
Premium Convenience Pkg., 2.5 S	3300	2862
Convenience Plus Pkg. plus Bose AM/FM radio w/in-dash 6-disc CD changer.		
Leather Pkg., 3.5 SE	3000	2727
Leather upholstery, heated front seats and mirrors, automatic climate control, Bose AM/FM radio w/in-dash 6-disc CD changer, power sunroof, automatic day/night rearview mirror, universal garage-door opener.		
Leather Sport Pkg., 3.5 SE	3900	3546
Leather Pkg. plus xenon headlights, rear spoiler.		
Sport Pkg., 3.5 SE	1250	1085
Power sunroof, rear spoiler.		

 Specifications begin on page 547.

OPTIONAL EQUIPMENT (cont.)

	RETAIL PRICE	DEALER INVOICE
Sport Plus Pkg., 3.5 SE	$2600	$2255
Sport Pkg. plus power sunroof, Bose AM/FM radio w/in-dash 6-disc CD changer, rear spoiler, xenon headlights.		
Braking and Airbag Pkg., 2.5 S, 3.5 SE manual	800	694
Antilock brakes, front side airbags, curtain side airbags.		
Traction Control and Airbag Pkg., 3.5 SE automatic, 3.5 SL, SE-R	800	694
Traction control, front side air bags, curtain side airbags.		
Navigation Pkg., 3.5 SE	5900	5272
2.5 S automatic, 3.5 SL	2000	1735
Navigation system, Sport Leather Pkg. (3.5 SE), speed-sensitive variable-intermittent wipers. 2.5 S requires SL Convenience Pkg., power sunroof.		
Safety		
Front side airbags and curtain side airbags, 2.5 S	500	433
Comfort & Convenience Features		
Power sunroof, 2.5 S automatic	850	738
Satellite radio	400	NA
Requires monthly fee.		
Appearance & Special Purpose		
Fog lights, 2.5 S	290	241
Chrome alloy wheels, 2.5 S	1310	926
3.5 SE	1360	962

Postproduction options also available.

NISSAN MAXIMA

CLASS: Midsize car
DRIVE WHEELS: Front-wheel drive
BASE PRICE RANGE: $27,100-$29,350. Built in USA.
ALSO CONSIDER: Honda Accord, Toyota Camry, Volkswagen Passat

Nissan's flagship sedan follows its 2004 redesign with minor changes to trim and some running gear. Maxima shares an underskin design with

Nissan's American-made Altima, which is slightly smaller and costs less. Maxima comes in sporty SE and luxury-oriented SL models with a 3.5-liter V6. Altima offers this same engine, but the Maxima's is tuned for extra horsepower. The SE comes with a 6-speed manual transmission, which Nissan says has improved shift action for '05. Optional for SE and standard for SL is a 5-speed automatic with manual shift gate. Both models include antilock 4-wheel disc brakes, head-protecting curtain side airbags, and front torso side airbags. Traction control is available. An antiskid system is optional with automatic transmission. The SL has 17-inch wheels, the SE 18s. Both models come with Nissan's Skyview roof—fixed tinted-glass panels over the front and rear seats. A conventional power sunroof is available. Also available are navigation system; heated front seats; and an Elite Package with full-length center console, twin rear bucket seats instead of a 3-passenger bench, and power rear-window sunshade. Other '05 changes include additional chrome interior accents and softer leather upholstery as standard for SL and optional for SE.

RATINGS	SE, man.	SE w/nav. sys., auto.	SL w/Elite Pkg., auto.
ACCELERATION	7	6	6
FUEL ECONOMY	5	5	5
RIDE QUALITY	6	6	7
STEERING/HANDLING	7	7	6
QUIETNESS	5	5	6
CONTROLS/MATERIALS	7	6	7
ROOM/COMFORT (FRONT)	7	7	7
ROOM/COMFORT (REAR)	6	6	6
CARGO ROOM	4	4	4
VALUE WITHIN CLASS	5	5	6

Nissan does an effective job separating Maxima from Altima. Differences in styling, size, and features make Maxima feel more substantial and more upscale. But Maxima's prices close in on the some luxury sedans. It has the performance to compete there, but not the polish, making this a sporty, if pricey, midsize choice.

TOTAL	59	57	60

Average total for midsize cars: 57.2

ENGINES

	dohc V6
Size, liters/cu. in.	3.5/214
Horsepower @ rpm	265 @ 5800
Torque (lb-ft) @ rpm	255 @ 4400
Availability	S
EPA city/highway mpg	
6-speed manual	20/29
4-speed automatic	20/27
5-speed automatic	20/28

PRICES

Nissan Maxima

	RETAIL PRICE	DEALER INVOICE
SE 4-door sedan, manual	$27100	$24780
SE 4-door sedan, automatic	27100	24780
SL 4-door sedan, automatic	29350	26836
Destination charge	560	560

STANDARD EQUIPMENT

SE: 3.5-liter V6 engine, 6-speed manual or 5-speed automatic transmission w/manual-shift capability, dual front airbags, front side airbags, curtain side airbags, antilock 4-wheel disc brakes, brake assist, front-seat active head restraints, emergency inside trunk release, air conditioning w/dual-zone automatic controls, power steering, tilt/telescope leather-wrapped steering wheel w/radio controls, cruise control, cloth upholstery, front bucket seats, 8-way power driver seat, center console, cupholders, split folding rear seat, power mirrors, power windows, power door locks, remote keyless entry, AM/FM/cassette/CD player, digital clock, tachometer, trip computer, automatic day/night rearview mirror, outside-temperature indicator, universal garage-door opener, illuminated visor mirrors, map lights, variable-intermittent wipers, rear defogger, automatic headlights, theft-deterrent system, glass roof panel, fog lights, cornering lights, sport suspension, 245/45VR18 tires, alloy wheels.

SL adds: leather upholstery, heated front seats, 4-way power passenger seat, heated power mirrors, Bose AM/FM radio w/in-dash 6-disc CD changer, compass, bi-xenon headlights, 225/55HR17 tires. *Deletes:* sport suspension.

OPTIONAL EQUIPMENT

Major Packages

	RETAIL PRICE	DEALER INVOICE
Sensory Pkg., SE	$2350	$2039
Leather upholstery, heated front seats and mirrors, 4-way power passenger seat, Bose AM/FM radio w/in-dash 6-disc CD changer, compass.		
Driver Preferred Pkg., SE	3650	3166
Sensory Pkg. plus power tilt/telescope and heated steering wheel, memory system (driver seat, mirrors, steering wheel), driver-seat power lumbar adjustment, driver-seat power entry/exit seat (automatic), power-folding mirrors, bi-xenon headlights, rear spoiler.		
Driver Preferred Pkg., SL	800	694
Power tilt/telescope and heated steering wheel, memory system (driver seat, mirrors, steering wheel), power entry/exit driver seat w/power lumbar adjustment, power-folding automatic day/night outside mirrors.		
Elite Pkg., SE	4600	3990
SL	1750	1519
Driver Preferred Pkg. plus heated rear bucket seats, rear center console, trunk pass-through, power rear sunshade, automatic up/down rear windows, rear auxiliary power outlet. Deletes split folding rear seat.		

Powertrain

Traction control	300	260
Requires Driver Preferred Pkg. or Elite Pkg.		

Safety

	RETAIL PRICE	DEALER INVOICE
Antiskid system	$900	$780

Includes traction control. Requires Driver Preferred Pkg. or Elite Pkg., power sunroof. NA SE w/manual transmission.

Comfort & Convenience Features

Power sunroof	900	780

Deletes glass roof panel.

Navigation system	2000	1735

Requires Driver Preferred Pkg. or Elite Pkg.

Bose AM/FM radio w/in-dash 6-disc CD changer, SE	1000	867
Satellite radio	400	346

Requires monthly fee.

Postproduction options also available.

NISSAN MURANO

CLASS: Midsize sport-utility vehicle
DRIVE WHEELS: Front-wheel drive, all-wheel drive
2004 BASE PRICE RANGE: $28,200-$30,750. Built in Japan.
ALSO CONSIDER: Ford Explorer, Honda Pilot, Toyota Highlander

A lower-priced model and new optional features highlight 2005 for this car-type SUV. Based on Nissan's Altima sedan platform, Murano is a 5-passenger wagon with no 3rd-row seating. An entry-level S model joins the SL and top-line SE versions for '05. All use a 3.5-liter V6 and a continuously variable automatic transmission providing a near-infinite range of gear ratios. SEs include a manual shift mode with preset "gears." All models offer front-wheel drive or all-wheel drive. Nissan leaves off-road duty to its truck-based Pathfinder SUV, so Murano's AWD lacks low-range gearing, though a console button can lock in a 50/50 power split for extra traction up to 30 mph. All Muranos come with ABS, front torso side airbags, and head-protecting curtain side airbags. Added for '05 is a rollover sensor designed to trigger the curtain airbags if a tip is imminent. All models have 18-inch wheels and a rear liftgate with fixed glass. SEs come with a firmer suspension and xenon headlamps. Antiskid/traction control is available. So is a navigation system, which now adds a camera that uses the navigation screen to display a rear view when backing up. Also new is a keyless entry/ignition system available for SL and SE. Other options include power-adjustable pedals, leather upholstery, heated front seats, and rear DVD entertainment.

 Specifications begin on page 547.

RATINGS

RATINGS	AWD SL	2WD SE w/nav. sys.
ACCELERATION	6	6
FUEL ECONOMY	4	5
RIDE QUALITY	5	5
STEERING/HANDLING	5	5
QUIETNESS	6	6
CONTROLS/MATERIALS	5	5
ROOM/COMFORT (FRONT)	7	7
ROOM/COMFORT (REAR)	7	7
CARGO ROOM	8	8
VALUE WITHIN CLASS	8	7

You may not love the design, but at least Murano brings some style to the conservative world of the family SUV. Its tangible assets include secure handling, good utility, and strong, efficient V6/CVT powertrain. Competitive pricing rounds out this Recommended pick's dossier.

TOTAL	61	61

Average total for midsize sport-utility vehicles: 54.7

ENGINES

	dohc V6
Size, liters/cu. in.	3.5/214
Horsepower @ rpm	245 @ 5800
Torque (lb-ft) @ rpm	246 @ 4400
Availability	S
EPA city/highway mpg	
CVT automatic	20/24[1]

1. 20/25 w/2WD.

2005 prices unavailable at time of publication.

2004 PRICES

Nissan Murano	RETAIL PRICE	DEALER INVOICE
2WD SL 4-door wagon	$28200	$25932
AWD SL 4-door wagon	29800	27404
2WD SE 4-door wagon	29150	26807
AWD SE 4-door wagon	30750	28278
Destination charge	560	560

STANDARD EQUIPMENT

SL: 3.5-liter V6 engine, continuously variable transmission (CVT), dual front airbags, front side airbags, curtain side airbags, front-seat active head restraints, antilock 4-wheel disc brakes, brake assist, air conditioning w/dual-zone automatic climate controls, power steering, tilt leather-wrapped steering wheel w/radio controls, cruise control, cloth upholstery, front bucket seats, 10-way power driver seat w/lumbar adjustment, center console, cupholders, split folding rear seat, power mirrors, power windows, power door locks, remote keyless entry, AM/FM/CD player, digital clock, tachometer, trip computer, outside-temperature indicator, compass, illuminated visor mirrors, automatic day/night rearview mirror, universal garage-door opener, map lights, variable-intermittent wipers, remote fuel-door/liftgate release, rear defogger, intermittent rear wiper, automatic headlights, theft-deterrent system, rear privacy glass, rear spoiler, fog lights, 235/65R18 tires, alloy wheels. **AWD** adds: all-wheel drive.

SE adds: manual-shift capability, xenon headlights, sport suspension. **AWD** adds: all-wheel drive.

OPTIONAL EQUIPMENT

Major Packages	RETAIL PRICE	DEALER INVOICE
Premium Pkg.	$1500	$1301
Power-adjustable pedals, Bose AM/FM/cassette w/in-dash 6-disc CD changer, cargo cover and net, roof rails.		
Leather Pkg., SL	3500	3036
Premium Pkg. plus leather upholstery, 4-way passenger seat, power sunroof, unique bumpers.		
Sunroof Pkg.	2500	2168
Premium Pkg. plus power sunroof.		
Touring Pkg., SL	4300	3730
Leather Pkg. plus heated front seats and mirrors, memory system (driver seat, pedals mirrors), xenon headlights w/manual leveler.		
Touring Pkg., SE	4000	3470
Premium Pkg. plus leather upholstery, memory system (driver seat, mirrors), power-adjustable pedals, heated front seats and mirrors, 4-way power passenger seat, power sunroof, cargo cover and net.		
Dynamic Control Pkg.	750	651
Antiskid system, traction control, tire-pressure monitor. Requires Touring Pkg.		
Tow Pkg.	580	481
Class II receiver hitch, ball mount.		
Comfort & Convenience Features		
Navigation system	2000	1735
Requires Touring Pkg., Dynamic Control Pkg.		
Rear-seat DVD entertainment system	1720	1361
SL requires Leather Pkg. SE requires Touring Pkg.		
Satellite radio	400	347
Requires monthly fee.		
Chrome alloy wheels, SL	1200	878
Requires Touring Pkg.		

Postproduction options also available.

NISSAN PATHFINDER

CLASS: Midsize sport-utility vehicle
DRIVE WHEELS: Rear-wheel drive, 4-wheel drive
BASE PRICE: NA. Built in USA.
ALSO CONSIDER: Ford Explorer, Honda Pilot, Toyota Highlander

Nissan redesigns its midsize SUV for 2005, giving it larger dimensions, more power, and seating for seven instead of five. Pathfinder retains a truck-type design, but adopts independent rear suspension. Compared to the

 Specifications begin on page 547.

1996-2004 model, it's 6.3 inches longer in wheelbase, 4.9 inches longer overall, 3.1 inches wider, and about 450 lb heavier. A V6 remains standard, but displacement increases to 4.0 liters and horsepower is up 30 to 270. A 5-speed automatic is the sole transmission. A 50/50 split folding 3rd-row seat is standard, with 40/20/40 split folding 2nd-row seats. Antilock 4-wheel disc brakes and antiskid/traction control are standard. Pathfinder is offered with rear-wheel drive or Nissan's All-Mode 4-wheel drive, which includes low-range gearing and can be left engaged on dry pavement. Four models are offered: XE, SE, SE Off-Road, and luxury-oriented LE. All have 16-inch wheels except LE, which has 17s. Front side airbags and head-protecting curtain side airbags that cover all three seating rows are standard on LE, optional on others. Exclusive to LE are driver-seat/mirror/pedal memory settings, wood-toned interior trim, and available navigation system. Standard on LE and optional on SE Off-Road are leather upholstery, heated outside mirrors, and power-adjustable front-passenger seat. Exclusive to SE Off-Road are standard all-terrain tires, Rancho-brand shock absorbers, chassis skid plates, and unique upholstery, plus Nissan's Hill Descent Control and Hill Start Assist braking systems. Other available features include power-adjustable pedals and rear DVD entertainment. This evaluation is based on preview test drives.

RATINGS	2WD SE Off-Road	4WD LE w/nav. sys.
ACCELERATION	5	5
FUEL ECONOMY	4	4
RIDE QUALITY	6	6
STEERING/HANDLING	4	4
QUIETNESS	5	5
CONTROLS/MATERIALS	6	6
ROOM/COMFORT (FRONT)	7	7
ROOM/COMFORT (REAR)	6	6
CARGO ROOM	8	8
VALUE WITHIN CLASS	6	6

Everyday driving ease and fuel economy won't match car-type competitors such as the Honda Pilot or Nissan's own Murano. But Pathfinder delivers a solid array of true-SUV attributes, such as towing ability and off-road capability. And features and road manners do compare favorably with those of such truck-type SUVs as the Dodge Durango and Ford Explorer.

TOTAL	57	57

Average total for midsize sport-utility vehicles: 54.7

ENGINES

	dohc V6
Size, liters/cu. in.	4.0/241
Horsepower @ rpm	270 @ 5600
Torque (lb-ft) @ rpm	291 @ 4000
Availability	S
EPA city/highway mpg	
5-speed automatic	15/21[1]

1. 16/23 with 2WD.

2005 prices unavailable at time of publication.

NISSAN QUEST

CLASS: Minivan
DRIVE WHEELS: Front-wheel drive
2004 BASE PRICE RANGE: $24,240-$32,240. Built in USA.
ALSO CONSIDER: Dodge Caravan, Honda Odyssey, Toyota Sienna

Optional satellite radio heads 2005 news for Nissan's minivans. Quest was redesigned last year with the longest wheelbase and overall length in its field. S, SL, and SE models return with a 240-hp V6 and automatic transmission. The SL now comes with a 5-speed automatic, like the top-line SE; the base S uses a 4-speed automatic. SEs have 17-inch wheels vs. 16s. All Quests carry seven with an available Seat Package, and have dual sliding rear side doors. SL and SE include power operation for one or both rear doors, plus the liftgate. Every Quest has ABS, traction control, tire-pressure monitor, and head-protecting curtain side airbags for all three seating rows. Front side airbags and an antiskid system are available. Newly standard are front head restraints designed to minimize whiplash injury, plus an antitheft/alarm system. The available Seat Package includes 2nd-row buckets and a 3rd-row bench that folds into the floor. The new satellite radio option joins available rear DVD entertainment with one or two screens, rear-obstacle detection, a full-length overhead console with air vents and reading lights, and Nissan's Skyview roof (four overhead glass roof panels). Other options include power-adjustable brake and accelerator pedals, power seat/pedal/mirror memory, heated front seats, leather upholstery, and a navigation system. The S gets a standard roof rack, like other Quests.

 Specifications begin on page 547.

RATINGS

RATINGS	SL	SE w/nav. sys.
ACCELERATION	6	6
FUEL ECONOMY	4	4
RIDE QUALITY	6	5
STEERING/HANDLING	5	5
QUIETNESS	4	4
CONTROLS/MATERIALS	4	4
ROOM/COMFORT (FRONT)	6	6
ROOM/COMFORT (REAR)	8	8
CARGO ROOM	9	9
VALUE WITHIN CLASS	6	6

Quest offers a versatile package with expected safety and convenience features, but isn't tops in minivan driving ease, refinement, and workmanship. And it gets quite pricey with options, though dealers should be discounting in light of weak 2004-model sales.

TOTAL	58	57

Average total for minivans: 58.0

ENGINES

	dohc V6
Size, liters/cu. in.	3.5/214
Horsepower @ rpm	240 @ 5800
Torque (lb-ft) @ rpm	242 @ 4400
Availability	S
EPA city/highway mpg	
4-speed automatic	19/26
5-speed automatic	18/25

2005 prices unavailable at time of publication.

2004 PRICES

Nissan Quest	RETAIL PRICE	DEALER INVOICE
S 4-door van	$24240	$22418
SL 4-door van	26740	24451
SE 4-door van	32240	29479
Destination charge	560	560

STANDARD EQUIPMENT

S: 3.5-liter V6 engine, 4-speed automatic transmission, traction control, dual front airbags, curtain side airbags, antilock 4-wheel disc brakes, brake assist, tire-pressure monitor, front and rear air conditioning w/rear controls, power steering, tilt steering wheel, cruise control, cloth upholstery, front bucket seats, driver-seat height and lumbar adjustment, cupholders, power mirrors, power front windows, power door locks, remote keyless entry, AM/FM/CD player, digital clock, tachometer, trip computer, illuminated visor mirrors, overhead console, variable-intermittent wipers, map lights, rear defogger, intermittent rear wiper/washer, automatic headlights, theft-deterrent system, rear privacy glass, cornering lights, 225/65HR16 tires, wheel covers.

SL adds: leather-wrapped steering wheel w/radio controls, 8-way power driver seat, power-adjustable pedals, passenger-side power door, power liftgate, heated power mirrors, power rear quarter windows, rear radio controls, automatic day/night rearview mirror, universal garage-door opener, roof rails, alloy wheels.

SE adds: 5-speed automatic transmission, front side airbags, antiskid system, rear-obstacle-detection system, dual-zone automatic climate controls, leather upholstery, heated front seats, 4-way power passenger seat, memory system (driver seat, mirrors, pedals), driver-side power door, Bose AM/FM radio w/in-dash 6-disc CD changer, power sunroof, glass roof panels, full-length overhead console, fog lights, roof rack, 225/60HR17 tires.

OPTIONAL EQUIPMENT

Major Packages	RETAIL PRICE	DEALER INVOICE
S Upgrade Pkg., S	$700	$607
Rear-obstacle-detection system, alloy wheels. Requires Seat Pkg.		
SL Upgrade Pkg., SL	750	651
Front side airbags, rear-obstacle-detection system, heated front seats. Requires Seat Pkg.		
Leather Pkg., SL	1500	1364
Leather upholstery, 4-way power passenger seat. Requires Seat Pkg., SL Upgrade Pkg.		
Seat Pkg., S, SL	350	322
SE	750	690
2nd-row fold-flat captain chairs, 3rd-row stowable bench seat.		
Towing Pkg.	540	459
Comfort & Convenience Features		
Navigation system, SE	2000	1735
Requires Seat Pkg., DVD Entertainment Pkg.		
Navigation system w/6-disc CD changer, SL	2300	1995
Requires Seat Pkg., DVD Entertainment Pkg.		
Single Screen DVD Entertainment Pkg.	1500	1301
Requires Seat Pkg.		
Dual Screen DVD Entertainment Pkg., SE	1900	1648
Requires Seat Pkg.		
Glass roof panels, SL	1500	1301
Requires SL Upgrade Pkg., Seat Pkg.		

NISSAN SENTRA

CLASS: Compact car
DRIVE WHEELS: Front-wheel drive
BASE PRICE RANGE: $12,500-$17,600. Built in Mexico.
ALSO CONSIDER: Ford Focus, Honda Civic, Toyota Corolla

Availability of satellite radio is among the few changes to Nissan's smallest sedans for 2005. Sentra comes in economy-oriented 1.8 and 1.8 S models,

 Specifications begin on page 547.

and in sporty SE-R and SE-R Spec V form. The 1.8 versions have a 126-hp 1.8-liter 4-cyl engine and a 5-speed manual transmission or optional 4-speed automatic. SE-Rs have a 165-hp 2.5-liter 4-cyl and automatic transmission. The SE-R Spec V has a 175-hp 2.5 and mandatory 6-speed manual. SE-R and Spec V come with 4-wheel disc brakes instead of rear drums, plus sport suspensions and 16- and 17-inch alloy wheels, respectively. Other Sentras come with 15-inch steel wheels. Sixteens are available for the 1.8 S in a new Sport Appearance Package that also includes a rear spoiler, fog lights, and leather-rim steering wheel. ABS packaged with front side airbags is optional for all but the base 1.8. The new satellite radio is also available for all but the base 1.8. The Spec V offers specific exterior and interior trim, sport seats, and available Brembo-brand brakes. All models get new upholstery fabrics for 2005, and the 1.8 S adds cruise control and a trip computer as standard.

RATINGS

	1.8, auto.	1.8 S, man.	SE-R Spec V
ACCELERATION	3	4	6
FUEL ECONOMY	6	7	5
RIDE QUALITY	5	5	3
STEERING/HANDLING	5	5	7
QUIETNESS	3	4	4
CONTROLS/MATERIALS	6	6	6
ROOM/COMFORT (FRONT)	4	4	5
ROOM/COMFORT (REAR)	3	3	3
CARGO ROOM	2	2	2
VALUE WITHIN CLASS	5	6	5

No Sentra matches Honda Civic and Volkswagen Jetta for refinement or Ford's Focus for roominess. But these are solid-enough small cars, and even the sporty SE-R and Spec V are competitively priced.

TOTAL	42	46	46

Average total for compact cars: 48.4

ENGINES

	dohc I4	dohc I4	dohc I4
Size, liters/cu. in.	1.8/110	2.5/152	2.5/152
Horsepower @ rpm	126 @ 6000	165 @ 6000	175 @ 6000
Torque (lb-ft) @ rpm	129 @ 2400	175 @ 4000	180 @ 4000
Availability	S[1]	S[2]	S[3]

ENGINES (cont.)

	dohc I4	dohc I4	dohc I4
EPA city/highway mpg			
5-speed manual	28/35		
6-speed manual			23/29
4-speed automatic	28/35	23/28	

1. 1.8, 1.8 S. 2. 2.5 S, SE-R. 3. SE-R Spec V.

PRICES

Nissan Sentra

	RETAIL PRICE	DEALER INVOICE
1.8 4-door sedan, manual	$12500	$11953
1.8 4-door sedan, automatic	13300	12718
1.8 S 4-door sedan, manual	14500	13486
1.8 S 4-door sedan, automatic	15300	14230
SE-R 4-door sedan, automatic	17400	16183
SE-R Spec V 4-door sedan, manual	17600	16389
Destination charge	560	560

STANDARD EQUIPMENT

1.8: 1.8-liter 4-cylinder engine, 5-speed manual or 4-speed automatic transmission, dual front airbags, emergency inside trunk release, power steering, tilt steering wheel, cloth upholstery, front bucket seats, center console, cupholders, passenger-side visor mirror, rear defogger, 195/60HR15 tires, wheel covers.

1.8 S adds: air conditioning, cruise control, height-adjustable driver seat, split folding rear seat, power mirrors, power windows, power door locks, remote keyless entry, AM/FM/CD player, digital clock, tachometer, trip computer, variable-intermittent wipers, visor mirrors, map lights.

SE-R adds to 1.8 S: 2.5-liter 4-cylinder 165-horsepower engine, 4-speed automatic transmission, 4-wheel disc brakes, leather-wrapped steering wheel, fog lights, rear spoiler, sport suspension, 195/55HR16 tires, alloy wheels.

SE-R Spec V adds: 2.5-liter 4-cylinder 175-horsepower engine, 6-speed manual transmission, limited-slip differential, Spec V suspension, 215/45ZR17 tires. *Deletes:* split folding rear seat.

OPTIONAL EQUIPMENT

Major Packages

	RETAIL PRICE	DEALER INVOICE
Convenience Pkg., 1.8	$1250	$1085
Air conditioning, AM/FM/CD player.		
ABS and Side Airbags Pkg., 1.8 S, SE-R, SE-R Spec V	600	520
Antilock brakes, front side airbags. SE-R, SE-R Spec V require Audio Fanatic Pkg., Sunroof Pkg.		
Spec V Brake Pkg., SE-R Spec V	1000	867
Brembo upgraded brakes, gold-painted front calipers. NA w/ABS and Side Airbags Pkg.		
Sunroof Pkg., 1.8 S, SE-R, SE-R Spec V	700	607
Power sunroof, illuminated visor mirrors. 1.8 S requires Special Edition Pkg., ABS and Side Airbags Pkg.		

Specifications begin on page 547.

OPTIONAL EQUIPMENT (cont.)

	RETAIL PRICE	DEALER INVOICE
Audio Pkg., 1.8 S	$900	$780
Rockford Fosgate AM/FM radio w/in-dash 6-disc CD changer, partial folding rear seat.		
Sport Appearance Pkg., 1.8 S	1100	954
Leather-wrapped steering wheel, fog lights, rear spoiler, special grille, 195/55R16 tires, alloy wheels.		
Special Edition Pkg., 1.8 S	500	433
Audio Pkg. and Sport Appearance Pkg.		
Audio Fanatic Pkg., SE-R, SE-R Spec V	550	478
Rockford Fosgate sound system, partial folding rear seat, theft-deterrent system w/alarm.		
Comfort & Convenience Features		
Satellite radio, 1.8 S, SE-R, SE-R Spec V	400	347
S requires Audio Pkg. or Special Edition Pkg.		
Appearance & Special Purpose		
Rear spoiler, 1.8 S	360	283

Postproduction options also available.

2004 NISSAN XTERRA

CLASS: Midsize sport-utility vehicle
DRIVE WHEELS: Rear-wheel drive, 4-wheel drive
BASE PRICE RANGE: $18,000-$28,000. Built in USA.
ALSO CONSIDER: Ford Explorer, Honda Pilot, Toyota Highlander

Altered wheel sizes for some models constitute the 2004 change of note for Nissan's youth-oriented SUV. Xterra's lineup starts with a price-leader XE model with a 143-hp 4-cyl engine, manual transmission, and rear-wheel drive. XE V6 and SE versions use a 180-hp V6. A 210-hp supercharged V6 powers top-line SE S/C models. Automatic transmission is optional on the XE V6, standard on other V6 Xterras. V6 models offer 2-wheel drive or 4-wheel drive that must be disengaged on dry pavement but includes low-range gearing. ABS and air conditioning are standard. For 2004, XE V6s trade 16-inch wheels for 15s, while nonsupercharged SEs get 17s instead of 16s. The 4-cyl XEs retain 15s and SE S/Cs continue with 17s. Head-protecting curtain side airbags are optional for any Xterra. The antiskid/traction-control system that is optional for automatic-transmission 4WD V6 models includes a tire-pressure monitor. Nissan begins selling redesigned 2005 Xterras in calendar '05 with new styling, larger dimensions and a larger, more-powerful V6. The underskin structure and many components will come from Nissan's redesigned 2005 Pathfinder SUVs.

RATINGS	2WD XE, 4-cyl man.	4WD SE	4WD SE S/C
ACCELERATION	2	3	4
FUEL ECONOMY	5	4	3
RIDE QUALITY	4	4	4
STEERING/HANDLING	3	3	4
QUIETNESS	3	3	3
CONTROLS/MATERIALS	5	5	5
ROOM/COMFORT (FRONT)	6	6	6
ROOM/COMFORT (REAR)	3	3	3
CARGO ROOM	7	7	7
VALUE WITHIN CLASS	4	6	5

Xterra is priced only slightly higher than car-based compact SUVs such as the Honda CR-V, Toyota RAV4, and Ford Escape/Mazda Tribute, and offers more room. It's less civilized than those vehicles in everyday driving, but pays back with its truck toughness, off-road ability, and available curtain side airbags.

TOTAL	42	44	44

Average total for midsize sport-utility vehicles: 54.7

ENGINES	dohc I4	sohc V6	Supercharged sohc V6
Size, liters/cu. in.	2.4/146	3.3/200	3.3/210
Horsepower @ rpm	143 @ 5200	180 @ 4800	210 @ 4800
Torque (lb-ft) @ rpm	154 @ 4000	202 @ 2800	246 @ 2800
Availability	S[1]	S[2]	S[3]
EPA city/highway mpg			
5-speed manual	19/24	17/20	
4-speed automatic		16/20[4]	15/18[5]

1. XE. 2. XE V6, SE. 3. SE S/C. 4. 17/21 w/2WD. 5. 15/19 w/2WD.

PRICES

Nissan Xterra	RETAIL PRICE	DEALER INVOICE
2WD XE 4-door wagon, manual	$18000	$17023
2WD XE V6 4-door wagon, manual	19400	18347
2WD XE V6 4-door wagon, automatic	20400	19293
4WD XE V6 4-door wagon, manual	21400	20239
4WD XE V6 4-door wagon, automatic	22400	21184
2WD SE 4-door wagon, automatic	24700	23102
4WD SE 4-door wagon, automatic	26700	24972
2WD SE S/C 4-door wagon, automatic	26000	24317
4WD SE S/C 4-door wagon, automatic	28000	26188
Destination charge	560	560

 Specifications begin on page 547.

STANDARD EQUIPMENT

XE: 2.4-liter 4-cylinder engine, 5-speed manual transmission, dual front airbags, antilock brakes, air conditioning, power steering, cloth upholstery, front bucket seats, center console, cupholders, split folding rear seat, AM/FM/CD player, digital clock, tachometer, rear defogger, intermittent rear wiper, roof rack, rear privacy glass, skid plates, full-size spare tire, 265/70R15 tires.

XE V6 adds: 3.3-liter V6 engine, 5-speed manual or 4-speed automatic transmission, height-adjustable driver seat w/lumbar adjustment. **4WD** adds: 4-wheel drive, 2-speed transfer case.

SE adds: 4-speed automatic transmission, limited-slip differential, tilt leather-wrapped steering wheel w/radio controls, cruise control, power mirrors, power windows, power door locks, remote keyless entry, Rockford Fosgate AM/FM radio w/in-dash 6-disc CD changer, compass, outside-temperature indicator, passenger-side visor mirror, variable-intermittent wipers, map lights, cargo cover, theft-deterrent system, fog lights, front tow hooks, 265/65R17 tires, alloy wheels. **4WD** adds: 4-wheel drive, 2-speed transfer case.

SE S/C adds: supercharged 3.3-liter V6 engine. **4WD** adds: 4-wheel drive, 2-speed transfer case.

OPTIONAL EQUIPMENT

Major Packages	RETAIL PRICE	DEALER INVOICE
Utility Pkg., XE	$900	$780
XE V6	1000	867
Tilt steering wheel, variable-intermittent wipers, cargo cover, first-aid kit, additional auxiliary power outlet, tubular side steps, 265/70R16 tires (XE V6), alloy wheels (XE V6).		
Power Pkg., XE	1000	867
Power mirrors, windows door locks; remote keyless entry; cruise control; cloth door inserts. Requires Utility Pkg.		
World Championship Value Pkg., XE V6	1300	1882
Utility Pkg. plus power mirrors and windows, power door locks, remote keyless entry, cruise control, map lights, cloth door inserts, triathlon backpack, theft-deterrent system w/alarm.		
Sport Pkg., XE V6	400	347
Limited-slip rear differential, additional auxiliary power outlets, fog lights, front tow hooks. Requires World Championship Pkg.		
Premium Audio Pkg., XE V6	800	694
Rockford Fosgate AM/FM radio w/in-dash 6-disc CD changer, steering-wheel radio controls. Requires World Championship Pkg.		
Rugged Leather Pkg., SE, SE S/C	1000	867
Leather upholstery, suedelike door inserts. Requires pop-up sunroof.		
Safety		
Curtain side airbags	500	433
XE requires Power Pkg. XE V6 requires Sport Pkg.		

OPTIONAL EQUIPMENT (cont.)	RETAIL PRICE	DEALER INVOICE
Antiskid system, 4WD w/automatic transmission	$550	$478
Includes traction control, tire-pressure monitor. SE and SE S/C delete limited-slip differential. Requires curtain side airbags.		
Comfort & Convenience Features		
Pop-up sunroof, SE, SE S/C	350	304
Automatic day/night rearview mirror, XE, XE V6	220	167
Appearance & Special Purpose		
Grille/taillight guards	620	492
Tow hitch	350	269
NA XE 4-cylinder.		

Postproduction options also available.

PONTIAC AZTEK

CLASS: Midsize sport-utility vehicle
DRIVE WHEELS: Front-wheel drive, all-wheel drive
BASE PRICE RANGE: $21,375-$24,290. Built in Mexico.
ALSO CONSIDER: Ford Explorer, Honda Pilot, Toyota Highlander

This slow-selling car-type SUV stands pat for '05. Aztek is based on GM's minivan, but has four swing-open side doors and a combination liftgate/tailgate. It's similar to the Buick Rendezvous, but that model has a longer body with different styling, one-piece liftgate, and seating for up to seven instead of five. Aztek comes only with a 3.4-liter V6, automatic transmission, and either front-wheel drive with optional traction control or GM's Versatrak all-wheel drive. Versatrak lacks low-range gearing and isn't designed for severe off-road use. Antilock 4-wheel disc brakes and front side airbags are included with AWD, available with 2WD. Among package options is the Rally Edition group with unique trim inside and out, lowered-ride-height suspension, and 17-inch alloy wheels vs. standard 16s. Also available: rear DVD entertainment, GM OnStar assistance, leather seating, satellite radio, in-dash CD changer, and CD/MP3 player. An optional trailering package allows towing up to 3500 lb. Available through dealers is a camping package with clip-on tent and fitted air mattress.

Specifications begin on page 547.

RATINGS

RATINGS	2WD	AWD
ACCELERATION	5	4
FUEL ECONOMY	5	5
RIDE QUALITY	5	4
STEERING/HANDLING	4	4
QUIETNESS	5	5
CONTROLS/MATERIALS	4	4
ROOM/COMFORT (FRONT)	7	7
ROOM/COMFORT (REAR)	7	7
CARGO ROOM	8	8
VALUE WITHIN CLASS	4	4

Aztek scores comfort points over most truck-type SUVs and offers lots of nifty features for active folks, but it can't go far off-road even with AWD. Worse, it lacks a "quality" look and feel, and 2WD buyers must pay extra for the safety of ABS and front side airbags. Continued slow sales mean ready discounts.

TOTAL	54	52

Average total for midsize sport-utility vehicles: 54.7

ENGINES

	ohv V6
Size, liters/cu. in.	3.4/204
Horsepower @ rpm	185 @ 5200
Torque (lb-ft) @ rpm	210 @ 4000
Availability	S
EPA city/highway mpg	
4-speed automatic	18/24[1]

1. 19/26 w/2WD.

PRICES

Pontiac Aztek	RETAIL PRICE	DEALER INVOICE
2WD Base 4-door hatchback	$21375	$19558
AWD Base 4-door hatchback	24290	22225
Destination charge	685	685

STANDARD EQUIPMENT

Base: 3.4-liter V6 engine, 4-speed automatic transmission, dual front airbags, daytime running lights, front air conditioning, power steering, tilt steering wheel, cloth upholstery, front bucket seats, center console, cupholders, split folding rear seat, power mirrors, power windows, power door locks, remote keyless entry, AM/FM/CD player, digital clock, tachometer, map lights, intermittent wipers, rear defogger, visor mirrors, power decklid release, automatic headlights, theft-deterrent system, roof rails, fog lights, 215/70R16 tires, wheel covers. **AWD** adds: all-wheel drive, front side airbags, antilock 4-wheel disc brakes, alloy wheels.

OPTIONAL EQUIPMENT

Major Packages

	RETAIL PRICE	DEALER INVOICE
1SB Option Group, 2WD	$1225	$1090
AWD	970	863

Cruise control, removable storage console/cooler, cargo nets and tie-downs, rear floormats, rear privacy glass, alloy wheels (2WD).

1SC Option Group, 2WD	3590	3195
AWD	3435	3057

Option Group 1SB plus traction control (2WD), front side airbags (2WD), antilock brakes (2WD), tire-pressure monitor, OnStar assistance system w/one-year service, upgraded upholstery, 6-way power driver seat, front-seat lumbar adjustment, leather-wrapped steering wheel w/radio controls, trip computer, compass, overhead console, driver information center, slide-out rear cargo tray, theft-deterrent system w/alarm, 225/60R17 tires.

Luxury Appointment Group	1395	1242

Leather upholstery, heated front seats, 6-way power passenger seat. Requires 1SC Option Group.

Rally Edition Appearance Pkg.	695	619

Unique front floormats, color-keyed grille, chrome exhaust tips, badging, lowered suspension, 225/60R17 tires, chrome alloy wheels. Requires Option Group.

Enhanced Storage Group	95	85

Cargo cover, front-door utility packs, roof rack. Requires Option Group.

Trailer Pkg.	450	401

Heavy-duty engine-oil cooler and alternator, load-leveling rear suspension, air-inflator kit. Requires Option Group.

Safety

Antilock brakes, 2WD	950	846

Includes front side airbags.

Comfort & Convenience Features

Power sunroof, w/1SB	695	619
w/1SC	285	254

Deletes OnStar assistance system.

Dual-zone manual climate controls	195	174

Includes rear climate controls and vents. Requires 1SC Option Group.

Rear-seat DVD Entertainment System	1295	1153

Requires 1SC Option Group. NA w/power sunroof.

AM/FM/CD/MP3 player, w/1SB	410	365
w/1SC	225	200

Includes leather-wrapped steering w/radio controls, rear-seat radio controls, upgraded speakers. Requires Option Group.

AM/FM w/in-dash 6-disc CD changer, w/1SB	805	716
w/1SC	695	619

Includes leather-wrapped steering wheel w/radio controls, cargo-area radio controls, upgraded speakers. Requires Option Group.

Satellite radio	325	289

Requires monthly fee after 3rd month. Requires Option Group.

Major Packages

	RETAIL PRICE	DEALER INVOICE
Cruise control	$550	$490
Includes rear privacy glass.		
6-way power driver seat	380	338
Includes sliding rear cargo tray. Requires 1SB Option Group.		
Removable storage console/cooler	125	111
Trailer hitch	310	276
Requires Option Group, Trailer Pkg.		
5-spoke alloy wheels	295	263
Includes 225/60R17 tires. Requires 1SB Option Group.		

PONTIAC BONNEVILLE

CLASS: Large car
DRIVE WHEELS: Front-wheel drive
BASE PRICE RANGE: $27,775-$35,395. Built in USA.
ALSO CONSIDER: Chrysler 300, Dodge Magnum, Toyota Avalon

Styling revisions for the midline model top 2005 news for Pontiac's largest sedans. Bonneville comes in three models. SE and SLE have a 205-hp V6. The performance-oriented GXP uses a 275-hp version of Cadillac's 4.6-liter Northstar V8. All have 4-speed automatic transmission, antilock 4-wheel disc brakes, tire-pressure monitor, load-leveling rear suspension, and front bucket seats. SE offers an optional front bench seat for 6-passenger capacity and now shares standard OnStar assistance with other models. Front side airbags are standard on GXP, optional for SE and SLE. Curtain side airbags are unavailable. Traction control is standard for SLE and GXP, optional for SE. Satellite radio is available for all. SEs ride on 16-inch wheels, SLEs 17s, GXPs have 18s. GXPs also have upgraded suspension and brakes, GM's Stabilitrak antiskid system, dual-zone climate control, 12-way power front seats, and leather/suede upholstery. For 2005, the SLE more closely resembles the GXP by virtue of revised nose and tail appearance and a new lower-bodyside treatment. Buick's LeSabre shares Bonneville's underskin design, but has different styling and doesn't offer a V8 model.

RATINGS	SE	SLE	GXP
ACCELERATION	6	6	7
FUEL ECONOMY	5	5	4
RIDE QUALITY	7	6	5

RATINGS (cont.)	SE	SLE	GXP
STEERING/HANDLING	5	6	7
QUIETNESS	6	5	5
CONTROLS/MATERIALS	5	5	5
ROOM/COMFORT (FRONT)	7	7	7
ROOM/COMFORT (REAR)	4	4	4
CARGO ROOM	6	6	6
VALUE WITHIN CLASS	6	5	4

Bonneville's SE model is a good big-car value. The SLE adds useful amenities for a bit more money. But ordering a few popular options pushes both into the price realm of cars with luxury-brand pedigrees, better interiors, and more refinement. The GXP appeals for its V8 power but suffers the same shortfalls as other Bonnevilles, so it doesn't compare well against newer sporty sedans of similar price.

TOTAL	57	55	54

Average total for large cars: 60.9

ENGINES

	ohv V6	dohc V8
Size, liters/cu. in.	3.8/231	4.6/278
Horsepower @ rpm	205 @ 5200	275 @ 5600
Torque (lb-ft) @ rpm	230 @ 4000	300 @ 4000
Availability	S[1]	S[2]
EPA city/highway mpg		
4-speed automatic	20/29	17/24

1. SE, SLE. 2. GXP.

PRICES

Pontiac Bonneville	RETAIL PRICE	DEALER INVOICE
SE 4-door sedan	$27775	$25414
SLE 4-door sedan	30160	27596
GXP 4-door sedan	35395	32386
Destination charge	725	725

STANDARD EQUIPMENT

SE: 3.8-liter V6 engine, 4-speed automatic transmission, dual front airbags, antilock 4-wheel disc brakes, daytime running lights, tire-pressure monitor, air conditioning, power steering, tilt steering wheel, cruise control, cloth upholstery, front bucket seats, 6-way power driver seat w/lumbar adjustment, center console, cupholders, trunk pass-through, power mirrors, power windows, power door locks, remote keyless entry, OnStar assistance system w/one-year service, AM/FM/CD player, digital clock, tachometer, map lights, intermittent wipers, automatic day/night rearview mirror, illuminated visor mirrors, rear defogger, remote decklid release, automatic headlights, floormats, theft-deterrent system, fog lights, load-leveling suspension, 225/60R16 tires.

SLE adds: traction control, leather-wrapped steering wheel w/radio controls, heated power mirrors, compass, rear spoiler, 235/55R17 tires, alloy wheels.

 Specifications begin on page 547.

GXP adds: 4.6-liter V8 engine, antiskid system, front side airbags, upgraded brakes, leather/suede upholstery, dual-zone automatic climate controls, 12-way power front seats, memory system (drive seat, mirrors), Monsoon AM/FM/cassette/CD player, outside-temperature indicator, air-inflator kit, performance suspension, 235/50WR18 tires.

OPTIONAL EQUIPMENT

Major Packages

	RETAIL PRICE	DEALER INVOICE
Option Group 1SC, SE	$1525	$1357
Manufacturer's Discount Price	*1325*	*1179*
Traction control, performance axle ratio, leather upholstery, driver-seat power lumbar support and recline, leather-wrapped steering wheel w/radio controls.		
Leather Appointment Pkg., SE	1025	912
Manufacturer's Discount Price	*850*	*757*
Leather upholstery, driver-seat power lumbar and recline, leather-wrapped steering wheel w/radio controls.		
Premier Edition Pkg., SLE	3985	3547
Manufacturer's Discount Price	*2735*	*2434*
Dual-zone automatic climate controls, leather upholstery, power sunroof, satellite radio (requires monthly fee after 3rd month), special paint, chrome alloy wheels.		
Special Edition Pkg., SLE	3235	2880
Manufacturer's Discount Price	*2735*	*2434*
Premier Edition Pkg. plus universal garage-door opener.		

Powertrain

Traction control, SE	175	156

Safety

Front side airbags, SE, SLE	350	312

Comfort & Convenience Features

Power sunroof	1100	979
Includes universal garage-door opener.		
Dual-zone automatic climate controls, SE, SLE	365	325
SE requires Option Group 1SC.		
Power passenger seat, SE, SLE	550	490
Includes heated front seats.		
Front split bench seat, SE	150	134
NA w/Option Group 1SC.		
Heated front seats, GXP	295	263
AM/FM/cassette/CD player, SE, SLE	150	134
12-disc CD changer, GXP	595	530
Satellite radio	325	289
Requires monthly fee after 3rd month.		
Head-up instrument display, GXP	325	289

Appearance & Special Purpose

Rear spoiler, SE	225	200
Alloy wheels, SE	375	334
Chrome alloy wheels, SLE	595	530

PONTIAC G6

CLASS: Midsize car
DRIVE WHEELS: Front-wheel drive
BASE PRICE RANGE: $20,675-$23,300. Built in USA.
ALSO CONSIDER: Honda Accord, Mazda 6, Nissan Altima

Pontiac begins replacing its best-selling car during the 2005 model year with the G6. This new midsize sedan takes over from the compact Grand Am, which comes only as a coupe for '05. G6 shares a basic front-wheel-drive design with the Chevrolet Malibu and the 9-3 from GM-owned Saab. G6 has a slightly longer wheelbase than Pontiac's other midsize car, the Grand Prix, but is 9.3-inches shorter in overall length. G6 offers base and sportier GT models. Both use the 200-hp 3.5-liter V6 and 4-speed automatic transmission offered in Malibu. The GT adds a manual shift gate and a firmer suspension with 17-inch wheels vs. the base's 16s. Both versions have 4-wheel disc brakes. The GT comes with antilock brakes, traction control, and power-adjustable pedals, all of which are available for the base G6. Front torso side airbags and head-protecting curtain side airbags are available as a single option. Leather upholstery and OnStar assistance are excluisve GT options. Satellite radio and remote starting are available on both models. So are a conventional sunroof or a "panoramic" power sunroof with a tilt-up front section and three rear-sliding panels that open to near the full length of the passenger compartment. Due later in calendar 2005 are coupe and retractable-hardtop convertible body styles, along with a 4-cyl SE model and a high-performance GTP with a 3.9-liter V6 and available 6-speed manual transmission. This evaluation is based on preview test drives.

RATINGS	Base w/ABS, sunroof	GT w/leather, panoramic sunroof
ACCELERATION	6	6
FUEL ECONOMY	6	6
RIDE QUALITY	6	6
STEERING/HANDLING	7	7
QUIETNESS	7	7
CONTROLS/MATERIALS	7	7
ROOM/COMFORT (FRONT)	7	7
ROOM/COMFORT (REAR)	6	6

 Specifications begin on page 547.

RATINGS (cont.)	Base w/ABS, sunroof	GT w/leather, panoramic sunroof
CARGO ROOM	3	3
VALUE WITHIN CLASS	6	6

G6 lacks the top-notch refinement of an Accord or Camry, but is competitive otherwise. It costs less than most V6 rivals, and a wide selection of safety and convenience features adds to its appeal.

TOTAL	61	61

Average total for midsize cars: 57.2

ENGINES

	ohv V6
Size, liters/cu. in.	3.5/213
Horsepower @ rpm	200 @ 4800
Torque (lb-ft) @ rpm	220 @ 4400
Availability	S
EPA city/highway mpg	
4-speed automatic	22/32[1]

1. Base; GT 21/29.

PRICES

Pontiac G6

	RETAIL PRICE	DEALER INVOICE
Base 4-door sedan	$20675	$18918
GT 4-door sedan	23300	21320
Destination charge	625	625

STANDARD EQUIPMENT

Base: 3.5-liter V6 engine, 4-speed automatic transmission, dual front airbags, 4-wheel disc brakes, daytime running lights, air conditioning, power steering, tilt/telescope steering wheel, cruise control, cloth upholstery, front bucket seats, center console, cupholders, split folding rear seat, power mirrors, power windows, power door locks, remote keyless entry, AM/FM/CD player, digital clock, tachometer, variable-intermittent wipers, visor mirrors, rear defogger, automatic headlights, theft-deterrent system, fog lights, 215/60R16 tires, wheel covers.

GT adds: 4-speed automatic transmission w/manual-shift capability, traction control, antilock 4-wheel disc brakes, 4-way power driver seat, power-adjustable pedals, Monsoon sound system, illuminated visor mirrors, floormats, rear spoiler, sport suspension, 225/50R17 tires, alloy wheels.

OPTIONAL EQUIPMENT

Major Packages

	RETAIL PRICE	DEALER INVOICE
Premium Value Pkg. w/power sunroof, Base	$1575	$1402
Manufacturer's Discount Price	*975*	*868*
GT	2345	2087
Manufacturer's Discount Price	*1345*	*1197*

Power sunroof, OnStar assistance system (GT), AM/FM radio w/in-dash 6-disc CD changer, alloy wheels (Base), chrome alloy wheels (GT).

OPTIONAL EQUIPMENT (cont.)

	RETAIL PRICE	DEALER INVOICE
Premium Value Pkg. w/power panoramic roof, Base	$2375	$2114
Manufacturer's Discount Price	*1775*	*1580*
GT	3145	2799
Manufacturer's Discount Price	*2145*	*1909*
Replaces power sunroof w/power panoramic roof.		
Convenience Pkg., Base	375	334
4-way power driver seat, power-adjustable pedals, cargo net, floormats.		
Driver's Pkg., Base	875	779
Manufacturer's Discount Price	*525*	*467*
Convenience Pkg. plus alloy wheels.		
Safety		
Curtain side airbags	690	614
Includes front side airbags. Base requires Convenience Pkg., antilock brakes.		
Antilock 4-wheel disc brakes, Base	400	356
Includes traction control.		
Comfort & Convenience Features		
OnStar assistance system, GT	695	619
Includes one-year service.		
Leather upholstery, GT	1365	1215
Includes 6-way power driver seat, leather-wrapped steering wheel.		
Power sunroof	700	623
Power panoramic roof	1500	1335
Remote starting	150	134
AM/FM radio w/in-dash 6-disc CD changer, Base	375	334
Upgraded sound system, Base	75	67
Requires satellite radio.		
Satellite radio	325	289
Requires monthly fee after 3rd month. Base requires upgraded sound system or AM/FM radio w/in-dash 6-disc CD changer. NA w/power panoramic roof.		
Appearance & Special Purpose		
Alloy wheels, Base	500	445
Chrome alloy wheels, GT	650	579

PONTIAC GRAND AM

CLASS: Midsize car
DRIVE WHEELS: Front-wheel drive
BASE PRICE RANGE: $22,365-$23,615. Built in USA.
ALSO CONSIDER: Hyundai Sonata, Mazda 6

Retail sales of the sedan body style cease during 2005 as Pontiac begins to phase-in Grand Am's replacement, a new car called the G6. Grand Am now offers only coupes in GT and GT1 trim. They come with a 175-hp V6, auto-

matic transmission, traction control, and antilock 4-wheel disc brakes. SC/T option packages include such features as a hood made of a plasticlike composite material, plus rear spoiler, chrome wheels and exhaust tips, SC/T logos, and satellite radio. The last is also a separate option, as is a CD/MP3 player. Side airbags are not offered.

RATINGS

	GT
ACCELERATION	6
FUEL ECONOMY	5
RIDE QUALITY	5
STEERING/HANDLING	6
QUIETNESS	4
CONTROLS/MATERIALS	3
ROOM/COMFORT (FRONT)	5
ROOM/COMFORT (REAR)	3
CARGO ROOM	4
VALUE WITHIN CLASS	4

Grand Am is overdue for replacement, lacking the refinement, build quality, and interior space of most import rivals. Main attractions are strong V6 power, competent road manners, and lots of equipment at attractive prices.

TOTAL	45

Average total for midsize cars: 57.2

ENGINES

	ohv V6
Size, liters/cu. in.	3.4/204
Horsepower @ rpm	175 @ 4800
Torque (lb-ft) @ rpm	205 @ 4000
Availability	S
EPA city/highway mpg	
4-speed automatic	20/29

PRICES

Pontiac Grand Am	RETAIL PRICE	DEALER INVOICE
GT 2-door coupe	$22365	$20464
GT1 2-door coupe	23615	21608
Destination charge	625	625

STANDARD EQUIPMENT

GT: 3.4-liter V6 engine, 4-speed automatic transmission, traction control, dual front airbags, antilock 4-wheel disc brakes, daytime running lights, air conditioning, power steering, tilt leather-wrapped steering wheel, cloth upholstery, front bucket seats, power height-adjustable driver seat, center console, cupholders, split folding rear seat, power mirrors, power windows, power door locks, remote keyless entry, Monsoon AM/FM/CD player, digital clock, tachometer, variable-intermittent wipers, driver-side visor mirror, rear defogger, automatic headlights, floormats, rear spoiler, 225/50R16 tires, alloy wheels.

GT1 adds: 6-way power driver seat, power sunroof, AM/FM/CD/MP3 player, steering-wheel radio controls.

OPTIONAL EQUIPMENT

Major Packages	RETAIL PRICE	DEALER INVOICE
Solid Value Appearance Pkg., GT	$1550	$1380
Manufacturer's Discount Price	*925*	*823*
AM/FM/CD/MP3 player, power sunroof, chrome alloy wheels.		
SC/T Solid Value Appearance Pkg., GT1	2960	2635
Manufacturer's Discount Price	*2250*	*2003*
SC/T Appearance Pkg. plus leather upholstery, satellite radio, chrome exhaust tips, chrome alloy wheels. Satellite radio requires monthly fee after 3rd month.		
SC/T Appearance Pkg.	1245	1108
Manufacturer's Discount Price	*1100*	*979*
Composite hood, aero rear spoiler.		
Comfort & Convenience Features		
Power sunroof, GT	700	623
Leather upholstery	595	530
AM/FM/CD/MP3 player, GT	200	178
Satellite radio	325	289
Requires monthly fee after 3rd month.		
Appearance & Special Purpose		
Chrome alloy wheels	650	579

PONTIAC GRAND PRIX

CLASS: Midsize car
DRIVE WHEELS: Front-wheel drive
BASE PRICE RANGE: $22,900-$26,560. Built in Canada.
ALSO CONSIDER: Honda Accord, Nissan Altima, Toyota Camry

Standard OnStar assistance and optional remote starting are among new 2005 features for the larger of Pontiac's midsize sedans. Grand Prix comes in three models, all with a 3.8-liter V6. Base and GT versions have 200 hp. The GTP is supercharged for 260 hp. A 4-speed automatic is the sole transmission. Steering-wheel paddles for manual shifting—Pontiac's TAPshift feature—

part of the GTP's available Competition Group. The option also includes a performance-tuned suspension and antiskid system. All models have 4-wheel disc brakes. ABS and traction control are optional for the base Grand Prix, standard otherwise. Base and GT have 16-inch wheels, the GTP has 17s. A tire-pressure monitor is standard on GT and GTP, available on base. All wheel designs are new for '05. Head-protecting curtain side airbags are available for GT and GTP; torso side airbags are not offered. The remote starting system operates from the keyfob and is joined as a new option by a navigation system and dual-zone automatic climate control. A CD/MP3 stereo is also newly available, and all models gain rear-seat cupholders as well as standard OnStar. Satellite radio and a head-up instrument display are also optional.

RATINGS	GT	GTP w/Competition Group
ACCELERATION	6	7
FUEL ECONOMY	5	4
RIDE QUALITY	7	6
STEERING/HANDLING	7	7
QUIETNESS	7	6
CONTROLS/MATERIALS	5	5
ROOM/COMFORT (FRONT)	7	7
ROOM/COMFORT (REAR)	3	3
CARGO ROOM	5	5
VALUE WITHIN CLASS	6	5

It trails our top-rated Honda Accord and Toyota Camry in quality of interior materials, and rear-seat comfort is substandard. But the competitively priced Grand Prix delivers good performance, a comfortable ride, cargo versatility, and plenty of features.

TOTAL	58	55

Average total for midsize cars: 57.2

ENGINES	ohv V6	Supercharged ohv V6
Size, liters/cu. in.	3.8/231	3.8/231
Horsepower @ rpm	200 @ 5200	260 @ 5400
Torque (lb-ft) @ rpm	230 @ 4000	280 @ 3600
Availability	S[1]	S[2]
EPA city/highway mpg		
4-speed automatic	20/30	18/28

1. Base, GT. 2. GTP.

PRICES

Pontiac Grand Prix

	RETAIL PRICE	DEALER INVOICE
Base 4-door sedan	$22900	$20954
GT 4-door sedan	24800	22692
GTP 4-door sedan	26560	24302
Destination charge	660	660

STANDARD EQUIPMENT

Base: 3.8-liter V6 engine, 4-speed automatic transmission, dual front airbags, 4-wheel disc brakes, daytime running lights, emergency inside trunk release, air conditioning, OnStar assistance system w/one-year service, power steering, tilt steering wheel, cruise control, cloth upholstery, front bucket seats, center console, cupholders, split folding rear seat, power mirrors, power windows, power door locks, remote keyless entry, AM/FM/CD player, digital clock, tachometer, intermittent wipers, rear defogger, automatic headlights, theft-deterrent system, rear spoiler, fog lights, 225/60R16 tires, wheel covers.

GT adds: traction control, antilock 4-wheel disc brakes, tire-pressure monitor, leather-wrapped steering wheel w/radio controls, 6-way power driver seat, fold-flat front passenger seat, AM/FM/CD/MP3 player, illuminated visor mirrors, map lights, floormats, alloy wheels.

GTP adds: 3.8-liter supercharged V6 engine, driver-seat power lumbar adjustment, AM/FM/CD player, 225/55HR17 tires.

OPTIONAL EQUIPMENT

Major Packages

	RETAIL PRICE	DEALER INVOICE
Competition Group, GTP	$1395	$1242
Antiskid system, upgraded variable-assist power steering, manual-shift capability, special axle ratio, head-up instrument display, trip computer, red-painted brake calipers, performance suspension, 225/55VR17 tires. NA w/chrome alloy wheels.		
Driver's Plus Pkg. PCM, Base	1250	1113
Manufacturer's Discount Price	*500*	*445*
6-way power driver seat, floormats, polished alloy wheels.		
Leather Trim Pkg., GT	795	708
GTP	665	592
Leather upholstery, heated front seats, driver-seat power lumbar adjustment (GT).		
Comfort and Info Pkg. PDE, GT, GTP	550	490
Dual-zone automatic climate controls, trip computer.		
Comfort and Infotech Pkg. PDF, GT, GTP	875	779
Dual-zone automatic climate controls, head-up instrument display, trip computer.		
Premium Audio Pkg., GT, GTP	695	619
AM/FM radio w/in-dash 6-disc CD changer, Monsoon sound system.		
Custom Accessories Pkg., GT, GTP	675	601
Unique rear spoiler, grille inserts, stainless-steel exhaust tips.		

 Specifications begin on page 547.

Safety	RETAIL PRICE	DEALER INVOICE
Curtain side airbags, GT, GTP	$395	$352
Antilock brakes, Base	600	534
Includes traction control, tire-pressure monitor.		
Comfort & Convenience Features		
Power sunroof, GT, GTP	895	797
Navigation system, GT, GTP	2390	2127
Includes Monsoon sound system. NA w/Premium Audio Pkg.		
Dual-zone automatic climate controls, GTP	275	245
AM/FM/CD/MP3 player, GTP	150	134
Satellite radio, GT, GTP	325	289
Requires monthly fee after 3rd month.		
Remote starting	150	133
Appearance & Special Purpose		
Polished alloy wheels, GT, GTP	495	440
GTP w/Comp. Group	275	245

PONTIAC GTO

CLASS: Sporty/performance car
DRIVE WHEELS: Rear-wheel drive
2004 BASE PRICE: $31,795. Built in Australia.
ALSO CONSIDER: Ford Mustang, Nissan 350Z

Pontiac's reborn muscle car gets more power for 2005. GTO is based on a car built by Holden, GM's Australian branch, and is offered only as a midsize coupe. A modified Chevrolet Corvette V8, now up from 5.7 to 6.0 liters and 350 to 400 horsepower, drives the GTO's rear wheels via a 4-speed automatic transmission or an available 6-speed manual. Antilock 4-wheel disc brakes, traction control, and a limited-slip differential are standard. Performance tires with 17-inch wheels are the only wheel-tire combination. GTO seats four and comes with leather upholstery, in-dash CD changer, and remote keyless entry. Side airbags, sunroof, and antiskid system are unavailable. New for '05 is a standard hood with twin open air scoops. Pontiac says the scoops provide engine cooling, but no performance advantage. A scoopless hood is a no-cost option.

RATINGS	Base, man.	Base, auto.
ACCELERATION	8	8

RATINGS (cont.)

	Base, man.	Base, auto.
FUEL ECONOMY	4	4
RIDE QUALITY	5	5
STEERING/HANDLING	8	8
QUIETNESS	4	4
CONTROLS/MATERIALS	6	6
ROOM/COMFORT (FRONT)	7	7
ROOM/COMFORT (REAR)	3	3
CARGO ROOM	2	2
VALUE WITHIN CLASS	9	9

A nicely appointed interior with a usable back seat are pluses in this class. But it is GTO's blend of American-V8 go and European road manners at a reasonable price that earn it our Best Buy rating.

TOTAL	56	56

Average total for sporty/performance cars: 48.5

ENGINES

	ohv V8
Size, liters/cu. in.	6.0/364
Horsepower @ rpm	400 @ 5200
Torque (lb-ft) @ rpm	395 @ 4000
Availability	S
EPA city/highway mpg	
6-speed manual	17/25
4-speed automatic	NA

2005 prices unavailable at time of publication.

2004 PRICES

Pontiac GTO

	RETAIL PRICE	DEALER INVOICE
Base 2-door coupe	$31795	$29410
Destination charge	700	700

Add $1000 Gas-Guzzler Tax w/standard automatic transmission.

STANDARD EQUIPMENT

Base: 5.7-liter V8 engine, 4-speed automatic transmission, traction control, limited-slip differential, dual front airbags, antilock 4-wheel disc brakes, daytime running lights, air conditioning, power steering, tilt/telescope steering wheel w/radio controls, cruise control, leather upholstery, 8-way power front bucket seats w/lumbar adjustment, rear bucket seats, center console, cupholders, power mirrors, power windows, power door locks, remote keyless entry, Blaupunkt AM/FM radio w/in-dash 6-disc CD changer, digital clock, tachometer, trip computer, variable-intermittent wipers, illuminated visor mirrors, map lights, rear defogger, automatic headlights, floormats, theft-deterrent system, fog lights, rear spoiler, 225/50WR17 tires, alloy wheels.

OPTIONAL EQUIPMENT

	RETAIL PRICE	DEALER INVOICE
6-speed manual transmission *Deletes Gas-Guzzler Tax.*	$695	$619

 Specifications begin on page 547.

PONTIAC MONTANA SV6

CLASS: Minivan
DRIVE WHEELS: Front-wheel drive, all-wheel drive
BASE PRICE RANGE: $24,520-$30,210. Built in USA.
ALSO CONSIDER: Chrysler Town & Country, Dodge Caravan, Honda Odyssey, Toyota Sienna

Pontiac's minivan becomes what GM calls a "crossover sport van" for 2005. Montana SV6 uses the 1997-2004 Pontiac Montana's extended-length body, but a new SUV-flavored nose adds slightly to length, wheelbase, and height. It retains a 4-speed automatic transmission, but replaces Montana's 185-hp 3.4-liter V6 with a 200-hp 3.5 V6.

SV6 offers 1SA and 1SB models, and is available with front-wheel drive with optional antiskid system or GM's Versatrak all-wheel drive. Antilock 4-wheel disc brakes are standard. Front side airbags with head and torso protection are optional, but curtain side airbags are not offered. OnStar assistance, air conditioning, power windows and locks, CD/MP3 player, and rear DVD entertainment are standard. Also standard are 17-inch wheels, sliding rear side doors, and 3-row seating for seven. Power sliding doors are available, as are 2nd-row bucket seats instead of the standard bench. The 3rd-row seat is a 50/50 split bench that folds flat atop the cargo floor. All 2nd- and 3rd-row seats can be removed. An included roof-rail system offers optional snap-on storage modules. Also available are satellite radio and a remote starting system that operates from the keyfob. SV6 shares its basic design with the Chevrolet Uplander, Buick Terraza, and Saturn Relay. We have not yet tested a Montana SV6, but performance and accommodations should be similar to those reported in our evaluation of the Relay.

ENGINES

	ohv V6
Size, liters/cu. in.	3.5/213
Horsepower @ rpm	200 @ 5200
Torque (lb-ft) @ rpm	220 @ 4400
Availability	S
EPA city/highway mpg	
4-speed automatic	NA

PRICES

Pontiac Montana SV6

	RETAIL PRICE	DEALER INVOICE
FWD 1SA 4-door van	$24520	$22191
AWD 1SA 4-door van	27700	25069
FWD 1SB 4-door van	27890	25240
AWD 1SB 4-door van	30210	27340
Destination charge	715	715

STANDARD EQUIPMENT

1SA: 3.5-liter V6 engine, 4-speed automatic transmission, dual front airbags, antilock 4-wheel disc brakes, daytime running lights, front air conditioning, power steering, tilt steering wheel, cruise control, 7-passenger seating, quad bucket seats, center console, cupholders, 3rd-row split folding seat, power mirrors, power windows, power door locks, remote keyless entry, OnStar assistance system w/one-year service, AM/FM/CD/MP3 player, rear radio controls, digital clock, tachometer, rear-seat DVD entertainment system, visor mirrors, automatic headlights, floormats, theft-deterrent system, roof rails, 225/60R17 white-letter tires, wheel covers. **AWD** adds: all-wheel drive, air-inflator kit, load-leveling rear suspension, alloy wheels.

1SB adds: rear air conditioning and heater, leather-wrapped steering wheel w/radio controls, 6-way power driver seat, 2nd-row center console, heated power mirrors, power sliding passenger-side door, illuminated visor mirrors, folding tray, rear defogger, intermittent rear wiper, rear privacy glass, air-inflator kit, performance suspension, load-leveling rear suspension, alloy wheels. **AWD**: all-wheel drive. *Deletes:* performance suspension.

OPTIONAL EQUIPMENT

Major Packages

	RETAIL PRICE	DEALER INVOICE
Climate Pkg., 1SA	$1055	$939

Rear air conditioning, heated power mirrors, rear defogger, intermittent rear wiper, rear privacy glass.

Storage and Convenience Pkg., 1SA	1110	988

Power sliding passenger-side door, leather-wrapped steering wheel w/radio controls, illuminated visor mirrors, 2nd-row center console, removable overhead console, cargo organizer. Requires Climate Pkg. Std. 1SB.

Premium Convenience Pkg., 1SB	815	725

Rear-obstacle-detection system, power sliding driver-side door, trip computer, universal garage-door opener, trip computer, driver information center, alarm.

Premium Seating Pkg., 1SB	1075	957

Leather upholstery, 6-way power passenger seat. Deletes 2nd-row center console. Requires front side airbags, quad captain chairs.

Powertrain

Traction control, FWD	195	174

 Specifications begin on page 547.

Safety	RETAIL PRICE	DEALER INVOICE
Front side airbags	$350	$312
Antiskid system, FWD 1SB	450	401
Requires traction control.		

Comfort & Convenience Features

6-way power driver seat, 1SA	355	316
Remote starting, 1SB	175	156
Removable overhead consoles	100	89
Two consoles, first-aid kit.		
AM/FM radio w/in-dash 6-disc CD changer, 1SB	295	263
Satellite radio	325	289
Requires monthly fee after 3rd month.		
Heated front seats, 1SB	275	245
Requires Premium Seating Pkg.		
Quad captain chairs ABD, 1SB	475	423
Deletes 2nd-row center console.		
2nd-row center console, 1SA	200	178
Rear 115-volt power outlet, 1SB	175	156

Appearance & Special Purpose

Rear spoiler, 1SB	250	223
Alloy wheels, FWD 1SA	325	289
Chrome alloy wheels, 1SB	650	579

PONTIAC SUNFIRE

CLASS: Compact car
DRIVE WHEELS: Front-wheel drive
BASE PRICE RANGE: $10,895-$15,085. Built in USA.
ALSO CONSIDER: Ford Focus, Honda Civic, Volkswagen Jetta and Golf

A sport package with larger tires and dress-up trim joins Sunfire's options list for 2005. Pontiac's smallest car comes as a 2-dr coupe. It shares an underskin design with Chevrolet's Cavalier sedans. Cavalier will be replaced during the 2005 model year by Chevy's new Cobalt coupes and sedans. Pontiac is not slated to get a version of the Cobalt. Sunfires use a 140-hp 4-cyl engine. A special-value model called 1SV comes with manual transmission and CD player, and cannot be ordered with any options. The costlier base coupe is available with option packages labeled 1SB and 1SC. They include automatic transmission, but allow manual transmission as a credit option. The 1SC package includes ABS and traction control, which are optional with 1SB. It also includes alloy instead of steel wheels, plus a firmer suspension. Front side airbags and OnStar assistance are available as part of the Protection Package option. Satellite radio is also available. Added midyear was a Sport Appearance Package option. It includes 16-inch chrome wheels vs. standard 15s, the firmer suspension, sport interior trim, and chrome-tipped dual exhausts. A sunroof bundled with CD/MP3 player is available and is required with the Protection Package. Sunfire performance mirrors that of comparably equipped Cavaliers.

RATINGS

	Base w/1SB, auto.	Base w/1SC, man.
ACCELERATION	4	5
FUEL ECONOMY	5	6
RIDE QUALITY	4	3
STEERING/HANDLING	5	6
QUIETNESS	3	3
CONTROLS/MATERIALS	4	4
ROOM/COMFORT (FRONT)	3	3
ROOM/COMFORT (REAR)	2	2
CARGO ROOM	3	3
VALUE WITHIN CLASS	3	3

Sunfire touts "expressive" styling and dollar value, but lacks the space efficiency, refinement, and workmanship of most rivals. Worse, ABS, traction control and front side airbags are available only in costly option groups. Cavalier charges far less for those safety musts and offers the sedan body style most small-car buyers prefer, but is also far from class-competitive.

TOTAL	36	38

Average total for compact cars: 48.4

ENGINES

	dohc I4
Size, liters/cu. in.	2.2/134
Horsepower @ rpm	140 @ 5600
Torque (lb-ft) @ rpm	150 @ 4000
Availability	S
EPA city/highway mpg	
5-speed manual	24/33
4-speed automatic	23/32

PRICES

Pontiac Sunfire	RETAIL PRICE	DEALER INVOICE
1SV 2-door coupe	$10895	$10187
Base 2-door coupe	15085	13954
Destination charge	565	565

 Specifications begin on page 547.

STANDARD EQUIPMENT

Base: 2.2-liter 4-cylinder engine, 5-speed manual transmission, dual front airbags, daytime running lights, air conditioning, power steering, cloth upholstery, bucket seats, center console, split folding rear seat, AM/FM radio, digital clock, tachometer, rear defogger, power decklid release, theft-deterrent system, fog lights, rear spoiler, 195/65R15 tires, wheel covers.

1SV adds: AM/FM/CD player.

OPTIONAL EQUIPMENT

Major Packages

	RETAIL PRICE	DEALER INVOICE
1SB Option Group, Base	$1200	$1068
4-speed automatic transmission, traction control (when ordered w/antilock brakes), tilt steering wheel, cupholder, AM/FM/CD player, easy-entry passenger-side seat, visor mirrors, floormats, chrome exhaust tip.		
1SC Option Group, Base	2495	2221
1SB Option Group plus traction control, antilock brakes, tilt leather-wrapped steering wheel, leather-wrapped shifter and parking-brake handle, cruise control, power door locks, remote keyless entry, sport bucket seats w/driver-side lumbar adjustment, variable-intermittent wipers, overhead console, map lights, cargo net, theft-deterrent system w/alarm, sport suspension, alloy wheels.		
Protection Pkg., Base	780	694
OnStar assistance system w/one-year service, front side airbags. Requires Sun and Sound Pkg. Requires 1SC Option Group or 1SB Option Group and Security Pkg.		
Sun and Sound Pkg., Base	875	779
Manufacturer's Discount Price	*585*	*521*
Power sunroof, AM/FM/CD/MP3 player. Requires 1SB or 1SC Option Group.		
Security Pkg., Base	465	414
Manufacturer's Discount Price	*365*	*325*
Power door locks, remote keyless entry, theft-deterrent system w/alarm. Requires 1SB Option Group.		
Power Pkg., Base	430	383
Manufacturer's Discount Price	*250*	*223*
Power mirrors and windows. Requires 1SC Option Group or 1SB Option Group and Security Pkg.		
Sport Appearance Pkg., Base w/1SB	795	708
Base w/1SC	595	530
Front sport seats, leather-wrapped steering wheel, chrome dual exhaust tips, sport suspension, 205/55R16 tires, chrome alloy wheels.		

Powertrain

5-speed manual transmission, Base (credit)	*(810)*	*(721)*
Requires 1SB or 1SC Option Group.		

Safety

Antilock brakes, Base	400	356
Requires 1SB Option Group.		

Comfort & Convenience Features	RETAIL PRICE	DEALER INVOICE
Cruise control, Base	$275	$245
Requires 1SB Option Group.		
Monsoon sound system, Base	195	174
Requires 1SC Option Group or 1SB Option Group, Security Pkg., and Sun and Sound Pkg.		
Satellite radio, Base	325	289
Requires 1SB Option Group or 1SC Option Group. Requires monthly service fee after 3rd month.		
Appearance & Special Purpose		
Alloy wheels, Base	375	334
Requires Option Group 1SB.		

PONTIAC VIBE

CLASS: Compact car
DRIVE WHEELS: Front-wheel drive, all-wheel drive
BASE PRICE RANGE: $17,000-$20,325. Built in USA.
ALSO CONSIDER: Chrysler PT Cruiser, Subaru Forester

Additional safety features and revised styling mark the 2005 edition of Pontiac's crossover wagon. Vibe shares its basic design with Toyota's Matrix and offers front- or all-wheel drive. Base and GT models are featured, both with a Toyota-sourced 4-cyl engine. The front-drive base model has 130 hp and a 5-speed manual transmission or optional 4-speed automatic. The AWD base model has 123 hp and automatic transmission only. The sportier Vibe GT has 170 hp, front-drive, and a 6-speed manual transmission. AWD Vibes are not intended for off-roading and lack low-range gearing. AWD and GT Vibes come with ABS and for '05 gain a standard tire-pressure monitor; that combination is optional on the base 2WD model. GTs include rear disc brakes instead of drums and, along with front-drive base models, are available for the first time with an antiskid system. Head-protecting curtain side airbags are another new '05 option; they team with carryover front torso side airbags. Front and rear styling are freshened, and leather upholstery and OnStar assistance are newly available. Vibes have a swing-up tailgate with separate-opening window. They come with 16-inch wheels; 17s are optional with front-drive. Among dealer-installed accessories is a supercharger for front-drive base models that boosts horsepower to 175. Vibe's performance and accommodations mirror those of comparably equipped Matrix models.

 Specifications begin on page 547.

RATINGS

	FWD Base, auto.	GT w/17-inch wheels
ACCELERATION	4	5
FUEL ECONOMY	7	6
RIDE QUALITY	5	4
STEERING/HANDLING	5	6
QUIETNESS	4	3
CONTROLS/MATERIALS	6	6
ROOM/COMFORT (FRONT)	6	6
ROOM/COMFORT (REAR)	5	5
CARGO ROOM	7	7
VALUE WITHIN CLASS	10	9

Any example of this Pontiac/Toyota crossover is a good alternative to a small wagon or compact SUV. High utility, Toyota-reliable engineering, and available AWD are assets, as are the new antiskid system and front curtain side airbags. On the downside, there's no surplus of power from engines that are somewhat noisy. And note that Vibes have higher base prices than the Matrix, though the Pontiacs generally have more standard equipment than comparable Matrix models and more-generous factory incentives.

TOTAL	59	57

Average total for compact cars: 48.4

ENGINES

	dohc I4	dohc I4
Size, liters/cu. in.	1.8/109	1.8/110
Horsepower @ rpm	130 @ 6000	170 @ 7600
Torque (lb-ft) @ rpm	125 @ 4200	127 @ 4400
Availability	S[1]	S[2]
EPA city/highway mpg		
5-speed manual	29/36	
6-speed manual		25/30
4-speed automatic	28/33[3]	

1. Base models; 123 hp and 118 lb-ft w/AWD. 2. GT. 3. 26/31 mpg w/AWD.

PRICES

Pontiac Vibe	RETAIL PRICE	DEALER INVOICE
FWD Base 4-door wagon	$17000	$15895
AWD Base 4-door wagon	20325	19004
GT 4-door wagon	19975	18677
Destination charge	560	560

Early production models require Premium Monotone Appearance Pkg.

STANDARD EQUIPMENT

Base: 1.8-liter 4-cylinder 130-horsepower engine, 5-speed manual transmission, dual front airbags, daytime running lights, air conditioning, power steering, tilt steering wheel, cloth upholstery, front bucket seats, height-adjustable driver seat, fold-flat passenger seat, center console, cupholders, split folding rear seat, power mirrors, AM/FM/CD player, digital clock, tachometer, outside-temperature indicator, variable-intermittent wipers, visor mirrors, map lights, cargo cover, rear defogger, variable-intermittent rear wiper, automatic headlights, floormats, roof rack, fog lights, 205/55R16 tires, wheel covers. **AWD** adds: all-wheel drive, 1.8-liter 4-cylinder 123-horsepower engine, 4-speed automatic transmission, antilock brakes, tire-pressure monitor.

GT adds: 1.8-liter 4-cylinder 170-horsepower engine, 6-speed manual transmission, antilock 4-wheel disc brakes, tire-pressure monitor, leather-wrapped steering wheel, alloy wheels.

OPTIONAL EQUIPMENT

Major Packages	RETAIL PRICE	DEALER INVOICE
Power Group Value Pkg.	$1150	$1024
Manufacturer's Discount Price	*850*	*757*
Cruise control, power windows and door locks, remote keyless entry.		
Moons and Tunes Value Pkg	1140	1015
Manufacturer's Discount Price	*840*	*748*
Power sunroof, premium sound system.		
Premium Monotone Appearance Pkg.	325	289
Color-keyed bodyside cladding, bumpers, and trim.		
Sport Pkg.	1890	1682
Manufacturer's Discount Price, ordered w/stainless steel exhaust tips	*1590*	*1416*
Fascia and rocker-panel extensions, two rear spoilers. Requires Premium Monotone Appearance Pkg.		
Powertrain		
4-speed automatic transmission, FWD Base	850	757
Safety		
Front side airbags	745	663
Includes curtain side airbags.		
Antilock brakes, FWD Base	525	467
Includes tire-pressure monitor.		
Antiskid system, FWD Base, GT	495	441
NA w/17-inch alloy wheels.		
Comfort & Convenience Features		
Navigation system	1650	1469
Includes AM/FM radio w/trunk-mounted 6-disc CD changer. NA w/Moon and Tunes Value Pkg., OnStar assistance system, satellite radio.		
OnStar assistance system	695	619
Requires Power Group Value Pkg.		
AM/FM radio w/in-dash 6-disc CD changer	325	289
Requires Moons and Tunes Value Pkg.		
Satellite radio	325	289
Requires monthly service fee after 3rd month.		
Leather upholstery	700	623

 Specifications begin on page 547.

Appearance & Special Features

	RETAIL PRICE	DEALER INVOICE
16-inch alloy wheels, Base	$440	$391
17-inch alloy wheels, FWD Base	825	734
GT	440	392
Include 215/50R17 tires.		

PORSCHE 911

CLASS: Premium sporty/performance car
DRIVE WHEELS: Rear-wheel drive, all-wheel drive
BASE PRICE: NA. Built in Germany.
ALSO CONSIDER: BMW 6-Series, Chevrolet Corvette, Mercedes-Benz SL-Class

This iconic sports car begins another design transition for 2005, blending new-generation rear-drive models into a lineup with carryover all-wheel-drive versions. All 911s have a rear-mounted, horizontally opposed 6-cyl engine. For '05, the base rear-drive coupe is redesigned with subtly altered styling and dimensions, plus revamped dashboard and seats. It's offered as the Carerra with a 325-hp 3.6-liter engine, and as the new Carerra S with a 355-hp 3.8. Retaining a vintage-1999 design are Turbo S coupe and cabriolet. These have a twin-turbocharged 3.6 liter and AWD. Turbo models have 444 hp. A 6-speed manual transmission is standard on all 911s. A 5-speed automatic with manual shift gate and steering-wheel buttons is optional.

Antilock 4-wheel disc brakes, antiskid/traction control, and front side airbags are standard. Carreras introduce additional side airbags that deploy from the window sills for head protection. Convertibles include a power top and heated glass rear window. Standard on Carrera S and optional for the base coupe is a new active suspension with a lower ride height, plus shock absorbers that adjust firmness within driver-selectable Normal and Sport modes. Carrera S also has 19-inch standard wheels vs. 18s for other models. Optional for both Carreras is a Sport Chrono Package Plus that allows altering various engine and chassis electronic controls for higher-performance driving. It includes a dashboard-mounted stopwatch. All 911s offer a navigation system. We have not yet tested the redesigned Carreras.

RATINGS

	Turbo S Cabriolet, man.
ACCELERATION	10
FUEL ECONOMY	4
RIDE QUALITY	2

RATINGS (cont.)

	Turbo S Cabriolet, man.
STEERING/HANDLING	10
QUIETNESS	2
CONTROLS/MATERIALS	4
ROOM/COMFORT (FRONT)	4
ROOM/COMFORT (REAR)	1
CARGO ROOM	1
VALUE WITHIN CLASS	4

Desirable for their high performance alone, 911s also offer prestige, solid construction, and proven reliability. You'll pay plenty, but these cars retain lots of value at resale time.

TOTAL	42

Average total for premium sporty/performance cars: 48.3

ENGINES

	dohc H6	dohc H6	Turbocharged dohc H6
Size, liters/cu. in.	3.6/219	3.8/233	3.6/220
Horsepower @ rpm	325 @ 6800	355 @ 6600	444 @ 5700
Torque (lb-ft) @ rpm	273 @ 4250	295 @ 4600	457 @ 3500
Availability	S[1]	S[2]	S[3]
EPA city/highway mpg			
6-speed manual	NA	NA	NA
5-speed automatic	NA	NA	NA

1. Carrera. 2. Carrera S. 3. Turbo models.

2005 prices unavailable at time of publication.

2004 PORSCHE BOXSTER

CLASS: Premium sporty/performance car
DRIVE WHEELS: Rear-wheel drive
BASE PRICE RANGE: $42,600-$59,900. Built in Germany.
ALSO CONSIDER: BMW Z4, Chevrolet Corvette, Honda S2000

Prosche's entry-level car is a 2-seat convertible that uses a midmounted, horizontally opposed 6-cyl engine. The base model comes with a 225-hp 2.7-liter and 5-speed manual transmission, the Boxster S with a 258-hp 3.2 and 6-speed manual. Both offer an optional 5-speed automatic with manual-shift steering-wheel buttons. Antilock 4-wheel disc brakes and side airbags are standard. Antiskid/traction control is optional. Also included is a power soft top with a heated glass rear window. A removable hardtop is optional. The base model has 16-inch wheels and is available with the S's 17s; 18s are optional for both, as is a sport exhaust system. A heavily revised 2005 Boxster is expected in the first half of calendar '05.

RATINGS	Base w/18-inch wheels, man.	S w/18-inch wheels, man.
ACCELERATION	7	8
FUEL ECONOMY	6	5
RIDE QUALITY	2	2
STEERING/HANDLING	10	10
QUIETNESS	2	2
CONTROLS/MATERIALS	5	5
ROOM/COMFORT (FRONT)	4	4
ROOM/COMFORT (REAR)	0	0
CARGO ROOM	2	2
VALUE WITHIN CLASS	6	6

Though more backroads-stormer than comfortable long-distance tourer, the Boxster is a highly capable yet fairly practical sports car. Even base models easily nudge $50,000 when popularly equipped, but this is still the most affordable way to live the "Porsche experience."

TOTAL	44	44

Average total for premium sporty/performance cars: 48.3

ENGINES

	dohc H6	dohc H6
Size, liters/cu. in.	2.7/164	3.2/194
Horsepower @ rpm	225 @ 6300	258 @ 6250
Torque (lb-ft) @ rpm	192 @ 4750	229 @ 4500
Availability	S[1]	S[2]
EPA city/highway mpg		
5-speed manual	20/29	
6-speed manual		18/26
5-speed automatic	18/26	17/26

1. Base. 2. S, SE; SE has 264 hp.

PRICES

Porsche Boxster	RETAIL PRICE	DEALER INVOICE
Base 2-door convertible	$42600	$37121
S 2-door convertible	51600	45001
SE 2-door convertible	59900	52267
Destination charge	765	765

STANDARD EQUIPMENT

Base: 2.7-liter 6-cylinder engine, 5-speed manual transmission, dual front airbags, side airbags, antilock 4-wheel disc brakes, integrated roll bars, air conditioning w/automatic climate control, interior air filter, power steering, telescope leather-wrapped steering wheel, partial leather upholstery, front bucket seats w/power recliners, center console, cupholder, heated power mirrors, power windows, power door locks, remote keyless entry, power convertible top, AM/FM/CD player, digital clock, tachometer, illuminated visor mirrors, rear defogger, heated washer nozzles, remote trunk releases, theft-deterrent system, rear spoiler, front and rear fog lights, 205/55ZR16 front tires, 225/50ZR16 rear tires, alloy wheels.

S adds: 3.2-liter 258-horsepower 6-cylinder engine, 6-speed manual transmission, variable-intermittent wipers, sport suspension, 205/50ZR17 front tires, 255/40ZR17 rear tires.

SE adds: 3.2-liter 264-horsepower engine, traction control, antiskid system, heated seats, upgraded sound system, trip computer, floormats, windblocker, xenon headlights, headlight washers, 225/40ZR18 front tires, 265/35ZR18 rear tires.

OPTIONAL EQUIPMENT

	RETAIL PRICE	DEALER INVOICE
Major Packages		
P70 Sport Design Pkg., Base, S	$1395	$1186
Black leather sport bucket seats, additional leather upholstery, aluminum-look interior accents.		
Powertrain		
5-speed automatic transmission w/manual-shift capability	3210	2729
2-stage sport exhaust system, S	2100	1785
Safety		
Antiskid/traction-control system, Base, S	1235	1050
Rear-obstacle-detection system, Base, S	530	451
Comfort & Convenience Features		
Navigation System	2680	2278
Includes trip computer.		
Cruise control	570	485
6-disc CD changer	715	608
Bose sound system, Base, S	1625	1381
SE	795	676
Trip computer, Base, S	280	238
Power Seat Pkg., Base, S	1550	1318
Power seats w/driver-seat memory. NA w/Sport Design Pkg.		
Heated seats, Base, S	410	349
Full leather upholstery, Base, S	2030	1726
Automatic day/night rearview and driver-side mirrors, Base, S	705	599
Includes rain-sensing wipers.		
Windblocker, Base, S	375	319

 Specifications begin on page 547.

Appearance & Special Purpose

	RETAIL PRICE	DEALER INVOICE
Removable hardtop, Base, S	$2345	$1993
Includes rear defogger.		
Luggage rack, Base, S	470	400
Xenon headlights, Base, S	1090	927
Includes headlight washers.		
Sport chassis, Base, S	705	599
Sport suspension, height-adjustable shock absorbers.		
Boxster-design alloy wheels, Base	1235	1050
Includes 205/50ZR17 front tires, 255/40ZR17 rear tires.		
Carrera alloy wheels, Base	2920	2482
S	1435	1220
Includes 225/40ZR18 front tires, 265/35ZR18 rear tires.		
Sport Design Wheels, S	2940	2499
Includes 225/40ZR18 front tires, 265/35ZR18 rear tires.		

PORSCHE CAYENNE

CLASS: Premium midsize sport-utility vehicle
DRIVE WHEELS: All-wheel drive
2004 BASE PRICE RANGE: $42,900-$88,900. Built in Germany.
ALSO CONSIDER: BMW X5, Cadillac SRX, Infiniti FX

An available manual transmission, rearview camera, and revised exterior trim are among 2005 additions to Porsche's SUV. Cayenne shares a basic design with the Volkswagen Touareg, but differs in styling and pricing, offers a different V8, and lacks a diesel-engine option. The base Cayenne uses a VW-sourced V6 that now offers a 6-speed manual transmission as well as 6-speed automatic. The manual includes a new Porsche Drive-Off Assistant system, designed to hold the brakes automatically on inclines until the clutch is engaged. The automatic, which has manual-shift capability, is standard on the V8 Cayenne S and Turbo. All models include ABS, antiskid/traction control, and all-wheel drive with low-range gearing and locking center differential. Optional for base and S and standard on the Turbo is a self-leveling air suspension with six driver-adjustable ride heights with up to 10.7 inches of ground clearance. Also included are 3-mode driver-adjustable shock absorbers that Porsche says are newly reprogrammed to enhance ride. The base model comes on 17-inch wheels vs. 18s; 19s and 20s are optional.

PORSCHE

For '05, Cayennes add a garage-door opener and power tailgate closer as standard. The base and S also get the Turbo's color-matched lower-body panels, replacing black. Voice control is newly available with the optional navigation system. Other new options include satellite radio, rearview camera, black instead of silver exterior trim, and a SportDesign package with flared side sills and deeper under-bumper fascias. Also available are heated steering wheel and seats, steering-linked bi-xenon headlamps, and an obstacle-detection system.

RATINGS	S w/18-inch wheels	S w/20-inch wheels	Turbo w/20-inch wheels
ACCELERATION	7	7	8
FUEL ECONOMY	3	3	3
RIDE QUALITY	6	4	4
STEERING/HANDLING	7	7	7
QUIETNESS	7	6	6
CONTROLS/MATERIALS	5	5	5
ROOM/COMFORT (FRONT)	7	7	7
ROOM/COMFORT (REAR)	5	5	5
CARGO ROOM	7	7	7
VALUE WITHIN CLASS	4	3	2

Cayenne impresses for engineering and solidity, and does many things well. But it's hardly cheap, and the V8 versions' sometimes-ragged power delivery is very un-Porsche. Unless you must have a 450-hp SUV, a V6 or V8 Touareg should satisfy as much—and save you money. But shop the competition, too.

TOTAL	58	54	54

Average total for premium midsize sport-utility vehicles: 59.6

ENGINES	dohc V6	dohc V8	Turbocharged dohc V8
Size, liters/cu. in.	3.2/195	4.5/275	4.5/275
Horsepower @ rpm	247 @ 6000	340 @ 6000	450 @ 6000
Torque (lb-ft) @ rpm	229 @ 2500	310 @ 2500	460 @ 2250
Availability	S[1]	S[2]	S[3]
EPA city/highway mpg			
6-speed manual	15/20		
6-speed automatic	15/19	14/18	13/18

1. Cayenne. 2. Cayenne S. 3. Cayenne Turbo.

2005 prices unavailable at time of publication.

2004 PRICES

Porsche Cayenne	RETAIL PRICE	DEALER INVOICE
Base 4-door wagon	$42900	$37384
S 4-door wagon	55900	48765
Turbo 4-door wagon	88900	77657
Destination charge	765	765

STANDARD EQUIPMENT

Base: 3.2-liter V6 engine, 6-speed automatic transmission w/manual-shift capability, all-wheel drive, 2-speed transfer case, locking center differen-

 Specifications begin on page 547.

tial, traction control, dual front airbags, front side airbags, curtain side airbags, antilock 4-wheel disc brakes, antiskid system, air conditioning, interior air filter, power steering, tilt/telescope leather-wrapped steering wheel w/radio controls, cruise control, leather upholstery, 12-way power front bucket seats, center console, cupholders, split folding rear seat, ski sack, heated power mirrors, power windows, power door locks, remote keyless entry, Bose AM/FM/CD player, digital clock, tachometer, trip computer, illuminated visor mirrors, variable-intermittent wipers, heated washers, map lights, cargo cover, rear defogger, rear wiper/washer, theft-deterrent system, rear privacy glass, fog lights, roof rails, 235/65R17 tires, alloy wheels.

S adds: 4.5-liter V8 engine, rear side airbags, dual-zone automatic climate controls, 255/55ZR18 tires.

Turbo adds: 4.5-liter turbocharged V8 engine, front- and rear-obstacle-detection system, navigation system, power tilt/telescope heated steering wheel, heated front and rear seats, memory system (front seats, mirrors, steering wheel, climate controls), steering-linked adaptive xenon headlights w/washers, height-adjustable and load-leveling active suspension.

OPTIONAL EQUIPMENT

Major Packages

	RETAIL PRICE	DEALER INVOICE
Electric Comfort Pkg.	$890	$757
Automatic day/night outside and rearview mirrors, universal garage-door opener, power rear-hatch release, programmable lighting.		
Convenience Pkg., S	3860	3282
Electric Comfort Pkg. plus power sunroof, variable-assist power steering, driver-seat and mirror memory, xenon headlights w/washers.		
Convenience Pkg., Turbo	1990	1692
Electric Comfort Pkg. plus power sunroof.		
Touring Pkg., S	4565	3881
Front- and rear-obstacle-detection system, navigation system, 6-disc CD changer, compass.		
Cold Weather Pkg., S	2680	2279
Heated front and rear seats, heated steering wheel, parking heater w/timer, all-season tires.		
Warm Weather Pkg., S, Turbo	2960	2517
4-zone air conditioning (including rear controls), thermal glass, rear sunshades.		
Off-Road Design Pkg., Base, S	3100	2635
Turbo	2850	2423
Running boards, fender trim, skid plates, enhanced drivetrain protection.		
Advanced Off-Road Tech Pkg., Base/S	4390	3732
Base/S w/xenon headlights, Turbo	4160	3536
Base/S w/Off-Road Design Pkg.	3520	2992
Base/S w/Off-Road Design Pkg. and xenon headlights, Turbo w/Off-Road Design Pkg	3290	2797
Locking rear differential, hydraulically disconnectable stabilizer bars, headlight washers, skid plates.		

OPTIONAL EQUIPMENT (cont.)

	RETAIL PRICE	DEALER INVOICE
Sports Aluminum Look Pkg., Base, S	$990	$842
Aluminum interior trim. Std. Turbo.		
Wood Pkg., Base, S	990	842
Turbo	NC	NC
Wood interior trim.		
Activity Pkg., S	3870	3290
Turbo	670	570
Height-adjustable and load-leveling active suspension (S), fire extinguisher, trailer hitch.		

Safety

Front- and rear-obstacle-detection system, Base, S	990	842
Tire-pressure monitor	590	502

Comfort & Convenience Features

Dual-zone automatic climate controls, Base	550	NA
4-zone air conditioning	1690	1437
Includes rear controls.		
Navigation system, Base, S	3050	2593
Power sunroof	1100	935
Variable-assist power steering, S	270	230
Std. Turbo.		
Proximity entry system	995	846
6-disc CD changer	715	608
Surround sound system, Base	1625	NA
Comfort seats, S	1290	1097
Includes driver-seat memory.		
Sport seats, Base, S	1290	1097
Turbo	NC	NC
S includes driver-seat memory.		
Heated front and rear seats, Base, S	960	NA

Appearance & Special Purpose

Xenon headlights, Base, S	1240	1054
Includes washers, cornering lights.		
Height-adjustable load-leveling active suspension, Base, S	3200	2720
18-inch wheels, Base	1800	NA
Includes 255/55ZR18 tires.		
Cayenne Design Wheels, Base	2190	NA
S, Turbo	1000	850
Includes 275/45ZR19 tires.		
Cayenne Sport Design Wheels, Base	3300	NA
S, Turbo	1960	1666
Includes 275/40ZR20 tires.		
Space-saver spare tire	170	145
Rear-mounted spare tire, Base	1450	NA
S, Turbo	1800	1530

SAAB 9-2X

CLASS: Premium compact car
DRIVE WHEELS: All-wheel drive
BASE PRICE RANGE: $22,990-$26,950. Built in Japan.
ALSO CONSIDER: Acura TSX, Audi A4, Volvo S40 and V50

Saab taps the holdings of parent-company General Motors for its new entry-level model: a 4-dr, all-wheel-drive wagon based on the Subaru Impreza. The 9-2X gets Saab-family styling alterations, but uses Impreza's bodyshell and powertrains. Two 9-2X models are offered, both with horizontally opposed 4-cyl engines and standard AWD. The base Linear has 165 hp. The turbocharged Aero mimics the sporty Impreza WRX with 227 hp and a functional hood scoop. Both offer a 5-speed manual transmission or optional 4-speed automatic. Antilock 4-wheel disc brakes, torso-and-head-protecting front side airbags, and 16-inch wheels are standard; the Aero is available with 17s. Leather upholstery and a sunroof are options. The 9-2X is aimed at a more upscale market than Impreza, and it has different nose, tail, and wheels. A roof rack is standard on Impreza, a dealer-supplied option on 9-2X. The interior design is shared, but the 9-2X gets different upholstery and Saab's active front-seat headrests designed to minimize whiplash injury. This evaluation is based on preview test drives.

RATINGS	Linear, man.	Linear w/Prem. Pkg., auto.	Aero w/Sport Pkg., man.
ACCELERATION	5	4	7
FUEL ECONOMY	5	5	4
RIDE QUALITY	5	5	4
STEERING/HANDLING	7	7	8
QUIETNESS	5	5	5
CONTROLS/MATERIALS	7	7	7
ROOM/COMFORT (FRONT)	5	5	5
ROOM/COMFORT (REAR)	3	3	3
CARGO ROOM	7	7	7
VALUE WITHIN CLASS	3	3	4

Saab's changes to exterior styling, sound deadening, and interior trim do their part to disguise this car's Impreza origins. And the versatile wagon body style and all-season AWD traction have some appeal. But there's no hiding the tepid base engine, the turbo's quirks, or the modest interior space. Still,

RATINGS (cont.)

	Linear, man.	Linear w/Prem. Pkg., auto.	Aero w/Sport Pkg., man.
9-2X, like Saab in general, lies off the beaten path, which should mean friendlier price breaks than you'll get on the more-mainstream competition.			
TOTAL	**52**	**51**	**54**
Average total for premium compact cars: 57.5			

ENGINES

	sohc H4	Turbocharged dohc H4
Size, liters/cu. in.	2.5/150	2.0/122
Horsepower @ rpm	165 @ 5500	227 @ 6000
Torque (lb-ft) @ rpm	166 @ 4000	217 @ 4000
Availability	S[1]	S[2]
EPA city/highway mpg		
5-speed manual	21/28	20/27
4-speed automatic	22/28	19/26

1. Linear. 2. Aero.

PRICES

Saab 9-2X	RETAIL PRICE	DEALER INVOICE
Linear 4-door wagon	$22990	$21841
Aero 4-door wagon	26950	25603
Destination charge	695	695

STANDARD EQUIPMENT

Linear: 2.5-liter 4-cylinder engine, 5-speed manual transmission, all-wheel drive, limited-slip differential, dual front airbags, front side airbags, front-seat active head restraints, antilock 4-wheel disc brakes, air conditioning, power steering, tilt steering wheel, cruise control, cloth upholstery, front bucket seats, height-adjustable driver seat, center console, cupholders, split folding rear seat, power mirrors, power windows, power door locks, remote keyless entry, AM/FM/CD player, digital clock, tachometer, map lights, variable-intermittent wipers w/deicer, visor mirrors, cargo cover, rear defogger, rear wiper/washer, rear spoiler, 205/55VR16 tires, alloy wheels.

Aero adds: 2.0-liter turbocharged 4-cylinder engine, automatic climate control, interior air filter, leather-wrapped steering wheel, AM/FM radio w/in-dash 6-disc CD changer, fog lights, sport suspension.

OPTIONAL EQUIPMENT

Major Packages	RETAIL PRICE	DEALER INVOICE
Premium Pkg., Linear	$2495	$2295
Leather upholstery, leather-wrapped steering wheel, AM/FM radio w/in-dash 6-disc CD changer, fog lights, xenon headlights.		
Premium Pkg., Aero	1695	1559
Leather upholstery, xenon headlights.		
Sport Pkg., Aero	1950	1794
Power sunroof, 215/45VR17 tires.		

OPTIONAL EQUIPMENT (cont.)

	RETAIL PRICE	DEALER INVOICE
Cold Weather Pkg.	$600	$552
Heated front seats and mirrors, rear wiper deicer.		
Powertrain		
4-speed automatic transmission	1250	1238
Comfort & Convenience Features		
Power sunroof, Linear	1200	1104

SAAB 9-3

CLASS: Premium compact car
DRIVE WHEELS: Front-wheel drive
BASE PRICE RANGE: $26,850-$42,600. Built in Sweden.
ALSO CONSIDER: Acura TSX, Audi A4, BMW 3-Series

Saab's best-selling line gains a base-trim convertible and an available navigation system for 2005, but loses some other features. The 9-3 comes as a 4-dr sedan and a 2-dr convertible with a power top, heated glass rear window, and a rollover bar that pops up if sensors detect an impending tip. Both body styles offer base Linear, luxury-oriented Arc, and sporty Aero models; the Linear convertible is new for '05. All use a turbocharged 2.0-liter 4-cyl engine with 175 hp in Linear models, 210 in Arc and Aero. A 5-speed manual transmission is standard; Aeros previously came with a 6-speed. A 5-speed automatic transmission with manual shift gate is optional; the Aero's includes steering-wheel-mounted shift paddles. Linear and Arc have 16-inch wheels; Linears previously came with 15s. Aeros have a sport suspension and 17-inch wheels. The 17s are an Arc option. All 9-3s have ABS and antiskid/traction control. Sedans get front side airbags and head-protecting curtain side airbags. Convertibles have front side airbags designed to protect the torso and head.

Leather upholstery is optional on the Linear convertible, standard on other 9-3s. On Arcs, wood interior trim is optional; it previously was standard. Sedans have a 60/40 split folding rear seatback with trunk pass-through. The navigation system is a new Arc and Aero option. A tire-pressure monitor and OnStar assistance are no longer available. Saab is owned by General Motors and the 9-3 shares its basic platform with the Chevrolet Malibu and Pontiac G6.

RATINGS	Linear sdn, auto.	Arc sdn, auto.	Arc conv, auto.	Aero sdn, man.
ACCELERATION	6	7	7	7
FUEL ECONOMY	6	5	5	5
RIDE QUALITY	8	7	7	5
STEERING/HANDLING	7	7	7	8
QUIETNESS	7	7	5	7
CONTROLS/MATERIALS	6	6	6	6
ROOM/COMFORT (FRONT)	7	7	7	7
ROOM/COMFORT (REAR)	4	4	2	4
CARGO ROOM	4	4	2	4
VALUE WITHIN CLASS	7	7	6	7

Its front-wheel-drive layout keeps the 9-3 from competing with its sportiest rear-drive rivals for ultimate handling prowess. And key competitors offer all-wheel drive for better all-season security. Still, this is a dynamically capable, fun-to-drive car, especially the solidly built convertible. As always, the 9-3 is the non-conformist alternative to premium compact rivals from Acura, Audi, and BMW.

TOTAL	62	61	54	60

Average total for premium compact cars: 57.5

ENGINES	Turbocharged dohc I4	Turbocharged dohc I4
Size, liters/cu. in.	2.0/121	2.0/121
Horsepower @ rpm	175 @ 5500	210 @ 5300
Torque (lb-ft) @ rpm	195 @ 2500	221 @ 2500
Availability	S[1]	S[2]
EPA city/highway mpg		
5-speed manual	22/31	21/29
5-speed automatic	21/30	18/28

1. Linear. 2. Arc, Aero.

PRICES

Saab 9-3	RETAIL PRICE	DEALER INVOICE
Linear 4-door sedan	$26850	$25330
Linear 2-door convertible	37100	34985
Arc 4-door sedan	30250	28538
Arc 2-door convertible	40100	37814
Aero 4-door sedan	32850	30922
Aero 2-door convertible	42600	40172
Destination charge	720	720

STANDARD EQUIPMENT

Linear: 2.0-liter turbocharged 4-cylinder 175-horsepower engine, 5-speed manual transmission, traction control, dual front airbags, front side airbags, curtain side airbags (sedan), front-seat active head restraints, automatic roll bar (convertible), antilock 4-wheel disc brakes, brake assist, antiskid system, emergency inside trunk release, daytime running lights, air conditioning, inte-

 Specifications begin on page 547.

rior air filter, power steering, tilt/telescope leather-wrapped steering wheel w/radio controls, cruise control, cloth upholstery (convertible), leather upholstery (sedan), front bucket seats, height-adjustable driver seat, center console, cupholders, split folding rear seat (sedan), trunk pass-through (sedan), heated power mirrors w/turn signals, power windows, power door locks, remote keyless entry, AM/FM/CD player, digital clock, tachometer, trip computer, outside-temperature indicator, variable-intermittent wipers, illuminated visor mirrors, map lights, rear defogger, power convertible top (convertible), automatic headlights, floormats, theft-deterrent system, rear fog light, 215/55HR16 tires, alloy wheels.

Arc adds: 2.0-liter turbocharged 4-cylinder 210-horsepower engine, automatic climate control, leather upholstery, 8-way power driver seat, upgraded sound system, front fog lights.

Aero adds: power sunroof (sedan), rear spoiler (convertible), sport suspension, 225/45ZR17 tires.

OPTIONAL EQUIPMENT

	RETAIL PRICE	DEALER INVOICE
Major Packages		
Premium Pkg., Linear sedan	$1895	$1706
Power sunroof, 8-way power driver seat, AM/FM radio w/in-dash 6-disc CD changer.		
Leather Pkg., Linear convertible	1895	1706
Leather upholstery, 8-way power driver seat.		
Driver's Pkg., Arc	1695	1526
Rear-obstacle-detection system, wood/leather-wrapped steering wheel (convertible), wood interior trim, driver-seat memory (sedan), remote top operation (convertible), remote window operation, AM/FM radio w/in-dash 6-disc CD changer, universal garage-door opener, automatic day/night rearview mirror, rain-sensing wipers.		
Touring Pkg., Aero	1495	1346
Rear-obstacle-detection system, driver-seat memory, universal garage-door opener, automatic day/night rearview, compass, remote power window operation, remote top operation (convertible), AM/FM radio w/in-dash 6-disc CD changer, rain-sensing wipers.		
Powertrain		
5-speed automatic transmission w/manual-shift capability	1350	1337
Aero includes steering-wheel shift paddles.		
Comfort & Convenience Features		
Navigation system, Arc, Aero	2295	2066
Power sunroof, Linear/Arc sedan	1200	1080
Heated front seats	500	450
Appearance & Special Purpose		
Xenon headlights, Arc, Aero	650	585
Includes washers.		
225/45VR17 tires, Arc	850	765

SAAB 9-5

CLASS: Premium midsize car
DRIVE WHEELS: Front-wheel drive
BASE PRICE RANGE: $32,550-$40,750. Built in Sweden.
ALSO CONSIDER: Acura TL, Audi A4, Infiniti G35

Saab's flagship gains an available navigation system for 2005. The 9-5 comes in three models: base Linear, luxury-oriented Arc, and sporty Aero. Arc and Aero come in both sedan and station wagon form, Linear as a wagon only. All have a turbocharged 2.3-liter 4-cyl engine. Linears have 185 hp, Arcs 220, Aeros 250. Aeros have a sport suspension, plus 17-inch wheels vs. the other models' 16s, though 17s are optional on Arc. Available are a 5-speed manual transmission or 5-speed automatic, which can be shifted manually via buttons on the steering-wheel spokes. Standard equipment includes ABS, antiskid/traction control, and front head-and-torso side airbags. Side curtain and rear side airbags are unavailable. All 9-5s have leather upholstery; Arc and Aero have heated front seats, which are optional on Linear. OnStar assistance and ventilated seats are available for Arc and Aero. Ventilated front seats are optional on Aero. Wagons do not offer 3rd-row seating.

RATINGS	Linear wgn, man.	Aero sdn, auto.
ACCELERATION	6	7
FUEL ECONOMY	6	5
RIDE QUALITY	8	6
STEERING/HANDLING	6	7
QUIETNESS	6	5
CONTROLS/MATERIALS	5	5
ROOM/COMFORT (FRONT)	7	7
ROOM/COMFORT (REAR)	7	7
CARGO ROOM	5	5
VALUE WITHIN CLASS	3	2

Even though Saab is owned by General Motors, the 9-5 retains its Scandinavian flavor. And few competitors offer a wagon body style. But this is among the oldest designs in the premium midsize class—a fact highlighted by the absence of curtain side airbags. These cars are also pricey for 4-cyl automobiles, and Japanese rivals beat Saab for reliability and resale value.

TOTAL	59	56

Average total for premium midsize cars: 61.7

 Specifications begin on page 547.

ENGINES

	Turbocharged dohc I4	Turbocharged dohc I4	Turbocharged dohc I4
Size, liters/cu. in.	2.3/140	2.3/140	2.3/140
Horsepower @ rpm	185 @ 5500	220 @ 5500	250 @ 5300
Torque (lb-ft) @ rpm	207 @ 1800	228 @ 1800	258 @ 1900
Availability	S[1]	S[2]	S[3]
EPA city/highway mpg			
5-speed manual	21/29	22/30[4]	22/30[6]
5-speed automatic	19/28	19/29[5]	19/28

1. Linear. 2. Arc. 3. Aero. 4. Sedan. SportWagon: 20/29. 5. Sedan. SportWagon: 19/29. 6. Sedan. SportWagon: 20/28.

PRICES

Saab 9-5	RETAIL PRICE	DEALER INVOICE
Linear 4-door wagon	$32550	$30610
Arc 4-door sedan	36250	33908
Arc 4-door wagon	37050	34653
Aero 4-door sedan	39950	37369
Aero 4-door wagon	40750	37113
Destination charge	720	720

STANDARD EQUIPMENT

Linear: 2.3-liter turbocharged 4-cylinder 185-horsepower engine, 5-speed manual transmission, traction control, dual front airbags, front side airbags, front-seat active head restraints, antilock 4-wheel disc brakes, antiskid system, daytime running lights, air conditioning w/dual-zone automatic climate controls, interior air filter, power steering, tilt/telescope leather-wrapped steering wheel w/radio controls, cruise control, leather upholstery, 8-way power front bucket seats, center console, cupholders, split folding rear seat, heated power mirrors w/turn signals, power windows, power door locks, remote keyless entry, AM/FM/cassette/CD player, digital clock, tachometer, outside-temperature indicator, trip computer, cooled glovebox, illuminated visor mirrors, variable-intermittent wipers, cargo cover, rear defogger, rear wiper/washer (wagon), rear defogger, automatic headlights, floormats, theft-deterrent system, rear fog light, 215/55HR16 tires, alloy wheels.

Arc adds: 2.3-liter turbocharged 4-cylinder 220-horsepower engine, 5-speed automatic transmission w/manual-shift capability, emergency inside trunk release (sedan), heated front seats, trunk pass-through (sedan), wood interior trim, power sunroof, front fog lights.

Aero adds: 2.3-liter turbocharged 4-cylinder 250-horsepower engine, 5-speed manual transmission, driver-seat memory, Harman/Kardon sound system, automatic day/night rearview mirror, compass, universal garage-door opener, sport suspension, 225/45VR17 tires. *Deletes:* wood interior trim.

OPTIONAL EQUIPMENT

Major Packages	RETAIL PRICE	DEALER INVOICE
Comfort Pkg., Linear	$1595	$1436
Heated front seats, power sunroof.		

OPTIONAL EQUIPMENT (cont.)

	RETAIL PRICE	DEALER INVOICE
Luxury Pkg., Arc	$1895	$1706
Driver-seat memory, automatic day/night rearview mirror, compass, universal garage-door opener, Harman/Kardon sound system.		
Executive Pkg., Aero	995	896
Heated rear seats, rain-sensing wipers, automatic day/night outside mirrors, xenon headlights w/washers.		
Sport Tech Pkg., Aero	595	536
Sport seats, carbon-fiber instrument panel, unique interior trim.		
Powertrain		
5-speed automatic transmission w/manual-shift capability, Linear, Aero	1350	1337
5-speed manual transmission, Arc	NC	NC
Comfort & Convenience Features		
Navigation system, Arc, Aero	2795	2516
Includes 6-disc CD changer.		
OnStar assistance system, Arc, Aero	699	629
Includes one-year service. Arc requires Luxury Pkg.		
Ventilated front seats, Arc, Aero	995	866
Arc requires Luxury Pkg.		
Appearance & Special Purpose		
Roof rails, wagon	250	225
Xenon headlights, Arc, Aero	650	585
225/45VR17 tires, Arc	850	765

SATURN ION

CLASS: Compact car
DRIVE WHEELS: Front-wheel drive
BASE PRICE RANGE: $11,430-$20,885. Built in USA.
ALSO CONSIDER: Ford Focus, Honda Civic, Hyundai Elantra, Toyota Corolla

Saturn's smallest cars get a new automatic transmission, freshened sedan front ends, and noise-reduction measures for 2005. Ion sedans and 4-dr Quad Coupes reprise a 140-hp 2.2-liter 4-cyl engine and standard 5-speed manual transmission. Automatic is optional, with a 4-speed unit replacing last year's 5-speed and continuously variable automatics. The sporty Red Line coupe returns with a manual transmission, a supercharged 205-hp 2.0-liter 4-cyl, and 4-wheel antilock disc brakes. Other Ions have rear drum brakes and offer optional ABS bundled with traction control. Head-protecting curtain side airbags are available for all; torso side airbags are not offered.

The base-trim Ion 1 sedan has 14-inch wheels, while midlevel 2s and top-line Ion 3s have 15- or 16-inch wheels. Steering and suspension are revised for '05, and all 2s and 3s gain new front and rear seats in retrimmed interiors. The Red Line boasts 17-inch wheels, sport suspension, and special interior and exterior styling. Red Lines have leather-trimmed seats, and leather upholstery is optional for Ion 3s. All models come with split folding rear seatbacks. Coupes add a folding front-passenger seat and have rear-hinged access doors that require opening the front doors first. A CD player is standard for Ion 2s, a CD/MP3 for 3s and Red Line. OnStar assistance are optional for all but 1s and Red Line. Satellite radio is optional for all but 1s. Sedans offer dealer-installed exterior roof-rail trim in colors to contrast with body paint. Ion shares powertrains and underskin design with Chevrolet's new 2005 Cobalt.

RATINGS

	2 sdn, auto.	3 sdn, man.	2 cpe, man.	Red Line
ACCELERATION	4	4	4	7
FUEL ECONOMY	6	7	7	6
RIDE QUALITY	5	5	5	4
STEERING/HANDLING	6	6	6	7
QUIETNESS	4	4	4	3
CONTROLS/MATERIALS	4	4	4	4
ROOM/COMFORT (FRONT)	5	5	5	5
ROOM/COMFORT (REAR)	4	4	4	4
CARGO ROOM	3	3	4	4
VALUE WITHIN CLASS	5	5	5	5

Ion matches most rivals for roominess and performance, though it trails them for interior refinement. Many buyers like the no-rust, ding-resistant plastic body panels, and the coupes offer the unique convenience of rear access doors. The Red Line is a genuine pocket rocket, though it is outperformed by the like-priced Dodge SRT-10. Note that contrary to long-standing policy, Saturn now offers rebates.

TOTAL	46	47	48	49

Average total for compact cars: 48.4

ENGINES

	dohc I4	Supercharged dohc I4
Size, liters/cu. in.	2.2/134	2.0/122
Horsepower @ rpm	140 @ 5800	205 @ 5600
Torque (lb-ft) @ rpm	145 @ 4400	200 @ 4400
Availability	S[1]	S[2]

ENGINES (cont.)

	dohc I4	Supercharged dohc I4
EPA city/highway mpg		
5-speed manual	26/35	23/29
4-speed automatic	25/33	

1. All exc. Red Line. 2. Red Line.

PRICES

Saturn Ion

	RETAIL PRICE	DEALER INVOICE
Ion 1 4-door sedan, manual	$11430	$10684
Ion 1 4-door sedan, automatic	12410	11595
Ion 2 4-door sedan, manual	14380	13427
Ion 2 4-door sedan, automatic	15280	14264
Ion 2 4-door coupe, manual	14930	13939
Ion 2 4-door coupe, automatic	15830	14776
Ion 3 4-door sedan, manual	15905	14846
Ion 3 4-door sedan, automatic	16805	15683
Ion 3 4-door coupe, manual	16680	15566
Ion 3 4-door coupe, automatic	17580	16403
Red Line 4-door coupe, manual	20885	19477
Destination charge	565	565

STANDARD EQUIPMENT

1: 2.2-liter 4-cylinder engine, 5-speed manual or 4-speed automatic transmission, dual front airbags, daytime running lights, emergency inside trunk release, power steering, tilt steering wheel, cloth upholstery, front bucket seats, center console, cupholders, split folding rear seat, AM/FM radio, digital clock, tachometer, visor mirrors, rear defogger, variable-intermittent wipers, theft-deterrent system, 185/70R14 tires, wheel covers.

2 adds: air conditioning, interior air filter, height-adjustable driver seat, fold-flat passenger seat (coupe), power door locks, rear-hinged rear doors (coupe), AM/FM/CD player, floormats, 195/60R15 tires.

3 adds: cruise control, power mirrors, power windows, remote keyless entry, AM/FM/CD/MP3 player, automatic headlights, rear spoiler (coupe), fog lights, sport suspension (coupe), 205/55R16 tires, alloy wheels.

Red Line adds: 2.0-liter supercharged 4-cylinder engine, antilock 4-wheel disc brakes, leather-wrapped steering wheel, cloth/leather upholstery, Red Line Suspension, 215/45WR17 tires. *Deletes:* floormats.

OPTIONAL EQUIPMENT

Major Packages

	RETAIL PRICE	DEALER INVOICE
Power Pkg., 2	$825	$767
Cruise control, power mirrors and windows, remote keyless entry, alarm.		
Travel Pkg., 2, 3	200	186
Automatic day/night rearview mirror, compass, outside-temperature indicator, map lights.		

 Specifications begin on page 547.

OPTIONAL EQUIPMENT (cont.)

	RETAIL PRICE	DEALER INVOICE
Safe and Sound Pkg., 2	$1215	$1130
3	1235	1149
Travel Pkg. plus traction control, curtain side airbags, antilock brakes, OnStar assistance system w/one-year service, AM/FM/CD/MP3 player (2), AM/FM radio w/in-dash 6-disc CD/MP3 changer (3).		
Safety		
Curtain side airbags	395	367
Antilock brakes, 1, 2, 3	400	372
Includes traction control.		
Comfort & Convenience Features		
OnStar assistance system, 2, 3	695	646
Includes one-year service. Requires Travel Pkg. 2 requires optional radio.		
Air conditioning, 1	960	893
Power sunroof, 2, 3, Red Line	725	674
2 requires Power Pkg.		
Leather upholstery, 3	700	651
Includes leather-wrapped steering wheel.		
AM/FM/CD player, 1	290	270
AM/FM/CD/MP3 player, 1	510	474
2	220	205
AM/FM radio w/in-dash 6-disc CD/MP3 changer, 2	460	428
3, Red Line	240	223
Satellite radio, 2, 3, Red Line	325	302
Requires monthly fee after 3rd month. 2 requires optional radio.		
Premium radio system, 2, 3, Red Line	290	270
2 requires Power Pkg., optional radio.		
Appearance & Special Purpose		
Rear spoiler, 2, 3 sedan	250	233
Aero wing rear spoiler, Red Line	380	353
Alloy wheels, 2	375	349

SATURN L300

CLASS: Midsize car
DRIVE WHEELS: Front-wheel drive
BASE PRICE: $21,370. Built in USA.
ALSO CONSIDER: Chevy Malibu, Honda Accord, Toyota Camry

This slow-selling midsize car drops wagons for a brief 2005 farewell. L300 sedans, unchanged except for fewer options, are due to end production by early calendar 2005. L300 features doors, front fenders, and bumper fascias made of Saturn's dent- and rust-resistant polymer plastic; other body parts are steel. The sole powertrain comprises a 182-hp V6 and 4-speed automatic transmission. Standard safety equipment includes antilock 4-wheel disc

brakes, traction control, and head-protecting curtain side airbags. Also standard are split folding rear seatback, 16-inch wheels, and heated power mirrors. A shortened options slate includes sunroof, power driver seat, and chrome alloy wheels. Deleted as options are heated front seats, leather upholstery, rear DVD entertainment, and GM OnStar assistance.

RATINGS

	L300
ACCELERATION	5
FUEL ECONOMY	5
RIDE QUALITY	6
STEERING/HANDLING	6
QUIETNESS	5
CONTROLS/MATERIALS	5
ROOM/COMFORT (FRONT)	5
ROOM/COMFORT (REAR)	4
CARGO ROOM	6
VALUE WITHIN CLASS	3

While Saturn's one-price stategy and plastic body panels are assets to some buyers, the L300 trails most competitors for quality and refinement. But Saturn has strayed from its long-standing no-rebates policy, so look for deep discounts on this little-loved lame duck.

TOTAL	50

Average total for midsize cars: 57.2

ENGINES

	dohc V6
Size, liters/cu. in.	3.0/183
Horsepower @ rpm	182 @ 5600
Torque (lb-ft) @ rpm	184 @ 3600
Availability	S
EPA city/highway mpg	
4-speed automatic	20/28

PRICES

Saturn L300	RETAIL PRICE	DEALER INVOICE
Base 4-door sedan	$21370	$19714
Destination charge	625	625

 Specifications begin on page 547.

STANDARD EQUIPMENT

Base: 3.0-liter V6 engine, 4-speed automatic transmission, traction control, dual front airbags, curtain side airbags, antilock 4-wheel disc brakes, daytime running lights, emergency inside trunk release, air conditioning, power steering, tilt steering wheel, cruise control, cloth upholstery, front bucket seats, center console, cupholders, split folding rear seat, heated power mirrors, power windows, power door locks, remote keyless entry, AM/FM/cassette/CD player, digital clock, variable-intermittent wipers, illuminated visor mirrors, rear defogger, map lights, automatic headlights, floormats, theft-deterrent system, 215/55R16 tires, alloy wheels.

OPTIONAL EQUIPMENT

Comfort & Convenience Features	RETAIL PRICE	DEALER INVOICE
Power sunroof	$725	$667
6-way power driver seat	325	299
Manufacturer's Discount Price	*NC*	*NC*
Appearance & Special Purpose		
Chrome alloy wheels	650	598
Manufacturer's Discount Price	*NC*	*NC*

SATURN RELAY

CLASS: Minivan
DRIVE WHEELS: Front-wheel drive, all-wheel drive
BASE PRICE: NA. Built in USA.
ALSO CONSIDER: Dodge Caravan, Honda Odyssey, Mazda MPV

Saturn gets its first minivan as one of four new GM "crossover sport vans." Relay shares its basic design with the 2005 Buick Terraza, Chevy Uplander, and Pontiac Montana SV6, all of which add an SUV-style nose to the 1997-2004 GM minivan design. Two trim levels are offered, Relay 2 and Relay 3, in a single body length with dual sliding rear side doors; power sliding doors are available. All Relays seat 7 via folding/removable 2nd-row bucket seats and a 50/50 fold-flat 3rd-row bench. The only powertrain is a 200-hp 3.5-liter V6 and 4-speed automatic transmission. There's a choice of front-wheel drive with available traction control, and all-wheel drive. GM's

Stabilitrak antiskid/traction control is also optional with front-drive. All models come with 4-wheel antilock brakes, 17-inch wheels, and OnStar assistance. Front side airbags providing head and torso protection are available, but curtain side airbags aren't offered. Also standard are a CD/MP3 player, rear DVD entertainment, and a roof-rail system with optional snap-on storage modules. Rear heating/air conditioning is optional on 2, standard on 3. Optional on both are satellite radio and a remote starting system that operates from the keyfob. Full pricing and equipment were unavailable in time for this report, but Saturn has announced a base price of $23,770, plus a $715 destination charge. This evaluation is based preview test drives.

RATINGS

	Relay 2	AWD Relay 3 w/leather
ACCELERATION	3	3
FUEL ECONOMY	4	4
RIDE QUALITY	6	6
STEERING/HANDLING	4	5
QUIETNESS	6	6
CONTROLS/MATERIALS	6	6
ROOM/COMFORT (FRONT)	6	6
ROOM/COMFORT (REAR)	6	6
CARGO ROOM	9	9
VALUE WITHIN CLASS	5	5

The lack of curtain side airbags is a big minus for safety conscious buyers, and the rear seating rows and cargo area aren't as convenient or as roomy as the minivans from Chrysler, Honda, or Toyota. However, fair prices and a comfortable ride make Relay a worthwhile option for value-conscious shoppers who want features such as available AWD and standard rear DVD entertainment.

TOTAL	55	56

Average total for minivans: 58.0

ENGINES

	ohv V6
Size, liters/cu. in.	3.5/213
Horsepower @ rpm	200 @ 5200
Torque (lb-ft) @ rpm	220 @ 4400
Availability	S
EPA city/highway mpg	
4-speed automatic	NA

2005 prices unavailable at time of publication.

SATURN VUE

CLASS: Compact sport-utility vehicle
DRIVE WHEELS: Front-wheel drive, all-wheel drive
2004 BASE PRICE RANGE: $16,920-$24,055. Built in USA.
ALSO CONSIDER: Ford Escape, Honda CR-V, Mazda Tribute

All-wheel drive is no longer available with the 4-cyl engine, and the continuously variable transmission (CVT) isn't available at all for 2005 on Saturn's car-type SUV. Vue seats five and uses Saturn's signature dent-resistant plastic-composite bodyside panels. It offers 4-cyl and V6 engines. For '05, the 4-cyl Vue comes only with front-wheel drive and either 5-speed manual transmission or, at extra cost, a conventional 4-speed automatic transmission. The conventional automatic replaces the CVT. V6 Vues use a Honda-sourced engine linked to a 5-speed automatic transmission. V6 versions come in front-drive or with AWD that lacks low-range gearing and is not designed for severe off-road use. ABS is standard with the V6 versions, optional on the 4-cyl. Head-protecting curtain side airbags and OnStar assistance are available for all. So are satellite radio and rear DVD entertainment. V6 Vues are available in Red Line versions that have specific exterior trim, a lowered sport supsension, and 18-inch wheels vs. other models' 16s or 17s. Rounding out '05 additions are detail interior revisions, and, for non-Red Line versions, chrome door handles, windowsill moldings, and headlamp bezels.

RATINGS

	AWD V6	AWD V6 Red Line
ACCELERATION	7	7
FUEL ECONOMY	4	4
RIDE QUALITY	5	5
STEERING/HANDLING	4	5
QUIETNESS	4	4
CONTROLS/MATERIALS	6	6
ROOM/COMFORT (FRONT)	6	7
ROOM/COMFORT (REAR)	6	6
CARGO ROOM	7	7
VALUE WITHIN CLASS	5	5

The outstanding performance and refinement of Honda's V6 almost offset Vue's deficits in handling, accomodations, and workmanship. Dent-resistant body panels, competitive prices, and Saturn's high customer-satisfaction ratings are other pluses, but we'd still scout the competition.

TOTAL	54	56

Average total for compact sport-utility vehicles: 49.0

ENGINES

	dohc I4	sohc V6
Size, liters/cu. in.	2.2/134	3.5/212
Horsepower @ rpm	143 @ 5400	250 @ 5800
Torque (lb-ft) @ rpm	152 @ 4000	242 @ 4500
Availability	S[1]	S[2]
EPA city/highway mpg		
5-speed manual	23/28	
4-speed automatic	22/26	
5-speed automatic		19/25[3]

1. 4-cyl model. 2. V6 models. 3. 20/28 w/2WD.

2005 prices unavailable at time of publication.

2004 PRICES

Saturn Vue	RETAIL PRICE	DEALER INVOICE
2WD 4-cylinder 4-door wagon, manual	$16920	$15790
2WD 4-cylinder 4-door wagon, CVT automatic	19005	17729
AWD 4-cylinder 4-door wagon, CVT automatic	20105	18751
2WD V6 4-door wagon, automatic	22405	20891
AWD V6 4-door wagon, automatic	24055	22425
Destination charge	575	575

STANDARD EQUIPMENT

4-cylinder: 2.2-liter 4-cylinder engine, 5-speed manual or continuously variable automatic transmission (CVT), dual front airbags, daytime running lights, air conditioning, interior air filter, power steering, tilt steering wheel, cloth upholstery, front bucket seats, height-adjustable driver seat, fold-flat passenger seat, center console, cupholders, split folding rear seat, AM/FM radio (manual), AM/FM/CD player (CVT), tachometer, visor mirrors, intermittent wipers, remote liftgate release, cargo organizer, rear defogger, intermittent rear wiper/washer, theft-deterrent system, rear privacy glass, roof rails, 215/70SR16 tires, wheel covers. **AWD** adds: all-wheel drive, 235/65SR16 tires.

V6 adds: 3.5-liter V6 engine, 5-speed automatic transmission, traction control, antilock brakes, leather-wrapped steering wheel, cruise control, power mirrors, power windows, power door locks, remote keyless entry, AM/FM/CD player, automatic day/night rearview mirror, compass, outside-temperature indicator, map lights, automatic headlights, fog lights, alloy wheels. **AWD** adds: all-wheel drive, 235/60SR17 tires. *Deletes:* traction control.

OPTIONAL EQUIPMENT

Major Packages	RETAIL PRICE	DEALER INVOICE
Power Pkg., 4-cylinder	$1385	$1288

Power mirrors and windows, power door locks, remote keyless entry, cruise control, automatic day/night rearview mirror, compass, outside-temperature indicator, map lights, automatic headlights, theft-deterrent system w/alarm.

OPTIONAL EQUIPMENT (cont.)

	RETAIL PRICE	DEALER INVOICE
Leather Pkg.,		
4-cylinder	$755	$702
V6	695	646
Leather upholstery, leather-wrapped steering wheel and shift knob. 4-cylinder requires Power Pkg.		
Comfort Pkg.	595	553
Heated front seats, 6-way power driver seat w/lumbar adjustment. 4-cylinder requires Power Pkg.		
Red Line Pkg., V6	1995	1855
Unique exterior trim, lowered sport suspension, 245/50SR18 tires.		

Safety

Curtain side airbags	395	367
Antilock brakes, 4-cylinder	600	558
2WD includes traction control.		

Comfort & Convenience Features

OnStar assistance system	695	646
Includes one-year service. Requires optional radio including an MP3 player. 4-cylinder requires Power Pkg. NA w/manual transmission.		
Power sunroof	725	675
4-cylinder requires Power Pkg.		
Rear-seat DVD entertainment system	995	925
Requires AM/FM/CD/MP3/DVD player. 4-cylinder requires Power Pkg. NA w/power sunroof.		
AM/FM/CD player, 4-cylinder manual	290	270
AM/FM/CD/MP3 player, 4-cylinder manual	440	409
4-cylinder CVT, V6	150	140
AM/FM/cassette w/in-dash 6-disc CD/MP3 changer,		
4-cylinder manual	940	874
4-cylinder CVT, V6	650	605
AM/FM/CD/MP3/DVD player, 4-cylinder manual	440	409
4-cylinder CVT, V6	150	140
Requires rear-seat DVD entertainment system. 4-cylinder requires Power Pkg.		
Advanced radio system	295	274
Upgraded sound system. Requires optional radio including an MP3 player. 4-cylinder requires Power Pkg.		
Satellite radio	325	302
Requires optional radio including an MP3 player. 4-cylinder requires Power Pkg. Requires monthly fee.		

Appearance & Special Purpose

Fog lights, AWD 4-cylinder	170	158
Alloy wheels, 4-cylinder	400	372
17-inch alloy wheels, FWD V6	300	279
Includes 235/60SR17 tires.		

SCION tC

CLASS: Sporty/performance car
DRIVE WHEELS: Front-wheel drive
BASE PRICE RANGE: $15,950-$16,750. Built in Japan.
ALSO CONSIDER: Acura RSX, Mini Cooper

Toyota's youth-oriented brand adds a third car to its line for 2005. The tC, a 2-dr hatchback coupe, joins the xA 4-dr hatchback and xB wagon under the Scion banner. It's longer and wider than those cars, and also larger than Toyota's Celica sporty coupe. The tC has a 160-hp 2.4-liter 4-cyl engine and a 5-speed manual transmission or 4-speed automatic. Antilock 4-wheel disc brakes, 17-inch wheels, and a driver-knee airbag are standard. Optional are front side airbags and head-protecting curtain side airbags covering both seating rows. Included in the $15,950 base price are air conditioning, power windows/locks/mirrors, sunroof, and cruise control. Also standard are a height-adjustable driver seat, split folding rear seatback, and front seatbacks that recline to form a flat load floor with the folded rear seatbacks. Dealer-installed options include 18- and 19-inch wheels, satellite radio, and special trim items. Scion says a supercharger option due later in the model year will yield about 200 hp.

RATINGS	Base, man.	Base w/18-inch wheels, man.	Base, auto.
ACCELERATION	6	6	5
FUEL ECONOMY	6	6	6
RIDE QUALITY	5	5	5
STEERING/HANDLING	7	7	7
QUIETNESS	4	4	4
CONTROLS/MATERIALS	6	6	6
ROOM/COMFORT (FRONT)	6	5	5
ROOM/COMFORT (REAR)	3	2	2
CARGO ROOM	6	6	6
VALUE WITHIN CLASS	8	8	8

Young people will be the most tolerant of its occasionally high noise levels, but anyone can recognize why the tC qualifies as a solid Recommended pick. It combines sporty performance, surprising space, Toyota quality, and a gen-

 Specifications begin on page 547.

RATINGS (cont.)	Base, man.	Base w/18-inch wheels, man.	Base, auto.

erous list of standard equipment at a bargain price. A smorgasbord of dealer-installed accessories allows an impressive degree of customization—though they quickly drive up the car's cost.

TOTAL	57	55	54
Average total for sporty/performance cars: 48.5			

ENGINES

	dohc I4
Size, liters/cu. in.	2.4/144
Horsepower @ rpm	160 @ 5700
Torque (lb-ft) @ rpm	163 @ 4000
Availability	S
EPA city/highway mpg	
5-speed manual	22/30
4-speed automatic	23/30

PRICES

Scion tC	RETAIL PRICE	DEALER INVOICE
Base 2-door hatchback coupe, manual	$15950	$15152
Base 2-door hatchback coupe, automatic	16750	15912
Destination charge	515	515

STANDARD EQUIPMENT

Base: 2.4-liter 4-cylinder engine, 5-speed manual or 4-speed automatic transmission, dual front airbags, driver-side knee airbag, antilock 4-wheel disc brakes, tire-pressure monitor, air conditioning, power steering, tilt steering wheel, cruise control, cloth upholstery, fold-flat front bucket seats, height-adjustable driver seat, center console, cupholders, split folding rear seat, power mirrors w/turn signals, power windows, power door locks, remote keyless entry, power sunroof, AM/FM/CD/MP3 player, digital clock, tachometer, outside-temperature indicator, visor mirrors, variable-intermittent wipers, rear defogger, cargo cover, automatic-off headlights, theft-deterrent system, 215/45ZR17 tires, alloy wheels.

OPTIONAL EQUIPMENT

Safety	RETAIL PRICE	DEALER INVOICE
Curtain side airbags *Includes front side airbags.*	$650	$559
Comfort & Convenience Features		
Pioneer AM/FM radio w/in-dash 6-disc CD/MP3 changer	395	305
Bazooka subwoofer	449	325
Satellite radio	695	600
Automatic day/night rearview mirror *Includes universal garage-door opener.*	310	225

Appearance & Special Purpose

	RETAIL PRICE	DEALER INVOICE
18-inch wheels	NA	NA
19-inch wheels	NA	NA

Postproduction options also available.

SCION xA

CLASS: Compact car
DRIVE WHEELS: Front-wheel drive
BASE PRICE RANGE: $12,480-$13,280. Built in Japan.
ALSO CONSIDER: Ford Focus, Honda Civic, Toyota Corolla

Scion is Toyota's youth-oriented line, and the xA 4-dr hatchback is Scion's least-expensive model. It carries over unchanged for 2005. Like its Scion siblings—a boxy wagon called the xB and a coupe called the tC—xA is a small front-wheel-drive model sold through Toyota dealers. The xA borrows from Toyota's Echo its 1.5-liter 4-cyl engine, manual and optional automatic transmissions, and other underskin components. Curtain side airbags bundled with front torso side airbags are available as the xA's only other major factory option. Standard equipment includes ABS, air conditioning, power windows/locks/mirrors, single-disc CD stereo, and 60/40 split folding rear seat. Dealers offer a variety of factory-approved functional upgrades and dress-up accessories for all Scions.

RATINGS	xA, man.	xA, auto.
ACCELERATION	4	3
FUEL ECONOMY	8	7
RIDE QUALITY	4	4
STEERING/HANDLING	5	5
QUIETNESS	5	5
CONTROLS/MATERIALS	5	5
ROOM/COMFORT (FRONT)	5	5
ROOM/COMFORT (REAR)	3	3
CARGO ROOM	2	2
VALUE WITHIN CLASS	6	6

Scion aspires to appeal to Generation-Y buyers, and the xA wraps the usual Toyota virtues in a fresh package. That means good workmanship and the

 Specifications begin on page 547.

RATINGS (cont.)

	xA, man.	xA, auto.

promise of good reliability and solid resale value. Standard ABS and available side airbags are added xA lures, as is keen pricing. But larger rivals such as the Ford Focus are more likely to be discounted, thus matching or beating xA for outright dollar value.

TOTAL	47	45
Average total for compact cars: 48.4		

ENGINES

	dohc I4
Size, liters/cu. in.	1.5/91
Horsepower @ rpm	108 @ 6000
Torque (lb-ft) @ rpm	105 @ 4200
Availability	S
EPA city/highway mpg	
5-speed manual	32/38
4-speed automatic	32/38

PRICES

Scion xA

	RETAIL PRICE	DEALER INVOICE
Base 4-door hatchback, manual	$12480	$11855
Base 4-door hatchback, automatic	13280	12615
Destination charge	515	515

STANDARD EQUIPMENT

Base: 1.5-liter 4-cylinder engine, 5-speed manual or 4-speed automatic transmission, dual front airbags, antilock brakes, air conditioning, power steering, tilt steering wheel, cloth upholstery, front bucket seats, split folding rear seat, power mirrors, power windows, power door locks, Pioneer AM/FM/CD/MP3 player, digital clock, tachometer, intermittent wipers, driver-side visor mirror, cargo cover, rear defogger, rear wiper, 185/60R15 tires, wheel covers.

OPTIONAL EQUIPMENT

	RETAIL PRICE	DEALER INVOICE
Safety		
Curtain side airbags and front side airbags	$650	$559
Comfort & Convenience Features		
Remote keyless entry	499	359
AM/FM radio w/in-dash 6-disc CD changer	395	305
Satellite radio	695	600
Requires monthly fee.		
Appearance & Special Purpose		
Fog lights	350	245
Rear spoiler	385	285
Front strut bar tie	225	159
Alloy wheels	665	459

SCION xB

CLASS: Compact car
DRIVE WHEELS: Front-wheel drive
BASE PRICE RANGE: $13,680-$14,480. Built in Japan.
ALSO CONSIDER: Ford Focus wagon, Honda Element

This boxy wagon from Toyota's new youth-oriented division carries into 2005 with no significant changes. The xB has front-wheel drive and a platform shared with Scion's smaller xA, but tops it with a taller vanlike body with a one-piece rear liftgate. Like the xA, the xB seats five and borrows its 1.5-liter 4-cyl engine, manual and optional automatic transmissions, and other underskin components from parent-company Toyota's small Echo sedan. ABS is standard. Also included is an antiskid/traction-control system that isn't available on the xA. However, the xA offers front side airbags and head-protecting curtain side airbags that aren't available on the xB. Scions are sold through Toyota dealers, who carry a number of factory-approved dress-up accessories, plus functional items including larger alloy wheels to replace the xB's standard 15-inch steel wheels.

RATINGS	xB, man.	xB, auto.
ACCELERATION	4	3
FUEL ECONOMY	6	7
RIDE QUALITY	5	5
STEERING/HANDLING	5	6
QUIETNESS	4	4
CONTROLS/MATERIALS	5	6
ROOM/COMFORT (FRONT)	6	7
ROOM/COMFORT (REAR)	7	7
CARGO ROOM	6	6
VALUE WITHIN CLASS	6	6

The xB melds hip-hop style with minivan practicality in a solid, pleasant little wagon bolstered by Toyota's reputation for reliability and high resale values. It's also priced right at under $13,700 to start, but be careful with the options or your xB could end up at over $18,000 like our test model.

TOTAL	54	57

Average total for compact cars: 48.4

 Specifications begin on page 547.

ENGINES

	dohc I4
Size, liters/cu. in.	1.5/91
Horsepower @ rpm	108 @ 6000
Torque (lb-ft) @ rpm	105 @ 4200
Availability	S
EPA city/highway mpg	
5-speed manual	31/35
4-speed automatic	30/34

PRICES

Scion xB	RETAIL PRICE	DEALER INVOICE
Base 4-door wagon, manual	$13680	$12995
Base 4-door wagon, automatic	14480	13755
Destination charge	515	515

STANDARD EQUIPMENT

Base: 1.5-liter 4-cylinder engine, 5-speed manual or 4-speed automatic transmission, traction control, dual front airbags, antilock brakes, antiskid system, air conditioning, power steering, tilt steering wheel, cloth upholstery, front bucket seats, cupholders, split folding rear seat, power mirrors, power windows, power door locks, Pioneer AM/FM/CD/MP3 player, digital clock, tachometer, intermittent wipers, driver-side visor mirror, rear defogger, rear wiper, rear privacy glass, 185/60R15 tires, wheel covers.

OPTIONAL EQUIPMENT

Comfort & Convenience Features	RETAIL PRICE	DEALER INVOICE
AM/FM radio w/in-dash 6-disc CD changer	$395	$305
Satellite radio	695	600
Requires monthly fee.		
Appearance & Special Purpose		
Fog lights	350	245
Rear spoiler	335	235
Alloy wheels	665	459

SUBARU BAJA

CLASS: Compact sport-utility vehicle
DRIVE WHEELS: All-wheel drive
BASE PRICE RANGE: $22,195-$27,095. Built in USA.
ALSO CONSIDER: Ford Escape, Honda CR-V, Mazda Tribute

This compact SUV is basically a small station wagon with a pickup-truck bed in place of an enclosed cargo area. It has a raised suspension and SUV-flavored styling, and like all Subarus, comes with all-wheel drive and a horizontally opposed 4-cyl engine. Two Baja models are offered. The Sport has a.

165-hp 2.5-liter. The Turbo has a 210-hp turbocharged 2.5. Both come with manual or automatic transmission. Antilock 4-wheel disc brakes are standard. Baja seats four and comes with a bedliner. The wall separating cargo bed from cabin has a panel that folds to create a pass-through beneath the fixed rear window. Roof lights and a bed-extender cage are options. For 2005, a bed cover is standard on Turbo models with leather upholstery.

RATINGS

	Baja Sport, auto.	Baja Turbo, auto.
ACCELERATION	4	6
FUEL ECONOMY	5	4
RIDE QUALITY	6	6
STEERING/HANDLING	6	6
QUIETNESS	4	4
CONTROLS/MATERIALS	5	5
ROOM/COMFORT (FRONT)	5	5
ROOM/COMFORT (REAR)	3	3
CARGO ROOM	4	4
VALUE WITHIN CLASS	5	4

Baja has less utility than a conventional compact pickup, but its versatility, features, and carlike behavior have appeal. Turbo models are somewhat pricey for their size, but furnish far better acceleration than Sport versions. With either, you get most of the AWD traction of a “real” SUV but with greater fuel efficiency and less unnecessary bulk.

TOTAL	47	47

Average total for compact sport-utility vehicles: 49.0

ENGINES

	sohc H4	Turbocharged dohc H4
Size, liters/cu. in.	2.5/150	2.5/150
Horsepower @ rpm	165 @ 5600	210 @ 5600
Torque (lb-ft) @ rpm	166 @ 4000	235 @ 3600
Availability	S[1]	S[2]
EPA city/highway mpg		
5-speed manual	21/27	19/25
4-speed automatic	21/28	18/23

1. Sport. 2. Turbo.

 Specifications begin on page 547.

PRICES

Subaru Baja

	RETAIL PRICE	DEALER INVOICE
Sport 4-door crew cab	$22195	$20399
Turbo 4-door crew cab	24195	22216
Turbo w/leather 4-door crew cab	27095	24852
Destination charge	575	575

Prices are for vehicles distributed by Subaru of America. Prices may vary in areas served by independent distributors.

STANDARD EQUIPMENT

Sport: 2.5-liter 4-cylinder engine, 5-speed manual transmission, all-wheel drive, limited-slip differential, dual front airbags, antilock 4-wheel disc brakes, daytime running lights, air conditioning, power steering, tilt steering wheel, cruise control, cloth upholstery, front bucket seats, cupholders, split folding rear seat, bed pass-through, power mirrors, power windows, power door locks, remote keyless entry, power sunroof, AM/FM/CD player, digital clock, tachometer, outside-temperature indicator, map lights, illuminated visor mirrors, variable-intermittent wipers, cargo-box light, rear defogger, automatic-off headlights, floormats, roof rack, rear privacy glass, fog lights, bedliner, raised suspension, 225/60HR16 white-letter tires, alloy wheels.

Turbo adds: 2.5-liter turbocharged 4-cylinder engine, leather-wrapped steering wheel, AM/FM radio w/in-dash 6-disc CD changer.

Turbo w/leather adds: 4-speed automatic transmission w/manual-shift capability, leather upholstery, heated front seats, 6-way power driver seat, cargo bed cover.

OPTIONAL EQUIPMENT

Major Packages

	RETAIL PRICE	DEALER INVOICE
Popular Equipment Group 8	$460	$301
Automatic day/night rearview mirror, compass, security-system upgrade kit, cargo nets.		
Premium Sound Pkg. 2, Sport	1020	717
Manufacturer's Discount Price	*795*	*467*
In-dash 6-disc CD changer, upgraded speakers, tweeter, subwoofer, amplifier.		
Premium Sound Pkg. 3, Sport	495	323
Manufacturer's Discount Price	*395*	*223*
Upgraded speakers, subwoofer, amplifier, tweeter kit.		
Active Lifestyle Pkg. 1, Sport	903	589
Upgraded sound system, splash-guard kit, bed extender.		
Active Lifestyle Pkg. 2, Sport	1198	781
Active Lifestyle Pkg. 1 plus trailer hitch.		
Bed Cargo Group	304	199
Bed extender, cargo net.		

Powertrain

4-speed automatic transmission, Sport	800	730
Turbo	1000	911
Turbo includes manual-shift capability.		

Comfort & Convenience Features	RETAIL PRICE	DEALER INVOICE
In-dash 6-disc CD changer, Sport	$525	$394
Appearance & Special Purpose		
Sport-activity lights	385	289
Cargo bed cover, Sport, Turbo	495	343

Postproduction options also available.

SUBARU FORESTER

CG RECOMMENDED AUTO

CLASS: Compact sport-utility vehicle
DRIVE WHEELS: All-wheel drive
BASE PRICE RANGE: $21,295-$27,395. Built in Japan.
ALSO CONSIDER: Ford Escape, Honda CR-V, Mazda Tribute

Addition of an L.L. Bean-themed model highlights 2005 changes to Subaru's compact SUV. Forester is basically a tall wagon built around the platform and powertrain of Subaru's Impreza compact car. It offers four models: 2.5 X, 2.5 XS, 2.5 XT, and the new 2.5 XS L.L. Bean Edition. Every Forester has all-wheel drive and a horizontally opposed 2.5-liter 4-cyl engine. The 2.5 XT is turbocharged and has 210 hp; other models have 165 hp. Automatic transmission is standard on the L.L. Bean and optional in place of manual transmission in the others. The manual transmission includes Subaru's Hill Holder feature designed to prevent rolling on inclines with the clutch disengaged. Head-and-chest-protecting front side airbags are standard, as is ABS; all but the 2.5 X have 4-wheel disc brakes. All Foresters have 16-inch wheels. For '05, wheels are of a new 8-spoke design on the 2.5 XS and a new 10-spoke style on L.L. Bean. The Bean also includes beige leather upholstery embossed with the outdoor outfitter's logo and is the only Forester with self-leveling rear suspension. Also for '05, all models get a new 3-spoke steering wheel. All but the 2.5 X gain a power driver seat. And the 2.5 XS now comes with monotone exterior appearance vs. contrasting-color cladding on others

RATINGS	XS, man.	XS L.L. Bean, auto.	XT w/Prem. Pkg., auto.
ACCELERATION	4	4	6
FUEL ECONOMY	6	6	5
RIDE QUALITY	5	5	5

 Specifications begin on page 547.

RATINGS (cont.)	XS, man.	XS L.L. Bean, auto.	XT w/Prem. Pkg., auto.
STEERING/HANDLING	6	6	6
QUIETNESS	5	5	5
CONTROLS/MATERIALS	6	6	6
ROOM/COMFORT (FRONT)	6	6	6
ROOM/COMFORT (REAR)	3	3	3
CARGO ROOM	7	7	7
VALUE WITHIN CLASS	7	7	7

If you can live with limited towing capacity and constrained rear-seat space, Forester is a highly rational alternative to any number of bulkier, less-efficient SUVs. This Recommended pick combines AWD security, plenty of cargo space, a stable ride, and respectable fuel economy in a pleasantly carlike package. Nonturbo models never feel spritely, but the 2.5 XT has impressive scoot.

TOTAL	55	55	56

Average total for compact sport-utility vehicles: 49.0

ENGINES	sohc H4	Turbocharged dohc H4
Size, liters/cu. in.	2.5/150	2.5/150
Horsepower @ rpm	165 @ 5600	210 @ 5600
Torque (lb-ft) @ rpm	166 @ 4000	235 @ 3600
Availability	S[1]	S[2]
EPA city/highway mpg		
5-speed manual	21/28	19/23
4-speed automatic	22/27	18/23

1. 2.5 X, 2.5 XS, 2.5 XS L.L. Bean. 2. 2.5 XT.

PRICES

Subaru Forester	RETAIL PRICE	DEALER INVOICE
2.5 X 4-door wagon	$21295	$19685
2.5 XS 4-door wagon	23695	21784
2.5 XS w/sunroof 4-door wagon	24695	22692
2.5 XS L.L. Bean Edition 4-door wagon	26395	24235
2.5 XT 4-door wagon	25695	23698
2.5 XT w/Premium Pkg. 4-door wagon	27395	25237
Destination charge	575	575

Prices are for vehicles distributed by Subaru of America. Prices may vary in areas served by independent distributors.

STANDARD EQUIPMENT

2.5 X: 2.5-liter 4-cylinder engine, 5-speed manual transmission, hill-holder clutch, all-wheel drive, dual front airbags, front side airbags, antilock brakes, daytime running lights, air conditioning, interior air filter, power steering, tilt steering wheel, cruise control, cloth upholstery, front bucket seats, height-adjustable driver seat w/lumbar adjustment, center console, cupholders, split folding rear seat, power mirrors, power windows, power door locks, remote keyless entry, AM/FM/weatherband/CD player, digital clock, tachometer, outside-temperature indicator, overhead console, map lights, visor mirrors, variable-intermittent wipers, cargo cover, rear defogger, rear wiper/washer, automatic-off headlights, floormats, fog lights, roof rack, full-size spare tire, 215/60HR16 tires.

2.5 XS adds: limited-slip differential, antilock 4-wheel disc brakes, automatic climate control, leather-wrapped steering wheel, heated front seats, 8-way power driver seat, heated power mirrors, AM/FM/weatherband radio w/in-dash 6-disc CD changer, windshield-wiper deicer, alloy wheels.

2.5 XS w/sunroof adds: power sunroof.

2.5 XS L.L. Bean Edition adds: 4-speed automatic transmission, leather upholstery, automatic day/night rearview mirror, compass, self-leveling rear suspension. *Deletes:* hill-holder clutch.

2.5 XT adds to XS: 2.5-liter turbocharged 4-cylinder engine.

2.5 XT w/Premium Pkg. adds: leather upholstery, power sunroof.

OPTIONAL EQUIPMENT

Major Packages	RETAIL PRICE	DEALER INVOICE
Popular Equipment Group 2	$429	$280
Automatic day/night rearview mirror, theft-deterrent system upgrade, tailpipe cover. NA XS L.L. Bean Edition, XT, XT Premium.		
Popular Equipment Group 4	170	105
Cargo bin, rubber floormats.		
Popular Equipment Group 7, XT, XT w/Premium	387	252
Automatic day/night rearview mirror, compass, theft-deterrent system upgrade.		
Protection Group	632	392
Brush guard, hood protector, rear dust deflector, differential protector.		
Powertrain		
4-speed automatic transmission	800	727
Std. XS L.L. Bean Edition. Deletes hill-holder clutch.		
Comfort & Convenience Features		
Premium Sound Pkg. 1, X	1101	770
In-dash 6-disc CD changer, upgraded sound system.		
Premium Sound Pkg. 2	375	245
Upgraded sound system. Std. XT, XT Premium.		
In-dash 6-disc CD changer, X	525	394
Appearance & Special Purpose		
Rear spoiler	353	230
Trailer hitch	295	192
Alloy wheels, X	659	495

Postproduction options also available.

SUBARU IMPREZA

CLASS: Compact car
DRIVE WHEELS: All-wheel drive
BASE PRICE RANGE: $18,095-$32,295. Built in Japan.
ALSO CONSIDER: Ford Focus, Honda Civic, Volkswagen Jetta and Golf

Interior revisions and two new appearance-enhanced models highlight 2005 for the smallest Subarus. Imprezas come as sedans and wagons and as the SUV-flavored Outback wagon. Each has all-wheel drive, ABS, and a horizontally opposed 4-cyl engine. The 2.5 RS sedans and wagons and the Outbacks have 165 hp. The WRX sedan and wagon are turbocharged for 227 hp and have a sport suspension, functional hood scoop, and special seats and trim. The WRX STi sedan has 300 hp and upgrades to suspension, brakes, and steering over regular WRXs. The STi comes only with 6-speed manual transmission; all other models have a 5-speed manual or optional 4-speed automatic. Front head/torso side airbags are standard for WRX and STi, unavailable otherwise. The STi has 17-inch wheels, all other models have 16s. For '05, Imprezas get upgraded interior materials and a new center console and door panels, and exchange a 4-spoke steering wheel for a 3-spoke design. WRX and STi gain automatic climate control and, along with the 2.5 RS Sport, an in-dash CD changer. The new 2.5 RS Sport sedan also gets WRX-style lower body trim, seats, steering wheel, and audio system. The new Outback Sport Special Edition has a rear spoiler, interior upgrades, and CD changer.

RATINGS	2.5 RS wgn, auto.	WRX sdn, man.	WRX wgn, man.	WRX STi
ACCELERATION	4	7	7	8
FUEL ECONOMY	6	5	5	4
RIDE QUALITY	5	4	4	1
STEERING/HANDLING	7	8	8	9
QUIETNESS	4	4	4	2
CONTROLS/MATERIALS	5	6	6	6
ROOM/COMFORT (FRONT)	4	5	5	5
ROOM/COMFORT (REAR)	3	3	3	3

RATINGS (cont.)	2.5 RS wgn, auto.	WRX sdn, man.	WRX wgn, man.	WRX STi
CARGO ROOM	7	2	7	2
VALUE WITHIN CLASS	4	5	6	5

Impreza is generally priced above Honda Civic and into Volkswagen Jetta territory, and Subaru is striving to elevate workmanship and refinement to justify this line's "premium small car" billing. Still, AWD is an asset for any model, and the STi and WRXs are fast—if rowdy—fun.

TOTAL	49	49	55	45

Average total for compact cars: 48.4

ENGINES	sohc H4	Turbocharged dohc H4	Turbocharged dohc H4
Size, liters/cu. in.	2.5/150	2.0/122	2.5/150
Horsepower @ rpm	165 @ 5600	227 @ 6000	300 @ 6000
Torque (lb-ft) @ rpm	166 @ 4000	217 @ 4000	300 @ 4000
Availability	S[1]	S[2]	S[3]
EPA city/highway mpg			
5-speed manual	21/28	20/27	
6-speed manual			18/24
4-speed automatic	22/28	19/26	

1. 2.5 RS, Outback Sport. 2. WRX. 3. WRX STi.

PRICES

Subaru Impreza	RETAIL PRICE	DEALER INVOICE
2.5 RS 4-door sedan	$18095	$16862
2.5 RS 4-door wagon	18095	16864
2.5 RS Sport 4-door sedan	19095	17781
Outback Sport 4-door wagon	18995	17683
Outback Sport Special Edition 4-door wagon	19495	18141
WRX 4-door sedan	24895	23098
WRX 4-door wagon	24395	22640
WRX Premium Pkg. 4-door sedan	26395	24475
WRX STi 4-door sedan	32295	30105
Destination charge	575	575

Prices are for vehicles distributed by Subaru of America. Prices may vary in areas served by independent distributors.

STANDARD EQUIPMENT

2.5 RS: 2.5-liter 4-cylinder engine, 5-speed manual transmission, all-wheel drive, dual front airbags, antilock 4-wheel disc brakes, daytime running lights, air conditioning, power steering, tilt steering wheel, cruise control, cloth upholstery, front bucket seats w/height-adjustable driver seat, center console, cupholders, split folding rear seat (wagon), trunk pass-through (sedan), power mirrors, power windows, power door locks, remote keyless entry, AM/FM/CD player, digital clock, tachometer, variable-intermittent wipers, illuminated visor mirrors, rear defogger, intermittent rear/wiper washer (wagon), cargo cover (wagon), floormats, roof rails (wagon), 205/55VR16 tires, alloy wheels.

 Specifications begin on page 547.

Outback Sport adds: outside-temperature indicator, cargo tray, fog lights, roof rack, raised heavy-duty suspension. *Deletes:* illuminated visor mirrors.

Outback Sport Special Edition adds: leather-wrapped steering wheel, AM/FM radio w/in-dash 6-disc CD changer, rear spoiler.

2.5 RS Sport adds to 2.5 RS: leather-wrapped steering wheel, AM/FM radio w/in-dash 6-disc CD changer.

WRX adds: 2.0-liter turbocharged 4-cylinder engine, limited-slip differential, front side airbags, automatic climate control, interior air filter, rear spoiler (wagon), fog lights, sport suspension. *Deletes:* illuminated visor mirrors.

WRX Premium Pkg. adds: power sunroof, heated front seats, heated power mirrors, windshield-wiper deicer, rear spoiler.

WRX STi adds to WRX: 2.5-liter turbocharged 4-cylinder engine, 6-speed manual transmission, upgraded brakes, outside-temperature indicator, illuminated visor mirrors, rear spoiler, xenon headlights, performance suspension, 225/45WR17 tires. *Deletes:* trunk pass-through, floormats, fog lights.

OPTIONAL EQUIPMENT

Major Packages	RETAIL PRICE	DEALER INVOICE
Popular Equipment Group 2, Outback, Outback Special Edition, WRX, WRX Premium, WRX STi	$415	$270
Automatic day/night rearview mirror, compass, security-system upgrade kit.		
Performance Group 2, WRX/WRX Premium manual	814	531
WRX STi	928	649
Short-throw shifter, titanium shift knob, turbo-boost gauge.		
Premium Sound Pkg. 1, RS, Outback	576	376
Upgraded speakers, tweeter kit, subwoofer, amplifier.		
Premium Sound Pkg. 2, RS, Outback	1096	766
Premium Sound Pkg. 1 plus in-dash 6-disc CD changer.		
Powertrain		
4-speed automatic transmission	800	733
NA WRX STi.		
Short-throw shifter, WRX STi	439	330
RS, RS Sport, Outback Special Edition, WRX, WRX Premium	345	225
NA w/automatic transmission.		
Comfort & Convenience Features		
Turbo-boost gauge, WRX, WRX Premium, WRX STi	310	202
Performance Gauge Pack, RS, RS Sport, Outback, Outback Special Edition, WRX, WRX Premium	725	518
WRX STi	740	529
Oil-pressure gauge, voltometer, vacuum gauge (RS, Outback), turbo-boost gauge (WRX). NA WRX STi.		
Automatic day/night rearview mirror	183	119
Includes compass. NA RS, RS Sport.		
In-dash 6-disc CD changer, RS, Outback	520	390

Appearance & Special Purpose

	RETAIL PRICE	DEALER INVOICE
Trailer hitch, wagon	$295	$192
Roof rack, RS wagon, WRX/WRX Premium wagon	179	111
Rear spoiler, RS/RS Sport/WRX sedan	399	300
RS/Outback/Outback Special Edition wagon	363	236
Fog lights, RS	317	207

Postproduction options also available.

SUBARU OUTBACK AND LEGACY

CLASS: Midsize car
DRIVE WHEELS: All-wheel drive
BASE PRICE RANGE: $21,295-$33,495. Built in USA.
ALSO CONSIDER: Hyundai Sonata, Mazda 6, Volkswagen Passat

Subaru redesigns its midsize cars for 2005, giving them new styling, additional features, and more power. Exterior dimensions grow fractionally. Both the Legacy and the SUV-flavored Outback come in sedan and wagon form They share the same platform, but the Outback has a slightly raised suspension. All-wheel drive is again standard, as are horizontally opposed engines. Legacy and Outback 2.5i models have a 168-hp 2.5-liter 4-cyl and come with manual transmission or 4-speed automatic. Legacy 2.5 GT and Outback 2.5 XT models have a new turbocharged version of that engine with 250 hp. They come with manual transmission or a 5-speed automatic with manual shift gate and steering-wheel-mounted shift buttons. Topping the line are the Outback 3.0 R sedan and wagon. They have a 3.0-liter 6-cyl engine with 250 hp, up from 212, and come only with the 5-speed automatic. Standard on all Legacys and Outbacks are ABS, front side airbags, and head-protecting curtain side airbags. The Outback 3.0 R VDC Limited wagon adds an antiskid system. Available features include leather upholstery, heated front seats, woodgrain interior trim, automatic climate control, and heated windshield wipers.

RATINGS	Legacy 2.5 GT Ltd. sdn, man.	Legacy 2.5 GT Ltd. wgn, auto.	Outback 2.5 XT Ltd. wgn, man.	Outback 3.0 R wgn
ACCELERATION	6	6	6	6
FUEL ECONOMY	4	4	4	5

RATINGS (cont.)	Legacy 2.5 GT Ltd. sdn, man.	Legacy 2.5 GT Ltd. wgn, auto.	Outback 2.5 XT Ltd. wgn, man.	Outback 3.0 R wgn
RIDE QUALITY	6	6	7	7
STEERING/HANDLING	7	7	6	6
QUIETNESS	7	7	7	7
CONTROLS/MATERIALS	7	7	7	7
ROOM/COMFORT (FRONT)	6	6	6	6
ROOM/COMFORT (REAR)	5	5	5	5
CARGO ROOM	3	7	7	7
VALUE WITHIN CLASS	6	6	7	7

Though pricey against front-wheel-drive competitors, Legacys appeal for all-wheel-drive capability and numerous standard safety features; for GTs, add turbocharged performance. Those same qualities apply to the Outback wagons, which offer the flavor of "real" SUVs but with carlike ride, handling, and fuel economy. The Outbacks are our Recommended picks.

TOTAL	57	61	62	63

Average total for midsize cars: 57.2

ENGINES	sohc H4	Turbocharged dohc H4	dohc H6
Size, liters/cu. in.	2.5/150	2.5/150	3.0/183
Horsepower @ rpm	168 @ 5600	250 @ 6000	250 @ 6600
Torque (lb-ft) @ rpm	166 @ 4000	250 @ 3600	219 @ 4200
Availability	S[1]	S[2]	S[3]
EPA city/highway mpg			
5-speed manual	23/28[4]	17/19[6]	
4-speed automatic	16/22[5]		
5-speed automatic		18/19[6]	19/19

1. Legacy 2.5i, Outback 2.5i. 2. Legacy 2.5 GT, Outback 2.5 XT. 3. Outback 3.0 R. 4. 23/30 for Legacy 2.5i. 5. 22/30 for Legacy 2.5i. 6. 19/25 for Legacy 2.5 GT.

PRICES

Subaru Outback and Legacy	RETAIL PRICE	DEALER INVOICE
Legacy 2.5i 4-door sedan	$21295	$19678
Legacy 2.5i 4-door wagon	22295	20589
Legacy 2.5i Limited 4-door sedan	24545	22607
Legacy 2.5i Limited 4-door wagon	25745	23701
Legacy 2.5 GT 4-door sedan	26095	24018
Legacy 2.5 GT 4-door wagon	27095	24929
Legacy 2.5 GT Limited 4-door sedan	28595	26294
Legacy 2.5 GT Limited 4-door wagon	29795	27386
Outback 2.5i 4-door wagon	24295	22409
Outback 2.5i Limited 4-door wagon	27095	24929
Outback 2.5 XT 4-door wagon	28095	25839
Outback 2.5 XT Limited 4-door wagon	30795	28296
Outback 3.0 R 4-door sedan	31095	28569

PRICES (cont.)

	RETAIL PRICE	DEALER INVOICE
Outback 3.0 R L.L. Bean Edition 4-door wagon	$32295	$29662
Outback 3.0 R VDC Limited 4-door wagon	33495	30754
Destination charge	575	575

Prices are for vehicles distributed by Subaru of America. Prices may vary in areas served by independent distributors.

STANDARD EQUIPMENT

Legacy 2.5i: 2.5-liter 4-cylinder engine, 5-speed manual transmission, all-wheel drive, dual front airbags, front side airbags, curtain side airbags, front-seat active head restraints, antilock 4-wheel disc brakes, daytime running lights, air conditioning, power steering, tilt steering wheel, cruise control, cloth upholstery, front bucket seats, height-adjustable driver seat, center console, cupholders, trunk pass-through (sedan), split folding rear seat (wagon), power mirrors, power windows, power door locks, remote keyless entry, AM/FM/CD player, digital clock, tachometer, outside-temperature indicator, map lights, illuminated visor mirrors, variable-intermittent wipers, cargo cover (wagon), rear defogger, intermittent rear wiper/washer (wagon), automatic-off headlights, floormats, theft-deterrent system, roof rails (wagon), 205/55HR16 tires, alloy wheels.

Legacy 2.5i Limited adds: leather upholstery, leather-wrapped steering wheel, heated front seats, 8-way power driver seat, dual-zone automatic climate controls, heated power mirrors, single power sunroof (sedan), dual power sunroofs (wagon), AM/FM radio w/in-dash 6-disc CD changer, wiper deicer, fog lights.

Legacy 2.5 GT adds to Legacy 2.5i: 2.5-liter turbocharged 4-cylinder engine, limited-slip differential, dual-zone automatic climate controls, leather-wrapped steering wheel, heated front seats, heated power mirrors w/turn signals, AM/FM radio w/in-dash 6-disc CD changer, wiper deicer, fog lights, 215/45ZR17 tires.

Legacy 2.5 GT Limited adds: leather upholstery, 4-way power passenger seat, single power sunroof (sedan), dual power sunroofs (wagon).

Outback 2.5i adds to Legacy 2.5i: limited-slip differential, heated front seats, 8-way power driver seat, heated power mirrors, cargo tray, wiper deicer, fog lights, roof rack, raised suspension, 225/60HR16 tires.

Outback 2.5i Limited adds: leather upholstery, leather-wrapped steering wheel, dual-zone automatic climate controls, dual power sunroofs, AM/FM radio w/in-dash 6-disc CD changer.

Outback 2.5 XT adds: 2.5-liter turbocharged 4-cylinder engine, 4-way power passenger seat, mirror-mounted turn signals, 225/55VR17 tires. *Deletes:* leather upholstery, dual power sunroofs.

Outback 2.5 XT Limited adds: leather upholstery, dual power sunroofs.

Outback 3.0 R/3.0 R L.L. Bean Edition adds: 3.0-liter 6-cylinder engine, 5-speed automatic transmission w/manual-shift capability, tire-pressure monitor, wood/leather-wrapped steering wheel, single power sunroof (sedan), dual power sunroofs (wagon), automatic day/night rearview mirror (L.L. Bean Edition).

Outback 3.0 VDC Limited adds: antiskid system, AM/FM radio w/in-dash 6-disc CD/MP3 changer, universal garage-door opener. *Deletes:* limited-slip differential, automatic day/night rearview mirror.

OPTIONAL EQUIPMENT

Major Packages	RETAIL PRICE	DEALER INVOICE
Outdoor Recreation Group 2, Legacy wagon	$675	$401
Outback wagon	525	316
Roof rack w/cargo basket and bike carrier.		
Powertrain		
4-speed automatic transmission w/manual-shift capability, 2.5i, 2.5i Limited	1000	911
5-speed automatic transmission w/manual-shift capability, 2.5 GT, 2.5 GT Limited, 2.5 XT, 2.5 XT Limited	1200	1094
Short-throw shifter	339	221
NA w/automatic transmission.		
Comfort & Convenience Features		
Automatic day/night rearview mirror	183	119
Includes compass. Std. 3.0 R L.L. Bean Edition.		
Appearance & Special Purpose		
Rear spoiler, sedan	380	285
Roof rack, Legacy wagon	150	85
Fog lights, Legacy 2.5i	365	274
Trailer hitch, Outback wagon	369	240

Postproduction options also available.

SUZUKI AERIO

CLASS: Compact car
DRIVE WHEELS: Front-wheel drive
2004 BASE PRICE RANGE: $12,999-$16,799. Built in Japan.
ALSO CONSIDER: Ford Focus, Honda Civic, Hyundai Elantra

Aerio gains front side airbags for 2005, along with revised styling inside and out. It comes in S and LX 4-dr sedans and an SX 4-dr wagon. All have a 155-hp 4-cyl engine with either manual transmission or optional automatic. Suzuki's QuadGrip all-wheel drive is optional in place of front-wheel drive for LX and SX with automatic transmission. ABS is optional on all models, front side airbags newly standard. All Aerios include air conditioning, power windows/locks/mirrors, keyless entry, tilt steering wheel, CD player, and split folding rear seats. The LX and SX use 15-inch alloy wheels, the S 14-inch steel wheels. Styling revisions for 2005 include clear-lens taillamps and new front bumper and grille. Inside, a new dashboard includes analog gauges to replace digital, and the steering wheel gains audio controls. Like other Suzukis, Aerio carries a 3-year/36,000-mile bumper-to-bumper warranty that includes roadside assistance, and transferable 7/100,000 powertrain coverage with provision for a free loaner car.

RATINGS	FWD LX sdn, man.	FWD SX wgn, man.	AWD SX wgn, auto.
ACCELERATION	4	4	3
FUEL ECONOMY	7	7	6
RIDE QUALITY	4	4	4
STEERING/HANDLING	5	5	5
QUIETNESS	4	3	3
CONTROLS/MATERIALS	6	6	6
ROOM/COMFORT (FRONT)	6	6	6
ROOM/COMFORT (REAR)	4	4	4
CARGO ROOM	4	7	7
VALUE WITHIN CLASS	4	5	5

Aerio makes sense as an efficient, low-price commuter car, and few others in this class offer the superior bad-weather traction of AWD. But its road manners don't match top-rated rivals, it's somewhat noisy, and Suzuki sells far fewer cars than most competitive brands, which hurts resale values.

TOTAL	48	51	49

Average total for compact cars: 48.4

ENGINES	dohc I4
Size, liters/cu. in.	2.3/140
Horsepower @ rpm	155 @ 5400
Torque (lb-ft) @ rpm	152 @ 3000
Availability	S
EPA city/highway mpg	
5-speed manual	25/31
4-speed automatic	25/31[1]

1. 24/29 w/AWD.

2005 prices unavailable at time of publication.

2004 PRICES

Suzuki Aerio	RETAIL PRICE	DEALER INVOICE
FWD S 4-door sedan, manual	$12999	$12219
FWD S 4-door sedan, automatic	13799	12971
FWD LX 4-door sedan, manual	14699	13817
FWD LX 4-door sedan, automatic	15499	14569

 Specifications begin on page 547.

PRICES (cont.)

	RETAIL PRICE	DEALER INVOICE
AWD LX 4-door sedan, automatic	$16499	$15509
FWD SX 4-door wagon, manual	14999	14099
FWD SX 4-door wagon, automatic	15799	14851
AWD SX 4-door wagon, automatic	16799	15791
Destination charge	500	500

AWD denotes all-wheel drive. FWD denotes front-wheel drive.

STANDARD EQUIPMENT

S: 2.3-liter 4-cylinder engine, 5-speed manual or 4-speed automatic transmission, dual front airbags, emergency inside trunk release, daytime running lights, air conditioning, interior air filter, power steering, tilt steering wheel, cloth upholstery, front bucket seats, center console, cupholders, split folding rear seat, power mirrors, power windows, rear defogger, AM/FM/CD player, digital clock, tachometer, outside-temperature indicator, map lights, intermittent wipers, visor mirrors, floormats, 185/65R14 tires, wheel covers.

LX/SX adds: leather-wrapped steering wheel, cruise control, height-adjustable driver seat, heated power mirrors, power door locks, remote keyless entry, AM/FM radio w/in-dash 6-disc CD changer, variable-intermittent wipers, cargo cover (SX), rear wiper/washer (SX), rear spoiler, fog lights, 195/55R15 tires, alloy wheels. **AWD** adds: all-wheel drive.

OPTIONAL EQUIPMENT

	RETAIL PRICE	DEALER INVOICE
ABS Auto Air Pkg.	$800	$752
Antilock brakes, automatic climate control.		

Other options available as dealer-installed accessories.

SUZUKI FORENZA AND RENO

CLASS: Compact car
DRIVE WHEELS: Front-wheel drive
BASE PRICE RANGE: $13,449-$17,449. Built in South Korea.
ALSO CONSIDER: Ford Focus, Honda Civic, Hyundai Elantra

Suzuki's South Korean-built compact Forenza sedan adds front side airbags for 2005, along with a wagon version and a 4-dr hatchback variant called the Reno. All are offered in S, LX, and top-line EX models, and have a 2.0-liter 4-cyl engine and 4-wheel disc brakes. Automatic transmission is standard for EX, optional for S and LX in place of manual. ABS is available for all. Standard on all models are air conditioning, power windows/locks/heated mirrors, tilt steering wheel, CD stereo with steering-wheel controls, and 15-inch wheels. LX adds cruise control and keyless entry. EX has leather upholstery instead of cloth. Like other Suzukis, Forenza and Reno carry a 3-year/36,000-mile bumper-to-bumper warranty that includes roadside assistance, and transferable 7/100,000 powertrain coverage with provision for a free loaner car. Forenza and Reno were designed by the bankrupt Daewoo Motor Company, Ltd., and are assembled by GM Daewoo Automotive Technologies, which was formed by General Motors after it bought parts of Daewoo. GM also owns a stake in Suzuki.

RATINGS	Forenza LX sdn, man.	Forenza EX sdn, auto.	Forenza EX wgn, auto.	Reno EX hatch, auto.
ACCELERATION	3	3	3	3
FUEL ECONOMY	7	6	6	6
RIDE QUALITY	4	4	4	4
STEERING/HANDLING	4	4	4	4
QUIETNESS	3	3	3	3
CONTROLS/MATERIALS	6	6	6	6
ROOM/COMFORT (FRONT)	6	6	6	6
ROOM/COMFORT (REAR)	4	4	4	4
CARGO ROOM	2	2	7	6
VALUE WITHIN CLASS	4	4	5	5

Forenza and Reno come with a host of standard features for an attractive price, and offer better interior accommodations than most compacts. Both fall behind competitors in performance and refinement, and Suzuki resale values don't yet match those of more-established Japanese makes.

TOTAL	43	42	48	47

Average total for compact cars: 48.4

ENGINES

	dohc I4
Size, liters/cu. in.	2.0/122
Horsepower @ rpm	126 @ 5600
Torque (lb-ft) @ rpm	131 @ 4000
Availability	S
EPA city/highway mpg	
5-speed manual	22/30[1]
4-speed automatic	22/30[2]

1. Wagon, 21/28. 2. Wagon, 20/26.

PRICES

Suzuki Forenza and Reno	RETAIL PRICE	DEALER INVOICE
Forenza S 4-door sedan, manual	$13449	$12776
Forenza S 4-door sedan, automatic	14249	13536
Forenza S 4-door wagon, manual	13949	13251
Forenza S 4-door wagon, automatic	14749	14011
Forenza LX 4-door sedan, manual	15349	14581

PRICES (cont.)

	RETAIL PRICE	DEALER INVOICE
Forenza LX 4-door sedan, automatic	$16149	$15341
Forenza LX 4-door wagon, manual	15849	15056
Forenza LX 4-door wagon, automatic	16649	15816
Forenza EX 4-door sedan, automatic	16949	16101
Forenza EX 4-door wagon, automatic	17449	16576
Reno S 4-door hatchback, manual	13449	12776
Reno S 4-door hatchback, automatic	14249	13536
Reno LX 4-door hatchback, manual	15349	15581
Reno LX 4-door hatchback, automatic	16149	15341
Reno EX 4-door hatchback, automatic	16949	16101
Destination charge	545	545

STANDARD EQUIPMENT

S: 2.0-liter 4-cylinder engine, 5-speed manual or 4-speed automatic transmission, dual front airbags, front side airbags, 4-wheel disc brakes, emergency inside trunk release, daytime running lights, air conditioning, interior air filter, power steering, tilt steering wheel w/radio controls, cloth upholstery, front bucket seats w/driver-side height and lumbar adjustment, center console, cupholders, split folding rear seat, heated power mirrors, power windows, power door locks, AM/FM/cassette/CD player (Forenza), AM/FM/CD/MP3 player (Reno), digital clock, tachometer, variable-intermittent wipers, map lights, visor mirrors, rear defogger, rear wiper/washer (wagon, Reno), floormats, roof rails (wagon), 195/55R15 tires, wheel covers.

LX adds: leather-wrapped steering wheel, cruise control, remote keyless entry, power sunroof, fog lights, alloy wheels.

EX adds: 4-speed automatic transmission, leather upholstery.

OPTIONAL EQUIPMENT

	RETAIL PRICE	DEALER INVOICE
Antilock brakes	$500	$475

SUZUKI GRAND VITARA

CLASS: Compact sport-utility vehicle
DRIVE WHEELS: Rear-wheel drive, 4-wheel drive
2004 BASE PRICE RANGE: $16,299-$21,999. Built in Japan.
ALSO CONSIDER: Ford Escape, Honda CR-V, Subaru Forester

Suzuki's smallest and oldest SUV loses its base Vitara model for 2005. Remaining is the Grand Vitara, a 4-dr wagon with a 165-hp V6 offered in LX and top-line EX trim. LX comes with manual transmission, EX with an automatic that's optional on LX. Both versions offer rear-wheel drive or 4WD that must be disengaged on dry pavement but includes low-range gearing. ABS is standard on EX 4WD, optional on the others. Neither front side airbags or curtain side airbags are offered. Like other Suzukis, Grand Vitara carries a 3-year/36,000-mile bumper-to-bumper warranty that includes roadside assistance, and transferable 7/100,000 powertrain coverage with provision for a free loaner car.

RATINGS

	4WD EX, auto.
ACCELERATION	3
FUEL ECONOMY	5
RIDE QUALITY	2
STEERING/HANDLING	3
QUIETNESS	2
CONTROLS/MATERIALS	3
ROOM/COMFORT (FRONT)	4
ROOM/COMFORT (REAR)	3
CARGO ROOM	6
VALUE WITHIN CLASS	2

The 4WD versions have some useful off-road ability, but Grand Vitara is a distant also-ran among compact SUVs for the kind of driving most people do. Most every class rival is roomier, more pleasant, and commands higher resale value.

TOTAL	33

Average total for compact sport-utility vehicles: 49.0

ENGINES

	dohc V6
Size, liters/cu. in.	2.5/152
Horsepower @ rpm	165 @ 6500
Torque (lb-ft) @ rpm	162 @ 4000
Availability	S
EPA city/highway mpg	
5-speed manual	19/22
4-speed automatic	19/22

2005 prices unavailable at time of publication.

2004 PRICES

Suzuki Grand Vitara	RETAIL PRICE	DEALER INVOICE
2WD Vitara V6 LX 4-door wagon, manual	$16299	$15321
2WD Vitara V6 LX 4-door wagon, automatic	17299	16261
4WD Vitara V6 LX 4-door wagon, manual	17499	16449
4WD Vitara V6 LX 4-door wagon, automatic	18499	17389

 Specifications begin on page 547.

PRICES (cont.)

	RETAIL PRICE	DEALER INVOICE
2WD Grand Vitara LX 4-door wagon, manual	$17499	$16449
2WD Grand Vitara LX 4-door wagon, automatic	18499	17389
4WD Grand Vitara LX 4-door wagon, manual	18999	17859
4WD Grand Vitara LX 4-door wagon, automatic	19999	18799
2WD Grand Vitara EX 4-door wagon, automatic	20299	19081
4WD Grand Vitara EX 4-door wagon, automatic	21999	20679
Destination charge	500	500

STANDARD EQUIPMENT

Vitara V6 LX: 2.5-liter V6 engine, 5-speed manual or 4-speed automatic transmission, dual front airbags, daytime running lights, air conditioning, interior air filter, power steering, tilt steering wheel, cruise control, cloth upholstery, front bucket seats, center console, cupholders, split folding rear seat, power mirrors, power windows, power door locks, remote keyless entry, AM/FM/CD player, tachometer, variable-intermittent wipers, passenger-side visor mirror, cargo cover, rear defogger, rear wiper/washer, automatic headlights, roof rails, full-size spare, 215/65R16 tires. **4WD** adds: 4-wheel drive, 2-speed transfer case.

Grand Vitara LX adds: automatic climate control, steering-wheel radio controls, outside-temperature indicator, map lights, visor mirrors, rear privacy glass, 235/60R16 tires. **4WD** adds: 4-wheel drive, 2-speed transfer case, cruise control, heated power mirrors.

Grand Vitara EX adds: 4-speed automatic transmission, cruise control, power sunroof, rear spoiler, fog lights, alloy wheels. **4WD** adds: 4-wheel drive, 2-speed transfer case, antilock brakes, heated power mirrors.

OPTIONAL EQUIPMENT

Safety

	RETAIL PRICE	DEALER INVOICE
Antilock brakes, LX, 2WD EX	$500	$470

Comfort & Convenience Features

	RETAIL PRICE	DEALER INVOICE
Cruise control, 2WD Grand LX	300	282
Alloy wheels, LX	500	470

Other options are available as dealer-installed accessories.

SUZUKI VERONA

CLASS: Midsize car
DRIVE WHEELS: Front-wheel drive
2004 BASE PRICE RANGE: $16,499-$19,499. Built in South Korea.
ALSO CONSIDER: Chevrolet Malibu, Hyundai Sonata, Mazda 6

Suzuki's largest car is a South Korean-built compact-size sedan that gains side airbags and a tire-pressure monitor for 2005. Verona offers S, LX, and top-line EX models. All come with a 2.5-liter inline 6-cyl engine plus a 4-speed automatic transmission and 4-wheel disc brakes. Standard on all models for '05 are front side airbags and a tire-pressure monitor. LX and EX include ABS, which is not

available on the S. EX also offers optional traction control. All Veronas include power windows/locks/heated mirrors, keyless entry, air conditioning, tilt steering wheel, CD/cassette stereo with steering-wheel controls, and split folding rear seat. The LX adds 16-inch alloy wheels to replace 15-inch steel wheels, plus automatic climate control and, for '05, a sunroof. EX adds leather upholstery, heated front seats, and power driver seat. Like other Suzukis, Verona carries a 3-year/36,000-mile bumper-to-bumper warranty that includes roadside assistance, and transferable 7/100,000 powertrain coverage with provision for a free loaner car. Verona was designed by the bankrupt Daewoo Motor Company, Ltd., and is built by GM Daewoo Automotive Technologies, which GM formed after buying parts of Daewoo. GM also owns a stake in Suzuki.

RATINGS

	EX w/trac. control
ACCELERATION	3
FUEL ECONOMY	5
RIDE QUALITY	6
STEERING/HANDLING	5
QUIETNESS	6
CONTROLS/MATERIALS	6
ROOM/COMFORT (FRONT)	6
ROOM/COMFORT (REAR)	6
CARGO ROOM	3
VALUE WITHIN CLASS	6

Verona is nicely equipped for its price and boasts a strong warranty, but it's plug-ordinary in performance, where its 6-cyl acts more like the 4-cyl engines of many rivals. Also, Suzuki is new to the compact class, and that, plus Verona's origins, imply a bigger depreciation hit and lower resale values vs. more-established competitors.

TOTAL	**52**

Average total for midsize cars: 57.2

ENGINES

	dohc I6
Size, liters/cu. in.	2.5/152
Horsepower @ rpm	155 @ 5800
Torque (lb-ft) @ rpm	177 @ 4000
Availability	S
EPA city/highway mpg	
4-speed automatic	20/28

2005 prices unavailable at time of publication.

2004 PRICES

Suzuki Verona	RETAIL PRICE	DEALER INVOICE
S 4-door sedan	$16499	$15344
LX 4-door sedan	17799	16553
EX 4-door sedan	19499	18134
Destination charge	500	500

STANDARD EQUIPMENT

S: 2.5-liter 6-cylinder engine, 4-speed automatic transmission, dual front airbags, 4-wheel disc brakes, daytime running lights, power steering, tilt leather-wrapped steering w/radio controls, cruise control, air conditioning, interior air filter, cloth upholstery, front bucket seats w/height adjustment, center console, cupholders, split folding rear seat, heated power mirrors, power windows, power door locks, remote keyless entry, AM/FM/cassette/CD player, digital clock, tachometer, variable-intermittent wipers, illuminated visor mirrors, map lights, rear defogger, floormats, theft-deterrent system, theft-deterrent system, fog lights, full-size spare tire, 205/65R15 tires, wheel covers.

LX adds: antilock 4-wheel disc brakes, automatic climate control, 205/55R16 tires, alloy wheels.

EX adds: leather upholstery, heated front seats, 8-way power driver seat, power sunroof, automatic day/night rearview mirror.

OPTIONAL EQUIPMENT	RETAIL PRICE	DEALER INVOICE
Traction control, EX	$500	$470

SUZUKI XL-7

CLASS: Midsize sport-utility vehicle
DRIVE WHEELS: Rear-wheel drive, 4-wheel drive
2004 BASE PRICE RANGE: $19,499-$26,899. Built in Japan.
ALSO CONSIDER: Ford Explorer, GMC Envoy, Toyota Highlander

SUZUKI

Suzuki's midsize SUV gets a tire-pressure monitor and new model names for 2005. XL-7 is basically a stretched version of Suzuki's compact Grand Vitara, with a 12.6-inch-longer wheelbase, 22.9 inches of added length, and a larger 2.7-liter V6. LX and uplevel EX models seat 5 passengers. Versions labeled LX III and EX III add a 3rd-row seat for 7-passenger capacity. LXs come with manual transmission, EXs with a 5-speed automatic that's optional on LXs. XL-7 offers rear-wheel drive or 4WD that should not be left engaged on dry pavement but has low-range gearing. All models include a tire-pressure monitor. ABS is standard on all but the 2WD LX, where it's optional. Neither front side airbags or curtain side airbags are offered. Leather upholstery and heated front seats are optional on EXs. Like other Suzukis, XL-7 carries a 3-year/36,000-mile bumper-to-bumper warranty that includes roadside assistance, and transferable 7/100,000 powertrain coverage with provision for a free loaner car.

RATINGS

	4WD LX III, man.	4WD EX III, auto.
ACCELERATION	4	3
FUEL ECONOMY	4	4
RIDE QUALITY	3	3
STEERING/HANDLING	3	3
QUIETNESS	3	3
CONTROLS/MATERIALS	7	7
ROOM/COMFORT (FRONT)	4	4
ROOM/COMFORT (REAR)	4	4
CARGO ROOM	7	7
VALUE WITHIN CLASS	3	3

Prices are attractive, particularly when compared with other 7-passenger SUVs. But XL-7 can't match the accommodations or on-road performance of top rivals, and can't match their resale value, either. Basically, it's a mediocre compact SUV stretched to become a mediocre midsize SUV with a cramped, available 3rd-row seat as its one asset.

TOTAL	**42**	**41**

Average total for midsize sport-utility vehicles: 54.7

ENGINES

	dohc V6
Size, liters/cu. in.	2.7/167
Horsepower @ rpm	185 @ 6000
Torque (lb-ft) @ rpm	184 @ 4000
Availability	S
EPA city/highway mpg	
5-speed manual	17/22
5-speed automatic	17/22[1]

1. 18/22 w/2WD.

2005 prices unavailable at time of publication.

2004 PRICES

Suzuki XL-7

	RETAIL PRICE	DEALER INVOICE
2WD LX 4-door wagon, manual	$19499	$18329
2WD LX 4-door wagon, automatic	20499	19269

PRICES (cont.)

	RETAIL PRICE	DEALER INVOICE
4WD LX 4-door wagon, manual	$21399	$20115
4WD LX 4-door wagon, automatic	22399	21055
2WD LX 4-door wagon w/3rd-row seat, automatic	21999	20679
4WD LX 4-door wagon w/3rd-row seat, automatic	23899	22465
2WD EX 4-door wagon, automatic	23199	21807
4WD EX 4-door wagon, automatic	24899	23405
2WD EX 4-door wagon w/3rd-row seat, automatic	25199	23687
4WD EX 4-door wagon w/3rd-row seat, automatic	26899	25285
Destination charge	500	500

STANDARD EQUIPMENT

LX: 2.7-liter V6 engine, 5-speed manual or 5-speed automatic transmission, dual front airbags, daytime running lights, front air conditioning, rear air conditioning (w/3rd-row seat), interior air filter, power steering, tilt steering wheel w/radio controls, cruise control, cloth upholstery, front bucket seats, center console, cupholders, 2nd-row split folding seat, 3rd-row split folding seat (w/3rd-row seat), heated power mirrors, power windows, power door locks, remote keyless entry, AM/FM/CD player, digital clock, tachometer, outside-temperature indicator, intermittent wipers, visor mirrors, map lights, cargo cover, rear defogger, rear wiper/washer, automatic headlights, floormats, rear privacy glass, roof rails, full-size spare tire, 235/60R16 tires, alloy wheels. **4WD** adds: 4-wheel drive, 2-speed transfer case, antilock brakes.

EX adds: 5-speed automatic transmission, antilock brakes, leather upholstery, leather-wrapped steering wheel, power sunroof, AM/FM radio w/in-dash 6-disc CD changer, rear spoiler, running boards (w/3rd-row seat), fog lights. **4WD** adds: 4-wheel drive, 2-speed transfer case, heated front seats.

OPTIONAL EQUIPMENT

	RETAIL PRICE	DEALER INVOICE
Antilock brakes, 2WD LX	$500	$470

Other options are available as dealer-installed accessories.

TOYOTA 4RUNNER

CLASS: Midsize sport-utility vehicle
DRIVE WHEELS: Rear-wheel drive, 4-wheel drive, all-wheel drive
BASE PRICE RANGE: $27,495-$37,495. Built in Japan.
ALSO CONSIDER: Acura MDX, Ford Explorer, Toyota Highlander

More V8 power and a new V6 transmission highlight 2005 for Toyota's truck-type midsize SUV. 4Runner comes in SR5, Sport, and Limited models, now with exterior styling touches specific to each. All offer a V6 or V8 with a 5-speed automatic transmission; the V6 had used a 4-speed automatic. The V8 has 270 hp, an increase of 35. Rear-wheel drive is standard. The V8 can be ordered with all-wheel drive, the V6 with 4WD that can be left engaged on dry pavement. Both systems have low-range gearing and also include hill descent control designed to limit speed down steep slopes. Hill ascent con-

trol—to avoid sliding backward—is standard for all models. So are anti-skid/traction control and antilock 4-wheel disc brakes. Front torso side airbags and head-protecting curtain side airbags are available linewide. The curtain airbags are designed to deploy when sensors detect an impending rollover. SR5s come on 16-inch wheels; the others have 17s. A firmer suspension is standard on Sports, optional for Limiteds. A rear load-leveling air-spring suspension is available for V8 Limiteds. Available on SR5 and Limited is a 3rd row for 7-passenger capacity vs. 5. Rear DVD entertainment is available for SR5s and Sports. Limiteds offer an optional navigation system with a camera that displays a rear view on the dashboard screen when backing up. A sunroof is optional on all models for '05; it had been standard on the Limited. Towing capacity is 5000 lb. Toyota's Lexus division sells a dressed-up V8 AWD 4Runner as the GX 470. It has different styling and 235 hp.

RATINGS	2WD SR5, V6	4WD SR5, V6	2WD Sport, V8	AWD Limited, V8
ACCELERATION	5	5	6	6
FUEL ECONOMY	4	4	4	3
RIDE QUALITY	5	5	4	5
STEERING/HANDLING	4	4	4	4
QUIETNESS	5	5	6	6
CONTROLS/MATERIALS	7	7	7	7
ROOM/COMFORT (FRONT)	7	7	7	7
ROOM/COMFORT (REAR)	7	7	7	7
CARGO ROOM	8	8	8	8
VALUE WITHIN CLASS	6	8	6	7

Some like-priced rivals offer a smoother ride and sharper on-road handling, but 4Runner is tough to beat for powertrain polish, off-road ability, and overall refinement. And few match its array of available safety features and traction enhancers, not to mention Toyota's reputation for reliability and high resale value. Those are Recommended-pick credentials.

TOTAL	58	60	59	60

Average total for midsize sport-utility vehicles: 54.7

 Specifications begin on page 547.

ENGINES

	dohc V6	dohc V8
Size, liters/cu. in.	4.0/241	4.7/285
Horsepower @ rpm	245 @ 5200	270 @ 5400
Torque (lb-ft) @ rpm	282 @ 3800	330 @ 3400
Availability	S[1]	S[2]
EPA city/highway mpg		
5-speed automatic	17/21[3]	15/19[4]

1. V6 models. 2. V8 models. 3. 18/21 w/2WD. 4. 16/20 w/2WD.

PRICES

Toyota 4Runner	RETAIL PRICE	DEALER INVOICE
2WD SR5 V6 4-door wagon	$27495	$24550
2WD SR5 V8 4-door wagon	28945	25846
4WD SR5 V6 4-door wagon	29770	26583
AWD SR5 V8 4-door wagon	31220	27879
2WD Sport V6 4-door wagon	28765	25618
2WD Sport V8 4-door wagon	30215	26914
4WD Sport V6 4-door wagon	31040	27650
AWD Sport V8 4-door wagon	32490	28944
2WD Limited V8 4-door wagon	35220	31451
2WD Limited V6 4-door wagon	33770	30155
4WD Limited V6 4-door wagon	36045	32186
AWD Limited V8 4-door wagon	37495	33480
Destination charge	565	565

Prices are for vehicles distributed by Toyota Motor Sales, U.S.A., Inc. The dealer invoice and destination charge may be higher in areas served by independent distributors.

STANDARD EQUIPMENT

SR5: 4.0-liter V6 or 4.7-liter V8 engine, 5-speed automatic transmission, traction control, limited-slip differential, dual front airbags, antilock 4-wheel disc brakes, brake assist, hill ascent control, antiskid system, tire-pressure monitor, air conditioning w/automatic climate control, interior air filter, power steering, tilt steering wheel, cruise control, cloth upholstery, front bucket seats, driver-seat height and power lumbar adjustment, center console, cupholders, split folding rear seat, power mirrors, power windows including tailgate window, power door locks, remote keyless entry, AM/FM/cassette/CD player, digital clock, tachometer, trip computer, variable-intermittent wipers, visor mirrors, map lights, rear defogger, intermittent rear wiper, cargo cover, power liftgate locking, automatic-off headlights, theft-deterrent system, running boards, rear privacy glass, fog lights, trailer hitch, skid plates, full-size spare tire, 265/70R16 tires, alloy wheels. **4WD/AWD** adds: 4-wheel drive/all-wheel drive, 2-speed transfer case, hill descent control.

Sport adds: tilt/telescope leather-wrapped steering wheel w/radio controls, heated power mirrors, roof rack, sport suspension, 265/65R17 white-letter tires. **4WD/AWD** adds: 4-wheel drive/all-wheel drive, 2-speed transfer case, hill descent control.

Limited adds: dual-zone automatic climate controls, leather upholstery, heated front seats, 8-way power driver seat, 4-way power passenger seat, rear radio controls, automatic day/night rearview mirror, compass, universal garage-door opener, illuminated visor mirrors, automatic headlights, 265/65R17 tires. *Deletes:* sport suspension. **4WD/AWD** adds: 4-wheel drive/all-wheel drive, 2-speed transfer case, hill descent control.

OPTIONAL EQUIPMENT

Major Packages

	RETAIL PRICE	DEALER INVOICE
Preferred Accessory Pkg.	$331	$220
First-aid kit, emergency-assistance kit, cargo mat, floormats.		

Safety

Front side airbags and curtain side airbags, SR5, Sport	680	583
Limited	650	559
SR5, Sport include illuminated visor mirrors.		

Comfort & Convenience Features

Power sunroof	900	720
Rear-seat DVD entertainment system, SR5, Sport	1997	1672
Includes rear radio controls. NA w/JBL sound system, JBL AM/FM/cassette w/in-dash 6-disc CD changer.		
Navigation system, Limited	2300	1917
Includes rearview camera, JBL sound system.		
JBL sound system, SR5, Sport	625	476
Limited	475	356
Includes rear radio controls. SR5 requires leather-wrapped steering wheel.		
JBL AM/FM/cassette w/in-dash 6-disc CD changer, SR5, Sport	875	664
Limited	725	544
Includes rear radio controls. SR5 requires leather-wrapped steering wheel. NA w/navigation system.		
Leather-wrapped steering wheel, SR5	220	176
Includes radio controls.		
3rd-row split folding seat, SR5	735	588
Limited	1195	956
NA w/power sunroof, JBL sound system, rear air suspension.		
Universal garage-door opener, SR5, Sport	125	100
Double-decker cargo system, SR5, Sport	125	100
Includes cargo net and mat. NA w/3rd-row seat. Std. Limited.		

Appearance & Special Purpose

Roof rack, SR5	220	176
Rear spoiler	200	160
Sport suspension, Limited	450	360
Rear air suspension, Limited V8	1400	1120
Includes sport suspension.		
265/65R17 tires, SR5	100	80

Postproduction options also available.

2004 TOYOTA AVALON

CLASS: Large car
DRIVE WHEELS: Front-wheel drive
BASE PRICE RANGE: $26,145-$30,605. Built in USA.
ALSO CONSIDER: Chrysler 300, Dodge Magnum

America's only import-brand 6-passenger sedan continues in 2004 form until early calendar 2005, when a redesigned replacement is expected. Avalon is based on Toyota's 1997-2001 Camry sedan. XL and uplevel XLS models include a 3.0-liter V6, automatic transmission, antilock 4-wheel disc brakes, and front side airbags. Both offer an antiskid system with traction control and full-power brake assist, plus either front bucket seats or a front bench for 6-passenger capacity. Exclusive to XLS is an optional DVD navigation system with dashboard screen and remote control for use by passengers.

RATINGS	XL w/bench seat	XLS w/bucket seats
ACCELERATION	5	5
FUEL ECONOMY	5	5
RIDE QUALITY	8	8
STEERING/HANDLING	5	5
QUIETNESS	7	7
CONTROLS/MATERIALS	7	7
ROOM/COMFORT (FRONT)	7	8
ROOM/COMFORT (REAR)	8	8
CARGO ROOM	4	4
VALUE WITHIN CLASS	10	10

Though not sporty or showy, the roomy, quiet, smooth-riding Avalon delivers everything a sedan in this class should. And it's more refined than many cars costing thousands more. Toyota's strong track record for quality, reliability, and resale value adds to the appeal.

TOTAL	66	67

Average total for large cars: 60.9

ENGINES

	dohc V6
Size, liters/cu. in.	3.0/181
Horsepower @ rpm	210 @ 5800
Torque (lb-ft) @ rpm	220 @ 4400
Availability	S
EPA city/highway mpg	
4-speed automatic	21/29

PRICES

Toyota Avalon

	RETAIL PRICE	DEALER INVOICE
XL 4-door sedan, front bench seat	$26965	$23997
XL 4-door sedan, front bucket seats	26145	23267
XLS 4-door sedan, front bench seat	30505	26844
XLS 4-door sedan, front bucket seats	30605	26932
Destination charge	515	515

Prices are for vehicles distributed by Toyota Motor Sales, U.S.A., Inc. The dealer invoice and destination charge may be higher in areas served by independent distributors.

STANDARD EQUIPMENT

XL: 3.0-liter V6 engine, 4-speed automatic transmission, dual front airbags, front side airbags, antilock 4-wheel disc brakes, daytime running lights, emergency inside trunk release, air conditioning w/dual-zone manual controls, interior air filter, power steering, tilt steering wheel, cruise control, cloth upholstery, manual front bucket seats w/center console or power split bench seat, cupholders, trunk pass-through, power mirrors, power windows, power door locks, AM/FM/cassette/CD player, digital clock, tachometer, outside-temperature indicator, rear defogger, illuminated visor mirrors, variable-intermittent wipers, remote fuel-door and decklid releases, automatic headlights, full-size spare tire, 205/65R15 tires, wheel covers.

XLS adds: dual-zone automatic climate controls, leather-wrapped steering wheel, power front seats, heated power mirrors w/driver-side automatic day/night, JBL sound system, remote keyless entry, trip computer, compass, automatic day/night rearview mirror, map lights, universal garage-door opener, rain-sensing wipers, theft-deterrent system, fog lights, alloy wheels.

OPTIONAL EQUIPMENT

Major Packages

	RETAIL PRICE	DEALER INVOICE
Pkg. 1, XL w/bucket seats *Power front seats, remote keyless entry.*	$1150	$920
Pkg. 2, XL w/bucket seats *Power front seats, remote keyless entry, alloy wheels.*	1540	1232
Pkg. 3, XL w/bench seat *Remote keyless entry, alloy wheels.*	705	564

OPTIONAL EQUIPMENT (cont.)	RETAIL PRICE	DEALER INVOICE
GU Premium Luxury Pkg., XLS	$580	$523
Leather upholstery, driver-seat and mirror memory, AM/FM/cassette w/in-dash 6-disc CD changer, 205/60R16 tires.		
GV Premium Luxury Pkg., XLS	895	806
GU Premium Luxury Pkg. plus heated front seats.		
Pkg. 8, XLS	440	340
In-dash 6-disc CD changer, 205/60R16 tires.		
Luxury Pkg., XL w/bucket seats	1995	1796
XL w/bench seat	1140	1026
Leather upholstery, leather-wrapped steering wheel and shift knob, power front seats (bucket seats), remote keyless entry, JBL sound system, alloy wheels.		
Sport Luxury Pkg., XL w/bucket seats	2264	2038
XL w/bench seat	1409	1268
Luxury Pkg. plus rear spoiler, painted alloy wheels.		
Safety		
Antiskid system	650	520
Includes traction control and brake assist.		
Comfort & Convenience Features		
Navigation system, XLS	2000	1700
XLS w/bench seat requires option pkg.		
Power sunroof	900	720
JBL sound system, XL	360	270
XL w/bucket seats requires Pkg. 1 or 2.		
Appearance & Special Purpose		
Rear spoiler	569	357

Postproduction options also available.

TOYOTA CAMRY

CLASS: Midsize car
DRIVE WHEELS: Front-wheel drive
BASE PRICE RANGE: $18,045-$25,405. Built in USA.
ALSO CONSIDER: Honda Accord, Mazda 6, Nissan Altima

Antilock brakes are standard on all models of this popular midsize sedan for 2005, and 4-cyl versions get a new transmission. The Camry line consists of Standard, LE, SE, and XLE models. The Standard model has a 157-hp 4-cyl engine. The others offer the 4-cyl or a V6 with 210 hp in LE and XLE versions, 225 in the SE. Four-cylinder Camrys come with manual transmission. V6s come with a 5-speed automatic, which for '05 replaces a 4-speed automatic as optional for 4-cyl models. All Camrys include ABS. It had been optional on Standard models and on the 4-cly LE and SE, though the 4-cyl LE retains rear drum brakes, while other Camrys have 4-wheel discs. Standards and LEs use 15-inch wheels, XLEs and 4-cyl SEs get 16s. V6 SEs have 17-inch alloys

and a firmer suspension. Front side airbags and head-protecting curtain side airbags are optional on all. An antiskid system is available for SEs and XLEs. The '05 Camrys get minor changes inside and out, including standard steering-wheel audio controls and a rear center headrest. SEs come with a specific new grille. Satellite radio joins an options list that also includes a navigation system and, for automatic-transmission models except the Standard, power-adjustable pedals. Leather upholstery is optional for SEs and 4-cyl XLEs, and newly standard for V6 XLEs. Camry's basic design is shared by the ES 330 at Toyota's luxury Lexus division.

RATINGS	LE, 4-cyl man.	LE, V6 auto.	XLE, 4-cyl auto.	SE w/nav. sys., V6
ACCELERATION	4	6	4	7
FUEL ECONOMY	6	5	6	5
RIDE QUALITY	8	8	8	8
STEERING/HANDLING	6	6	6	6
QUIETNESS	7	8	7	8
CONTROLS/MATERIALS	10	10	10	8
ROOM/COMFORT (FRONT)	7	7	7	7
ROOM/COMFORT (REAR)	6	6	6	6
CARGO ROOM	5	5	5	5
VALUE WITHIN CLASS	9	9	10	8

Few rivals match Camry's blend of family sedan pace, space, and refinement, plus laudable safety features and Toyota's proven reliability and strong resale values. Competitive pricing and available incentives clinch the case for this perennial Best Buy.

TOTAL	68	70	69	68

Average total for midsize cars: 57.2

ENGINES	dohc I4	dohc V6	dohc V6
Size, liters/cu. in.	2.4/144	3.0/183	3.3/202
Horsepower @ rpm	157 @ 5600	210 @ 5800	225 @ 5600
Torque (lb-ft) @ rpm	162 @ 4000	220 @ 4400	240 @ 3600
Availability	S[1]	S[2]	S[3]
EPA city/highway mpg			
5-speed manual	24/33		
5-speed automatic	24/34	20/28	21/29

1. 4-cyl models. 2. LE, XLE V6. 3. SE V6.

Specifications begin on page 547.

PRICES

Toyota Camry

	RETAIL PRICE	DEALER INVOICE
Standard 4-cylinder 4-door sedan, manual	$18045	$16509
Standard 4-cylinder 4-door sedan, automatic	18875	17268
LE 4-cylinder 4-door sedan, manual	19145	17133
LE 4-cylinder 4-door sedan, automatic	19975	17876
LE V6 4-door sedan, automatic	22380	19916
SE 4-cylinder 4-door sedan, manual	19975	17776
SE 4-cylinder 4-door sedan, automatic	20805	18516
SE V6 4-door sedan, automatic	23625	21025
XLE 4-cylinder 4-door sedan, automatic	22395	19929
XLE V6 4-door sedan, automatic	25405	22610
Destination charge	540	540

Prices are for vehicles distributed by Toyota Motor Sales, U.S.A., Inc. The dealer invoice and destination charge may be higher in areas served by independent distributors.

STANDARD EQUIPMENT

Standard: 2.4-liter 4-cylinder engine, 5-speed manual or 5-speed automatic transmission, dual front airbags, antilock 4-wheel disc brakes, daytime running lights, emergency inside trunk release, air conditioning, interior air filter, power steering, tilt steering wheel w/radio controls, cruise control, cloth upholstery, front bucket seats, height-adjustable driver seat, center console, cupholders, split folding rear seat, power mirrors, power windows, power door locks, AM/FM/CD player, digital clock, tachometer, outside-temperature indicator, visor mirrors, map lights, variable-intermittent wipers, rear defogger, automatic headlights, wheel covers, 205/65R15 tires.

LE adds: 2.4-liter 4-cylinder engine or 3.0-liter V6 engine, power front seats, remote keyless entry, theft-deterrent system (V6), full-size spare tire, alloy wheels (V6). *Deletes:* 4-wheel disc brakes (4-cylinder).

SE adds: 2.4-liter 4-cylinder or 3.3-liter V6 engine, antilock 4-wheel disc brakes, power sunroof, leather-wrapped steering wheel, fog lights, sport suspension, 215/60R16 tires (4-cylinder), 215/55R17 tires (V6), alloy wheels (V6).

XLE 4-cylinder adds to LE: 5-speed automatic transmission, antilock 4-wheel disc brakes, heated power mirrors, automatic climate control, JBL AM/FM/cassette w/in-dash 6-disc CD changer, automatic day/night rearview mirror, compass, trip computer, universal garage-door opener, illuminated visor mirrors, rear sunshade, fog lights, 215/60R16 tires.

XLE V6 adds: 3.0-liter V6 engine, leather upholstery, power sunroof, alloy wheels.

OPTIONAL EQUIPMENT

Major Packages

	RETAIL PRICE	DEALER INVOICE
Convenience Plus Pkg. B, LE	$1480	$1160
SE	580	440

Power sunroof (LE), JBL AM/FM/cassette w/in-dash 6-disc CD changer, rear sunshade, cargo net.

OPTIONAL EQUIPMENT (cont.)

	RETAIL PRICE	DEALER INVOICE
VSC and Side Airbag Pkg., LE, SE, XLE	$1300	$1079
Antiskid system, front side airbags, curtain side airbags. NA w/power-adjustable pedals.		
Premium Pkg., SE	1630	1280
Leather upholstery, JBL AM/FM/cassette w/in-dash 6-disc CD changer, rear sunshade, cargo net.		
Navigation Pkg., SE V6	3205	2633
Navigation system, leather upholstery, JBL AM/FM/CD player, universal garage-door opener, rear sunshade, cargo net.		
Navigation Pkg., XLE V6	1450	1243
Navigation system, JBL AM/FM/CD player.		
Premium Pkg., XLE 4-cylinder	1630	1304
Leather upholstery, alloy wheels.		
Premium Plus Pkg., XLE 4-cylinder	2530	2024
Premium Pkg. plus power sunroof.		

Safety

Front side airbags/curtain side airbags	650	559
Antiskid system, SE, XLE	650	520

Comfort & Convenience Features

Power sunroof, LE, XLE 4-cylinder	900	720
JBL AM/FM/cassette w/in-dash 6-disc CD changer, LE, SE	290	218
Satellite radio	449	359
LE requires Convenience Plus Pkg. B. SE requires Convenience Plus Pkg. B or Premium Pkg. NA Standard.		
Power-adjustable pedals, automatics	120	96
NA Standard.		
Heated front seats, SE V6, XLE	315	252
SE V6, XLE 4-cylinder require Premium Pkg., Premium Plus Pkg., or Navigation Pkg.		

Appearance & Special Purpose

Rear spoiler, SE	435	348
Alloy wheels, SE/XLE 4-cylinder	410	328

Postproduction options also available.

TOYOTA CELICA

CLASS: Sporty/performance car
DRIVE WHEELS: Front-wheel drive
BASE PRICE RANGE: $17,670-$23,035. Built in Japan.
ALSO CONSIDER: Acura RSX, Honda Civic Si, Mini Cooper

These sporty 4-cyl hatchback coupes are virtually unchanged for 2005, which Toyota says will be their final model year. Celica offers a 140-hp

model with standard 5-speed manual transmission and a 180-hp GT-S with 6-speed manual. Automatic transmission is available for both and provides the GT-S with steering-wheel buttons for manual shifting. Other shared options include ABS, front side airbags, xenon headlamps, remote keyless entry, sunroof, and rear spoiler. Both also offer an Action Package with adjustable rear spoiler and "aero" lower-body panels. Exclusive GT-S options include leather upholstery and 16-inch wheels instead of 15s. Reflecting sluggish U.S. sales in recent years, Toyota says no 2006 Celica is planned.

RATINGS

	GT, auto.	GT-S, man.
ACCELERATION	5	6
FUEL ECONOMY	7	6
RIDE QUALITY	4	4
STEERING/HANDLING	7	7
QUIETNESS	3	3
CONTROLS/MATERIALS	6	6
ROOM/COMFORT (FRONT)	4	4
ROOM/COMFORT (REAR)	1	1
CARGO ROOM	5	5
VALUE WITHIN CLASS	5	5

Toyotas are known for quality, durability, and high resale value, yet Celica has been a tough sell in a harsh, fickle market segment. That's why it's going away. At least dealers should be offering attractive end-of-model discounts while supplies last.

TOTAL	47	47

Average total for sporty/performance cars: 48.5

ENGINES

	dohc I4	dohc I4
Size, liters/cu. in.	1.8/109	1.8/110
Horsepower @ rpm	140 @ 6400	180 @ 7600
Torque (lb-ft) @ rpm	125 @ 4200	130 @ 6800
Availability	S[1]	S[2]
EPA city/highway mpg		
5-speed manual	27/33	
6-speed manual		23/32
4-speed automatic	29/36	23/30

1. GT. 2. GT-S.

PRICES

Toyota Celica

	RETAIL PRICE	DEALER INVOICE
GT 2-door hatchback, manual	$17670	$15990
GT 2-door hatchback, automatic	18470	16714
GT-S 2-door hatchback, manual	22335	20100
GT-S 2-door hatchback, automatic	23035	20730
Destination charge	540	540

Prices are for vehicles distributed by Toyota Motor Sales, U.S.A., Inc. The dealer invoice and destination charge may be higher in areas served by independent distributors.

STANDARD EQUIPMENT

GT: 1.8-liter 4-cylinder 140-horsepower engine, 5-speed manual or 4-speed automatic transmission, dual front airbags, daytime running lights, air conditioning, power steering, tilt steering wheel, cloth upholstery, front bucket seats, center console, cupholders, split folding rear seat, power mirrors, AM/FM/CD player, digital clock, tachometer, rear defogger, intermittent wipers, visor mirrors, automatic headlights, 195/60R15 tires, wheel covers.

GT-S adds: 1.8-liter 4-cylinder 180-horsepower engine, 6-speed manual or 4-speed automatic transmission w/manual-shift capability, 4-wheel disc brakes, leather-wrapped steering wheel, cruise control, power windows, power door locks, AM/FM radio w/in-dash 6-disc CD changer, intermittent rear wiper, fog lights, 205/55R15 tires, alloy wheels.

OPTIONAL EQUIPMENT

Major Packages

	RETAIL PRICE	DEALER INVOICE
Upgrade Pkg., GT	$820	$656
Cruise control, power windows and door locks.		
All Weather Guard Pkg., GT	270	223
Intermittent rear wiper, heavy-duty rear defogger, heavy-duty battery and starter. Std. GT-S.		
Action Pkg., GT	1965	1700
GT-S	1875	1613
Bodyside cladding, fog lights (GT), rear spoiler.		

Safety

Antilock brakes	300	258
Front side airbags	250	215

Comfort & Convenience Features

Power sunroof	900	720
GT requires Upgrade Pkg.		
Remote keyless entry	230	184
GT requires Upgrade Pkg.		
Leather upholstery, GT-S	660	528
Requires power sunroof.		

 Specifications begin on page 547.

OPTIONAL EQUIPMENT (cont.)

	RETAIL PRICE	DEALER INVOICE
JBL sound system, GT-S	$510	$383
AM/FM radio w/in-dash 6-disc CD changer, GT	315	236
Automatic day/night rearview mirror	295	204
Appearance & Special Purpose		
Rear spoiler, GT	545	436
GT-S	435	348
GT includes fog lights.		
Fog lights, GT	110	88
Xenon headlights	515	412
Alloy wheels, GT	385	308
205/50R16 tires, GT-S	60	48

Postproduction options also available.

TOYOTA COROLLA

CLASS: Compact car
DRIVE WHEELS: Front-wheel drive
BASE PRICE RANGE: $13,680-$17,455. Built in Canada.
ALSO CONSIDER: Ford Focus, Honda Civic, Mazda 3

Toyota's popular small sedan gains optional curtain side airbags, a high-performance model, and mild styling changes for 2005. Corolla lends its platform to the company's Matrix wagon and the similar Pontiac Vibe. Corolla offers base CE, sporty S, luxury LE, and new performance-oriented XRS models. All use a 1.8-liter 4-cyl engine. In the CE, S, and LE, it produces 130 hp and comes with 5-speed manual or 4-speed automatic transmission. In the XRS, it makes 170 hp and comes only with 6-speed manual. XRS also gets unique interior and exterior trim, sport suspension, and 16-inch wheels vs. 15s on other models. ABS is standard on XRS, optional on other Corollas, and comes with a tire-pressure monitor. Head-protecting curtain side airbags and front side airbags are optional on all models. An antiskid system is optional on S and LE. Leather upholstery is optional on the LE. All Corollas get revised front and rear styling for 2005, and LEs get new gauges.

RATINGS

RATINGS	CE, man.	S, man.	LE, auto.	XRS
ACCELERATION	4	4	4	5
FUEL ECONOMY	8	8	7	7
RIDE QUALITY	5	5	5	4
STEERING/HANDLING	5	5	5	6
QUIETNESS	5	5	5	4
CONTROLS/MATERIALS	6	6	6	6
ROOM/COMFORT (FRONT)	5	5	5	5
ROOM/COMFORT (REAR)	3	3	3	3
CARGO ROOM	3	3	3	3
VALUE WITHIN CLASS	8	7	8	6

It's not as refined as it could be, but fine value for money and Toyota reliability qualify Corolla for Recommended status. Honda Civic, Ford Focus, and Mazda 3 sedans have more spice, but no more utility.

TOTAL	52	51	51	49

Average total for compact cars: 48.4

ENGINES

	dohc I4	dohc I4
Size, liters/cu. in.	1.8/110	1.8/110
Horsepower @ rpm	130 @ 6000	170 @ 7600
Torque (lb-ft) @ rpm	125 @ 4200	127 @ 4400
Availability	S[1]	S[2]
EPA city/highway mpg		
5-speed manual	32/41	
6-speed manual		26/34
4-speed automatic	30/38	

1. CE, S, LE. 2. XRS.

PRICES

Toyota Corolla

	RETAIL PRICE	DEALER INVOICE
CE 4-door sedan, manual	$13680	$12652
CE 4-door sedan, automatic	14480	13392
S 4-door sedan, manual	14725	13325
S 4-door sedan, automatic	15525	14049
LE 4-door sedan, manual	14890	13473
LE 4-door sedan, automatic	15690	14197
XRS 4-door sedan, manual	17455	15796
Destination charge	540	540

Prices are for vehicles distributed by Toyota Motor Sales, U.S.A., Inc. The dealer invoice and destination charge may be higher in areas served by independent distributors.

STANDARD EQUIPMENT

CE: 1.8-liter 130-horsepower 4-cylinder engine, 5-speed manual or 4-speed automatic transmission, dual front airbags, daytime running lights, emergency inside trunk release, air conditioning, interior air filter, power steering, tilt steering wheel, cloth upholstery, front bucket seats, height-adjustable driver seat, center console, cupholders, split folding rear seat, power mirrors, AM/FM/CD player, digital clock, tachometer, outside-temperature indicator, intermittent wipers, rear defogger, remote fuel-door and decklid release, 185/65R15 tires, wheel covers.

LE adds: tire-pressure monitor, power windows, power door locks, remote keyless entry, variable-intermittent wipers, map lights, 195/65R15 tires.

S adds to CE: leather-wrapped steering wheel, power door locks, map lights, fog lights, 195/65R15 tires.

XRS adds: 1.8-liter 170-horsepower 4-cylinder engine, 6-speed manual transmission, antilock 4-wheel disc brakes, tire-pressure monitor, cruise control, rear spoiler, sport suspension, 195/55R16 tires, alloy wheels. *Deletes:* split folding rear seat.

OPTIONAL EQUIPMENT

Major Packages	RETAIL PRICE	DEALER INVOICE
Convenience Pkg., CE manual	$345	$310
CE automatic	375	337
Cruise control, power door locks.		
Power Pkg., S, XRS	605	484
Power windows, remote keyless entry.		
Enhanced Power Pkg., S	500	450
Power Pkg. plus cruise control.		
Sport Plus Pkg., S	825	660
Rear spoiler, alloy wheels.		
Extra Value Pkg. 1, S	900	810
Power windows, remote keyless entry, rear spoiler, alloy wheels.		
Audio Value Pkg., LE	200	180
Cruise control, AM/FM radio w/in-dash 6-disc CD changer.		
JBL Value Pkg., LE	510	459
Cruise control, JBL AM/FM radio w/in-dash 6-disc CD changer.		
Leather Pkg., LE	900	720
Leather upholstery, leather-wrapped steering wheel, cruise control.		
Moon Roof/Side Airbags Pkg., S, LE, XRS	1400	1159
Front side airbags, curtain side airbags, power sunroof.		
All Weather Guard Pkg	70	59
Heavy-duty heater, rear heat ducts.		
Safety		
Front side airbags	655	563
Includes curtain side airbags.		
Antilock brakes, CE, S, LE	390	335
Includes tire-pressure monitor.		
Antiskid system, S, LE	650	559
Includes traction control. Requires automatic transmission, antilock brakes.		

	RETAIL PRICE	DEALER INVOICE
Comfort & Convenience Features		
Power sunroof, S, LE, XRS	$750	$600
Appearance & Special Purpose		
Alloy wheels, LE	390	312

Postproduction options also available.

TOYOTA ECHO

CLASS: Compact car
DRIVE WHEELS: Front-wheel drive
BASE PRICE RANGE: $10,355-$11,685. Built in Japan.
ALSO CONSIDER: Ford Focus, Hyundai Elantra

Toyota's smallest cars are unchanged for 2005. Echo offers 2-dr coupes and 4-dr sedans with a 4-cyl engine and manual or optional automatic transmission. ABS, front side airbags, and power steering are optional. Also available are 15-inch wheels to replace the standard 14s, a power windows/door locks package, tachometer, in-dash CD changer, and split folding rear seatbacks.

RATINGS	Base cpe, man.	Base sdn, auto.
ACCELERATION	4	3
FUEL ECONOMY	8	8
RIDE QUALITY	5	5
STEERING/HANDLING	4	4
QUIETNESS	4	4
CONTROLS/MATERIALS	4	4
ROOM/COMFORT (FRONT)	5	5
ROOM/COMFORT (REAR)	3	4
CARGO ROOM	3	3
VALUE WITHIN CLASS	4	4

This is an efficient small car with keen pricing and Toyota's strong reputation for quality and reliability. Its modest power, crosswind-sensitive tall shape, and light weight don't inspire confidence on today's busy interstates, how-

 Specifications begin on page 547.

RATINGS (cont.)

	Base cpe, man.	Base sdn, auto.

ever. Competition from a strong field of less-quirky entry-level rivals has rendered Echo a sales dud, so dealers should be willing to discount.

TOTAL	44	44
Average total for compact cars: 48.4		

ENGINES

	dohc I4
Size, liters/cu. in.	1.5/91
Horsepower @ rpm	108 @ 6000
Torque (lb-ft) @ rpm	105 @ 4200
Availability	S
EPA city/highway mpg	
5-speed manual	35/42
4-speed automatic	33/39

PRICES

Toyota Echo	RETAIL PRICE	DEALER INVOICE
Base 2-door coupe, manual	$10355	$9733
Base 2-door coupe, automatic	11155	10485
Base 4-door sedan, manual	10885	10230
Base 4-door sedan, automatic	11685	10982
Destination charge	540	540

Prices are for vehicles distributed by Toyota Motor Sales, U.S.A., Inc. The dealer invoice and destination charge may be higher in areas served by independent distributors.

STANDARD EQUIPMENT

Base: 1.5-liter 4-cylinder engine, 5-speed manual or 4-speed automatic transmission, dual front airbags, tilt steering wheel, cloth upholstery, front bucket seats, center console, cupholders, AM/FM radio, driver-side visor mirror, 175/65R14 tires, wheel covers.

OPTIONAL EQUIPMENT

Major Packages	RETAIL PRICE	DEALER INVOICE
Appearance Pkg.	$1060	$864
Power steering, tachometer, digital clock, intermittent wipers, bodyside cladding.		
Upgrade Pkg. 1	1095	892
Appearance Pkg. plus remote control outside mirrors, split folding rear seat.		
Upgrade Pkg. 2	1165	920
Air conditioning, AM/FM/cassette/CD player. Requires Appearance Pkg. or bodyside cladding.		
Upgrade Pkg. 3, sedan	575	460
Power windows, power door locks. Requires Upgrade Pkg. 1 and 2.		

OPTIONAL EQUIPMENT (cont.)

	RETAIL PRICE	DEALER INVOICE
All Weather Pkg.	$275	$220
Rear defogger, heavy-duty battery, rear-seat heater ducts. Requires Appearance Pkg. or Upgrade Pkg. 1.		
Safety		
Antilock brakes	340	290
Includes daytime running lights. Requires Upgrade Pkg. 2 and All Weather Pkg.		
Front side airbags	250	215
Comfort & Convenience Features		
Power steering	270	231
Air conditioning	925	740
AM/FM/CD player	140	105
AM/FM/cassette/CD player	240	180
In-dash 6-disc CD changer	589	414
NA w/Upgrade Pkg. 2 or AM/FM/cassette/CD player.		
Tachometer	75	60
Power door locks, coupe	180	144
sedan	275	220
Requires Upgrade Pkg. 1.		
Remote keyless entry	175	140
Requires power door locks.		
Rear defogger	205	164
Split folding rear seat	165	132
Appearance & Special Purpose		
Rear spoiler	300	240
Fog lights	110	88
Sport bodyside cladding	400	320
Alloy wheels	499	375
185/60R15 tires	90	72

Postproduction options also available.

TOYOTA HIGHLANDER

CLASS: Premium midsize sport-utility vehicle
DRIVE WHEELS: Front-wheel drive, all-wheel drive
BASE PRICE RANGE: $24,080-$31,380. Built in Japan.
ALSO CONSIDER: Ford Explorer, Honda Pilot, Nissan Murano

More standard equipment for the base model highlights 2005 for this midsize SUV based on Toyota's Camry sedan platform. The RX 330 from Toyota's luxury Lexus division also shares this underskin structure. Highlander comes in base trim with a 160-hp 4-cyl engine and in base and Limited models with a 230-hp V6. Both engines use an automatic transmission, a 4-speed with the 4-cyl, a 5-speed with the V6. All Highlanders are available with front-wheel drive or with all-wheel drive without low-range gearing. Unlike the 5-passenger RX 330, Highlander can be ordered with a 2-passenger 3rd-row seat for up to 7-passen-

 Specifications begin on page 547.

ger capacity. The 3rd-row seat folds flush into the floor. Also optional for the Toyota, but standard on the Lexus, are head-protecting curtain side airbags covering the 1st and 2nd seating rows; front torso side airbags are included. All Highlanders have antilock 4-wheel disc brakes, antiskid system, and tire-pressure monitor. Limiteds add 17-inch alloy wheels vs. 16-inch steel wheels for base versions. For '05, base models gain as standard a roof rack and remote keyless entry; those features had been options and continue as standard on Limiteds. Limiteds gain a windshield-deicer grid for '05; it's optional for other models. A navigation system is an exclusive Limited option. Sunroof, leather upholstery, heated seats, and rear DVD entertainment are available for all Highlanders.

RATINGS

	AWD Limited w/nav. sys.
ACCELERATION	5
FUEL ECONOMY	4
RIDE QUALITY	6
STEERING/HANDLING	4
QUIETNESS	6
CONTROLS/MATERIALS	7
ROOM/COMFORT (FRONT)	7
ROOM/COMFORT (REAR)	7
CARGO ROOM	8
VALUE WITHIN CLASS	10

Any V6 Highlander is among the top choices in a car-type midsize SUV. This wagon does most everything well and has all the expected family focused features. High refinement, solid workmanship, and Toyota's good reputation for reliability are more reasons for Best Buy honors.

TOTAL	64

Average total for midsize sport-utility vehicles: 54.7

ENGINES

	dohc I4	dohc V6
Size, liters/cu. in.	2.4/144	3.3/202
Horsepower @ rpm	160 @ 5700	230 @ 5600
Torque (lb-ft) @ rpm	165 @ 4000	242 @ 4400
Availability	S[1]	S[2]
EPA city/highway mpg		
4-speed automatic	21/25[3]	
5-speed automatic		18/24[4]

1. Base 4-cyl. 2. Base V6 and Limited. 3. 22/27 w/2WD. 4. 19/25 w/2WD.

PRICES

Toyota Highlander

	RETAIL PRICE	DEALER INVOICE
2WD Base 4-cylinder 4-door wagon	$24080	$21429
AWD Base 4-cylinder 4-door wagon	25480	22675
2WD Base 4-cylinder w/3rd-row seat 4-door wagon	24930	22187
2WD Base V6 4-door wagon	25140	22373
2WD Base V6 w/3rd-row seat 4-door wagon	25990	23129
AWD Base V6 w/3rd-row seat 4-door wagon	27390	24375
2WD Limited 4-door wagon	29980	26680
AWD Limited 4-door wagon	31380	27926
Destination charge	540	540

Prices are for vehicles distributed by Toyota Motor Sales, U.S.A., Inc. The dealer invoice and destination charge may be higher in areas served by independent distributors.

STANDARD EQUIPMENT

Base: 2.4-liter 4-cylinder or 3.3-liter V6 engine, 4-speed automatic transmission (4-cylinder), 5-speed automatic transmission (V6), traction control, dual front airbags, antilock 4-wheel disc brakes, brake assist, antiskid system, tire-pressure monitor, air conditioning, power steering, tilt steering wheel, cruise control, cloth upholstery, front captain chairs, center console, cupholders, split folding rear seat, power mirrors, power windows, power door locks, remote keyless entry, AM/FM/cassette/CD player, digital clock, tachometer, map light, variable-intermittent wipers, visor mirrors, cargo cover, rear defogger, intermittent rear wiper, automatic-off headlights, roof rack, full-size spare tire, 225/70R16 tires. **AWD** adds: all-wheel drive.

Base w/3rd-row seat adds: 3rd-row folding seat, rear heater, rear privacy glass. **AWD** adds: all-wheel drive.

Limited adds: 3.3-liter V6 engine, 5-speed automatic transmission, daytime running lights, automatic climate control, leather-wrapped steering wheel w/radio controls, 8-way power driver seat, 4-way power passenger seat, heated power mirrors, JBL sound system, illuminated visor mirrors, universal garage-door opener, automatic day/night rearview mirror, compass, outside-temperature indicator, wiper deicer, automatic headlights, theft-deterrent system, rear spoiler, fog lights, 225/65R17 tires, alloy wheels. **AWD** adds: all-wheel drive.

OPTIONAL EQUIPMENT

Major Packages

	RETAIL PRICE	DEALER INVOICE
Leather Pkg., Base	$1935	$1548
Base w/3rd-row seat	2285	1828

Leather upholstery, 8-way power driver seat, leather-wrapped steering wheel w/radio controls, universal garage-door opener, illuminated visor mirrors, theft-deterrent system. Requires optional radio.

	RETAIL PRICE	DEALER INVOICE
Leather Pkg., Limited	1400	1120

Leather upholstery.

OPTIONAL EQUIPMENT (cont.)

	RETAIL PRICE	DEALER INVOICE
Preferred Pkg., Base	$665	$532
8-way power driver seat, universal garage-door opener, theft-deterrent system.		
Convenience Pkg., Base	1438	963
Running boards, rear spoiler, exhaust tip, tow hitch.		
Value Pkg., Limited	560	504
Power sunroof, JBL AM/FM/cassette w/in-dash 6-disc CD changer.		
Appearance Pkg.,		
Base V6	910	728
Base V6 w/3rd-row seat	600	480
Rear privacy glass, mud guards, alloy wheels.		
Cold Weather Pkg., Base	60	48
Heated power mirrors, wiper deicer.		
Towing Prep Pkg.	160	128
Heavy-duty radiator and fan, transmission-oil cooler, trailer wiring.		

Safety

Front and 2nd-row curtain side airbags, Base	680	583
Base w/Leather Pkg., Limited	650	559
Includes front side airbags. Base includes illuminated visor mirrors.		

Comfort & Convenience Features

Navigation system,		
Limited	2000	1700
Includes AM/FM/cassette w/in-dash 6-disc CD changer.		
8-way power driver seat, Base	410	328
Heated front seats	440	352
Requires Leather Pkg.		
Power sunroof	900	720
Base requires alloy wheels.		
Rear-seat DVD entertainment system	1770	1416
Requires power sunroof. Base requires alloy wheels, optional radio.		
JBL AM/FM/cassette/CD player, Base	395	296
Base requires Leather Pkg. or steering-wheel radio controls.		
JBL AM/FM radio w/in-dash 6-disc CD changer, Base	595	446
Limited	200	150
Base requires Leather Pkg. or steering-wheel radio controls.		
Steering-wheel radio controls, Base	50	40

Appearance & Special Purpose

Fog lights, Base	110	88
Rear spoiler, Base	200	160
Side steps	459	295
Rear privacy glass, Base	310	248
Std. Base w/3rd-row seat, Limited.		
Alloy wheels, Base	520	416

Postproduction options also available.

TOYOTA LAND CRUISER

CG BEST BUY AUTO

CLASS: Premium large sport-utility vehicle
DRIVE WHEELS: All-wheel drive
2004 BASE PRICE: $54,725. Built in Japan.
ALSO CONSIDER: Cadillac Escalade, Infiniti QX56, Lincoln Navigator

Standard wheel size increases from 17 inches to 18 as the only 2005 change to this Japanese-built SUV. Land Cruiser is somewhat smaller but much costlier than Toyota's American-made Sequoia. The Lexus LX 470 is a luxury Land Cruiser with several exclusive features. Land Cruiser comes with V8, 5-speed automatic transmission, and all-wheel drive that includes low-range gearing. Also standard: ABS, antiskid/traction control, power tilt/telescope steering column, and 3-row seating for eight. Front torso side airbags are optional, but include head-protecting curtain side airbags covering the 1st and 2nd rows. Also available are rear DVD entertainment and a navigation system with CD changer and rearview camera. The navigation's dashboard screen can display DVD video with the transmission in Park and shows a view of what's behind when backing up. Land Cruiser's performance and accommodations mirror those of comparable LX 470s.

RATINGS

	Base
ACCELERATION	5
FUEL ECONOMY	2
RIDE QUALITY	7
STEERING/HANDLING	3
QUIETNESS	8
CONTROLS/MATERIALS	7
ROOM/COMFORT (FRONT)	8
ROOM/COMFORT (REAR)	8
CARGO ROOM	8
VALUE WITHIN CLASS	7

Aged they may be, but these SUVs are true premium products—capable off-road, comfortable on-road, built to a high standard. A Best Buy in this class,

 Specifications begin on page 547.

RATINGS (cont.)

	Base
Land Cruiser offers better dollar value than its costlier cousin, though the LX 470 benefits from Lexus's longer warranty and reputation for superior customer care.	
TOTAL	**63**
Average total for premium large sport-utility vehicles: 63.0	

ENGINES

	dohc V8
Size, liters/cu. in.	4.7/285
Horsepower @ rpm	235 @ 4800
Torque (lb-ft) @ rpm	320 @ 3400
Availability	S
EPA city/highway mpg	
5-speed automatic	13/17

2005 prices unavailable at time of publication.

2004 PRICES

Toyota Land Cruiser	RETAIL PRICE	DEALER INVOICE
4WD Base 4-door wagon	$54725	$47883
Destination charge	540	540

Prices are for vehicles distributed by Toyota Motor Sales, U.S.A., Inc. The dealer invoice and destination charge may be higher in areas served by independent distributors.

STANDARD EQUIPMENT

Base: 4.7-liter V8 engine, 5-speed automatic transmission, all-wheel drive, 2-speed transfer case, limited-slip center differential, traction control, dual front airbags, antilock 4-wheel disc brakes, brake assist, antiskid system, daytime running lights, front and rear air conditioning w/front and rear automatic climate controls, interior air filter, rear heater, power steering, power tilt/telescope leather-wrapped steering wheel w/radio controls, cruise control, leather upholstery, heated front bucket seats w/power lumbar support, 10-way power driver seat, 8-way power passenger seat, center console, cupholders, 2nd-row split folding seat, 3rd-row split folding seat, heated power mirrors, power windows, power door locks, remote keyless entry, power sunroof, JBL AM/FM/cassette w/in-dash 6-disc CD changer, rear radio controls, power antenna, digital clock, tachometer, map lights, illuminated visor mirrors, universal garage-door opener, variable-intermittent wipers, automatic day/night rearview mirror, compass, outside-temperature indicator, rear defogger, rear variable-intermittent wiper/washer, automatic headlights, theft-deterrent system, fog lights, rear privacy glass, front and rear tow hooks, skid plates, full-size spare tire, 275/65R17 tires, alloy wheels.

OPTIONAL EQUIPMENT

Major Packages	RETAIL PRICE	DEALER INVOICE
Convenience Pkg.	$1236	$771
First-aid kit, dashboard inserts, cargo mat and net, floormats, glass-breakage sensor, rear wind deflector, wheel locks.		
Roof Rack Pkg.	565	452
Includes running boards.		
Safety		
Front side airbags	650	520
Includes front and 2nd-row curtain side airbags.		
Comfort & Convenience Features		
Navigation system	3350	2848
Includes DVD player, rearview camera.		
Rear-seat DVD entertainment system	2097	1767
Includes wireless headphones.		
Tow-hitch receiver	379	259
275/60R18 tires	80	64

Postproduction options also available.

TOYOTA MATRIX

CLASS: Compact car
DRIVE WHEELS: Front-wheel drive, all-wheel drive
BASE PRICE RANGE: $14,760-$18,750. Built in Canada.
ALSO CONSIDER: Chrysler PT Cruiser, Ford Focus, Subaru Forester

Freshened styling and newly available safety features mark the 2005 Matrix. This crossover wagon shares its basic design and Toyota powertrain with the Pontiac Vibe, which differs slightly in appearance. Matrix has a swing-up tailgate with separate-opening window and a 1.8-liter 4-cyl engine. Three models are offered. Standard and XR versions offer front- or all-wheel drive. They have 130 hp in front-drive form, 123 with AWD. The sporty XRS model comes only with front-wheel drive and has 170 hp. AWD versions have a 4-speed automatic transmission. Front-drive Standard and XR models come with a 5-speed manual transmission or optional automatic. A 6-speed manual is the only XRS transmission. AWD versions have the same ride height as front-drive equivalents and are not designed for off-road use. ABS is standard for XRS and AWD versions, optional otherwise. XRSs have rear disc brakes vs. drums. An antiskid system is a new-for-'05 option and is available on front-drive, automatic-transmission models. Also newly available are head-protecting curtain side airbags; they're included in an option that carries over front torso side airbags. All models get a new front bumper and grille and new clear-lens taillamps. Wheels are 16 inch, with 17s available for XRS and the front-drive XR.

RATINGS	Standard FWD, man.	XR AWD, auto.	XRS w/17-inch wheels
ACCELERATION	4	3	5
FUEL ECONOMY	7	7	6
RIDE QUALITY	5	5	4
STEERING/HANDLING	5	5	6
QUIETNESS	4	4	3
CONTROLS/MATERIALS	6	6	6
ROOM/COMFORT (FRONT)	6	6	6
ROOM/COMFORT (REAR)	5	5	5
CARGO ROOM	7	7	7
VALUE WITHIN CLASS	10	9	9

Matrix and Vibe are appealing alternatives to conventional small wagons and compact SUVs. We like their utility, good road manners, available AWD, and Toyota-grade reliability. We don't like the needlessly noisy engines and the harsher, high-strung nature of the Matrix XRS and Vibe GT models. Note that Matrix base prices are generally a bit lower than those of comparable Vibes, but Pontiac more frequently offers factory rebates and incentives.

TOTAL	59	57	57

Average total for compact cars: 48.4

ENGINES

	dohc I4	dohc I4
Size, liters/cu. in.	1.8/110	1.8/110
Horsepower @ rpm	130 @ 6000	170 @ 7600
Torque (lb-ft) @ rpm	125 @ 4200	127 @ 4400
Availability	S[1]	S[2]
EPA city/highway mpg		
5-speed manual	30/36	
6-speed manual		25/32
4-speed automatic	28/34[3]	

1. Standard and XR; 123 hp and 118 lb-ft w/AWD. 2. XRS. 3. 26/31 mpg w/AWD.

PRICES

Toyota Matrix	RETAIL PRICE	DEALER INVOICE
FWD Standard 4-door wagon, manual	$14760	$13652
FWD Standard 4-door wagon, automatic	15560	14392
AWD Standard 4-door wagon, automatic	17295	15995
FWD XR 4-door wagon, manual	16240	14696
FWD XR 4-door wagon, automatic	17070	15447

PRICES (cont.)

	RETAIL PRICE	DEALER INVOICE
AWD XR 4-door wagon, automatic	$18635	$16863
FWD XRS 4-door wagon, manual	18750	16968
Destination charge	540	540

Prices are for vehicles distributed by Toyota Motor Sales, U.S.A., Inc. The dealer invoice and destination charge may be higher in areas served by independent distributors. FWD denotes front-wheel drive. AWD denotes all-wheel drive.

STANDARD EQUIPMENT

Standard: 1.8-liter 4-cylinder 130-horsepower engine, 5-speed manual or 4-speed automatic transmission, dual front airbags, daytime running lights, air conditioning, interior air filter, power steering, tilt steering wheel, cloth upholstery, front bucket seats, fold-flat passenger seat, center console, cupholders, split folding rear seat, AM/FM/CD player, digital clock, tachometer, outside-temperature indicator, intermittent wipers, cargo cover, rear defogger, theft-deterrent system, 205/55R16 tires, wheel covers. **AWD** adds: all-wheel drive, 1.8-liter 4-cylinder 123-horsepower engine, 4-speed automatic transmission, antilock brakes, intermittent rear wiper.

XR adds: power mirrors, power windows, power door locks, remote keyless entry, height-adjustable driver seat, variable-intermittent wipers, map lights, intermittent rear wiper. **AWD** adds: all-wheel drive, 1.8-liter 4-cylinder 123-horsepower engine, 4-speed automatic transmission, antilock brakes.

XRS adds: 1.8-liter 4-cylinder 170-horsepower engine, 6-speed manual transmission, antilock 4-wheel disc brakes, tire-pressure monitor, cruise control, fog lights, alloy wheels.

OPTIONAL EQUIPMENT

Major Packages

	RETAIL PRICE	DEALER INVOICE
Power Pkg., Standard automatic	$510	$459
Standard manual	480	432
Power windows and door locks, remote keyless entry.		
Extra Value Pkg. 1, XR	270	243
Cruise control, front and rear underbody spoilers, fog lights.		
Extra Value Pkg. 2, XR	880	792
Extra Value Pkg. 1 plus power sunroof, alloy wheels.		
All Weather Guard Pkg., Standard FWD	250	207
XR FWD, XRS FWD	70	59
Heavy-duty heater, rear heat ducts, intermittent rear wiper (Standard). Std. AWD.		

Safety

Front side impact airbags	645	555
Includes curtain side airbags.		
Antilock brakes, Standard FWD, XR FWD	390	335
Includes tire-pressure monitor.		
Antiskid system, Standard, XR	650	559
Requires Power Pkg., antilock brakes. NA w/manual transmission, AWD.		

Comfort & Convenience Features

	RETAIL PRICE	DEALER INVOICE
Power sunroof, XR, XRS	$750	$600
AM/FM radio w/in-dash 6-disc CD changer, XR, XRS	240	180
JBL AM/FM radio w/in-dash 6-disc CD changer, XRS	540	405
Cruise control, Standard	250	200
Intermittent rear wiper, Standard FWD	180	148

Appearance & Special Purpose

16-inch alloy wheels, Standard, XR	410	328
17-inch alloy wheels, XR FWD	560	448
XRS	150	120

Includes 215/50R17 tires. XR requires antilock brakes. NA w/antiskid system.

Postproduction options also available.

TOYOTA MR2 SPYDER

CLASS: Sporty/performance car
DRIVE WHEELS: Rear-wheel drive
BASE PRICE RANGE: $25,145-$26,145. Built in Japan.
ALSO CONSIDER: Honda S2000, Mazda Miata, Mini Cooper

This midengine 2-seat sports car is essentially unchanged for 2005, which is its final year. MR2 teams a 1.8-liter 4-cyl engine with 5-speed manual transmission or an optional 6-speed sequential manual transmission. The SMT uses computer control to eliminate the clutch pedal. A floor-mounted lever moves forward for upshifts, back for downshifts; steering-wheel buttons can also control shifting. Toyota's SMT has no automatic shift mode, and no conventional automatic transmission is offered. Antilock 4-wheel disc brakes are standard, as is a manual folding top with heated glass rear window. Leather upholstery and limited-slip differential are optional. Side airbags are unavailable. Reflecting minuscule U.S. demand in recent years, Toyota says MR2 will end production in January 2005, with sales continuing until inventory is exhausted.

RATINGS

	Base, man.
ACCELERATION	6
FUEL ECONOMY	7
RIDE QUALITY	4

RATINGS (cont.)

	Base, man.
STEERING/HANDLING	9
QUIETNESS	3
CONTROLS/MATERIALS	7
ROOM/COMFORT (FRONT)	4
ROOM/COMFORT (REAR)	0
CARGO ROOM	1
VALUE WITHIN CLASS	6

MR2 is a hoot to drive, but less practical than most every other sports car. That largely explains the paltry U.S. sales—and why Toyota is giving up on this design. Toyota says it will build only some 1500 of the '05s, but most dealers should offer end-of-model discounts.

TOTAL	47

Average total for sporty/performance cars: 48.5

ENGINES

	dohc I4
Size, liters/cu. in.	1.8/109
Horsepower @ rpm	138 @ 6400
Torque (lb-ft) @ rpm	125 @ 4400
Availability	S
EPA city/highway mpg	
6-speed SMT	25/30
5-speed manual	25/31

PRICES

Toyota MR2 Spyder

	RETAIL PRICE	DEALER INVOICE
Base 2-door convertible, manual	$25145	$22754
Base 2-door convertible, SMT	26145	23659
Destination charge	540	540

Prices are for vehicles distributed by Toyota Motor Sales, U.S.A., Inc. The dealer invoice and destination charge may be higher in areas served by independent distributors.

STANDARD EQUIPMENT

Base manual: 1.8-liter 4-cylinder engine, 5-speed manual transmission, dual front airbags, antilock 4-wheel disc brakes, daytime running lights, air conditioning, power steering, tilt leather-wrapped steering wheel, cloth upholstery, bucket seats, center console, cupholders, power mirrors, power windows, power door locks, remote keyless entry, AM/FM radio w/in-dash 6-disc CD changer, power antenna, digital clock, tachometer, map lights, variable-intermittent wipers, visor mirrors, rear defogger, wind deflector, fog lights, full-size spare tire, 185/55R15 front tires, 215/45R16 rear tires, alloy wheels.

Base SMT adds: 6-speed sequential-shift manual transmission (SMT), cruise control.

 Specifications begin on page 547.

OPTIONAL EQUIPMENT

Major Packages	RETAIL PRICE	DEALER INVOICE
Leather Pkg.	$660	$528
Leather upholstery, tan or black convertible top.		
Preferred Accessory Pkg.	795	476
Simulated carbon-fiber dashboard, first-aid kit, floormats, theft-deterrent system.		
Powertrain		
Limited-slip differential	275	220

Postproduction options also available.

TOYOTA PRIUS

CLASS: Compact car
DRIVE WHEELS: Front-wheel drive
2004 BASE PRICE: $20,295. Built in Japan.
ALSO CONSIDER: Honda Civic Hybrid, Volkswagen Golf/Jetta TDI

Toyota's hybrid-power car adds a standard rear-window wiper for 2005. Prius was redesigned last year as a 4-dr hatchback with more size and power than the original sedan model. A 4-cyl gasoline engine links by computer control to an electric motor powered by a battery pack. The system makes a total 110 hp, which goes to the front wheels through a continuously variable automatic transmission (CVT) providing near-infinite drive ratios. The electric motor helps save fuel by moving the car at low speeds and by assisting the gas engine for acceleration and other needs. Coasting and decelerating recharge the motor's batteries, so there's no plugging-in. Prius comes with antilock brakes, traction control, electric power steering, and now the rear-window wiper/washer, formerly a $180 option. An antiskid system is available, as are front torso side airbags and head-protecting curtain side airbags. Other options include xenon headlamps, a navigation system with voice control, and a keyless entry/starting system with carry-along transmitter. Prius includes special warranty coverage of 3-years/36,000-mi. bumper-to-bumper, 5/60,000 powertrain, and 8/100,000 for the motor, battery pack, and other hybrid-related components.

RATINGS

	Base w/nav. sys.
ACCELERATION	3
FUEL ECONOMY	9
RIDE QUALITY	7
STEERING/HANDLING	4
QUIETNESS	6
CONTROLS/MATERIALS	5
ROOM/COMFORT (FRONT)	6
ROOM/COMFORT (REAR)	6
CARGO ROOM	5
VALUE WITHIN CLASS	6

Prius trumps the more-orthodox Civic Hybrid for room and performance, and both get great mpg. But all the high tech means relatively high initial prices vs. regular economy cars, a cost that will take time to recoup in fuel savings even with the federal tax deduction allowed on hybrid-vehicle purchases. And battery life and replacement cost are unknown. Otherwise, Toyota's "green machine" is a pleasant, practical, all-around family car. Unhappily for shoppers, it's much in demand with today's stiff gas prices, so expect a dealer markup and a long wait, though Toyota is promising to increase supply.

TOTAL	57

Average total for compact cars: 48.4

ENGINES

	dohc I4/electric
Size, liters/cu. in.	1.5/91
Horsepower @ rpm	76 @ 4500
Torque (lb-ft) @ rpm	82 @ 4200
Availability	S[1]
EPA city/highway mpg	
CVT automatic	60/55

1. Gas engine; electric motor has 67 hp @ 1200 rpm and 295 lb-ft @ 0-1200 rpm.

2005 prices unavailable at time of publication.

2004 PRICES

Toyota Prius	RETAIL PRICE	DEALER INVOICE
Base 4-door sedan	$20295	$18687
Destination charge	515	515

Prices are for vehicles distributed by Toyota Motor Sales, U.S.A., Inc. The dealer invoice and destination charge may be higher in areas served by independent distributors.

STANDARD EQUIPMENT

Base: 1.5-liter 4-cylinder engine, electric drive motor, continuously variable transmission (CVT), traction control, dual front airbags, antilock brakes, brake assist, emergency inside trunk release, air conditioning w/automatic climate control, power steering, tilt steering wheel w/radio and climate controls, cruise control, cloth upholstery, front bucket seats, center console, cupholders, split folding rear seat, heated power mirrors, power windows, power door locks, remote keyless entry, AM/FM/CD player, digital clock, outside-temperature indicator, variable-intermittent wipers, rear defogger, visor mirrors, theft-deterrent system, rear spoiler, 185/65R15 tires, alloy wheels.

OPTIONAL EQUIPMENT

Major Packages

	RETAIL PRICE	DEALER INVOICE
Pkg. 1	$180	$144
Intermittent rear wiper.		
Pkg. 2	650	559
Front side airbags, curtain side airbags.		
Pkg. 3	830	703
Front side airbags, curtain side airbags, rear intermittent wiper.		
Pkg. 4	1100	880
Smart keyless entry/starting, universal garage-door opener, intermittent rear wiper, alarm.		
Pkg. 5	1920	1544
Front side airbags, curtain side airbags, JBL AM/FM/cassette w/in-dash 6-disc CD changer, intermittent rear wiper, alarm.		
Pkg. 6	1280	1063
Front side airbags, curtain side airbags, smart keyless entry/starting, intermittent rear wiper.		
Pkg. 7	2255	1864
Front side airbags, curtain side airbags, antiskid system, smart keyless entry/starting, xenon headlights, fog lights, intermittent rear wiper.		
Pkg. 8	3150	2584
Navigation system, smart keyless entry/starting, JBL AM/FM/cassette w/in-dash 6-disc CD changer, intermittent rear wiper.		
Pkg. 9	5245	4320
Pkg. 7 plus navigation system, AM/FM/cassette w/in-dash 6-disc CD changer, universal garage-door opener, alarm.		
Preferred Accessory Pkg.	262	167
First-aid kit, floormats, cargo mat and net.		

Postproduction options also available.

TOYOTA RAV4

CLASS: Compact sport-utility vehicle
DRIVE WHEELS: Front-wheel drive, all-wheel drive
2004 BASE PRICE RANGE: $18,450-$20,900. Built in Japan.
ALSO CONSIDER: Honda CR-V, Subaru Forester

Toyota's smallest SUV is little-changed after its 2004 update. RAV4 returns with a 2.4-liter 4-cyl engine and manual transmission or extra-cost automatic. It offers front-wheel drive or all-wheel drive without low-range gearing. Four-wheel antilock disc brakes and antiskid system are standard, as is a tire-

pressure monitor. Options include front torso side airbags and head-protecting curtain side airbags, plus leather upholstery, alloy wheels, and sunroof. A CD/cassette stereo option is dropped, but an in-dash CD changer remains available. In the only other '05 news, RAV4's available Sport Package adds a unique mesh grille and metal-trimmed foot pedals to carryover features that include a hood scoop, heated mirrors, and sport-cloth upholstery.

RATINGS

	2WD Base, man.
ACCELERATION	5
FUEL ECONOMY	6
RIDE QUALITY	5
STEERING/HANDLING	5
QUIETNESS	4
CONTROLS/MATERIALS	7
ROOM/COMFORT (FRONT)	5
ROOM/COMFORT (REAR)	3
CARGO ROOM	7
VALUE WITHIN CLASS	6

Honda's CR-V has more usable room and feels more stable in gusty crosswinds. RAV4 is at its best as an urban errand-runner, with the bonuses of sound ergonomics and Toyota's reputation for quality, durability, and high resale value.

TOTAL	53

Average total for compact sport-utility vehicles: 50.4

ENGINES

	dohc I4
Size, liters/cu. in.	2.4/144
Horsepower @ rpm	161 @ 5700
Torque (lb-ft) @ rpm	165 @ 4000
Availability	S
EPA city/highway mpg	
5-speed manual	22/27[1]
4-speed automatic	22/27[2]

1. 24/30 w/2WD. 2. 24/29 w/2WD.

 Specifications begin on page 547.

2005 prices unavailable at time of publication.

2004 PRICES

Toyota RAV4

	RETAIL PRICE	DEALER INVOICE
2WD Base 4-door wagon, manual	$18450	$17086
2WD Base 4-door wagon, automatic	19500	18059
AWD Base 4-door wagon, manual	19850	18104
AWD Base 4-door wagon, automatic	20900	19061
Destination charge	540	540

Prices are for vehicles distributed by Toyota Motor Sales, U.S.A., Inc. The dealer invoice and destination charge may be higher in areas served by independent distributors.

STANDARD EQUIPMENT

Base: 2.4-liter 4-cylinder engine, 5-speed manual or 4-speed automatic transmission, traction control, dual front airbags, antilock 4-wheel disc brakes, brake assist, antiskid system, tire-pressure monitor, air conditioning, interior air filter, power steering, tilt steering wheel w/radio controls, cruise control, cloth upholstery, front bucket seats w/height-adjustable driver seat, center console, cupholders, split folding rear seat, power mirrors, power windows, power door locks, AM/FM/CD player, digital clock, tachometer, variable-intermittent wipers, visor mirrors, map lights, rear defogger, intermittent rear wiper, rear-mounted full-size spare tire, 215/70R16 tires. **AWD** adds: all-wheel drive, skid plates.

OPTIONAL EQUIPMENT

Major Packages

	RETAIL PRICE	DEALER INVOICE
Sport Pkg.	$625	$500
Heated color-keyed mirrors, sport upholstery, color-keyed door handles, roof rack, overfenders, hood scoop. NA w/Upgrade Pkg. L.		
Upgrade Pkg. L.	1030	824
Heated color-keyed mirrors, leather-wrapped steering wheel and shift knob, rear privacy glass, fog lights, color-keyed spare-tire cover and bumpers. Requires alloy wheels.		

Safety

Front side airbags and curtain side airbags	680	583
Includes illuminated visor mirrors.		

Comfort & Convenience Features

Power sunroof	900	720
Leather upholstery	670	536
Requires Upgrade Pkg. L.		
Heated front seats	440	352
Requires leather upholstery.		
Leather-wrapped steering wheel	170	136
Requires Sport Pkg.		

OPTIONAL EQUIPMENT (cont.)

	RETAIL PRICE	DEALER INVOICE
Universal garage-door opener	$125	$100
Requires Sport Pkg. or Upgrade Pkg. L.		
Automatic day/night rearview mirror	125	100
Requires Sport Pkg. or Upgrade Pkg. L.		
Remote keyless entry	230	184
AM/FM/cassette/CD player	380	285
Requires Sport Pkg. or Upgrade Pkg. L.		
AM/FM/cassette w/in-dash 6-disc CD changer	580	435
Requires Sport Pkg., or Upgrade Pkg. L.		
Appearance & Special Purpose		
Roof rack	220	176
Side steps	445	219
Rear spoiler	200	160
Rear privacy glass	310	248
Alloy wheels AW	400	346

Postproduction options also available.

TOYOTA SIENNA

CG RECOMMENDED AUTO

CLASS: Minivan
DRIVE WHEELS: Front-wheel drive, all-wheel drive
2004 BASE PRICE RANGE: \$22,955-\$37,150. Built in USA.
ALSO CONSIDER: Dodge Caravan, Honda Odyssey, Mazda MPV

Sienna gets only minor changes for 2005. Models ascend through CE, LE, XLE, and leather-trimmed XLE Limited. All have a 230-hp V6 and a 5-speed automatic transmission. Front-wheel drive is standard. All but the CE are available with all-wheel drive. Antilock brakes and a tire-pressure monitor are standard. AWD versions have run-flat tires. All Siennas have a tilt/telescope steering wheel, remote keyless entry, and rear air conditioning. The sliding side doors have power-down windows. A power right-side sliding door is optional for LEs. XLEs and Limiteds come with dual power doors, power liftgate, and—new for '05—dual power front seats (vs. driver only). Seating for seven is standard and includes 2nd-row buckets and a 60/40 split folding 3rd-row bench that folds into the floor. CE and LE can carry eight via an optional 2nd-row bench; its middle section is sized for a child-safety seat. Standard on Limited are front torso airbags and head-protecting curtain side airbags covering all three seating rows. Other models offer packages that group the airbags with various features. Limiteds and AWD Siennas have 17-inch wheels vs. 16s. Exclusive to Limiteds are standard xenon headlamps, front/rear-obstacle warning, and radar cruise control. A navigation system and rear DVD entertainment are optional for most Siennas.

RATINGS	AWD LE	FWD XLE	AWD XLE Limited
ACCELERATION	5	5	5
FUEL ECONOMY	4	5	4
RIDE QUALITY	6	7	6
STEERING/HANDLING	5	4	5
QUIETNESS	6	6	6
CONTROLS/MATERIALS	6	6	6
ROOM/COMFORT (FRONT)	7	7	7
ROOM/COMFORT (REAR)	7	7	7
CARGO ROOM	9	9	9
VALUE WITHIN CLASS	8	8	7

Sienna combines good ideas from rival minivans with its own appealing pluses, including first-rate refinement, build quality, and carlike road manners. Prices get steep on loaded models, but that's partly offset by Toyota's strong reputation for reliability and resale. This is an easy Recommended value.

TOTAL	63	64	62

Average total for minivans: 58.0

ENGINES

	dohc V6
Size, liters/cu. in.	3.3/202
Horsepower @ rpm	230 @ 5600
Torque (lb-ft) @ rpm	242 @ 3600
Availability	S
EPA city/highway mpg	
5-speed automatic	19/27[1]

1. 18/24 w/AWD.

2005 prices unavailable at time of publication.

2004 PRICES

Toyota Sienna	RETAIL PRICE	DEALER INVOICE
FWD CE 4-door van, 7 passenger	$22955	$20658
FWD CE 4-door van, 8 passenger	23575	21216
FWD LE 4-door van, 7 passenger	24480	22030
FWD LE 4-door van, 8 passenger	24630	22166
AWD LE 4-door van, 7 passenger	28095	25283
FWD XLE 4-door van, 7 passenger	28480	25345
AWD XLE 4-door van, 7 passenger	31685	28197

PRICES (cont.)

	RETAIL PRICE	DEALER INVOICE
FWD XLE Limited 4-door van, 7 passenger	$34700	$30883
AWD XLE Limited 4-door van, 7 passenger	37150	33062
Destination charge	540	540

Prices are for vehicles distributed by Toyota Motor Sales, U.S.A., Inc. The dealer invoice and destination charge may be higher in areas served by independent distributors.

STANDARD EQUIPMENT

CE: 3.3-liter V6 engine, 5-speed automatic transmission, dual front airbags, antilock brakes, brake assist, tire-pressure monitor, front and rear air conditioning w/rear controls, power steering, tilt/telescope steering wheel, cruise control (8 passenger), cloth upholstery, front bucket seats, cupholders, 2nd-row bucket seats (7 passenger), 2nd-row split folding seat (8 passenger), 3rd-row stowable split folding seat, power mirrors, power windows, power door locks, remote keyless entry, AM/FM/cassette/CD player, digital clock, tachometer, visor mirrors, variable-intermittent wipers, conversation mirror, rear defogger, rear wiper/washer, automatic-off headlights, roof rack (8 passenger), 215/65R16 tires, wheel covers.

LE adds: interior air filter, steering-wheel radio controls, cruise control, driver-seat lumbar adjustment, fold-flat front passenger seat, power rear quarter windows, heated power mirrors, illuminated visor mirrors, theft-deterrent system, rear privacy glass, roof rack. **AWD** adds: all-wheel drive, traction control, antilock 4-wheel disc brakes, antiskid system, daytime running lights, windshield-wiper deicer, 225/60R17 run-flat tires, alloy wheels.

XLE adds: tri-zone automatic climate controls, leather-wrapped steering wheel, 8-way power driver seat, dual power sliding rear doors, power liftgate, removable center console, JBL sound system, rear radio controls, outside-temperature indicator, universal garage-door opener, automatic headlights, fog lights, alloy wheels. **AWD** adds: all-wheel drive, traction control, antilock 4-wheel disc brakes, antiskid system, daytime running lights, windshield-wiper deicer, 225/60R17 run-flat tires.

XLE Limited adds: traction control, front side airbags, curtain side airbags, antilock 4-wheel disc brakes, antiskid system, front- and rear-obstacle-detection system, daytime running lights, leather upholstery, heated front seats, woodgrain/leather-wrapped steering wheel, radar cruise control, power sunroof, automatic day/night rearview and driver-side mirrors, 2nd- and 3rd-row sunshades, windshield-wiper deicer, tray table, xenon headlights, 225/60R17 tires. **AWD** adds: all-wheel drive, center console box, rear spoiler, 225/60R17 run-flat tires.

OPTIONAL EQUIPMENT

Major Packages

	RETAIL PRICE	DEALER INVOICE
CE Pkg. 2, CE 7 passenger	$470	$376
Cruise control, roof rack. Std. 8 passenger.		
CE Pkg. 3, CE 7 passenger	2145	1764
CE 8 passenger	1675	1388
Cruise control (7 passenger), traction control, front side airbags, curtain side airbags, antiskid system, daytime running lights, antilock 4-wheel disc brakes, windshield-wiper deicer, roof rack (7 passenger).		

OPTIONAL EQUIPMENT (cont.)

	RETAIL PRICE	DEALER INVOICE
LE Pkg. 1, LE	$810	$648
Power sliding passenger-side door, trip computer, universal garage-door opener, rear radio controls.		
LE Pkg. 2, FWD LE	1220	976
LE Pkg. 1 plus alloy wheels.		
LE Pkg. 3, LE	1435	1117
LE Pkg. 1 plus JBL sound system.		
LE Pkg. 4, LE	1610	1336
LE Pkg. 1 plus front side airbags, curtain side airbags.		
LE Pkg. 5, FWD LE	1845	1445
LE Pkg. 3 plus alloy wheels.		
LE Pkg. 6, FWD LE	2645	2133
LE Pkg. 5 plus front side airbags, curtain side airbags.		
LE Pkg. 7, FWD LE	2895	2364
LE Pkg. 4 plus traction control, antilock 4-wheel disc brakes, antiskid system, daytime running lights, windshield-wiper deicer, alloy wheels.		
LE Pkg. 8, FWD LE	3545	2805
LE Pkg. 5 plus rear DVD player.		
LE Pkg. 9, FWD LE	4345	3493
LE Pkg. 6 plus rear DVD player.		
LE Pkg. 10, FWD LE	3520	2833
LE Pkg. 6 plus traction control, antilock 4-wheel disc brakes, antiskid system, daytime running lights, windshield-wiper deicer.		
LE Pkg. 11, FWD LE	4810	3865
LE Pkg. 10 plus rear DVD player.		
LE Pkg. 12, AWD LE	3935	3165
LE Pkg. 3 plus front side airbags, curtain side airbags, rear DVD player.		
XLE Pkg. 1, FWD XLE	875	700
Traction control, antilock 4-wheel disc brakes, antiskid system, daytime running lights, windshield-wiper deicer.		
XLE Pkg. 2, FWD XLE	900	720
Power sunroof.		
XLE Pkg. 3, FWD XLE	1630	1304
Leather upholstery, 2nd- and 3rd-row sunshades.		
XLE Pkg. 4, XLE	2070	1656
XLE Pkg. 3 plus heated front seats.		
XLE Pkg. 5, FWD XLE	2575	2108
XLE Pkg. 1 and XLE Pkg. 2 plus front side airbags, curtain side airbags.		
XLE Pkg. 6, FWD XLE	2530	2024
XLE Pkg. 2 and XLE Pkg. 3.		
XLE Pkg. 7, FWD XLE	2860	2278
XLE Pkg. 6 plus JBL AM/FM/cassette w/in-dash 6-disc CD changer, 225/60R17 tires.		
XLE Pkg. 8, FWD XLE	2970	2376
XLE Pkg. 6 plus heated front seats.		

OPTIONAL EQUIPMENT (cont.)

	RETAIL PRICE	DEALER INVOICE
XLE Pkg. 9, FWD XLE	$3170	$2526
XLE Pkg. 8 plus JBL AM/FM/cassette w/in-dash 6-disc CD changer.		
XLE Pkg. 10, FWD XLE	3300	2630
XLE Pkg. 9 plus 225/60R17 tires.		
XLE Pkg. 11, FWD XLE	3460	2816
XLE Pkg. 7 plus front side airbags, curtain side airbags.		
XLE Pkg. 12, FWD XLE	3875	3148
XLE Pkg. 1 and XLE Pkg. 4 plus front side airbags, curtain side airbags.		
XLE Pkg. 13, FWD XLE	5000	3990
XLE Pkg. 10 plus rear DVD player.		
XLE Pkg. 14, FWD XLE	4845	3914
XLE Pkg. 1 and XLE Pkg. 9 plus front side airbags, curtain side airbags.		
XLE Pkg. 15, FWD XLE	4960	4016
XLE Pkg. 11 plus rear DVD player.		
XLE Pkg. 16, FWD XLE	6545	5274
XLE Pkg. 14 plus rear DVD player.		
XLE Pkg. 17, XLE	2870	2344
XLE Pkg. 4 plus front side airbags, curtain side airbags.		
XLE Pkg. 18, AWD XLE	3530	2814
Leather upholstery, rear DVD player, JBL AM/FM/cassette w/in-dash 6-disc CD changer.		
XLE Pkg. 19, FWD XLE	7040	5784
XLE Pkg. 15 plus navigation system.		
XLE Pkg. 20, FWD XLE	1700	1408
XLE Pkg. 2 plus front side airbags, curtain side airbags.		
XLE Pkg. 21, AWD XLE	5410	4432
Leather upholstery, rear DVD player, navigation system.		
Limited Pkg. 2, FWD XLE Limited	50	40
Center console box.		
Limited Pkg. 3, FWD XLE Limited	250	200
Center console box, rear spoiler.		
Limited Pkg. 4, FWD XLE Limited	1750	1400
AWD XLE Limited	1500	1200
Center console box (FWD), rear DVD player.		
Limited Pkg. 5, FWD XLE Limited	1950	1560
Center console box, rear DVD player, rear spoiler.		
Limited Pkg. 6, FWD XLE Limited	3630	3018
AWD XLE Limited	3380	2818
Center console (FWD), rear DVD player, navigation system.		

Appearance & Special Purpose

	RETAIL PRICE	DEALER INVOICE
Running boards	599	399
Tow-hitch receiver	415	315
Includes wiring harness, ball mount.		
Alloy wheels, CE, FWD LE	699	550

Postproduction options are also available.

TOYOTA SOLARA

CLASS: Midsize car
DRIVE WHEELS: Front-wheel drive
BASE PRICE RANGE: $19,220-$29,650. Built in USA.
ALSO CONSIDER: Chrysler Sebring coupe, Dodge Stratus coupe, Honda Accord coupe

Redesigned for 2004, these 2-dr spinoffs of Toyota's Camry sedan are unchanged for 2005. Solara offers coupes in SE, SE Sport, and luxury SLE trim, plus SE and SLE convertibles with a standard power top and heated glass rear window. Coupes come with a 4-cyl or V6 engine; convertibles are V6 only. Four-cyl models offer 5-speed manual transmission or optional 4-speed automatic. V6s have standard 5-speed automatic. SE Sports feature unique lower-body styling, performance-tuned suspension, and 17-inch wheels. SLE V6 coupes and both convertibles also have 17-inch wheels; SE and 4-cyl coupes have 16s. All Solaras come with antilock 4-wheel disc brakes and front side airbags. Options include curtain side airbags for coupes and navigation system.

RATINGS	SE 4-cyl cpe, auto.	SE Sport V6 cpe	SLE V6 cpe w/nav. sys.	SLE V6 conv w/nav. sys.
ACCELERATION	4	6	6	6
FUEL ECONOMY	6	5	5	5
RIDE QUALITY	7	5	6	6
STEERING/HANDLING	5	6	6	5
QUIETNESS	7	6	7	5
CONTROLS/MATERIALS	7	7	7	7
ROOM/COMFORT (FRONT)	7	7	7	7
ROOM/COMFORT (REAR)	4	4	4	3
CARGO ROOM	3	3	3	2
VALUE WITHIN CLASS	4	4	4	4

Solara inherits many virtues from its Camry parent, but trades 4-dr practicality for 2-dr style and is no more entertaining to drive. Accord coupes have more spirit, but Solara matches the Honda's reputation for reliability and high resale value, and offers a convertible body style that Accord does not.

TOTAL	54	53	55	50

Average total for midsize cars: 57.2

ENGINES

	dohc I4	dohc V6
Size, liters/cu. in.	2.4/144	3.3/202
Horsepower @ rpm	157 @ 5600	225 @ 5600
Torque (lb-ft) @ rpm	162 @ 4000	240 @ 3600
Availability	S[1]	S[2]
EPA city/highway mpg		
5-speed manual	24/33	
4-speed automatic	23/32	
5-speed automatic		21/29

1. 4-cyl models. 2. V6 models.

PRICES

Toyota Solara	RETAIL PRICE	DEALER INVOICE
SE 4-cylinder 2-door coupe, manual	$19220	$17297
SE 4-cylinder 2-door coupe, automatic	20050	18044
SE V6 2-door coupe, automatic	21550	19394
SE V6 2-door convertible, automatic	26380	23740
SE Sport 4-cylinder 2-door coupe, manual	20715	18643
SE Sport 4-cylinder 2-door coupe, automatic	21545	19389
SE Sport V6 2-door coupe, automatic	23045	20739
SLE 4-cylinder 2-door coupe, automatic	23095	20783
SLE V6 2-door coupe, automatic	26095	23483
SLE V6 2-door convertible, automatic	29650	26684
Destination charge	540	540

Prices are for vehicles distributed by Toyota Motor Sales, U.S.A., Inc. The dealer invoice and destination charge may be higher in areas served by independent distributors. Convertible prices and equipment not available at time of publication.

STANDARD EQUIPMENT

SE 4-cylinder: 2.4-liter 4-cylinder engine, 5-speed manual or 4-speed automatic transmission, dual front airbags, front side airbags, antilock 4-wheel disc brakes, tire-pressure monitor, daytime running lights, emergency inside trunk release, air conditioning, interior air filter, power steering, tilt/telescope steering wheel w/radio controls, cruise control, cloth upholstery, front bucket seats, height-adjustable driver seat, center console, cupholders, split folding rear seat, power mirrors, power windows, power door locks, remote keyless entry, AM/FM/CD player, digital clock, tachometer, trip computer, outside-temperature indicator, illuminated visor mirrors, map lights, variable-intermittent wipers, rear defogger, automatic headlights, theft-deterrent system, fog lights, 215/60R16 tires, alloy wheels.

SE V6 adds: 3.3-liter V6 engine, 5-speed automatic transmission, power convertible top (convertible), leather-wrapped steering wheel (convertible), heated power mirrors w/driver-side automatic day/night (convertible), rear spoiler (convertible), 215/55R17 tires (convertible). *Deletes:* split folding rear seat (convertible).

SE Sport 4-cylinder adds to SE 4-cylinder: leather-wrapped steering wheel, rear spoiler, sport suspension, 215/55R17 tires.

SE Sport V6 adds: 3.3-liter V6 engine, 5-speed automatic transmission.

SLE 4-cylinder adds to SE 4-cylinder: 4-speed automatic transmission, leather-wrapped steering wheel, 8-way power driver seat w/power lumbar adjustment, automatic climate control, heated power mirrors w/driver-side automatic day/night, power sunroof, JBL AM/FM/cassette w/in-dash 6-disc CD changer, automatic day/night rearview mirror, compass, universal garage-door opener.

SLE V6 adds: 3.3-liter V6 engine, 5-speed automatic transmission, leather upholstery, heated front seats, power convertible top (convertible), rear spoiler (convertible), 215/55R17 tires. *Deletes:* split folding rear seat (convertible), power sunroof (convertible).

OPTIONAL EQUIPMENT

### Major Packages	RETAIL PRICE	DEALER INVOICE
Convenience Pkg., SE V6 coupe	$1205	$933
SE V6 convertible	1115	860
8-way power driver seat w/power lumbar adjustment, JBL AM/FM/cassette w/in-dash 6-disc CD changer, 215/55R17 tires (coupe).		
Exterior Pkg., SE V6 coupe	300	240
Rear spoiler, 215/55R17 tires.		
Leather Pkg., SE Sport	1525	1220
Leather upholstery, power driver seat w/power lumbar adjustment.		
Leather Pkg., SLE 4-cylinder	1365	1092
Leather upholstery, heated front seats.		
Safety		
Curtain side airbags, coupe	400	344
SLE V6 requires antiskid system.		
Antiskid system, SLE V6	650	559
Includes traction control. Coupe requires curtain side airbags.		
Comfort & Convenience Features		
Navigation system, SLE V6	1350	1163
Requires antiskid system. Coupe requires curtain side airbags.		
Power sunroof, SE/SE Sport coupe	900	720
SE 4-cylinder requires 8-way power driver seat, rear spoiler. SE V6 requires Convenience Pkg. or Exterior Pkg. NA w/curtain side airbags.		
JBL AM/FM/cassette w/in-dash 6-disc CD changer, SE Sport	630	473
Requires power sunroof.		
8-way power driver seat, SE 4-cylinder	475	380
Includes power lumbar adjustment.		
Windblocker, convertible	395	295
Appearance & Special Purpose		
Rear spoiler, SE/SLE coupe	200	160

Postproduction options also available.

VOLKSWAGEN JETTA AND GOLF

CLASS: Compact car
DRIVE WHEELS: Front-wheel drive
BASE PRICE RANGE: $15,830-$25,045. Built in Mexico.
ALSO CONSIDER: Ford Focus, Honda Civic, Toyota Corolla

Volkswagen's best-selling line mostly marks time for 2005, as redesigned models begin arriving in spring of 2005. Jettas are 4-dr sedans and wagons that far outsell Golf 2- and 4-dr hatchbacks. Roughly parallel lineups offer identical front-wheel-drive powertrains. GL and GLS models use a 2.0-liter 4-cyl engine. A turbo 1.8 4-cyl powers 1.8T models, Jetta GLI 1.8T sedan and 2-dr Golf GTI. A 2.8-liter V6 is reserved for the Golf GTI VR6. TDI models use a 4-cyl 1.9-liter turbodiesel. Dropped for '05 are Jetta's GLI VR6 sedan and the limited-edition all-wheel-drive V6 Golf R32. All models offer 5-speed manual transmission or optional automatic except GTI VR6, which comes only with 6-speed manual. The automatic for 2.0-liter models is a 4-speed unit; 1.8Ts offer a 5-speed automatic with manual shift gate. All Jettas and Golfs include antilock 4-wheel disc brakes, front torso side airbags, and head-protecting curtain side airbags. Traction control is standard except on 2.0 and TDI models, where it's unavailable. An antiskid system is standard for GTI VR6, optional elsewhere. OnStar assistance is available for all. VW says redesigned Jettas bow next April as "late" 2005 models. A redesigned 2006 GTI is due in October 2005, redesigned mainstream Golfs in early calendar 2006.

RATINGS	Golf GLS TDI, man.	Golf GTI VR6	Jetta GL sdn, man.	Jetta GLS 1.8T wgn w/Sport Pkg., auto.
ACCELERATION	4	6	3	5
FUEL ECONOMY	9	6	7	7
RIDE QUALITY	6	4	6	5
STEERING/HANDLING	6	8	6	7
QUIETNESS	5	5	6	5
CONTROLS/MATERIALS	7	7	7	7
ROOM/COMFORT (FRONT)	6	6	6	6
ROOM/COMFORT (REAR)	3	2	3	3
CARGO ROOM	6	6	3	7

 Specifications begin on page 547.

RATINGS (cont.)	Golf GLS TDI, man.	Golf GTI VR6	Jetta GL sdn, man.	Jetta GLS 1.8T wgn w/Sport Pkg., auto.
VALUE WITHIN CLASS	6	5	6	6

These VWs are rather pricey for small cars, so they're not outstanding dollar values. But all are satisfying to drive and come with a laudable list of standard safety features. The available diesel engine and range of body styles are other assets. VW's high-grade interior materials are the industry standard, but the company also gets below-average customer-satisfaction scores for vehicle reliability and dealer service.

TOTAL	58	55	53	58

Average total for compact cars: 48.4

ENGINES	sohc I4	Turbocharged dohc I4	dohc V6	Turbodiesel sohc I4
Size, liters/cu. in.	2.0/121	1.8/109	2.8/170	1.9/116
Horsepower @ rpm	115 @ 5200	180 @ 5500	200 @ 6200	100 @ 4000
Torque (lb-ft) @ rpm	122 @ 2600	173 @ 1950	195 @ 3200	177 @ 1800
Availability	S[1]	S[2]	S[3]	S[4]
EPA city/highway mpg				
5-speed manual	24/31	24/31		38/46
6-speed manual			21/30	
4-speed automatic	24/30			
5-speed automatic		22/29		33/44

1. Jetta GL and GLS, Golf GL and GLS. 2. Jetta GL 1.8T and GLS 1.8T, Golf GTI. 3. Golf GTI VR6. 4. TDI models.

PRICES

Volkswagen Jetta and Golf	RETAIL PRICE	DEALER INVOICE
Golf GL 2-door hatchback, manual	$15830	$14824
Golf GL 2-door hatchback, automatic	16705	15688
Golf GL 4-door hatchback, manual	16030	15009
Golf GL 4-door hatchback, automatic	16905	15873
Golf GL TDI 4-door hatchback, manual	17450	16321
Golf GL TDI 4-door hatchback, automatic	18525	17394
Golf GLS 4-door hatchback, manual	18390	17189
Golf GLS 4-door hatchback, automatic	19265	18053
Golf GLS TDI 4-door hatchback, manual	19580	18287
Golf GLS TDI 4-door hatchback, automatic	20655	19360
Golf GTI 2-door hatchback, manual	19510	17827
Golf GTI 2-door hatchback, automatic	20585	18900
Golf GTI VR6 2-door hatchback, manual	22330	20375
Jetta GL 4-door sedan, manual	17680	16174
Jetta GL 4-door sedan, automatic	18555	17038
Jetta GL 4-door wagon, manual	18680	17077
Jetta GL 4-door wagon, automatic	19555	17941
Jetta GL TDI 4-door wagon, manual	19930	18611

PRICES (cont.)

	RETAIL PRICE	DEALER INVOICE
Jetta GL TDI 4-door wagon, automatic	$21005	$19864
Jetta GLS 4-door sedan, manual	19720	18017
Jetta GLS 4-door sedan, automatic	20595	18881
Jetta GLS 4-door wagon, manual	20720	18921
Jetta GLS 4-door wagon, automatic	21595	19785
Jetta GLS TDI 4-door sedan, manual	20740	19359
Jetta GLS TDI 4-door sedan, automatic	21815	20432
Jetta GLS TDI 4-door wagon, manual	21740	20283
Jetta GLS TDI 4-door wagon, automatic	22815	21356
Jetta GLS 1.8T 4-door wagon, manual	22200	20257
Jetta GLS 1.8T 4-door wagon, automatic	23275	21330
Jetta GLI 1.8T 4-door sedan, manual	24070	21946
Jetta GLI 1.8T 4-door sedan, automatic	25045	22914
Destination charge	575	575

TDI not available in Calif., Mass., Maine, N.Y., Vt.

STANDARD EQUIPMENT

Golf/Jetta GL: 2.0-liter 4-cylinder engine, 1.9-liter turbodiesel 4-cylinder engine (TDI), 5-speed manual or 4-speed automatic transmission, 5-speed manual or 5-speed automatic transmission w/manual-shift capability (TDI), dual front airbags, front side airbags, curtain side airbags, antilock 4-wheel disc brakes, daytime running lights, emergency inside trunk release (Jetta sedan), air conditioning, interior air filter, power steering, tilt/telescope steering wheel, cruise control, cloth upholstery, height-adjustable front bucket seats, center console, cupholders, split folding rear seat, heated power mirrors, power windows, power door locks, remote keyless entry, AM/FM/cassette/CD player, digital clock, tachometer, map lights, variable-intermittent wipers, illuminated visor mirrors (Golf, Jetta wagon), rear defogger, intermittent rear wiper/washer (Golf, Jetta wagon), cargo cover (Golf, Jetta wagon), floormats, theft-deterrent system, roof rails (Jetta wagon), full-size spare tire, 195/65HR15 tires, wheel covers.

Golf/Jetta GLS adds: power sunroof, Monsoon sound system, illuminated visor mirrors, alloy wheels.

Jetta GLS 1.8T adds: 1.8-liter 4-cylinder turbocharged engine, 5-speed manual or 5-speed automatic transmission w/manual-shift capability, traction control.

Jetta GLI adds: 6-speed manual or 5-speed automatic transmission w/manual-shift capability, leather-wrapped steering wheel, trip computer, outside-temperature indicator, sport suspension, 225/40YR18 tires.

Golf GTI adds to Golf/Jetta GL: 1.8-liter turbocharged 4-cylinder engine, 5-speed manual or 5-speed automatic transmission w/manual-shift capability, traction control, leather-wrapped steering wheel, illuminated visor mirrors, sport suspension, 205/55HR16 tires, alloy wheels.

Golf GTI VR6 adds: 2.8-liter V6 engine, 6-speed manual transmission, brake assist, antiskid system, trip computer, 225/45HR17 tires.

 Specifications begin on page 547.

OPTIONAL EQUIPMENT

Major Packages

	RETAIL PRICE	DEALER INVOICE
Leather Pkg., Jetta GLS/GLS TDI/GLS 1.8T	$1050	$929
GTI, GTI VR6	800	706
Leather upholstery, heated front seats and washer nozzles, leather-wrapped steering wheel w/cruise and radio controls (Jetta).		
Luxury Pkg., GTI, GTI VR6	1240	1095
Power sunroof, Monsoon sound system.		
Technology Pkg., GTI VR6	755	667
Automatic climate control, automatic day/night rearview mirror, rain-sensing wipers.		
Sport Pkg., GLS 1.8T	800	706
Sport suspension, 225/45HR17 tires.		
Cold Weather Pkg.	150	133
Heated front seats, heated washer jets. NA GL, GL TDI, GL 1.8T, GLI.		

Safety

Antiskid system	280	247
Includes brake assist. Std. GTI VR6.		

Comfort & Convenience Features

OnStar assistance system	699	617
Jetta GL sedan includes illuminated visor mirrors.		
6-disc CD changer	499	323

Appearance & Special Purpose

Rear spoiler, Jetta sedan	479	298
17-inch alloy wheels, GTI	400	353
Includes 225/45HR17 tires.		

VOLKSWAGEN NEW BEETLE

CLASS: Sporty/performance car
DRIVE WHEELS: Front-wheel drive
BASE PRICE RANGE: $16,570-$26,525. Built in Mexico.
ALSO CONSIDER: Acura RSX, Mini Cooper, Toyota Celica

Optional satellite radio and linewide availability of 6-speed automatic transmission lead changes for Volkswagen's 2005 retro-styled cars. New Beetles are 2-dr hatchbacks and convertibles with 4-cyl power. GL and GLS models have a 115-hp 2.0-liter engine. GLS 1.8T versions use a 150-hp turbocharged 1.8. Available only as a hatchbacks is the GLS TDI model with a 100-hp 1.9-liter turbodiesel. A 5-speed manual transmission is standard. A 6-speed automatic transmission with manual-shift gate replaces last year's 4-speed option on non-TDI models. Every New Beetle includes antilock 4-wheel disc brakes and front side airbags with head and torso protection. An antiskid system is standard for the GLS 1.8T convertible, optional elsewhere. Also new for '05, factory audio systems add a jack for connecting digital music players, and satellite radio is available for all models. Also optional are OnStar assistance, leather upholstery, heated front seats, and xenon headlamps. Among convertibles, the GL has a manual-folding top, the GLS a power top; both include a heated glass rear window and rollover bars that deploy if sensors detect an imminent tip.

RATINGS	GL hatch, man.	GLS TDI hatch, man.	GLS 1.8T hatch w/17-inch wheels, auto.	GLS conv, auto.
ACCELERATION	5	3	6	2
FUEL ECONOMY	7	9	6	7
RIDE QUALITY	6	6	4	6
STEERING/HANDLING	6	6	7	6
QUIETNESS	5	5	5	4
CONTROLS/MATERIALS	6	6	6	6
ROOM/COMFORT (FRONT)	7	7	7	6
ROOM/COMFORT (REAR)	2	2	2	2
CARGO ROOM	6	6	6	1
VALUE WITHIN CLASS	6	6	7	5

The retro styling has its drawbacks, but New Beetles are entertaining, well-built, and reasonably practical funmobiles, though convertibles sacrifice some of the hatchback's passenger and cargo space. Waning buyer interest should mean attractive dealer discounts on any model.

TOTAL	56	56	56	45

Average total for sporty/performance cars: 48.5

ENGINES	sohc I4	Turbodiesel sohc I4	Turbocharged dohc I4
Size, liters/cu. in.	2.0/121	1.9/116	1.8/109
Horsepower @ rpm	115 @ 5200	100 @ 4000	150 @ 5800
Torque (lb-ft) @ rpm	122 @ 2600	177 @ 1800	162 @ 2200
Availability	S[1]	S[2]	S[3]
EPA city/highway mpg			
5-speed manual	24/30	38/46	24/31
6-speed automatic	21/31	36/42	23/30

1. GL, GLS. Torque is 125@3200 in convertible. 2. GL TDI, GLS TDI. 3. GLS 1.8T.

PRICES

Volkswagen New Beetle	RETAIL PRICE	DEALER INVOICE
GL 2-door hatchback, manual	$16570	$15844
GL 2-door hatchback, automatic	17645	16917

Specifications begin on page 547.

PRICES (cont.)	RETAIL PRICE	DEALER INVOICE
GL 2-door convertible, manual	$21290	$20300
GL 2-door convertible, automatic	22365	21373
GLS 2-door hatchback, manual	18770	17540
GLS 2-door hatchback, automatic	19845	18613
GLS 2-door convertible, manual	23040	21483
GLS 2-door convertible, automatic	24115	22556
GLS TDI 2-door hatchback, manual	20010	18685
GLS TDI 2-door hatchback, automatic	21085	19758
GLS 1.8T 2-door hatchback, manual	20940	19544
GLS 1.8T 2-door hatchback, automatic	22015	20617
GLS 1.8T 2-door convertible, manual	25450	23710
GLS 1.8T 2-door convertible, automatic	26525	24783
Destination charge	575	575

TDI not available in Calif., Mass., Maine, N.Y., Vt.

STANDARD EQUIPMENT

GL: 2.0-liter 4-cylinder engine, 5-speed manual or 6-speed automatic transmission w/manual-shift capability, dual front airbags, front side airbags, antilock 4-wheel disc brakes, automatic roll bars (convertible), front-seat active head restraints, emergency inside trunk release (convertible), daytime running lights, air conditioning, interior air filter, power steering, tilt/telescope steering wheel, cruise control, cloth upholstery (hatchback), vinyl upholstery (convertible), front bucket seats w/height adjustment, center console, cupholders, folding rear seat (hatchback), trunk pass-through (convertible), heated power mirrors w/turn signals, power windows, power door locks, remote keyless entry, AM/FM/cassette, digital clock, tachometer, outside-temperature indicator, illuminated visor mirrors, map lights, variable-intermittent wipers, rear defogger, cargo cover (hatchback), manual convertible top (convertible), floormats, theft-deterrent system, full-size spare tire, 205/55HR16 tires.

GLS adds: 1.9-liter 4-cylinder turbodiesel engine (TDI), 1.8-liter turbocharged 4-cylinder engine (1.8T), traction control (1.8T), brake assist (1.8T convertible), antiskid system (1.8T convertible), Monsoon sound system, power sunroof (hatchback), power convertible top (convertible), fog lights, rear spoiler (1.8T hatchback), alloy wheels.

OPTIONAL EQUIPMENT

Major Packages	RETAIL PRICE	DEALER INVOICE
Leather Pkg., GLS	$900	$795
Leather upholstery, heated front seats, leather-wrapped steering wheel, heated washer nozzles.		
Leather Sport Seats Pkg., GLS 1.8T convertible	1100	971
Leather Pkg. plus front sport seats w/lumbar adjustment, unique interior trim.		
Cold Weather Pkg., GLS	150	133
Heated front seats, heated washer nozzles.		

Safety	RETAIL PRICE	DEALER INVOICE
Antiskid system	$280	$247
Std. GLS 1.8T convertible.		
Comfort & Convenience Features		
OnStar assistance system	730	645
Includes one-year service, automatic day/night rearview mirror. NA convertible.		
6-disc CD changer, GL convertible, GLS	575	485
Satellite radio	375	331
Requires monthly fee.		
Wind blocker, GLS convertible	250	221
Ski sack, GLS convertible	185	163
Appearance & Special Purpose		
Xenon headlights, GLS	600	530
Includes washers.		
17-inch alloy wheels, GLS 1.8T	400	353
Includes 225/45R17 tires.		

VOLKSWAGEN PASSAT

CLASS: Midsize car
DRIVE WHEELS: Front-wheel drive, all-wheel drive
BASE PRICE RANGE: $23,360-$33,615. Built in Germany.
ALSO CONSIDER: Honda Accord, Nissan Altima, Toyota Camry

Passat sheds its unpopular W8 models, but makes few other changes for this final year of its current design. Volkswagen's midsize car line comprises sedans and wagons in GL, GLS, and GLX trim. All include front side airbags, head-protecting curtain side airbags, and antilock 4-wheel disc brakes. GLS models use a 170-hp 1.8-liter turbo 4-cyl engine; TDI versions substitute a 134-hp 2.0-liter 4-cyl turbodiesel. For '05 GL models are available only with the turbodiesel engine. Top-line GLX models have a 190-hp V6. A 5-speed automatic transmission with manual shift gate is standard on all models except the GLS 1.8T, where it is optional. The GLS 1.8T comes with a 5-speed manual. Most Passats have front-wheel drive with traction control. GLX and non-TDI GLS models also offer VW's 4Motion all-wheel drive. An antiskid system is standard for GLX and GLS models, optional for GLs. OnStar assistance is available for all but the GL. Also for 2005, GLS models exchange 15-inch alloy wheels for standard 16s, while GLX models swap 16s for standard 17-inch alloy wheels. The discontinued W8 had a 270-hp 8-cyl engine. VW says redesigned 2006 Passats begin sale in late 2005.

RATINGS	GLS sdn, man.	GLS TDI turbodiesel sdn	GLX sdn, auto.	GLX 4Motion wgn
ACCELERATION	5	3	5	5
FUEL ECONOMY	6	8	5	4
RIDE QUALITY	7	7	7	7
STEERING/HANDLING	6	6	7	7
QUIETNESS	6	5	7	7
CONTROLS/MATERIALS	8	8	8	8
ROOM/COMFORT (FRONT)	7	7	7	7
ROOM/COMFORT (REAR)	6	6	6	6
CARGO ROOM	4	4	4	7
VALUE WITHIN CLASS	7	6	6	6

These solid sedans and wagons match some costlier cars for quality, refinement, and features. And no rival midsize delivers Passat's European flair, available AWD, or turbodiesel engine. Within this lineup, the GLS models are the best choices on price. Passat doesn't offer the reliability and low pricing set by class-leading Honda Accord and Toyota Camry.

TOTAL	**62**	**60**	**62**	**64**

Average total for midsize cars: 57.2

ENGINES	Turbocharged dohc I4	Turbodiesel sohc I4	dohc V6
Size, liters/cu. in.	1.8/109	2.0/121	2.8/169
Horsepower @ rpm	170 @ 5900	134 @ 4000	190 @ 6000
Torque (lb-ft) @ rpm	166 @ 1950	247 @ 1800	206 @ 3200
Availability	S[1]	S[2]	S[3]
EPA city/highway mpg			
5-speed manual	22/31		
5-speed automatic	21/30	27/38	19/27[4]

1. GL, GLS. 2. GL TDI, GLS TDI. 3. GLX. 4. 19/26 w/4Motion.

PRICES

Volkswagen Passat	RETAIL PRICE	DEALER INVOICE
GL TDI 4-door sedan, automatic	$23360	$21408
GL TDI 4-door wagon, automatic	24360	22311
GLS 4-door sedan, manual	24380	22226
GLS 4-door sedan, automatic	25455	23299
GLS TDI 4-door sedan, automatic	25660	23485
GLS 4-door wagon, manual	25380	23130
GLS 4-door wagon, automatic	26455	24203
GLS TDI 4-door wagon, automatic	26660	24389
AWD GLS 4Motion 4-door sedan, automatic	27205	25129
AWD GLS 4Motion 4-door wagon, automatic	28205	26033

PRICES (cont.)

	RETAIL PRICE	DEALER INVOICE
GLX 4-door sedan, automatic	$30865	$28187
GLX 4-door wagon, automatic	31865	29090
AWD GLX 4Motion 4-door sedan, automatic	32615	30017
AWD GLX 4Motion 4-door wagon, automatic	33615	30920
Destination charge	575	575

TDI not available in Calif., Mass., Maine, N.Y., Vt.

STANDARD EQUIPMENT

GL: 2.0-liter turbodiesel 4-cylinder engine, 5-speed automatic transmission w/manual-shift capability, traction control, dual front airbags, front side airbags, curtain side airbags, antilock 4-wheel disc brakes, daytime running lights, emergency inside trunk release, air conditioning, interior air filter, power steering, tilt/telescope steering wheel, cruise control, cloth upholstery, height-adjustable front bucket seats w/lumbar adjustment, center console, cupholders, split folding rear seat, heated power mirrors, power windows, power door locks, remote keyless entry, AM/FM/cassette/CD player, digital clock, tachometer, trip computer, outside-temperature indicator, map lights, variable-intermittent wipers, illuminated visor mirrors, rear defogger, cargo cover (wagon), intermittent rear wiper/washer (wagon), floormats, theft-deterrent system, roof rails (wagon), full-size spare tire, 195/65HR15 tires, wheel covers.

GLS adds: 1.8-liter 4-cylinder turbocharged engine or 2.0-liter turbodiesel 4-cylinder engine (TDI), 5-speed manual or 5-speed automatic transmission w/manual-shift capability, antiskid system, brake assist, power sunroof, Monsoon sound system, universal garage-door opener, fog lights, 205/55HR16 tires, alloy wheels. **AWD** adds: all-wheel drive. *Deletes:* traction control.

GLX adds: 2.8-liter V6 engine, leather upholstery, heated 8-way power front seats, memory system (driver seat, mirrors), leather-wrapped steering wheel w/radio controls, wood interior trim, automatic climate control, passenger-side mirror tilt-down back-up aid, automatic day/night rearview mirror, rear-window sunshade (sedan), rain-sensing wipers, heated windshield-washer nozzles, 225/45HR17 tires. *Deletes:* full-size spare tire. **AWD** adds: all-wheel drive. *Deletes:* traction control.

OPTIONAL EQUIPMENT

Major Packages

	RETAIL PRICE	DEALER INVOICE
Leather and Wood Pkg., GLS sedans	$1590	$1405
GLS wagons	1475	1302

Leather upholstery, heated front seats and windshield-washer nozzles, leather-wrapped steering wheel w/radio controls, wood interior trim, rear sun shade (sedan).

Safety

Antiskid system , GL	280	247

Includes brake assist.

 Specifications begin on page 547.

Comfort & Convenience Features	RETAIL PRICE	DEALER INVOICE
OnStar assistance system, GLS, GLX	$699	$617
Includes one-year service.		
6-disc CD changer	499	323

Appearance & Special Purpose

225/45HR17 tires, GLS	400	353
Replaces full-size spare tire w/compact spare tire.		

VOLKSWAGEN PHAETON

CLASS: Premium large car
DRIVE WHEELS: All-wheel drive
2004 BASE PRICE RANGE: $64,600-$94,600. Built in Germany.
ALSO CONSIDER: Lexus LS 430, Mercedes-Benz S-Class

The largest, costliest car in Volkswagen history is a virtual rerun for its second season. Phaeton (FAY-a-ton) is sized and equipped to compete with premium sedans like the Mercedes-Benz S-Class and BMW 7-Series. It also targets the A8 at VW's own Audi brand, with which it shares a basic chassis, standard all-wheel drive, and a 335-hp 4.2-liter V8. Phaeton also offers a 420-hp 6.0-liter W12 engine, essentially a mating of two narrow-angle V6s. The W12 model comes with 5-speed automatic transmission, the V8 with a 6-speed; both include manual shift gate. Phaetons have ABS, antiskid system, and 18-inch wheels (replacing standard 17s for V8s). Also included are front and rear torso side airbags and head-protecting curtain side airbags. A standard air suspension is designed to automatically adjust firmness within four driver-selectable levels. Other features include leather, wood, and brushed-metal interior trim, plus xenon headlamps, OnStar assistance, and 4-zone climate control. An optional 4-seat package replaces the 3-passenger rear bench with a pair of adjustable buckets and a center console. Phaeton's one notable change for 2005 is adding standard "soft close" doors, which snug-in automatically without slamming. VW says active cruise control, designed to maintain a safe following distance, will be offered later in the model year.

RATINGS	V8	V8 w/4-seater Pkg.	W12
ACCELERATION	7	7	8
FUEL ECONOMY	4	3	2

RATINGS (cont.)	V8	V8 w/4-seater Pkg.	W12
RIDE QUALITY	8	8	9
STEERING/HANDLING	7	7	7
QUIETNESS	8	8	9
CONTROLS/MATERIALS	7	7	7
ROOM/COMFORT (FRONT)	9	9	9
ROOM/COMFORT (REAR)	8	9	8
CARGO ROOM	4	4	4
VALUE WITHIN CLASS	7	6	2

Phaeton at first glance has much going against it. Its lofty prices and limousine opulence don't square with Volkswagen's sensible-shoes image. And most rivals offer higher brand prestige, residual values, and customer-satisfaction scores, plus the personalized dealer attention monied buyers expect—something else for which VW isn't known. Phaeton nonetheless earns our Recommended nod as a good premium large-car value for those willing to give it a chance. They'll enjoy understated refinement, benchmark materials quality, and performance that stands up to the like-priced competition, with the added bonus of standard all-wheel drive. Note: Slow sales mean discounts are available.

TOTAL	69	68	65

Average total for premium large cars: 67.8

ENGINES

	dohc V8	dohc W12
Size, liters/cu. in.	4.2/252	6.0/366
Horsepower @ rpm	335 @ 6500	420 @ 6000
Torque (lb-ft) @ rpm	317 @ 3500	406 @ 3250
Availability	S[1]	S[2]
EPA city/highway mpg		
5-speed automatic		12/19
6-speed automatic	16/22	

1. V8 model. 2. W12 model.

2005 prices unavailable at time of publication.

2004 PRICES

Volkswagen Phaeton	RETAIL PRICE	DEALER INVOICE
V8 4-door sedan	$64600	$59276
W12 4-door sedan	94600	86681
Destination charge	615	615

V8 adds $1300 Gas-Guzzler Tax. W12 adds $3000 Gas-Guzzler Tax.

STANDARD EQUIPMENT

V8: 4.2-liter V8 engine, 6-speed automatic transmission w/manual-shift capability, all-wheel drive, traction control, locking center differential, dual front airbags, front and rear side airbags, curtain side airbags, antilock 4-wheel disc brakes, brake assist, antiskid system, tire-pressure monitor,

 Specifications begin on page 547.

emergency inside trunk release, daytime running lights, air conditioning w/4-zone automatic climate controls w/rear controls, navigation system, OnStar assistance system w/one-year service, power steering, power tilt/telescope leather-wrapped steering wheel w/radio controls, cruise control, leather upholstery, heated/cooled massaging front seats, 18-way power driver seat, 16-way power passenger seat, memory system (front seats, outside and rearview mirrors, steering wheel), center console, cupholders, trunk pass-through, wood interior trim, heated power mirrors w/automatic day/night, turn signals, passenger-side tilt-down back-up aid, power windows, power door locks, remote keyless entry, power sunroof, AM/FM radio, 6-disc CD changer, analog clock, tachometer, trip computer, automatic day/night rearview mirror, outside-temperature indicator, illuminated visor mirrors, universal garage-door opener, rain-sensing variable-intermittent wipers w/heated washer nozzles, power rear sunshade, manual rear side sunshades, rear defogger, automatic headlights, floormats, theft-deterrent system, xenon headlights w/washers, fog lights, adjustable and load-leveling air suspension, full-size spare tire, 235/55HR17 tires, alloy wheels.

W12 adds: 6.0-liter W12 engine, 5-speed automatic transmission w/manual-shift capability, heated steering wheel, heated rear seats, power trunk closer, 255/45HR18 tires.

OPTIONAL EQUIPMENT

Major Packages

	RETAIL PRICE	DEALER INVOICE
Comfort and Cold Weather Pkg.,		
V8	$2900	$2590
W12	1790	1600
Heated steering wheel (V8), heated/cooled massaging rear seats, rear power lumbar adjustment, power rear headrests, rear climate-control display.		
4-Seater Pkg., V8	5750	5136
W12	4700	4198
Comfort and Cold Weather Pkg. plus 10-way power rear bucket seats, rear center console, rear controls for front-passenger seat, screen for climate controls.		
Technology Pkg., V8	1150	1027
Rear-obstacle-detection system, power trunk closer.		

Safety

Rear-obstacle-detection system, W12	700	625

Comfort & Convenience Features

Keyless access	500	447
Upgraded sound system	1000	893

Appearance & Special Purpose

235/55HR17 tires, W12	NC	NC
255/45HR4518 tires, V8	NC	NC

VOLKSWAGEN TOUAREG

CLASS: Premium midsize sport-utility vehicle
DRIVE WHEELS: All-wheel drive
2004 BASE PRICE RANGE: $35,900-$57,800. Built in Slovakia.
ALSO CONSIDER: Acura MDX, Cadillac SRX, Lexus RX 330

Volkswagen's sole SUV gets more V6 power and new options for 2005. Named for a nomadic tribe of the Sahara, Touareg (TOUR-regg) is a 4-dr 5-passenger luxury wagon with rear liftgate and no 3rd-row seating available. It offers a base V6 engine that now makes 240 hp, up 20, plus a 310-hp V8 and 310-hp turbodiesel V10. All use a 6-speed automatic transmission with manual shift gate and an all-wheel-drive system designed for severe off-road conditions. The AWD includes low-range gearing and a locking center differential; a locking rear differential is optional. Touaregs come with ABS and antiskid system. The V10 adds a height-adjusting air suspension, which is available for other models. The V6 comes on 17-inch wheels; others use 18s or optional 19s. All Touaregs include front side airbags and head-protecting curtain side airbags for both seating rows, plus wood and aluminum interior trim and a sunroof. Added for 2005 is standard OnStar assistance, optional before, plus self-dimming exterior mirrors. Leather upholstery is optional for the V6, standard otherwise. Newly available for all models are satellite radio and tire-pressure monitor. Other options include navigation system, obstacle detection, 4-zone climate control, and heated steering wheel and rear seats. An external spare tire is available for the V10 and now the V8. Towing capacity is 7716 lb for all models. Touareg was developed with Porsche, which offers costlier versions called Cayenne.

RATINGS	V6	V8 w/Prem. Plus Pkg.	V8 w/Prem. Plus Pkg., 19-in. whls.	V10 turbodiesel
ACCELERATION	4	6	6	6
FUEL ECONOMY	3	2	2	4
RIDE QUALITY	5	5	4	5
STEERING/HANDLING	5	5	6	5
QUIETNESS	7	7	6	5
CONTROLS/MATERIALS	6	6	6	7
ROOM/COMFORT (FRONT)	7	8	8	7
ROOM/COMFORT (REAR)	5	5	5	5

 Specifications begin on page 547.

RATINGS (cont.)	V6	V8 w/Prem. Plus Pkg.	V8 w/Prem. Plus Pkg., 19-in. whls.	V10 turbodiesel
CARGO ROOM	7	7	7	7
VALUE WITHIN CLASS	6	5	4	5

Touareg offers first-class cabin decor, solid construction, and more-than-competent SUV road manners. And it's an off-road wizard. But it's pricey for a Volkswagen, on par with BMW and Mercedes-Benz rivals offering superior brand prestige, resale values, and customer care. The turbodiesel really costs—far more than its higher potential fuel economy will repay—and isn't widely available. The V6 and V8 Touaregs are worth a look, though, if only as budget-label stand-ins for their Porsche Cayenne cousins.

TOTAL	55	56	54	56

Average total for premium midsize sport-utility vehicles: 59.6

ENGINES	dohc V6	dohc V8	Turbodiesel sohc V10
Size, liters/cu. in.	3.2/195	4.2/252	4.9/300
Horsepower @ rpm	240 @ 5400	310 @ 6200	310 @ 3750
Torque (lb-ft) @ rpm	229 @ 3200	302 @ 3000	553 @ 2000
Availability	S[1]	S[2]	S[3]
EPA city/highway mpg			
6-speed automatic	16/21	14/18	17/23

1. V6 model. 2. V8 model. 3. V10 model.

2005 prices unavailable at time of publication.

2004 PRICES

Volkswagen Touareg	RETAIL PRICE	DEALER INVOICE
V6 4-door wagon	$35900	$32532
V8 4-door wagon	42640	38620
V10 4-door wagon	57800	52315
Destination charge	615	615

V10 not available in Calif., Mass., Maine, N.Y., Vt.

STANDARD EQUIPMENT

V6: 3.2-liter V6 engine, 6-speed automatic transmission w/manual-shift capability, all-wheel drive, 2-speed transfer case, locking center differential, hill ascent/descent control, dual front airbags, front side airbags, curtain side airbags, antilock 4-wheel disc brakes, brake assist, antiskid system, tire-pressure monitor, daytime running lights, air conditioning w/dual-zone automatic climate controls, power steering, cruise control, tilt/telescope leather-wrapped steering wheel w/radio controls, vinyl upholstery, heated height-adjustable front seats, center console, cupholders, split folding rear seat, wood/aluminum interior trim, heated power mirrors w/passenger-side tilt-down back-up aid, power windows, power door locks, remote keyless entry, power sunroof, AM/FM/CD player, digital clock, tachometer, trip computer, outside-temperature indicator, compass, automatic day/night rearview mirror, universal garage-door opener, illuminated visor mirrors, rain-sensing intermittent wipers w/heated nozzles, map lights, rear defogger, intermittent rear wiper, automatic headlights, floormats, theft-deterrent system, fog lights, rear privacy glass, roof rack, 255/60HR17 tires, alloy wheels.

V8 adds: 4.2-liter V8 engine, leather upholstery, 12-way power front seats w/lumbar adjustment, memory system (driver seat, mirrors), automatic day/night outside mirrors, rear side sunshades, 255/55VR18 tires.

V10 adds: 4.9-liter tubodiesel V10 engine, OnStar assistance system, xenon headlights, height-adjustable suspension.

OPTIONAL EQUIPMENT

Major Packages

	RETAIL PRICE	DEALER INVOICE
Premium Pkg., V6	$2200	$1943
Leather upholstery, 12-way power front seats, memory system (driver seat, mirrors), power-folding outside mirrors, center console wood trim and sliding armrest.		
Premium Pkg. II, V6	2440	2155
Premium Pkg. plus rear side sunshades.		
Premium Plus Pkg., V8	7600	6711
V10	3800	3356
Navigation system, 6-disc CD changer, Convenience Pkg., upgraded leather upholstery and wood interior trim, xenon headlights (V8), silver-colored roof rack (V8), height-adjustable air suspension (V8).		
Convenience Pkg., V8, V10	850	751
Keyless access, power tilt/telescope steering wheel w/memory, passenger-seat memory.		
Winter Pkg., V8, V10	600	530
Heated steering wheel and rear seats, ski sack.		

Powertrain

Locking rear differential	550	486

Safety

Obstacle-detection system	600	530

Comfort & Convenience Features

Navigation system	2650	2340
Includes upgraded sound system.		
OnStar assistance system, V6, V8	699	617
Sound System I	500	442
Upgraded sound system. NA w/navigation system, Premium Plus Pkg.		
4-zone automatic climate controls, V8, V10	1200	1060
Requires Premium Plus Pkg.		

Appearance & Special Purpose

Xenon headlights, V6, V8	750	663
Height-adjustable air suspension, V6, V8	2600	2296
Requires xenon headlights.		
275/45YR19 summer performance tires, V8, V10	1200	1060

2004 VOLVO C70

CLASS: Premium sporty/performance car
DRIVE WHEELS: Front-wheel drive
BASE PRICE RANGE: $39,880-$41,880. Built in Sweden.
ALSO CONSIDER: Audi A4, BMW 3-Series

A substantial price cut marks the swan-song season for Volvo's C70 convertible. This 4-seat ragtop comes with a power top and heated glass rear window. Two models are offered, both with a turbo inline 5-cyl engine. The C70 2.4 has 197 hp; the C70 2.3 has a higher-pressure turbo and 242 hp. The 2.4 comes only with automatic transmission. The 2.3 comes with a 5-speed manual or optional automatic. Standard on both are traction control, antilock 4-wheel disc brakes, front side airbags, leather upholstery, and heated front seats. Base prices for '04 are cut by $4245 vs. final '03 prices.

RATINGS	2.4	2.3 w/17-in. whls., man.
ACCELERATION	6	7
FUEL ECONOMY	5	5
RIDE QUALITY	4	3
STEERING/HANDLING	6	6
QUIETNESS	4	4
CONTROLS/MATERIALS	5	5
ROOM/COMFORT (FRONT)	6	6
ROOM/COMFORT (REAR)	2	2
CARGO ROOM	2	2
VALUE WITHIN CLASS	2	2

C70s are high style—for Volvo. But their basic 1993-vintage design shows its age in mediocre chassis rigidity for the class, and turbo throttle lag aggravates. Audi A4 and BMW 3-Series rivals are better cars, and even with C70's '04 price cuts, also better values.

TOTAL	42	42

Average total for premium sporty/performance cars: 48.3

Prices accurate at publication.

ENGINES

	Turbocharged dohc I5	Turbocharged dohc I5
Size, liters/cu. in.	2.4/149	2.3/141
Horsepower @ rpm	197 @ 5700	242 @ 5400
Torque (lb-ft) @ rpm	210 @ 1800	243 @ 2400
Availability	S[1]	S[2]
EPA city/highway mpg		
5-speed manual		18/25
5-speed automatic	18/27	20/26

1. C70 2.4. 2. C70 2.3.

PRICES

Volvo C70	RETAIL PRICE	DEALER INVOICE
2.4-liter 2-door convertible	$39880	$37518
2.3-liter 2-door convertible	41880	39398
Destination charge	685	685

STANDARD EQUIPMENT

2.4-liter: 2.4-liter turbocharged 5-cylinder 197-horsepower engine, 5-speed automatic transmission, traction control, dual front airbags, front side airbags, front-seat active head restraints, rollover-protection system, antilock 4-wheel disc brakes, daytime running lights, emergency inside trunk release, air conditioning w/dual-zone automatic climate controls, interior air filter, power steering, tilt/telescope leather-wrapped steering wheel, cruise control, leather upholstery, heated 8-way power front bucket seats w/driver-seat memory, center console, cupholders, trunk pass-through, heated power mirrors, power windows, power door locks, remote keyless entry, AM/FM/cassette/CD player, digital clock, tachometer, rear defogger, illuminated visor mirrors, intermittent wipers, map lights, rear defogger, power convertible top, remote fuel-door and decklid release, floormats, theft-deterrent system, front and rear fog lights, headlight wiper/washer, 205/55ZR16 tires, alloy wheels.

2.3-liter adds: 2.3-liter turbocharged 242-horsepower 5-cylinder engine, 5-speed manual transmission, AM/FM/cassette w/in-dash 3-disc CD changer, trip computer, automatic day/night rearview mirror, outside-temperature indicator, wood interior trim, 225/50ZR16 tires.

OPTIONAL EQUIPMENT

Major Packages	RETAIL PRICE	DEALER INVOICE
Touring Pkg., 2.4-liter	$765	$657
Manufacturer's Discount Price	*595*	*511*

Trip computer, automatic day/night rearview mirror, wood or aluminum interior trim.

Powertrain		
5-speed automatic transmission, 2.3 liter	1000	1000

 Specifications begin on page 547.

Comfort & Convenience Features

	RETAIL PRICE	DEALER INVOICE
AM/FM/cassette w/in-dash 3-disc CD changer, 2.4-liter	$1200	$1032
Includes Dolby Prologic Surround Sound System.		
Dolby Prologic Surround Sound System, 2.3 liter	600	516
Wood/leather-wrapped steering wheel	250	215

Appearance & Special Purpose

Cratos alloy wheels	500	430
Includes 225/45ZR17 tires.		
Propus alloy wheels	975	838
Includes 225/45ZR17 tires.		

VOLVO S40 AND V50

CLASS: Premium compact car
DRIVE WHEELS: Front-wheel drive, all-wheel drive
BASE PRICE RANGE: $23,260-$28,910. Built in Belgium.
ALSO CONSIDER: Acura TSX, Audi A4, BMW 3-Series

Volvo's entry-level line adds wagon and all-wheel-drive variants for 2005. The S40 sedan is joined by a wagon called the V50. Both have a 5-cyl engine. They come in two trim levels: base 2.4i and sporty T5. The 2.4i versions are front-drive and have 168 hp. T5s have 218 hp and come with front- or all-wheel drive. The S40 2.4i is available with a 5-speed manual transmission or a 5-speed automatic with manual shift gate. The V50 2.4i comes only with the automatic. T5 models have front-drive or AWD and are turbocharged for 218 hp. T5s offer a 6-speed manual transmission or the 5-speed automatic. Standard on every S40 and V50 are antilock 4-wheel disc brakes, front side airbags, head-protecting curtain side airbags, and traction control. AWD versions come with a sport suspension that is optional on other models. Other options include an antiskid system, 17-inch wheels to replace standard 16s, navigation system with pop-up dashboard screen, and in-dash CD changer. Leather upholstery, sunroof, and heated seats are also available.

RATINGS	S40 2.4i, man.	S40 T5 w/Sport Pkg., man.	S40 T5, auto.	V50 T5, man.
ACCELERATION	5	7	6	6
FUEL ECONOMY	6	5	5	5
RIDE QUALITY	7	6	7	7
STEERING/HANDLING	6	7	6	6

RATINGS (cont.)	S40 2.4i, man.	S40 T5 w/Sport Pkg., man.	S40 T5, auto.	V50 T5, man.
QUIETNESS	6	5	6	6
CONTROLS/MATERIALS	7	7	7	7
ROOM/COMFORT (FRONT)	7	7	7	7
ROOM/COMFORT (REAR)	4	4	4	4
CARGO ROOM	3	3	3	7
VALUE WITHIN CLASS	5	5	6	6

They may be a little too pricey and not quite sporty enough to bring in the younger buyers Volvo targets. But S40 and V50 are solid, capable, and comfortable small cars offering most big-Volvo features in appealing compact packages. And AWD versions widen appeal considerably.

TOTAL	56	56	57	61

Average total for premium compact cars: 57.5

ENGINES

	dohc I5	Turbocharged dohc I5
Size, liters/cu. in.	2.4/149	2.5/154
Horsepower @ rpm	168 @ 6000	218 @ 5000
Torque (lb-ft) @ rpm	170 @ 4400	236 @ 1500
Availability	S[1]	S[2]
EPA city/highway mpg		
5-speed manual	22/30	
6-speed manual		22/31
5-speed automatic	22/30	22/31

1. 2.4i models. 2. T5 models.

PRICES

Volvo S40 and V50	RETAIL PRICE	DEALER INVOICE
FWD S40 2.4i 4-door sedan, manual	$23260	$21900
FWD V50 2.4i 4-door wagon, automatic	25660	24156
FWD S40 T5 4-door sedan, manual	26060	24532
FWD V50 T5 4-door wagon, manual	27260	25660
AWD S40 T5 4-door sedan, manual	27710	26083
AWD V50 T5 4-door wagon, automatic	28910	27200
Destination charge	685	685

FWD denotes front-wheel drive. AWD denotes all-wheel drive.

STANDARD EQUIPMENT

2.4i: 2.4-liter 5-cylinder engine, 5-speed manual or 5-speed automatic transmission w/manual-shift capability, traction control, dual front airbags, front side airbags, curtain side airbags, front-seat active head restraints, antilock 4-wheel disc brakes, brake assist, daytime running lights, emergency inside trunk release, air conditioning, interior air filter, power steering, tilt/telescope leather-wrapped steering wheel, cruise control, cloth upholstery, front bucket seats, folding front-passenger seat, center console, cupholders, split folding rear seat, heated power mirrors, power windows, power door locks, remote keyless entry, AM/FM/CD player, digital clock, tachometer, outside-temperature indicator, variable-intermittent wipers, map lights, illuminated visor mirrors, cargo cover (wagon), rear defogger, rear wiper/washer (wagon), floormats, theft-deterrent system, rear fog light, 205/55R16 tires, alloy wheels.

T5 adds: 2.5-liter turbocharged 5-cylinder engine, 6-speed manual or 5-speed automatic transmission w/manual-shift capability, automatic climate control, 8-way power driver seat, aluminum interior trim, steering-wheel radio controls, trip computer, front fog lights. **AWD** adds: all-wheel drive, sport suspension.

OPTIONAL EQUIPMENT

Major Packages	RETAIL PRICE	DEALER INVOICE
Premium Pkg., 2.4i	$3525	$3031
Manufacturer's Discount Price	*2295*	*1973*
2.4i w/Sport Pkg.	3444	2961
Manufacturer's Discount Price	*2214*	*1903*
Power sunroof, automatic climate control, leather upholstery, 8-way power driver seat, steering-wheel radio controls, leather shift knob, woodgrain interior trim.		
Premium Pkg., T5	3000	2580
Manufacturer's Discount Price	*2195*	*1887*
Power sunroof, leather upholstery, power passenger seat, driver-seat memory.		
Sport Pkg., 2.4i	1175	881
Manufacturer's Discount Price	*850*	*731*
T5 FWD	775	666
Manufacturer's Discount Price	*750*	*645*
Aluminum interior trim (2.4i), front fog lights (2.4i), sport suspension, 205/50R17 tires, unique alloy wheels.		
Dynamic Trim Pkg., T5	2025	1741
Body cladding, rear spoiler, sport suspension (FWD), 205/50R17 tires, unique alloy wheels.		
Climate Pkg	975	838
Manufacturer's Discount Price	*625*	*537*
ordered w/bi-zenon	718	617
Manufacturer's Discount Price	*368*	*316*
Heated front seats, rain-sensing wipers, headlight washers.		
Convenience Pkg., 2.4i wagon	1175	1009
Manufacturer's Discount Price	*605*	*520*
2.4i sedan, T5 wagon	850	730
Manufacturer's Discount Price	*505*	*434*
T5 sedan	425	365
Manufacturer's Discount Price	*305*	*262*
Universal garage-door opener, trip computer (2.4i), automatic day/night rearview mirror, compass, cargo-area auxiliary power outlet (wagon), grocery-bag holder, roof rails (wagon).		

OPTIONAL EQUIPMENT (cont.)

	RETAIL PRICE	DEALER INVOICE
Audio Pkg., 2.4i	$1325	$1138
Manufacturer's Discount Price	*895*	*769*
2.4i w/Premium Pkg.	1274	1095
Manufacturer's Discount Price	*844*	*726*
T5	1250	1074
Manufacturer's Discount Price	*850*	*731*
AM/FM radio w/in-dash 6-disc CD changer, steering-wheel radio controls (2.4i), upgraded sound system.		
Powertrain		
5-speed automatic transmission w/manual-shift capability, 2.4i sedan, T5 sedan, T5 FWD wagon	1200	1200
Safety		
Antiskid system	695	597
Integrated child seats	300	258
Comfort & Convenience Features		
Navigation system	2120	1823
Requires Audio Pkg.		
Power sunroof	1200	1032
Leather upholstery	1200	1032
Appearance & Special Purpose		
Bi-xenon headlights	700	602
Includes headlight washers.		
Laminated side windows	300	258
Sagitta alloy wheels, T5 AWD	500	430
Includes 205/50R17 tires.		

2004 VOLVO S60

CLASS: Premium midsize car
DRIVE WHEELS: Front-wheel drive, all-wheel drive
BASE PRICE RANGE: $26,960-$37,250. Built in Sweden.
ALSO CONSIDER: Acura TL, Cadillac CTS, Lexus ES 330

A 300-hp high-performance model highlights 2004 additions to Volvo's best-selling line. The S60 is the sedan variant of Volvo's V70 wagon. All S60s use an inline 5-cyl engine and all but the 168-hp base model are turbocharged. The 2.5T models have 208 hp, the T5 has 247, And the new S60 R has 300. The 2.5T AWD and the R have all-wheel drive. Other S60s have front-wheel drive. Base, T5, and R come with manual transmission—a 5-speed on base and T5, a 6-speed on the R. A 5-speed automatic is standard on the 2.5T models and optional on the others. Wheel diameter ranges from 15 inches on the base model to optional 18s on the R. Front side airbags, head-protecting curtain side airbags, traction control, and antilock 4-wheel disc brakes are standard. An antiskid system is standard on T5 and R, optional for other S60s. The R's suspension has three driver-selectable settings to emphasize ride or handling. Optional on all is a navigation system with pop-up dashboard screen. Among '04 changes, the standard remote locking system uses an integrated key transmitter, and cabin appearance is revised with charcoal-colored trim and watch-bezel-style instrument surrounds. All S60s are available with Volvo's On-Call Plus assistance system.

RATINGS	AWD 2.5T	T5 w/nav. sys., man.	R w/18-inch wheels, man.
ACCELERATION	6	6	8
FUEL ECONOMY	5	4	4
RIDE QUALITY	7	5	4
STEERING/HANDLING	7	7	8
QUIETNESS	5	5	4
CONTROLS/MATERIALS	7	6	7
ROOM/COMFORT (FRONT)	7	7	7
ROOM/COMFORT (REAR)	5	5	5
CARGO ROOM	3	3	3
VALUE WITHIN CLASS	5	3	3

These are arguably the most-stylish Volvos ever and certainly the best-handling Volvo sedans yet. But compromised powertrain smoothness relative to other near-luxury cars is hard to overlook. The all-season capability of available AWD is an asset to this line, but it doesn't help the S60 match the Acura TL or Lexus ES 330 for overall value, or the Audi A4 and BMW 3-Series for driving satisfaction.

TOTAL	57	51	53

Average total for premium midsize cars: 61.7

ENGINES	dohc I5	Turbocharged dohc I5	Turbocharged dohc I5	Turbocharged dohc I5
Size, liters/cu. in.	2.4/149	2.5/153	2.3/141	2.5/153
Horsepower @ rpm	168 @ 5900	208 @ 6000	247 @ 5200	300 @ 5250
Torque (lb-ft) @ rpm	170 @ 4500	236 @ 1500	243 @ 2400	295 @ 1950
Availability	S[1]	S[2]	S[3]	S[4]
EPA city/highway mpg				
5-speed manual	22/30		21/27	
6-speed manual				18/25
5-speed automatic	22/31	20/27	20/28	22/30

1. Base. 2. 2.5T, 2.5T AWD. 3. T5. 4. R (258 lb-ft w/automatic).

PRICES

Volvo S60

	RETAIL PRICE	DEALER INVOICE
Base 4-door sedan	$26960	$25377
FWD 2.5T 4-door sedan	29610	27870
AWD 2.5T 4-door sedan	31385	29537
T5 4-door sedan	33285	31323
R 4-door sedan	37250	35050
Destination charge	685	685

STANDARD EQUIPMENT

Base: 2.4-liter 5-cylinder engine, 5-speed manual transmission, traction control, dual front airbags, front side airbags, curtain side airbags, front-seat active head restraints, antilock 4-wheel disc brakes, emergency inside trunk release, daytime running lights, air conditioning w/dual-zone manual climate controls, interior air filter, power steering, tilt/telescope leather-wrapped steering wheel w/radio controls, cruise control, cloth upholstery, front bucket seats, center console, cupholders, split folding rear seat, power-folding rear headrests, heated power mirrors, power windows, power door locks, remote keyless entry, AM/FM/cassette/CD player, digital clock, tachometer, outside-temperature indicator, rear defogger, illuminated visor mirrors, map lights, variable-intermittent wipers, floormats, theft-deterrent system, rear fog light, 195/65HR15 tires, alloy wheels.

2.5T FWD adds: 2.5-liter turbocharged 208-horsepower 5-cylinder engine, 5-speed automatic transmission, 8-way power driver seat, memory system (driver seat, mirrors), dual-zone automatic climate controls, front fog lights, 215/55HR16 tires.

2.5T AWD adds: all-wheel drive, heated front seats, rain-sensing wipers, headlight wiper/washer, 205/55HR16 tires.

T5 adds to 2.5T 2WD: 2.3-liter turbocharged 247-horsepower 5-cylinder engine, 5-speed manual transmission, antiskid system, cloth/vinyl upholstery, 8-way power passenger seat, trip computer, universal garage-door opener, automatic day/night rearview mirror.

R adds: 2.5-liter turbocharged 300-horsepower 5-cylinder engine, 6-speed manual transmission, all-wheel drive, brake assist, leather upholstery, xenon headlights w/washers, rear spoiler, adjustable-damping suspension, 235/45ZR17 tires.

OPTIONAL EQUIPMENT

Major Packages

	RETAIL PRICE	DEALER INVOICE
Premium Pkg., Base	$3785	$3255
Manufacturer's Discount Price	*2995*	*2575*
Leather upholstery, 8-way power driver seat, memory system (driver seat, mirrors), power sunroof, dual-zone automatic climate controls, trip computer, simulated-wood interior trim.		
Premium Pkg., 2.5T	3335	2868
Manufacturer's Discount Price	*2595*	*2231*
Leather upholstery, power passenger seat, power sunroof, trip computer, simulated-wood interior trim.		

 Specifications begin on page 547.

OPTIONAL EQUIPMENT (cont.)

	RETAIL PRICE	DEALER INVOICE
Premium Pkg., T5	$2650	$2279
Manufacturer's Discount Price	*1995*	*1715*
Leather upholstery, power sunroof, simulated-wood interior trim.		
Premium Pkg., R	2400	2064
Manufacturer's Discount Price	*1995*	*1715*
Power sunroof, AM/FM radio w/in-dash 4-disc CD changer, upgraded sound system.		
Touring Pkg., Base, 2.5T	775	665
Manufacturer's Discount Price	*595*	*511*
Automatic day/night rearview mirror, universal garage-door opener, interior air-quality system, grocery-bag holder, security-laminated side windows. Base requires Premium Pkg. 2.5T AWD requires power sunroof.		
Touring Pkg., T5, R	550	472
Manufacturer's Discount Price	*495*	*425*
Interior air-quality system, grocery-bag holder, security-laminated side windows.		
Sport Pkg., Base	795	683
Front fog lights, 215/55HR16 tires. Requires automatic transmission power sunroof.		
Sport Pkg., 2.5T	950	817
Manufacturer's Discount Price	*795*	*683*
Manual-shift capability, front and rear sport seats, 235/45HR17 tires. Requires Premium Pkg.		
Sport Pkg., T5	775	666
Sport suspension, 235/45HR17 tires.		
Climate Pkg., Base, 2.5T 2WD, T5	550	473
R	400	344
Heated front seats, headlight washers (Base, 2.5T, T5), rain-sensing wipers. Base requires automatic transmission, power sunroof.		

Powertrain

5-speed automatic transmission, Base	1000	1000
5-speed automatic transmission w/manual-shift capability,		
T5	1200	1200
R	1250	1250

Safety

Dynamic Stability Traction Control, Base, 2.5T	695	597
Antiskid system. Requires Premium Pkg.		

Comfort & Convenience Features

Power sunroof	1200	1032
Navigation system	1995	1715
Base requires automatic transmission, power sunroof. 2.5T AWD requires power sunroof.		
On-Call Plus	835	718
On-Call Plus Assistance system. Includes one-year service. Base requires automatic transmission, power sunroof. 2.5T AWD requires power sunroof.		

OPTIONAL EQUIPMENT (cont.)

	RETAIL PRICE	DEALER INVOICE
Leather upholstery, Base, 2.5T	$1400	$1204
T5	1450	1247
Base requires automatic transmission, power sunroof. 2.5T AWD requires power sunroof.		
Upgraded leather upholstery, R	1550	1333
Leather/cloth upholstery, 2.5T AWD, T5	1050	903
2.5T requires power sunroof.		
AM/FM radio w/in-dash 4-disc CD changer, 2.5T, T5, R	1200	1032
Includes upgraded sound system. 2.5T requires Premium Pkg.		

Appearance & Special Purpose

Xenon headlights, Base, 2.5T, T5	500	430
Includes washers. Base, 2.5T 2WD, T5 require Climate Pkg. 2.5T AWD requires power sunroof.		
235/40ZR18 tires, R	995	855

2004 VOLVO S80

CLASS: Premium large car
DRIVE WHEELS: Front-wheel drive
BASE PRICE RANGE: $35,450-$48,515. Built in Sweden.
ALSO CONSIDER: Acura RL, Lexus LS 430, Volkswagen Phaeton

Midyear addition of a new base model completes the 2004 changes to Volvo's flagship sedan. S80 kicked off the model year with freshened styling and newly available all-wheel drive. Offered are 2.5T and T6 models, both with turbocharged engines. The 2.5T versions have a 208-hp 5 cyl and a 5-speed automatic transmission. They come with front-wheel drive or AWD. T6s have a 268-hp inline 6-cyl, 4-speed automatic with manual shift gate, and come only with front-drive. The front-drive 2.5T was a midyear replacement for the prior entry-level S80, the 194-hp 2.9 model. Traction control, ABS, front side airbags, and head-protecting curtain side airbags are standard on all S80s. Leather upholstery, sunroof, and an antiskid system are standard on T6s, optional on 2.5Ts. A navigation system, rain-sensing wipers, and Volvo's On-Call Plus assistance system are available. The T6 Premier's rear seat is heated and angled for 2 inches more leg room. It includes a power sunshade and dual-screen video with DVD and tuner; a refrigerator is optional. For '04, front and rear fascias and taillamps are revised, as are interior door panels

 Specifications begin on page 547.

and gauge graphics. Volvo's Four-C (Continuously Controlled Chassis Concept) adjustable suspension option for T6s has driver-selectable Comfort or Sport settings.

RATINGS	AWD 2.5T	T6 w/Four-C, nav. sys.	T6 Premier
ACCELERATION	6	7	7
FUEL ECONOMY	5	5	5
RIDE QUALITY	7	8	7
STEERING/HANDLING	7	7	7
QUIETNESS	7	7	7
CONTROLS/MATERIALS	6	4	6
ROOM/COMFORT (FRONT)	8	8	8
ROOM/COMFORT (REAR)	7	7	9
CARGO ROOM	4	4	4
VALUE WITHIN CLASS	3	4	3

The base 2.5T model feels larger and more substantial than many like-priced upscale sedans, though amenties such as leather upholstery and sunroof are optional here and standard on most rivals. The 2.5T AWD adds the security of AWD, but is hard to recommend over AWD competitors or even Volvo's own AWD S60. The T6 is the best all-around luxury value in this line, while the Premier pampers rear-seaters for less than other makers charge for similar features.

TOTAL	60	61	63

Average total for premium large cars: 67.8

ENGINES	Turbocharged dohc I5	Turbocharged dohc I6
Size, liters/cu. in.	2.5/153	2.9/178
Horsepower @ rpm	208 @ 5000	268 @ 5200
Torque (lb-ft) @ rpm	236 @ 1500	280 @ 1800
Availability	S[1]	S[2]
EPA city/highway mpg		
4-speed automatic		19/26
5-speed automatic	20/27	

1. 2.5T models. 2. T6 models.

PRICES

Volvo S80	RETAIL PRICE	DEALER INVOICE
FWD 2.5T 4-door sedan	$35450	$33358
AWD 2.5T 4-door sedan	37200	35003
FWD T6 4-door sedan	44525	41888
FWD T6 Premier 4-door sedan	48515	45639
Destination charge	685	685

STANDARD EQUIPMENT

2.5T: 2.5-liter turbocharged 5-cylinder engine, 5-speed automatic transmission, traction control, dual front airbags, front side airbags, curtain side airbags, front-seat active head restraints, antilock 4-wheel disc brakes, daytime running lights, emergency inside trunk release, air conditioning w/dual-zone automatic climate controls, interior air filter, power steering, tilt/telescope leather-wrapped steering wheel w/radio controls, cruise control, cloth upholstery, front bucket seats, 8-way power driver w/memory, fold-flat passenger seat, center console, cupholders, split folding rear seat w/trunk pass-through, power-folding rear headrests, heated power mirrors w/memory, power windows, power door locks, remote keyless entry, AM/FM/cassette/CD player, digital clock, tachometer, trip computer, variable-intermittent wipers, rear defogger, illuminated visor mirrors, outside-temperature indicator, universal garage-door opener, map lights, floormats, theft-deterrent system, rear fog light, 215/55HR16 tires, alloy wheels. **AWD** adds: all-wheel drive, heated front seats, rain-sensing wipers, headlight wiper/washer.

T6 adds: 2.9-liter turbocharged 6-cylinder engine, 4-speed automatic transmission w/manual-shift capability, antiskid system, On-Call Plus assistance system w/one-year service, leather upholstery, 8-way power passenger seat, power sunroof, automatic day/night rearview mirror, front fog lights, 225/50HR17 tires.

T6 Premier adds: heated front and rear seats, DVD player, tuner, 2 rear screens, wireless headphones, power rear sunshade, rain-sensing wipers, headlight wiper/washer.

OPTIONAL EQUIPMENT

Major Packages

	RETAIL PRICE	DEALER INVOICE
Premium Pkg., 2.5T	$3050	$2623
Manufacturer's Discount Price	*2495*	*2145*
Leather upholstery, power passenger seat, power sunroof.		
Warm Weather Pkg., T6	825	709
Manufacturer's Discount Price	*575*	*494*
T6 w/Climate Pkg.	750	642
Manufacturer's Discount Price	*500*	*430*
Infrared-reflective windshield, rear and side sunshades, interior air-quality system.		
Climate Pkg., T6	675	580
Manufacturer's Discount Price	*650*	*559*
2.5T 2WD	550	473
Heated front seats, rain-sensing wipers, headlight wipers/washers, interior air-quality system (T6).		
Four-C Chassis, T6, T6 Premier	995	855
Driver-selectable and computer-controlled adjustable shock absorbers.		
Touring Pkg., 2.5T	690	592
Manufacturer's Discount Price	*625*	*537*
Automatic day/night rearview mirror, interior air-quality system, security-laminated side windows, grocery-bag holder.		

Safety

Dynamic Stability Traction Control, 2.5T	695	597
Antiskid system.		
Rear-obstacle-detection system	400	344

 Specifications begin on page 547.

Comfort & Convenience Features

	RETAIL PRICE	DEALER INVOICE
Navigation system	$1995	$1715
On-Call Plus, 2.5T	835	718
On Call Plus Assistance system. Includes one-year service.		
Refrigerator, T6 Premier	900	774
Mounted in back-seat center armrest.		
In-dash 4-disc CD changer	1200	1032
Deletes cassette player.		

Appearance & Special Purpose

Xenon headlights	500	430
2.5T 2WD, T6 require Climate Pkg.		
Interceptor/Stentor alloy wheels, 2.5T	500	430
T6 Premier	250	215
2.5T includes variable-assist power steering, 225/50HR17 tires. Std. T6.		

2004 VOLVO V70/XC70

CLASS: Premium midsize car
DRIVE WHEELS: Front-wheel drive, all-wheel drive
BASE PRICE RANGE: $28,460-$38,750. Built in Sweden.
ALSO CONSIDER: Audi allroad quattro, Mercedes-Benz E-Class

A 300-hp high-performance model highlights 2004 changes for Volvo's near-luxury station wagons. All V70 and XC70 models have an inline 5-cyl engine, and all but the 168-hp base 2.4 model are turbocharged. The V70 2.5T models and the XC70 have 208 hp. The T5 has 247 hp. The new V70 R has 300. The 2.4, 2.5T, and T5 have front-wheel drive. The 2.5T AWD, XC70, and V70 R have all-wheel drive. The XC70 is distinguished by its raised suspension and SUV-flavored trim. The 2.4 and T5 come with a 5-speed manual transmission, the R with a 6-speed manual. A 5-speed automatic is optional on those models and standard elsewhere. The R's suspension is driver-adjustable for ride and handling. Traction control and antilock 4-wheel disc brakes are standard on all models. An antiskid system is standard on the T5 and R, optional on the others. All models come with front side airbags and head-protecting curtain side airbags. Dual integrated rear child seats, a rear-facing 3rd-row seat, navigation system, and Volvo's On-Call Plus assistance system are optional. New for 2004 is a Special Titanium Package for the 2.5T that includes specific equipment and a silver/gray color scheme. Also, the standard remote locking system gets an integrated key transmitter, and cabin appearance is revised with charcoal-colored trim and watch-bezel-style instrument surrounds.

RATINGS	2.4 auto.	AWD 2.5T	AWD XC70 w/nav. sys.	AWD, auto.
ACCELERATION	4	5	5	6
FUEL ECONOMY	5	5	5	4
RIDE QUALITY	7	7	6	4
STEERING/HANDLING	6	7	5	7
QUIETNESS	6	5	5	5
CONTROLS/MATERIALS	7	7	6	7
ROOM/COMFORT (FRONT)	7	7	7	7
ROOM/COMFORT (REAR)	5	5	5	5
CARGO ROOM	7	7	7	7
VALUE WITHIN CLASS	4	6	4	3

Not as refined or well-built as Audi, Mercedes, and BMW competitors, and less fuel efficient than you might expect. Examples we tested also had some loose interior panels and other quality gaffes. Still, this is Volvo's best wagon yet. The XC70 provides some SUV flavor without SUV drawbacks, but the best values are the 2.5T models—the all-season-capable 2.5T AWD in particular.

TOTAL	58	61	55	55

Average total for premium midsize cars: 61.7

ENGINES	dohc I5	Turbocharged dohc I5	Turbocharged dohc I5	Turbocharged dohc I5
Size, liters/cu. in.	2.4/149	2.5/153	2.3/141	2.5/153
Horsepower @ rpm	168 @ 5900	208 @ 5000	247 @ 5200	300 @ 5250
Torque (lb-ft) @ rpm	170 @ 4500	236 @ 1500	243 @ 2400	295 @ 1950
Availability	S[1]	S[2]	S[3]	S[4]
EPA city/highway mpg				
5-speed manual	22/30		20/26	
6-speed manual				18/24
5-speed automatic	22/30	20/27[5]	20/26	18/24

1. 2.4. 2. 2.5T, XC70. 3. T5. 4. R 258 lb-ft w/automatic. 5. XC70 19/24.

PRICES

Volvo V70/XC70	RETAIL PRICE	DEALER INVOICE
FWD 2.4 4-door wagon	$28460	$26787
FWD 2.5T 4-door wagon	31785	29913
AWD 2.5T 4-door wagon	33560	31582

 Specifications begin on page 547.

PRICES (cont.)

	RETAIL PRICE	DEALER INVOICE
AWD XC70 4-door wagon	$34810	$32757
FWD T5 4-door wagon	34810	32757
AWD R 4-door wagon	38750	36460
Destination charge	685	685

FWD denotes front-wheel drive. AWD denotes all-wheel drive.

STANDARD EQUIPMENT

2.4: 2.4-liter 5-cylinder engine, 5-speed manual transmission, traction control, dual front airbags, front side airbags, curtain side airbags, front-seat active head restraints, antilock 4-wheel disc brakes, daytime running lights, air conditioning w/manual dual-zone controls, interior air filter, power steering, tilt/telescope leather-wrapped steering wheel w/radio controls, cruise control, cloth upholstery, front bucket seats, center console, cupholders, split folding rear seat, heated power mirrors, power windows, power door locks, remote keyless entry, AM/FM/cassette/CD player, digital clock, tachometer, outside-temperature indicator, intermittent wipers, illuminated visor mirrors, map lights, rear defogger, cargo cover, intermittent rear wiper, remote fuel-door/tailgate release, floormats, theft-deterrent system, rear fog light, 195/65HR15 tires, alloy wheels.

2.5T FWD adds: 2.5-liter turbocharged 5-cylinder 208-horsepower engine, 5-speed automatic transmission, dual-zone automatic climate controls, 8-way power driver seat, memory system (driver seat, mirrors), 205/55HR16 tires.

2.5T AWD adds: all-wheel drive, heated front seats, rain-sensing wipers, headlight washers.

XC adds: 3rd-row split folding seat, front fog lights, roof rails, raised ride height, 215/65HR16 tires.

T5 adds to 2.5T FWD: 2.3-liter turbocharged 5-cylinder 247-hp engine, 5-speed manual transmission, antiskid system, cloth/vinyl upholstery, 8-way power passenger seat, trip computer, automatic day/night rearview mirror, universal garage-door opener, front fog lights, 215/55HR16 tires.

R adds: 2.5-liter turbocharged 5-cylinder 300-horsepower engine, 6-speed manual transmission, all-wheel drive, brake assist, leather upholstery, headlight wiper/washer, xenon headlights, rear spoiler, adjustable-damping suspension, 235/45ZR17 tires.

OPTIONAL EQUIPMENT

Major Packages

	RETAIL PRICE	DEALER INVOICE
Premium Pkg., 2.4	$3750	$3225
Manufacturer's Discount Price	*2995*	*2575*

Leather upholstery, power sunroof, 8-way power driver seat w/memory, mirror memory, dual-zone automatic climate controls, trip computer, simulated-wood interior trim.

OPTIONAL EQUIPMENT (cont.)

	RETAIL PRICE	DEALER INVOICE
Premium Pkg., 2.5T	$3300	$2838
Manufacturer's Discount Price	*2595*	*2231*
XC	3350	2881
Manufacturer's Discount Price	*2650*	*2279*
Leather upholstery, 8-way power passenger seat, power sunroof, trip computer.		
Premium Pkg., T5	2650	2279
Manufacturer's Discount Price	*1995*	*1715*
Leather upholstery, power sunroof.		
Premium Pkg., R	2400	2064
Manufacturer's Discount Price	*1995*	*1715*
Power sunroof, AM/FM radio w/in-dash 4-disc CD changer.		
Touring Pkg., 2.4, 2.5T, XC	1075	923
Manufacturer's Discount Price	*795*	*683*
Automatic day/night rearview mirror, universal garage-door opener, interior air-quality system, grocery-bag holder, cargo net, security-laminated side windows. 2.4 requires Premium Pkg. XC requires power sunroof.		
Touring Pkg., R	875	751
Manufacturer's Discount Price	*695*	*597*
T5	850	730
Manufacturer's Discount Price	*695*	*597*
Interior air-quality system, grocery-bag holder, cargo net, cargo-area auxiliary power outlet (R), security-laminated side windows.		
Sport Pkg., 2.5T	950	817
Manufacturer's Discount Price	*795*	*683*
T5	850	731
Manufacturer's Discount Price	*775*	*666*
Front and rear sport seats, automatic transmission manual-shift capability (2.5T), rear spoiler (T5), 235/45HR17 tires, special alloy wheels. Requires Premium Pkg.		
Special Titanium Pkg., 2.5T FWD	7350	6321
Manufacturer's Discount Price	*5850*	*5031*
Automatic transmission w/manual-shift capability, leather upholstery, heated front sport seats, power passenger seat, power sunroof, power-folding mirrors, trip computer, rain-sensing wipers, dual booster seats, cargo net, rear spoiler, silver-colored roof rails and bodyside moldings, Titanium Gray paint, xenon headlights w/washers and wipers, 235/45HR17 tires, unique alloy wheels.		
Convenience Pkg., 2.5T FWD	1000	858
Universal garage-door opener, automatic day/night rearview mirror, interior air-quality system, grocery-bag holder, folding table, cargo-area auxiliary-power outlet. Requires Special Titanium Pkg.		

OPTIONAL EQUIPMENT (cont.)

	RETAIL PRICE	DEALER INVOICE
Versatility Pkg., 2.4, 2.5T, T5	$1675	$1440
Manufacturer's Discount Price	*1300*	*1118*
XC	1500	1290
Manufacturer's Discount Price	*1250*	*1075*
Rear-facing 3rd-row seat, integrated child-booster seats, folding table (2.4, 2.5T, T5), cargo-area auxiliary-power outlet. Deletes Touring Pkg. grocery-bag holder. 2.4, XC require power sunroof.		
Climate Pkg., 2.4, 2.5T FWD, T5	550	473
R	400	344
Heated front seats, rain-sensing wipers, headlight wipers/washers (2.4, 2.5T FWD, T5). 2.4 requires power sunroof.		
Powertrain		
5-speed automatic transmission, 2.4	1000	1000
5-speed automatic transmission w/manual-shift capability, T5	1200	1200
R	1250	1250
Safety		
Antiskid system, 2.4, 2.5T, XC	695	597
Requires Premium Pkg.		
Dual booster seats	300	258
2.4, XC require power sunroof.		
Comfort & Convenience Features		
Navigation system	1995	1715
2.4, XC require power sunroof.		
On-Call Plus	835	718
On Call Plus Assistance system. Includes one-year service. 2.4, XC require power sunroof.		
Power sunroof	1200	1032
Leather upholstery, 2.4, 2.5T	1400	1204
XC	1450	1247
2.4, XC require power sunroof.		
Upgraded leather upholstery, R	1550	1333
Rear-facing 3rd-row seat, 2.5T FWD, R	1150	989
2.5T requires Special Titanium Pkg.		
AM/FM w/in-dash 4-disc CD changer, 2.5T, T5, XC, R	1200	1032
Includes premium sound system. XC requires power sunroof.		
Appearance & Special Purpose		
Xenon headlights, 2.4, 2.5T, T5, XC	500	430
Includes washers. 2.4, XC require power sunroof. 2.4 requires Premium Pkg.		
Mimas alloy wheels, 2.4	550	473
Includes 205/55HR16 tires. Requires power sunroof.		
Xenia alloy wheels, XC	250	215
Includes 215/65HR16 tires. Requires power sunroof.		

2004 VOLVO XC90

CLASS: Premium midsize sport-utility vehicle
DRIVE WHEELS: Front-wheel drive, all-wheel drive
BASE PRICE RANGE: $34,790-$40,965. Built in Sweden.
ALSO CONSIDER: Acura MDX, Lexus RX 330

Volvo's first SUV is an upscale wagon based on its S80 car platform. XC90 seats up to seven and is close in size to the Acura MDX. It comes in two models, both with a turbocharged engine, standard seating for five, and a combination rear liftgate/drop-down tailgate. The 2.5T offers front-wheel drive or all-wheel drive and uses a 208-hp 5 cyl and a 5-speed automatic transmission. The T6 has AWD, a 268-hp 6-cyl, and a 4-speed automatic. Both transmissions have a manual shift gate. XC90's AWD lacks low-range gearing and isn't intended for severe off-road use. Antilock 4-wheel disc brakes and antiskid/traction control are standard. So is Volvo's Roll Stability Control, designed to detect an impending tip and activate the antiskid system to reduce chances of a rollover. Also included are front torso side airbags and head-protecting curtain side airbags covering the first two seating rows. The 3rd-row seat is part of the optional Versatility Package, which includes rear load-leveling suspension and 3rd-row climate and audio controls. The 2nd-row bench splits 40/20/40 and offers an optional integrated child-booster seat for its middle section. All XC90s have wood interior trim. Leather upholstery is optional on the 2.5T, standard on T6. Seventeen-inch wheels are standard and are restyled for 2004; 18s are optional. Other options include rear-obstacle detection, navigation system, and heated front seats.

RATINGS	AWD 2.5T	AWD T6 w/nav. sys.	AWD T6 w/Premium Pkg.
ACCELERATION	5	5	5
FUEL ECONOMY	4	3	3
RIDE QUALITY	6	6	5
STEERING/HANDLING	6	6	6
QUIETNESS	5	6	6
CONTROLS/MATERIALS	6	4	6
ROOM/COMFORT (FRONT)	7	7	7
ROOM/COMFORT (REAR)	4	4	4
CARGO ROOM	8	8	8

Specifications begin on page 547.

RATINGS (cont.)	AWD 2.5T	AWD T6 w/nav. sys.	AWD T6 w/Premium Pkg.
VALUE WITHIN CLASS	5	5	5

Carlike road manners, solid feel, and numerous safety features are the XC90's strengths. Handling-conscious drivers will wish for sharper steering. And the 5-cyl engine's level of refinement disappoints. But prices are low enough to tempt MDX and Lexus RX 330 intenders, while those considering BMW X3, Volkswagen Touareg, and Mercedes ML350 would do well to look here, too.

TOTAL	56	54	55

Average total for premium midsize sport-utility vehicles: 59.6

ENGINES	Turbocharged dohc I5	Turbocharged dohc I6
Size, liters/cu. in.	2.5/153	2.9/178
Horsepower @ rpm	208 @ 5000	268 @ 5200
Torque (lb-ft) @ rpm	236 @ 1500	280 @ 1800
Availability	S[1]	S[2]
EPA city/highway mpg		
4-speed automatic		15/20
5-speed automatic	18/24	

1. 2.5T. 2. T6.

PRICES

Volvo XC90	RETAIL PRICE	DEALER INVOICE
2.5T 4-door wagon	$34790	$32738
AWD T6 4-door wagon	40965	38543
Destination charge	685	685

STANDARD EQUIPMENT

2.5T: 2.5-liter 5-cylinder turbocharged engine, 5-speed automatic transmission w/manual-shift capability, traction control, dual front airbags, front side airbags, front- and 2nd-row curtain side airbags, antilock 4-wheel disc brakes, antiskid system, roll stability control, daytime running lights, air conditioning w/dual-zone automatic climate controls, power steering, tilt/telescope steering wheel w/radio controls, cruise control, cloth/vinyl upholstery, front bucket seats, 8-way power driver seat w/memory, center console, cupholders, 2nd-row split folding seat, wood interior trim, heated power mirrors, power windows, power door locks, remote keyless entry, AM/FM/CD player, digital clock, tachometer, trip computer, intermittent wipers, illuminated visor mirrors, map lights, cargo cover, rear defogger, rear wiper/washer, floormats, theft-deterrent system, front and rear fog lights, roof rails, 235/65R17 tires, alloy wheels.

T6 AWD adds: 2.9-liter 6-cylinder turbocharged engine, 4-speed automatic transmission w/manual-shift capability, all-wheel drive, leather upholstery, 8-way power passenger seat, automatic day/night outside mirrors w/memory, power sunroof, AM/FM radio w/in-dash 6-disc CD changer, automatic day/night rearview mirror, universal garage-door opener.

OPTIONAL EQUIPMENT

Major Packages

	RETAIL PRICE	DEALER INVOICE
Premium Pkg., 2.5T	$3825	$3288
Manufacturer's Discount Price	*2575*	*2214*
Leather upholstery, 8-way power passenger seat, memory mirrors, power sunroof, AM/FM radio w/in-dash 6-disc CD changer, automatic day/night rearview mirror, universal garage-door opener.		
Premium Pkg., T6	1675	1440
Manufacturer's Discount Price	*1300*	*1118*
Prologic Surround Sound System, power-retractable mirrors, 235/60R18 tires.		
Versatility Pkg.	2200	1892
Manufacturer's Discount Price	*1700*	*1462*
3rd-row seat, rear air conditioning and radio controls, integrated child-booster seat, load-leveling rear suspension. 2.5T requires Premium Pkg. NA w/subwoofer radio equipment.		
Climate Pkg	675	580
Manufacturer's Discount Price	*625*	*537*
Heated front seats, air-quality system, rain-sensing wipers, headlight washer/wiper.		
Security Pkg	810	696
Manufacturer's Discount Price	*675*	*580*
Security-laminated side windows, level sensor.		

Powertrain

All-wheel drive, 2.5T	1775	1526

Safety

Rear-obstacle-detection system	400	344
Integrated child-booster seat	150	129

Comfort & Convenience Features

Navigation system	1995	1715
2.5T requires Premium Pkg.		
Rear-seat DVD player	750	645
Prologic Surround Sound	775	666
2.5T requires Premium Pkg.		
Rear radio controls	100	86
2.5T requires Premium Pkg.		
Subwoofer radio equipment	300	258
2.5T requires Premium Pkg.		
Wood/leather-wrapped steering wheel	325	279
Leather shift knob	50	43
Cargo net	300	258

Appearance & Special Purpose

Xenon headlights	500	430
Requires Climate Pkg.		
235/60R18 tires, 2.5T	750	645

 Specifications begin on page 547.

VEHICLE SPECIFICATIONS

Dimensions and capacities are supplied by the vehicle manufacturers. Pickup-truck specifications are for the half-ton 2WD model. **Body types:** 2-door coupe or 4-door sedan = a standard-body car with a separate trunk; hatchback = car with a rear liftgate; wagon = car or sport-utility vehicle with an enclosed cargo bay; regular-cab pickup truck = standard-length cab with room for one row of front seats; extended-cab pickup truck = lengthened cab with seating positions behind the front seats; crew-cab pickup truck = lengthened cab with four forward-opening doors. **Wheelbase:** Distance between the front and rear axles. **Curb weight:** Weight of base model, not including optional equipment. Weight listed for sport-utility vehicles is for the 4-wheel-drive version. **Height:** Overall height of the base model, not including optional equipment. Height listed for SUVs is for 4WD model. **Cargo volume:** *(Does not apply to pickup trucks)* Coupes and sedans = maximum volume of the trunk; hatchbacks and station wagons = maximum volume with the rear seat folded; minivans and sport-utility vehicles = maximum volume with all rear seats folded or removed, when possible. **Maximum payload:** *(Applies to pickup trucks)* Maximum weight the listed model can carry, including passengers. **NA**= Not available. **(—)**= not applicable.

COMPACT CARS	Wheelbase, in.	Overall length, in.	Overall width, in.	Overall height, in.	Curb weight, lb	Cargo volume, cu ft	Fuel capacity, gal	Seating capacity	Front head room, in.	Max. front leg room, in.	Rear head room, in.	Min. rear leg room, in.
Chevrolet Aveo 4-door hatchback	97.6	152.8	65.8	58.9	2348	42.0	11.9	5	39.3	41.3	37.6	35.4
Chevrolet Aveo 4-door sedan	97.6	166.7	65.7	58.9	2370	11.7	11.9	5	39.3	41.3	37.6	35.4
Chevrolet Cavalier 2-door coupe	104.1	182.7	68.7	53.0	2617	13.2	14.1	5	37.6	41.9	36.6	32.7
Chevrolet Cavalier 4-door sedan	104.1	182.7	67.9	54.7	2676	13.6	14.1	5	38.9	41.9	37.2	34.4
Chevrolet Cobalt 2-door coupe	103.3	180.3	67.9	55.7	2808	13.9	13.2	5	38.7	42.0	35.7	32.2
Chevrolet Cobalt 4-door sedan	103.3	180.5	67.9	57.1	2868	13.9	13.2	5	38.5	41.8	37.7	33.7
Chrysler PT Cruiser 4-door wagon	103.0	168.8	67.1	63.0	3101	64.2	15.0	5	39.2	40.6	39.5	40.9
Chrysler PT Cruiser 2-door convertible	103.0	168.8	67.1	60.6	3303	7.4	15.0	4	38.7	40.6	36.4	40.9
Dodge Neon 4-door sedan	105.0	174.4	67.4	56.0	2581	13.1	12.5	5	38.4	42.2	36.7	34.8
Ford Focus 2-door hatchback	103.0	168.5	66.9	56.3	2614	28.0	14.1	5	39.1	40.7	38.6	37.6
Ford Focus 4-door hatchback	103.0	168.5	66.9	56.3	2693	28.0	14.1	5	39.1	40.7	38.6	37.6
Ford Focus 4-door sedan	103.0	175.2	66.9	56.3	2643	14.0	14.1	5	39.1	40.7	38.6	37.6

COMPACT CARS (cont.)

COMPACT CARS (cont.)	Wheelbase, in.	Overall length, in.	Overall width, in.	Overall height, in.	Curb weight, lb	Cargo volume, cu ft	Fuel capacity, gal	Seating capacity	Front head room, in.	Max. front leg room, in.	Rear head room, in.	Min. rear leg room, in.
Ford Focus 4-door wagon	103.0	178.4	66.9	56.3	2790	73.0	14.1	5	39.1	40.7	39.8	37.6
Honda Civic 2-door hatchback	101.2	165.7	66.7	56.7	2782	35.7	13.2	5	37.8	42.2	36.7	33.0
Honda Civic 2-door coupe	103.1	175.4	66.7	55.1	2449	12.9	13.2	5	39.0	42.5	35.4	32.8
Honda Civic 4-door sedan	103.1	175.4	67.5	56.7	2449	12.9	13.2	5	39.8	42.2	37.2	36.0
Honda Insight 2-door hatchback	94.5	155.1	66.7	53.3	1850	16.3	10.6	2	38.8	42.9	—	—
Hyundai Accent 2-door hatchback	96.1	166.7	65.7	54.9	2255	16.9	11.9	5	38.9	42.6	38.0	32.8
Hyundai Accent 4-door sedan	96.1	166.7	65.7	54.9	2290	11.8	11.9	5	38.9	42.6	38.0	32.8
Hyundai Elantra 4-door sedan	102.7	178.1	67.9	56.1	2635	12.9	14.5	5	39.6	43.2	38.0	35.0
Hyundai Elantra 4-door hatchback	102.7	177.9	67.7	56.1	2635	37.0	14.5	5	39.6	43.2	38.0	35.0
Kia Rio 4-door sedan	94.9	166.9	65.9	56.7	2242	9.2	11.9	5	39.4	42.8	37.6	32.7
Kia Rio 4-door wagon	94.9	166.9	65.9	56.7	2236	44.3	11.9	5	39.4	42.8	37.6	32.7
Kia Spectra 4-door sedan	102.8	176.4	68.3	57.9	2701	12.2	14.5	5	40.0	42.8	38.2	35.4
Kia Spectra5 4-door wagon	102.8	170.9	68.3	57.9	2844	18.3	14.5	5	40.0	42.8	38.8	35.4
Mazda 3 4-door hatchback	103.9	176.6	69.1	57.7	2762	31.2	14.5	5	39.1	41.9	38.4	36.3
Mazda 3 4-door sedan	103.9	178.3	69.1	57.7	2696	11.4	14.5	5	39.1	41.9	37.4	36.3
Mitsubishi Lancer 4-door sedan	102.4	180.5	66.8	54.1	2656	11.3	13.2	5	38.8	43.2	36.7	36.6
Mitsubishi Lancer 4-door wagon	102.4	181.3	66.8	58.1	3020	60.7	13.2	5	38.8	43.2	37.2	36.6
Nissan Sentra 4-door sedan	99.8	177.5	67.3	55.5	2513	11.6	13.2	5	39.9	41.6	37.0	33.7
Pontiac Sunfire 2-door coupe	104.1	182.0	68.4	53.0	2771	12.4	14.1	5	37.6	42.1	36.6	32.6
Pontiac Vibe FWD 4-door wagon	102.4	171.9	69.9	62.2	2701	53.2	13.2	5	40.6	41.8	39.8	36.3
Pontiac Vibe AWD 4-door wagon	102.4	171.9	69.9	62.2	2976	53.2	11.9	5	40.6	41.8	39.8	36.3
Saturn Ion 4-door coupe	103.2	185.0	67.9	56.0	2751	14.2	13.2	4	38.9	42.2	36.5	32.7
Saturn Ion 4-door sedan	103.2	184.5	67.2	57.4	2692	14.7	13.2	5	40.0	42.2	37.0	33.3
Scion xA 4-door hatchback	93.3	154.1	66.7	60.2	2340	11.7	11.9	5	39.6	41.3	38.8	37.6

COMPACT CARS (cont.)	Wheelbase, in.	Overall length, in.	Overall width, in.	Overall height, in.	Curb weight, lb	Cargo volume, cu ft	Fuel capacity, gal	Seating capacity	Front head room, in.	Max. front leg room, in.	Rear head room, in.	Min. rear leg room, in.
Scion xB 4-door wagon	98.4	155.3	66.5	64.6	2395	21.2	11.9	5	46.1	45.3	45.7	38.0
Subaru Impreza 4-door sedan	99.4	173.8	68.1	56.7	2972	11.0	15.9	5	38.6	42.9	36.7	33.0
Subaru Impreza 4-door wagon	99.4	173.8	66.7	58.5	3024	61.6	15.9	5	39.7	42.9	37.3	33.7
Suzuki Aerio 4-door sedan	97.6	171.3	67.7	60.8	2661	14.6	13.2	5	40.6	41.4	37.6	36.0
Suzuki Aerio SX 4-door hatchback	97.6	166.5	67.7	61.0	2698	63.7	13.2	5	40.6	41.4	39.0	35.2
Suzuki Forenza 4-door sedan	102.4	177.2	67.9	56.9	2701	12.4	14.5	5	39.1	42.0	37.8	36.7
Suzuki Forenza 4-door wagon	102.4	179.7	67.9	59.1	2849	61.8	14.5	5	39.4	42.0	39.3	36.7
Suzuki Reno 4-door hatchback	102.4	169.1	67.9	56.9	2739	45.4	14.5	5	39.1	42.1	37.9	36.7
Toyota Corolla 4-door sedan	102.4	178.3	66.9	58.3	2530	13.6	13.2	5	39.1	41.3	37.1	35.4
Toyota Echo 2-door coupe	93.3	164.6	65.4	59.4	2035	13.6	11.9	5	39.9	41.1	37.6	35.2
Toyota Echo 4-door sedan	93.3	164.6	65.4	59.4	2055	13.6	11.9	5	39.9	41.1	37.6	35.2
Toyota Matrix 4-door wagon	102.4	171.3	69.9	61.6	2679	53.2	13.2	5	40.6	41.8	39.8	36.3
Toyota Matrix AWD 4-door wagon	102.4	171.3	69.9	61.6	2943	53.2	11.9	5	40.6	41.8	39.8	36.3
Toyota Prius 4-door hatchback	106.3	175.0	67.9	58.1	2890	16.1	11.9	5	39.1	41.9	37.1	38.6
Volkswagen Golf 2-door hatchback	98.9	164.9	68.3	56.7	2771	41.8	14.5	5	38.6	41.5	37.4	33.5
Volkswagen Golf 4-door hatchback	98.9	164.9	68.3	56.7	2857	41.8	14.5	5	38.6	41.5	37.4	33.5
Volkswagen Jetta 4-door sedan	98.9	172.3	68.3	56.7	2895	13.0	14.5	5	38.6	41.5	36.9	33.5
Volkswagen Jetta 4-door wagon	99.0	173.6	68.3	58.5	3034	51.9	14.5	5	38.6	41.5	38.1	33.5

PREMIUM COMPACT CARS	Wheelbase, in.	Overall length, in.	Overall width, in.	Overall height, in.	Curb weight, lb	Cargo volume, cu ft	Fuel capacity, gal	Seating capacity	Front head room, in.	Max. front leg room, in.	Rear head room, in.	Min. rear leg room, in.
Acura TSX 4-door sedan	105.1	183.3	69.4	57.3	3230	13.0	17.1	5	37.8	42.4	37.3	34.2
Audi A4 4-door sedan	104.3	179.0	69.5	56.2	3252	13.4	18.5	5	38.4	41.3	37.2	34.2
Audi A4 4-door wagon	104.3	179.0	69.5	56.2	3516	60.6	18.5	5	38.4	41.3	37.2	34.2
Audi A4 2-door convertible	104.5	180.0	70.0	54.8	3638	10.2	18.5	4	37.9	41.3	36.3	32.4

PREMIUM COMPACT CARS (cont.)

PREMIUM COMPACT CARS (cont.)	Wheelbase, in.	Overall length, in.	Overall width, in.	Overall height, in.	Curb weight, lb	Cargo volume, cu ft	Fuel capacity, gal	Seating capacity	Front head room, in.	Max. front leg room, in.	Rear head room, in.	Min. rear leg room, in.
BMW 3-Series 2-door coupe	107.3	176.7	69.2	53.9	3197	9.5	16.6	5	37.5	41.7	36.5	33.2
BMW 3-Series 2-door convertible	107.3	176.7	69.2	54.0	3560	7.7	16.6	4	38.0	41.7	36.4	32.0
BMW 3-Series 4-door sedan	107.3	176.0	68.5	55.7	3219	10.7	16.6	5	38.4	41.4	37.5	34.6
BMW 3-Series 4-door wagon	107.3	176.3	68.5	55.5	3362	48.0	16.6	5	38.4	41.4	37.7	34.4
Jaguar X-Type 4-door sedan	106.7	183.9	70.4	56.7	3496	16.0	16.0	5	37.2	42.4	37.5	34.4
Jaguar X-Type 4-door wagon	106.7	185.6	70.4	58.4	3761	49.9	16.0	5	37.2	42.4	38.5	34.4
Lexus IS 300 4-door sedan	105.1	176.6	67.9	55.5	3255	10.1	17.5	5	39.1	42.7	37.7	30.2
Lexus IS 300 4-door wagon	105.1	177.0	67.9	56.7	3410	21.8	17.5	5	39.1	42.7	37.7	30.2
Mercedes-Benz C-Class 2-door hatchback	106.9	171.0	68.0	54.3	3250	38.1	16.4	4	38.5	42.0	36.3	33.0
Mercedes-Benz C-Class 4-door sedan	106.9	178.3	68.0	55.2	3310	12.2	16.4	5	38.9	41.7	37.3	33.0
Mercedes-Benz C-Class 4-door wagon	106.9	178.3	68.0	55.2	3415	63.6	16.4	5	38.9	41.7	37.3	33.0
Saab 9-2X 4-door wagon	99.4	175.6	66.7	57.7	3070	61.6	15.9	5	39.7	42.9	37.3	33.7
Saab 9-3 4-door sedan	105.3	182.5	69.0	56.8	3175	14.8	16.4	5	38.9	42.3	37.0	35.1
Saab 9-3 2-door convertible	105.3	182.5	69.4	56.5	3480	12.4	16.4	4	38.0	41.5	37.1	31.9
Volvo S40 4-door sedan	103.9	175.9	69.7	57.2	3084	14.3	16.3	5	38.9	41.6	37.2	34.4
Volvo V50 4-door wagon	103.9	177.7	69.7	57.2	3269	62.7	15.9	5	38.9	41.6	38.1	34.4

MIDSIZE CARS

MIDSIZE CARS	Wheelbase, in.	Overall length, in.	Overall width, in.	Overall height, in.	Curb weight, lb	Cargo volume, cu ft	Fuel capacity, gal	Seating capacity	Front head room, in.	Max. front leg room, in.	Rear head room, in.	Min. rear leg room, in.
Buick LaCrosse 4-door sedan	110.5	198.1	73.0	57.4	3495	16.0	17.5	6	39.4	42.3	37.2	37.6
Chevrolet Malibu 4-door sedan	106.3	188.3	69.9	57.5	3174	15.4	16.3	5	39.6	41.9	37.6	38.5
Chevrolet Malibu Maxx 4-door hatchback	112.3	187.8	69.8	58.1	3458	41.0	16.4	5	39.4	41.9	39.4	41.0
Chevrolet Monte Carlo 2-door coupe	110.5	197.9	72.7	55.2	3340	15.8	17.0	5	38.1	42.4	36.5	35.8
Chrysler Sebring 2-door coupe	103.7	191.9	69.9	53.9	3133	16.3	16.3	5	38.5	42.3	36.0	34.0
Chrysler Sebring 2-door convertible	106.0	193.7	69.4	55.0	3357	11.3	16.0	4	38.7	42.4	37.0	35.2

MIDSIZE CARS (cont.)	Wheelbase, in.	Overall length, in.	Overall width, in.	Overall height, in.	Curb weight, lb	Cargo volume, cu ft	Fuel capacity, gal	Seating capacity	Front head room, in.	Max. front leg room, in.	Rear head room, in.	Min. rear leg room, in.
Chrysler Sebring 4-door sedan	108.0	190.7	70.6	54.9	3173	16.0	16.0	5	37.6	42.3	35.8	38.1
Dodge Stratus 2-door coupe	103.7	190.9	70.3	53.9	3051	16.3	16.3	5	38.5	42.3	36.0	34.0
Dodge Stratus 4-door sedan	108.0	191.2	70.6	54.9	3175	16.0	16.0	5	37.6	42.3	35.8	38.1
Ford Taurus 4-door sedan	108.5	197.6	73.0	56.1	3306	17.0	18.0	6	40.0	42.2	38.1	38.9
Ford Taurus 4-door wagon	108.5	197.7	73.0	57.8	3497	81.3	18.0	8	39.4	42.2	38.9	38.5
Honda Accord 2-door coupe	105.1	187.6	71.3	55.7	2994	12.8	17.1	5	39.8	43.1	36.1	31.9
Honda Accord 4-door sedan	107.9	189.5	71.5	57.1	3059	14.0	17.1	5	40.4	42.6	38.5	36.8
Hyundai Sonata 4-door sedan	106.3	186.9	71.7	56.0	3181	14.1	17.2	5	39.3	43.3	37.6	36.2
Hyundai XG350 4-door sedan	108.3	191.9	71.9	55.9	3651	14.5	18.5	5	39.7	43.4	38.0	37.2
Kia Optima 4-door sedan	106.3	186.2	71.7	55.5	3157	13.6	17.2	5	39.0	43.3	37.6	36.2
Mazda 6 4-door sedan	105.3	186.8	70.1	56.7	3102	15.2	18.0	5	38.7	42.3	37.1	36.5
Mazda 6 4-door hatchback	105.3	186.8	70.1	56.7	3172	58.7	18.0	5	38.7	42.3	36.7	36.5
Mazda 6 4-door wagon	105.3	187.8	70.1	57.3	3404	60.4	18.0	5	38.7	42.3	38.6	36.5
Mercury Sable 4-door sedan	108.5	199.8	73.0	55.5	3308	16.0	18.0	6	39.8	42.2	36.7	38.9
Mercury Sable 4-door wagon	108.5	197.8	73.0	57.8	3294	81.3	18.0	8	39.4	42.2	38.9	38.5
Mitsubishi Galant 4-door sedan	108.3	190.6	72.4	57.9	3351	13.3	17.7	5	39.6	42.6	37.0	37.0
Nissan Altima 4-door sedan	110.2	192.3	70.4	57.9	3001	15.6	20.0	5	40.8	43.9	37.6	36.4
Nissan Maxima 4-door sedan	111.2	193.5	71.7	58.3	3432	15.5	20.0	5	39.7	43.6	37.1	36.5
Pontiac G6 4-door sedan	112.3	189.0	70.6	57.0	3380	14.0	16.4	5	39.5	42.2	36.3	37.6
Pontiac Grand Am 2-door coupe	107.2	186.3	70.4	55.1	3066	14.6	14.1	5	38.3	42.1	37.3	35.5
Pontiac Grand Prix 4-door sedan	110.5	198.3	73.8	55.9	3477	16.0	17.0	5	38.5	42.4	36.5	36.5
Saturn L300 4-door sedan	106.5	190.4	68.5	56.4	3033	17.5	15.7	5	39.3	42.3	38.0	35.4
Subaru Legacy 4-door sedan	105.1	186.2	68.1	56.1	3200	11.4	16.9	5	39.5	44.1	36.5	33.9
Subaru Legacy 4-door wagon	105.1	188.7	68.1	58.1	3255	66.2	16.9	5	40.5	44.1	39.1	33.9

MIDSIZE CARS (cont.)	Wheelbase, in.	Overall length, in.	Overall width, in.	Overall height, in.	Curb weight, lb	Cargo volume, cu ft	Fuel capacity, gal	Seating capacity	Front head room, in.	Max. front leg room, in.	Rear head room, in.	Min. rear leg room, in.
Subaru Outback 4-door sedan	105.1	188.7	69.7	59.1	3545	11.4	16.9	5	37.5	44.1	36.5	33.9
Subaru Outback 4-door wagon	105.1	188.7	69.7	61.6	3310	66.2	16.9	5	38.7	44.1	37.1	33.9
Suzuki Verona 4-door sedan	106.3	187.8	71.5	57.1	3380	13.4	17.2	5	39.1	42.2	37.3	37.8
Toyota Camry 4-door sedan	107.1	189.2	70.7	58.3	3108	16.7	18.5	5	39.2	41.5	38.3	37.8
Toyota Solara 2-door coupe	107.1	192.5	71.5	56.1	3175	13.8	18.5	5	38.0	42.0	36.4	35.4
Toyota Solara 2-door convertible	107.1	192.5	71.5	56.5	3549	12.0	18.5	4	38.5	42.0	38.4	35.0
Volkswagen Passat 4-door sedan	106.4	185.2	68.7	57.6	3212	15.0	16.4	5	39.7	41.5	37.8	35.3
Volkswagen Passat 4-door sedan 4Motion	106.4	185.2	68.7	57.6	3721	10.0	16.4	5	37.8	41.5	37.3	35.3
Volkswagen Passat 4-door wagon	106.4	184.3	68.7	59.0	3307	56.5	16.4	5	39.7	41.5	39.7	35.3

PREMIUM MIDSIZE CARS	Wheelbase, in.	Overall length, in.	Overall width, in.	Overall height, in.	Curb weight, lb	Cargo volume, cu ft	Fuel capacity, gal	Seating capacity	Front head room, in.	Max. front leg room, in.	Rear head room, in.	Min. rear leg room, in.
Acura RL 4-door sedan	110.2	193.6	72.7	57.1	3984	13.1	19.4	5	38.5	42.4	37.2	36.3
Acura TL 4-door sedan	107.9	189.3	72.2	56.7	3482	12.5	17.0	5	38.7	42.8	37.2	34.9
Audi A6 4-door sedan	110.9	191.7	72.3	56.9	3957	15.9	18.5	5	38.3	41.3	37.4	36.9
Audi allroad quattro 4-door sedan	108.5	189.4	74.6	62.0	4178	73.2	18.5	5	37.5	41.3	38.4	37.3
BMW 5-Series 4-door sedan	113.7	189.6	72.7	58.0	3428	14.0	18.5	5	37.7	41.5	37.9	36.0
Cadillac CTS 4-door sedan	113.4	190.1	70.6	56.7	3568	12.8	17.5	5	38.9	42.4	36.9	37.0
Cadillac STS 4-door sedan	116.4	196.3	72.6	57.6	3857	13.8	17.5	5	38.7	42.6	37.9	38.3
Infiniti G35 2-door coupe	112.2	182.2	71.5	54.8	3486	7.8	20.0	4	39.2	43.8	34.7	31.4
Infiniti G35 4-door sedan	112.2	186.5	69.0	57.7	3468	14.8	20.0	5	40.1	43.6	37.9	33.6
Jaguar S-Type 4-door sedan	114.5	193.4	71.6	56.0	3771	14.1	18.4	5	40.5	43.1	36.9	37.0
Lexus ES 330 4-door sedan	107.1	191.1	71.3	57.3	3472	14.5	18.5	5	38.5	42.2	37.4	35.6
Lexus GS 4-door sedan	110.2	189.2	70.9	55.9	3649	14.8	19.8	5	39.0	44.5	37.4	34.3

PREMIUM MIDSIZE CARS (cont.)	Wheelbase, in.	Overall length, in.	Overall width, in.	Overall height, in.	Curb weight, lb	Cargo volume, cu ft	Fuel capacity, gal	Seating capacity	Front head room, in.	Max. front leg room, in.	Rear head room, in.	Min. rear leg room, in.
Lincoln LS 4-door sedan	114.5	194.3	73.2	56.1	3681	13.5	18.0	5	40.5	42.8	37.3	36.0
Mercedes-Benz E-Class 4-door sedan	112.4	189.7	71.3	57.2	3635	15.9	21.1	5	37.4	41.9	37.7	35.6
Mercedes-Benz E-Class 4-door wagon	112.4	191.7	71.7	58.9	3966	68.9	21.1	7	37.9	41.9	38.0	36.0
Saab 9-5 4-door sedan	106.4	190.1	70.5	57.0	3470	15.9	18.5	5	38.7	42.4	37.0	36.6
Saab 9-5 4-door wagon	106.4	190.1	70.5	57.0	3620	73.0	18.5	5	38.7	42.4	38.2	36.6
Volvo S60 4-door sedan	107.0	180.2	71.0	56.2	3276	13.9	18.5	5	38.7	42.6	37.9	33.3
Volvo V70 4-door wagon	108.5	185.4	71.0	57.7	3369	71.5	18.5	5	39.3	42.6	38.9	38.7
Volvo XC70 4-door wagon	108.8	186.3	73.2	61.5	3827	71.5	18.5	5	39.3	42.6	38.9	38.7

LARGE CARS	Wheelbase, in.	Overall length, in.	Overall width, in.	Overall height, in.	Curb weight, lb	Cargo volume, cu ft	Fuel capacity, gal	Seating capacity	Front head room, in.	Max. front leg room, in.	Rear head room, in.	Min. rear leg room, in.
Buick LeSabre 4-door sedan	112.2	200.0	73.5	57.0	3567	18.0	18.5	6	38.8	42.4	37.8	39.9
Buick Park Avenue 4-door sedan	113.8	206.8	74.7	57.4	3778	19.1	18.0	6	39.8	42.4	38.0	41.4
Chevrolet Impala 4-door sedan	110.5	200.0	73.0	57.3	3465	18.6	17.0	6	39.2	42.2	36.8	38.4
Chrysler 300 4-door sedan	120.0	196.8	74.1	58.4	3721	15.6	18.0	5	38.7	41.8	38.0	40.2
Dodge Magnum 4-door wagon	120.0	197.7	74.1	58.4	3855	71.6	18.0	5	38.4	41.8	38.1	40.2
Ford Crown Victoria 4-door sedan	114.7	212.0	78.2	58.3	4101	20.6	19.0	6	39.5	41.6	37.7	38.4
Ford Five Hundred 4-door sedan	112.9	200.7	74.5	61.5	3664	21.2	19.0	5	39.4	41.3	38.7	41.3
Kia Amanti 4-door sedan	110.2	196.0	72.8	58.5	4021	15.5	18.5	5	40.0	43.7	38.4	37.8
Mercury Grand Marquis 4-door sedan	114.6	211.9	78.2	58.4	4135	20.6	19.0	6	39.5	41.6	37.7	38.4
Mercury Montego 4-door sedan	112.9	200.7	74.5	60.1	3650	21.0	19.0	5	39.4	41.3	38.6	41.3
Pontiac Bonneville 4-door sedan	112.2	202.6	74.2	56.6	3590	18.0	18.5	6	38.7	42.6	37.3	38.0
Toyota Avalon 4-door sedan	107.1	191.9	71.7	57.1	3417	15.9	18.5	6	38.7	41.7	37.9	40.1

PREMIUM LARGE CARS	Wheelbase, in.	Overall length, in.	Overall width, in.	Overall height, in.	Curb weight, lb	Cargo volume, cu ft	Fuel capacity, gal	Seating capacity	Front head room, in.	Max. front leg room, in.	Rear head room, in.	Min. rear leg room, in.
Cadillac DeVille 4-door sedan	115.3	207.0	74.4	56.7	3984	19.1	18.5	6	39.1	42.4	38.3	43.2
Lexus LS 430 4-door sedan	115.2	197.4	72.0	58.7	3990	20.2	22.2	5	38.1	44.0	37.9	37.6
Lincoln Town Car 4-door sedan	117.7	216.2	78.2	59.0	4345	21.0	19.0	6	39.4	41.6	37.4	41.1
Lincoln Town Car (L) 4-door sedan	123.7	221.4	78.2	59.1	4518	21.0	19.0	6	39.4	41.6	37.4	47.0
Volkswagen Phaeton 4-door sedan	118.1	203.7	74.9	57.1	5194	13.0	23.8	5	37.2	41.7	38.1	43.1
Volvo S80 4-door sedan	109.9	189.8	72.1	57.2	3626	14.4	21.1	5	38.9	42.2	37.6	35.9
Volvo S80 T6 Premier 4-door sedan	109.9	189.8	72.1	57.2	3703	14.4	21.1	5	38.9	42.2	37.6	37.8

SPORTY/PERFORMANCE CARS	Wheelbase, in.	Overall length, in.	Overall width, in.	Overall height, in.	Curb weight, lb	Cargo volume, cu ft	Fuel capacity, gal	Seating capacity	Front head room, in.	Max. front leg room, in.	Rear head room, in.	Min. rear leg room, in.
Acura RSX 2-door hatchback	101.2	172.4	67.9	54.9	2734	16.0	13.2	4	37.8	43.1	34.1	29.2
Ford Mustang 2-door coupe	107.1	187.6	73.9	54.5	3300	13.0	16.0	4	38.6	42.7	35.0	31.0
Honda S2000 2-door convertible	94.5	162.2	68.9	50.0	2835	5.0	13.2	2	34.6	44.3	—	—
Hyundai Tiburon 2-door hatchback	99.6	173.0	69.3	52.3	2940	14.7	14.2	4	38.0	43.0	34.4	29.9
Mazda Miata 2-door convertible	89.2	155.7	66.0	48.4	2387	5.1	12.7	2	37.1	42.8	—	—
Mazda RX-8 4-door coupe	106.3	174.2	69.7	52.8	3029	7.6	15.8	4	38.2	42.6	36.8	32.2
Mini Cooper 2-door hatchback	97.1	142.8	66.5	55.4	2524	23.7	13.2	4	38.8	41.3	37.6	31.3
Mini Cooper 2-door convertible	97.1	143.1	66.5	55.7	2700	4.2	13.2	4	38.4	41.3	38.1	27.7
Mitsubishi Eclipse 2-door hatchback	100.8	176.8	68.9	51.6	2910	16.9	16.4	4	37.9	42.3	34.9	30.2
Mitsubishi Eclipse 2-door convertible	100.8	176.8	68.9	52.8	3097	7.2	16.4	4	39.4	42.3	34.5	29.4
Nissan 350Z 2-door hatchback	104.3	169.6	71.5	51.9	3188	6.8	20.0	2	38.2	42.6	—	—
Nissan 350Z 2-door convertible	104.3	169.4	71.5	52.3	3428	4.1	20.0	2	39.2	42.6	—	—
Pontiac GTO 2-door coupe	109.8	189.8	72.5	54.9	NA	7.0	18.5	4	37.3	42.2	37.3	37.1
Scion tC 2-door hatchback	106.3	174.0	69.1	55.7	2905	12.8	14.5	5	37.6	41.6	36.6	33.6
Toyota Celica 2-door hatchback	102.4	170.5	68.3	51.4	2425	16.9	14.5	4	38.4	43.6	35.0	27.0

SPORTY/PERFORMANCE CARS (cont.)	Wheelbase, in.	Overall length, in.	Overall width, in.	Overall height, in.	Curb weight, lb	Cargo volume, cu ft	Fuel capacity, gal	Seating capacity	Front head room, in.	Max. front leg room, in.	Rear head room, in.	Min. rear leg room, in.
Toyota MR2 Spyder 2-door convertible	96.5	153.0	66.7	48.8	2195	48.8	12.7	2	37.3	42.2	—	—
Volkswagen New Beetle 2-door hatchback	98.7	161.1	67.9	59.0	2743	27.1	14.5	4	41.3	39.4	36.7	33.5
Volkswagen New Beetle 2-door convertible	98.8	161.1	67.9	59.1	3075	5.0	14.5	4	40.7	39.4	37.2	31.5

PREM. SPORTY/PERFORMANCE CARS	Wheelbase, in.	Overall length, in.	Overall width, in.	Overall height, in.	Curb weight, lb	Cargo volume, cu ft	Fuel capacity, gal	Seating capacity	Front head room, in.	Max. front leg room, in.	Rear head room, in.	Min. rear leg room, in.
Acura NSX 2-door coupe	99.6	174.2	71.3	46.1	3153	5.0	18.5	2	36.3	44.3	—	—
Audi TT 2-door hatchback	95.4	159.1	73.1	53.0	2921	24.2	14.5	4	37.8	41.2	32.6	20.2
Audi TT 2-door convertible	95.4	159.1	73.1	53.0	3131	7.8	14.5	2	38.3	41.2	—	—
BMW 6-Series 2-door convertible	109.4	190.2	73.0	54.1	3781	13.0	18.5	4	37.8	42.0	35.5	28.8
BMW 6-Series 2-door coupe	109.4	190.2	73.0	54.1	4178	10.6	18.5	4	37.8	42.0	36.7	28.8
BMW Z4 2-door convertible	98.2	161.1	70.1	50.1	2932	9.5	14.5	2	37.3	42.0	—	—
Cadillac XLR 2-door convertible	105.7	177.7	72.3	50.4	3647	11.6	18.0	2	37.6	42.6	—	—
Chevrolet Corvette 2-door hatchback	106.0	175.0	73.0	49.0	3179	22.0	18.0	2	38.0	43.0	—	—
Chevrolet Corvette 2-door convertible	106.0	175.0	73.0	49.0	3199	11.0	18.0	2	38.0	43.0	—	—
Chevrolet SSR regular cab convertible	116.0	191.4	78.6	64.2	4760	23.7	25.0	2	40.0	42.1	—	—
Chrysler Crossfire 2-door hatchback	94.5	159.8	69.5	51.4	3060	7.6	15.9	2	36.9	42.7	—	—
Chrysler Crossfire 2-door convertible	94.5	159.8	69.5	51.8	3140	6.5	15.9	2	37.3	42.7	—	—
Dodge Viper 2-door convertible	98.8	175.6	75.2	47.6	3410	8.4	18.5	2	36.5	42.4	—	—
Ford Thunderbird 2-door convertible	107.2	186.3	72.0	52.1	3780	8.5	18.0	2	37.2	42.7	—	—
Jaguar XK Series 2-door coupe	101.9	187.8	70.8	50.5	3779	11.5	19.9	4	37.4	43.0	33.3	23.7
Jaguar XK Series 2-door convertible	101.9	187.8	70.8	51.0	3980	10.8	19.9	4	37.0	43.0	33.2	23.1
Lexus SC 430 2-door convertible	103.1	177.8	72.0	53.1	3840	8.8	19.8	4	37.2	43.6	33.9	27.1
Mercedes-Benz CLK 2-door coupe	106.9	182.6	68.5	55.4	3515	10.4	16.4	4	37.1	42.0	35.8	33.0
Mercedes-Benz CLK 2-door convertible	106.9	182.6	68.5	54.4	3770	8.6	16.4	4	38.4	42.0	36.3	30.4

PREM. SPORTY/ PERFORMANCE CARS (cont.)

PREM. SPORTY/ PERFORMANCE CARS (cont.)	Wheelbase, in.	Overall length, in.	Overall width, in.	Overall height, in.	Curb weight, lb	Cargo volume, cu ft	Fuel capacity, gal	Seating capacity	Front head room, in.	Max. front leg room, in.	Rear head room, in.	Min. rear leg room, in.
Mercedes-Benz SL-Class 2-door convertible	100.8	178.5	71.5	51.0	4045	10.2	21.1	2	37.7	42.9	—	—
Mercedes-Benz SLK-Class 2-door convertible	95.7	160.7	70.4	51.1	3231	9.8	18.4	2	37.9	42.5	—	—
Porsche 911 2-door coupe	92.5	175.6	71.2	51.6	3075	4.8	16.9	4	NA	NA	NA	NA
Porsche Turbo 2-door coupe	92.5	174.6	72.1	51.0	3505	3.5	16.6	4	38.0	41.6	NA	NA
Porsche Turbo 2-door convertible	92.5	174.6	72.1	51.0	3660	3.5	16.6	4	38.0	41.6	NA	NA
Porsche Boxster 2-door convertible	95.1	170.1	70.1	50.8	2911	9.1	16.9	2	38.4	41.6	—	—
Volvo C70 2-door convertible	104.9	185.7	71.5	56.3	3450	8.1	17.9	4	39.2	41.4	36.6	34.6

COMPACT SUVS

COMPACT SUVS	Wheelbase, in.	Overall length, in.	Overall width, in.	Overall height, in.	Curb weight, lb	Cargo volume, cu ft	Fuel capacity, gal	Seating capacity	Front head room, in.	Max. front leg room, in.	Rear head room, in.	Min. rear leg room, in.
BMW X3 4-door wagon	110.1	179.7	73.0	66.0	4001	71.0	17.7	5	39.3	40.2	39.4	35.8
Ford Escape 4-door wagon	103.1	174.9	70.1	69.7	3340	66.3	16.5	5	40.4	41.6	39.2	36.3
Honda CR-V 4-door wagon	103.3	181.0	70.2	66.2	3428	72.0	15.3	5	40.9	41.3	39.1	39.4
Honda Element 4-door wagon	101.4	166.5	71.5	70.4	3525	77.1	15.9	4	43.3	41.0	39.4	39.1
Hyundai Santa Fe 4-door wagon	103.1	177.2	72.7	66.0	3752	77.7	19.0	5	39.6	41.6	39.2	36.8
Hyundai Tucson 4-door wagon	103.5	170.3	70.7	66.1	3425	65.5	17.2	5	40.3	42.1	38.8	37.2
Jeep Liberty 4-door wagon	104.3	174.4	71.6	70.2	3851	69.0	20.5	5	40.7	40.8	42.1	37.2
Jeep Wrangler 2-door convertible	93.4	154.9	66.7	70.9	3200	47.1	19.0	4	42.5	40.9	39.7	35.3
Jeep Wrangler Unlimited 2-door convertible	103.4	171.0	66.7	70.9	3721	63.3	19.0	4	41.9	41.1	40.6	36.7
Land Rover Freelander 2-door wagon	101.0	174.7	71.2	71.2	3640	42.2	16.9	5	38.4	41.8	38.9	36.8
Land Rover Freelander 4-door wagon	101.0	174.7	71.2	72.0	3699	46.6	16.9	5	38.4	41.8	38.9	36.8
Mazda Tribute 4-door wagon	103.1	174.4	72.0	70.0	3346	66.8	16.5	5	40.4	41.6	39.2	36.3
Mercury Mariner 4-door wagon	103.1	174.9	70.1	70.7	3409	66.4	16.5	5	40.4	41.6	39.2	36.2
Mitsubishi Outlander 4-door wagon	103.3	179.1	68.9	66.3	3461	60.3	15.7	5	38.9	42.3	38.2	35.5

COMPACT SUVS (cont.)

COMPACT SUVS (cont.)	Wheelbase, in.	Overall length, in.	Overall width, in.	Overall height, in.	Curb weight, lb	Cargo volume, cu ft	Fuel capacity, gal	Seating capacity	Front head room, in.	Max. front leg room, in.	Rear head room, in.	Min. rear leg room, in.
Saturn Vue 4-door wagon	106.6	181.3	71.5	66.5	3630	63.5	16.3	5	40.4	41.2	40.3	36.8
Subaru Baja 4-door crew cab	104.3	193.3	70.1	62.1	3480	—	16.9	4	38.3	43.3	37.3	33.5
Subaru Forester 4-door wagon	99.4	175.2	68.3	62.6	3090	64.1	15.9	5	39.8	43.6	39.8	33.7
Suzuki Grand Vitara 4-door wagon	97.6	164.5	70.1	67.8	3230	50.2	16.9	5	39.9	41.4	39.6	30.6
Toyota RAV4 4-door wagon	98.0	166.6	68.3	66.1	3119	68.3	14.7	5	41.3	42.3	38.4	32.6

MIDSIZE SUVS

MIDSIZE SUVS	Wheelbase, in.	Overall length, in.	Overall width, in.	Overall height, in.	Curb weight, lb	Cargo volume, cu ft	Fuel capacity, gal	Seating capacity	Front head room, in.	Max. front leg room, in.	Rear head room, in.	Min. rear leg room, in.
Buick Rendezvous 4-door wagon	112.2	186.5	73.6	68.9	4250	108.9	18.0	7	40.9	40.5	40.1	39.0
Chevrolet Blazer 2-door wagon	100.5	176.8	67.8	64.3	3866	60.6	18.7	4	39.6	42.4	38.3	35.6
Chevrolet Equinox 4-door wagon	112.5	188.8	71.4	67.0	3776	68.6	16.6	5	40.9	41.2	40.1	40.2
Chevrolet TrailBlazer 4-door wagon	113.0	191.8	74.6	74.5	4594	80.1	22.0	5	40.2	42.9	39.6	37.0
Chevrolet TrailBlazer EXT 4-door wagon	129.0	207.8	74.7	77.1	4954	107.0	25.0	7	40.2	42.9	39.6	37.0
Chrysler Pacifica 4-door wagon	116.3	198.9	79.3	66.5	4675	79.5	23.0	6	39.2	40.9	40.4	38.9
Dodge Durango 4-door wagon	119.2	200.8	76.0	74.3	5015	102.4	27.0	7	40.8	41.4	39.3	37.4
Ford Explorer 4-door wagon	113.7	189.6	72.1	72.1	4301	87.8	22.5	7	39.8	42.4	38.8	36.8
Ford Explorer Sport Trac 4-door crew cab	125.9	205.9	71.8	70.5	4349	—	22.5	5	39.4	42.5	38.6	37.8
Ford Freestyle 4-door wagon	112.9	199.8	74.4	64.9	4112	86.5	19.0	7	39.4	40.8	39.4	39.8
GMC Envoy 4-door wagon	113.0	191.6	74.7	71.9	4612	80.1	22.0	5	40.2	41.4	39.6	37.0
GMC Envoy XL 4-door wagon	129.0	207.6	74.7	75.5	4954	107.4	25.0	7	40.2	41.4	39.6	37.0
GMC Envoy XUV 4-door wagon	129.0	208.4	74.7	72.6	5042	108.8	25.0	5	40.2	41.4	39.4	37.0
Honda Pilot 4-door wagon	106.3	188.0	77.3	70.6	4414	90.3	20.4	8	41.9	41.4	40.9	37.4
Isuzu Ascender 4-door wagon	129.0	207.6	76.1	75.5	4967	100.2	25.0	7	40.2	43.1	39.6	37.5
Jeep Grand Cherokee 4-door wagon	109.5	186.6	73.3	67.7	4441	67.4	20.8	5	39.7	41.7	39.3	35.5
Kia Sorento 4-door wagon	106.7	179.8	73.3	68.1	4255	66.4	21.1	5	39.7	42.6	39.5	36.1

MIDSIZE SUVS (cont.)	Wheelbase, in.	Overall length, in.	Overall width, in.	Overall height, in.	Curb weight, lb	Cargo volume, cu ft	Fuel capacity, gal	Seating capacity	Front head room, in.	Max. front leg room, in.	Rear head room, in.	Min. rear leg room, in.
Mercury Mountaineer 4-door wagon	113.8	180.9	72.3	71.5	4566	81.4	22.5	7	39.8	42.4	38.8	36.8
Mitsubishi Endeavor 4-door wagon	108.7	190.2	73.6	67.3	4079	76.4	21.4	5	39.6	41.4	38.7	38.5
Mitsubishi Montero 4-door wagon	109.7	190.2	74.8	71.5	4787	91.7	23.8	7	39.8	42.3	40.6	35.2
Nissan Murano 4-door wagon	111.2	187.6	74.0	66.5	3955	81.6	21.7	5	40.7	43.4	39.7	36.1
Nissan Pathfinder 4-door wagon	112.2	187.6	72.8	69.1	4586	79.2	21.1	7	40.0	42.4	39.0	34.2
Nissan Xterra 4-door wagon	104.3	178.0	70.4	74.0	4034	65.6	19.4	5	38.6	41.4	37.8	32.8
Pontiac Aztek 4-door wagon	108.3	182.2	73.6	66.9	4043	95.1	18.0	5	39.7	40.5	39.1	35.6
Suzuki XL-7 4-door wagon	110.2	187.4	70.1	68.5	3704	75.1	16.9	7	40.0	41.4	39.2	31.4
Toyota 4Runner 4-door wagon	109.8	189.0	73.8	68.5	4300	75.1	23.0	7	39.7	41.8	39.1	34.6
Toyota Highlander 4-door wagon	106.9	184.6	71.9	66.1	3750	80.6	19.1	7	40.0	40.7	39.8	36.4

PREMIUM MIDSIZE SUVS	Wheelbase, in.	Overall length, in.	Overall width, in.	Overall height, in.	Curb weight, lb	Cargo volume, cu ft	Fuel capacity, gal	Seating capacity	Front head room, in.	Max. front leg room, in.	Rear head room, in.	Min. rear leg room, in.
Acura MDX 4-door wagon	106.3	188.7	77.0	68.7	4451	81.5	20.4	7	38.4	41.5	39.0	37.8
BMW X5 4-door wagon	111.0	183.7	73.7	67.5	4652	69.0	24.6	5	39.9	39.3	38.5	35.4
Buick Rainier 4-door wagon	113.0	193.4	75.4	71.9	4628	80.1	22.0	5	40.2	44.6	39.6	37.1
Cadillac SRX 4-door wagon	116.0	195.0	72.6	67.8	4438	69.5	20.0	7	40.3	42.1	38.4	41.0
Infiniti FX 4-door wagon	112.2	189.1	75.8	65.0	4268	64.5	23.8	5	40.8	43.9	39.5	35.2
Land Rover LR3 4-door wagon	113.6	190.9	75.4	74.1	5426	90.3	22.8	7	40.4	42.4	42.4	37.6
Lexus GX 470 4-door wagon	109.8	188.2	74.0	73.0	4675	77.5	23.0	8	41.0	41.8	40.4	36.8
Lexus RX 330 4-door wagon	106.9	186.2	72.6	66.1	4065	84.7	19.2	5	39.3	42.5	38.6	36.4
Lincoln Aviator 4-door wagon	113.7	193.3	76.0	71.4	4818	81.7	22.5	7	39.9	42.4	38.4	36.8
Mercedes-Benz M-Class 4-door wagon	111.0	182.6	72.4	71.7	4819	81.2	22.6	7	39.8	40.3	39.7	38.0
Porsche Cayenne 4-door wagon	112.4	188.2	75.9	66.9	4762	62.5	26.4	5	39.6	40.6	38.8	35.9

PREMIUM MIDSIZE SUVS (cont.)

	Wheelbase, in.	Overall length, in.	Overall width, in.	Overall height, in.	Curb weight, lb	Cargo volume, cu ft	Fuel capacity, gal	Seating capacity	Front head room, in.	Max. front leg room, in.	Rear head room, in.	Min. rear leg room, in.
Toyota Land Cruiser 4-door wagon	112.2	192.5	76.4	73.2	5390	90.8	25.4	8	39.2	42.3	39.1	34.3
Volkswagen Touareg 4-door wagon	112.4	187.2	75.9	68.0	5086	71.0	26.4	5	38.7	41.3	38.3	35.6
Volvo XC90 4-door wagon	112.6	188.9	74.7	70.2	4450	93.2	19.0	7	40.1	41.0	39.5	36.4

MINIVANS

	Wheelbase, in.	Overall length, in.	Overall width, in.	Overall height, in.	Curb weight, lb	Cargo volume, cu ft	Fuel capacity, gal	Seating capacity	Front head room, in.	Max. front leg room, in.	Rear head room, in.	Min. rear leg room, in.
Buick Terraza 4-door van	121.1	205.0	72.0	72.0	4470	136.5	25.0	7	39.8	39.9	38.9	38.9
Chevrolet Astro 3-door van	111.2	189.8	77.5	75.0	4321	170.4	27.0	8	39.2	41.6	37.9	36.5
Chevrolet Uplander 4-door van	121.1	204.0	72.0	72.0	3838	136.7	25.0	7	39.8	39.9	38.9	38.9
Chrysler Town & Country 4-door van	113.3	189.3	78.6	68.8	3899	146.7	20.0	7	39.6	40.8	39.7	36.5
Chrysler Town & Country (ext.) 4-door van	119.3	200.5	78.6	68.9	4239	160.7	20.0	7	39.6	40.6	39.6	37.5
Dodge Caravan 4-door van	113.3	189.1	78.6	68.9	3908	146.7	20.0	7	39.6	40.6	39.9	36.5
Dodge Grand Caravan 4-door van	119.3	200.5	78.6	68.9	3960	167.9	20.0	7	39.6	40.6	39.1	39.0
Ford Freestar 4-door van	120.8	201.0	76.6	70.8	4275	130.6	26.0	7	38.9	40.7	40.1	38.0
GMC Safari 3-door van	111.2	189.8	77.5	75.0	4321	170.4	27.0	8	39.2	41.6	37.9	36.5
Honda Odyssey 4-door van	118.1	201.0	77.1	68.8	4377	147.4	21.0	8	40.9	40.8	40.0	39.6
Kia Sedona 4-door van	114.6	194.1	74.6	69.3	4709	127.5	19.8	7	39.4	40.6	39.2	37.2
Mazda MPV 4-door van	111.8	187.8	72.1	68.7	3794	127.0	19.8	7	41.0	40.8	39.3	37.0
Mercury Monterey 4-door van	120.8	201.0	76.4	70.8	4434	131.5	26.0	7	38.9	40.7	39.7	37.9
Nissan Quest 4-door van	124.0	204.1	77.6	70.0	4012	148.7	20.1	7	41.9	41.6	41.7	41.3
Pontiac Montana SV6 4-door van	121.1	205.0	72.0	72.0	NA	136.5	25.0	7	39.8	39.9	38.9	38.9
Saturn Relay 4-door wagon	121.1	204.9	72.0	72.0	4272	136.5	25.0	7	39.8	39.9	38.9	38.9
Toyota Sienna 4-door van	119.3	200.0	77.4	68.9	4120	148.9	20.0	8	42.0	42.9	40.2	39.6

MANUFACTURERS' WARRANTIES

Brand	Bumper-To-Bumper Warranty (Years/miles)	Powertrain Warranty (Years/miles)	Corrosion Warranty (Years/miles)	Roadside Assistance (Years/miles)
Acura	4/50,000	—	5/unlimited	4/50,000
Audi	4/50,000	—	12/unlimited	4/50,000
BMW	4/50,000	—	12/unlimited	4/50,000
Buick	3/36,000	—	6/100,000	3/36,000
Cadillac	4/50,000	—	6/100,000	4/50,000
Chevrolet	3/36,000	[1]	6/100,000	3/36,000
Chrysler	3/36,000	7/70,000 [2]	5/100,000	3/36,000
Dodge	3/36,000	7/70,000 [2]	5/100,000	3/36,000
Ford	3/36,000	[4]	5/unlimited	3/36,000
GMC	3/36,000	—	6/100,000	3/36,000
Honda	3/36,000	[4]	5/unlimited	—
Hummer	3/36,000	—	6/100,000	3/36,000
Hyundai	5/60,000	10/100,000	5/100,000	5/unlimited
Infiniti	4/60,000	6/70,000	7/unlimited	4/unlimited
Isuzu	3/50,000	7/75,000	6/100,000	7/75,000
Jaguar	4/50,000	—	6/unlimited	4/50,000
Jeep	3/36,000	7/70,000 [2]	5/100,000	3/36,000
Kia	5/60,000	10/100,000	5/100,000	5/unlimited
Land Rover	4/50,000	—	6/unlimited	4/50,000
Lexus	4/50,000	6/70,000	6/unlimited	4/unlimited
Lincoln	4/50,000	—	5/unlimited	4/50,000
Mazda	4/50,000	—	5/unlimited	4/50,000
Mercedes-Benz	4/50,000	4/50,000	Unlimited	
Mercury	3/36,000	—	5/unlimited	3/36,000
Mini	4/50,000	—	12/unlimited	4/50,000
Mitsubishi	5/60,000	10/100,000	7/100,000	5/unlimited
Nissan	3/36,000	5/60,000	5/unlimited	extra cost [5]
Pontiac	3/36,000	—	6/100,000	3/36,000
Porsche	4/50,000	—	10/unlimited	4/50,000
Saab	4/50,000	—	6/unlimited [6]	4/50,000
Saturn [7]	3/36,000 [8]	—	6/100,000	3/36,000
Subaru	3/36,000	5/60,000	5/unlimited	3/36,000
Suzuki	3/36,000	7/100,000	3/unlimited	3/36,000
Toyota	3/36,000	5/60,000 [9]	5/unlimited	—
Volkswagen	4/50,000	5/60,000	12/unlimited	4/50,000
Volvo	4/50,000	—	8/unlimited	4/unlimited

Note: Manufacturers may periodcally offer additional coverage as a purchase incentive. These offers are not reflected on this chart.

1. 5/60,000 on Aveo and Cobalt. 2. $100 deductible per visit. 3. 5/100,000 on Focus; 8/100,000 on Escape Hybrid battery pack. 4. 8/80,000 on Civic Hybrid battery pack; 10/100,000 on PZEV vehicles. 5. Security Plus. 6. 10/unlimited for 9-3 sedan. 7. Saturns have a 30-day, 1500-mile vehicle-exchange program. 8. Buyers can choose 5/60,000 bumper-to-bumper coverage or $1000-$1250 purchase credit. 9.Prius includes 8/100,000 on hybrid-related compontents, first three service visits up to 30 months/37,500 miles, and 3/36,000 roadside assistance.